# Cost Control and Information Systems

# COST CONTROL AND INFORMATION SYSTEMS

## A Complete Guide to Effective Design and Implementation

Pravin P. Shah

MCGRAW-HILL BOOK COMPANY
New York St. Louis San Francisco Auckland
Bogotá Hamburg Johannesburg London Madrid Mexico
Montreal New Delhi Panama Paris São Paulo
Singapore Sydney Tokyo Toronto

Dedicated to
my father,
the late Mr. Pranlal L. Shah,
who would have been extremely
jubilant to see this book,
and to my son, Anup,
whose love inspired me
to write this book.

Library of Congress Cataloging in Publication Data

Shah, Pravin P
Cost control and information systems.

Bibliography: p.
Includes index.
1. Information storage and retrieval systems—
Cost accounting. I. Title.
HF5686.C8S455 657′.42 80-25587
ISBN 0-07-0056369-1



1234567890 DODO 8987654321

The editors for this book were Kiril Sokoloff and Beatrice E. Eckes, the designer was Blaise Zito Associates, and the production supervisor was Sally Fliess. It was set in Baskerville by Bi-Comp, Incorporated. Printed and bound by R. R. Donnelley & Sons Company.

# CONTENTS

# EXHIBITS

# PREFACE

Cost accounting has long been recognized as an essential management tool; in the present inflationary era it is becoming more and more popular, both for its functional utility and for its application to various organizations. It is now widely recognized that cost accounting is a valuable tool not only for inventory and cost control but also for decision making and profit planning. Cost data are now regarded as an important resource. Similarly, it is no longer believed that cost accounting is useful only to a manufacturing organization. The usefulness of cost accounting has been recognized even by nonmanufacturing organizations such as hotels, restaurants, banks, insurance companies, communications companies, retail organizations, public utilities, and stock and commodity brokerage houses. Even not-for-profit organizations need cost information and cost control systems. Further, the proliferation of various laws and government regulations in the past few years has created a direct or indirect legal necessity for several industries to install cost accounting systems. The phenomenal growth in the use of cost accounting has occurred not only in the United States but also in many other countries.

This wider recognition of the need or usefulness of cost accounting has also brought a growth in the literature on the subject of cost accounting. However, most of this literature deals with (1) *descriptions* of cost accounting procedures, methods, etc., in general; (2) *descriptions* of cost accounting systems used by specific industries; and (3) the *use* of various cost techniques for managerial decisions and so on. The literature dealing with the state of the art of *design and implementation* of cost systems is small in number and narrow in scope. The books falling under the three categories listed above are not intended to provide know-how for the design and implementation of a custom-made cost system. Providing that know-how is the objective of this book. Thus, this book will fill a recognized gap.

The book provides practical, step-by-step, comprehensive know-how for the successful design and implementation of effective cost systems from scratch or for the improvement or modification of an existing cost system. It explains in clear, concise, and simple language not only *what* to do but also *how, why,* and in what *sequence* the steps should be taken and *who* should take them. It also deals at length with the important subject of system implementation. Thus, its focus is on providing a structured approach to developing and implementing a modern cost system.

The book not only deals with technical aspects but also with the practical problems, including people problems, associated with various phases of the design and implementation of a cost system. It provides the know-how for designing a cost system for any type of entity, manufacturing or nonmanufacturing, profit-seeking or not-for-profit, small, medium-size, or large. Throughout the book, detailed checklists, practical guidelines, specimen forms, and actual company practices are presented for every phase of cost system design.

The book consists of twenty chapters, which are divided into five parts representing a natural learning process: "Introduction and Road Map," "System Analysis," "System Design," "System Implementation," and "Other Aspects." Chapter 1 gives a road map of the entire book. The system analysis phase, Chapters 2 through 4, explains how to gain an understanding of a company's business and determine its cost information needs. The system design phase, Chapters 5 through 16, explains how to design a cost control and information system to satisfy preset objectives. Once a cost system has been designed, it is necessary to test it, sell it to the users, implement it, operate it, refine it, maintain it, and sometimes even to revise it. These subjects are treated in the system implementation phase, Chapters 17 through 19. To make the book comprehensive, special points for designing cost systems for nonmanufacturing and not-for-profit organizations are dealt with in Chapter 20.

This book has multiple uses and users. It is designed for busy controllers, management consultants, and others responsible for the design and implementation of cost systems or for the revision of existing cost systems. They can use this book as a reference work or as a source of complete information on the design and implementation of cost systems. They can also use it to guide and train their assistants and thereby make an effective delegation of their work. The book is also meant for persons desiring to learn the subject by self-study or to supplement classroom instruction at colleges, in-house training courses, or refresher courses in accounting systems and procedures or advanced cost accounting.

In some chapters masculine pronouns are used for succinctness and are intended to refer to both males and females.

### Acknowledgements

I owe a great deal to more than 100 controllers and cost accounting executives of *Fortune* 1000 companies for sharing their experiences and knowledge with me by responding to my survey questionnaire. Besides them, several persons assisted directly or indirectly in the preparation of this book. I am grateful to all of them. Two persons, however, need special mention. My brother, Mr. Ishwar Shah, an expert in designing computer systems, reviewed the portion relating to computerized cost systems and offered valuable suggestions. Of course, I will take all responsibility for the final contents. My wife, Pragna, cheerfully, patiently, and painstakingly typed the entire manuscript, prepared the index, and checked the proofs.

PRAVIN P. SHAH

# Chapter 1

# Introduction and Road Map

There is always a first time for everything.

Cost *data* are a valuable resource for any organization. They are required for planning, budgeting, decision making, cost control, performance measurement and evaluation, profitability determination by profit centers, inventory valuation, and various other purposes. For effective use of this important resource, it is essential to manage cost data properly, i.e., properly to classify, accumulate, process, and report the cost data generated within an organization. For the proper management of cost data, a *cost accounting system* is required. Since the output of a cost accounting system is cost information, the system is also called a *cost information system.*

Accounting data are a species of business data with two subsets: financial data and cost data. Similarly, an accounting information system is a species of management information system, and the two subsets of an accounting system are a financial accounting system and a cost accounting system. Both of these accounting information systems provide information for external users as well as for internal management. Sometimes the accounting system concerned with providing the accounting information required by management is called a *management accounting system.*

A financial accounting system is intended to record and report financial transactions—transactions relating to assets, liabilities, revenues, and expenses. The end products of a financial accounting system are the balance sheet, income statement, statement of changes in financial condition, status of accounts receivable, etc. A cost accounting system deals only with the recording and reporting of cost data. The basic difference between financial accounting and cost accounting lies in the nature of classification, accumulation, processing, and reporting of expenses. In financial accounting, expenses are normally classified according to their nature, e.g., salaries, wages, payroll taxes, material, rent, electricity, depreciation, etc. In cost accounting, expenses may *additionally* be classified by causes (maintenance, sales, etc.), by geographic locations, by sources (department, division, etc.), by processes, by products, by cost behavior (variable or fixed), by controllability, and by any other segment of a business unit.

*A cost control system* requires more than cost information. For example, for cost control purposes, it is essential to define policy on the incurrence of various costs, to set forth authorization procedures, and to establish some sort of standards, budgets, or norms for the incurrence of various expenses. Hence, a cost control system goes beyond the bounds of a basic cost accounting system.

## FOCUS OF THE BOOK

First, this book explains the science and the art of designing and implementing a cost system. It not only provides a structured approach for developing and implementing a cost system, but it also deals with the practical problems, including people problems, associated with various phases of the design and implementation of the system. Second, practical, step-by-step, comprehensive know-how is provided not only for designing and implementing a cost system *from scratch* but also for *improving* or modifying an existing cost system. Third, this book does not give a recipe of a cost system for a specific company or a specific industry, but it deals with the design and implementation of a cost system for commercial and noncommercial organizations in general. Thus, its approach has a universal application. Though the discussion generally centers in designing a manufacturing cost system, the approach is valid even for nonmanufacturing concerns such as service companies or retailers. To make the book comprehensive, special aspects of cost systems for nonmanufacturing and even not-for-profit organizations are discussed in Chapter 20.

A cost accounting system is a species of management information system, and, like any other management information system, it may be *manual* or *computer-based.* To design a manual cost system, the designer must know (1) cost accounting principles, techniques, concepts, etc., and (2) cost system design. To design a computer-based cost system, the designer must, in addition, have knowledge of computer system design and of available computer equipment and its capability. It is uncommon to find a person who knows all these subjects. Hence, a computer-based cost system usually is designed by a team of at least two persons, one having knowledge of designing a cost system and the other having knowledge of designing a computer-based system in general. However, so that the cost system designer can communicate well with the computer system designer and together they can develop an effective cost system, the cost system designer should be generally familiar with the process of designing a computerized system and with the capability and limitations of a computer. Similarly, the computer specialist should have general familiarity with cost accounting and with the process of designing a cost system. This book provides this general familiarity required by both persons and shows the interconnection between their work.

Further, most of the steps in the design and implementation of a cost system are common to both a manual cost system and a computer-based cost system. Hence, unless otherwise specified, the discussions throughout the book relate to a manual as well as to a computerized cost system. The special points for designing a computerized cost system with which the cost system designer should be familiar are dealt with at appropriate places throughout the book.

## ARRANGEMENT OF THE BOOK

The approach of the book in explaining the process of designing a cost system is the same as that adopted in designing a cost system. There are three well-defined phases for designing a cost information system: system analysis, system design, and system implementation. The book itself is divided into these three phases. Within each phase, there are several subphases, which are dealt with in separate chapters.

To appreciate the logical division of the book into its various chapters and the sequence of chapters, it is necessary to recognize two facts:

1. The process of designing a cost system is *iterative* in nature; i.e., the various tasks involved are completed through several iterations, or repetitive steps. Hence, in designing a cost system, a *building-block,* or *modular,* approach is adopted under which all the necessary tasks are first identified, then completed through several iterations, and finally synthesized to develop a unified cost system. For example, the starting point in designing a cost system is to define the objectives and the scope of the proposed system. However, during the design phase, the objectives or the scope may be modified for several reasons; e.g., it may be too expensive to design the proposed system. Thus, initially most tasks are completed only tentatively, and later they are modified if necessary. Similarly, interdependent tasks are completed in two or more installments because initially each of these tasks can be completed only partially, and later they are finished

after the prerequisite part of the interdependent tasks has been completed.

2. A cost system consists of *several subcost systems.* For example, the cost system of a manufacturing company consists of a direct material cost system, a direct labor cost system, a manufacturing overhead cost system, a marketing cost system, and an administrative cost system. Several subcost systems are needed because of differences in classification, accumulation, allocation, absorption, and control procedures for various kinds of costs. As a result of the differences in subcost systems, the considerations, issues, procedures, and methods in designing the various systems also differ. In other words, though the basic design procedure and methods are common to all subcost systems, there are differences in their applications, and there are problems peculiar to the design of each subcost system. Hence, each subcost system is also treated as a building block in designing a cost system. Thus, there are two types of building blocks: the first set of blocks is common to the entire cost system, and the second set relates to the individual subcost systems.

To give a proper perspective to the reader, the total tasks involved in designing and implementing a cost system are first summarized in this chapter. Then, each of the blocks or tasks is dealt with, in detail, in a separate chapter. The arrangement of chapters follows the order in which various tasks are performed, though through several iterative steps. Each chapter discusses the issues which arise in performing the relevant task. The book contains a continuing case study of ACME Company that illustrates various aspects of designing a cost system so that the reader can see the application of the subjects under discussion to a real-life situation.

## SUMMARY OF TASKS INVOLVED

As mentioned before, the entire project of developing a cost system can be conveniently divided into three phases:

System analysis
System design
System implementation

Each of these phases involves several tasks, which are enumerated below.

*First Phase: System Analysis*

1. Define the objectives and the scope of the proposed cost system.
2. Gather pertinent background information to gain an understanding of the company, its business, and its existing cost system, if any.

3. On the basis of the objectives, the understanding of the company's business, and the study of the existing system, crystallize the detailed requirements of the cost system—what exactly the system is expected to do.

Chapters 2 through 4 are devoted to the system analysis phase.

*Second Phase: System Design*

1. Select cost methods and techniques suitable for the company.
2. Prepare a broad conceptual outline of the system and determine the gap between the desired system and the existing system, if any.
3. Conduct a systems feasibility study which involves consideration of various alternatives and a cost-benefit analysis.
4. Establish the necessary responsibility centers and cost centers.
5. Design a cost accounting system separately for direct materials, direct labor, manufacturing overhead, and nonmanufacturing costs, covering the following aspects:
    *a.* Classification and accumulation of costs.
    *b.* Allocation of costs.
    *c.* Absorption of costs.
    *d.* Control over costs. (This may involve setting standards, developing expense budgets, developing procedures for cost control, etc.)
    *e.* Documents, records, and reports to be used or prepared.
    *f.* Clerical and operating procedure to be followed for processing each transaction.
6. Develop a comprehensive chart of accounts.

Chapters 5 through 16 are devoted to the system design phase; the arrangement of these chapters is logical. Chapter 5 gives an overview of the system design phase. Chapter 6 is devoted exclusively to designing a cost control system. Since the procedures for classification, standards setting, budget preparation, etc., are different for direct materials, direct labor, manufacturing overhead, and nonmanufacturing costs, they are dealt with separately for each of these cost elements in Chapters 9 through 13. On the other hand, subjects such as selection of cost methods, establishment of cost centers, design of cost reports, and development of a chart of accounts, which are common to all cost elements, are dealt with in Chapters 7, 8, 14, 15, and 16.

*Third Phase: System Implementation*

1. Synthesize various parts of the system and develop a unified system.
2. Review and test the entire system to verify whether it will meet

previously defined objectives and information needs, and give it a finishing touch.

3. Present and sell the system to the company management and other internal users.
4. Prepare a manual, if required.
5. Implement the system.
6. Follow up and iron out any wrinkles in the system.
7. Keep the system current by modifying it in accordance with changes in the business environment.
8. Introduce refinements and sophistications in the system.

The system implementation phase is discussed in Chapters 17 through 19.

In addition to the above tasks, the following major tasks are involved in designing and implementing a computer-based cost system:

1. Selection, acquisition, and installation of electronic data processing equipment
2. Acquisition of preexisting software or development of the system's own software
3. Developing operating procedure for the computer system

These tasks are dealt with at appropriate places in the book.

In short, this chapter gives the entire road map in brief, and Chapters 2 through 20 give detailed maps of the individual aspects of system design work. This arrangement enables the reader to take a capsule look at the total efforts involved in designing a cost system and to understand the relationship of each task to the total system design efforts. Thus, this chapter also serves as a frame of reference during the reading of other chapters. A graphic view of the arrangement and of the building blocks of the project for designing and implementing a cost system is given in Exhibit 1-1.

For a better understanding of the process involved in developing a cost system, it is useful to compare this process with that of constructing a building. First, the architect determines the owner's requirements or expectations from the building and also understands the nature of the land on which the building is to be constructed, the climate of the area, the applicable regulations, etc. Then, the architect prepares a plan or an outline of the building to be constructed, which plan will show the building as it will look when completed. Once the initial plan has been approved by the owner, the contractor divides the construction work into recognizable parts or blocks (excavation, foundation, plinth, slabs, walls, doors, windows, etc.), constructs the building in a modular fashion, and, finally, gives it a finishing touch.

**EXHIBIT 1-1**

**Graphic View of the Building Blocks of Cost System Design and Implementation**

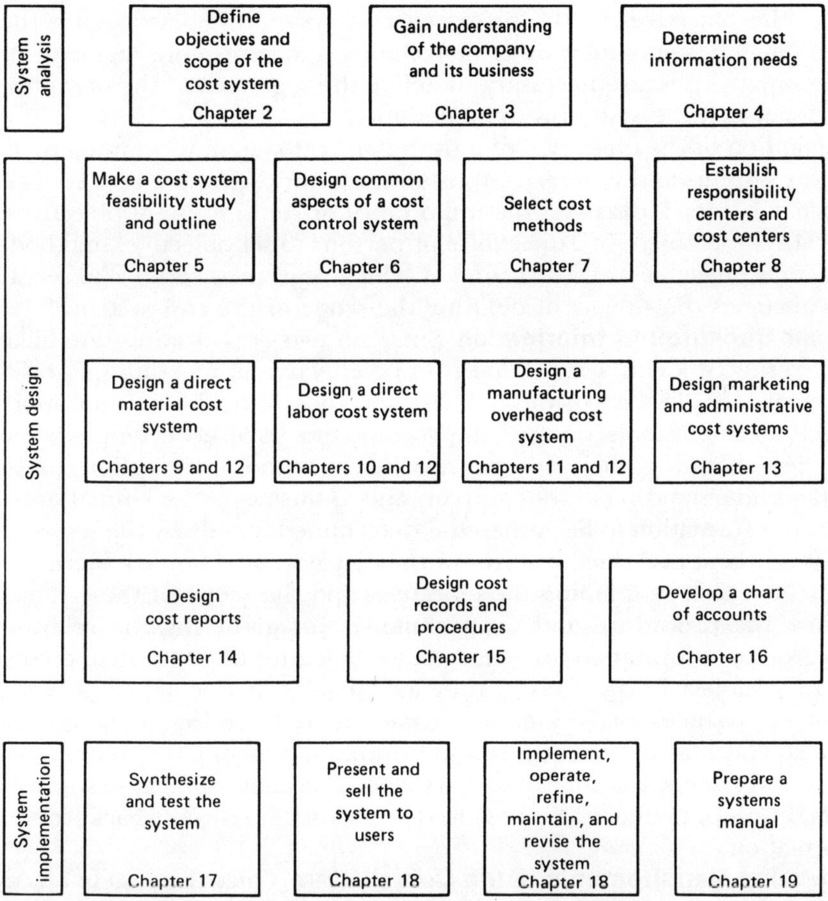


NOTE:
Chapter 20 deals with the special aspects of designing a cost system for nonmanufacturing and not-for-profit organizations.

The three phases and the various subphases within them that have been enumerated above are summarized below.

**Define Objectives and Scope of the Cost System** The basic purpose of all cost systems is to generate cost information. This information may be required to satisfy internal requirements, such as cost control, product pricing, or inventory valuation, or to comply with legal requirements, such as justifying price discrimination based on cost differentiation under the Robinson-Patman Act. Since different types of cost information are required for different objectives and since different cost methods and techniques may be suitable for different purposes, it is essential to define the objectives of the proposed cost system. Similarly, since the system may be companywide or be confined to one or more segments of the company, it is also necessary to define the segments of the organization for which the system is to be designed.

Definition of the objectives of a proposed cost system is common to all subcost systems and is a very important task in designing a cost system. Hence, Chapter 2 discusses the importance of setting system objectives, typical system objectives, the choice of persons to set objectives, methods of setting objectives, and the time at which objectives should be set. It also discusses the subject of defining the scope of the cost system.

**Gather Background Information** Since no two organizations are alike in all respects, a cost system that is to be effective in meeting its preset objectives should be custom-tailored for the particular organization. Hence, once the objectives of the cost system have been defined, the designer should gather the relevant background information for a proper understanding of the company and its business. The kind of background information to be gathered is determined mainly by the scope of the assignment and the objectives of the cost system. This task therefore follows the task of defining the objectives and the scope of the system.

Since the procedure and the techniques for gathering the relevant background information are common to the entire cost system and constitute a subject in themselves, they are dealt with in Chapter 3. That chapter also discusses the kind of information to be collected and gives a detailed checklist of the background information for the cost system as a whole and for each of the subcost systems. The continuing case study of ACME Company illustrates how to document the relevant background information.

**Determine Requirements of the Cost System** Once the system objectives (the reasons for which a cost system is required) have been defined, it is necessary to determine, in specific terms, what the system is expected to do to satisfy each of its objectives. To be precise, for each objective the designer should assess (1) what information is required, (2) who requires it, (3) to what time period the information should pertain, (4) when and how frequently it is required, and (5) the specific form, if any, in which it is required.

Chapter 4 explains how to determine the requirements of a cost system and illustrates it with the help of the continuing case study of ACME Company. To facilitate the task of determining the items of cost information which should be provided by the cost system, a checklist of usually required cost information is presented.

**Design a Cost Control System** There are significant differences in the design of a cost system for cost control and that of a system for product costing. For example, for cost control purposes, it is necessary to define policy on the incurrence of various costs, set forth the authorization procedure, select cost control techniques, lay out the procedure for the development of standards and budgets for various cost items (where standard costing and budgetary control techniques are selected), establish responsibility centers, and design a responsibility reporting and follow-up system.

Because of these issues and of the growing importance of a cost control system, Chapter 6 is devoted exclusively to explaining the process of designing a cost control system. That chapter deals with all the tasks peculiar to designing a cost control system as a whole. The subjects of setting standards and preparing budgets for direct materials, direct labor, manufacturing overhead, and nonmanufacturing costs are discussed in Chapters 9 through 13 and illustrated with the help of the continuing case study of ACME Company.

**Select Appropriate Cost Methods** Several methods of costing (standard costing, job order costing, etc.) are available for product costing, cost control, and cost analysis. Each method has its own characteristics. The method selected affects the classification, accumulation, allocation, absorption, and reporting of costs. It also influences the establishment of cost centers and the development of a chart of accounts. Most important, it determines the kind of cost information that will be generated. Because of these differences, each cost method has its own suitability. For cost control, for example, standard costing is generally more suitable than historical costing. Thus, great care is required in selecting the appropriate cost method. Moreover, because the type of cost method selected has an impact on practically every other task of system design, selection of a method should be the first task in the system design phase.

To enable the designer to make a rational choice of the appropriate cost method, Chapter 7 discusses the pros and cons of each of the methods and gives selection guidelines.

**Prepare an Outline of the Proposed System and Conduct a Feasibility Study** Once the cost information need has been determined and appropriate cost methods and techniques have been tentatively selected, the designer should prepare an outline of the proposed cost system and determine the gap between the proposed system and the existing system. Next, the designer should estimate the efforts and costs involved in designing, implementing, and operating a system to bridge that gap. Because of cost considerations, sometimes either the cost method selected may be changed or the cost information requirements may be modified.

For the sake of convenience, this subject is dealt with in Chapter 5, "Cost System Design: An Overview."

**Establish Necessary Cost Centers and Responsibility Centers** For cost control or responsibility accounting, it is necessary to classify costs by the organizational segments responsible for incurring and controlling various costs. For product costing and cost analysis, it is necessary to classify costs by the various departments, activities, products, etc., incurring or benefiting from various costs. Since different cost conditions exist in different segments of an organization and since more than one person within an organization will be responsible for the different costs which it incurs, the organization must be subdivided into smaller segments called *cost centers* and *responsibility centers.* A cost center is the lowest *accounting entity* established for the accumulation and allocation of costs. A responsibility center is the lowest *organization unit* established for placing responsibility for controlling costs.

The process of establishing cost centers and responsibility centers is explained and illustrated in Chapter 8.

**Determine the Classification of Costs and Select Bases for the Allocation and Absorption of Costs** For accumulation, allocation, absorption or product costing, reporting, standard setting, and budgeting, it is necessary to classify costs. Costs can be classified by nature, functions, cost behavior, or cost centers or in other ways. The types of cost classification adopted depend upon the objectives of the cost information required and the cost methods, techniques, and concepts selected.

For product costing and, to some extent, for responsibility accounting, it becomes necessary to allocate common expenses and charge expenses to production units or user cost centers. For these purposes, it is necessary to select bases for the allocation and absorption (charging) of costs.

Since the classification, allocation, and absorption of costs are different for each of the subcost systems, these topics have been dealt with in Chapters 9, 10, 11, and 13: direct materials in Chapter 9, direct labor in Chapter 10, manufacturing overhead in Chapter 11, and selling, distribution, and administrative costs in Chapter 13. These topics are exemplified by the continuing case study of ACME Company given in Chapters 12 and 13.

**Design a Cost Reporting System** The output of a cost accounting system is cost reports, which may be product cost statements, cost control and performance reports by responsibility centers, cost analyses statements, etc. As discussed before, the type of cost information required is determined during the system analysis phase itself. Then, during the system design phase, a system is developed for the classification, accumulation, allocation, and absorption of costs to generate the desired cost information. In addition, standards, budgets, and control procedures may be established for cost control purposes. The next step is to design cost report forms in which the desired output information will be reported and to establish a procedure for the timely preparation and distribution of cost reports.

Chapter 14 explains reporting principles and guidelines, the means of determining the type of reports to be prepared, the responsibility reporting system, the design of a report form, and procedural aspects of cost reports. It also contains a few specimen cost reports.

**Design Cost Records and Procedures** After determining the classification of costs, establishing cost centers and responsibility centers, and selecting bases for allocation and absorption of costs, the next step is to design cost records for the accumulation, allocation, and absorption of costs by cost items and by cost centers. This task involves determining whether there should be an integrated cost and financial accounting system or two separate systems, the division of cost records into double-entry bookkeeping records and memorandum records, and the subdivision of double-entry-bookkeeping records into a general ledger and subsidiary ledgers. It also becomes necessary to design supporting documents, worksheets, procedures, and work schedules specifying who (title or position) is to do what, when, and how and with what forms.

The design of cost records and procedures is influenced by, among other things, the objectives of the cost system, the kind of cost information required, the cost method selected, the number of cost centers and responsibility centers established, and the cost reports designed. Chapter 15 deals with this subject separately for each of the cost methods (standard costing, job order costing, etc.) and for each of the subcost systems.

**Develop a Comprehensive Chart of Accounts** For consistency and uniformity in recording costs according to their predetermined classification, it is essential to develop a chart of accounts. Such a chart gives a distinct descriptive title to each account and arranges the various accounts in some logical order. In addition, each account may be given a distinct code, and the use of each account may be explained briefly. If the cost accounting system is integrated with the financial accounting system, it is necessary to develop an integrated chart of accounts for assets, liabilities, revenue, expenses (for financial accounting), and subclassification of expenses (for cost accounting).

Chapter 16 is devoted to explaining and illustrating the process of developing a comprehensive chart of accounts.

**Synthesize and Test the System** Since a modular, or building-block, approach is adopted in designing a cost system, it is necessary to bring together all the blocks and develop a unified system. Also, the system should be tested to ensure that it will meet the objectives for which it has been designed and that it is technically sound and practical. No system should ever be implemented before it is thoroughly tested because a defective system may cost time and money and create frustration and distrust among the concerned employees before the defects can be corrected.

Chapter 17 explains the areas to be tested, the persons who should conduct the testing, methods of testing, and the time at which a system should be tested.

**Implement the System** Before the system is implemented, it should be presented and sold to the company management and users. Since people, by their very nature, resist change, the designer should not overlook human considerations in designing and implementing a cost system. He should take steps to prevent user resistance and must also know how to overcome any resistance that may occur. Further, the designer must decide whether to implement the entire system in one shot or in a phased manner. To smooth the implementation of the new system, the system implementation work must be carefully planned. Once the system is operational, it should be kept current by making minor modifications or even by overhauling it when necessary.

These subjects are discussed in Chapter 18, but human considerations are so important to the entire project that they are discussed briefly here.

## PEOPLE INVOLVED

Several people are associated with a cost accounting system. For the design of an effective cost system, the designer must have a thorough understanding of the roles and needs of these people. In other words, the designer must know all the players of the game. The various persons associated with a cost accounting system are described here by their roles.

**Initiator** First, someone in the organization must recognize the need or usefulness of a cost accounting system or the need for revising such a system if it already exists; that person may be from top management or middle management or from staff or line management. The recognition may arise from voluntary acceptance of such a system's usefulness or from direct or indirect legal necessity.

Often, the controller or the chief financial officer of an organization is the initiator. This officer may recognize the need or usefulness of a cost accounting system for valuing inventory or from difficulties experienced in conducting the cost-benefit analyses required by management for making various business decisions, such as whether to make or buy a product or to continue or discontinue a product line. Sometimes, the president may recognize the need for a cost control system. One company manufacturing custom-made equipment realized the need for a cost accounting system when it received a substantial order for the first time. Even an outside consultant may recommend a cost accounting system to solve some problems. For example, while assisting a company in justifying price discrimination based on cost differentiation under the Robinson-Patman Act, an outside cost consultant made the company management aware of the need for a cost system.

**Sponsor** Once the usefulness of a cost accounting system has been recognized, someone must sponsor the project for designing the system and someone must approve that project. The initiator, the sponsor, and the person approving the project may be different persons or be one and the same person. For designing a cost system for inventory valuation only, it is not uncommon to find that the controller initiates, sponsors, and approves the project. On other hand, if cost control and cost analysis for decision making are the purposes of the cost system, approval from upper management is desirable for several reasons. First, every cost information and control system should reflect the philosophy of upper management toward cost control and decision making. For example, where management is not likely to use objective data for decision making, a cost information system would be useless. Hence, before designing the system, it is well to find out whether or not company management will use the cost information generated by the system. The best way to find that out is to ask upper management to approve the project. Second, the successful design, implementation, and operation of a cost control system require involvement and support from upper management and the cooperation of people from several departments. Upper management's involvement is necessary, for example, in selecting appropriate methods and techniques of cost control or in clearly defining the authority and responsibility of various managers for responsibility accounting. The user departments must specify the kind of cost information they need, participate in setting cost standards when a standard cost system is to be employed, provide input data, study cost control reports, explain variances, and take corrective action. Without continuous support from top management, it often becomes difficult to obtain users' cooperation. Once upper management has approved the project, it is comparatively easy to get its involvement and support for the system. Third, for design and operation of the system, it is necessary to budget some resources. The amount depends upon whether the system will be manual or computerized, whether it will be designed in-house or by an outside consultant, and how much manpower will be needed to operate the system. If the amount involved is large, it is necessary or desirable to obtain the prior approval of upper management. Thus, the approval of upper management may be required for securing its involvement and support, for resource allocation, and for ensuring that company management will use the information generated by the cost system.

**Designer** Company management (often the controller) must decide whether the cost accounting system should be designed by an outside consultant or by in-house expertise. An outside consultant may be a certified public accounting firm or a non-CPA firm. The in-house designer may be the controller or his subordinate. In the case of a computerized cost system, a computer specialist will also be required. The computer specialist may be a system analyst or a computer programmer, or both.

Several cost and noncost considerations are involved in reaching this decision. An outside consultant is necessary or desirable when the company lacks capable personnel for designing a cost accounting system. Once the system has been designed, however, the company will need someone to be responsible for the cost accounting function and one or more persons to operate the system. Hence, if a company does not have someone who will ultimately be responsible for the cost accounting function, it may hire a capable cost accountant to design and implement a cost accounting system and then make this accountant responsible for the cost accounting function, provided the company can afford a person with this dual capability. Further, a large company with a continuous need for designing and revising cost systems may have an in-house capability for designing and implementing these systems.

Whenever a choice is involved, the major selection criteria are the cost involved, the completion time, and the degree of objectivity and reliability desired. An outside consultant is likely to be more objective than an in-house designer because he is not a part of the organization and, if experienced, has broad-based experience in designing a cost system. This objectivity is essential for designing a cost control system because the job involves such controversial issues as the classification of costs into variable and fixed categories and into controllable and noncontrollable categories. Further, users are likely to have greater faith in a system designed by an outside consultant, particularly a reputable consultant, than in one designed by an in-house designer. If the system is being designed for regulatory or statutory compliance, such as for rate regulation or for providing cost justification for price discrimination under the Robinson-Patman Act, an outside consultant may be preferable to an in-house designer because the bases for cost allocations and classifications are likely to be accepted more readily when the system has been designed by a reputable professional consultant. Further, his help may be needed in proving the company's case should such an occasion arise.

An outside consultant may require more time to gain understanding of the client company's business than an in-house designer (unless the latter is new to the company). On the other hand, because of his experience, an outside consultant may take less time to design the system. Further, an outside consultant can generally dedicate all his time to the project, whereas an in-house designer may not be able to do so. In this case, there will be a difference in elapsed time: the time gap between commencing and completing the project.

For cost comparison purposes, the fees quoted by an outside consultant should be compared with all the costs to be incurred specifically for designing the system in-house. Such costs, when appropriate, will include the salaries of the designer and of any assistants, employee benefit costs, etc. Much depends upon the facts of each case. For example, if a designer is already available in-house and has spare time to design the system, the company will not be required to incur additional cost on the in-house designer. In such a situation, the final decision can be made by weighing the noncost benefits, if any, of choosing an outside consultant against the cost of the consultant's services. It may be mentioned that the approach to system design work and the tasks involved are more or less the same irrespective of who designs the system.

When an outside consultant is engaged to design a cost system, he must allow cost accounting department personnel to participate in the system design process so that they will become familiar with the system while it is being designed and their training period will be reduced.

Sometimes, even if a company itself undertakes to design a cost system, it may engage an outside consultant to supervise the system design work, to provide consultation on specific problems which may be encountered by the in-house designer, or to review the system once it has been designed in-house.

**Implementer** The system, once designed, may be implemented by the designer or by the cost accountant who will be responsible for running it. This subject is dealt with in detail in Chapter 18.

**System Users** The users are the people for whose benefit the cost system is being designed, and they vary with the objectives and the scope of the system. The system users may be external, such as regulatory agencies, or internal. Internal users may be the controller's department itself or various line and staff departments. The designer must bear in mind that the success of the system will depend upon the extent to which it will satisfy the users' needs for cost information.

**Persons Subject to Performance Evaluation** If a cost system is being designed for cost control, the designer must ascertain the persons whose performance will be evaluated with the help of the information generated by the cost system. Depending upon the scope of the system, these persons may be direct labor, supervisors, purchasing officers, quality controllers, salespersons, or others. The same person may be a user as well as a person subject to performance evaluation. For example, supervisors will need cost information for controlling the performance of the individual workers reporting to them, and their superiors will use cost information to judge supervisors' performance.

Once the designer knows the persons subject to performance evaluation, he can, when appropriate, involve them in designing the system and ensure that the control reports used for evaluating their performance will be understandable by them. In the case of a standard cost system, it is also essential that all these people accept the standards applicable to them.

**Providers of Input Data** These people are either users of the system or persons whose performance will be evaluated with the help of the information generated by the system, or both. Since the reliability, accuracy, and timely availability of the required input data are essential to the success of a cost system, the ability of these people to provide the required input data should be considered by the designer while designing the system.

**System Operators** These are the people from the cost accounting department who must run the system and provide cost information once the system has been designed and implemented. Usually, a cost accounting department is a part of the controller's department, though sometimes it may be separate from that department. In the case of a computerized system, besides the cost accounting department the electronic data processing department will be responsible for operating it. The ability, experience, education, and number of personnel available to run the system (and the type of computer system available) must be considered in designing the system.

**Liaison Person** When an outside consultant has been engaged to design a cost system, it usually is necessary to designate a person who will act as a liaison person between the company and the consultant. When an in-house staff member is designing a system, there may or may not be a need for designating a liaison person. For example, in a multidivision or multibranch company, it may be necessary to have a liaison person from each division or branch, but such a person may not be necessary in a smaller company.

Depending upon the organization of the company and the importance of the project, the liaison person may be the controller, the chief financial officer, the general manager, the assistant to the president, or some other executive. Since setting up a cost accounting system, particularly a cost control system, requires the cooperation of persons from several departments, the liaison person must be a well-placed individual.

## PROJECT MANAGEMENT

Designing a cost system from scratch is a sizable job often extending over several months and, in some cases, over several years. Hence, it is essential that the entire project be managed in a systematic manner. The subject of project management is discussed here under these headings: (1) scope of the project, (2) role of designer and others, (3) order of approach, (4) project management techniques, (5) announcement of the project, and (6) progress reports.

**Scope of the Project** Irrespective of whether the designer is an in-house expert or an outside consultant, he must, before starting the project, clearly ascertain the total scope of the assignment. In particular, the designer must have a very clear understanding of the following aspects:

1. Whether a new system must be designed or the existing system be redesigned or improved
2. Whether the designer must also implement the system which he has designed or redesigned
3. Whether the designer must prepare a manual of the cost accounting system or only a detailed report explaining the proposed system or recommending changes in the existing system
4. The objectives of the cost system
5. Segments of the organization for which the system is to be designed or redesigned

**Role of Designer and Others** As discussed earlier, various people are involved in designing and implementing a cost system. The designer must identify who those people are in a given organization and what specific roles they will play in system analysis, design, and implementation. In particular, the designer must clarify what is decidedly not his job (e.g., setting of standards) and reach a clear understanding about tasks which are in gray areas (e.g., whether the designer will be responsible also for system implementation, whether he must prepare a detailed systems manual, etc.). Preferably, responsibility for significant tasks should be reduced to writing.

In computer-based cost systems, it is essential to define the respective roles of the cost system designer and the computer specialist. Though their respective roles will depend upon their knowledge and expertise, the division of work given below is commonly adopted.

The *cost system designer* will be exclusively responsible for the following tasks:

- Defining system objectives
- Selecting cost methods and cost control techniques
- Establishing responsibility centers and cost centers

- Designing a budgetary control system and a standard cost system
- Classifying costs
- Determining bases for allocation and absorption of costs
- Specifying types, formats, contents, frequency, and timing of cost reports
- Resolving all other cost accounting issues

The cost system designer and the computer specialist will *jointly* perform the following tasks:

- Conducting a preliminary survey
- Determining the requirements of the proposed cost system
- Making a selection between separate cost accounting, financial accounting, and other applications and an integrated system
- Preparing a feasibility study report for obtaining management's approval
- Designing cost records and input documents
- Developing a chart of accounts, account title and arrangement of accounts by the cost system designer, and coding by the computer specialist
- Testing and implementating the system
- Preparing a systems manual

The *computer specialist* will be responsible for the following tasks:

- Selection of electronic data processing and telecommunications equipment and their configuration
- Selection of programming language
- Developing or acquiring software
- File contents and layout, file arrangement, input layout, storage and retrieval systems, data processing checks to be applied, and similar tasks
- Processing run specifications, i.e., specifying what each computer run is supposed to do

**Order of Approach** Two of the most perplexing questions which arise in the mind of a designer are "Where should we start?" and "In what sequence should we proceed?" There is no one best answer to each of these questions because the answer depends, among other things, upon the complexity of the organization, the nature of business operations of the company, and the kind of cost information required. However, the following guidelines would be useful:

1. As stated before, the entire process is iterative, involving going back and forth. The number of iterations required for completing a given task

may be one, two, or several, but since the entire work cannot be started simultaneously and since most steps depend on the completion of other steps, some sequence should be established.

2. First, list the required steps or activities under each task or block. Then, classify these steps into independent, dependent, and interdependent steps. Arrange the steps in some logical sequence. Steps which are independent of other steps can be undertaken in any sequence, but dependent steps can be undertaken only after the steps on which they depend have been completed. Interdependent steps may have to be completed in two or more installments.

3. Of the various steps to be taken, certain ones are technical, while others are mechanical or routine. Usually, the technical steps are more critical than the mechanical steps, which, in fact, are influenced by the technical steps. For example, policy issues, such as the selection of a cost method or an inventory pricing method, are more important than the design of a stores ledger or a material requisition distribution journal. Logically, the more important steps should be undertaken first.

**Project Management Techniques** The project of designing and implementing a cost system involves many steps, ranging from a few scores to a few hundreds, depending upon the complexity of the system. Further, the project is time-consuming and involves more than one person. Hence, cost system design requires a systematic approach. Various techniques available for managing any type of project can also be used to manage the project of cost system development. The simplest technique is to prepare a work and time schedule that shows who is to do what, when, and in what sequence. Such a schedule will enable all persons involved in the system project to understand not only their own and other persons' roles but also what work precedes their work and what work succeeds their work. It will also enable all concerned to do advance planning of their work. Thus, a time-bound work schedule will facilitate an effective coordination of the work of various people.

A specimen work and time schedule is given in Exhibit 1-2. This schedule will also serve as a progress report for the appropriate management. The chart is self-explanatory. Periodically, the last two columns will be completed with the actual dates or with the latest forecast dates if these differ from the original target dates. Thus, this schedule will also enable the designer to keep track of the project and will serve as a progress report for the appropriate management.

If the system design work is very complex or if several persons are involved in the work, a program evaluation and review technique (PERT) and a critical path method (CPM) are very useful. A PERT chart clearly depicts the interrelationships of various steps and of the work of

**EXHIBIT 1-2**

**Program and Status Report on Design and Implementation of Cost System**

| Company | | Sponsor | | Designer | | | Date prepared | |
|---|---|---|---|---|---|---|---|---|
| Activity no. | Activity or event description | Depends on activity no. | Dependent activity no. | Responsibility of | Target dates | | Latest forecast as of ______ or actual dates | |
| | | | | | Start | Finish | Start | Finish |
| | | | | | | | | |

various persons. It also enables the designer to measure and control the progress of the entire project.

A specimen PERT chart is given in Exhibit 1-3. This is a partial chart for an actual project. The basis of its preparation was the work and time schedule shown in Exhibit 1-2. The number in the center of each circle indicates the activity number, and the letter beside each circle indicates the person responsible for a given activity. In each circle, in the space above and below the activity number, the target start and finish dates will be entered. The activities are arranged in the order in which they should be undertaken. The activities appearing at the same level can be undertaken simultaneously. The actual start and finish dates, as well as revised dates, may be entered on the same chart or on a copy. A typical PERT chart for designing a standard cost system is given in the Appendix.

The critical path method enables the designer to estimate from the PERT chart the total time required to complete the project by finding the longest continuous time path.

Another useful technique of project management is the Gantt chart, which graphically shows the duration of various activities and their interdependence. Usually, a Gantt chart is good for a summary graphic display and control over each block of the system project, whereas the PERT chart is good for detailed planning and control of the project. A specimen Gantt chart is given in Exhibit 1-4.

**Announcement of the Project** Once a decision has been made to undertake a project for designing a cost system, it should be communicated to all concerned. The project announcement should cover the reasons for undertaking the project, the persons who will design and implement the system, the persons who will assist the designer and in what manner, the dates on which the project will commence and be completed, and other relevant points. Sometimes this information may be communicated in installments. For example, the initial announcement may cover only the fact that an outside consultant has been engaged to design and implement a cost control and information system and that the necessary details will be announced in due course.

The announcement of the project serves several purposes. First, it takes away all guesswork and fear among employees. Second, it informs the people concerned of what is expected of them and thereby enables them to make advance preparation when necessary. It also increases the degree of participation and cooperation of the concerned personnel. Hence, the announcement should be made by as high-ranking an executive as possible.

**Progress Reports** A project for designing a cost system is time-consuming. The *elapsed time,* the time interval between commencing and completing a project, lasts at least several months. The *effective time,* the

**EXHIBIT 1-3**

**Partial PERT Chart for Cost System Project**

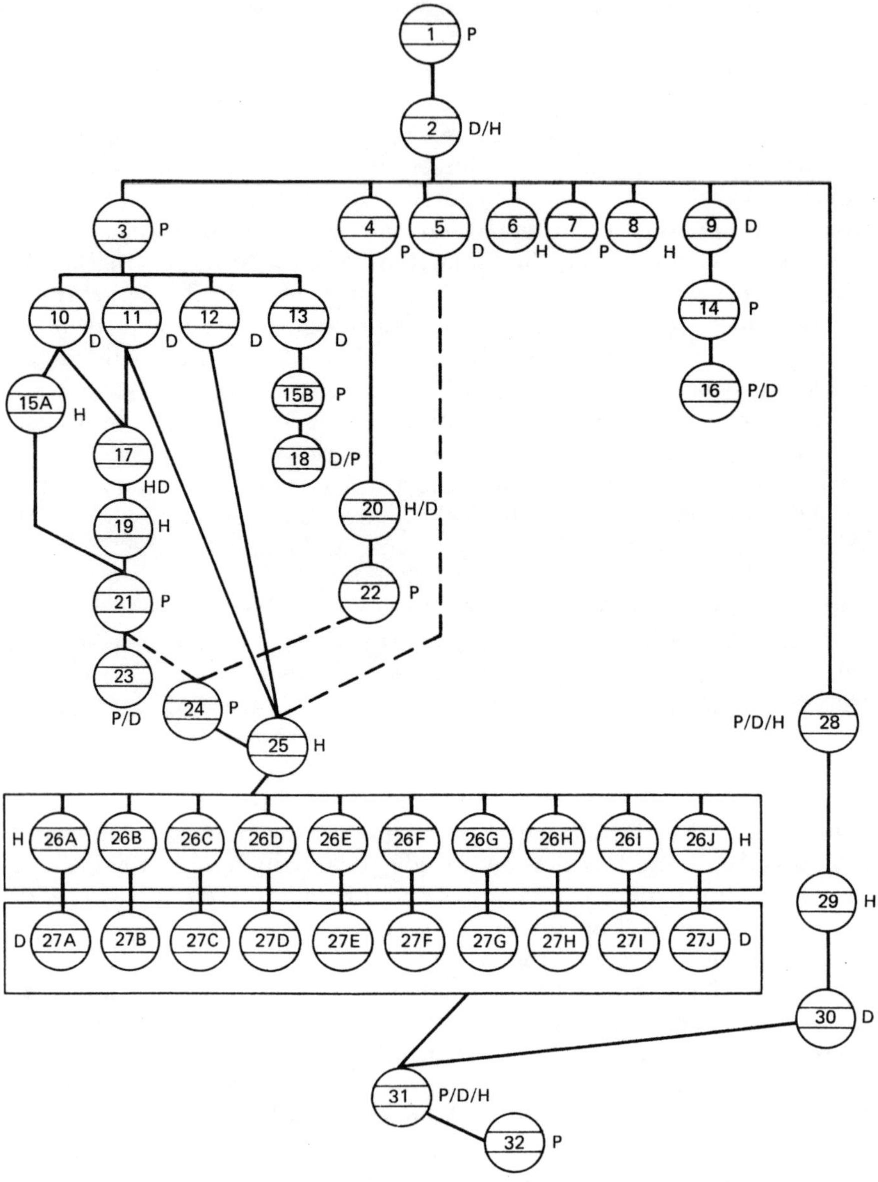

**EXHIBIT 1-4**

**Illustrative Gantt Chart for Cost System Project**

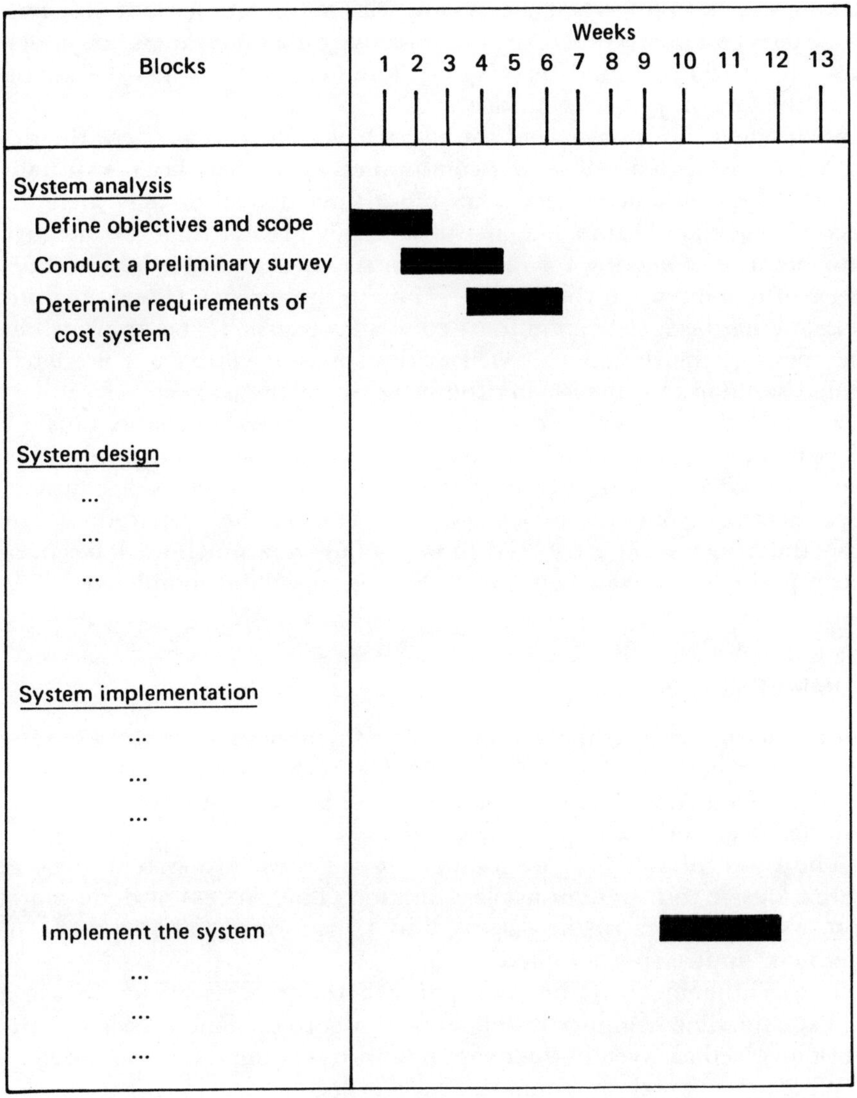

time actually spent on the project, also extends to several person-months or even more, depending upon the complexity, the objectives, and the scope of the system. Hence, the sponsor and the users will be interested in knowing not only when the system will be operational but also how much effective time it will take. The effective time determines how much the project will cost, and the elapsed time determines when the payoff from the system project will start.

Even when the sponsor and the users have not so requested, the designer should set a deadline and communicate it to them because usually a cost system design project takes more time than they may imagine. Second, the elapsed time may be substantially greater than the effective time because of waiting for information from users and others and because of inability to devote all one's time to the project. Once a realistic deadline has been set, communicated to all concerned, and approved by the sponsor, the designer as well as the sponsor will have a predetermined standard for measuring the progress of the project.

Further, the sponsor, users, and other concerned personnel must be informed periodically of the status of the project. For this purpose, either the status report form given in Exhibit 1-2 may be used or a summary report showing only the major system blocks may be prepared. In any case, the progress report should show not only how much work has been accomplished but also when the entire project will be completed.

## SUMMARY

For proper management of cost data, a cost system is required. Designing and implementing a cost system constitute both a science and an art. A computerized cost system is designed by a team consisting of a cost system designer and a computer specialist.

The three phases for developing a cost system are system analysis, system design, and system implementation. The process of designing a cost system is iterative in nature, and therefore a building-block, or modular, approach is adopted.

The arrangement of the book parallels the process of developing a cost system. The beginner is well-advised first to gain an overview of the work involved as given in this chapter before reading the other chapters.

Whether manual or computerized, a cost system is designed for human beings and operated by human beings, and its output is used by human beings. Hence, the designer must understand all the people concerned with the cost system and their respective roles. According to their roles, these people can be described as initiator, sponsor, designer, implementer, users, persons subject to performance evaluation, providers of input data, system operators, and liaison person.

A project for designing a cost system should be managed systematically. The designer must define the scope of the assignment, clarify his role and that of other persons, organize the work in some logical order, use one or more project management techniques, and ensure that all concerned are informed about the project and its progress.

# PHASE I

# System Analysis

# Chapter 2

# Defining Objectives and Scope of the Cost System

If you don't know where you are going, any road is good for you.

One of the important tasks that the designer must perform during the system analysis phase is to define the objectives and the scope of the proposed cost system.

## SYSTEM OBJECTIVES

Every cost system exists to serve some purpose. Hence, the task of setting the objectives of the proposed cost system involves understanding the purpose or purposes that management is trying to achieve with the help of the system. For example, the objective of a cost system could be to assist management in controlling costs or to provide the accounting department with the necessary cost data for inventory valuation.

## SCOPE OF THE SYSTEM

This task involves defining the segment of the organization or the business for which the system is to be designed or redesigned. The scope of a system may extend to (1) the entire organization, (2) all or some of the divisions or subsidiary companies within the organization, (3) all or some of the products, (4) all or some of the functions such as manufacturing, selling, and distribution, (5) all or some of the geographic locations or branches, and (6) all or some of the cost elements (e.g., a standard cost system may be confined to direct materials and direct labor).

The scope should be defined separately for each objective, or objectives should be defined separately for each segment because certain objectives may be relevant for one segment but not for another. For example, the objective of inventory valuation is relevant for a production division but not for a service division that does not use a significant amount of materials.

This leads us to discussion of the following topics:

Why set system objectives?
A few specific objectives of a cost system
Who should set objectives and scope?
How to set objectives and scope
When to set system objectives and scope

## WHY SET SYSTEM OBJECTIVES?

A cost system, being only a management tool, is a means to an end and not an end in itself. And the ends to which it is a means may differ from industry to industry and, within an industry, from company to company. The kind, timing, frequency, and accuracy of the cost information required will vary with the objective for which it is required. For product pricing, for example, information about production as well as marketing and distribution costs is required, whereas for inventory valuation information about only production costs is required.

Second, any information system, be it cost accounting, financial accounting, or any other system, should provide not as much information as possible but as much as is *needed* or *useful.* A lack or inadequacy of diet may cause an anemic condition, and an excess of food may cause indigestion. The case of the excess or inadequacy of cost information is similar. As one company aptly put it in reply to the author's survey questionnaire, "It is very easy to design a system that produces more data than can be utilized." Further, the more cost information generated, the greater the cost of generating information.

Third, of the various cost methods, concepts, and techniques available, some are suitable for one purpose but not for another. On the other hand, several alternative cost methods, concepts, or techniques may be available for a given purpose. For example, for cost control, standard costing is more appropriate than historical costing; in a specific-order type of industry (e.g., a custom furniture shop or a company manufacturing custom equipment), only job order costing, and not process costing, is suitable. Thus, unless the objectives for which a cost system is being designed are defined, it is not possible to select appropriate cost methods, concepts, and techniques. As someone has said, if you don't know where you are going, any road will take you there. Similarly, it can be said that if the designer does not know why he is designing a cost system, any cost method or technique will be appropriate.

Fourth, setting objectives works to the advantage of management as well as of the designer. Once a cost system has been implemented, management can evaluate the effectiveness of the system in providing the required cost information to meet each of the preset objectives. The designer, on the other hand, will not be blamed for the failure of the system to provide cost data to serve objectives not envisaged by management while the system was being designed. Thus, system objectives become the commonly agreed-upon yardsticks for evaluating the actual system.

In addition to knowing or setting present objectives, it is preferable to ascertain possible additional objectives for the near future, say, for the next 3 to 5 years. It is not the intention to make a wild guess but to reckon only known or predictable objectives so that frequent revisions in the system can be avoided. For example, a company designing a cost accounting system should first ascertain the proposals, relevant to the cost accounting system, for additional accounting requirements or for amendments to exisitng accounting requirements by the Cost Accounting Standards Board (CASB), Financial Accounting Standards Board (FASB), Securities and Exchange Commission (SEC), or any other applicable regulatory agency. Requirements which are likely to be effective and applicable to the company should be included in the objectives of the proposed cost system.

## A FEW SPECIFIC OBJECTIVES OF A COST SYSTEM

The basic purpose of all cost systems is to generate cost information. The cost information may be required to satisfy internal (managerial) requirements or to comply with some external (often legal) requirements. The typical objectives of a cost system falling under these two broad categories are discussed below:

### Internal Requirements

**Data Base for Profit Planning and Operating Budgeting** Profit planning and the preparation of operating budgets require a multitude of cost data, such as costs by functions, costs by product lines, unit and total costs, and variability of costs with changes in the volume of production and sales. Though a cost accounting system is not absolutely indispensable for these two purposes, a good cost accounting system definitely adds to their effectiveness. For example, profit planning and budgeting require forecasting of costs. A good cost accounting system facilitates this task by providing the past trend of costs and by classifying costs by nature, by cost behavior, by function, etc. If the required cost information is not available from a cost accounting system, it may have to be developed from the financial accounting data or be estimated. Both these approaches may take more time and may not provide very reliable and accurate information.

**Cost Control** For cost control purposes, management needs timely and reliable feedback information on costs incurred by various responsibility centers. Further, for better cost control it is also essential to determine costs before they are incurred, compare the actual costs against predetermined costs, and analyze variances for further management action. A good cost accounting system can serve both these purposes.

**Profitability Appraisal by Segments** This requires the accumulation and allocation of costs by segments, which may be different products, divisions, geographic locations, etc.

**Performance Evaluation** For appraising the performance of the research and development department, for example, management needs information not only on the outcome of research and development activities but also on the costs incurred.

**Managerial Decision Making** To enable management to make rational routine and nonroutine decisions, often it is necessary to conduct cost-benefit analyses or to weigh the cost of various alternatives. A cost accounting system is very helpful, if not essential, for providing the relevant data needed for cost-benefit analyses.

Some of the typical decision areas for which cost information is needed are listed below (the designer may use this list as a checklist to determine the decision areas applicable to a given company):

- ☐ Selection of the most profitable product mix when there is a shortage of a common direct material, plant capacity, or any other resources or of the demand itself
- ☐ Making or buying a product, parts, or a component
- ☐ Choice of overtime versus an additional shift
- ☐ Expansion of capacity versus subcontracting
- ☐ Deciding whether to drop or continue a product, a division, etc.
- ☐ Selecting the most economical sales channel, modes of distribution, etc.
- ☐ Setting goals in terms of volume and market share

**Product Pricing** Besides the market forces of demand and supply, the costs of producing and marketing a product constitute an important factor in setting product prices. Similarly, cost information is required for special-order pricing, for cost-plus pricing, and for deciding whether to increase or decrease a price in order to increase overall sales revenue. Further, cost information is required for setting transfer pricing for valuing the internal transfer of goods and services.

**Cost Reduction** A cost reduction effort requires knowledge of significant cost items, the cost of each major activity, segregation of controllable and noncontrollable costs, effects of reduction in each cost item on revenue and profit, and the like. A cost accounting system can be designed to provide these types of information.

### External Requirements

**Inventory Valuation for Income Determination** For external reporting purposes—to stockholders, the SEC in the United States, the Registrar of Companies in India, an income tax department, etc.—it is necessary to value inventory. Usually, inventory is valued at cost or at the lower of the cost or market value. Hence, a cost accounting system may be designed to provide cost data by various products, jobs, parts, assemblies, etc. When a cost accounting system is designed for inventory valuation, it is an extension of the financial accounting system.

**Prescribed Accounting** Various government agencies and regulatory bodies from time to time prescribe either accounting systems or accounting requirements for different industries for regulating one or more aspects of those industries. For example, the Federal Communications Commission (FCC) has prescribed accounting systems for certain communications companies, the objective of which is to obtain reliable and accurate cost and other data on a uniform basis for regulating the rates charged by those communications companies. Similarly, the CASB has prescribed cost accounting standards for certain types of negotiated defense contracts and subcontracts. In India, the government has prescribed compulsory cost accounting records for companies manufacturing cement, sugar, bicycles, and various other products.

**Indirect Statutory Compulsion** Sometimes, there may be an indirect statutory compulsion to maintain elaborate cost records, for example, to justify price discrimination based on cost differentiation under the Robinson-Patman Act.

**Requirements of the Financial Accounting Standards Board Statement No. 14** This statement requires that financial statements of a business enterprise include profitability and other information about the enterprise's operations in different industries, its foreign operations, its export sales, and its major customers. To comply with this requirement, it is necessary to maintain records by reporting segments and to allocate common operating expenses among these segments on some equitable basis.

**Labor Negotiations** Cost information may be required for labor negotiations.

**Loans** For obtaining loans from financial institutions, it is necessary to prepare a projection of profits for the next 5 to 10 years. A cost accounting system provides a valuable data base for this purpose.

**Providing Cost Information to a Trade Association** Sometimes a cost system may be designed to provide cost information to an industry or trade association. These data may be utilized for making representations before the government or for the exchange of summary information among members on a voluntary basis.

## WHO SHOULD SET SYSTEM OBJECTIVES AND SCOPE?

Usually, several people in the organization participate or contribute in setting the objectives and scope of a cost system. These people include top management, the controller, the cost accountant, the chief financial officer, various line managers, and the designer of the cost system. Often, the controller and the designer themselves will be able to set most of the objectives. Sometimes a governing regulation, for example, a prescribed accounting system, may set the system objectives.

There are two advantages in allowing users of cost information to participate in setting system objectives. First, they have firsthand knowledge of their problems and needs for cost information (though they may not know what kind of information they need). Second, once they participate in setting system objectives and in designing the system, they will have a greater sense of commitment to the system. Hence, the designer should involve the users in setting system objectives, and even if the designer takes a lead in setting those objectives, he should have them validated by the users.

## HOW TO SET SYSTEM OBJECTIVES AND SCOPE

Initially, someone in the organization will recognize the need or usefulness of a cost system. That person usually will have in mind some objective of such a system. Sometimes, an outside consultant may have recommended a cost system to solve a particular management problem. This objective becomes a starting point for setting the objectives of the proposed cost system. However, even when a cost system is proposed to be designed for one or more prime objectives, it is not uncommon to try to achieve other incidental objectives too.

Whether or not management knows the objectives for which a cost system is required, the designer has an important role to play in setting system objectives. If management does not know or knows only vaguely why it needs a cost system, the designer should help management define the objectives of the proposed cost system. He can do this by asking key management personnel about the nature of the usual decisions they make or the problems they encounter. For this purpose, the list of typical cost objectives given earlier in this chapter may be used as a checklist. Similarly, the designer should inquire about the applicable laws and the type of cost information required to comply with them. From the analysis of the results of these inquiries, the designer should be able to develop a list of the possible objectives.

On the basis of the foregoing steps, the designer should draw up a list of the possible objectives of the proposed cost system. If there are several system objectives, the designer should classify them into primary and secondary objectives or arrange them in the order of importance so that the more important objectives can be given greater attention in designing the system.

Usually, the scope of the cost system is set by the sponsor of the system. If it is not, the designer should ask the sponsor to define the scope of the proposed system. Often, the designer must advise management on what should be the scope of the system. In so doing, he should remember certain points. First, a cost system should be designed only for those business segments or functions which need it or can use it. Second, in case of a multidivision company, it is advisable initially to confine the system to one or two divisions. Once the system has become operational in those initially chosen divisions, it may be extended to other divisions. On the other hand, the system may be designed for the entire organization but implemented in a phased manner. In short, do not attempt to do too much too soon. Third, the scope and the objectives of a cost system are intertwined. Hence, the foregoing discussion about setting of system objectives will also be useful in setting the scope of the system. Next, the designer should discuss the possible objectives and scope with the key users of the system as well as with the cost accountant and the controller and, after considering their comments, finalize the objectives and the scope of the system. The final list should be approved by the appropriate management.

## Impact of a Computer on the Objectives and Scope of a Cost System

A computer can do what may be difficult to do manually. For example, with a computer it is possible or easy to use various mathematical models and operation research techniques for cost allocations, cost-volume-profit analysis, separation of costs into fixed and variable elements, and various other purposes. Further, a computer may be able to serve more objectives or departments with little extra cost. Consequently, in the case of a computerized cost system, the objectives may be more refined and the scope may be wider than those in the case of a manual cost system. However, since human beings cannot change their way of thinking overnight, the objectives and the scope should be expanded at a pace consistent with the ability of the company's personnel.

## WHEN TO SET SYSTEM OBJECTIVES AND SCOPE

The very first task during the system analysis phase should be to set the objectives (at least the prime objectives) and the scope of the system. However, the designer, particularly if he is an outside consultant or is relatively new to the company, faces a chicken-and-egg type of problem. To set system objectives and scope, the designer must understand the company and its business by conducting a systematic survey (which is the subject of Chapter 3). But to make the effort goal-directed while conducting the survey, it is desirable that the designer know the objectives and the scope of the cost system.

To solve this problem, the system objectives and scope initially should be defined tentatively and be finalized only after the designer has gained an adequate understanding of the company and its business. It may be noted that even in the process of setting objectives, the designer will gain a general understanding of the company's business. Thus, the order of tasks may be something like this: gain a general understanding of the company's business ⟶ tentatively define system objectives and scope ⟶ conduct a systematic survey of the company's business ⟶ finalize the objectives and define the scope of each objective. Further, as we will see in Chapter 5, after completing the system analysis phase, the designer must conduct a feasibility study. On the basis of the feasibility study, it may be found that it is not cost-beneficial to have certain objectives or to extend the scope of the cost system to certain segments or functions. In this case the scope or the objectives of the cost system should be suitably modified.

This discussion illustrates the point that the system design process is iterative in nature and that it may be necessary to go back and forth a few times before completing a particular task.

## SUMMARY

The designer must define the objectives for which a cost system is being designed. He must also define the organizational segments, functions, and activities which will be covered by the cost system. A cost system may be designed to satisfy internal or external requirements for cost information. When it is designed to satisfy internal requirements, the internal users must be involved in setting the system objectives and scope. One or more iterations may be necessary before the final objectives and the scope of the cost system are determined.

# Chapter 3

# Understanding the Company and Its Business

. . . fact-finding is more effective than fault-finding.
Carl Becker

Having defined, at least tentatively, the objectives for which the proposed cost system is being designed and its scope, it is necessary to gather the relevant background information to understand properly the company and its business and to determine its cost information needs. In fact, background information forms the *foundation* for the design and implementation of the cost system. To gather the relevant background information, the designer should conduct a fact-finding survey as described in this chapter. This survey is similar to the diagnostic examination conducted by a physician to evaluate a patient's health and to determine the nature of the problem or disease.

The following questions which arise concerning a fact-finding survey are discussed in this chapter.

- Why should background information be gathered?
- What background information should be collected?
- What are the sources of background information?
- How should a fact-finding survey be conducted?
- How should background information be documented?

## NEED FOR BACKGROUND INFORMATION

For a cost system to be effective in serving the preset objectives, it must suit the environment of the company for which it is designed. Companies in different industries differ in the nature of their businesses, and even in the same industry no two companies are alike. There may be differences in size, organization structure, management style, education and experience of personnel, and mode of conducting business. Further, differences may be found even among different divisions of a multidivision company.

These differences determine or influence the type and the amount of costs incurred by the company, the distribution of authority-responsibility for the incurrence of and control over costs, and the kinds of business decisions which arise and the kinds of cost information which are used or required. For example, a company manufacturing custom-made equipment needs a capability for *estimating* the costs of different types of equipment so as to be able to quote prices. This capability is not required by a company manufacturing standard equipment. Hence, these two companies need different cost systems. Similarly, a cost system for a centralized organization differs from that for a decentralized organization. In a decentralized organization, for example, the need for accountability is greater, and hence there are more responsibility reports than in a centralized organization of the same size. Further, if management is accustomed to informed decision making rather than deciding by the seat of its pants, a cost system can be more sophisticated.

Thus, an understanding of the company and its business is necessary not only for defining or refining the objectives and the scope of the cost system but also for determining the exact requirements of the system. Further, this information is essential for designing an effective cost system for the accumulation, allocation, analysis, summarization, and reporting of cost data.

## WHAT INFORMATION SHOULD BE GATHERED?

The nature of the background information to be gathered is not a matter of an exact formula but properly one of judgment. It is determined mainly by the scope of the assignment, the objectives of the cost system, and the complexity of the company's business. Much more background information is required for designing a cost system from scratch than for improving an existing system. Similarly, the background information required for designing a cost control system is much more extensive than that required for designing a product cost system.

As a matter of strategy, the designer should go from general information to specific information, from a business overview to a detailed view. In other words, the designer should first try to gain a broad understanding of the company and its business from various angles without going into the details of any aspect. Then, during the system design phase, he should examine the relevant aspects in depth.

Broadly speaking, the background information to be gathered for designing a cost system may be grouped as follows:

1. The company, its organization structure, and its personnel
2. The company's business
3. The company's mode of operation, i.e., its various operating systems and procedures, cost and noncost information systems, etc.

A checklist of the background information to be collected is given in Exhibit 3-1. It itemizes the information to be collected for the cost system as a whole and for each of the subcost systems, such as the direct material cost system, direct labor cost system, marketing cost system, etc. The designer should customize this checklist after taking into account the scope of the assignment, the objectives of the proposed system, and the type and complexity of the business. Not all the items given in the checklist may be relevant in every case. *Further, when appropriate, some of the information may be collected while the cost system is being designed.* For example, details about direct material cost, direct labor cost, etc., may be obtained while the respective subcost systems are being designed. Any reader who has ever designed a cost system will recognize the need for most of the information contained in Exhibit 3-1. Further, the checklist itself explains the need for certain items where the need may not be obvious. To a beginner, however, the need for some of the items listed in the exhibit may not be obvious. As the beginner reads through the subsequent chapters, the need will become clearer. In addition, the importance of knowing the history and stages of growth of the company is illustrated by the following case study adapted from an actual situation.

A diversified company consisted of five divisions, including an engineering division and a textile division. In all the divisions except the engineering division, the financial and cost control and reporting systems were satisfactory. A consulting firm of certified public accountants was engaged to redesign the financial and cost accounting systems for the engineering division. On studying the history and the stages of growth of the division, the consultant learned that initially the division was only a repairs and maintenance department of the company. Gradually, it started manufacturing small parts and, later, even textile machinery for the textile division of the company. After some time, it also started manufacturing textile machines to be sold outside, and in the course of time it became one of the major production divisions of the company. Thus, there was a significant *change* in the *status* of the engineering division. It had grown from a *service unit* to a *production unit* or from a *cost center* to a *profit center.*

These facts made the consultant suspect, based on his considerable experience, that improvements in management and in the accounting

**EXHIBIT 3-1**

**Checklist of Background Information Required for Designing a Cost System**

1. *Information Common to the Entire Cost System*
   1.1 History and stages of growth of the company.
   1.2 General description of the company's business, e.g., manufacturing consumer goods, communications, transportation.
   1.3 Lines of business, i.e., a list of products or services provided. When the products are numerous, they should be suitably grouped and subgrouped.
   1.4 Industry background, particularly the number and size of various companies in the industry and the relative position of the company in the industry.
   1.5 Organization structure and key executives of the company. The number of employees should be classified by suitable functions (e.g., management, sales, operations, clerical) in various departments.
   1.6 Geographical location of production, sales, and administrative facilities.
   1.7 Analysis of profit and cost structures, i.e., each major cost element expressed in dollar amount and as a percentage of total costs and profit as a percentage of revenue by product lines. If exact figures are not available, they should be estimated.
   1.8 Key internal and external factors having a direct or indirect bearing on the business of the company. Usually, these areas require greater attention by management, and hence management requires more information on these areas. *External factors* include government regulations (such as the regulations of the Securities and Exchange Commission and the Federal Communications Commission), economic factors, and government policies. Shortage of raw materials, shortage of skilled labor, stiff competition, price regulations, extent of market demand, and government import policy are examples of external factors affecting the business. *Internal factors* include the type and location of production facilities, production capacity, availability of technical know-how, marketing strength, and so on.

Note the favorable or adverse impact of these factors in each of the following areas and the consequent business decisions which may require cost information:

Production (When production capacity is limited, for example, there may be a need to decide whether to make or buy a part.)

Sales

Product pricing (When product prices are regulated by a government agency, for example, the basis of computing product costs used by the agency should be understood.)

Direct materials

Labor

Other costs

Working capital

**EXHIBIT 3-1**

**Checklist of Background Information Required for Designing a Cost System (*Continued*)**

Long-term funds
Plant and equipment
Inventory
Distribution
Profit
Accounting and record keeping
Reporting

1.9 Corporate objectives, policies, and plans, to the extent that these are relevant to the system design project. For example, if it is the company's policy to treat individual product lines and individual geographical branches as separate profit centers, that information is relevant for establishing the necessary profit centers and cost centers.

2. *Manufacturing Cost Systems (Direct Materials, Direct Labor, and Manufacturing Overhead Cost Systems)*
   2.1 Manufacturing organization structure. Is it functional, geographical, or organized along product lines?
   2.2 Physical layout of production facilities, description of production processes employed by the concern, length of the production cycle, and sequence of physical flow of materials starting with materials receiving at the factory gate and ending with transfer of finished goods to the warehouse or the packing department. Note the departments through which materials flow and the operations performed in each of the concerned departments. Prepare a flowchart for better understanding.
   2.3 List of service departments, such as maintenance, production planning, etc., and their activities.
   2.4 List of direct materials and components used for each product together with the classification of items into those manufactured in the company and those bought outside. In some companies, the number of items can run into hundreds or thousands, in which case a list of the major items should be obtained.
   2.5 Is any material bought for resale, wholly or partly? This information is necessary to charge part of the purchasing and handling overhead to the material bought for resale and also to segregate it from the materials used for production. Similarly, note separately any own-manufactured material which is consumed for production and also is sold outside.
   2.6 Obtain or prepare a list of the total value of each item of material consumed during the most recent year so as to identify the high-value items.
   2.7 Obtain a present classification, if available, of materials into direct and indirect materials.

**EXHIBIT 3-1**

**Checklist of Background Information Required for Designing a Cost System (*Continued*)**

2.8 Obtain a list of materials recovered during production or materials having significant scrap, waste, etc.

2.9 Obtain or prepare a table showing the number of workers in each production and service center. If a production department has more than one identifiable operation, obtain a breakdown of workers by each operation.

2.10 Obtain the classification, if any, of the workers in each department into supervisors, clerks, direct workers, and indirect workers, and incorporate the classification in the above-mentioned table.

2.11 List the operations performed by direct and indirect workers in each department.

2.12 Ascertain the types of wage systems (e.g., time-rated system, piece-rated system, incentive plan) for regular and overtime work adopted by the concern. In particular, inquire whether different systems are adopted for *different types of workers* in different departments or even in the same department.

2.13 Ascertain the elements of labor-related costs, e.g., regular-time pay, overtime pay, piece-rated pay, bonus, payroll taxes, and fringe benefits.

2.14 Study the manufacturing overhead cost incurred by the company, particularly in the following respects:

- Total manufacturing overhead costs in dollar amount and as a percentage of the total cost of production
- Composition of the manufacturing overhead costs by cost factors, departments, products, regions, etc., to the extent that this information is available
- Purpose of each major expense
- Present policies and procedures for incurrence of and control over various manufacturing overhead costs

2.15 Bases for valuation of inventory of direct materials, work in process, and finished products.

2.16 Thoroughly examine various functional systems (purchasing, receiving, inspection, etc.) concerning direct materials, direct labor, and manufacturing overhead, and note for each of them the following aspects in particular:

- Departments involved, e.g., production planning and control, purchasing, receiving and handling, inspection, storekeeping, production, personnel, and other service departments.
- Functions performed by each department in relation to material, labor, and manufacturing overhead, e.g., preparing purchase requisitions, placing purchase orders, receiving materials, hiring, preparing payroll, and distributing wages.

**EXHIBIT 3-1**

**Checklist of Background Information Required for Designing a Cost System *(Continued)***

- Operating controls, e.g., material control, scrap control, and labor control, in force.
- Functional procedures relating to material, labor, and overhead for preparing purchase requisitions, placing purchase orders, timekeeping, etc. Prepare a flowchart, which may be combined with the flowchart of the physical movement of materials.
- Note the documents and the records prepared in each department for each physical movement of material, for each labor operation, for each functional procedure, and for each operating control. The notations may be made on the flowchart itself. Obtain a specimen copy of each document (or a complete set, if multiple copies are prepared). Note also the purpose, procedure, and time of preparation and distribution or routing of each type of document to other departments.
- Volume of each type of transaction, e.g., number of purchase orders, material requisitions, and so on.

As mentioned before, during the preliminary survey only a broad view of the concern's operations may be obtained and the relevant aspects may be studied in depth while the cost system is being designed.

The major reasons for studying various functional systems are as follows:

- A cost accounting system does not exist in a vacuum; rather, it must be an integral part of various functional systems within the company, such as production, purchasing, storekeeping, payroll, and marketing. Hence, the designer should thoroughly understand the various operations of the company and their interrelations.
- A sound cost accounting system requires sound functional systems. For example, a weak material issue procedure may result in incorrect material cost allocation to various production orders or products. After reviewing various functional systems operating within the concern, the designer will be in a position to recommend changes in those systems, which changes may be necessary for a sound cost accounting system.
- Many of the documents used for various functional systems may also be useful for the cost accounting system. For better internal control and lower clerical costs, those documents should be used also for cost record keeping to the extent possible.

**EXHIBIT 3-1**

**Checklist of Background Information Required for Designing a Cost System (*Continued*)**

3. *Marketing Cost System*

3.1 Understand the company's marketing function, particularly in terms of:

- Products sold and their variety, e.g., various brands or models, different packaging, sizes, and the like. Group the products in suitable categories whenever appropriate.
- Customers served, classified in some logical manner, e.g., as government, industrial, and others, according to the number of orders placed per month, or by size of the individual orders placed.
- Territories served and their groupings, if any.
- Marketing organization. Is it functional, territorial, or organized along product lines, customer types, or some other facet of the marketing function?
- Sales channels, e.g., distributors, retailers, mail order, direct, and so on.
- Methods of solicitation, e.g., by telephone, through sales representatives, by mail, etc.
- Marketing policies relating to pricing, terms of sale (cash or credit), period of credit, discounts, returns, and allowances, to name a few.
- Size of orders by products, territories, sales channels, customers, distribution channels, credit terms, etc. Only relevant and significant correlations should be studied.
- Channels of distribution employed, e.g., own transportation, outside trucking company, rail, sea, or air.
- Volume and amount of sales returns, allowances, and discounts allowed, classified by products, territories, or any other marketing aspect.

All the above information may not be applicable or *relevant* in every case. Second, all the requisite quantitative data may not be readily available because of the absence of a cost accounting system. In the latter case, an attempt should be made to obtain approximate figures.

3.2 Examine the present marketing functional systems (e.g., warehousing, order getting, distribution, billing, collection) and note, in particular, the following:

- Procedures employed
- Documents and records prepared or used (e.g., sales orders, dispatch orders, delivery notes, sales invoices, sales order register, delivery register)

**EXHIBIT 3-1**

**Checklist of Background Information Required for Designing a Cost System (*Continued*)**

- Controls instituted and their effectiveness
- Positions and personnel involved and their authority-responsibility

3.3 Study the marketing expenses incurred by the company, with special attention to the following:

- Nature and purpose of each type of expense
- Present policies on the incurrence and control of marketing expenses, whether marketing expense budget is prepared, basis on which traveling expenses are reimbursed to sales representatives, and so on

4. *General and Administrative Expenses*

4.1 Various administrative and general departments of the company and their activities.

4.2 Kind and amount of costs incurred by each of the major administrative departments.

4.3 Present policies and procedures for incurrence and control of various administrative costs.

5. *Existing Accounting and Reporting Systems*

5.1 Chart of accounts, account codes, and accounting manual, if available; otherwise, the latest trial balance.

5.2 List of books of account, registers, and memorandum records maintained for the concern as a whole and for its individual segments. Note, in particular, the extent of centralization or decentralization of the accounting system.

5.3 Financial and nonfinancial reports prepared, with details on by whom prepared, purpose of preparation, frequency of preparation, distribution, etc.

5.4 Specimen copies of accounting documents, forms, and reports used.

5.5 Type of accounting machines and computer used for record keeping and report preparation.

5.6 Existing cost accounting system, if any.

6. *Future Business Environments*

Note all known or predictable future business environments which may influence the design of the costing system, for example:

- Expansion, diversification, or divestment plans
- Pending regulations concerning cost accounting information to be provided
- If, for the present, the system is to be manual, whether mechanization or automation of accounting applications in the near future is contemplated

Consideration of the impact of impending events on the cost system will avoid the need for undue revisions in the system.

system might not have kept pace with the change in the status of the engineering division. Consequently, the consultant focused his attention on the evolution in various aspects of the division. He found that problems were not confined to the accounting system but also were present in all aspects of management of that division. For example, the engineering division continued to be regarded as a part of the textile division and continued to provide repairs and maintenance services to other divisions. There was not much change in the attitude of the managerial personnel of the engineering division, materials and labor required for production and repairs were not distinguished, and so on. The organization structure and the accounting system had not been developed systematically but only as a patchwork of various pieces, some connecting with others, some overlapping, some duplicating, and many working at cross-purposes. From these facts, the designer realized that a mere redesign of the accounting system would not improve the situation until the root cause of the problem was also removed. He therefore strongly recommended that while the new system was being designed, the engineering division be given a face-lift by making it a self-contained operating unit and a profit center and by staffing it appropriately. Had the consultant not discovered the root cause of the problem by studying the growth of the engineering division, he would have given it only a symptomatic treatment, which perhaps would not have solved the problem to any significant extent.

## Additional Background Information to Be Gathered in the Case of a Computerized Cost System

Irrespective of whether a cost system is to be manual or computerized, the background information listed in Exhibit 3-1 is necessary. However, in the case of a computerized cost system, the following additional information will be needed:

1. Does the organization use a computer in any of its current operations, and if so, what is the specific role of the computer? If the organization has found a computer useful even for a nonaccounting application, it will be comparatively easy to sell the use of a computer for a cost system. If the computer is being used for accounting applications, the types of accounting records maintained on the computer and the types of accounting reports generated by the computer should also be ascertained.

2. The kind and capability of the computer equipment and the peripheral equipment. Often it is advisable to build around what exists. In any case, the starting point is the present system.

3. The present unused capacity of the computer and the peripheral equipment and the potential for expansion of their capacity.

4. The attitude of personnel toward the role of a computer in managing the business. The employees' understanding of the computer's capability determines the degree of sophistication of the cost system that can be adopted at the present time.

## SOURCES OF BACKGROUND INFORMATION

From the list of background information required for design and implementation of a cost system, it is apparent that this information will not be available in a readily recognizable form and that it will be necessary to gather it from various sources. These sources may be grouped under the headings of company personnel, internal records and publications, and external publications. Company personnel constitute the most important source of information. The major sources of information falling under each of the other two headings are listed below:

*Internal Records and Publications*

1. Manual of company's goals, policies, and procedures
2. Annual reports to stockholders, Securities and Exchange Commission, etc., for the past few years
3. Chairman's speeches
4. Organization charts and authority-responsibility manual
5. Catalog of products sold by the company
6. Flowcharts of production processes
7. Accounting and other records, and management reports
8. Chart of accounts and accounting manual, if any
9. Reports of internal auditors
10. Bill of materials or product formula sheets
11. Marketing literature describing products, services, etc.

*External Records and Publications*

1. Industry and trade publications
2. Moody's *Industrial Manual,* Standard & Poor's *Standard Corporation Descriptions,* and the like
3. Uniform system of accounts prescribed by law or recommended by the industry association, e.g., the uniform system of accounts prescribed by the Federal Communications Commission for wire-line communications companies in the United States or the cost accounting records rules prescribed for cement, sugar, bicycle, and other industries in India

4. Accounting systems and procedures suggested for the concerned industry in an encyclopedia or handbook of accounting systems

## HOW SHOULD A FACT-FINDING SURVEY BE CONDUCTED?

Having defined what background information should be gathered and the possible sources for it, the designer should next decide how to gather it. The methods commonly employed for this purpose are as follows:

- *Interviewing,* i.e., seeking information by discussions with the appropriate personnel in the organization
- *Questionnaire,* i.e., preparing a questionnaire soliciting the pertinent information and sending it to the relevant personnel in the organization
- *Self-study,* i.e., reading, examining, observing, or researching the available records, documents, publications, facilities, operations, etc.

The selection among these alternatives should be made with regard to the characteristics of the organization and its personnel as well as the nature of the information required and the merits and demerits of each method. In gathering background information, an outside consultant can expect greater assistance from company personnel than can an in-house designer.

The following summary of the merits and demerits of each method will serve as a checklist for the designer:

**Clarity of Communication** If the questions or answers are not clear, the party to an interview can always ask supplementary questions or repeat the questions or answers. Facial expressions, gestures, etc., also help in making communication clear. On the other hand, in the case of the questionnaire method, written questions may not be clear, and the prospect may have to refer them back to the designer. If the prospect misunderstands the question, he may furnish an inaccurate or misleading answer. In such a case, the designer may have to return to the prospect; otherwise the picture may be misleading.

**Ease of Remembering** Information collected during an interview may not be remembered completely even though notes of major points have been made. Also, the designer cannot replay the interview. On the other hand, in the case of the questionnaire method, the designer need not remember the replies, as he can refer to them as often as he wishes.

**Time Factor** Compared with the questionnaire method, the interview method demands more time of the designer and less time of management. Overall, it may take less time because normally interviews can be obtained more rapidly than written replies. Self-study, on the other hand, requires maximum time of the designer and saves the time of management.

**Cost Considerations** When many persons are to be interviewed or when the persons to be interviewed are located at different places, the questionnaire method will be less expensive than the interview method.

**Other Factors** The questionnaire method is regarded as more formal than the interview method. People are, therefore, normally reluctant to furnish replies in writing and may never disclose certain information in writing. Many valuable comments, suggestions, etc., can be obtained during an oral discussion. Further, persons such as the president of the company may not have time to furnish written replies.

## The Best Approach

In practice, some combination of the three methods is used. The best approach will more or less be as described below:

1. To start with, the designer should discuss the subject with a person who is acting as a liaison person or who is well versed with the problem. Normally, that person will be the controller or the controller's assistant.
2. On the basis of the discussion with the liaison person and his own knowledge, the designer should draw up a list of possible sources of collecting the background information.
3. The designer should collect as much information as possible by self-study. The questionnaire and the interviewing methods should be used only as supplemental to the self-study method. In almost all cases, however, interviewing is inevitable, but the questionnaire method may not be necessary.
4. Then, the designer should prepare a list of the rest of the information to be collected by issuing a questionnaire or by conducting interviews. Usually, it is preferable to have a personal (group or individual) discussion before sending out a questionnaire so as to establish the ground for mutual trust and understanding. In fact, both methods could be combined; i.e., instead of asking company personnel to fill out the questionnaire, the designer may do so during the personal discussion.
5. Since the objective at this stage is to collect broad-based information and not details, it is a good plan first to interview department heads, who usually have a broader perspective of the business, and later approach their assistants for details, if necessary.
6. If the questionnaire method is selected as one of the methods for data gathering, it should be followed up with personal discussions

whenever necessary either to collect supplementary information or to clarify replies.

### Some Dos and Don'ts

Collecting information through a questionnaire and interviews requires considerable skill and tact, the discussion of which is beyond the scope of this book. However, a few useful dos and don'ts are given below:

- Generally, ask open-ended questions instead of yes - no types of questions so as to get complete and unbiased replies.
- Interview all concerned persons even if the same questions must be repeated because multiple sources of information validate the information collected.
- Distinguish between facts and opinion.
- Remember that one of the objectives of the interview is to secure cooperation from those who must use and run the system. When those people feel that their views have been taken into account, their cooperation flows readily. Hence, whenever possible, ask for their suggestions, opinions, views, etc.
- The questionnaire must be sent out with a covering letter signed by a fairly senior person, preferably one who is higher in rank than the persons to whom it is sent.

### A Specimen Questionnaire

A specimen questionnaire for gathering the background information for the design of a cost system, adapted from the very effective actual questionnaire used by the author, is given in Exhibit 3-2. This questionnaire can be used for obtaining written replies as well as for interviews.

## DOCUMENT BACKGROUND INFORMATION

Background information is the foundation for the design and implementation of a cost system. It will be necessary to refer to this information several times during the system design and implementation phases of the system life cycle. During the implementation phase, it will be necessary to refer to this information to provide explanations or justifications for various aspects of the proposed system. Proper documentation of the background information will also help the task of modifying or improving the system in the future. Thus, proper documentation of the background information is essential.

**EXHIBIT 3-2**

**Specimen Questionnaire for Gathering Background Information**

Memo to
From
Subject Development of Cost Information and Control System

As announced by ( name ) in his (her) memorandum of ( date ), the Controller's Department has undertaken the project of developing a cost information and control system. This project has been undertaken to satisfy several requirements for various types of cost information and for exercising control over costs. This will be a companywide system and is intended to provide the cost information and controls required for every cost element by every department throughout the company.

Your department has a significant role in this system. Therefore, we will need your and your department's assistance and cooperation in (1) gathering certain basic data relating to your department and (2) determining your expectations of the system. For this purpose a *questionnaire,* two copies of which are enclosed herewith, has been prepared.

You will appreciate that since this is going to be a companywide system, we will be involved in discussions with a number of persons and departments in the company. We want to ensure that your requirements and views are properly understood and not overlooked. Hence, please submit the information requested in writing on the enclosed questionnaire. There is a separate page for each question. If the space below each question is not sufficient for your answer, please use a separate sheet of paper.

In case you need clarification on any question, please feel free to call ( name ) at Extension _____.

Upon receiving your replies to the questionnaire, we plan to meet with you for a discussion. However, if after reading through the questionnaire, you would like to discuss it in its entirety, we will be glad to do so.

We would appreciate it if you could submit your replies to the questionnaire by ( month and date ).

(Signature)

*Enclosures*

Questionnaire

(In actual practice, each question should be typed on a separate page so that the respondent can reply below each question itself.)

1. What are the various *functions,* operations, or duties performed within your department for which costs are incurred or cost information is required? Please indicate separately the *decision-making areas* (for example, whether to repair or replace a piece of equipment) and the key areas or functions for which *perfor-*

**EXHIBIT 3-2**

**Specimen Questionnaire for Gathering Background Information (*Continued*)**

*mance measurement* and *control* are necessary (for example, direct labor cost control, control over consumption of direct materials, etc.).

2. Please list in sufficient detail the *steps* involved in performing each of the above functions and their *sequence*.

3. Please list in detail the *items of information* that your department needs from time to time in order to carry out effectively each of the above functions or to make the above decisions or to measure, review, and control performance. Please also specify the *purpose* for which and the *frequency* at which each item or group of items of information may be needed. Also, state whether the information is available from within your department or from outside the department, and if the latter, please specify its source. Preferably, give this information in the attached table (Annex A) or in any other suitable tabular form.

4. Provide details regarding *documents* (external or internal) and *records* prepared or used by your department in the attached Annex B following the instructions for preparing it. Please attach a specimen copy of each of the documents and records prepared by your department.

5. Are there any *written instructions,* procedures, or guidelines in respect of any of the above items? If so, please attach a copy thereof.

6. (where appropriate) In your opinion, is the *present system* inadequate or defective, or does it need revision or improvement in respect of:

*a.* Procedures involved
*b.* Documentation, recording, and reporting
*c.* Information supplied
*d.* Controls provided
*e.* Any other aspect

If so, please explain in detail.

7. The *objectives* of the proposed cost system, as visualized by us, from the viewpoint of the company as a whole, are listed below. Please state whether and in what respect the list should be modified.

Objectives of the Proposed Cost System

*a.* Internal requirements
   i. To provide a data base for profit planning and operating budgeting
   ii. To provide information needed for managerial decisions, such as
      ■ Make or buy a component
      ■ Special order pricing
   iii. To provide a system for exercising control over cost throughout the company

*b.* External requirements
   i. For valuation of inventory for income determination
   ii. To comply with the segment reporting requirements prescribed by Financial Accounting Standards Board Statement No. 14
   iii. Income tax substantiation

**EXHIBIT 3-2**

**Specimen Questionnaire for Gathering Background Information** ***(Continued)***

8. Please also give any additional information, comments, suggestions, or opinions, whether or not pertaining to your department, which in your opinion may be relevant or useful to this project.

Annex A

Cost Information Required (see Question 3)

Department

| Information required (1) | Purpose (2) | Required by (title) (3) | Frequency (4) | When required (5) | Present source document, record (if known) (6) | Presently prepared by (if known) (7) | Title of report, if any (8) |
|---|---|---|---|---|---|---|---|
| 1. | | | | | | | |
| 2. | | | | | | | |
| . . . | | | | | | | |
| 18. | | | | | | | |
| 19. | | | | | | | |
| 20. | | | | | | | |

Annex B
Page 1 of 2

Details of Document or Record Prepared (see Question 4)

(See instructions on the back of this form)

1. Title
2. Sequence no.
3. Department
4. Prepared by
5. Approved by
6. When prepared
7. Number of copies
8. Volume per year
9. Purpose(s) of the document or record (if necessary, continue on the back)

10. Sources of information

11. Distribution or routing

| Copy No. | Distributed or Routed to Department or person | Basic Purpose |
|---|---|---|

12. Remarks, if any

**EXHIBIT 3-2**

**Specimen Questionnaire for Gathering Background Information (*Continued*)**

Annex B
Page 2 of 2

Instructions for Filling "Details of Document or Record Prepared"

| Item No. | Instructions |
|---|---|
| General | Use a separate page for each document or record. |
| 1 | Name of the document or record. |
| 2 | Leave blank. |
| 3 | Name of the originating department. |
| 4 | Name of the person preparing it. |
| 5 | Fill out where applicable. |
| 6 | Daily, weekly, monthly, as and when necessary, etc. |
| 7 | Please attach a complete set of the document and a specimen page of the record. |
| 8 | Number of documents prepared. Leave blank in case of a record. |
| 9 | Uses made of document or record by your or other departments (if covered by item 11, say so). |
| 10 | Documents, record, or file from which the source information is obtained in preparing it. (Alternatively this may be indicated on the specimen document or record itself.) |
| 11 | Explain the basic purpose of sending it to each person or department. |
| 12 | Please insert here any suggestions, comments, or additional information which you may wish to furnish. |

In addition to background information, a system analysis documentation should also cover the following:

- Scope of assignment
- System objectives
- Specific information needs

The information should be suitably classified and arranged. It should then be documented in the form of notes, organization charts, flowcharts, tables, matrices, specimen documents, etc. In particular, matrices are very helpful for proper understanding of the relationship among, say, marketing expenses, marketing activities, marketing organization, and marketing methods.

**EXHIBIT 3-3**

**Partial Organization Chart of ACME Company**

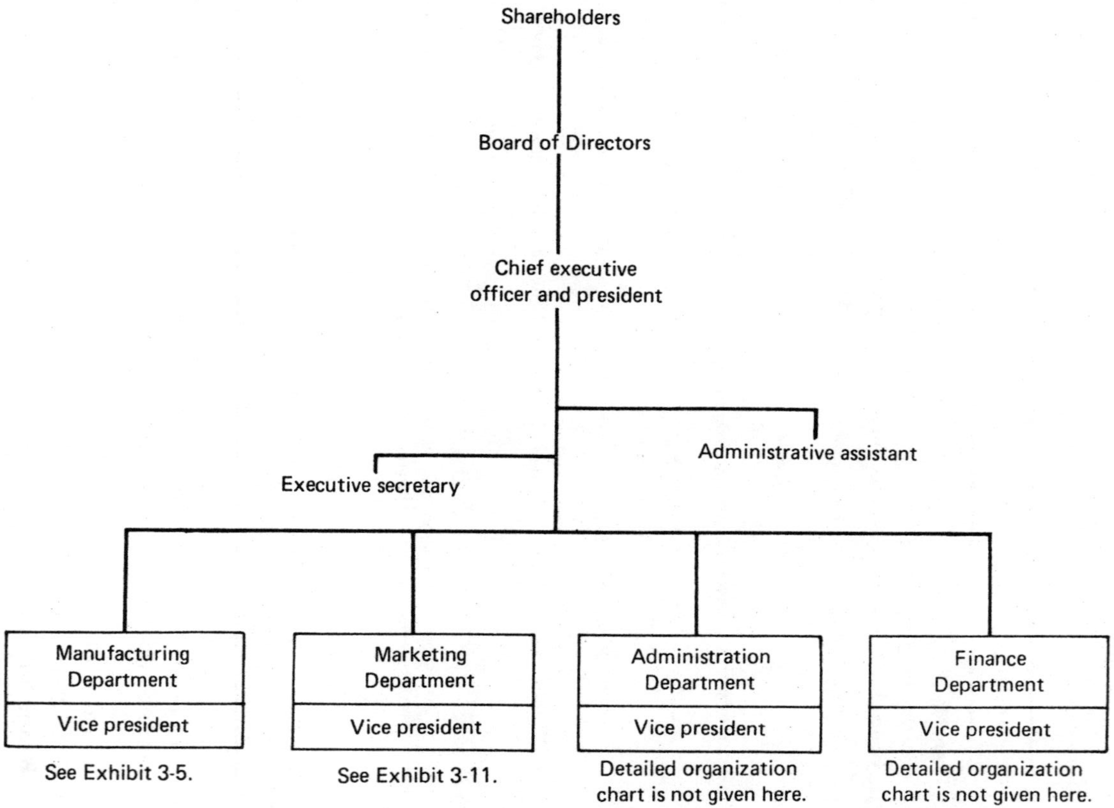

## Case Example

An example of how to document the relevant background information required for designing a cost system is given below. Though the illustration covers all the major aspects, it is not exhaustive. This case study is a part of the continuing case study of a *hypothetical* ACME Company used throughout the book.

1. *Information Common to the Entire Cost System*
   1.1 Company's name: ACME Company, Inc.
   1.2 History: Established in 1970.
   1.3 Line of business: Manufacturing and selling products X and Y, which are used by automotive, aerospace, and other industries as components for their products. Both products are of standard specifications and are manufactured for inventory. Only occasionally does the company receive orders for product X with different specifications.
   1.4 Industry background: Competition is stiff from both domestic and foreign manufacturers. ACME Company has about 25 percent of the domestic market share. The company does not sell any part of its production in the foreign market. Two other large domestic manufacturers control respectively 15 and 10 percent of the domestic market. Three large foreign suppliers control about 10 to 15 percent of the domestic market. The remaining 35 to 40 percent of the domestic market is shared by some twenty-five domestic and foreign manufacturers.
   1.5 Organization chart of ACME Company is given in Exhibit 3-3 (only a partial organization chart is given here).
   1.6 Profit centers: There is only one profit center, ACME Company as a whole.
   1.7 Geographic locations of operation:

      Production: Plant in New York
      Sales: Two regional offices, Memphis and New York
      Warehousing and distribution: The products are warehoused and distributed from the two distribution centers, Memphis and New York.
      Corporate and administrative offices: New York

   1.8 Revenue, cost, and profit structures for the last completed year; i.e., the year 1979 is given in Exhibit 3-4.

2. *Production and Production Costs*
   2.1 The organization chart of the manufacturing department of ACME Company along with the title of the person responsible for each organizational segment is given in Exhibit 3-5. The pur-

*(Text continues on page 64)*

**EXHIBIT 3-4**

**Revenue, Cost, and Profit Structure of ACME Company**

Revenue, Profits before Tax, and Sales Units ($ in millions)

| | 1979 | | | 1978 | | | 1977 | | |
|---|---|---|---|---|---|---|---|---|---|
| | Revenue | Profit | Units | Revenue | Profit | Units | Revenue | Profit | Units |
| Product X | $5.1 | | 21,000 | $4.45 | | 18,200 | $3.95 | | 16,500 |
| Product Y | 3.4 | | 13,700 | 2.80 | | 12,000 | 2.55 | | 10,500 |
| Total | $8.5 | $0.82 | 34,700 | $7.25 | $0.70 | 30,200 | $6.50 | $0.62 | 27,000 |

1979 Cost and Profit Structure

| | $000 | Percent of Total Revenue |
|---|---|---|
| Direct materials | $2000 | 24 |
| Direct labor | 1300 | 15 |
| Manufacturing overhead costs | 1886 | 22 |
| Total manufacturing costs | 5186 | 61 |
| Decrease in finished goods and work-in-process inventories | (100) | (1) |
| Warehousing and distribution | 1440 | 16 |
| Selling | 400 | 5 |
| Advertising | 210 | 3 |
| Total marketing costs | 2050 | 24 |
| General and administrative costs | 540 | 6 |
| Total costs | 7676 | 90 |
| Pretax operating income | 824 | 10 |
| Total revenue | $8500 | 100 |

**EXHIBIT 3-5**

**Manufacturing Organization Chart of ACME Company**

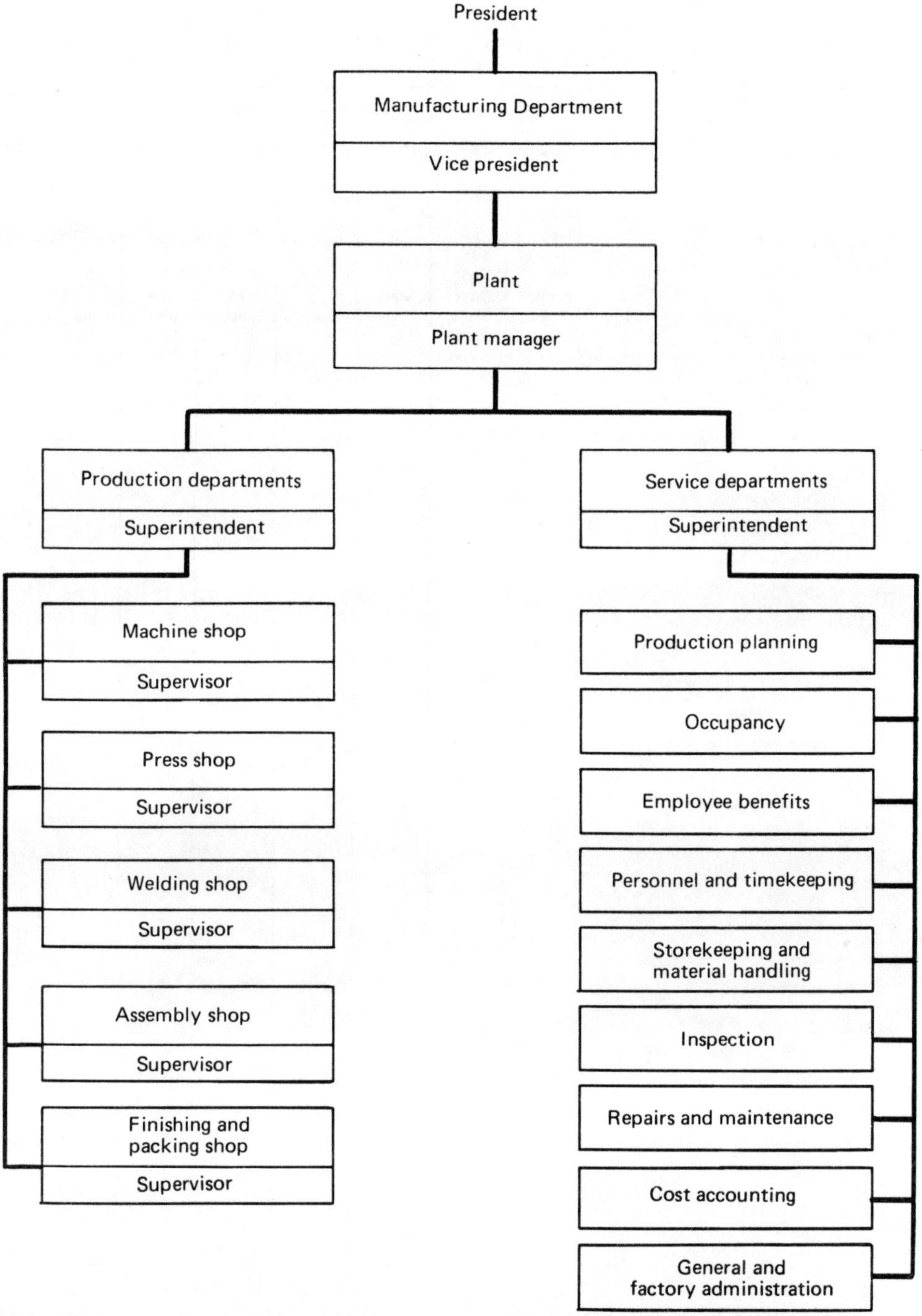

**EXHIBIT 3-6**

## Manufacturing Resource-Expense Matrix

As of April 8, 1980

| Resources or Expense | | Office of Vice President, Manufacturing, and Plant Manager | Production Departments | | | | | |
|---|---|---|---|---|---|---|---|---|
| | | | Production Superintendent | Machine Shop | Press Shop | Welding Shop | Assembly Shop | Finishing and Packing Shop |
| *A. Plant, equipment, etc.* | | | | | | | | |
| 1. Building | | X | X | X | X | X | X | X |
| 2. Each type or group of equipment: | | | | | | | | |
| Lathes | | | | X | | | | |
| Drill presses | | | | | X | | | |
| Milling machines | | | | X | | | | |
| Benches | | | | X | | X | X | X |
| ... | | | | | | | | |
| ... | | | | | | | | |
| ... | | | | | | | | |
| 3. Furniture and fixtures | | X | X | X | X | X | X | X |
| *B. Personnel* (number) | | | | | | | | |
| 1. Management and clerical | (27) | 5 | 2 | 1 | 1 | 1 | 2 | 1 |
| 2. Direct labor | (140) | | | 38 | 12 | 29 | 46 | 15 |
| 3. Indirect labor | (11) | | | | | | | |
| *C. Expenses incurred* | | | | | | | | |
| 1. Direct materials | | | | X | X | X | X | X |
| 2. Supplies | | | | X | X | X | X | X |
| 3. Tools | | | | X | X | X | X | X |
| 4. Direct labor | | | | X | X | X | X | X |
| 5. Indirect labor | | | | X | X | X | X | X |
| 6. Occupancy expenses | | X | X | X | X | X | X | X |
| 7. Repairs and maintenance | | | | X | X | X | X | X |
| 8. Electricity and fuel | | X | X | X | X | X | X | X |
| 9. Other utilities | | | | X | X | X | X | X |
| 10. Insurance | | | | X | X | X | X | X |
| 11. Depreciation | | X | X | X | X | X | X | X |
| 12. Salaries | | X | X | X | X | X | X | X |
| 13. Others | | X | X | X | X | X | X | X |

| Service Departments & Objective Expense Accounts | | | | | | | | | | |
|---|---|---|---|---|---|---|---|---|---|---|
| Service Superintendent | Production Planning | Building | Personnel and Timekeeping | Employee Benefits | Inspection | Storekeeping and Material Handling | Utilities | Repairs and Maintenance | Cost Accounting | General Factory Expenses |
| X | X | X | X | | X | X | | X | X | X |
| X | X | X | X | | X | X | | X | X | X |
| 2 | 2 | | 3 | | 3 | 1 | | 1 | 2 | |
| | | 2 | | | | 2 | | 7 | | |
| | | X | | | X | X | X | X | | |
| | | X | | | X | | | X | | |
| | | X | | | | X | | X | | |
| X | X | X | X | | X | X | | X | X | X |
| | | X | | | | | | | | X |
| X | X | X | X | | X | X | X | X | X | X |
| | | X | | | | | X | X | | |
| | | X | | | | X | | X | | |
| X | X | X | X | | X | X | | X | X | X |
| X | X | | X | | X | X | | X | X | |
| X | X | X | X | X | X | X | | X | X | X |

**EXHIBIT 3-7**

**Breakdown of Direct Material Cost of ACME Company, 1979**

| | Product X | | Product Y | |
|---|---|---|---|---|
| Material Consumed | $000 | Percent | $000 | Percent |
| A | $ 408 | 30 | $224 | 35 |
| B | 680 | 50 | 128 | 20 |
| C | ... | .. | 160 | 25 |
| Other materials | 272 | 20 | 128 | 20 |
| Total direct material cost | $1360 | 100 | $640 | 100 |

NOTE: In the absence of adequate cost records, this breakdown is compiled from various analyses and estimates.

**EXHIBIT 3-8**

**Breakdown of Direct Labor Cost of ACME Company, 1979**

| | Product X | | Product Y | |
|---|---|---|---|---|
| Production Departments | $000 | Percent | $000 | Percent |
| Machine shop | $261 | 30 | $108 | 25 |
| Welding shop | 174 | 20 | 86 | 20 |
| Assembly shop | 304 | 35 | 172 | 40 |
| Other shops | 131 | 15 | 64 | 15 |
| Total direct labor cost | $870 | 100 | $430 | 100 |

NOTE: In the absence of adequate cost records, this breakdown is compiled from various analyses and estimates.

**EXHIBIT 3-9**

**Material Flowchart of ACME Company**

| Activity or Transaction | Document Prepared or Used | Elapsed Time | |
|---|---|---|---|
| 1. Receipt of materials from vendors at factory gate | Delivery note from vendors | | |
| 2. Weighing or counting of materials at factory gate | Material received notes by gatekeeper<br>Copy 1: vendor<br>Copy 2: storeroom<br>Copy 3: accounts payable<br>Copy 4: gatekeeper | Same day | |
| 3. Interim storage in storeroom; kept aside for inspection | | 3–8 days | |
| 4. Inspection by Inspection Department | Inspection report on storeroom's copy of material received note | | |
| 5. Materials transferred to regular storage area or returned to vendor | | Q: How is accounts payable informed about material returned? | |
| 6. Issue of material to Production Department | Material requisition | Inventory equal to 60 days' consumption is maintained. | |
| 7. Production | | | |
| Production processes: | | Product X: | Product Y: |
| Machine shop | | 3 days | 2 days |
| Press shop | | 2 days | 2 days |
| Welding shop | | 2–10 days | 3–10 days* |
| Assembly shop | | 4–8 days | 3–6 days* |
| Paint shop | | 4 days | 4 days |
| Finishing, Testing, and Packing shop | | 3 days | 3 days |
| | | 18–30 days | 17–27 days |
| 8. Finished goods warehousing and packing | Finished goods receipt memorandum and packing slip | 8 days | |
| 9. Sent to distribution centers and storage at centers | Delivery memorandum (distribution centers) | Inventory equal to 30 days' sale | |
| 10. Dispatch to customers | Sales order and delivery note | 2 days | |
| Total material cycle | | Product X: 121 to 138 days<br>Product Y: 120 to 135 days | |

* Bottleneck due to capacity imbalance.

**EXHIBIT 3-10**

**Breakdown of Manufacturing Overhead Cost (ACME Company)**

| | $000 | Percent |
|---|---|---|
| Supervisory and clerical salaries | $388 | 20.6 |
| Indirect labor | 71 | 3.8 |
| Costs related to direct labor | 78 | 4.1 |
| Employee benefits costs | 520 | 27.6 |
| Indirect materials | 213 | 11.3 |
| Depreciation | 261 | 13.8 |
| Repairs and maintenance | 102 | 5.4 |
| Power, heat, and light | 121 | 6.4 |
| Insurance | 40 | 2.1 |
| Property taxes | 21 | 1.1 |
| Miscellaneous | 71 | 3.8 |
| Total manufacturing overhead cost | $1886 | 100 |

chasing officer reports to the vice president, administration, and not to the vice president, manufacturing.

2.2 The manufacturing resource-expense matrix given in Exhibit 3-6 identifies fixed assets, personnel, and expense items concerning the manufacturing plant with various segments of the manufacturing organization. To denote the type of resources utilized by each department and to indicate the kind of expenses incurred by each department, an *X* is placed in the appropriate column-row of the matrix. (NOTE: In actual practice, if necessary, each department may be divided into two columns or each expense item into two rows to show whether the expense is fixed or variable, or both.)

2.3 Direct materials used: ACME Company consumes ten materials, of which materials A, B, and C are the major materials. See Exhibit 3-7 for a breakdown of direct material costs for products X and Y.

2.4 Indirect materials used: As per list (not attached here).

2.5 Direct labor: See Exhibit 3-8 for a breakdown of direct labor costs for products X and Y.

2.6 Physical layout: As per diagram (not attached here).

2.7 Material flowchart is given in Exhibit 3-9.

2.8 Manufacturing overhead costs: See Exhibit 3-10 for a breakdown of manufacturing overhead costs for 1979.

2.9 Basis for valuation of inventory: direct materials: first in, first out; work in process: full absorption costing, computed at yearly average costs; finished goods: full absorption costing, computed at yearly average costs.

3. *Marketing Costs*
   3.1 The marketing organization chart of ACME Company is given in Exhibit 3-11.
   3.2 The marketing resource-expense matrix given in Exhibit 3-12 identifies fixed assets, personnel, and expense items with various segments of the marketing organization. This matrix is prepared in the same manner as the manufacturing resource-expense matrix.
   3.3 Marketing costs: See Exhibit 3-13 for a breakdown of marketing costs for 1979.

**EXHIBIT 3-11**

**Partial Marketing Organization Chart of ACME Company**

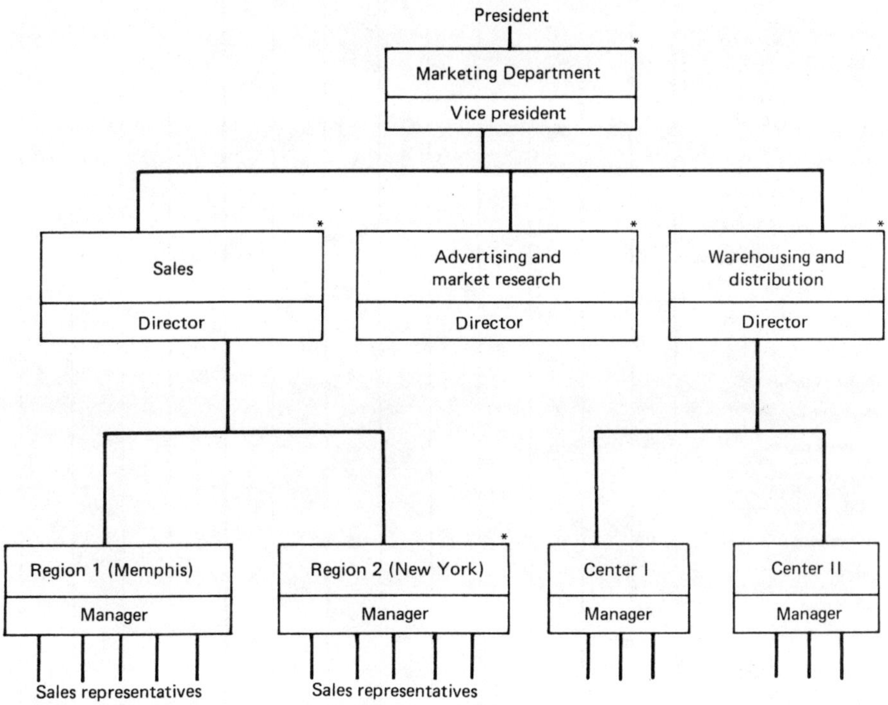


* Located in corporate office in New York.

**EXHIBIT 3-12**

**Marketing Cost Matrix: ACME Company**

| | Functional Departments, Regions, and Products | | | | | | | | | | | | |
|---|---|---|---|---|---|---|---|---|---|---|---|---|---|
| | Advertising and Market Research | | | | | | | | | Sales | | | |
| | R1 | | R2 | | Common | | | | | R1 | | R2 | |
| Cost Factors | Px | Py | Px | Py | Px | Py | R1 | R2 | C | Px | Py | Px | Py |
| Salaries, payroll taxes, and allowances | | | | | | | | | | | | | |
| Vice president | | | | | | | | | | | | | |
| Directors | | | | | | | | | X | | | | |
| Managers | | | | | | | | | | | | | |
| Supervisors | | | | | | | | | | | | | |
| Staff | | | | | | | | | X | | | | |
| Salespersons | | | | | | | | | | | | | |
| Truck drivers and helpers | | | | | | | | | | | | | |
| Others | | | | | | | | | X | | | | |
| Sales commission | | | | | | | | | | | | | |
| Managers | | | | | | | | | | | | | |
| Salespersons | | | | | | | | | | X | X | X | X |
| Newspaper advertisements | | | | | | | | | | | | | |
| Local | X | X | X | X | | | X | X | | | | | |
| National | | | | | X | X | X | X | X | | | | |
| Television advertisements | | | | | | | | | X | | | | |
| Radio advertisements | | | | | | | | | | | | | |
| Travel and entertainment | | | | | | | X | X | X | | | | |
| Warehouse rent | | | | | | | | | | | | | |
| Freight: outside trucks | | | | | | | | | | | | | |
| Freight: rail | | | | | | | | | | | | | |
| Trucking expenses | | | | | | | | | | | | | |
| Depreciation | | | | | | | | | X | | | | |
| Property taxes | | | | | | | | | X | | | | |
| Telephone | | | | | | | | | X | | | | |
| Postage and printing | | | | | | | | | X | | | | |
| Insurance | | | | | | | | | X | | | | |
| Office rent | | | | | | | | | X | | | | |
| Office supplies | | | | | | | | | X | | | | |
| Utilities | | | | | | | | | X | | | | |
| Miscellaneous expenses | | | | | | | | | X | | | | |

NOTE: R1 = Region 1; R2 = Region 2; PX = product X; PY = product Y; C = company as a whole; C1 = Center I; C2 = Center II.

Functional Departments, Regions, and Products

| Sales | | | | | Warehousing and Distribution | | | | | | | | | Office of Vice President, Marketing |
|---|---|---|---|---|---|---|---|---|---|---|---|---|---|---|
| Common | | | | | C1 | | C2 | | Common | | | | | |
| Px | Py | R1 | R2 | C | Px | Py | Px | Py | Px | Py | C1 | C2 | C | |
| | | | | | | | | | | | | | | X |
| | | | | X | | | | | | | | | X | |
| | | X | X | | | | | | | | X | X | | |
| | | | | | | | | | | | X | X | | |
| | | X | X | X | | | | | | | | | | X |
| | | X | X | | | | | | | | | | | |
| | | | | | | | | | | | X | X | | |
| | | | | | | | | | | | X | X | | |
| | | X | X | X | | | | | | | X | X | X | X |
| | | | | | | | | | | | | | | |
| | | X | X | | | | | | | | | | | |
| | | | | | | | | | | | | | | |
| | | | | | | | | | | | | | | |
| | | | | | | | | | | | | | | |
| | | | | | | | | | | | | | | |
| | | | | | | | | | | | | | | |
| | | | | | | | | | | | | | | |
| | | X | X | X | | | | | | | X | X | X | X |
| | | | | | X | X | X | X | | | X | X | | |
| | | | | | X | X | X | X | | | | | | |
| | | | | | X | X | X | X | | | | | | |
| | | | | | | | | | | | X | X | | |
| | | X | X | X | | | | | | | X | X | X | X |
| | | X | X | X | | | | | | | X | X | X | X |
| | | X | X | X | | | | | | | X | X | X | X |
| | | X | X | X | | | | | | | X | X | X | X |
| | | X | X | X | X | X | X | X | | | X | X | X | X |
| | | X | X | X | | | | | | | X | X | X | X |
| | | X | X | X | | | | | | | X | X | X | X |
| | | X | X | X | | | | | | | X | X | X | X |
| | | X | X | X | | | | | | | X | X | X | X |

**EXHIBIT 3-13**

**Marketing Costs: ACME Company (Combined for Products X and Y), 1979**

| | $000 | Percent |
|---|---|---|
| *Warehousing and distribution* | | |
| Salaries | $ 150 | 10.4 |
| Drivers' wages | 200 | 13.9 |
| Helpers' wages | 80 | 5.6 |
| Truck depreciation | 200 | 13.9 |
| Gas, oil, and tools | 40 | 2.8 |
| Repairs and maintenance | 150 | 10.4 |
| Vehicle and property taxes | 15 | 1.0 |
| Insurance | 40 | 2.8 |
| Freight: outside trucks | 200 | 13.9 |
| Freight: rail | 250 | 17.3 |
| Other | 115 | 8.0 |
| Subtotal | $1440 | 100 |
| *Selling expenses* | | |
| Salaries | $ 220 | 55.0 |
| Commission | 40 | 10.0 |
| Allowances | 15 | 3.8 |
| Traveling | 40 | 10.0 |
| Rent | 24 | 6.0 |
| Telephone | 30 | 7.5 |
| Other | 31 | 7.7 |
| Subtotal | $ 400 | 100 |
| *Advertising and marketing research* | | |
| Salaries | $ 50 | 23.8 |
| Media advertising | 50 | 71.4 |
| Rent | 10 | 4.8 |
| Subtotal | $ 210 | 100 |
| Total marketing costs | $2050 | |

3.4 Customers' composition for 1979:

| Customer Type | Number of Customers | Sales as Percentage of Total Revenue ($ in millions) Product X ($5.1) | Product Y ($3.4) | Total ($8.5) |
|---|---|---|---|---|
| Automotive | 30 | 50 | 40 | 47 |
| Aerospace | 20 | 24 | 30 | 26 |
| Leisure industry products | 15 | 10 | 20 | 13 |
| Other | 10 | 16 | 10 | 14 |
| Total | 75 | 100 | 100 | 100 |

3.5 Sales channel: Both products are sold through the company's own sales representatives. The sales organization chart is given in Exhibit 3-11.

3.6 Distribution channels: Own trucks, outside trucking company and rail, as may be appropriate.

4. *Administrative Costs*
Not given here for the sake of brevity.

5. *Existing Accounting and Reporting Systems*

5.1 Accounting system: Formal cost accounting system is not maintained. Cost data are compiled on a limited basis from general accounting records as and when needed.

5.2 Accounting and reporting are centralized in New York except that each office keeps petty cash records. Each office sends the relevant expense vouchers to New York.

5.3 Chart of accounts and accounting manual: None.

5.4 Books of account and other relevant records maintained:

| Financial Accounting Records | Other Records |
|---|---|
| General ledger | Production register |
| Accounts receivable ledger | Material cards at plant |
| Accounts payable ledger | Finished goods cards |
| Sales register | Finished goods cards by distribution centers |
| Purchase register | Memorandum cost records (these records are very brief and unsystematic) |
| Cash books (receipts and disbursements) | |
| Petty cash books (three) | |

5.5 Vouchers prepared (relevant to the cost system) and volume of major transactions are as follows:

| | 1979 | 1978 |
|---|---|---|
| Production orders | 22 | 20 |
| Purchase requisitions | 2500 | 2000 |
| Purchase orders | 2000 | 1800 |
| Goods receipt memoranda | 2300 | 2100 |
| Inspection reports | 2300 | 2100 |
| Material rejection memoranda | 200 | 150 |
| Material requisitions | 4000 | 3700 |
| Material return memoranda | 300 | 300 |
| Finished goods receipts (transfer to finished goods warehouse) | 520 | 600 |
| Finished goods packing slips | 1000 | 850 |
| Sales orders | 800 | 700 |
| Sales dispatch orders | 760 | 670 |
| Sales delivery slips | 650 | 600 |
| Shipment trips made by own trucks | 100 (8 trucks) | 70 (6 trucks) |
| Rail receipts (for shipment through railways) | 300 | 280 |
| Sales return memoranda | 50 | 45 |
| Sales invoices | 650 | 600 |

5.6 Financial and nonfinancial reports, etc., prepared:

Current month versus last month costs comparison report (the report lists expenses by nature without identifying them with organizational segments).

Capital budget

Balance sheet

Income statement

Production report (by products)

Sales report (by products)

Accounts receivable (by customers)

Unit product cost statement (by products on total cost basis from financial accounting and memorandum records)

5.7 Accounting machines used: None, but the company is contemplating using a minicomputer for payroll, accounts receivable, and general accounting. Later on, the computer may also be used for inventory control and cost accounting.

6. *General*

6.1 Key internal and external factors affecting ACME Company are:

- Stiff competition.
- Prices of materials A, B, and C fluctuate frequently and significantly.
- Consumption of material B per unit of finished product X as well as product Y varies from time to time.
- Supply of material A is erratic, and sometimes the company faces a hand-to-mouth situation.

# Chapter 4

# Determining Requirements of the Cost System

> Creative efforts can be made more goal-directed if they are properly disciplined.
>
> Pravin P. Shah

A cost system exists to satisfy certain predetermined objectives. To design an effective cost system to satisfy those objectives, the designer must have a clear-cut understanding of the requirements of the proposed system. Chapter 2 has dealt with the subject of defining system objectives. This chapter deals with the subject of determining system requirements for each objective.

## MEANING OF SYSTEM REQUIREMENTS

Determining requirements of the proposed cost system entails assessment, in specific terms, of what the system is expected to do to satisfy each of its objectives. For example, if a cost system is being designed for cost control, it is necessary to define, among other things, what cost information is required and by whom for effectively controlling costs. The emphasis during this phase is on *what* results the system must achieve and not on *how* those results are to be achieved. The latter part is considered during the system design phase. The simplified example given in Exhibit 4-1 will help clarify the meaning of the phrase *system requirements* as it applies to a cost control system.

The two obvious questions which arise are:

- What are the different elements of requirements of a cost system?
- How should the requirements of a cost system be determined?

**EXHIBIT 4-1**

**Illustration of Requirements of a Cost System**

Objective of the Proposed Cost System

To provide information for controlling the cost of direct materials consumed for production.

Statement of Requirements of the Proposed Cost System

The proposed cost system should provide the following information to the production manager:

1. Daily consumption of the three major (of ten) direct materials:
   - In total and separately for each material
   - In terms of quantity, price, and cost
   - On actual and standard cost bases along with variances from the standards

   This information should be available in the form of a written report which should be submitted by 9 A.M. of the following day.
2. Weekly material cost variance analysis, together with the causes of variances, for the three major direct materials. This report should be submitted by the end of the first day of the following week.

These two subjects are explained at length and are illustrated by a comprehensive case study in this chapter. In addition, to help the designer and management in crystallizing the requirements of a given cost system, a detailed checklist of the typical requirements of cost systems is given at the end of the chapter.

## ELEMENTS OF THE REQUIREMENTS OF A COST SYSTEM

An analysis of the illustration in Exhibit 4-1 will reveal that there are seven closely interrelated elements of requirements of a cost system:

1. *Why?* A system is designed to meet some predetermined objectives or purposes, such as cost control, inventory valuation, etc.
2. *What?* To satisfy each objective, certain information is required.
3. *Who?* The information is needed by a designated person.
4. *Time period.* The information relates to a specified time period, such as a week, a month, or a quarter.
5. *Timing.* The regularly required information is expected at a specified frequency and by a certain time.
6. *Accuracy.* The extent of accuracy desired may vary from information to information.
7. *Form and mode.* The information is reported in some form and conveyed by some mode (orally, in writing, etc.).

**EXHIBIT 4-2**

**Elements of Requirements of a Cost System**

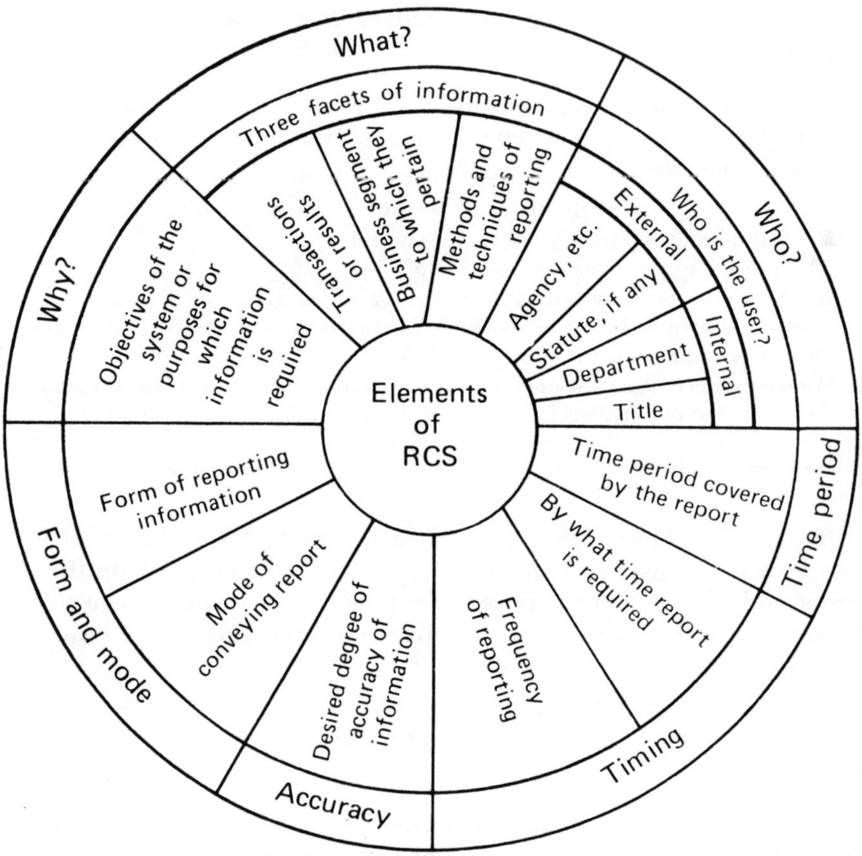


These elements are depicted diagrammatically in Exhibit 4-2 and explained later in this chapter.

## HOW SHOULD THE REQUIREMENTS OF A COST SYSTEM BE DETERMINED?

Reducing the requirements of the proposed cost system to clear and comprehensive statements is the single most important task of the system analysis phase. It is also the most difficult task because it involves a highly analytical, creative, and iterative process not amenable to any set procedure.

### Prior Steps

It may be remembered that before the designer begins to determine requirements of the new cost system, he has already:

- Defined system objectives, at least, in broad terms.
- Conducted a survey to gain an understanding of the company, its business, its major activities, and the amount and types of costs incurred.
- Gained an understanding of the present system in whatever form it may exist.

From these raw data, the designer must formulate specific requirements of the proposed cost system through several iterative steps. The number of iterations depends upon the objectives of the proposed system and the complexity of the organization.

### Major Tasks Involved

Since there is no step-by-step procedure for developing the requirements of a cost system, it is not possible to describe the procedure involved. However, to make the effort goal-directed, the seven major tasks to be performed in developing system requirements are identified and explained below.

**Task 1: Refine System Objectives** System requirements must be developed objective by objective. For this purpose, each broadly defined objective of the proposed cost system should be made more specific and clear-cut by analyzing, defining, and modifying it in the light of the background information gathered during the fact-finding survey. The purposes for which cost information is required should be stated as specifically as possible. For example, in Exhibit 4-1 not only is it specified that the information is required for controlling costs, but it also is made explicit that the costs to be controlled are the costs of materials. Further, if in that illustration more than one product is manufactured, the statement should specify whether the material costs of each product or of only certain products need be controlled.

**Task 2: Analyze Background Information** The background information should be analyzed in the perspective of each objective of the proposed cost system. If this information must be supplemented, additional information may be gathered by employing any of the techniques discussed in Chapter 3.

The purpose of analyzing the background information is to identify:

- Major profit centers and cost centers
- Major decision areas and problem areas, such as make or buy, capacity planning, etc.
- Major profit-making and loss-making factors

These are the areas about which management will require cost information, and the cost accounting system should therefore be built around them. For example, management will like to have more detailed, accurate, and frequent information about the purchases, prices, consumption, waste, and inventory of significant direct materials than that of insignificant direct materials. Similarly, if there are two divisions, one with stable business and the other with fluctuating business, management will need more information about the second division than about the first division.

**Task 3: Determine System Requirements** With the help of analysis of the background information, the designer can determine system requirements in terms of each of the remaining six elements. For this purpose, the designer should seek answers to the following questions *separately* for each objective.

**What Information Is Required to Meet the Objective?** Different cost information may be required to satisfy different objectives. Hence, for each objective it is essential to segregate relevant and irrelevant information. Further, even if certain information is relevant for a given purpose, it may not be significant enough to be considered, and it is also necessary therefore to sift significant and insignificant information. Thus, only those items of information which are both *relevant* and *significant* for a given objective should be selected. For instance, in the illustration given in Exhibit 4-1, information relating to the three major materials alone would be sufficient to satisfy the user's requirements. Further, a careful analysis of any item of cost information will reveal that it has *three facets,* as shown diagrammatically in Exhibit 4-3, which also gives a few examples of each facet.

*Transactions* (or events) and *results* can be reported individually, in groups, or in total. Further, they may be expressed in quantitative or monetary terms, or both. Moreover, transactions or events such as production, sales, and consumption can be reported more frequently than results (e.g., profit or loss, unit cost, etc.) and analysis of results (e.g., causes of variation in material usage or labor yield). Usually, operating personnel are interested in individual transactions for day-to-day control over a given activity, whereas management personnel are interested in the overall control of an activity and hence in results or, at best, in aggregate transactions. For example, a production supervisor will be interested in knowing the consumption and variances in consumption of direct materials by production orders, whereas a plant manager will be interested in knowing the consumption and variances in consumption of direct materials for a week or a month.

Transactions, events, and results relate to some *segment of business* or its subdivision. For example, direct material consumption and variances in

**EXHIBIT 4-3**

**Three Facets of Cost Information**

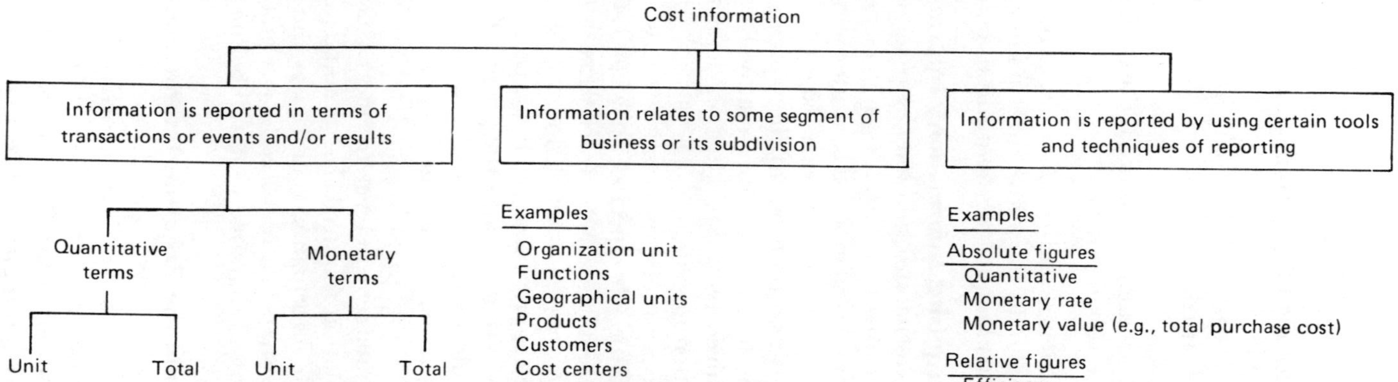


Examples

- Cost amount
- Production quantity
- Material quantity
- Labor time
- Machine capacity
- Inventory quantity and value
- Profits

Examples

- Organization unit
- Functions
- Geographical units
- Products
- Customers
- Cost centers
- Sales channels
- Distribution channels
- Terms of sales
- Order sizes
- Sales representatives

Examples

Absolute figures
- Quantitative
- Monetary rate
- Monetary value (e.g., total purchase cost)

Relative figures
- Efficiency
- Cost per unit of production
- Percent capacity utilized
- Turnover
- Etc.

Comparative figures
- Same segment, different periods
- Different segments, same period
- Same segment, same period, but actual versus budgeted or standard figures and variances
- Absolute or relative figures

Analysis of results
- E.g., causes of cost variances

consumption are identified with individual production centers as well as with individual products.

The tools and *techniques of reporting* to be used depend to a large extent upon the methods and techniques of costing employed. For example, if standard costing is used, actual costs will be compared with standard costs, but if historical costing is used, they will be compared with past actual costs.

Thus, to determine what information is required, the designer should actually ask the following three subquestions:

- What are the transactions (events) and results to be reported?
- To what business segments should the above information relate?
- What are the methods and techniques of reporting to be employed?

**Who Is the User of the Requisite Information?** Information users may be external or internal. External information needs should be identified with the agencies, government authorities, or persons requiring them and the governing statutes, regulations, etc., under which the cost information is to be furnished. Internal information needs should be identified with the departments and positions of the persons within the organization. For example, in Exhibit 4-1, the information is required for an internal purpose: it is required by the production department, and the title of the user is production manager.

External users normally specify their information needs in terms of what, why, when, how often, for what period, in what form, etc., in the governing statutes, rules, regulations, etc. In contrast, the information needs of internal users are not well-defined, and the designer therefore must help these users determine their needs for cost information. This by no means is an easy task. To determine the potential users of cost information, the designer should inquire about the persons responsible for incurring and controlling costs, measuring or accounting for performance, business decision making, planning, and similar activities.

Ordinarily, the higher the management level, the more condensed and the less frequent is the information required. For example, even within the production department the information required by the production manager will be more detailed than that required by the manufacturing vice president but more condensed than that required by the production supervisors.

**To What Time Period Should the Requisite Information Relate?** A report may cover a time period of a day, a week, a month, a quarter, a half year, the year to date, and so on. The report period should be chosen according to the purpose and users of the report. For example, the period of cost control reports required by lower-level management will be shorter than that required by higher-level management. Similarly, cost control reports for direct materials and direct labor are usually prepared daily or weekly, whereas overhead control reports are usually prepared monthly.

**At What Frequency and by What Time Period at the Latest Should the Requisite Information Be Provided to the Users?** Information may be furnished daily, weekly, monthly, quarterly, semiannually, or annually. The timing may be any one or more of the following:

- At the end or the beginning of each day, week, month, etc.
- Within a certain number of days, weeks, or months
- As soon as possible
- On or before a certain event (e.g., with some other report, on the completion of a contract, etc.)

Often the report period and the frequency of reporting will be the same. For example, if the report period is a month, the frequency of reporting will be monthly. However, there may be exceptions. For example, if manufacturing overhead for the last quarter of the year is used for inventory valuation, this information will be prepared only once a year.

The following *guidelines* will be helpful in selecting the frequency and the timing of reporting:

1. The frequency at which information is required depends mainly upon the *purpose* for which it is required and the *importance* of the information. For example, among different materials, information on price fluctuations in major items should be made available more frequently than that in minor items. Usually, information for cost control should be made available more frequently than that for most of the other purposes, and it should be furnished well in time to take corrective action.

2. As a general rule, the higher the *management level,* the lower the frequency of reporting because the information becomes more and more condensed as it travels upward in the management hierarchy. For example, a supervisor will be interested in knowing daily material and labor usage, but a production manager will be interested in knowing weekly or monthly usage or only abnormal variations in usage.

3. The timing of submitting a report is governed not only by the earliest time at which it is needed but also by the earliest *time* at which it can be *prepared.* That time depends upon the availability of personnel, the volume of the information and the complexity of processing it, the degree of accuracy desired, and the like.

4. Usually, it is better to start with a less frequent reporting schedule for internal reports and gradually to increase the frequency as the employees become accustomed to the routine.

5. Costs such as direct materials or direct labor, which need to be

controlled on an activity-by-activity basis, should be reported more frequently than costs such as advertising or research and development, which are controlled in the aggregate.

**How Accurate Should the Information Be?** The degree of accuracy desired depends upon the purpose for which information is required and the frequency at which it is required. Information needed for a more significant purpose should be more reliable than that needed for a less significant purpose. For example, information required for quoting the price of a contract worth $1 million should be much more reliable than that of a contract amounting to only a few thousand dollars. Generally, information for operational controls should be more accurate than that for management controls. For example, reports on shortages in materials received from vendors should be more accurate than reports on monthly consumption of materials submitted to the vice president, manufacturing. Similarly, flash reports may be less accurate than regular reports.

Further, speed with reasonable accuracy is preferable to precision with delay. For example, to prepare a monthly cost statement and an income statement by the first day of the following month, the variable expenses for the last 2 days of the month may be estimated, and any difference between estimated and actual expenses for these days may be adjusted in the following month's statements.

**What Are the Best Form and Mode of Reporting the Requisite Information?** The form of reporting refers to the arrangement of information in a report, whereas the mode refers to the manner in which the report is conveyed. For example, the mode may be oral or written. An oral report may be given at a meeting or by telephone. To convey important events or transactions, flash reports containing a rough estimate of important events or transactions may be used. Flash reports may also be prepared for reporting monthly unit costs, profit or loss, and similar important results while the regular reports are being prepared.

The designer should repeat tasks 1 through 3 until the system requirements are refined. In developing and refining the system requirements, the designer must use considerable judgment and imagination and consider not only what is *useful* but also what is likely to be *used.*

**Task 4: Document System Requirements** Once developed, the requirements of the proposed cost system should be documented in some suitable form. Usually, a tabular form (see Exhibit 4-4 below) is best.

**Task 5: Outline of Report Forms** On the basis of the system requirements developed, the designer should prepare an outline of each cost report to be used, clearly showing what significant information is to appear in each report (see Exhibits 4-5 through 4-10 below). The final report forms should be designed after the other aspects of the system have been designed.

**Task 6: Approval of System Requirements** The designer should remember that the cost system is being designed to satisfy users' requirements for certain cost information, and therefore he should encourage users to participate in developing and refining the system requirements. Also, once the designer has refined the system requirements, the system must be presented to the concerned users for their review and approval. There are two advantages of users' participation and acceptance. First, because of their firsthand knowledge of the company's business, users may be able to point out deficiencies, errors, a need for additions, deletions, or improvements in the system requirements developed by the designer. Second, once the users have approved the system requirements, there will be less resistance at implementation time and greater commitment to the system after it has been implemented. However, both participation and acceptance should be *real* and not pseudo.

It is the cost accounting department which will be responsible for operating the cost system once it has been designed and implemented. Hence, unless the system is being designed by the department itself, the designer should also encourage the controller or the cost accountants who will be responsible for operating the system to participate in system specifications. For example, they should be consulted on the feasibility of the timing of submission of various reports.

**Task 7: Modifying System Requirements** During the system design phase and even during the system implementation phase, the need to modify system requirements may become evident. This may happen for several reasons, such as the following:

- Facts and circumstances may have changed in the interim; e.g., a new product line may have been added.
- Certain relevant facts may not have been considered while developing the system requirements because the designer either was not aware of them or inadvertently ignored them.
- It may be too burdensome for the cost accounting department to generate certain output information.
- The particular computer system selected may not be able to generate the required output or to generate it at the specified time.

Any radical change in the already-approved system requirements must be approved by management. Before beginning to design a cost system, the designer should attempt to give as much concrete shape to the system requirements as possible so that subsequent modifications will be minimal.

## DETERMINING THE REQUIREMENTS OF A COMPUTERIZED COST SYSTEM

Theoretically, first the requirements of the cost system should be specified, and then it should be decided whether a computerized cost system is essential or a manual cost system will be adequate. Though this approach sometimes is adopted, usually the designer has some indication at the outset whether or not the cost system will be computerized. If the designer does not know whether or not a computer will be used, he should first define the minimum requirements of the cost system and later expand or modify them if it is decided to use a computer.

Though the process of determining the requirements of a computerized cost system is more or less the same as explained in Chapter 3, a computer has impact on practically every element of the cost system requirements, as explained below.

1. Computerized reports can be more informative and analytical than manually prepared reports. For example, from the material usage data file a computer can generate usage reports by parts, products, and production shops. Similarly, a computer can easily generate exception reports, such as a report showing the higher of more than 5 percent or $1000 unfavorable variances in individual cost items by responsibility centers. Exception reports can be generated in a manual system too, but generating them is time-consuming. In a manual system, it is necessary first to generate complete cost reports by responsibility centers and then, by going over each item, to select the variances outside the acceptable limit.

Further, because a computer can easily handle tedious and complex calculations, information on ratios, percentages, trends, etc., can readily be included in the computerized reports. Similarly, a computer facilitates special cost analysis for nonroutine managerial decisions, provided the required data are already in the computer and appropriate programs to generate the special cost analysis reports are available.

2. Since a computer can process a large amount of data in a relatively short time and with a low error rate, the computerized cost reporting system is superior to the manual cost reporting system in the following respects:

- Reports can be generated for a greater number of levels of the organization.
- Report periods can be made shorter and be varied.
- Reports can be made more frequent and timely.
- Reports will be more accurate.

3. Computerized reports can be in a printed form or be displayed

visually on a cathode-ray-tube (CRT) screen. Further, a computer itself can generate graphs, charts, etc.

4. Because of these features, a greater number of objectives can be achieved with a computerized cost system than with a manual cost system.

Thus, a computerized cost system is much more flexible in generating cost information than a manual cost system.

Because of the expanded capability of the computerized system, there is often a tendency to generate more information than is necessary or can be used. Thus, the designer should exercise restraint and be selective in defining what information should be generated, when it should be generated, and so on. Further, there is greater need than with a manual system to be very specific in defining present and future requirements because changes in the requirements may require changes in the software and even in the hardware.

## CASE STUDY: DETERMINING THE REQUIREMENTS OF A COST SYSTEM FOR ACME COMPANY

Using the background information developed for ACME Company in Chapter 3, the following case study illustrates the first five tasks in the process of developing the requirements of a cost system (this is a part of the continuing illustration of ACME Company used throughout the book). For the purpose of this study, we will take one of the major objectives of the proposed cost system for ACME Company and demonstrate how to determine the requirements of the system to meet that objective.

### Tasks Already Completed

1. *Preliminary statement of objective of the proposed cost system.* The management of ACME Company has specified the following objective as one of the major objectives of the proposed cost system: "To control costs more effectively throughout the company."

2. *Preliminary survey.* The preliminary survey of ACME Company, its business, and its accounting system has been conducted and documented in Chapter 3.

### Major Tasks to Be Performed

By using the above information, the five major tasks will be performed as explained below:

**Task 3 (Partial): Frame the Relevant Questions for Determining System Requirements** To refine the preliminary statement of objective and to develop clear-cut system requirements, the designer prepares the following questions, which deal with the remaining six aspects of the system requirements of the cost system:

**What Information Is Required?** Since there are three facets of every item of information, there are three questions:

*Q-1.* What cost factors are controllable and significant enough to be controlled?

*Q-2.* What are the individual business segments to which the cost factors determined by Q-1 should relate?

*Q-3.* What methods and techniques of cost control are to be used?

**By Whom Is the Information Required?**

*Q-4.* Who has the authority in the relevant business segments (Q-2) to control the significant controllable cost factors (Q-1)?

**Time Period**

*Q-5.* To what time period should each of the significant controllable cost factors (Q-1) in the relevant business segments (Q-2) relate so as to ensure that meaningful cost information is furnished?

**Frequency and Timing of Reporting**

*Q-6.* At what frequency and by what time at the latest should the required information be submitted to the user to enable the user to take timely action for effectively controlling costs?

**Degree of Accuracy**

*Q-7.* How accurate should the information be? What margin of error is acceptable? Where are estimates and approximations permissible?

**Form of Reporting**

*Q-8.* What are the best mode and form of reporting which will quickly apprise recipients of the situation?

**Task 2: Analyze Background Information** To make the system objective more specific and to find suitable answers to the above questions, the designer analyzes the information gathered during the survey of ACME Company. The analysis reveals that the following background information is more relevant to the objective of controlling costs within ACME Company:

*a.* Major cost factors are analyzed in the following table:

| Major Cost Factors (in $000) | Product X | Product Y | Total |
|---|---|---|---|
| Direct material | | | |
| A | $408 | $224 | $632 |
| B | 680 | 128 | 808 |
| C | . . . | 160 | 160 |
| Direct labor | | | |
| Machine shop | 261 | 108 | 369 |
| Welding shop | 174 | 86 | 260 |
| Assembly shop | 304 | 172 | 476 |
| Manufacturing overhead costs | | | 1886 |
| Warehousing and distribution expenses | | | 1440 |
| Subtotal, major cost factors | | | 6031 |
| Other costs | | | 2469 |
| Total costs | | | $8500 |
| Major cost factors as percent of total costs | | | 53 |

*b.* Consumption of material B per unit of finished product X as well as of product Y varies from one production batch to another.

*c.* Prices of materials A, B, and C fluctuate frequently and significantly.

*d.* Supply of material A is erratic, and sometimes the company faces a hand-to-mouth situation.

*e.* Direct materials inventory level is uniformly at 60 days' consumption.

*f.* Often there are bottlenecks in the welding and assembly shops.

**Task 1: Make the Preliminary Objective More Specific** On the basis of the preceding tasks, the designer refines the statement of objective to read as follows: "The objective of the cost control system is to control all costs more effectively throughout the organization, particularly the following costs:

- "Cost of materials A and B for product X
- "Cost of materials A, B, and C for product Y
- "Direct labor costs in machine, welding, and assembly shops for both products
- "Distribution costs for both products
- "Selling expenses for both products"

**Task 3: Determine System Requirements** That is, answer the eight questions framed earlier. With the help of the users, the designer develops the following answers to those questions:

| Controllable and Significant Cost Factors (Q-1) | Business Segments (Q-2) | By Whom Controllable (Q-4) |
|---|---|---|
| 1. Quantity of material B (for products X and Y) | Production departments | Supervisors and production superintendent |
| 2. Prices of materials A, B, and C (for product X, materials A and B; for product Y, materials A, B, and C) | Purchasing department<br>Production departments | Purchasing officer<br>Production planner (because this person lays down the material specifications which influence material costs) |
| 3. Direct labor costs of assembly shop, machine shop, and welding shop (for Products X and Y) | Respective shops at the plant | Supervisors of the respective shops |
| 4. Distribution costs (for Products X and Y and two distribution centers) | Respective distribution centers | Managers of the respective distribution centers |
| 5. Selling expenses and sales performance | Sales department | Regional sales managers |
| 6. Direct material inventory | Plant | Plant manager, production planner, and purchasing officer |

**Q-3: Control Methods and Techniques** It has tentatively been decided that some sort of standard costs and budgets will be employed for controlling costs.

**Q-5 and Q-6: Time Period and Timing of Reporting** The fundamental principle of reporting for cost control is that the user be furnished the information in good time to take corrective action. This principle governed the time period and the timing of reporting determined for ACME Company as noted below in the table (Exhibit 4-5) under task 4. For example, the designer has determined that

- Information about consumption (actual, standard, and variance) of material B for Products X and Y should be available to the production supervisors on a daily basis so that they can take immediate corrective action. However, the production superintendent and the plant manager should be furnished only weekly summaries, and the vice president, manufacturing, should be given only monthly reports on this factor.

- Direct labor costs (actual, standard, and variance) by products for the three major shops should be reported to the respective supervisors on a daily basis.

**Q-7: Degree of Accuracy** Following the general rule, it has been decided that information will be as accurate as possible and that estimates and approximations will be introduced only to the extent necessary. The latter aspect can and will be decided only after the entire cost system has been designed.

**Q-8: Form and Mode of Reporting** Regularly required control reports will be in writing, but matters demanding immediate attention should be reported orally and covered later by appropriate written reports. Outlines of written cost reports are discussed below under "Task 5."

**Task 4: Document System Requirements** On the basis of the preceding tasks, the system requirements are tabulated as shown in Exhibit 4-4. The requirements tabulated there are illustrative and not exhaustive. For example, for controlling the inventory of direct materials, it would be necessary to establish safety stock levels, lead time, reorder points, economic order quantity, and minimum-maximum levels, which requirements are not included in Exhibit 4-4.

**Task 5: Outline of Cost Reports** On the basis of the system requirements tabulated in Exhibit 4-4, the designer draws outlines of cost reports clearly showing what significant information is to appear in each cost report. The cost reports in outline form are given in Exhibits 4-5 through 4-9. The final forms will be designed once the other aspects of the cost system have been designed.

## CHECKLIST OF TYPICAL COST INFORMATION REQUIRED

To facilitate the task of determining the items of cost information which should be provided by the cost system, a checklist of the usually required cost data is given in Exhibit 4-10. The checklist also includes typical quantitative information which may be available from various operating systems, such as production control, purchasing. labor control, etc. There are two reasons for including them in the list. First, since a cost accounting system should be an integral part of various operating systems, it is difficult to segregate information available from various operating systems and the cost accounting system. Second, even if various information can be identified with individual systems, it is necessary to consider them together because usually cost reports also require or contain quantitative information.

**EXHIBIT 4-4**

**Tabulating System Requirements of ACME Company**

| What Information | Report Period | Timing of Reporting | Required by | Report Reference |
|---|---|---|---|---|
| 1. Consumption of material B for products X and Y: quantity and cost (actual, standard, and variance) | Day | By 9 A.M. of the following day | Supervisors of production shops | Exhibit 4-5 |
| 2. Consumption of materials A, B, and C for products X and Y: quantity, price, and cost (actual, standard, and variance) along with causes of quantity variances and actions planned | Week | Every Monday | Supervisors, production superintendent, and plant manager | Exhibits 4-5 and 4-9 |
| 3. Causes of variances in prices of materials A, B, and C for products X and Y and actions planned | Two weeks | First and sixteenth of the month | Purchasing officer and plant manager | Exhibits 4-5 and 4-9 |
| 4. Summary of reports 2 and 3 above | Month | Third day of the following month | Production superintendent, plant manager, and vice president, manufacturing | Exhibits 4-5 and 4-9 |
| 5. Quarterly summary of report 3 only if unfavorable variances in the prices of individual materials exceed 10 percent | Quarter | First week of January, April, July, and October | Purchasing officer, vice president, manufacturing, and president | Exhibits 4-5 and 4-9 |
| 6. Consumption of remaining seven materials (actual, standard, and variance); variance analysis (if variance exceeds 10 percent) and actions planned | Month | Third day of the following month | Supervisors, production superintendent, plant manager, and vice president, manufacturing | Exhibits 4-5 and 4-9 |
| 7. Inventory of direct materials A, B, and C (actual, standard, and variance) | | As soon as the inventory level reaches the reorder point or exceeds the maximum level | Purchasing officer and plant manager; report to vice president, manufacturing, if the situation continues beyond 4 weeks | None |

| | | | | |
|---|---|---|---|---|
| 8. Direct labor cost of machine shop, welding shop, and assembly shop (actual, standard, and variance) | Day | By 9 A.M. of the following day | Respective supervisors | Exhibit 4-6 |
| 9. Direct labor cost of machine shop, welding shop, and assembly shop (actual, standard, and variance), with causes of variances and actions planned | Week | Every Tuesday | Respective supervisors and production superintendent | Exhibits 4-6 and 4-9 |
| 10. Direct labor cost of machine shop, welding shop, and assembly shop (actual, standard, and variance), with causes of variances and actions planned | Month | Third day of the following month | Plant manager and vice president, manufacturing | Exhibits 4-6 and 4-9 |
| 11. Direct labor cost of other shops, along with causes of variances (if variance exceeds 10 percent) and actions planned | Week | Every Tuesday | Respective supervisors | Exhibits 4-6 and 4-9 |
| 12. Direct labor cost of other shops, along with causes of variances (if variance exceeds 10 percent) and actions planned | Month | Third day of the following month | Respective supervisors, production superintendent, plant manager, and vice president, manufacturing | Exhibits 4-6 and 4-9 |
| 13. Distribution cost report for each center showing:<br>■ Costs by mode of distribution and cost factors<br>■ Cost per unit of product distributed, separately for each mode of distribution, actual and variance (compared with flexible budget) | Week | Every Monday | Distribution center managers | Exhibit 4-7 |
| 14. Same as item 13, with causes of variances and actions planned | Month | Third day of the following month | Distribution center managers, director, warehousing and distribution, and vice president, marketing | Exhibits 4-7 4-9 |
| 15. Cost statements by responsibility centers (actual, standard, and variance) for costs other than those mentioned above and actions planned | Month | Fifth day of the following month | Persons responsible for respective responsibility centers | Exhibits 4-8 and 4-9 |

**EXHIBIT 4-5**

**Outline of Material Consumption Report**

**ACME Company**

Product __________

Report period ________________

| Direct material | Actual consumption | | | Standard | | | Variance | | |
|---|---|---|---|---|---|---|---|---|---|
| | Quantity | Rate | Cost | Quantity | Rate | Cost | Quantity | Rate | Cost |
| A | | | | | | | | | |
| B | | | | | | | | | |
| C | | | | | | | | | |
| D | | | | | | | | | |
| E | | | | | | | | | |
| F | | | | | | | | | |
| G | | | | | | | | | |
| H | | | | | | | | | |
| I | | | | | | | | | |
| J | | | | | | | | | |
| Total | X | X | | X | X | | X | X | |

Causes of variances:

Prepared by ____________________ Date ____________

Distribution:

1. Daily report on consumption of material B for products X and Y to production superintendent.
2. Weekly report on consumption of materials A, B, and C for products X and Y together with causes of quantity variances to respective supervisors, production superintendent, and plant manager.
3. Semimonthly report on causes of variances in prices of materials A, B, and C to purchasing officer and production plant manager.
4. Monthly summary of reports in Paragraphs 2 and 3 to vice president, manufacturing, plant manager, and production superintendent.
5. Quarterly summary of report in Paragraph 3 to president only if unfavorable variances in prices of individual materials exceed 10 percent, and copies to vice president, manufacturing, and purchasing officer.
6. Monthly consumption report of remaining seven materials along with variance analysis, if variance exceeds 10 percent, to vice president, manufacturing, plant manager, production superintendent, and concerned supervisors.

**EXHIBIT 4-6**

**Outline of Direct Labor Cost Report**

**ACME Company**

Shop ________________

Report Period ______________

| Job description | Actual | | | Standard | | | Variance | | |
|---|---|---|---|---|---|---|---|---|---|
| | Unit or hours | Rate | Cost | Unit or hours | Rate | Cost | Unit or hours | Rate | Cost |
| Product X | | | | | | | | | |
| ... | | | | | | | | | |
| ... | | | | | | | | | |
| Subtotal | | | | | | | | | |
| Product Y | | | | | | | | | |
| ... | | | | | | | | | |
| ... | | | | | | | | | |
| Subtotal | | | | | | | | | |
| Total | X | X | | X | X | | X | X | |

Causes of variances:

Prepared by ________________ Date ____________

Distribution:

1. Daily reports of direct labor cost of machine shop, welding shop, and assembly shop to respective supervisors.
2. Weekly summary of report in Paragraph 1 with causes of variances to respective supervisors and production superintendent.
3. Monthly summary of report in Paragraph 2 to vice president, manufacturing, and plant manager.
4. Weekly summary of direct labor cost of other shops, along with causes of variances if variance exceeds 10 percent, to respective supervisors.
5. Monthly summary of report in Paragraph 4 to vice president, manufacturing, and plant manager, production superintendent, and concerned supervisors.

## EXHIBIT 4-7

## Outline of Distribution Cost Report

ACME Company

| | | | | | | | | | | | | |
|---|---|---|---|---|---|---|---|---|---|---|---|---|
| Week or Month | | | | | | | | | | | | |
| Actual | | | | | | | Variances compared with flexible budget | | | | | |
| Current week or month | | | Year to date | | | | Current week or month | | | Year to date | | |
| Center I | Center II | Total | Center I | Center II | Total | Details | Center I | Center II | Total | Center I | Center II | Total |
| | | | | | | 1. Own truck expenses | | | | | | |
| | | | | | | . . . | | | | | | |
| | | | | | | . . . | | | | | | |
| | | | | | | . . . | | | | | | |
| | | | | | | 2. Statistical data: own trucks | | | | | | |
| | | | | | | . . . | | | | | | |
| | | | | | | 3. Average cost of own trucks | | | | | | |
| | | | | | | a. Per trip | | | | | | |
| | | | | | | b. . . . | | | | | | |
| | | | | | | . . . | | | | | | |
| | | | | | | 4. Outside truck freight | | | | | | |
| | | | | | | Product X | | | | | | |
| | | | | | | Product Y | | | | | | |
| | | | | | | 5. Rail freight | | | | | | |
| | | | | | | Product X | | | | | | |
| | | | | | | Product Y | | | | | | |
| | | | | | | 6. Total distribution cost (1 + 4 + 5) | | | | | | |
| | | | | | | 7. Statistical data: distribution | | | | | | |
| | | | | | | 8. Average distribution cost | | | | | | |
| | | | | | | a. Per unit delivered | | | | | | |
| | | | | | | . . . | | | | | | |
| | | | | | | 9. Packing expenses | | | | | | |
| | | | | | | . . . | | | | | | |
| | | | | | | 10. Warehousing expenses | | | | | | |
| | | | | | | . . . | | | | | | |
| | | | | | | 11. Common expenses | | | | | | |
| | | | | | | . . . | | | | | | |
| | | | | | | 12. Total warehousing and distribution costs (6 + 9 + 10 + 11) | | | | | | |

Causes of variances:

Prepared by ___________ Date _________

Distribution:

1. Weekly reports to distribution center managers.
2. Monthly reports to distribution center managers, director, warehousing and distribution, and vice president, marketing.

**EXHIBIT 4-8**

**Outline of Cost Control Reports by Cost Centers**

ACME Company

Responsibility center ______________ Month ______________

| Description | Current month | | | Year to date | | |
|---|---|---|---|---|---|---|
| | Actual | Standard (budget) | Variance | Actual | Standard (budget) | Variance |
| Activity volume | | | | | | |
| ... | | | | | | |
| ... | | | | | | |
| ... | | | | | | |
| Costs elements | | | | | | |
| ... | | | | | | |
| ... | | | | | | |
| Total | | | | | | |

Causes of variances:

Prepared by ______________ Date ______________

Distribution: Persons responsible for respective responsibility centers.

**EXHIBIT 4-9**

**Variance Explanation and Action Report**

ACME Company

Responsibility center ________________ Week or month __________

Responsibility of ________________

| Variance | Explanation | Action planned or taken |
|---|---|---|
| | | |

Prepared by ________________________ Date ________

Distribution: All recipients of the relevant cost report.

The checklist includes the cost and quantitative data required in the following areas:

1. Capacity and production
2. Product cost information
3. Direct materials
4. Direct labor
5. Manufacturing overhead costs
6. Sales
7. Distribution expenses
8. General and administrative expenses
9. Profitability
10. Inventory and purchases

The checklist includes the information required for both product costing and cost control. For these two purposes the following types of information are required:

- What resources are available or employed? Examples of resources available with a manufacturing company are production capacity, inventory, and number of employees.
- To what extent are available resources *utilized*? The measurement devices used are percentage production capacity used, turnover of inventory, etc.
- How *efficiently* are the resources utilized? For example, direct labor efficiency and direct material usage ratios are the indicators of efficiency in the use of these two resources.
- How effective is the company in achieving its predetermined goals of production, sales, etc.?
- How much does it cost to produce various products and to carry out various activities?
- How do actual performance and costs compare with predetermined performance and costs? This step results in computing variances.
- What are the *causes* of *variances* from the predetermined performance and costs? The variance analysis provides direction for correcting or preventing unacceptable performance and costs as well as for revising unreasonable standards.

**EXHIBIT 4-10**

**Checklist of Typical Cost Information Required**

1. *Capacity and Production*

Capacity
- Theoretical
- Practical
- Normal
- Actual utilized
- Overutilization or underutilization of capacity compared with planned utilization

Machine efficiency (production ÷ machine-hours)
- Actual
- Standard or expected
- Variances from standard or expected efficiency

Production of each production unit, which may be one or more of the following:
- Each product
- Each group of products
- Each job, batch, process, or operation
- Each component or part of a group of components or parts
- Each subassembly
- Each assembly
- Others

(Actual as well as planned production figures may be given. Production of each production unit may be accumulated by departments, workers, operations, etc.)

Production quantity, classified into:
- Good quality (actual, expected, and variance)
- Defective (normal and abnormal)
- Spoiled (normal and abnormal)
- Substandard (normal and abnormal)

Causes of defective, spoiled, or substandard production
- Defective or substandard material
- Inexperienced labor
- Careless labor
- Defective machine or tools
- Power cut
- Others

Causes of below-normal good-quality production
- Higher defective, spoiled, or substandard production
- Material, labor, or power shortage
- Poor production planning
- Machine breakdown
- Production bottleneck
- Others

**EXHIBIT 4-10**

**Checklist of Typical Cost Information Required (*Continued*)**

Work in process
- Percent completed or equivalent units produced
- Cost

Turnover ratios, etc.
- Finished goods produced ÷ work in process
- Length of production cycle
- Length of each process, operation, or job cycle

2. *Product Cost Information*

Total and unit costs of each of the production units. Total and unit costs may be broken down into cost elements, major cost elements, or the appropriate classification of various cost elements (e.g., direct materials, direct labor, and manufacturing overhead; fixed and variable costs; etc.).

3. *Direct Materials*

The following information concerning direct materials may be required (*a*) in total for *all* direct materials or separately for each material or a *group* of materials or only for significant items of material; (*b*) in total for *all* production units or separately for *each* production unit:

Consumption and cost (in quantitative and monetary terms):
- Actual
- Variance from standard or estimated consumption and cost:
  - Price variance and quantity variance

Yield (production ÷ consumption)
- Actual
- Variance from standard or estimated yield

Causes of variance in consumption and yield
- Defective material
- Improper specifications
- Substandard or superior material
- Improper mix of materials
- Substandard or superior labor
- Inadequate training
- Faulty workmanship
- Machine breakdown or defect
- Power cut
- Production interruption due to material, labor, or power shortage
- Old standards
- Material loss or gain
- Others

Material losses (in quantitative and monetary terms)
- Scrap (normal and abnormal)
- Waste (normal and abnormal)
- Natural loss or gain due to shrinkage, evaporation, etc. (normal and abnormal)

**EXHIBIT 4-10**

**Checklist of Typical Cost Information Required (*Continued*)**

Damage, deterioration, theft, etc., during transit, storage in stockroom, or material handling in factory
Defective material
Obsolete material
Slow-moving material (aging analysis)
Ratios (in quantitative and monetary terms)
Material consumed ÷ material consumption
Material loss ÷ good production
Material requirements (monthly, weekly, etc.)
Material on hand

4. *Direct Labor*

The following information concerning direct labor may be required:

*a.* In total for all direct workers or separately for each worker or a group of workers
*b.* In total for all production units or separately for each production unit or a group of production units
*c.* For the company as a whole and separately for each department or division

Availability (required or actually available)
Number of direct workers
Number of direct person-hours or person-days
Both classified into:
Permanent and temporary
Skilled and unskilled

Direct labor cost
Total
Breakdown by cost elements, e.g.:
Wages on time basis
Bonus or incentive payments
Piece-rate payments
Normal and overtime payments
Fringe benefits (e.g., payroll taxes, pensions, etc.)
Comparison with predetermined costs
Classified into:
Payments to permanent and temporary workers
Payments to skilled and unskilled workers
Average hourly or daily rate

Labor utilization and idle time (in terms of time and cost)
Actual productive and idle time
Variances from standard or estimate, i.e., normal and abnormal idle time
Utilization and idle time may be expressed as a percentage of total time or cost paid.
Cost and causes of idle time

**EXHIBIT 4-10**

**Checklist of Typical Cost Information Required (*Continued*)**

Causes
- Waiting for work
- Waiting for instructions
- Waiting for fellow workers
- Lack of material
- Machine breakdown
- Waiting for machine and tools
- Others

Labor efficiency (production ÷ labor time or cost)
- Actual
- Variance from standard or estimate

Causes of labor efficiency variances
- Excess or lack of workers
- Inefficient or superior labor
- Trainees or new workers
- Improper or better supervision
- Defective or superior material
- Defective or superior machine or tools
- Go-slow action by workers
- Improper or better production scheduling or better plant layout
- Outdated standards
- Others (e.g., absenteeism due to bad weather, flood, etc.)

Miscellaneous
- Labor turnover rate
- Cost of labor turnover (with details; e.g., costs of hiring, training, production losses, etc.)
- Causes of labor turnover
- Absenteeism rate
- Others

5. *Manufacturing Overhead Costs*

The following information in total and separately for each cost center and responsibility center:

Cost of each of the cost elements or a group of them
- Indirect material (quantity and cost)
- Indirect labor (time or number of employees and cost), with breakdown into managerial, supervisory, etc.
- Other expenses, with classification by nature of expenses
- Only actual cost figures
- Actual, budgeted or estimated, and variances
  - Budget may be based on standard costs and may be fixed or flexible.
  - Causes of variances
- Classification of each cost item by controllability, i.e., separation of controllable and noncontrollable costs

**EXHIBIT 4-10**

**Checklist of Typical Cost Information Required (*Continued*)**

Classification of each cost element by behavior, i.e., separation of fixed, variable, and semivariable costs
Overhead cost absorption rates
Actual or predetermined overhead cost per production unit

6. *Sales*
The following information separately for each product or a group of products:
Sales (quantity, price, and total amount)
Actual
Comparison with budgets or goals
Variances
Analysis of sales variance
Quantity
Price
Product mix
Ratios
Sales turnover ratio (to reveal slow-moving products, excessive inventory, or inadequate inventory) = sales ÷ finished goods inventory

7. *Distribution Expenses*
Classification of expenses by nature, e.g., salaries, advertisement, traveling, etc.
Classification of expenses by functions, e.g., warehousing, advertising, order getting, order filling, billing, etc.
Each of the above classifications of expenses identified with segments and methods of marketing, as for example:
Territories
Products or group of products (in total and per unit of product sold)
Customers or types of customers
Sales channels
Sales representatives
Methods of distribution
Size of orders (to determine economic order size, charge extra cost for smaller orders, or give discount for larger orders)
Special orders
Terms of sale (cash or credit, different credit periods, etc.)
For cost control, the above data are identified with persons responsible:
Only actual cost figures
Actual, budgeted, variances
Budget may be fixed or flexible.
Causes of variances
Each cost element may be classified into fixed, semifixed, and variable categories.

**EXHIBIT 4-10**

**Checklist of Typical Cost Information Required (*Continued*)**

8. *General and Administrative Expenses*
   Classification of expenses by
   Nature, e.g., salaries, donations, audit fees, etc.
   Functions, e.g., accounting, finance, legal, secretarial, personnel, etc.
   Only actual cost figures or
   actual, budgeted and variances. Usually, administrative expenses are controlled through a fixed budget.
9. *Profitability*

   Profit for the company as a whole classified by profit centers, which may be:
   Divisions
   Products or product groups
   Territories
   Customers
   Channels of sales
   Channels of distribution
   Sales representatives
   Others

   Profits may be computed on:
   *a.* Total cost basis or direct cost basis, i.e., on contribution margin approach
   *b.* Actual or standard cost method. Actual profits may be compared with budgeted profits or actual profits of past period.

   Profit margin may be expressed as:
   Gross profit on sales (in total, per unit, and as a percentage of sales or cost of goods sold)
   Operating income on sales (in total, per unit, and as a percentage of sales or cost of goods sold)

   Profit per unit of key or limiting factor (e.g., profit by products, per machine-hour, per unit of direct material in short supply, etc.)
10. *Inventory and Purchases*
    Quantity, cost, and value of inventory of direct materials, work in process, finished goods, packing material, spare parts, tools, etc.:
    In total
    Separately for each major material, product, etc.
    Identified with each manufacturing division, profit center, or cost center
    Comparison of actual quantity and costs with budgeted quantity and costs

    Slow-moving and obsolete inventory

    Inventory variances from the minimum-maximum levels

    Purchases of direct materials
    Orders placed, delivery awaited with expected time of delivery
    Purchases of total direct materials, with or without comparison with material purchase budget and analysis of variances
    Purchase price fluctuation report on major direct materials

# PHASE II

# System Design

# Chapter 5

# Cost System Design: An Overview

Thinking is the hardest work there is, which is the probable reason why so few engage in it.

Henry Ford

During the *system analysis phase,* the designer analyzes and determines the exact cost information required by the concern. During the *system design phase,* in the light of the first phase and using his expert knowledge, the designer designs a cost system for providing the required information. Thus, during the system analysis phase, the designer is concerned with *what is required* and, during the system design phase, with *how to satisfy* that requirement.

An overview of the system design phase is given in this chapter, and the individual blocks of this phase are dealt with in Chapters 6 through 16. To enable the designer to gain an overview, this chapter

1. Explains the relationship between the system analysis and the system design phases.
2. Describes the cost accounting process.
3. Identifies the various facets of a cost system.
4. Explains how to ascertain and deal with the system constraints to design a practical cost system.
5. Explains the most common approach to designing a manual cost system.
6. Discusses the additional tasks involved in designing a computerized cost system.
7. Discusses a feasibility study for a proposed cost system.

## RELATIONSHIP BETWEEN THE SYSTEM ANALYSIS AND THE SYSTEM DESIGN PHASES

Exhibit 5-1 shows the relationship between the system analysis phase and the system design phase and the transition from the first to the second. During the system analysis phase, the designer (1) studies the present system and determines what cost information is available from it and (2) determines what cost information is required.

At the outset of the system design phase, the designer prepares a broad outline of the desired system from the requirements defined during the system analysis phase. Then, he compares the present and the proposed systems to determine the gap between them. Next, the designer defines the various tasks to be completed to bridge the gap. Finally, he completes those tasks and develops the desired system. In understanding the relationship between these two phases, the following points should be noted.

First, every concern except a new concern has some features of a cost system even if it lacks a formal system. For example, for financial accounting purposes it will maintain records of direct material inventory and accumulate various expenses. Hence, the designer must identify those features.

Second, the gap between the two systems may exist for all or for some of the subcost systems such as direct materials and direct labor. Further, the gap may be present for standards, budgets, cost reports, etc. For example, a concern may have direct material standards but not direct labor standards, or its cost accumulation and allocation system may be adequate while its cost reporting system may need an overhaul. Unless the designer carefully ascertains what is available from the present system, duplications and overlappings may adversely impact the quality of the new system. Thus, the designer should carefully determine the gap.

Third, the gap between the present and the proposed systems need not be defined at the outset of the system design phase. It can be defined while each block of the system is being designed.

Fourth, if the outline of the proposed system is modified while the system is being designed, the gap determined earlier will also change, and so also the tasks required to bridge the gap. In other words, the process of development of a cost system is iterative in nature.

### Documenting the Cost System Gap

Since a cost system consists of many elements, a methodical approach should be adopted not only in determining the gap between the desirable system and the current system but also in documenting the gap. Exhibit 5-2 is a specimen form for documenting the gap. The exhibit contains

**EXHIBIT 5-1**

**Relationship between System Analysis Phase and System Design Phase**

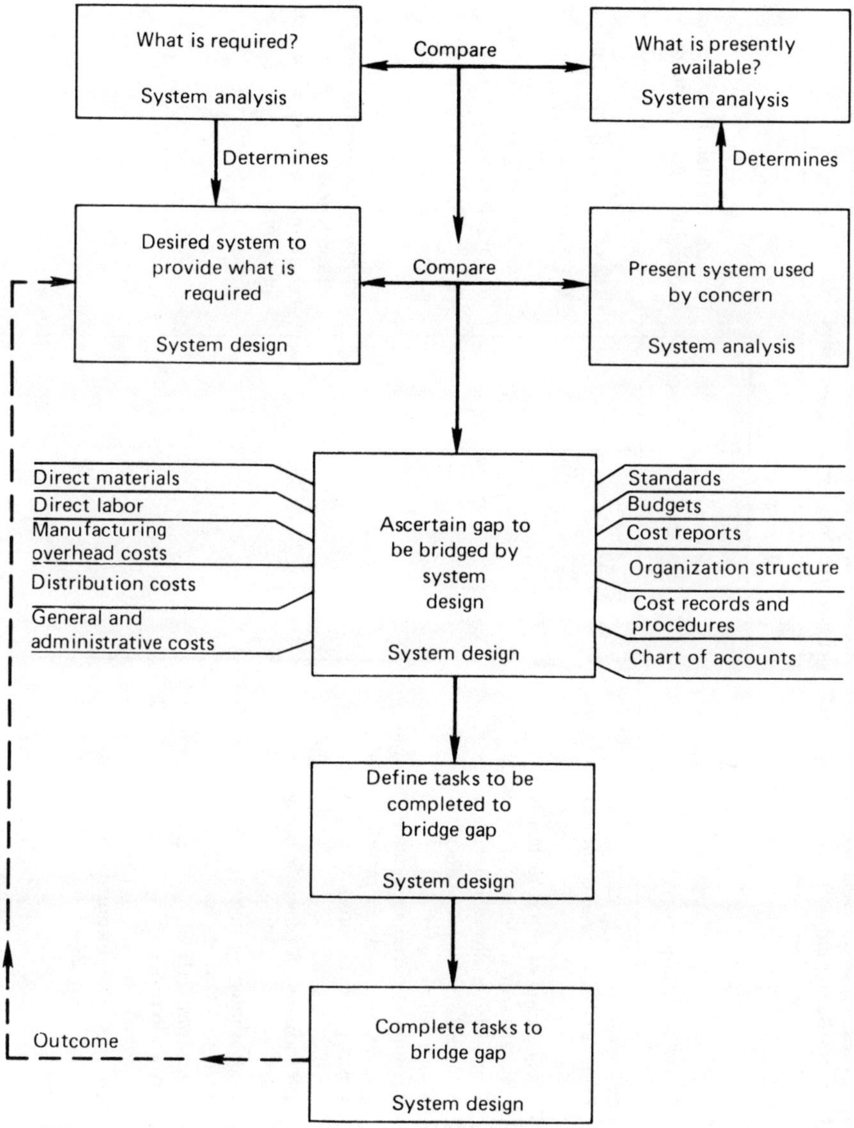

**EXHIBIT 5-2**

**Specimen Form for Documenting the Gap between Desirable and Present Cost Systems**

| Number | Desirable Features | Current Status | | | Remarks (explain improvements desired and seriousness of deficiency) |
|---|---|---|---|---|---|
| | | OK | Needs Improvement | Absent | |
| | *Direct materials* | | | | |
| 1 | Definition of direct and indirect materials | | √ | | Classify small-value items like glue as indirect materials. |
| 2 | Classification of direct materials | √ | | | |
| 3 | Standards for direct materials usage | | | √ | Initially, set standards for five major materials. |
| 4 | Standards for direct materials losses | | | √ | Initially, set standards for five major materials. |
| 5 | Standards for direct materials prices | | | √ | Initially, set standards for five major materials. |
| 6 | Use of bill of materials | √ | | | |
| 7 | Accounting treatment of cash and trade discounts and direct materials losses | √ | | | |
| 8 | Direct materials consumption budget | | √ | | For five major materials, use standards instead of estimates. |
| 9 | Direct materials purchase budget | | √ | | For five major materials, use standards instead of estimates. |
| 10 | Establishment of inventory standards | | | | |
| 11 | Inventory budgets for<br>Direct materials<br>Work in process<br>Finished goods | | | | |
| 12 | Use of source documents for material requisitions, issues, transfers, and material losses | | | | |
| 13 | Inventory records for receipts, issues, and transfers of direct materials | | | | |

|  |  |  |  |  |  |  |
|---|---|---|---|---|---|---|
| 14 | Cost accounting records of consumption and loss of direct materials |  |  |  |  |  |
| 15 | Classification of direct materials accounts in the chart of accounts |  |  |  |  |  |
| 16 | Direct materials cost reports on consumption, losses, inventory, cost, and prices |  |  |  |  |  |
|  | *Direct labor* |  |  |  |  |  |
| 17 | Standards for direct labor time |  |  |  |  |  |
| 18 | Standards for direct labor time losses |  |  |  |  |  |
| 19 | Standards for direct labor rates |  |  |  |  |  |
| 20 | Manning table |  |  |  |  |  |
| 21 | Direct labor cost budget |  |  |  |  |  |
|  | *Organization structure* |  |  |  |  |  |
| 22 | Establishment of responsibility centers |  |  |  |  |  |
| 23 | Definition of authority-responsibility |  |  |  |  |  |
| 24 | Establishment of cost centers |  |  |  |  |  |
| 25 | Classification of manufacturing cost centers into production centers and service centers |  |  |  |  |  |
|  | *Manufacturing overhead costs* |  |  |  |  |  |
| 26 | Classification of manufacturing overhead items by<br>Nature of expenses<br>Responsibility centers<br>Cost behavior<br>Controllability |  |  |  |  |  |
| 27 | Standards for<br>Equipment-hours<br>Maintenance time<br>Setup time<br>Inspection quantity and time<br>Indirect materials usage |  |  |  |  |  |
| 28 | Budget for manufacturing overhead by responsibility centers |  |  |  |  |  |

NOTE: The items listed in the "Desirable features" column are illustrative only.

most of the desirable features found in the cost system of a manufacturing concern that uses standards and budgets. Before employing it for a particular company, the designer should list all the desirable features of the proposed cost system. As the designer reviews the current system, he should enter check marks in the appropriate subcolumns under "Current Status." Whenever improvements are needed, a suitable explanation should be provided in the "Remarks" column. This exhibit can be used even when the designer has not determined the desired features of the system. For example, if the present system does not have standards for direct materials usage, the designer should put a check mark in the subcolumn "Absent" against item 3. Later, he can decide whether or not standards for direct materials usage should be developed.

In designing a cost system, the designer should (1) understand the cost accounting process and (2) know various aspects of a cost accounting system. Both topics are explained below.

## THE COST ACCOUNTING PROCESS

To design an efficient and effective cost system, the designer must thoroughly understand the entire cost accounting process, i.e., what is normally done in compiling and reporting costs. Since the designer is supposed to know this aspect well, it is only briefly discussed here.

The end result of financial accounting is the preparation of the balance sheet, the income statement, and similar statements. The end result of cost accounting is product costing (i.e., costing a product, job, process, operation, activity, etc.) or responsibility accounting (i.e., compiling and reporting costs incurred by areas of responsibility such as departments or divisions), or both. Because of this difference in objectives there is a significant difference in the *classification of expenses* for these two systems. In financial accounting, expenses are normally classified according to their nature, such as salaries, wages, rent, electricity, traveling, etc. In cost accounting, expenses may *additionally* be classified by function (manufacturing, selling, etc.), location, process, job, department, cost behavior, etc.

For responsibility accounting, all costs are ultimately charged to organizational segments responsible for incurring and controlling them. For product costing, all costs are ultimately charged to production or sales. For example, for responsibility accounting occupancy costs are charged only to the occupancy cost center, but for product costing they are ultimately charged to the products benefiting from the occupancy costs. Thus, in the ultimate analysis, a cost accounting system analyzes and identifies cost information with one or more segments (products, departments, activities, etc.), depending upon its purpose. To compute costs by segments, it is necessary to

- Identify and define various segments by which cost information is required
- Record (or accumulate) costs by the defined segments

Some costs (e.g., direct materials) can be directly identified with various segments. Others may not be identifiable with any segment because they are common costs (e.g., indirect materials) or joint costs (administrative expenses, financial expenses, etc.); these costs are also known as overhead costs. Hence, it is necessary first to *accumulate* overhead costs separately and then to *allocate* or *apportion* them on some rational basis.

Usually, in a manufacturing organization the manufacturing department is divided into production departments and service departments (personnel, inspection, etc.). All overhead costs are first accumulated by the nature of expenses. Then, all manufacturing overhead costs are allocated to the relevant production and service departments. This process is called *primary allocation* of overhead. Next, the service departments' costs are allocated to the production departments benefiting from them. This process is known as *secondary allocation* of overhead. Ultimately, the production departments' overhead costs are charged to the various products, jobs, etc., benefiting from them. This process is called *absorption* of overhead.

The primary allocation of overhead costs is necessary for product costing as well as for responsibility accounting, but the secondary allocation and absorption of overhead are necessary only for product costing.

In essence, any cost system involves conversion of the source data (input) into the desired cost information (output). The conversion steps vary depending upon whether the cost accounting system is designed for responsibility accounting or for product costing.

A simple flow diagram of a cost accounting process is given in Exhibit 5-3. Direct labor and direct materials can be directly charged to products, whereas overhead costs such as power and occupancy expenses cannot be charged directly to various products. Hence, overhead costs are first accumulated separately, then allocated to various cost centers, and finally absorbed by various products. For cost control purposes, cost accounting ends at the primary allocation stage, and the cost data flow to the cost control reports by areas of responsibility. For product costing, the cost accounting process continues further and culminates at the stage of preparation of the costing profit and loss account (income statement).

**EXHIBIT 5-3**

**Flow Diagram of Cost Accounting Process**

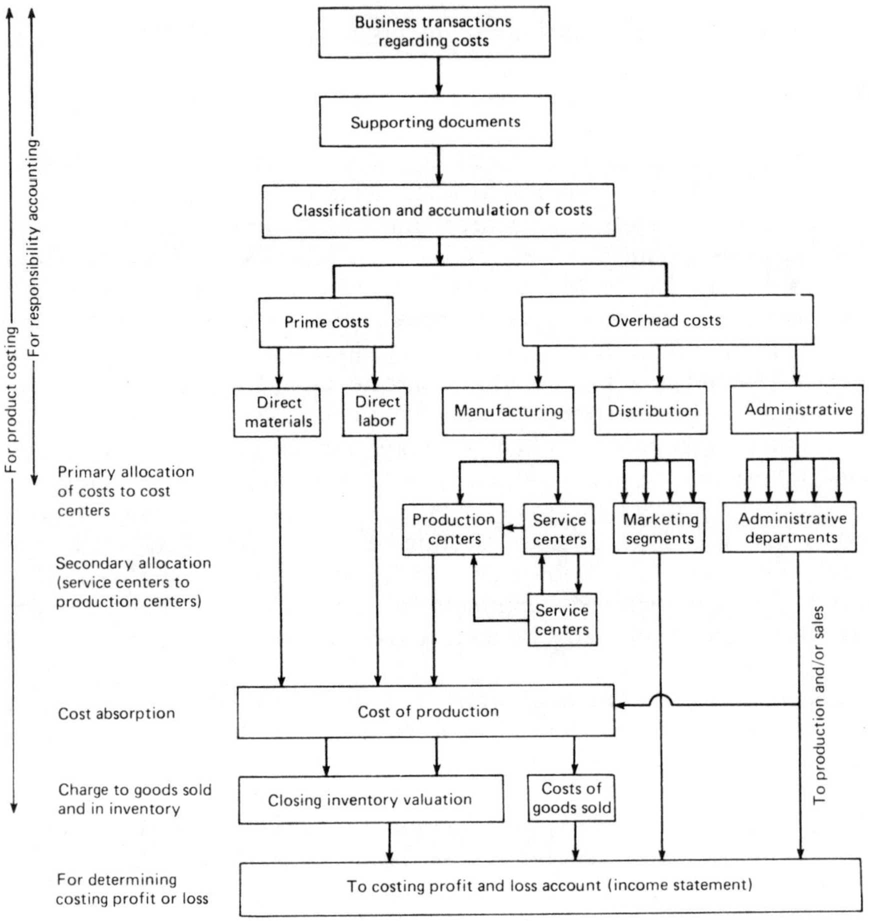


## FACETS OF A COST SYSTEM

From a design point of view, a cost accounting system has the following three aspects or facets:

1. *Policy aspect.* For example, selecting the cost techniques, concepts, and methods to be used, e.g., standard or actual costing, total or direct costing, and bases for allocation of costs

2. *Structural aspect.* Components or anatomy of a cost system, which includes a chart of accounts, a list of responsibility centers, a list of cost centers, supporting documents, accounting and other records, and cost reports

3. *Procedural aspect.* For example, flow of papers, sequence and method of recording and summarizing transactions, timing and frequency of submission of cost reports, and the persons who are to do which part of the cost accounting work, when, and how

Knowledge of various aspects of a cost system enables the designer to determine the method and the order of approach to system design work and to check whether all aspects of the work have been taken care of.

Though a cost system enters into various functional areas, the designer must consider the above-listed aspects only insofar as they pertain to the cost system. For example, the designer is not supposed to develop or design purchasing policy, the purchase order, or purchasing procedures. However, since a cost system must be integrated with various functional systems, he may have to suggest changes in these systems. For example, the designer may have to ask the purchasing department to provide space on the purchase requisition and purchase order for writing the department or the cost center code on these two documents.

## SYSTEM CONSTRAINTS

Let us suppose that a tailor makes a good suit from a superior-quality fabric. What good will that suit be if it does not fit its user well? Even when suits are made to be sold as ready-made suits, they are not made in the abstract. First, a correlation between height, arm length, chest size, and the like is established from an empirical study, and suits in different sizes are made with sufficient margin for alterations. Then, each suit is altered to fit the individual customer.

Similarly, a designer of a cost system cannot design it in the abstract because a given system must not only be *technically sound* but also be *compatible* with the company's environment. Every company, even within the same industry, has its own chemistry, culture, and limitations. Further, even the various divisions of one company may have their own peculiarities. Hence, for a cost system to become an effective management tool it must either be custom-made or, at least, be customized. To design a custom-made cost system, two factors ought to be considered: system objectives and system constraints. The first factor has been explained in Chapter 2; the second is discussed in this chapter.

System constraints are those factors which influence or limit the final design of a cost system. Though constraints do put limitations on a cost system, they need not necessarily be looked upon as negative, because their due consideration imparts a touch of realism to the resulting system. A simple but common example will illustrate the point. Let us suppose that a custom-designed cost system for a given company is technically sound and capable of achieving all the set objectives *provided* five persons are assigned to operate it. If, however, management will not assign more than three persons and will not allow overtime payments, the system is not likely to succeed. Either management must assign more personnel, or the designer must so modify the system that it can be operated by three persons. The second alternative may involve cutting some of the features of the system or making it less sophisticated.

## Examples of System Constraints

System constraints may be internal or external. Some of the most common examples of system constraints of each type are given below.

### Internal Constraints

1. *Attitude and philosophy of top management.* This is a vital constraint because it is responsible for the absence or the existence of many other internal constraints. It is said that you can take a horse to water but you cannot make it drink. Similarly, however good a system may be, unless management appreciates its value and is inclined to use the information generated by the system, there is no point in designing it.

2. *Preferences and attitude of controller in charge of the accounting department.* This constraint is as important as the first one.

3. *Organization structure.* The basic structure of a cost system must follow the company's organization structure. This factor is particularly relevant in determining cost centers and the bases for allocating overhead costs. It is also relevant for establishing responsibility centers for a cost control system.

4. *Availability of personnel.* This constraint refers not only to the numbe of persons but also to their qualifications, experience, abilities, and attitude. Further, it refers to the personnel available not only to operate a system but also to design and implement it. For example, if because of budget constraints an adequate staff is not allocated for designing a cost system, the company may have to be content with a less sophisticated system.

5. *Extent of mechanization of accounting.* This constraint is relevant even if the cost accounting system is primarily manual, because even in such a system it is possible to mechanize or computerize some accounting applications. For example, if a company proposing to design a manual cost system has computerized payroll and fixed assets and depreciation

acccounting, these will greatly facilitate the detailed cost allocation of labor and depreciation costs as well as costs which are allocated in the ratio of labor costs.

### External Constraints

1. *Requirements of applicable laws and regulations.* For example, the accounting record rules of the Federal Communications Commission (FCC) require concerned communications companies to compute depreciation by the straight-line method. If company management feels that for performance evaluation depreciation ought to be computed by the declining-balance method, the designer will have to provide two different methods of computation and allocation of depreciation for achieving different purposes. Similarly, if a cost system is intended primarily to facilitate price or rate setting by statutory bodies, their accounting requirements and price- or rate-setting practices will be important considerations.

2. *Prevailing accounting standards and practices.* For example, the Cost Accounting Standards Board of the United States has prescribed several costing standards for use by certain defense contractors, which they are required to follow.

### Procedure

Having discussed the importance and the nature of system constraints, we are left with two questions:

1. How are system constraints ascertained?
2. How should knowledge of prevailing system constraints be used in designing a cost system?

If during such prior stages as objective setting, preliminary survey, study of the existing accounting system, and determination of the requirements of the cost system the designer has kept his eyes and ears open and looked specifically for possible system constraints, he will be in a position to list most of the constraints prevailing in the company. Some constraints will also surface during the system design phase and the system implementation phase. The best course for the designer is to continue listing separately the possible system constraints as they come to notice. Also, the designer should analyze the background information to identify system constraints.

Having prepared a preliminary list of system constraints, the designer may adopt the following procedure:

1. Prepare, *without* regard to system constraints, the conceptual design of the system, i.e., the broad outline of the system which will best achieve the given objectives.

2. Then consider the effect of the major constraints upon the broad outline of the system, and identify the areas where one or more constraints may require changes in the proposed system.

3. Consider whether, how, and at what cost any of the constraints can be removed. Some constraints are so fundamental to achieving a given objective that they cannot be removed. In fact, such constraints prescribe the conditions under which the objective can be achieved. For example, the uniform system of accounts prescribed by the FCC for the communications industry lays down the account heads and the account numbers which every company must maintain and allows a company only to divide these accounts into subaccounts and sub-subaccounts. Obviously, in this case it is not possible to ignore the prescribed accounting system.

4. Next consider whether and how the proposed system should be modified to take care of the constraints and the impact of such modifications on the system objectives. This step may involve the deletion, substitution, consolidation, or expansion of certain aspects of the proposed system. For example, in designing a cost system for a communications company, we found that the desired accounts classification for internal purposes was different from that prescribed by the uniform system of accounts. To solve this problem, we classified the accounts in greater detail than that prescribed by the FCC. The account code for each account indicated FCC's account number and the company's account number. For the FCC's purposes, the accounts were summarized according to the FCC's account numbers, and for the company's internal purposes they were summarized according to the company's account numbers.

5. If steps 3 and 4 do not produce a commonly acceptable solution, compare the results of the two steps and decide which one is easier and less unfavorable to accept. Thus, either the constraints should be removed, or the design of the system should be so modified that the objectives are achieved without violating the constraints, or the objectives should be suitably modified. Usually, the end result will be a combination of these three alternatives.

6. The procedure mentioned in steps 1 through 5 is to be applied also while each aspect of the system design is considered in detail. For example, while determining cost centers, the designer should ask the question "Are there any constraints which will affect the determination of cost centers?" Then each of the above steps should be followed.

The above procedure explains the iterative nature of system design work.

## DIVISION OF MANUAL COST SYSTEM DESIGN WORK

Since developing a cost system is a very complex task, it is necessary to divide the system design work into various components, design each component, and then synthesize or assemble the components to make a unified cost system.

The most common approach to the design of a cost system for a manufacturing concern, which is used in this book, is given below:

1. Select the cost accounting method (standard costing, direct costing, etc.) to be employed (Chapter 7).
2. Classify the entire organization into segments, which are commonly known as cost centers and responsibility centers (Chapter 8).
3. For direct materials, direct labor, manufacturing overhead, and nonmanufacturing expenses, (*a*) determine their classification by nature, cost centers, cost behavior, controllability, etc.; (*b*) set cost standards; and (*c*) design a budgetary cost control system (Chapter 6 and Chapters 9 through 13).
4. Determine the bases for allocation and absorption of overhead to products (Chapters 11 and 13).
5. Design the reports to be prepared, and lay down the procedure for report preparation from the input stage to the output stage (Chapter 14).
6. For each cost factor, (*a*) set forth the procedure for recording, allocation, and absorption of costs; and (*b*) design appropriate cost documents, records, and worksheets (Chapter 15).
7. Classify various expenses of the entire organization into various account heads, which are collectively referred to as a chart of accounts (Chapter 16).

Since the entire process is iterative, each step will be completed only tentatively at first and be finalized in the second or the third round.

Exhibit 5-4 summarizes the cost system development process and its outcome. On the left-hand side all the tasks (or blocks) under the three phases of system development are listed. These tasks result in developing a cost system that contains the various facets or aspects listed on the right-hand side. To the extent that any aspect already exists and is satisfactory, the designer need not develop it. Further, if the cost system does not employ standard costs and budgets, the aspects relating to them will not be developed. If a cost systems manual is prepared, all the facets mentioned on the right will be included in the manual.

**EXHIBIT 5-4**

**Graphic View of Cost System Development and Its Outcome**

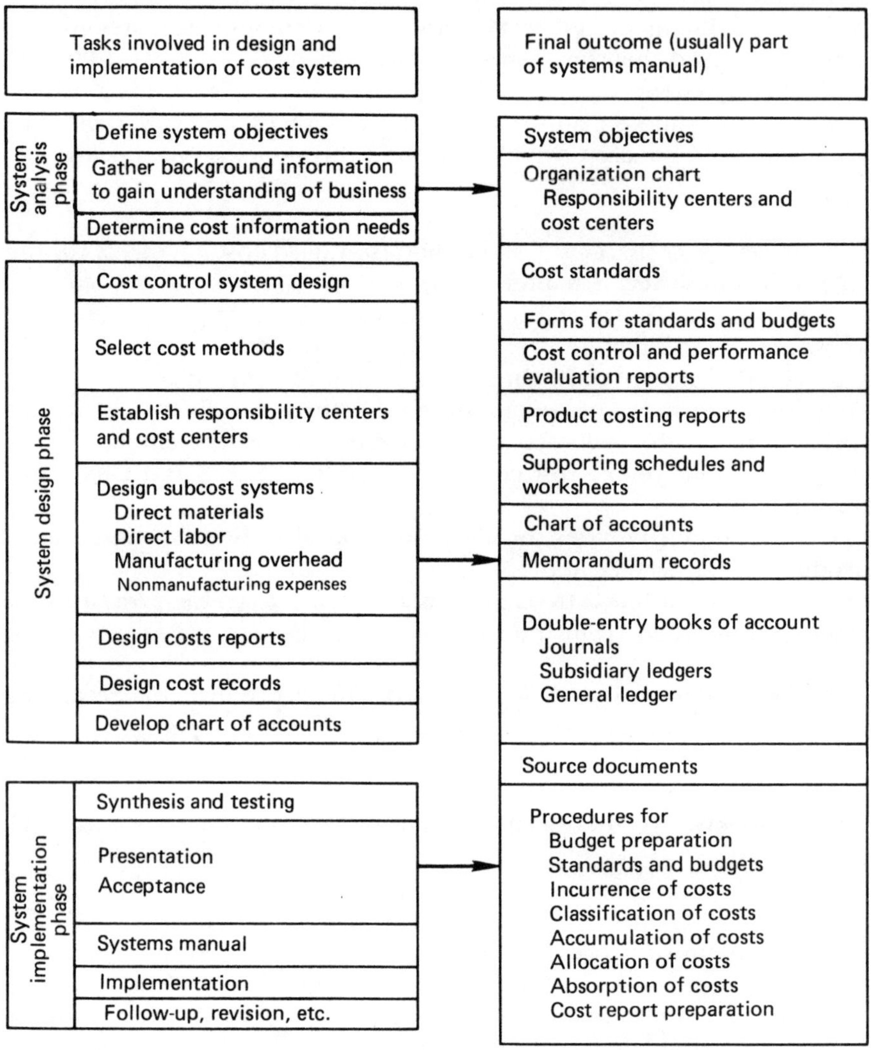


## OVERVIEW OF A COMPUTERIZED COST SYSTEM

The basic cost accounting process in a computerized cost system is the same as that in a manual cost system which has been explained earlier. However, in a computerized system most or some of the manual cost accounting functions are done by a computer. The involvement of a computer adds a whole new dimension to the cost system design process. In particular, there are the following additional major issues to be resolved or tasks to be performed in designing a computerized cost system:

1. As explained earlier, a computerized cost system usually is designed by a team consisting of a cost system designer and a computer specialist. Hence, it is necessary to define their respective *roles* and coordinate their work.

2. Determine which tasks or jobs will be *computerized* and which will be handled *manually*. For example, if the technique of budgeting is used for cost control, the computer may be employed to prepare budgets or budgets may be prepared manually and the budget data then entered in the computer. For this purpose, the cost system designer must know the general potential of a computer.

3. Select the computer and the peripheral equipment (generally known as *hardware*) and their configuration. Equipment is required for capturing input data, storage of data, processing, and generating output. A simple model of a computerized system is shown in Exhibit 5-5.

There are many makes and models of computers and peripheral equipment with widely varying capability, limitations, cost, and reliability. Basically, computers are classified into small computers, minicomputers, and main-frame computers. Further, computer technology is rapidly changing to serve data processing needs better. The multiple choice, on the one hand, offers a great deal of flexibility and, on the other hand, makes selection of data processing equipment and its configuration difficult.

4. Select the *location* of the data processing equipment. Location has an impact on the equipment configuration and the personnel required. This choice is important particularly in a multilocation company, in which three alternatives are available:

   a. *Centralized system.* All data processing functions are performed at one location. The various locations send their input to the central computer system, which generates the required output and distributes it as specified.
   b. *Stand-alone (decentralized) system.* Individual locations have their own computer systems, which function independently of one another. In a stand-alone system, any exchange of data between locations is done manually.
   c. *Dispersed (distributed) data processing system.* The data processing function is distributed among various locations. In a true network of data processing systems, the various systems are linked via telecommunication devices. There are several ways in which

**EXHIBIT 5-5**

**Simple Model of a Computer System**

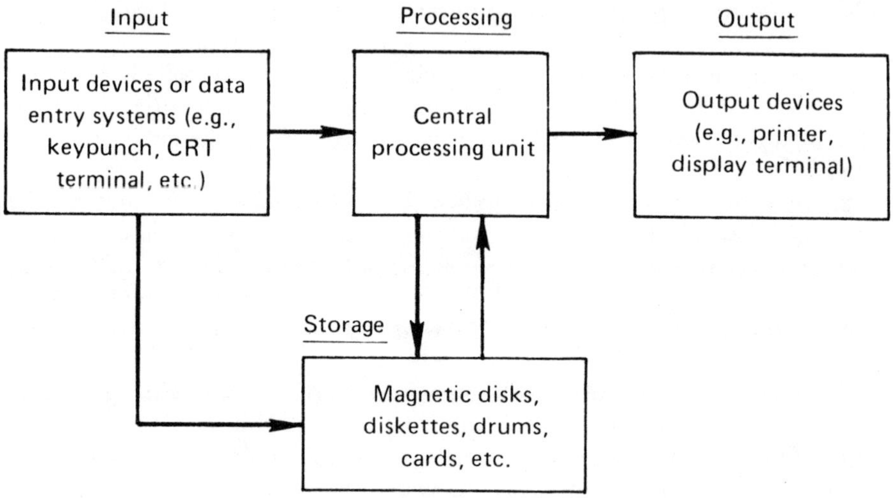


Explanation:

1. A computer system has input media and device, a central processing unit, storage media and device, and an output device.
2. Input media and device are used for entering input data in the computer system.
3. The central processing unit is used for processing (e.g., calculating, sorting, classifying, summarizing, etc.) various input data.
4. Storage media and device are used for storing input data as well as processed data.
5. An output device is used to generate reports for users.

the data processing function can be distributed among different locations. Any or all of the four functions of input, processing, storage, and output can be distributed. When minimum dispersion is made of the data processing function, the remote locations have only input devices to enter input data directly in the central computer, which handles all other functions. When maximum dispersion is made of the data processing function, the remote locations have their own computer system linked to the central computer. A local computer system handles all or most of the data processing needs of each location, and the central computer system performs consolidation work and monitors individual systems. Through the central computer, headquarters personnel can directly access the data in any of the local computers to control the performance of individual locations.

5. Develop or obtain the appropriate *software* to perform the necessary data processing functions. There are two types of software; *operating software* and *application software*. Operating software is required for operating and controlling the computer itself and is usually supplied by the computer manufacturer. Application software is required for the conversion of input data to generate the desired output. For example, there will be application software for the cost accounting system, financial accounting, accounts payable, etc. A company may develop application software from scratch or buy canned or prewritten software from a software house. Prewritten software may need modest to extensive modifications (called *customization*) to suit the individual company's requirements.

The development of application software costs considerable time and money. Hence, every company should investigate available application software to see whether some ready-made software will satisfy most of its needs. If satisfactory prewritten software is available, a cost-benefit analysis should be conducted to make a rational choice between developing one's own software and buying prewritten software.

The application software and hardware should be compatible with each other.

6. When the company is *already using* a computer for non-cost accounting applications, consider whether and how the available equipment can also be used for cost accounting and whether and how the output of the present applications will be useful for the cost system. For example, if general ledger and financial reporting are already computerized, it will be better to integrate a computerized cost accounting system with them because both will have many common input data. If, however, only accounts receivable are computerized, there is not much scope for integrating them with a cost accounting system.

## FEASIBILITY STUDY

The purpose of a feasibility study is to evaluate the economics of the cost system or to weigh the costs to be incurred and the benefits to be derived from the proposed cost system. When there is no obvious case favoring a cost system, the feasibility study will focus on (1) whether it will be worthwhile to have a cost system, (2) how broad its scope should be, (3) how sophisticated it should be, and (4) which of alternative systems should be selected. When, however, there is a clear-cut case favoring a cost system (e.g., if it is needed to comply with a statutory requirement), the feasibility study will focus on the remaining three questions. The benefits should include both cost and noncost benefits, such as speedier cost estimation on nonstandard jobs, reduction in management time spent on operational control because of a more effective cost reporting system, etc. Often, top management's judgment will be involved in valuing the intangible benefits.

### Cost of the Proposed System

The validity of the feasibility study depends upon how carefully the various costs are estimated. The following are major cost factors, some or all of which may be relevant in a given case.

**Hardware** In a computerized cost system, the hardware will include the central processing unit, input-output devices (printer, CRT terminal, etc.), storage devices, and, if appropriate, communications equipment. Even in a manual system, some mechanical devices may be used, and their cost should be estimated.

**Software** If prewritten software is to be acquired, its acquisition cost can easily be ascertained. In addition, the costs of customizing should be estimated even if the software will be customized in-house.

If the software is to be developed by an outside consultant, cost estimates should be obtained from the consultant. If the software is to be developed in-house, all relevant costs, including salaries of existing personnel, should be estimated. However, for deciding whether to buy prewritten software, have it developed by an outside consultant, or develop it in-house, only the incremental in-house costs may be considered if in-house personnel have spare time in which to develop the software.

In addition, the cost of developing the manual portion of the cost system should be estimated.

**Site Preparation** The data processing equipment may require special air conditioning or wiring, a raised floor, or other provisions. All these costs should be estimated.

**Training** In a computerized cost system, operators will have to be trained to operate the hardware, and the system analyst and the programmer will have to be trained in the programming language, prewritten software, and technical features of the hardware. Usually, the training will be provided by the hardware and the software vendors.

In a manual cost system, training will be handled on the job; usually it is difficult to estimate its cost. However, specific expenses such as traveling and fees for attending outside training classes should be estimated.

**Testing, Parallel Run, and Implementation** These costs will consist of:

1. Implementation and testing of hardware.
2. Implementation and testing of software. Testing may involve running the new system parallel with the present system, if any. Further, testing may be done on a third party's computer, which will involve some charges.
3. Entering the existing useful data in the computer or the storage media. For example, the balances in various accounts will have to be entered. Similarly, the past years' actual data may be entered for trend analysis and other purposes. Even in a manual cost system, some conversion work will be involved.

**Operating Costs** Operating costs will include the costs of hardware and software maintenance, communications, manpower, stationery, insurance of hardware, storage cost, utility cost, and rent.

An illustrative cost estimation form for a dispersed data processing system is given in Exhibit 5-6. In this case, the total cost of the purchasing option was computed first.

## Financing Options

Several financing options may be available for acquiring hardware and, in some cases, even software. These options can be grouped as follows:

- Outright purchase
- Leasing from vendors or from a third party
- Renting hardware from the vendors

For evaluating various financing options as well as hardware and software options, the total costs under each option should be reduced to a common denominator. An evaluation of financing options will inevitably include an analysis of leasing versus buying, which is beyond the scope of this book. It may, however, be noted that the cost differentials of various alternative systems may vary from one financing option to another.

An illustrative form for summarizing various options is given in Exhibit 5-7. Since the duration of payment under different financing options varied from option to option, it was considered appropriate in this case to compute the total costs for the first 5 years only and to explain by notes instances in which payment beyond 5 years was involved.

**EXHIBIT 5-6**

**Estimation of the Cost of a Proposed Computerized Cost System under Outright-Purchase Option**

(In thousands of dollars)

| | ER | CR | WR | HQ | Total |
|---|---|---|---|---|---|
| I. *One-time costs* | | | | | |
| *Hardware* | | | | | |
| 6600 CPU with 120,000 of memory, etc. | 56.0 | 56.0 | 56.0 | 56.0 | 224.0 |
| 600 LPM printer (Model 9260) | 17.2 | 17.3 | 17.2 | ... | 51.7 |
| CRTs at $1450 each (Model 8200) | (3) 4.4 | (3) 4.3 | (3) 4.4 | (1) 1.4 | (10) 14.5 |
| Installation | 1.2 | 1.2 | 1.2 | 1.0 | 4.6 |
| Disks and decollators | 1.9 | 1.9 | 1.9 | 1.9 | 7.6 |
| Subtotal | 80.7 | 80.7 | 80.7 | 60.3 | 302.4 |
| CRTs and modems at cities at $2850 each | (8) 22.8 | (6) 17.1 | (3) 8.6 | ... | (17) 48.5 |
| Total, hardware, .....A | 103.5 | 97.8 | 89.3 | 60.3 | 350.9 |
| *Software: one-time* | | | | | |
| Cost accounting, financial accounting, and reporting, ......B | 36.0 | 36.0 | 36.0 | ... | 108.0 |
| *Site preparation*, .......C | 5.0 | 10.0 | 10.0 | 5.0 | 30.0 |
| *Training* | | | | | |
| Hardware, software, and programming: HQ, regions, and cities, ..............D | ... | 5.5 | 5.5 | 1.0 | 12.0 |
| *Testing, conversion, parallel run*, etc., .....E | 2.0 | 2.0 | 2.0 | ... | 6.0 |
| Total, one-time costs, A + B + C + D + E | 146.5 | 151.3 | 142.8 | 66.3 | 506.9 |
| II. *Yearly operating costs* | | | | | |
| H/W maintenance: HQ and regions | 8.6 | 8.6 | 8.6 | 5.9 | 31.7 |
| CRT maintenance: cities at $264 per CRT | 2.1 | 1.6 | 0.8 | ... | 4.5 |
| Subtotal, ............F | 10.7 | 10.2 | 9.4 | 5.9 | 36.2 |

**EXHIBIT 5-6**

**Estimation of the Cost of a Proposed Computerized Cost System under Outright-Purchase Option (*Continued*)**

| | ER | CR | WR | HQ | Total |
|---|---|---|---|---|---|
| Communications: regions | 23.4 | 23.4 | 23.4 | ... | 70.2 |
| Communications: cities at $3480 per CRT | 27.8 | 20.9 | 10.4 | ... | 59.1 |
| Subtotal, ...........G | 51.2 | 44.3 | 33.8 | ... | 129.3 |
| Salaries (additional only) | | | | | 20.0 |
| Taxes and other | | | | | 12.0 |
| Rent | | | | | 13.2 |
| Utilities, etc. | | | | | 10.8 |
| Stationery | | | | | 8.4 |
| Insurance | | | | | 0.5 |
| Subtotal, ...........H | 11.0 | 11.0 | 11.0 | 31.9 | 64.9 |
| Total operating costs per year, F + G + H | 72.9 | 65.5 | 54.2 | 37.8 | 230.4 |

NOTE: ER = Eastern Region; CR = Central Region; WR = Western Region; HQ = headquarters; H/W = hardware.

## EXHIBIT 5-7

### Cost Comparison of Two Computer Systems and Different Financing Options (ABC Company)

(In thousands of dollars)

| | | Annual Cost | | | | | | | Ranking Based on | | | Possibility of Increase in Charges for | | | |
|---|---|---|---|---|---|---|---|---|---|---|---|---|---|---|---|
| Options | One-Time Cost | Year 1 | Year 2 | Year 3 | Year 4 | Year 5 | Total Costs in 5 Years | Present Value of Total Costs at 8 Percent | 5-Year Costs | Present Value of 5-Year Costs | Will ABC Own Equipment? | H/W Lease | H/W Rent | S/W Rent | Maintenance |
| *Datapoint (DP)* | | | | | | | | | | | | | | | |
| A. Purchase | | | | | | | | | | | | | | | |
| B. Third-party $1 buy-back: 1-year lease | | | | | | | | | | | | | | | |
| C. Third-party $1 buy-back: 3-year lease | | | | | | | | | | | | | | | |
| D. Third-party $1 buy-back: 5-year lease | | | | | | | | | | | | | | | |
| E. DP lease: 3 years | | | | | | | | | | | | | | | |
| F. DP lease: 2 years | | | | | | | | | | | | | | | |
| G. DP lease: 1 year | | | | | | | | | | | | | | | |
| *IBM* | | | | | | | | | | | | | | | |
| H. Purchase | | | | | | | | | | | | | | | |
| I. Third-party $1 buy-back: 1-year lease | | | | | | | | | | | | | | | |
| J. IBM lease: 3 years | | | | | | | | | | | | | | | |
| K. Third-party $1 buy-back: 3-year lease | | | | | | | | | | | | | | | |
| L. Third-party $1 buy-back: 5-year lease | | | | | | | | | | | | | | | |
| M. IBM rental | | | | | | | | | | | | | | | |

NOTE: H/W = hardware; S/W = software.

# Chapter 6

# Designing a Cost Control System

Without a yardstick, there is no measurement.
And without measurement, there can be no control.
Pravin P. Shah

If we compare the job of a business manager with that of a physician, an airplane pilot, or even an automobile driver, we will find that each of them manages or controls something. However, there is a striking difference in the way they manage. A physician uses devices from those of simple measurement, such as a stethoscope, to more advanced devices, such as x-ray equipment. An airplane pilot has many control gadgets to use. Further, no one would think of driving an automobile without a speedometer or a fuel-level indicator. In contrast, a business manager often plunges into a business without having adequate control tools and techniques. Ironically, management controls are introduced after some damage has been done. Cost controls, which are a species of management controls, are no exception to this general phenomenon. For example, as reported by Alfred P. Sloan, Jr., in his book *My Years with General Motors* (1964), financial controls in General Motors came out of the ruins of 1920, when the corporation wrote off one-sixth of its total assets.

## COST CONTROL SYSTEM VERSUS PRODUCT COSTING SYSTEM

A cost accounting system may be developed for product costing or cost control, or both. A cost control system goes beyond the bounds of a cost accounting system for product costing. For example, for cost control purposes it is necessary to define policy on the incurrence of various costs, set forth authorization procedures, set standards for costs which may be incurred for a given objective, and the like. The general procedure for developing a cost control system is discussed in this chapter. As in the case of product costing, special points for designing material, labor, and overhead cost control systems will be dealt with in Chapters 9 through 13.

## TYPES OF CONTROL SYSTEMS

A cost control system is a species of management control system. Management control mechanisms can be classified into *preventive* and *feedback* mechanisms. Internal checks and controls which are applied before an event are a part of the preventive mechanism. For example, the requirement of prior approval by higher authority for issuing materials in excess of the standard quantity is intended to prevent excessive consumption of materials. It is an advance-warning system. However, *after-the-fact* reporting of excessive consumption of materials is a feedback mechanism. Every company needs both types of control mechanisms.

Another way to classify controls is to relate them to the levels of organization at which they are exercised. Controls exercised at operating levels are called *operational controls;* they are applied on a day-to-day basis and a transaction-to-transaction basis. Controls exercised at the management level are called *management controls;* they are applied on an overall basis and to a group of transactions. For example, the supervisor of a production shop will be interested in controlling the consumption of individual items of direct materials on a daily basis, whereas a plant manager will be interested in controlling direct material consumption in the aggregate and on a weekly or bimonthly basis. Further, besides cost controls there are production controls, marketing controls, and various other controls.

All these types of controls should be closely integrated with one another so that they will be effective. For example, without direct material standards (preventive control), direct material cost reports (feedback control) will not be very effective. Similarly, without feedback reports, the effectiveness of preventive controls will not be known.

## NATURE OF COST CONTROL

A few important reminders about cost control will be useful. First, cost control is not tantamount to downward pressure on cost in the abstract. The purpose of a cost control system is, and should be, to achieve the company's *objectives* at the *lowest possible cost.* For example, to achieve the objective of higher net profit, it may be necessary to increase advertising expenses. Similarly, to increase market share, it may be necessary, say, to improve the quality of the products, the cost of which may exceed the additional profit from the incremental revenue. In the same way, cheaper materials will reduce cost but may affect the organization's goal of providing high-quality products. In short, cost control should not be applied in a vacuum or without considering the company's objectives.

Second, not only the short-term but also the long-term effects of cost control should be considered. For example, it will be necessary to incur costs in the short run on a project for improving the design of an automobile with a view to reducing the cost of production, but the benefit from the improved design may not start flowing for a year or more. If the project for improving the car design is pruned, there will be short-term cost savings but a loss of potentially greater cost savings in the long term. In other words, current performance, costs, and profits should not be overemphasized.

Third, cost control and cost reduction are not synonymous. *Cost reduction* means doing the same thing at a cost lower than the past actual cost or the past standard cost. *Cost control* means containing costs within predetermined limits. Cost reduction may be accomplished by finding less expensive material, labor, or other items, by reducing the quantity of material or labor used, by improving the product design or production methods, etc. Once an item of cost has been reduced, it becomes a new standard until it is changed.

Fourth, a cost control system is a management tool, and as in the case of any other management tool, it is management's decision whether and to what extent to employ it. There is no use in designing a cost control system if management is not going to use it. Similarly, management acceptance and support for the system should not be presumed. Management must be educated about the usefulness of a cost control system.

Fifth, every business, small or large, needs a cost control system. A small business may need a simple system, whereas a large business may need an elaborate and sophisticated system. A profitable business needs a cost control system as much as a loss-making business needs it.

Sixth, for effective cost control, attention should be paid not only to the monetary amount but also to nonmonetary factors such as quantity of materials, labor time, quantity of power, number of employees, and so on.

Seventh, and this is the most important point, a cost control system is useful not only for controlling *costs* but also for controlling various activities and *operations*. For example, the establishment of direct materials standards and the preparation of direct materials consumption documents, records, and reports help to improve the materials management function. Often, poor cost control is a sign of poor management.

## ESSENTIALS OF EFFECTIVE COST CONTROL

To design an effective cost system, the designer must understand the essential requirements for achieving cost control. These essentials are briefly discussed below with a view to giving the reader an overview of the cost control system. This discussion will also enable the reader to appreciate the importance of each of the tasks in designing such a system. Later, these essentials will be expanded while the process of designing a cost control system is explained.

**Appropriate Organization Structure** The functions and activities of the organization should be clearly defined and organized. The responsibility for accomplishing various functions should be assigned to specific individuals, who must also be given the necessary authority for carrying out assigned duties and for the incurrence of costs. The entire organization should be divided into segments according to areas of responsibility.

**Staffing** The organization should be staffed with competent managers and other employees, and they should either have the necessary experience or be provided adequate training. A good manager can compensate for poor organization and a poor control system.

**Leadership** Effective leadership is a must for cost control. Systems and reports by themselves will not bring about cost control. How well the leader enforces the discipline for controlling costs will have a profound impact on the effectiveness of the cost control system.

**Planning** For controlling expenses, it is necessary to plan the activities of the company and to determine how much the company wants to spend on each of its planned objectives and activities. The importance of planning in controlling expenses may not be obvious. An example will make the point clear. Unless sales activities are planned, the production department will not know what to produce and how much to produce, and there may be either excess production or a shortage of products available for sale. Excess production means higher inventory carrying costs and a greater risk of obsolescence. A shortage of products means loss of revenue and underutilization of available sales facilities. Further, if the production department does not plan its activities in terms of what, how much, and when to produce, the purchasing department will not know what, how much, and when to buy, and it may be required to buy materials at premium prices or may not be able to procure required materials on time. Both these situations mean higher costs. Thus, planning is an important *prerequisite* of effective cost control.

**Standards** Goals or desirable performance should be defined in advance by establishing performance targets as well as cost standards and budgets. These standards should be established separately for individual responsibility centers. For example, if we know only that 2 kilograms of direct material is used to produce one unit of finished product, we cannot tell whether or not the material is being used efficiently. However, if it has been predetermined that only 1.9 kilograms of direct material should be consumed, we can tell that there has been an excess consumption of the material. Thus, some sort of predetermined standards are essential for cost control.

**Policies and Procedures** There should be appropriate policies and procedures for the incurrence, authorization, and payment of expenditures.

**Measurement** Costs actually incurred by various responsibility centers should be accumulated because without measurement there is no control.

**Comparison against Standards** Actual costs should be compared against standards, and variances should be computed and identified with the persons responsible for them.

**Cost Control Reports** Actual costs and their variances from standard costs should be reported to the individual responsibility center managers responsible for those variances. Without feedback reports, the center managers will have no means of knowing how well they have performed.

**Corrective or Preventive Actions** The responsibility center managers should investigate the causes of variances and take appropriate corrective or preventive action. In most cases, control is a day-to-day, item-by-item function; i.e., responsibility center managers and their subordinates should be able to notice many deviations from the individual transactions themselves. For example, vigilant supervisors may notice excessive consumption of direct materials and direct labor. Hence, they should initiate corrective or preventive action on the spot without waiting for a report.

**Self-Propelling Mechanism** The cost control mechanism should be self-propelling; i.e., it should be so structured that successive steps are taken as a matter of routine. For example, once responsibility reports have been submitted to responsibility center managers, the managers should explain the causes of significant variances and also the actions taken or planned to correct or prevent the variances. They should not wait for the controller's department or their superiors to request explanations. For this purpose, the system should define significant variances; e.g., variances in excess of $1000 and 10 percent of the standard cost may be considered significant.

**Measure Efficiency and Effectiveness** Each responsibility center is responsible for achieving some *result* (*output*), such as production, sales, provision of repair services, etc. To enable it to achieve that result, it is allowed to use certain *resources* (*input*). If a responsibility center achieves or exceeds the predetermined result, it is said to be *effective;* otherwise, it is said to be ineffective or less effective. If it spends resources within the predetermined limits, it is said to be *efficient;* otherwise, it is said to be inefficient or less efficient.

Naturally, a responsibility center should be not only efficient but also effective; otherwise the company cannot achieve its goal. For example, let us assume that the budgeted sales of Region A totaled 1500 units and that its advertising budget was $30,000, or $20 per unit of sales. If the region spends only $18,000 on advertising and achieves sales of 1000 units, its advertising cost per unit of sales will be $18. Thus, though Region A *appears* to be efficient in spending the advertising money, it is not effective in achieving its sales goal of 1500 units. Hence, the saving of $12,000 in the advertising cost is a false economy because the company will lose the profit that it would have made from the sale of an additional 500 units. This example shows the importance of measuring both efficiency in using resources and effectiveness in achieving desired results.

**Human Factor in Cost Control** Often a cost control system is viewed as a mechanical system involving the establishment of standards, budgets, the preparation of variance reports, obtaining explanations for variances, etc. It would be a grave mistake to ignore the fact that human beings are at the center of a cost control system. Ultimately, cost control must be *personalized;* i.e., responsibility for cost control should rest with individuals, and variances of actual costs from predetermined costs should be identified with the individuals responsible for controlling them. For example, the standards established for direct materials, equipment-hours, etc., are to be achieved by individuals and not by machines.

Further, there is always an interaction of human beings and machines, human beings and materials, internal and external factors, two or more individuals, and so on. When something is out of control, the normal tendency is to blame inanimate things (machine, material, etc.), external factors (vendors, customers, the weather), and even other persons in the company. To check this blame passing, the lines of responsibility-authority of each responsibility center and its personnel should be defined as clearly as possible, and to the extent possible objective standards of their performance should be set.

To achieve the above two purposes, concerned individuals should be allowed to participate in setting standards and should accept the standards. Further, they should be motivated to achieve control and be given the needed direction and guidance by their superiors. Everyone concerned must be enabled to understand the company's budgeting process, classification of expenses, report forms, items included in the reports, what those items do or do not convey, and so on.

## MAJOR TASKS INVOLVED IN DESIGNING A COST CONTROL SYSTEM

The process of designing a cost control system involves the nine major tasks shown in Exhibit 6-1. The process is iterative in nature, and the number of iterations required depends upon the complexity of the business, the experience of the designer, and the sophistication of the cost control system to be designed. Each of the major tasks is explained separately.

### Task 1: Defining Scope of Cost Control System

In designing a cost control system, the designer should have a clear idea about the scope of the system. Ideally, a cost control system should pervade all segments of the company, all layers of management, and all functional areas. However, this ideal situation may not always be feasible or even advisable, as in the following situations:

■ The need for control may be more pressing in some segments or functional areas than in others. In such cases, the segments or areas

**EXHIBIT 6-1**

**Major Tasks Involved in Designing a Cost Control System**

9. Designing a cost recording system
8. Designing a responsibility reporting and follow-up system
7. Developing expense control policy and procedure
6. Establishing procedure for developing cost standards and/or preparing expense budgets
5. Determining cost information required for cost control
4. Establishing responsibility centers
3. Studying cost characteristics
2. Gaining understanding of company's business
1. Defining scope of cost control system

with a more pressing need may be given priority. For instance, if the company management feels that manufacturing costs are fairly stable but marketing costs are rising disproportionately, the cost system may be developed first for controlling marketing costs.

- If the development of an all-pervasive cost control system requires considerable time, it may be advisable to develop it in a phased manner so that benefits start flowing sooner and the entire project becomes more manageable. In a small organization the entire cost control system usually may be designed at one time, but in a large organization it is necessary to design and implement the system in a phased manner.
- If a budgetary control system or a standard cost system is to be employed for the first time, management may be skeptical about its usefulness to the company and may not be willing to commit all the resources necessary for the development of a full-fledged budgetary control system or a standard cost system.
- Even though management is convinced of the practical value of an all-pervasive cost control system, the company may not be in a position to commit the necessary resources at one time.
- If the company management is very tradition-bound, the designer may feel that it is desirable to develop a cost control system segment by segment.
- If the required number of qualified people are not available, it may not be possible to develop a full-fledged cost control system.

In these situations, a cost control system may be developed first for one or more profit centers, divisions, branches, departments, functional areas, or cost elements. For example, the system may be developed for the manufacturing departments of all the profit centers within the company. However, if it is decided eventually to have a full-fledged cost control system, the designer should first develop a broad design of the system and then develop it in phases to ensure that the entire system will be cohesive.

## Task 2: Gaining Understanding of Company's Business

The designer should understand the business and various activities of the company for which the cost control system is being designed. He should also study the company's organization structure and cost structure and identify the costs incurred with each major activity and major segment of the company. Since this subject has been dealt with in detail in Chapter 3, it is not repeated here.

## Task 3: Studying Cost Characteristics

Next, the designer should study two characteristics of each cost factor: its cost behavior and its controllability.

**Cost Behavior** As we shall see later in this chapter, different techniques are available for cost control, and the suitability of each technique depends mainly upon the behavior of the cost to be controlled. For example, though the fixed-budgeting technique is suitable for controlling fixed costs, the techniques of flexible budgeting and standard costing are more appropriate for controlling variable costs. Separation of costs into variable and fixed categories is necessary also for product costing based on direct costing.

Variable costs are those costs which remain constant *per unit of production* or sales but vary *in total* in direct proportion to the volume of production or sales. Direct materials and direct labor are variable costs.

Fixed costs are those costs the total amount of which remains constant during a given period. Consequently, fixed costs per unit of production or sales decrease with an increase in the volume of production or sales, and vice versa. Depreciation, rent of premises, managerial and supervisory salaries, property taxes, and insurance are fixed costs.

Classification of costs into variable and fixed costs poses two major problems. First, the separation of semivariable or semifixed costs, such as indirect materials, supplies, maintenance, tools, and indirect labor, is not a cut-and-dried issue. These costs should be separated into fixed and variable elements by using any of the techniques of scatter diagram, high-low method, regression analysis, etc. Since an explanation of these techniques is available from any standard textbook on cost accounting, it is not given here.

Second, most fixed costs remain constant only over a certain range called a *relevant range,* of production or sales, and this range may differ from one item of fixed cost to another. Hence, it is necessary to determine the relevant range of production or sales separately for each fixed-cost item. Even some of the variable costs per unit may change beyond a certain range of production or sales. For example, at a higher volume of production, the direct material cost may decrease because of a quantity discount. Hence, even for variable costs the relevant range of production may have to be determined.

**Non-Volume-Related Changes in Costs** The distinction between fixed and variable costs is based only on their behavior pattern in relation to volume of production or sales. There may be non-volume-related changes in both fixed and variable costs. For example, owing to inflation, both variable and fixed costs may rise even at the same volume of production or sales. For effective cost control, even non-volume-related changes in costs should be controlled.

**Controllability** Though variable costs are usually controllable, they may not be fully controllable. Further, fixed costs are not necessarily noncontrollable. For example, though the direct material cost is variable, the direct material price may not be controllable. On the other hand, though clerical salaries are fixed in nature, they are usually controllable. Hence, to design an effective cost control system, it is necessary to determine which costs are controllable and which costs are noncontrollable, to what extent each of the controllable costs is controllable, and by whom it is controllable.

**Need** It is essential to separate controllable and noncontrollable costs because it is a waste of effort and money to set up an elaborate control mechanism for controlling a noncontrollable cost element. Instead, cost control efforts should be focused on reducing the element of noncontrollability and, until that goal is achieved, on controlling the controllable costs. For instance, if there is a single source of supply for one of the direct materials consumed by the company and if the price of that material is subject to frequent upward revisions, this price is noncontrollable by the company. Hence, setting up an elaborate purchase authorization policy requiring multilevel approval for purchasing that material would be a waste of valuable management time and talent. Instead, management should attempt to reduce the element of noncontrollability by entering into a long-term contract with the supplier, developing alternative sources of supply of the material, or changing the product design either to replace the material by another material more amenable to control or to reduce the usage of the material so that it does not form a significant portion of the total cost, and so on.

**Meaning** A cost item should be regarded as controllable by the company if the company can determine whether or not to incur it or can determine or influence its amount. Otherwise, the item should be regarded as noncontrollable. Often, a company has greater control over the quantity of the cost factor used and less control over its rates or prices. For example, usually a company has greater control over the quantity of direct materials consumed but less control over their prices. Hence, for each controllable cost factor, what precisely is controllable should be ascertained.

**By Whom Are Costs Controllable?** Costs can be controlled, if at all, by the departments and the individuals who have the authority to incur them. For effective cost control, controllable costs should be identified with the departments and the specific individuals within each department who are responsible for controlling them. Then only will it be possible to personalize cost variances and hold the responsible individuals accountable for those variances. In responsibility accounting, these departments are known as responsibility centers.

In practice, the identification of costs by responsibility centers is not always easy, particularly when responsibility for a cost item is shared by two or more centers or individuals. For example, responsibility for the cost of power generated in-house is shared by the power-consuming departments and the power-generating department. The former are responsible for the costs related to the volume of power consumed and the latter for the unit cost of generating power. Similarly, the responsibility for the direct material cost lies with the purchasing department (for the material prices) and with the production departments (for the quantity of materials consumed). However, both the price and the quantity of material are influenced by the material specifications, which in turn are governed by the product design and the company's objectives regarding product quality.

As we shall see, a few techniques are available to deal with the problem of assigning responsibility for cost control in case of shared responsibility. Suffice it to say here that one should be very careful in determining the individuals responsible for various costs.

**Relation to Time** Cost controllability is relative not only to persons but also to time. What is noncontrollable in the short run may be controllable in the long run. For example, a monthly lease of premises is controllable from month to month, but usually a long-term lease is not cancelable at any time without incurring a penalty and therefore is not controllable in the short run. However, rent under a long-term lease is controllable before the lease is signed and therefore will be controllable when the lease is due for renewal.

## Engineered, Discretionary, and Committed Costs

On the basis of the above two characteristics of costs, we can classify costs, from the standpoint of cost control, into three categories: (1) engineered costs, (2) discretionary costs, and (3) committed costs.

*Engineered costs* are those costs which bear a physical relation to output, and their amount can therefore be determined by engineering standards. For example, direct materials, direct labor, indirect materials, power, etc., bear some quantifiable relation to production and hence can be called engineered costs. These costs may be variable, semivariable, or fixed in nature for a given range of production or sales. Usually, the techniques of standard costing and flexible budgeting are employed to control engineered costs.

*Discretionary costs* are those costs which are incurred at the discretion of management. For example, sales promotion, advertising, and research and development are discretionary costs because whether and to what extent to incur them are left to management. These costs are also known as *policy costs* or *managed costs.* Usually, they are controlled through fixed or appropriation budgets.

*Committed costs* are those costs which are committed for a period of time. For example, rent under a long-term lease is a committed cost because it is committed to be incurred for the duration of the lease. Committed costs are usually noncontrollable during the period of commitment or are controllable subject to the incurrence of a penalty for breaking the commitment.

Depreciation is another example of committed costs. It is also known as sunk cost because an investment has already been made in the purchase of a fixed asset and depreciation is just a process of allocating the sunk cost of the fixed asset.

Though the company cannot influence the amount of committed costs once commitments have been made, it can certainly control the benefits from committed costs. For example, once a machine has been purchased, the company should endeavor to make the best possible use of it.

The three categories of costs are not mutually exclusive. For example, though research and development costs are discretionary, some of their recurring cost items may be amenable to engineering standards, and the depreciation of research equipment is a sunk cost.

### Cost Characteristics Matrix

After studying the cost characteristics of each cost factor, it is advisable to prepare a cost characteristics matrix as illustrated by Exhibit 6-2. For each cost factor, this matrix shows cost behavior as well as cost controllability.

## Task 4: Establishing Responsibility Centers

As we saw earlier, for effective cost control costs should be identified with the departments and the individuals responsible for controlling various costs. Hence, the entire organization must be segmented according to the areas of responsibility for cost control and an individual be placed in charge of each segment. These organizational segments are known as responsibility centers. When the technique of budgeting is employed, the responsibility centers are also called budget centers.

The process of establishing responsibility centers is a subject by itself and is dealt with in Chapter 8.

## Task 5: Determining Cost Information Required for Cost Control

From the study of the characteristics of the costs incurred by the company, the designer should determine what cost information is required for cost control. Generally, cost information for cost control should be confined to the controllable cost items which are significant enough to be controlled. Further, it should be related to the responsibility centers and to the individuals who have the responsibility as well as the authority for controlling those cost items. Since the procedure for determining the cost information required for the various objectives of a cost system has been explained in Chapter 4, it is not repeated here.

### Task 6: Establishing Procedure for Developing Cost Standards and for Preparing Expense Budgets

Once the responsibility centers have been established, it is essential to determine how much cost each center is authorized to incur and for what purpose. These predetermined cost amounts become standards, yardsticks, or benchmarks against which actual costs can be measured. Without some sort of standards, it is difficult to institute cost control and measure the performance of the responsibility center managers. Though current costs can be compared with past costs, the latter do not provide a valid basis for comparison because they may include inefficiencies and do not reflect changes in current cost conditions caused by changes in internal and external factors affecting the company.

Standard costs and budgets are two well-known forms of expressing predetermined costs. If a cost control system is based on standard costs, it is called a *standard cost control system,* and if it is based on budgets, it is called a *budgetary cost control system.* For employing these two systems, it is necessary to design procedures for the development of standard costs and the preparation of budgets. These two important subjects are dealt with in detail later in this chapter.

### Task 7: Developing Expense Control Policy and Procedure

For proper control over expenses, it is necessary to have well-defined policies and procedures on the incurrence as well as the payment of various expenses. These policies and procedures are preventive control mechanisms, rather than feedback control mechanisms. Expense control policies and procedures are necessary whether or not the techniques of budgeting and standard costing are employed. It is also worthwhile to remember that the incurrence of an expense and its payment are not synonymous. An expense can be controlled, if at all, before and not after it has been incurred. For example, traveling expenses should be controlled before a journey is undertaken. Control over payment after an expense has been incurred merely verifies compliance with the policy and procedure for the incurrence of an expense. However, both types of control are necessary.

**EXHIBIT 6-2**

**Illustrative Cost Characteristics Matrix (XYZ Company)**

| Cost factor | Controllability: By Whom Controllable | Controllability: When Controllable | Cost Behavior (Whether Variable and Factor of Variability) |
|---|---|---|---|
| 1. *Direct materials* | | | |
| Usage | Product Engineering Department and Production Department | While designing products and while manufacturing products | Varies with quantity of finished products produced |
| Price | Product Engineering Department | At the time of determining specifications while designing a product | Varies with quantity bought and specifications of direct materials |
| | Purchasing Department | While purchasing | |
| 2. *Bought out electricity* | | | |
| Volume | Production and other consuming departments | Before its consumption (i.e., on day-to-day basis) | In Production Department; varies with volume of production |

| | | | |
|---|---|---|---|
| Rate | Electricity company (i.e., noncontrollable) | | Base amount of $100,000 per month is fixed. The variable amount at the rate of 10 cents per kilowatthour depends upon the volume of electricity consumed. |
| 3. *Rent* | | | |
| Factory buildings on 5-year lease | Office Administration Department | Not controllable until expiration of present lease | Once lease is entered into, it is fixed in nature; i.e., it becomes a committed cost. |
| Branch offices on monthly lease | Branch managers | Month-to-month basis | More or less fixed during a year |
| 4. *Advertising* | Marketing Department and company president | Before incurring it | Discretionary cost. Usually, the company spends 3 percent of its revenue on advertising. |
| 5. *Research and development* (60 percent consists of salaries) | R&D department manager and company president | Before undertaking an R&D project, but in-house R&D projects can be stopped at any time. | Discretionary cost. Usually the company spends 1.5 percent of its revenue on R&D. |

Setting policies for expense controls is the responsibility of management and not of the designer. However, the designer should make management aware of the need for expense control policies and, if so required by management, even define the necessary elements of the policies. Depending upon his expertise and the scope of the assignment, the designer may or may not be responsible for developing procedures for the incurrence and payment of various expenses. But the discussion of these subjects is certainly beyond the scope of this book.

At a minimum, the designer should know that the policy and procedure on the incurrence of each item of expense should include the following major elements:

- Under what circumstances can the expense be incurred?
- Who can incur it?
- Who should approve its incurrence?
- When should it be approved?
- In what form should approval be obtained?
- On which form, if any, should the actual expense be reported, and what vouchers should be prepared in support of it?
- Who should scrutinize compliance with the set policy and procedure before the payment of the expense?
- Who should approve the expense before its payment?

## Task 8: Developing a Responsibility Reporting and Follow-up System

Approved cost budgets and standards represent commitment by responsibility center managers to achieve their centers' objectives within the limits of their budgets and standards. However, to ensure that actual costs do not exceed budgeted or standard costs, it is necessary periodically to compute variances between actual and budgeted or standard costs, report them to responsibility center managers, and use the reports as a basis for corrective or preventive action. Thus, responsibility reports feed back information to the responsibility center managers *after the fact.* Consequently, responsibility reporting is a *feedback control system* and not a preventive control system. However, responsibility reports may be the basis for action to prevent the recurrence of unfavorable variances in the future.

A responsibility report provides a measurement of the performance of the responsibility center in controlling costs and achieving predefined objectives.

### Operational Reports versus Management Reports

There are two types of responsibility reports: operational reports and management reports. Operational reports are required by operating personnel and focus on individual transactions, events, or activities. For example, for controlling direct materials usage, each material issue should be controlled; for controlling direct labor time, the activities of each worker should be controlled on a continuous basis; and so on. Management reports are required by middle and upper management and focus either on a summary of transactions or results or on exceptional transactions or results. Thus, first-line supervisors need detailed reports, middle management needs summary reports, and upper management needs exception reports. Sometimes, exception reports may also be submitted to middle management, and summary reports may be submitted to upper management. For example, upper management receives a summary income statement.

Because of the difference in the focus of operational and management reports, there is also a difference in the frequency of reporting. Operational reports are prepared daily or weekly, and management reports are prepared monthly or at best weekly.

### Essential Features of Responsibility Reporting System

A responsibility reporting system, should contain the following essential features:

1. The cost accounting department should compare *actual* costs with *budgeted* or *standard* costs and compute variances. In comparing actual expenses with flexible budgets, budgeted expenses should be adjusted for the volume of activity actually attained; i.e., if the actual activity level is higher than that planned for a particular month, budgeted expenses should be increased appropriately, and vice versa. Similarly, budgeted expenses should be adjusted for changes in goals in nonrecurring programs. If, for example, there is a significant budget allowance for putting a manual inventory system on a computer and if that program has been put off during the budget year, the budget allowance for the project should be deleted; otherwise, the concerned department's budget will incorrectly show a favorable budget variance. In a fixed budget, the comparison will be made with budgeted expenses without any adjustment.

2. Then, the cost accounting department should *analyze variances by causes;* direct materials and direct labor variances into usage and price or rate variances; fixed overhead variances into volume variance, efficiency variance, and spending variance; and variable overhead variances into efficiency variance and spending variance. The types of variances computed will depend upon the cost control techniques used and the significance of each type of variance.

3. The cost accounting department should next *identify variances* with

the individual responsibility centers and prepare responsibility *reports* by responsibility centers. Specimen responsibility reports are given in Exhibits 4-5 through 4-9 and in Exhibit 6-3. The following guidelines will be helpful for this purpose.

*a.* For the cost items to be included in a responsibility report, two approaches are possible. Under the first approach, a responsibility report contains only those items for which the responsibility center is responsible. In other words, the costs of one center are *not allocated* to other centers because no element of control is added by the allocation of costs. For example, all occupancy costs are charged to the occupancy center and are not allocated to other centers on the basis of the space occupied by them. This type of allocation is necessary for product costing but not for cost control. Under this approach, a budget center will not be responsible for a volume variance. If, for example, expansion of the packing department requires renting additional space, the responsibility for the rise in occupancy costs will lie not with the occupancy center manager but with the packing department head.

   Under the second approach, the costs of each responsibility center are classified into (i) controllable and/or direct costs and (ii) noncontrollable and/or allocated costs. The costs of one center are allocated to other centers whenever this is appropriate. All allocated costs are treated as controllable by the charging centers and as noncontrollable by the user centers. There is one exception to this rule: it occurs when a sold-service concept is adopted for controlling the cost of certain service centers such as repairs and maintenance, the powerhouse, etc. This concept is explained in detail in Chapter 11. In either case, the costs controllable by each cost center are clearly identified to the extent possible. However, this is by no means an easy task and often calls for judgment and controversial decisions.

*b.* A responsibility report should show the variance analysis or causes of variances, such as usage variance, rate variance, or efficiency variance.

*c.* The report should contain nonmonetary data, such as the quantity of materials consumed, labor-hours, and machine-hours which were used in developing the budgeted or standard costs. It should also contain all information which may be useful in explaining variances and which may be known to the cost accounting department. For example, information on actual and standard rates, the use of a substitute material, excessive waste, etc., should be included.

*d.* The report should indicate significant variances which require explanation and identify the departments responsible for explaining them.

*e.* A *pyramid structure* of reporting should be adopted; i.e., the information submitted at a lower level of organization should be more detailed than that at a higher level. Further, the report for each successive level of responsibility centers should contain a summary by *responsibility centers,* not by *nature of expenses.* The accompanying illustration will clarify this point. Let us say that the ABC Company's Manufacturing Department is organized as shown. The responsibility reports for the Manufacturing Department will be as shown in Exhibit 6-3.

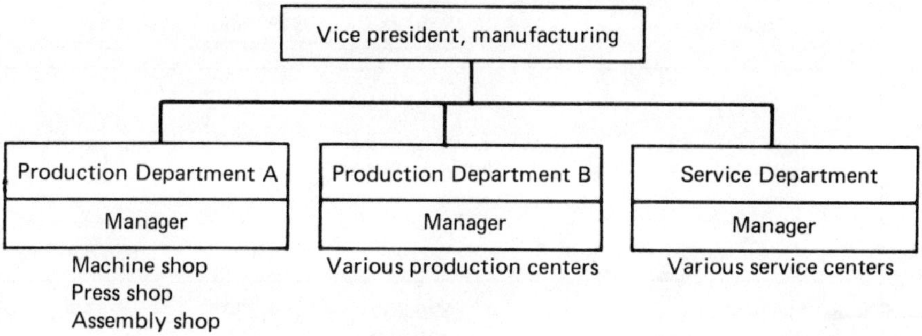


The first level of responsibility reports for Production Department A are for the machine shop, press shop, and assembly shop. Each of these responsibility reports contains all the controllable costs by nature of expenses. The total of each of these reports is carried to the responsibility report for Production Department A. The manager of Production Department A can judge the performance of each center from his own responsibility report and whenever necessary can be supplied with the details of the individual center's performance. For example, from the responsibility report given in Exhibit 6-3, the manager of Production Department A learns that the machine shop and the assembly shop exceeded their budgets respectively by $1400 and $1000 and that the press shop achieved savings of $600. Hence, the manager knows that attention should be focused on the machine shop and the assembly shop to stay within the budget. Had the responsibility reports for Production Department A contained the total of each expense item for various centers, the production manager would not have been able to judge the extent to which the individual shops were responsible for not meeting the department's budget without studying the report for each shop.

Similarly, from the responsibility report given in Exhibit 6-3,

**EXHIBIT 6-3**

**Pyramid Structure of Responsibility Reports**

Report No. 1

Responsibility center: Manufacturing Department

| Controllable costs of | Actual | Budget | Better (worse) than budget |
|---|---|---|---|
| Production Department A | $ 71,600 | $ 69,800 | $(1800) |
| Production Department B | 75,000 | 76,000 | 1000 |
| Service departments | 50,400 | 53,000 | 2600 |
| Total | $197,000 | $198,800 | $ 1800 |

Report No. 2

Responsibility center: Production Department A

| Controllable costs of | Actual | Budget | Better (worse) than budget |
|---|---|---|---|
| Machine shop | $26,200 | $24,800 | $(1400) |
| Press shop | 23,400 | 24,000 | 600 |
| Assembly shop | 22,000 | 21,000 | (1000) |
| Total | $71,600 | $69,800 | $(1800) |

Report No. 3

Responsibility center: Machine shop

| Controllable costs | Actual | Budget | Better (worse) than budget |
|---|---|---|---|
| Indirect labor | $10,000 | $ 9,000 | $(1000) |
| Indirect material | 5,500 | 6,000 | 500 |
| Employee benefits costs | 6,000 | 5,500 | (500) |
| Power | 2,500 | 2,400 | (100) |
| Maintenance | 1,000 | 1,100 | 100 |
| Other | 1,200 | 800 | (400) |
| Total | $26,200 | $24,800 | $(1400) |

the vice president, manufacturing, can learn immediately that Production Department A exceeded its budget by $1800 and that Production Department B and the service departments effected savings respectively of $1000 and $2600.

For reporting the costs of each responsibility manager's own department, three approaches are possible. For example, the costs incurred by the office of the manager of Production Department A may be reported to him in a report similar to Exhibit 6-3, report 3, and also be included as a separate responsibility center in report 2. Alternatively, they may be included in responsibility report 2 in Exhibit 6-3, which contains the data on the performance of the departments reporting to the manager. The third alternative is to regard the office of the manager of Production Department A as a part of the Office of the Vice President, Manufacturing, and accordingly to include the costs of the former in the responsibility report of the latter.

*f.* The controller's department should *red-flag* exceptionally high unfavorable variances and even bring them specifically to the attention of the concerned responsibility center manager and appropriate upper management.

4. The responsibility reports should be sent to the concerned responsibility center managers, who should be *asked to explain:*

- The causes of all significant variances (favorable or unfavorable) in expenses
- How they propose to correct unfavorable variances
- How, if at all, major unfavorable variances could have been avoided

An unfavorable variance does not necessarily mean poor performance, and a favorable variance does not necessarily mean good performance. Both variances could be the result or the indicator of a problem. For example, repairs higher than the budgeted amount could be the result of deteriorating plant conditions. Similarly, favorable variances in costs could be the result of a poor forecast of expenses or of false economy and not necessarily of better control over expenses or better performance. Hence, the causes of both favorable and unfavorable variances should be determined. Thus, a variance analysis may serve as a diagnostic tool.

It is necessary to define what should be regarded as a *significant variance.* Such a definition depends upon the size of the company and its cost structure. For example, a variance may be regarded as significant if it exceeds the lower of $1000 or 10 percent of the budgeted or standard cost. Separate limits may be set for different expense items.

5. Once the responsible managers have explained the significant vari-

ances and the corrective or preventive actions taken or planned, there may be *review meetings* among the controller or budget director, the president, and the concerned responsibility center managers to evaluate the reasonableness of the explanations and the adequacy of the actions taken or planned. Such meetings are necessary particularly if a planned action requires the cooperation of more than one department. If the responsibility centers are at different locations, written reports may take the place of review meetings.

Though the purpose of the responsibility reporting system is to pin down the responsibility for variances, the task is not always easy. In such cases it should be remembered that determining who is responsible for a variance is not as important as determining how it can be corrected.

6. There should be a periodic *follow-up* of planned actions to see that they have been implemented and are effective. The follow-up is the job of the line manager and not of the controller.

## Role of the Controller's Department

Often, the controller's department misunderstands its role in the cost control process. The controller's job is to accumulate actual cost data, compare them with budgets or standards, interpret variances, and report actual and budgeted costs and variances to the individual responsibility center managers. Once the controller's department has submitted the responsibility reports, it is left to line management and the president to see that proper actions are taken to correct deviations.

Of course, the controller's department should see that the responsibility center managers have explained all the variances and that their explanations contain no errors of accounting or arithmetic. Further, the controller, as a part of the management team, may express his views. But he should not sit in judgment on the line managers and evaluate their judgment or actions.

A good reporting and follow-up system also requires good rapport between the controller's department and line management. There should be an atmosphere of mutual trust and understanding. Line management should trust the controller's accounting data, and the controller should present the situation truly. The controller's analysis should be objective and unbiased.

## Task 9: Designing a Cost Recording System

Once the responsibility reporting system has been designed, it is necessary to design a cost recording system for accumulation and allocation of cost data. Since the cost recording system supports the responsibility reporting system, the structure of cost accounting must parallel the responsibility reporting structure and the budgeting structure. These three systems should be closely integrated so that the classification and summarization of expenses by nature of expenses, by responsibility centers, and by cost behavior are uniform in the three. These systems should also parallel the organization structure of the company.

The design of cost records is dealt with in Chapter 15.

## COST CONTROL TECHNIQUES

In this section, we will discuss the issues which arise in developing standard costing and budgeting, two well-known techniques for controlling costs. Most of this discussion also applies to the development of these techniques for product costing. Several good books deal with the other aspects of the two techniques.

### Meaning and Suitability of Standard Costing and Budgeting

Standard costs are predetermined costs; i.e., they are determined before the relevant activities are undertaken. Budgeted costs are also predetermined costs. Though both are predetermined costs, they are not equally effective in controlling the costs of every cost element.

Standard costs are used predominantly for controlling direct materials and direct labor, while budgets are used for controlling manufacturing overhead and marketing and administrative expenses. The reason for this distinction is that it is easier to apply standard costing to direct materials and direct labor than to manufacturing overhead and marketing and administrative expenses. A standard cost represents the unit cost of a product, activity, work, etc., whereas a budget represents the total amount budgeted for a given product, activity, work, etc. Since the unit costs of direct materials and direct labor do not change with a change in the volume of production, standard costs can be used effectively for controlling the costs of those items. Manufacturing overhead costs consist of variable, semivariable, and fixed costs, and the unit manufacturing overhead therefore will not remain constant with a change in the volume of production. Similarly, the unit marketing and administrative expenses will not remain constant with a change in the volume of sales and other activities. Consequently, different techniques are required to control different direct and indirect costs.

Standard costing and budgeting are interrelated techniques, and hence both can be employed simultaneously. Since a standard cost represents a unit cost and a budget represents the total amount, when standard costs are based on *current standards,* total standard costs will mean the total budget allowance. In this sense, even if standard costing is used to control direct materials and direct labor, it is necessary to prepare direct materials and direct labor budgets for controlling these costs in the aggregate. Similarly, even if budgeting is used to control manufacturing overhead costs, marketing costs, and administrative expenses, it is necessary to establish some sort of standards for each expense item. These standards may either be scientifically set or be based on past experience. For example, engineered standards can be set for indirect materials, indirect labor, power, and several other items of manufacturing overhead costs. These standards usually will be set separately for different volumes of production because most of these costs are semivariable. These standards will then form the basis for preparing the manufacturing overhead budget. In the absence of these standards, it will be necessary to estimate the cost of these items based on past experience. Further, concerns not employing standard costing often prepare direct materials and direct labor budgets on the basis of the manufacturing department's estimates. It is obvious that a budget based on standards will be more scientific than one based on estimates. Hence, both these techniques often are used together.

Since the techniques of standard costing and budgeting can be used independently of each other, the designer should understand and explain to company management the distinguishing features of each technique. For ready reference, these features are summarized in Exhibit 6-4.

**EXHIBIT 6-4**

**Summary Comparison of Budgeting and Standard Costing Techniques**

| Budgeting | Standard costing |
|---|---|
| 1. Budgeting can be used for planning and control of total resources, cash, capital expenditures, revenue, and operating expenses. Budgeting can also help in income determination and inventory valuation by enabling computation of predetermined manufacturing overhead rates. | Standard costing has a limited scope: it can be used for cost control, product costing, inventory valuation, and income determination. But standard costs provide a data base for planning, budgeting, measurement, control, and reporting. |
| 2. Budgeting is more appropriate for controlling manufacturing overhead, marketing expenses, administrative expenses, research and development expenses, and vari- | Standard costing is more suitable for controlling direct materials and direct labor. |

**EXHIBIT 6-4**

**Summary Comparison of Budgeting and Standard Costing Techniques (*Continued*)**

| Budgeting | Standard costing |
|---|---|
| ous fixed or discretionary expenses. | |
| 3. Budgeting is suitable even for nonrepetitive activities or functions. | Standard costing is suitable only for repetitive activities or functions. |
| 4. The two techniques are interrelated and hence can be used simultaneously for repetitive activities or functions. | |
| 5. Budgets reflect allocation of resources to various functions and expenses. | Standards reflect set methods and predetermined costs of performing various functions. |
| 6. Usually, a budget allowance connotes the total amount. | A standard cost connotes a unit cost. |
| 7. Budgets are usually expressed in monetary and quantitative terms. | Standards can be for quality, weight, time, procedure, method, price, rate, amount, quantity, etc. |
| 8. Budgets are less precise than standards. | |
| 9. More time and effort are required to develop a standard cost system than a budgetary cost control system. | |
| 10. Budgets are based on a forecast of conditions expected to prevail during the budget period and hence are reasonably attainable. | Standard costs can be basic, ideal, or current. |
| 11. Budgeting is not normally used as a basis for employee remuneration, though it can be so used. | Standard costing is often used as a basis for incentive payment to workers. |
| 12. Budgeting is not a method of cost accounting. However, it is desirable to adopt a uniform classification of costs (by nature of expenses and by budget centers) in budgets and in cost records. | Standard costing is a method of cost accounting, and cost accounting records hence can be based on standard costs, and cost accounting and financial accounting records can be integrated to avoid duplication. However, standard costing can also be maintained on a memorandum basis or independently of financial accounting. |
| 13. Usually, budgets are more frequently revised than standards. | |

## DEVELOPMENT OF STANDARD COSTS FOR COST CONTROL

The process of developing standard costs to be used for cost control involves the following major tasks:

1. Determine the products and the cost elements for which the standard costs are to be developed.
2. Determine the kind of standards to be used.
3. Define what specific standards are to be set and by whom.
4. Establish individual cost standards.
5. Set forth the policy and the procedure for the revision of standards.

Each of these tasks is explained below. The process of developing standard costs for product costing is the same except for possible differences in the tightness of the standards for these two purposes.

### Scope of the Standard Costs System

Standard costs may be developed for all products and for all cost elements or be confined to some of them. Here are two examples:

- A large aluminum company uses a standard cost system only for all direct costs and budgets for overhead.
- A medium-sized cable-manufacturing company employs a full-absorption standard cost system and has 38,000 standard costs.

### Kinds of Standards

Three kinds of standards can be used for developing standard costs: basic standards, ideal standards, and current standards.

*Basic standards* are the standards which, once set, remain unchanged until there is a change in the products manufactured, production processes, or similar fundamental conditions. Hence, a comparison of actual costs with basic standard costs will reveal a trend of variation in costs since the last change in basic standard costs. Obviously, basic standards are inappropriate for cost control because they provide an outdated yardstick for comparing actual costs and performance. For example, even if the purchase price has risen because of inflation, the standard material cost based on basic standards will remain unchanged and thus will be unrealistic and meaningless for measuring the performance of the purchasing department in controlling purchase prices.

*Ideal standards* are the standards which can be achieved only under ideal conditions, such as the most efficient use of personnel, machines, and materials. Since ideal conditions seldom exist, ideal standards are unattainable and hence will usually show unfavorable variances. Thus, ideal standards are inappropriate for cost control, although they can be used as long-term cost reduction and cost control goals. In using ideal standards as long-term standards, it should be made explicit that though they may not be currently attainable, they should be achieved in the long run. For example, one company manufacturing rayon yarn had been experiencing a decline in the rate of consumption of wood pulp per ton of rayon yarn produced, and it predicted that the declining trend would continue for the next few years. Hence, it set the following wood-pulp consumption standards for the ensuing 5 years:

| | |
|---|---|
| Year 1 | 1.25 |
| Year 2 | 1.20 |
| Year 3 | 1.15 |
| Year 4 | 1.1 |
| Year 5 | 1.1 |

The standard industry ratio for wood-pulp consumption was 1.1. Hence, company management made it explicit that the goal of the company was to reach the ratio of 1.1 as soon as possible but no later than the fourth year from the date of setting the standards. Thus, though the ratio of 1.1 would be regarded as ideal for years 1 through 3, it would be regarded as achievable for years 4 and 5.

*Current standards* are the standards which are currently attainable because they are based on the conditions expected to prevail during the period for which they are set. Current standards allow for normal spoilage, wastage, inefficiency, etc., even though these factors may be undesirable. For example, though the ideal wood-pulp consumption ratio for the company manufacturing rayon yarn was 1.1, higher standards were allowed during years 1 through 3 because those standards were considered reasonably attainable during the first 3 years. Thus, it is clear that for current cost control as opposed to a long-term cost reduction goal, current standards are the best of the three types of standards.

**Example of Actual Company Practice** One large multiproduct and multidivision United States company's accounting policy and procedures manual provides as follows:

> Cost standards must be realistic and attainable so as to reflect unfavorable variances from standards. Excess waste and inefficiencies should obviously not be built into them. The standards must be as current as possible to reflect prevailing price levels, labor rates and operating practices.

The kind of standards to be used is a management choice, while the role of the designer is to explain to management the pros and cons of each kind of standards. In any event, the kind of standards used must be consistent with the objective to be achieved from the standard cost system. If more than one objective are to be achieved, more than one kind of standards may be used for the same cost element. For example, for meeting the objectives of current cost control and long-term cost reduction concerning material consumption, both currently attainable standards and ideal standards may be set. A comparison between actual material consumption and standard consumption based on current standards will reveal the degree of control currently being achieved, whereas a comparison between actual consumption and standard consumption based on ideal standards will reveal how close current performance is to the long-term goal of reducing material consumption.

### Specific Standards to Be Set and Responsibility for Setting Standards

Once the scope of the standard cost system has been defined and the kind of standards to be used has been selected, the designer should determine what specific standards are to be set. For responsibility accounting, standards should be set by responsibility centers, and within a responsibility center by products, activities, and cost elements. Insofar as possible, cost standards should be separated into quantity standards and rate or price standards. For example, in designing a standard cost system for ACME Company (our assumed company for the continuing case study), which produces products X and Y in five production shops and consumes ten direct materials, the following standards will be set for direct materials:

- Separate cost standards will be set for each of the ten direct materials consumed for products X and Y.
- For each direct material, both quantity and price standards will be set. In setting material quantity standards, allowances will be made for material losses, or material loss standards will be set separately.
- Each of the direct materials will be identified with the production shops consuming it so that responsibility can be established for variances in actual consumption from standard consumption.
- Usually, the purchasing department will be responsible for material price variances.

For determining the specific standards to be set, the designer should study the product cost structure and the flow of various costs within the organization. Once the designer has prepared a list of specific standards to be developed, he should, with the help of the company management, also define the persons responsible for setting those standards.

A very important point is that standard setting is *not the designer's responsibility:* it is the responsibility of industrial engineering and operating personnel. There are two reasons for this. First, standard setting requires knowledge (technical, industrial engineering, etc.) beyond the bounds of cost accounting. The second and more important reason is that when standards have been developed on a scientific basis and the users have participated in setting them, the standards will be accepted by the users with less resistance. However, as we will see later, the designer has a role to play in setting standards.

When feasible and worthwhile, standards should be developed by industrial engineers. If this is not feasible or worthwhile, operating departments should set the standards. However, standards should not be set by those who are responsible for attaining them, though those people should be allowed to participate in setting them. For example, standards for direct labor should not be set by direct labor but may be set by supervisors and approved by the production superintendent or the production manager. In any case, all significant standards must be reviewed by the manufacturing department head.

A list of some of the typical standards required in a manufacturing company along with the responsibility for their setting is given in Exhibit 6-5.

**Actual Company Practices** In 1976, the author conducted a survey of the approach adopted by some of the *Fortune* 1000 companies and large nonindustrial companies in designing cost systems. The following excerpts from their replies or their cost system manuals demonstrate typical practice:

1. *An industrial products company:*

> We have made a very heavy investment in method study and standards development by Industrial Engineering. . . . In most instances, the system was "sold" and explained to all of the users from line foremen to division managers. In some cases, operating supervisors were detached to assist in the design and later returned to production or mill planning duties.

2. *A consumer products company:*

> . . . Industrial Engineering has the joint or sole responsibility for approval in many areas. . . . In cases where engineered standards have not been established or are not to be used, the Manufacturing Department will generally issue the necessary directives.

3. *A multicompany conglomerate:*

> 6. Engineering department specifies bills of materials, and industrial engineering specifies raw materials quantities *including engineered loss factors.*

In some companies the bills of materials prepared by engineering are not in a suitable form for cost purposes. The cost department should not take the responsibility of supplying needed information.

It is the design or product engineering department's responsibility to provide usable documentation for all users of this information. Similarly, for fabricated piece parts, it is the industrial engineering department's responsibility to supply engineered data on material requirements.

*Corporate Manufacturing Policy MF 15* clearly states that engineering has the responsibility to provide engineering material usage data.

**EXHIBIT 6-5**

**Typical Standards in a Manufacturing Company and Standard-Setting Responsibility**

| Standard | Responsibility |
|---|---|
| 1. Direct material standards including type, specifications, quantity, and allowable loss factor | Industrial engineering, research and development, process engineering, product engineering, or production department |
| 2. Standard usage of indirect materials | Industrial engineering and/or production department |
| 3. Standard packing material usage | Industrial engineering and/or packing department |
| 4. Standard purchase prices for all materials | Purchasing department subject to audit by cost department |
| 5. Standard methods and standard speeds | Industrial engineering and/or production department |
| 6. Standard setup and start-up times | Industrial engineering and/or production department |
| 7. Standard time for direct labor, repairs, shipping, etc. | Industrial engineering and/or production, maintenance, shipping, etc., departments |
| 8. Standard labor rates | Personnel department (labor contracts) and cost department |

## Establishment of Individual Cost Standards

In designing a standard cost system, standards setting is the most important but the most difficult task because (1) standards apply to the future, (2) different techniques and considerations are involved in setting standards for different cost elements, and (3) participation of several persons is required in setting standards. Because of this complexity, the procedures involved in setting standards for direct materials, direct labor, manufacturing overhead, and nonmanufacturing overhead are explained in Chapters 9 through 13. However, *common guidelines* are given below:

1. Standards set for cost control purposes should be *neither too tight nor too loose.* If standards are so tight that it is very difficult to achieve them, persistently negative cost variances will appear; the operating people will lose faith in the standards as a realistic yardstick for measuring their performance and will disown their responsibility for negative variances. On the other hand, if standards are so loose that it is very easy to achieve them and normally favorable cost variances are appearing, the value of standard costs as a means of cost control will be reduced because they will not enable the company to keep costs at the minimum level possible. Thus, though standards should post a real challenge, they should be realistic and reasonably attainable.

2. To be realistic, standards should be based on the *cost conditions expected to prevail* during the period for which the standards are to be applied. For example, the persons setting standards should take into account the condition and age of plant and equipment, the direct material supply situation, the labor situation, etc. On the basis of this evaluation, they should make appropriate allowances for wastage, spoilage, scrap, evaporation, inefficiency, learning time, downtime, defective production, etc.

3. To pose a real challenge, standards should incorporate *all current cost reduction goals or claims.* For example, if a company has set up a program to increase direct labor productivity by 5 percent during the coming year, direct labor cost standards set for the year should reflect increased labor productivity by 5 percent.

4. Standards should be *set scientifically* and be based on *objective data.* As far as possible, industrial engineering techniques should be used. Though some judgment and estimates are inevitably required, they should be kept to a minimum. Some of the areas in which judgment or estimation is involved are availability of direct material of particular specifications, price trends, and learning time in the case of relatively new processes. Further, though past data may be used as a guide, they should not automatically be regarded as standards.

The time and the money spent on setting standards should be commensurate with the importance of the cost item for cost control purposes. For example, for setting standards for major controllable cost factors sophisticated techniques may be employed, while for minor items current actual costs with due adjustments may be used as standards.

5. Standards should be expressed in units meaningful to first-line supervisors.

6. If standards are to be set, a *selective approach* may be used and

standards developed according to the priority assigned by the designer and the company management. Until standards have been set for a cost element, the actual cost for that cost factor will be measured against existing standards, however imperfect they may be, but with a clear understanding of the nature of standards on the part of concerned employees and company management.

7. Unless the structure of accumulation of actual costs and noncost data parallels that of standard costs, it will be difficult to investigate the causes of variances and standard costs will not be very useful for controlling costs. Hence, in developing any standards, the feasibility of accumulating actual cost and noncost data on the bases on which standard costs are being developed should be considered.

8. All standards must be "sold" to the persons whose performance will be measured against them. The persons concerned should also understand the standards, because if they accept a standard without understanding it, they may later oppose it.

9. An accurate and complete record of each standard developed should be kept. The record should show the basis, computations, the person who developed the standard, when it was developed, who approved it, the procedure followed, and other relevant information. This record will be useful in selling standards to the users and also in revising the standards.

### Role of Designer in Setting Standards

Though the establishment of cost standards is not the responsibility of the cost system designer, he has an important role to play. The designer should contribute to the process of setting standards by providing needed guidance, specifying what standards are to be set, and auditing the standards once they have been set. In particular, the designer must ensure that

1. The kind of standards used (i.e., current, ideal, or basic) and the degree of tightness of standards are the same as initially agreed to by management.
2. Standards have been set for all cost items except those items for which standards are not to be set at this time.
3. The methods and techniques used for establishing standards are logical and appropriate insofar as the designer can judge. The best course is to ask the person responsible for setting each standard what alternative methods were available and the person's reasons for selecting a particular method.
4. The data and assumptions used for setting standards are appropri-

ate, reliable, and accurate or reasonable. The accuracy of computations should also be verified. Remember: "Garbage in, garbage out."

5. Standards have been set, supervised, reviewed, and approved by persons designated as responsible for these tasks.

6. Standards have been set after giving effect to current cost reduction goals set by management or to current cost reduction claims made by operating departments. For example, in one case, on examining the capital budget for the ensuing year, the designer found that in justifying a certain capital expenditure it was claimed that it would reduce direct labor in the assembly department by 10 percent. However, in setting direct labor standards for the assembly department, without any valid reason this claim was not considered.

7. The controller's department or the designer has compared past usage, rates, and amounts with the standards set by the engineering and operating departments and analyzed all significant differences to verify that the standards are reasonable and contain no errors. Whenever the controller's department or the designer is not convinced of the reasonableness of any standard, the person who set it should be asked to review it, and if a difference of opinion persists, the matter should be referred to appropriate management for resolution. Of course, past data should be used only as a guide.

8. Supervisors, direct labor, and management have accepted the standards as being reasonable.

## Revision of Standards

To maintain the integrity of standards, it is necessary to define the following aspects concerning their revision:

- Circumstances under which the standards once set should be revised or updated
- Form for computing revision in standards
- Persons who should initiate the action and review and approve the revised standards
- Persons who should be informed of the revised standards

Current standards should be revised at least annually. Ideal standards may or may not be revised, depending upon the nature of the change. For example, if there is a price change, the standard will probably not be changed, but if the material itself has changed, both the standard quantity and the standard price may be revised.

Revisions during the year should be as few as possible so as not to reduce the value of standard costs for controlling costs. In any event, insignificant changes should not be made during the year even though they are otherwise warranted. Considerable judgment is called for in deciding when to revise standards. Further, if both standard costs and budgets are used for cost control, revision policy should be the same for both.

## DEVELOPMENT OF BUDGETS FOR COST CONTROL

The technique of budgeting can be used for several objectives, such as (1) profit planning and control, (2) forecasting profit, cash, etc., (3) cost control, and (4) product costing. Consequently, there are different types of budgets, among them the operating budget, the cost budget, the cash budget, and the capital budget. Since this book focuses on cost systems, it deals only with the process of developing cost budgets. Further, the discussion in this chapter is confined to the development of cost budgets for cost control. However, most of this discussion will also be useful in developing budgets for product costing.

The process of developing budgets for cost control involves the following major tasks:

1. Determine whether fixed or flexible budgets are to be used.
2. Determine how tight the budgets should be.
3. Define the length of the budget period.
4. Prepare a skeleton of the budgetary cost control system.
5. Define organizational responsibility for the preparation and monitoring of budgets.
6. Lay down procedures and guidelines for preparing individual budgets.
7. Set forth policies and procedures for budget revisions.

### Fixed versus Flexible Budgets

A budget may be fixed (static) or flexible (variable). A fixed budget is prepared for only one forecast level of activity, and actual costs are compared with fixed budgeted costs even if the level of activity attained differs from the forecast level.

Under flexible budgeting, it is recognized that certain costs will increase with an increase in the level of activity, and vice versa. Consequently, under flexible budgeting, budget allowances for fixed and variable costs are established on different bases. For fixed costs, budget allowances are established in terms of total dollars for a period, and these allowances remain constant regardless of the volume of activity actually attained. For variable costs, budget allowances are developed in terms of rate per unit of activity, work, or output, and their total dollar amount varies with the volume of activity, etc., actually attained. For a given level of activity, total budget allowances for a budget center consist of budgeted variable costs (computed by multiplying the volume of activity attained with the expense rates of individual variable cost items) *plus* budgeted fixed costs (not adjusted for the volume of activity attained). Hence, total budget allowances will increase with an increase in the level of activity and decrease with a decrease in the level of activity.

Thus, it is obvious that under both types of budgets, the treatment of fixed costs is the same and that it is the treatment of variable costs which differs. Further, in preparing even fixed budgets, cost behavior is recognized. For example, a fixed budget may be higher for 10,000 units of production than for 8000 units and be exactly the same as the flexible budget at the forecast level of activity. However, for the purpose of comparing actual versus budgeted costs, the fixed budget, once it is prepared, is not adjusted for fluctuations in the volume of activity. It is in this respect that the flexible budget differs from the fixed budget. For the purpose of comparing actual and budgeted costs, the flexible budget is adjusted for fluctuations in the volume of activity. A corollary is that if there are no variable costs, there is no difference whatsoever between a fixed budget and a flexible budget.

**Suitability of Fixed and Flexible Budgets** In actual practice, some concerns use flexible budgets and some use fixed budgets for cost control. Though the choice between fixed and flexible budgets is ultimately a management decision, the designer must recommend to management what type of budget is suitable for a given company. In this regard, the designer and management will find the following guidelines useful:

1. The prime consideration in selecting the type of budget should be the type of costs to be controlled. For controlling variable costs, a flexible budget is usually inevitable because it permits comparing actual costs with budget allowances *adjusted* for the *actual* level of activity attained. Thus, it permits comparing like with like. An illustration will clarify the point. Let us suppose that during a particular month budgeted power consumption was \$20,000 (200,000 kilowatthours at 10 cents per kilowatthour) based on the budgeted production of 100,000 units. However, actual production and power consumption were respectively 80,000 units and \$17,000 (170,000 kilowatthours at 10 cents per kilowatthour). Under fixed budgeting, power consumption will show a favorable budget variance of \$3000, whereas under flexible budgeting there will be an unfavorable budget variance of \$1000 because of excess power consumption by 10,000 (170,000 − 160,000) kilowatthours for the actual production of 80,000 units. Obviously, comparison with the flexible budget

reveals the true picture. Because flexible budgeting increases the budget allowance with an increase in the activity level, and vice versa, it is fair both to the company and to the employees.

2. A fixed budget is appropriate for controlling fixed costs. In fact, for fixed costs the question of using a flexible budget does not arise. Fixed costs are either more or less constant irrespective of the volume of activity or are governed by the good judgment of management. For example, the cost of office security and various general and administrative expenses are fixed in nature. On the other hand, amounts of research and development, donations, litigation expenses, nonroutine maintenance, and various other expenses are left to management's discretion. Both these types of costs can be better controlled by fixed budgets.

3. Even for controlling variable costs, fixed budgets are appropriate if there is not much *unpredictable* fluctuation in activities during a year or if variable costs form a small portion of total costs.

4. Even if flexible budgets are considered better than fixed budgets for controlling variable costs, fixed budgets may be used because of various practical considerations. First, a flexible budget requires the separation of costs into variable and fixed categories and the determination of the variable budget rate for each variable cost in each budget center. These tasks are by no means simple and often involve controversial issues. Also, it takes more time and money to design and implement a flexible budgetary control system than a fixed budgetary control system. Second, operating people find that, compared with a flexible budget, a fixed budget is relatively easy to prepare and understand. Third, flexible budgeting requires the monthly adjustment of budget allowances on the basis of the actual level of activity attained. Thus, compared with fixed budgeting, flexible budgeting takes more time and money to prepare a monthly budget comparison report. Because of these three factors, management sometimes prefers fixed budgeting to flexible budgeting, especially when budgeting is being implemented for the first time and the company does not have professional managers. In such a case, fixed budgeting may be replaced by flexible budgeting once management becomes used to budgeting and realizes the usefulness of flexible budgeting.

## Zero-Base Budgeting

Recently, there has been a great deal of interest in another concept of budgeting known as *zero-base budgeting*. The traditional method of budgeting is incremental budgeting, under which the last year's activities and expenditures are taken for granted and a budget is prepared by making plus or minus adjustments only for known or predictable changes in activities or expenditures. Under zero-base budgeting, every year fresh justification is required for every activity and every expenditure. The total planned activities of the budget year are divided into separate *decision packages,* each package contains a detailed cost-benefit analysis, and the packages are ranked in the order of importance.

In 1977 the American Management Associations (AMA) conducted a survey among forty-eight enterprises that had been using zero-base budgeting and/or had attended seminars on zero-base budgeting. Below is a relevant excerpt from the summary of the survey findings, as given in the AMA survey report:

> 1. The largest single class of users of ZBB within the responding group are manufacturers.
> 2. The most significant objectives for implementing ZBB were (in declining order) to better allocate resources, to improve decision making, and to facilitate planning; the least important objective was to reduce costs or personnel.
> 3. Of the implementing respondents, 94 percent reported that objectives were fully-to-fairly well achieved; only 6 percent reported that objectives were poorly or not at all achieved.
> 4. The objectives that were best achieved were to facilitate planning, to improve decision making, and to better allocate resources. The least achieved objective was to reorganize.
> 5. Organizations implementing ZBB tended to implement at all organizational levels simultaneously (48 percent did so). The breakdown of those implementing ZBB on a restricted level was as follows: 25 percent implemented the system in headquarters, 13 percent at the division level, and 15 percent in departments.

It is important to note that

> ZBB is not a technique that can be universally applied. In manufacturing, for example, technology determines the mix and levels of inputs, and standard costing provides the basis for budgeting—so there is no need for zero-base methods. On the other hand, ZBB is applicable and needed where standard costing and traditional budgeting techniques do not work, in, for example, service, support, and other staff functions. Traditional budgeting methods apply primarily to manufacturing and other production oriented functions.[1]

## Tightness of Budgets

Irrespective of whether fixed or flexible budgets are used for cost control, management must decide how tight the budgets should be. Budgets

[1] L. Allan Austin, *Zero-Base Budgeting: Organization Impact and Effect,* AMA survey report, American Management Associations, New York, 1977, p. 25.

can be pessimistic (conservative), most likely, or optimistic. On one hand, the budget center manager would like to have a liberal budget to be on the safe side. On the other hand, management would like to have a tight budget so that wasteful expenditures are kept to a minimum. Hence a middle road is the best.

Of course, it is easier said than done that most likely or realistic budgets should be prepared for cost control. Much depends upon the attitude of the budget center managers and of upper management. For example, if managers are penalized for unfavorable variances or their compensation is tied to their achieving the budgets, they will tend to provide more padding in their budgets. If, however, upper management does not look upon *justifiable* unfavorable variances harshly and if budget achievement and compensation are not directly linked, budgets will tend to approximate the most likely cost conditions. Thus, to make budgets an effective tool for cost control, management must understand these human behavioral aspects and also the chemistry of the company's organization.

### Length of Budget Period

For planning purposes, a long-range budget covering a period of more than a year is useful. For cost control purposes, the appropriate length of the budget period depends upon the circumstances of each company. Usually an annual budget is adequate for cost control, but there may be certain cost items whose lead time (the time between the decision to incur an expense and the actual incurrence of the expense) is longer than 1 year. For example, an action for importing certain direct materials may have to be initiated more than 12 months in advance.

Similarly, a builder who undertakes several construction projects simultaneously can follow this procedure: The builder should prepare a separate budget for each construction project and make the period of a project budget coextensive with the length of the concerned construction project. Then, from the individual project budgets, the builder should prepare an annual budget coinciding with the firm's accounting year. The annual budget should be used for overall planning and control, particularly of overhead costs, and the project budgets for detailed project planning and control.

Another question of importance is whether to have a periodic budget (for 1 or more accounting years) or a rolling budget (e.g., as a month is over, it is deleted from the budget and a new month added, so that there is always a full 12-month budget). For cost control, a periodic budget is more widely used than a rolling budget for two reasons. First, it enables a company to tie its budget period to its accounting year. Second, a periodic budget requires budget centers to achieve their budgets monthly, quarterly, for the year to date, and for the year as a whole. For example, if a budget center is over its budget in a particular month, it will be required, as far as possible, to make up for the excess in the remaining months of the year. This control feature will be lost under a rolling budget, because once a completed month has been deleted, the budget variance will also be forgotten. In most cases, an ideal situation will be to have a 2-year budget: a detailed budget for the coming year and a less detailed and, perhaps, a little less accurate budget for the following year.

One more issue to be decided is whether and how the budget period should be broken down into smaller time intervals. Usually, a budget period is divided into months and quarters and, in some cases, into weeks. A company may be selective and prepare weekly budgets only for those expenses (e.g., direct materials) which are significant and need a shorter reporting interval.

## Outline of the Budgetary Control System

Costs (i.e., input) are incurred to achieve production, inventory, sales, profits, etc. (i.e., output or results). Hence, for effective cost control, cost budgets should be an integral part of the operating budget as well as the capital and cash budgets. To ensure that cost budgets are well tied to one another and also to other budgets, the designer should prepare a conceptual outline of the entire budgetary control system.

If the designer has properly conducted the system analysis, it will not be difficult to prepare an outline of the budgetary control system. The structure of budgeting should follow the organization structure, and components of the budgets will depend upon the nature of the concern's business. For example, a multiproduct and multidivision company will prepare budgets by divisions and, within a division, by product lines and functions. A specimen outline of a budgetary control system for a manufacturing company producing only one product is given in Exhibit 6-6. The second part of Exhibit 6-6 shows the structure of the budgeted income statement.

The process of preparing an operating budget is iterative and varies with the complexity of the company. However, the general procedure is as described here. From an analysis of internal and external situations, profit and other goals are established. On the basis of these goals, a sales budget is prepared, and the desired levels of finished goods inventory are established. From these budgets, the production budget is prepared. The production budget becomes the basis for direct labor, direct materials, other direct expenses, and manufacturing overhead budgets. Simultaneously, the adequacy of plant capacity is examined, and the capi-

## EXHIBIT 6-6

**Specimen Skeleton of Budgetary Control System for a Single-Division Manufacturing Company**

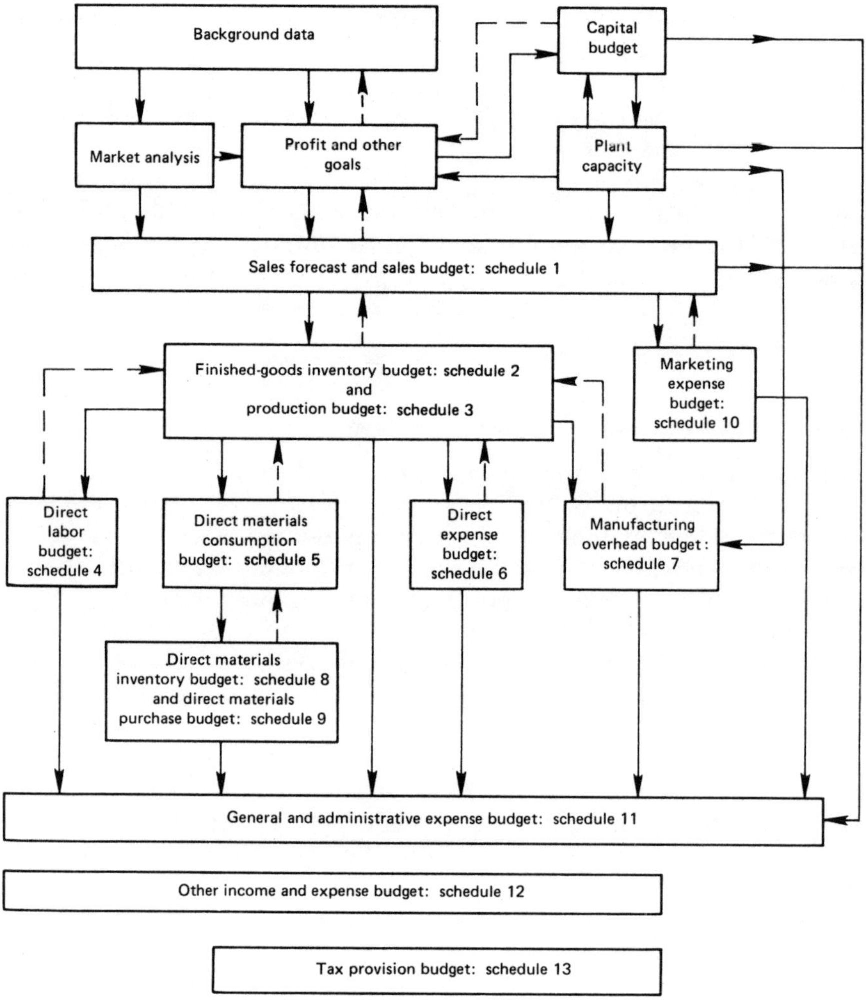


NOTES:

1. It would also be necessary to tie the operating and the capital budgets with the cash budget.
2. — —➤indicates the sequence of changes in the tentative budgets which may be necessary for several reasons.
3. Schedules 12 and 13 are necessary to compute net income though they are not part of the operating budget.

**EXHIBIT 6-6**

**Specimen Skeleton of Budgetary Control System for a Single-Division Manufacturing Company (*Continued*)**

The following budgeted income statement is the final result of the various budget schedules indicated in the first part of Exhibit 6-6:

Budgeted income statement

| | | Schedule |
|---|---|---|
| Budgeted sales | | 1 |
| Budgeted direct materials | | 5 |
| Budgeted direct labor | | 4 |
| Budgeted direct expenses | | 6 |
| Budgeted manufacturing overhead costs | | 7 |
| Budgeted decrease (increase) in work-in-process inventory | | 3 |
| Budgeted cost of production (5 + 4 + 6 + 7 +3) | A | |
| Budgeted decrease (increase) in finished-goods inventory | | 2 |
| Budgeted cost of goods sold (A + 2) | B | |
| Budgeted gross profit (1 – B) | C | |
| Budgeted marketing expenses | | 10 |
| Budgeted general and administrative expenses | | 11 |
| Budgeted operating profit (loss) (C – 10 – 11) | D | |
| Budgeted other net income (expenses) | | 12 |
| Budgeted pretax profit (loss) (D – 12) | E | |
| Budgeted tax provision | | 13 |
| Budgeted aftertax net profit (loss) (E – 13) | F | |

tal budget is prepared. From the sales budget, the marketing expense budget is prepared. From all other budgets, the general and administrative expense budget is prepared. Also, other income and expenses are budgeted, income taxes are computed, and the budgeted aftertax income or loss is ascertained. If this aftertax income falls short of the profit goal, the sales budget may be increased, and various cost budgets may be reduced to the extent possible. The profit goal itself may be reduced if it is found to be unattainable because of inadequate plant capacity, competition, lack of adequate demand, or inability to reduce costs. Thus, it is seen that cost budgets and other budgets are interrelated and interdependent and that they cannot be prepared without each other.

### Who Should Prepare Budgets?

In any organization, small or large, neither a bottom-up nor a top-down approach but a participative approach should be adopted in preparing budgets. Under a participative approach, top management issues important directions and policy guidelines for the preparation of budgets. Following these guidelines, individual budget center managers prepare budgets for their respective centers. Individual budgets are then reviewed and revised by upper management in consultation with the individual budget center managers. Finalized budgets are then consolidated into the company budget. Under a top-down approach, a budget for each budget center is prepared by upper management or by the controller's department, and the individual budget center managers are asked to operate within their budgets. A top-down budget is inappropriate for cost control (for that matter, even for profit planning and control) for two reasons. First, since the budget center managers are not allowed to participate in developing budgets for their centers, they lack the necessary sense of commitment and enthusiasm for adhering to the budgets. Second, whereas the individual center managers lack an overall view of the business, upper management often is not familiar with the details essential in developing a realistic and accurate budget. If budgets are unrealistic, budget center managers, however diligent they may be, cannot stay within their budgets.

### Preparation of Individual Cost Budgets

Once the various cost budgets to be prepared have been defined and the persons responsible for preparing them have been identified, it is necessary to set forth procedures and guidelines for the preparation of individual cost budgets. This subject will be dealt with in Chapters 9 through 13, which treat individual subcost systems.

### Revision of Budgets

During the year, several changes may occur which were not anticipated or planned for while the budget was being prepared. For example, there may be changes in product designs, production processes, plant layout, plant and equipment, material prices, wage rates, material supply, etc., or even errors in the preparation of budgets. A knotty question is whether the budget should be changed once it has been approved. There is no cut-and-dried answer to this question which would be applicable to all situations. A factor which compounds the complexity of this issue is that a budget is a multipurpose management tool: it can be used for projecting profits, profit planning, and controlling expenses. Though there is a considerable similarity, there are also some fundamental differences in the use of the budgeting technique for each of these three objectives. The purpose for which a budgeting technique is used is one of the important factors in determining whether and when a budget should be revised.

**Budgeting for Profit Projections** When a budget is prepared for forecasting profits, it is intended to show what will happen rather than what should happen, as in the case of a budget prepared for profit planning. Initially, the forecast budget may be the same as the planning budget, but as the year progresses, the forecast will probably change. Since the objective of the forecast budget is to know what will happen, it is appropriate to revise it frequently. Usually, companies prepare three *forward looks* during the first three quarters of a year. In preparing a forward look, they take the actual figures for the past months and the revised projections for the remaining months. If significant fluctuations occur from month to month, some companies even make monthly revisions. In addition, even flash reports may be issued to show the impact of an important unplanned and unpredicted event as soon as that event occurs. In short, a forecast budget should be revised for every major change irrespective of the reason for the change.

**Planning Budget** A planning budget specifies the profit and other goals to be achieved during the year and the actions to achieve them. It should not be revised as frequently as a forecast budget. In fact, the planning budget should not be revised unless some significant economic or other changes have made existing goals and plans less meaningful. In deciding whether to revise a planning budget, it is important to distinguish between changes in goals and changes in a planned course of action. Though changes in circumstances may necessitate changes in the planned course of action, a change in the goal does not necessarily follow. Further, when events which were not forecast while budgets were being prepared occur, management usually will not be a silent spectator but will take corrective action. Hence, the combined effect of an unforeseen event and consequent management actions should be considered in deciding whether a revision is called for in the budgets and what the revision should be. A few examples will make these points clear.

- Let us suppose that in the middle of a year a company finds that the prices of some major direct materials have gone up by 10 percent above budgeted costs. If company management decides that the purchasing department should find alternative sources of supply or that the product engineering department should change material specifications to permit less expensive substitute materials, the planning budget should not be changed.

- If, for some reason, sales are expected to be significantly above budgeted sales, the planning budget should be revised; otherwise the company will not be able to achieve the higher sales.
- If production capacity has been seriously impaired by fire, flood, or other natural calamities, causing changes in planned production or sales, then also the planning budget should be changed. If the company has enough inventory to meet the current year's sales, perhaps the profit goal will not change, though there will be changes in various components of the budget.

**Budgeting for Cost Control** It is well to remember that the purpose of a cost control budget is to control expenses within a predetermined amount and not to forecast expenses. Hence, a cost control budget should not be so revised as to defeat its purpose. For setting policies for budget revision, we recommend two alternative approaches. Let us call these approaches the *microapproach* and the *macroapproach,* or *global approach.* Under the microapproach, each cost item is treated separately for the purpose of cost control. Under the macroapproach various expense items are dealt with separately as well as in total. Budget revision criteria under the two approaches are explained below.

**Microapproach** Under this approach, there are five considerations in deciding whether or not to change an expense budget (for the current month and future months) because of changes in operating conditions:

- Is the change related to the volume or the goal?
- Was the event predictable or unpredictable while the budget was being prepared?
- Was the event which caused the change in expense levels controllable or noncontrollable?
- Is the change favorable or unfavorable?
- What is the company policy on expense budgeting?

The application of these criteria is shown diagrammatically in Exhibit 6-7 and illustrated below:

1. In comparing actual expenses with budgeted expenses, the latter should be adjusted for the volume of activity actually attained; i.e., if the actual activity level is higher than that planned for a particular month, budgeted expenses should be increased appropriately, and vice versa. Naturally, only variable and semivariable expenses will change.

**EXHIBIT 6-7**

**Model for Budget Revision under Microapproach to Expense Control**

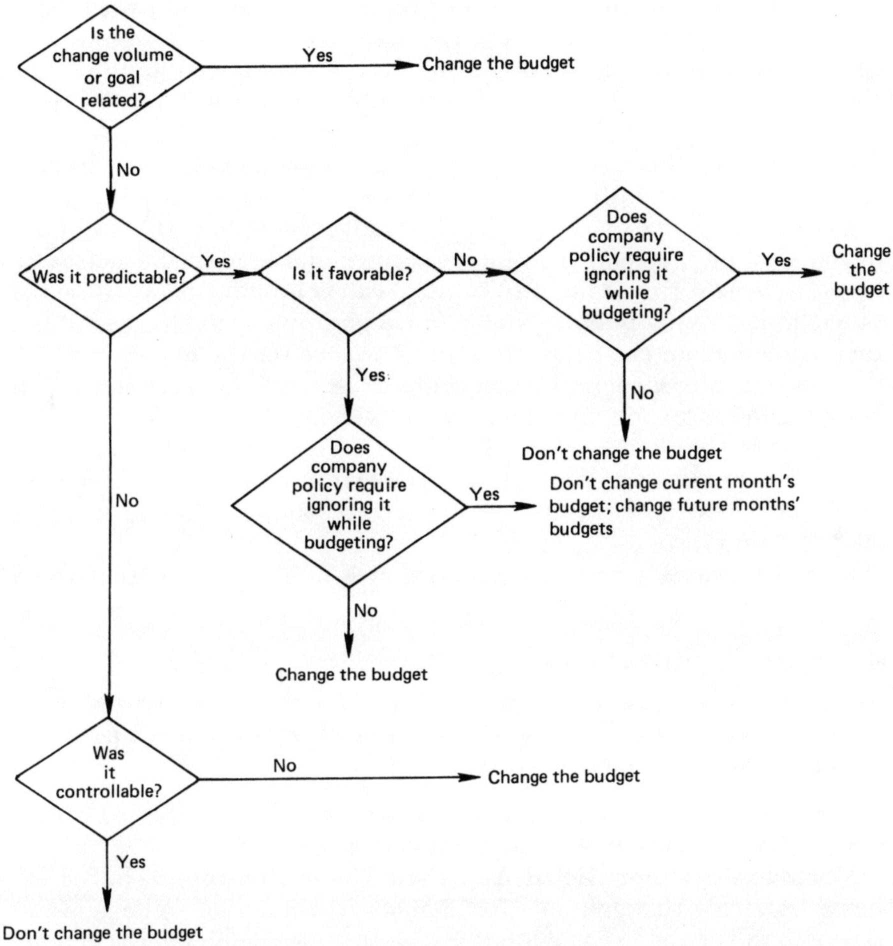


2. Similarly, budgeted expenses should be adjusted for changes in goals in the nature of nonrecurring programs if there is a significant impact on expenses. This stricture applies mainly to discretionary costs or proposed committed costs. For example, if a company has budgeted expenses for converting its manual inventory system to a computerized inventory system and if that program has been abandoned or postponed, the budget allowances for this project should be deleted; otherwise, the concerned department's budget will show a favorable budget variance.

3. An increase in the price of a direct material or a shortage of a direct material as a result of a strike at the supplier's plant, which strike had been threatened at the time of preparing a budget, is a predictable event. If company policy requires that in preparing budgets all unfavorable impacts of predictable events, even though uncertain, be taken into account, the direct materials budget should not be changed and the purchasing department should be held responsible for the unfavorable price variance.

4. If, as a result of a cost reduction program under way, a reduction in cost was predictable, though it was not certain, and if company policy required budgeting such changes, the budget allowance should be reduced because the concerned budget center manager should not be allowed to benefit from failure to comply with company policy. If, on the other hand, company policy did require ignoring such changes unless they actually materialized, the budget allowance for the month in which the cost reduction program became effective should not be changed, but budget allowances for subsequent months should be reduced.

5. An increase in the prices of direct materials due to an oil embargo or the outbreak of war is an unpredictable and usually noncontrollable event, and it is therefore proper to increase budget allowances under such circumstances.

6. An increase in defective production is a non-volume-related and unpredictable but controllable event. Hence, budget allowances should not be changed.

7. To get approval of their projects, some people deliberately underestimate or ignore noncontrollable costs which were known or predictable while the budget was being prepared. If such cases come to light, the budget should not be changed.

Undeniably, it is difficult to apply these rules to every single change, but they can be applied to significant changes.

**Macroapproach, or Global Approach** Under this approach, the expense budget is changed only for changes in volume or some goals, as shown in the model in Exhibit 6-8. Except for the changes in the volume of activity or goals, budgeted expenses are *not* changed even if the increase (or decrease) in expenses is beyond the control of the individual department concerned. However, to establish responsibility for variances, these should be separated into controllable and noncontrollable variances.

The reason for not changing budgeted expenses even if there are noncontrollable increases or decreases in expenses lies in the concept of *total resource management*. Every department head is allowed budgeted resources for achieving certain objectives. If there is an increase in one of the cost items, the department concerned should endeavor to make sav-

**EXHIBIT 6-8**

**Expense Budget Revision Model under Macroapproach**

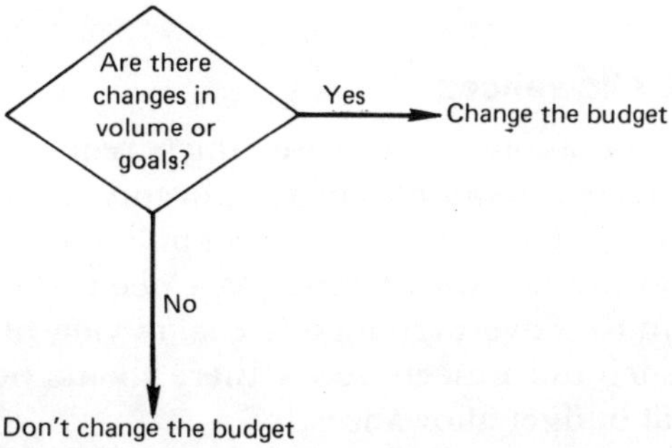


ings in other cost items either for the same objective or for other objectives to be undertaken by it in the coming months. If the budget is changed for an increase in expenses, the concerned department head will feel that he is within the budget and may not try to find avenues for achieving offsetting cost savings. If, on the other hand, unfavorable variances appear month after month, the department head will be motivated to take steps to be within the budget. If it is not possible for the department to make offsetting savings in costs, the president should look for possible cost savings in other departments or possible revenue increases so as to achieve the predetermined profit goal. If, however, far-reaching changes have taken place because of conscious decisions made by upper management or by other departments, it may not be advisable to adhere to the old budgeted allowances. Typical examples of this situation are changes in production processes, product design, substitution of the existing material by some other material, etc. Hence, even under the second approach, management should use discretion and change budget allowances under exceptional circumstances.

**Multipurpose Budgeting** If a company employs the technique of budgeting for all three purposes, the following approach, which is also the most commonly used approach, is recommended:

- Actual performance is compared with the original budget to measure the degree of success in achieving the plan. The original budget may be modified in exceptional circumstances as explained in the section "Planning Budget" above.
- Actual performance is compared with the flexible budget, revised as

explained in the section "Budgeting for Cost Control" above, for measuring the effectiveness in controlling costs.

- A monthly or a quarterly forward look is prepared for forecasting the profits for the year.

## Special Budget Allowances

During the year, occasions often arise which require the incurring of expenses not budgeted. Examples of such events are the announcement of an important trade fair in the company's line of business, the opening up of trade opportunities with China, or a need to undertake a crash research program to convert from oil to coal in view of the energy crisis. To take care of such unforeseen needs, there should be a procedure for approving special budget allowances.

In reporting actual versus budgeted expenses, the special budget allowances and the expenditures against them should be shown separately so that the benefits from such expenses can be measured. Further, if the amount of the special budget allowance is significant and will not directly or immediately increase profits, separate reporting of this amount will alert management to the need for making offsetting cost savings.

# Chapter 7

# Selecting Appropriate Cost Methods

Selecting the right things to do is more important than doing things right.
Pravin P. Shah

Several methods of costing are available for product costing, cost control, and cost analysis for managerial decision making. The method selected affects the classification, accumulation, allocation, and reporting of costs, and it also influences the establishment of cost centers and the development of a chart of accounts. Most important of all, the method of costing determines the kind of cost information that will be generated and will influence business decisions based on that information. For all these reasons, it is necessary to select an appropriate method of costing at quite an early stage of the system design phase. Further, once one method of costing has been employed, it is not easy to change to another method. Hence, it is essential to exercise great care in selecting the method of costing.

To enable the designer to make an appropriate selection, in this chapter we will discuss the alternative methods of costing available, examine the pros and cons of each method, and offer selection guidelines.

## DIFFERENT METHODS OF COSTING

There are three aspects of any method of costing, and for each aspect two or more alternative methods are available, as shown in Exhibit 7-1. Any cost system includes at least one alternative concerning each of the three aspects. For example, the cost system of a company may be job order–actual–full absorption costing, process–actual–full absorption

**EXHIBIT 7-1**

**Three Aspects of a Costing Method with Alternatives for Each Aspect**

| Aspect | Alternatives |
|---|---|
| A. Production process or service-oriented | 1. Job order costing<br>2. Process costing (or unit costing)<br>3. Batch costing<br>4. Operating costing (or functional or unit costing) |
| B. Time factor-oriented | 1. Actual (or historical) costing<br>2. Standard (or predetermined) costing |
| C. Cost composition-oriented | 1. Full absorption (or total) costing<br>2. Direct (or marginal) costing |

costing, job order–standard–direct costing, and so on. In all, there are sixteen options.

The designer must make a selection from these sixteen choices. However, these sixteen methods of costing are not mutually exclusive; i.e., a company can employ more than one method simultaneously. For example, a company can, and many companies do, employ job order–full absorption costing on an actual as well as a standard cost basis or job order–actual costing on a full absorption as well as a direct cost basis. Similarly, a company may use process costing for one product (say, rolled-steel products) and job order costing for another product (say, fabricated steel, forgings, castings, etc.). It may use two different methods of costing even for different components of the same product. For example, a company manufacturing television sets may employ job order costing for major components like picture tubes, receivers, etc., and process costing for minor components like knobs, buttons, switches, etc.

**Actual Company Practices** In 1976, the author conducted a survey of the costing methods employed by some of the *Fortune* 1000 companies and large nonindustrial companies. The result of the survey is summarized in Exhibit 7-2.

Since the designer must choose one or more alternatives from each of the three aspects of a costing method, let us consider the characteristics, pros and cons, and suitability of various alternatives available for each aspect.

## FIRST ASPECT: JOB ORDER–PROCESS–BATCH–OPERATING COSTING

Under the job order cost method, the cost of each job is costed separately. A job may consist of a single unit of a product or multiple units of a product. Under the process cost method, the cost of each process for a month, a quarter, or any other period is computed separately, and a unit cost of production is then worked out. Under the operating cost method, each operation, activity, or function is costed separately. Operating costing is similar to process costing and is used mainly in service industries.

Normally, a manufacturing company employs either a job order cost method or a process cost method, but sometimes a company may employ or need a hybrid method, i.e., a combination of the two methods. For example, a pharmaceutical company uses what is often referred to as batch costing, which is basically a process cost method but partakes of the character of a job order cost method because each production batch, like each job order, is costed separately. Let us take, for instance, the costing of tablets in a pharmaceutical company. First, granules are prepared by mixing different ingredients, then from the granules powder is made, and from the powder tablets are made. The tablets are then packed in bottles, which, in turn, are packed in cartons. To compute the cost of packed tablets, the company can use either batch costing or process costing:

1. Under *batch costing,* first compute the average cost of manufacturing tablets for each production batch. Then, to compute the total cost of each packing size, cost the tablets at the average tablet-manufacturing cost of the batch from which the tablets are used, and add to it the

**EXHIBIT 7-2**

**Costing Methods Employed by Certain Companies**

| Product Manufactured or Activities | Company's Annual Revenue | Method of Costing Employed |
|---|---|---|
| 1. Aircraft and related products | $1.3 billion | Job order–actual–full absorption costing (Company describes its system as "costing by standards," wherein actual costs are distributed by the relationship of the standard costs to the work output.) |
| 2. Rolled-steel products | $5 billion | Process–historical–full absorption costing |
| Fabricated steel, forgings, castings, and ships | | Job order–actual–full absorption costing |
| Industrial fasteners | | Job order–standard–full absorption costing |
| 3. Primary and fabricated aluminum products | $2.3 billion | Single-process, multiprocess, job order–actual, and standard–full absorption costing |
| 4. Primary aluminum and aluminum products | $1.6 billion | Process–standard–full absorption costing |
| 5. Large-scale computer systems, computer peripheral products, and various computer-related services | $1.3 billion | Job order–actual–full absorption costing |
| 6. Television and other products | $900 million | Process–actual and standard–full absorption costing |
| 7. Electrical appliances | $1.5 billion | Job order and process–standard–full absorption (direct when applicable) costing |
| 8. Packaging, chemicals, and consumer products | $2.9 billion | Job order and process–standard–full absorption costing |
| 9. Specialty chemicals and machinery | Not available | Job order–actual and standard–direct costing |
| 10. Pharmaceuticals and health care, chemicals, agricultural products, and consumer products | $1.5 billion | Multiprocess–standard–full absorption costing |
| 11. Pharmaceuticals, cosmetics, toiletries, and household products | $900 million | Multiprocess–standard–full absorption costing |
| 12. Health care | $1 billion | Multiprocess–standard–full absorption and direct costing |

relevant costs of packing. This method may give different costs of packed tablets from batch to batch.

2. Alternatively, the company can use a *pure process cost method* under which an average cost of tablets of a particular kind manufactured during the costing period will be computed. Similarly, the average costs of packing material, packing labor, and packing overhead for each size will be computed. The total of tablet-manufacturing costs and packing costs will give the total costs of packed tablets by the size of the package.

### Illustration of Job Order Costing and Process Costing

To discuss the pros and cons of job order costing and process costing, the following simplified illustration is used:

XYZ Company manufactures a single product called radio pager of only one kind. There are only two manufacturing processes, which are performed respectively in Department A and Department B. During the month of January 1980, the company undertook two production orders of, respectively, 3000 pagers and 2000 pagers. There was neither beginning nor ending work in process. The total cost of production was as follows:

| | |
|---|---:|
| Direct materials | $300,000 |
| Direct labor | 175,000 |
| Manufacturing overhead | 125,000 |
| Total cost of production | $600,000 |
| Number of units produced | 5000 |
| Unit cost | $120 |

If the company uses process costing, its cost statement will be as shown in Exhibit 7-3. If it employs job order costing, it will cost each production order separately, as shown in Exhibit 7-4.

### Comparison of Job Order Costing and Process Costing

Selecting job order versus process costing involves several major considerations: (1) cost control; (2) profit determination; (3) price quotation and price determination; (4) costs of designing, implementing, and operating a cost system; and (5) nature of the business. These are explained below. The first three considerations stem from the objectives for designing a cost system. The last consideration is often the most impor-

**EXHIBIT 7-3**

**Process Cost Statement**

Product: Radio pagers

Month: January 1980

| | Process 1 (Department A) | | Process 2 (Department B) | | Total | |
|---|---|---|---|---|---|---|
| | Total cost | Unit cost | Total cost | Unit cost | Total cost | Unit cost |
| A. Cost of production | | | | | | |
| Transferred from process 1 | | | $375,000 | $ 75 | | |
| Added into present process | | | | | | |
| Materials | $200,000 | $40 | $100,000 | $ 20 | $300,000 | $ 60 |
| Labor | 100,000 | 20 | 75,000 | 15 | 175,000 | 35 |
| Manufacturing overhead | 75,000 | 15 | 50,000 | 10 | 125,000 | 25 |
| Subtotal | $375,000 | $75 | $225,000 | $ 45 | | |
| Total costs | $375,000 | $75 | $600,000 | $120 | $600,000 | $120 |
| B. Units of production | | | | | | |
| Equivalent opening units | ..... | | ..... | | | |
| Received in process | 5,000 | | 5,000 | | | |
| Completed and transferred | 5,000 | | 5,000 | | 5,000 | |
| Remaining in process | ..... | | ..... | | | |
| Equivalent completed units | 5,000 | | 5,000 | | | |
| C. Cost of production apportioned | | | | | | |
| To completed production | $375,000 | $75 | $600,000 | $120 | $600,000 | $120 |
| To work in process | ........ | ... | ........ | .... | ........ | .... |
| Total cost of production | $375,000 | $75 | $600,000 | $120 | $600,000 | $120 |

tant one. For example, for industries manufacturing joint products and by-products, process costing is the only suitable method of costing. Hence, the first four considerations are relevant only when a choice of at least two methods of costing is available.

**EXHIBIT 7-4**

**Job Order Cost Statements**

Production Order No. 1 Month started January 1980 Month Completed January 1980

| | Department A | | Department B | | Total | |
|---|---|---|---|---|---|---|
| | Total cost | Unit cost | Total cost | Unit cost | Total cost | Unit cost |
| Direct materials | $126,000 | $42 | $ 69,000 | $23 | $195,000 | $ 65 |
| Direct labor | 54,000 | 18 | 48,000 | 16 | 102,000 | 34 |
| Manufacturing overhead | 45,000 | 15 | 30,000 | 10 | 75,000 | 25 |
| Total cost of production | $225,000 | $75 | $147,000 | $49 | $372,000 | $124 |
| Number of units produced | 3000 | | 3000 | | 3000 | |

Production Order No. 2 Month started January 1980 Month completed January 1980

| | Department A | | Department B | | Total | |
|---|---|---|---|---|---|---|
| | Total cost | Unit cost | Total cost | Unit cost | Total cost | Unit cost |
| Direct materials | $ 74,000 | $37 | $30,000 | $15 | $105,000 | $ 52 |
| Direct labor | 46,000 | 23 | 28,000 | 14 | 73,000 | 37 |
| Manufacturing overhead | 30,000 | 15 | 20,000 | 10 | 50,000 | 25 |
| Total cost of production | $150,000 | $75 | $78,000 | $39 | $228,000 | $114 |
| Number of units produced | 2000 | | 2000 | | 2000 | |

Since batch costing is a combination of job costing and process costing, its merits and demerits fall between those of job costing and those of process costing. Its exact pros and cons depend upon whether it resembles more closely job costing or process costing. Hence, its pros and cons are not discussed here, but the types of industries for which it is suitable are given later in this chapter.

**Cost Control** For cost control, job order costing is more suitable than process costing for two reasons:

1. Job order costing enables the accumulation of material, labor, and overhead costs by jobs and by cost centers. Hence, it is possible to compare the costs of various jobs by cost elements and by cost centers and to locate areas of inefficiency and waste in the use of material, labor, and machines by jobs and cost centers. Process costing, on the other hand, accumulates material, labor, and overhead costs by processes or departments only and hence provides information in terms of an *average cost* of production undertaken during the costing period. Areas of cost efficiency and inefficiency are buried in the average cost generated by the process cost method.

For example, Exhibit 7-4, based on job order costing, reveals that the unit cost of Production Order Number 1 exceeded that of Production Order Number 2 by $10, which was made up of the following:

| *Department A* | *$ per unit* |
|---|---|
| Excess direct materials | 5.00 |
| Excess direct labor | (5.00) |
| Excess cost in Department A | .... |
| *Department B* | |
| Excess direct materials | 8.00 |
| Excess direct labor | 2.00 |
| Excess cost in Department B | 10.00 |
| Total excess cost of Order Number 1 | 10.00 |

This analysis would lead an alert management to make the following inquiries:

- Why was the direct material cost for Order Number 1 higher than that for Order Number 2 in both Departments A and Department B?
- Why was the direct labor cost in Department B higher for Order Number 1 than for Order Number 2?
- Why was the direct labor cost in Department A higher for Order Number 2 than for Order Number 1?

Such inquiries enable management to learn if labor productivity is lower or if spoiled, defective, or substandard work is greater than usual, say, during the night shift, for rush orders, or for certain types of jobs.

Information of this kind is very valuable not only for cost control but also for price quoting or price setting. For example, if labor productivity is lower for rush orders, management will try either to pass on the cost of lower labor productivity to customers placing rush orders or to reduce the impact of rush orders by inventorying more goods to meet such orders, provided the volume of rush orders can be forecast on the basis of past experience.

On the other hand, Exhibit 7-3, based on process costing, shows only the average production cost for the month of January 1980. Unlike Exhibit 7-4, it does not show variances in the cost of production of two production orders during that month. Thus, cost inefficiencies are buried in the average cost for the month.

Cost comparison among various jobs also brings to light ways to improve productivity and reduce costs. For example, in one company the unit labor cost of a particular operation was always estimated at 25 hours times the current wage rate for that operation, and the actual labor cost always turned out to be between 24 and 27 hours times the prevailing wage rate. For one rush order, the unit labor cost was only $200 (20 hours times $10), as against the estimated cost of $250 (25 hours times $10). On inquiring into the causes for the 20 percent lower labor cost, company management found that closer supervision and better planning for that job had reduced waiting time and idle time. Thereupon, company management took steps to apply the better planning technique to all jobs and to tighten supervision. Under process costing, such cost efficiencies (and also cost inefficiencies) would have been buried in an average cost.

It is true that if process costing is used in conjunction with standard costs and if the standards are reasonable, the disadvantages mentioned above would be alleviated to some extent because a comparison of the actual average cost with the standard cost would reveal the areas of efficiencies and inefficiencies. However, in comparison with job order costing, it would still be much more difficult to investigate the causes of variances and pin down responsibility for them.

2. The job order cost method identifies costs (except common overhead) with the respective jobs on a continuous basis and hence can provide information on variances from the estimated or expected cost soon after the variances have taken place. Timely information on cost variances enables management to take timely corrective action. Under the process cost method, management may not learn about cost variances until the end of the month, when the process cost statement is prepared. For instance, let us assume that in the illustration given in Exhibit 7-4 the company has estimated the unit material cost in Department A to be $35. Soon after the manufacturing operation in Department A is over for Production Order Number 1, management will be alerted that the actual

unit material cost has exceeded the estimate by $7. This will prompt management to take steps to bring the material cost of subsequent orders within control as far as possible. If there has been an uncontrollable increase in the cost of material, management may consider increasing prices or may try to save costs in other areas.

3. For proper cost control, it is essential to personalize cost variances. The job order cost method enables management to place responsibility for cost inefficiency and for defective, spoiled, and substandard work. Once cost variances have been identified with job orders and cost centers, it is easy to track down the individuals responsible for cost variances. Since the process cost method does not identify costs with individual production orders, it usually is not possible to personalize cost variances.

Further, the job order cost method facilitates control over the physical progress of a job because the costs and the progress of the work are recorded on the job cost card as the work passes through various stages of production. Hence, the physical progress of the job can be ascertained at any time from the job cost card.

**Profit Determination** Job order costing enables profit to be determined by jobs, and if production is undertaken against an order, profit can be determined as soon as a job has been completed and the total job cost has been computed. Under the process cost method, profit from individual jobs can be computed only on an average basis, and normally profit cannot be determined until the process cost statement has been prepared for the costing period.

For companies manufacturing custom-made products such as custom-made equipment or furniture, the cost of production as well as profit will vary from job to job. Hence, usually it will be desirable to compute profits by jobs. For this type of company, the job order cost method is more suitable than the process cost method.

**Price Quotation and Price Determination** For quoting or setting the price of a standard product, an average cost of the product is required. Hence, the process cost system serves the purpose, and there is no need for an elaborate job order cost system. For quoting the price of a nonstandard product, however, the job order cost method is better than the process cost method because it facilitates cost estimating. Further, because under job order costing costs and profits are computed by jobs, variances between estimates and actual costs help improve price estimation in the future. If a company gets many rush orders requiring subcontracting for aspects of a job, the job order cost method is more advantageous than the process cost method.

For cost-plus contracts, the job order cost method is virtually inevitable, although process costing may be employed for common parts manufactured for several cost-plus contracts.

**Design, Implementation, and Operation Costs** Since the job order cost method identifies the costs of material, labor, and overhead with jobs and cost centers, it is more elaborate than the process cost method. Hence, compared with the process cost method, it requires more time and cost not only to design and implement it but also to operate it. In particular, the increased clerical cost of operating the job order cost method may far outweigh its benefits for many concerns. For example, for a company manufacturing standard products, say, nails, and employing simple processes, it is not worthwhile to have a job order cost method because a process cost method will serve all the same purposes. Normally, job order costing is more appropriate in concerns producing products with a high unit cost and a low volume of production. And for low-unit-cost and high-volume products, process costing is decidedly better. For example, job order costing is preferable for shipbuilding, whereas process costing is better for nail manufacturing.

Thus, a cost-benefit analysis should be made in selecting a cost system. There is no point in having a Cadillac if a Pinto will do the job.

**Suitability by Industries** In selecting the appropriate cost method, the designer should also bear in mind that for each industry one type of costing usually is more appropriate than the other. In fact, in some cases no choice is available. Hence, the designer should understand the nature of the company's business and, in particular, ascertain whether the production processes are continuous or discrete and whether the products are standard or custom-made. The impact of these two factors on the selection of the appropriate cost method is explained in the guidelines given below. Whenever a choice is available, the final selection should be made after weighing the other four considerations:

**Process Costing** This method is used when it is impossible, difficult, or impractical to trace costs to individual production units. The following types of industries fall in this category:

- Continuous-process industries, such as chemical and cement factories.
- Industries manufacturing standard products on a mass scale. Usually, industries of this type manufacture products with a high volume and a low unit cost. Hence, from the cost angle process costing is more appropriate.
- Industries manufacturing either joint products or main products and by-products. Examples of such industries are meat packing and petroleum refining.

*Process industries manufacturing nonstandard products* may employ either process costing or job order costing, though usually process costing will serve the purpose. For example, foundries and machine shops normally use process costing under which costs are computed on the weighted-average basis. In textile mills producing printed cloth according to prints furnished or selected by customers, the cost of artwork (e.g., an artist's sketches and printing rolls) and the cost of color may vary from order to order. Usually, however, the mills neither cost each order separately nor set prices according to the print selected. The normal practice is to compute the average cost by using the process cost method.

**Batch Costing** This method can be used when production either is taken up in batches or can be divided into suitable batches. As explained earlier, in a pharmaceutical company, drugs are manufactured in batches, and hence batch costing usually is employed.

Even in *continuous-process industries* in which production is taken up *in batches,* it may be possible to employ batch costing instead of process costing. For example, the artificial-fiber industry employs a combination of batch costing and process costing:

- For the prespinning process (for manufacturing viscose, polymers, etc., from wood pulp and various chemicals), either batch costing or process costing is employed.
- For the spinning and cone-winding processes, process costing is employed.

Whenever batch costing can be employed, process costing can be employed, but it may not be possible to use batch costing whenever process costing is used. For example, in the artificial-fiber industry, though either batch costing or process costing can be employed for the prespinning process, only process costing can be employed for costing the other two processes.

**Job Order Costing** This method can be used when costs can be traced or assigned to individual units of production. This is possible in industries with discrete production processes, such as the radio- and television-manufacturing industries. However, in most of these industries it is also possible to use batch costing or process costing. Hence, final selection will depend upon the four considerations mentioned earlier. To explain this point, we will classify the discrete-process industries into three categories according to the nature of their products.

1. For industries manufacturing *custom-made products* (e.g., shipbuilding) or providing *individual services* (e.g., repair shops), job order costing usually is more appropriate than process costing. However, if the variation in the unit cost from order to order is not significant, process costing may be used instead of job costing. For example, a concern manufacturing custom-made shirts may use process costing except, perhaps, for the cost of cloth if prices vary significantly from one type of cloth to another.

Fashion industries (e.g., those manufacturing garments, jewelry, furniture, etc.) manufacturing *nonstandard products* for *inventory* and employing *discrete* processes may use process costing, batch costing, operating costing, or job costing, depending upon the differences in the cost of manufacturing an individual variety of articles. If, for instance, a concern manufactures shirts of only one pattern, in different sizes, but from cloth of different prints and colors, the only cost which may vary from one type of shirt to another will be that of cloth, and hence either process costing or operating costing will be suitable. If, on the other hand, the concern manufactures shirts of different patterns (e.g., tapered and untapered, long-sleeved and short-sleeved, with or without cuffs, and with or without darts) from the same or different cloth, it is better to employ job order costing or batch costing because the cost will vary from pattern to pattern. If in the latter case process costing is employed, only the combined average cost of all patterns of shirts will be available; this will not be of much use for price setting, profit measurement by individual patterns of shirts, cost control, and inventory valuation.

2. For industries manufacturing *standard products* and employing *discrete production processes,* two choices are available:

- If the *number of operations* required in manufacturing a product is relatively *few,* batch costing or job order costing is more appropriate, though process costing is employed in some cases. Examples of such industries are companies manufacturing bicycles, furniture (of standard sizes and varieties), briefcases, suitcases, mechanical and electrical toys, and sport and leisure industry products such as tennis rackets and ice skates.
- If a *large number of operations* is required in producing a product and if the end product is produced in a large quantity, either operating costing or batch costing is employed. For example, concerns manufacturing radios, television sets, automobiles, typewriters, and the like fall in this category. On the other hand, for high-unit-cost and low-volume products such as aircraft and ships job order costing is more appropriate. Even in these types of industries, batch costing or process costing may be employed for parts produced on a mass scale.

3. If a concern manufactures *both standard products and custom-made products,* it can employ a combination of job order and process costing. For example, a company manufacturing standard as well as custom-made equipment may use process costing for standard equipment as well as for components common to standard and custom-made equipment and job order costing for custom-made equipment. In computing the cost of the custom-made equipment, the cost of the common components will be taken at the unit cost derived from process costing.

Exhibit 7-5 shows the method of costing used by some major industries.

**EXHIBIT 7-5**

**Method of Costing Used by Various Industries**

### Examples of Industries Usually Employing Process Costing

Chemical plants
Paper mills
Lumber mills
Pulp mills
Rolled-steel mills
Food processors
Paint factories
Glass factories
Sugar factories
Flour mills
Tire and rubber plants
Cement factories
Mines
Electricity-generating companies
Breweries
Wineries
Bakeries
Confectioneries
Hosieries
Bottling plants
Artificial-fiber plants (For prespinning stage, even batch costing can be used.)
Textile mills (Batch costing can also be used.)
Plants producing primary aluminum and aluminum products like rods, sheets, etc.

### Examples of Joint Products and By-Products Industries Using Process Costing

Meat packers
Oil and gas producers
Petroleum refiners
Certain chemical factories (e.g., a company manufacturing fatty acid and its by-products)
Dairy plants
Extractive industries

### Examples of Industries Usually Employing Batch Costing

Bakeries
Plants producing pharmaceuticals and health care products
Canneries (Job order costing may also be employed.)

**EXHIBIT 7-5**

**Method of Costing Used by Various Industries (*Continued*)**

Examples of Industries Usually Employing Batch Costing (*continued*)

Artificial-fiber plants (rayon, nylon, etc.), for prespinning process, i.e., for making cellulose from wood pulp, chemicals, etc. (Alternatively, process costing can be used.)

Diamond manufacturing (for industrial use as well as for making jewelry)

Plants producing standard equipment, appliances, and parts

Examples of Industries Usually Employing Job Order Costing (Process Costing or Batch Costing Can Also Be Used.)

Furniture-manufacturing plants
Shipbuilders
Plants producing custom-made equipment
Construction companies
Repair shops
Printing shops
Concerns producing artwork
Companies manufacturing custom-made machine tools
Companies constructing transmission towers
Contractors
Companies manufacturing packing materials (boxes, containers, etc.)
Drilling contractors (oil, water, etc.)
Custom-made equipment manufacturers
Software consultants for custom-made software
Folding-box industry

Fabricators of plastics against specific orders (If production is for inventory, batch costing or process costing is used.)

Research, engineering, and development services (Since costing is done by projects, this is also known as *project costing*.)

Plants fabricating steel, forgings, and castings
Plants manufacturing industrial fasteners
Film-producing companies

## Operating Costing

Service industries such as the banking, transportation, communications, hospital, and hotel industries use operating costing. Under this method, the costs of different operations are separately determined, and then the unit cost of each operation is computed. For example, in the hotel industry, the cost for rooms of different sizes and the cost for meals of different kinds are worked out. In a transportation company, the cost of operating a bus between any two destinations is computed. We will discuss this method in detail in Chapter 20, which treats special points for designing cost systems for nonmanufacturing companies.

The operating cost method is very similar to the process cost method and, therefore, can be used also in manufacturing industries in combination with the job order method or the process cost method. For example, in a job order industry, the direct labor cost may be accumulated by operations and then charged to various jobs by using the average cost of operation (e.g., a machine-hour rate) and the actual time devoted to each job. In any case, operating costing is used to accumulate and allocate the costs of the service departments of a manufacturing company.

Operating costing is also useful for establishing a standard cost system in the future. In establishing a standard cost system, it is necessary to set standards for each operation and suboperation. If historical operating costing is in use, it will provide useful basic data for setting standards.

## SECOND ASPECT: ACTUAL VERSUS STANDARD COSTING

The second aspect of the cost system to be decided is time-oriented; i.e., a choice must be made between actual (historical) costing and standard costing. Under actual costing, costs are accumulated, allocated, and absorbed on an actual basis and after the fact. Under a full-fledged standard cost system, costs are predetermined, recorded on a standard basis, and used as a basis for performance measurement and planning. Besides the two extremes of a pure actual cost system and a full-fledged standard cost system, two other options are available: either actual and standard costing may be used simultaneously, or some combination of these two costing methods may be employed. Even when full-fledged standard costing is employed, it is also necessary to accumulate actual costs for computing variances and for external reporting. However, it is not necessary to accumulate the actual costs by jobs, processes, or individual production units, as with a pure historical cost method.

A combination of the actual cost and the standard cost methods may take one or more of the following forms:

- For certain divisions or products, standard costing may be used, and for other divisions or products actual costing may be used.
- Standard costing may be used for certain cost elements (usually direct costs), and actual costing for other cost elements.
- Standard costs may be used for certain objectives, and actual costs for certain other purposes. For example, standard costs may be used as

a data base for planning and as a yardstick for cost control but not for inventory valuation or for product pricing.

- Standard cost information may not form part of accounting records but be compiled only statistically. All accounting records may be based on actual costs.

**Actual Company Practices** In actual practice, several variations are found, as is clear from Exhibit 7-2. One outstanding fact revealed by that exhibit is that not all large companies necessarily employ standard costing.

The following information about the practices of three companies using standard costing is interesting:

- In describing its cost system, a company manufacturing aircraft and related products stated that it does not use *standard costs*. It uses *costing by standards* "wherein the standard is not used as a recorded amount of cost itself, but rather as a measuring device. In effect, actual costs are distributed by the relationship of standard costs to the work output."
- A large aluminum company uses a standard cost system only for direct costs and budgets for overhead.
- A medium-size company manufacturing cables employs a full absorption standard cost system and has 38,000 standard costs.

As explained earlier (see Exhibit 7-1), standard costing and actual costing are not cost methods by themselves. They are used in conjunction with job order, process, batch, or operating costing on the one hand and direct costing or full absorption costing on the other hand.

## Comparison of Actual Costing and Standard Costing

To enable the designer to make a proper selection between actual costing and standard costing, the pros and cons and the suitability of the two cost systems are discussed below.

**Cost Control** Standard costing is far superior to actual costing for cost control for two reasons:

1. Predetermined or planned costs and various nonmonetary standards developed under the standard cost system provide objective yardsticks or benchmarks with which actual costs and performance can be compared. The variances show performance above or below the standard and help place responsibility for below-standard performance. Thus, variance reports under standard costing trigger corrective action.

Under actual costing, comparison at best will be made with past actual costs and performance, which inherently are defective as a basis for comparison for two reasons. First, the comparison of actual costs with actual costs shows only the cost efficiency or inefficiency between two time periods and is not relative to the standards. If past performance was inefficient, inefficiencies in current performance will not be revealed. Further, if current performance is better than the last period's performance, the extent of improvement will be shown but the *potential* for improvement will not be shown. Second, operating conditions do not always remain static. There may be changes, say, in specifications of materials, product design, or production processes. Hence, even if past performance was efficient, the past cost may become invalid as a basis for evaluating current performance if current operating conditions have significantly changed. Since under standard costing standards are updated with major changes in operating conditions, standard costing provides a valid basis for performance evaluation and cost control.

2. Normally, employees subject to various standards are allowed to participate in the development of those standards, and their acceptance of the standards is obtained. Consequently, employees have a strong sense of commitment to the standards. Once accepted by the employees, the standards can be used as a means of motivating them to equal or better standard performance. Some companies base their wages and incentive-bonus plans on the engineering standards developed under standard costing. Under actual costing, the basis for motivating employees is past actual performance, which may or may not reflect currently attainable performance.

However, unless the standards set are reasonably attainable, they may do more harm than good. Too loose standards will fail to achieve cost control at the desirable level, while too tight standards will not achieve control because employees will lose their faith in the standards.

**Data Base for Profit Planning and Budgeting** Standard costing provides an excellent data base for profit planning and budgeting. For example, since the quantity and price standards for material, labor, and overhead are established, it is easy and less time-consuming to develop an operating budget for any given volume of activity. Second, the data base under standard costing provides information for measuring the effect of price, mix, volume, and cost on profits by products, divisions, regions, and other segments of the business. These types of information enable company management to select the best volume of production and the most profitable product mix. Third, the data base generated by actual costing needs updating for profit planning and budgeting because what will happen in the future may not be the same as what has actually happened in the past. Standard costs, on the other hand, provide the current data base at any given time because they either are usually updated on a continuing basis or can be updated very easily.

**Product Pricing** Usually, it is necessary to determine product prices before actual production and distribution take place. This is inevitable for quoting the price of custom-made products or for bidding or quoting prices even on standard products. Even companies manufacturing products for inventory must determine product prices in advance in order to decide on the volume of production because at a given price only a certain quantity of the product can be sold. Though product-pricing decisions involve several factors, the costs of production and distribution constitute an important input even in a competitive market. And for product pricing, standard costing, when based on current standards, is decidedly better than actual costing because it provides more appropriate and accurate cost data on a timely basis for pricing decisions. However, in cost-plus contracts, actual cost data may be required.

**Financial Accounting and Reporting** Usually, a cost accounting system also provides certain data required for financial accounting and reporting purposes. In this regard, standard costing is better suited than actual costing. A few examples will make the point clear:

- Valuing inventory at standard costs will save considerable time and effort because the standard unit prices to be applied to actual quantities are readily available. Under actual costing, it is necessary to compute the actual product cost at the time of inventory valuation. However, in valuing inventory at standard costs the requirements of the income tax laws must be taken into account.
- Standard costs readily provide nonmonetary information required for management reporting.
- Profitability reporting can be more detailed and frequent if standard costing is employed than if actual costing is employed.

**Design, Implementation, and Operation** A standard cost system is difficult and more time-consuming to design and implement because standard setting is an elaborate process. Second, standards must be kept up to date to be meaningful for cost control. Once a standard cost system has been implemented, however, it will involve less clerical cost than a historical cost system. For example, in television, radio, or automobile companies manufacturing and assembling scores or even hundreds of parts and components, it is difficult and time-consuming to cost those parts and components on an actual basis; but if they are costed on a standard cost basis, considerable time and clerical cost will be saved. Standard costing offers greater advantages in a job order industry, because of the greater opportunities for saving clerical labor, than in a process industry, but it is easier to implement in a process cost industry than in a job order industry because there are fewer standards to be established. In a new company, it may be difficult to use a standard cost method because it is hard to establish various engineering standards and specifications unless industry standards are available and are used. Even in an existing company, it may be difficult to introduce, for the first time, a cost system based on standard costing because the lack of cost data by cost centers for the past few years will make standard setting difficult.

**Suitability** A standard cost system is suitable when production processes and other activities are repetitive. Hence, it is more commonly found in industries manufacturing standard products than in industries manufacturing nonstandard or custom-made products.

If the manufacture of custom-made articles involves certain common operations or materials though their contents vary, it will be possible to use standard costing. In such cases, a standard cost will be set for each of the commonly used operations and direct materials, and the standard cost of an article will be computed by taking the standard costs of the required materials and operations.

As explained in Chapter 6, standard costing is suitable for controlling variable costs but not for discretionary or committed costs. Hence, if variable costs are fairly stable, a standard cost system may not be necessary.

Further, standard costing is unsuitable when actual cost data are required. Generally, the actual cost system can be employed in almost all industries, but it may not be as appropriate as the standard cost system.

## THIRD ASPECT: DIRECT COSTING VERSUS FULL ABSORPTION COSTING

The third and last aspect of the cost system involves selection between direct costing and full absorption costing. Both are methods of product costing, and the basic difference between them lies in the treatment of fixed manufacturing overhead. Under direct costing, fixed manufacturing overhead is treated as *period costs* and therefore is not included in the valuation of inventory but is written off to costing profit and loss account. Under full absorption costing, fixed manufacturing overhead is treated as product costs and hence is included in the valuation of inventory. In other words, under direct costing, only those production costs which vary with the volume of production are included in product costing. Hence, direct costing is also known as *variable costing* or *marginal costing*.

Though direct costing and full absorption costing are primarily methods of product costing and inventory valuation, the underlying concept can be applied also to nonproduct costs such as selling, general, and administrative expenses. In this broader sense, direct costing includes all variable costs—manufacturing as well as selling, general, and administrative expenses. Full absorption costing (often called *total costing* in the broader sense) includes all costs, variable as well as fixed, and manufacturing as well as selling, general, and administrative expenses. The broader definition of the terms direct costing and full absorption costing has no impact on product costing and inventory valuation. It makes a difference only in the reporting of cost and profit information. For example, an income statement prepared on direct costing will separate all variable and fixed costs and show profit both before and after deducting fixed costs. On the other hand, an income statement prepared on full absorption costing will not make this distinction but will show gross profit (i.e., sales less manufacturing cost of goods sold) and operating income (i.e., gross profit less selling, general, and administrative expenses).

## Comparison of Direct Costing and Full Absorption Costing

To enable the designer to make a proper selection between direct costing and full absorption costing, the pros and cons and the suitability of these two methods are discussed below.

**Cost Control** As we have shown in Chapter 6, the classification of costs according to their variability is essential for using the responsibility accounting system, budgeting technique, and standard costing technique for effectively controlling costs. Since under direct costing fixed and variable costs are separated, direct costing usually is better suited for cost control than full absorption costing.

Sometimes it is argued that both fixed and variable costs need to be controlled and that therefore full-absorption costing is superior to direct costing for cost control. However, the point is that direct costing merely separates variable and fixed costs; it does not ignore fixed costs. Hence, the argument has no validity.

**Data Base for Profit Planning and Decision Making** For profit planning, it is essential to forecast costs and profits at various levels of sales and production. For this purpose, it is necessary to know which costs will vary with changes in the volume of production and sales and which costs will not so vary. Since direct costing separates fixed and variable costs, it provides an excellent data base for profit planning. It also enables a "what if" type of analysis (What would be the impact of profit if we, say, increase prices by 10 percent?), which is required for profit planning and certain management decisions.

Similarly, for several managerial decisions such as whether to make or buy an item, drop a product line, or discontinue a division, direct costing provides an excellent data base because understanding cost behavior is essential for these decisions.

Thus, by separating costs into fixed and variable categories direct costing makes possible the use of several cost accounting techniques, such as cost-volume-profit relationship, breakeven analysis, what-if analysis, differential costing or incremental costing, and the like. All these techniques provide valuable cost information to management. For a further discussion of these techniques the reader may refer to any standard textbook on cost accounting.

**Product Pricing** For regular product pricing, total cost is relevant, and hence full absorption costing is better than direct costing. On the other hand, direct costing is more appropriate for special-order pricing, particularly when the objective is to determine the lowest price that the company can accept without incurring losses.

**Inventory Valuation and Profit Determination** Direct costing and full absorption costing are alternative methods of valuing inventory and determining profits. There are several pros and cons of these two methods of valuing inventory, but a complete discussion of them is beyond the scope of this book. Hence, only the important points are summarized below.

1. The value of inventory under the two methods will be different. Hence, depending upon the levels of sales, production, and inventory, the pretax profit under the two methods may also differ.
2. In the United States, full absorption costing is the only acceptable method of inventory valuation for external reporting and for the purpose of federal income taxation. However, in countries such as the United Kingdom and India direct costing is acceptable for tax purposes. Even in the United States direct costing can be used for internal management reporting, and many companies do so use it. In that case, it is necessary to adjust the inventory based on direct costing to include the proportionate fixed manufacturing overhead.
3. Because full absorption costing involves the allocation of fixed manufacturing overhead for inventory valuation, inventory valuation and income determination take more time than under direct costing. Even the use of predetermined overhead absorption rates does not significantly reduce the time because it is necessary to compute the underabsorbed or overabsorbed overhead and to dispose of it.

**Design, Implementation, and Operation** The separation of fixed and variable costs required under direct costing is fraught with several practical difficulties because the separation is not always black and white. Usually, there are two problems. First, separation of semivariable costs into fixed and variable costs is difficult. Second, even many fixed costs remain fixed only within a certain range of production or sales. Determining that range of production or sales for each fixed cost is time-consuming and difficult. Though full absorption costing does not involve the problems of separation of fixed and variable costs, it involves the equally challenging task of allocating fixed manufacturing overhead to different products. Thus, it is difficult to generalize about which method is more difficult to design and implement.

Generally, compared with full absorption costing, direct costing takes less time to operate because it does not require allocation of fixed manufacturing overhead. However, if direct costing is used for internal reporting and full absorption for external reporting, then the additional work of adjusting the inventory valuation to full absorption costing is involved.

Whatever the costing method used, the controller or the cost accountants have an important role to play. They must interpret the cost information generated under any of these methods.

**Suitability** Unlike the suitability of job order costing and process costing, the suitability of direct costing and full absorption costing does not depend upon the nature of the business: it depends upon the purpose for which cost information is required and upon management philosophy. Further, both these methods can very easily coexist. Hence, whenever necessary, both methods should be employed to make the cost system flexible enough to provide cost information on either basis for different objectives.

When both costing methods are employed, the basic cost accounting records will generally be maintained on one of the two bases and a supplementary analysis made on the other basis as and when required. But the basic cost records will be so maintained that the supplementary analysis on the other basis can be undertaken without undue trouble.

Before we close the discussion of these two methods of costing, it is also necessary to differentiate them from the term *direct costs.*

### Direct Costing and Full Absorption Costing versus Direct Costs

In cost accounting literature, there is some confusion about the terms *direct costing* and *direct costs.* These two terms are not synonyms, and it is essential for the designer to understand the distinction between them.

*Direct costing* is a method of product costing, and the product cost computed under direct costing consists of direct materials, direct labor, and *variable* manufacturing overhead. *Direct costs,* on the other hand, are those costs which can be directly identified with a product, department, operation, responsibility center, etc. They include both *variable costs* and *fixed costs.* Costs which are not directly identifiable are called *indirect costs* or *joint costs.* It will be obvious that costs which are direct, say, to a department may be indirect to products processed by that department.

In short, product costs computed under direct costing exclude fixed manufacturing overhead, but direct product costs include even fixed manufacturing overhead which can be charged directly (i.e., without allocation) to individual products. The distinction between direct product costs and product costs computed under full absorption costing is that the former will exclude the fixed manufacturing overhead (e.g., general plant expenses) which cannot be directly charged to individual products, whereas the latter will include it. Thus, product costs computed on a direct cost basis will be more than those under direct costing, but less than those under full absorption costing.

Direct costs as such are not the method of valuing inventory. However, direct product costs may be computed for managerial decisions, such as whether to make or buy a product. Further, as explained here, sometimes the inventory valuation on absorption costing may be equal to the direct costs of production. Even under absorption costing, it is not necessary (at least for internal reporting) to include all the fixed manufacturing overhead in product costing. For example, only directly chargeable fixed manufacturing overhead may be included in the inventory valuation, and the joint overhead may be written off as period costs. If this approach is adopted, the product costs under absorption costing will be equal to direct (manufacturing) costs.

As in the case of direct costing and full absorption costing, the term direct costs is applicable not only to manufacturing costs but also to selling, general, and administrative expenses.

## Usefulness of Direct Costs Information

The classification of costs into direct and indirect categories is useful for cost control, segment profitability evaluation, and several other purposes. For example, for cost control it is essential to identify and assign all direct costs to individual responsibility centers and to keep all indirect costs out of allocation because their inclusion in cost control reports does not add any element of control. Similarly, segment profit computed by considering only the costs directly incurred by the particular segment provides a better measure of the segment's profitability and its contribution to the overall profits of the company. This is called a *contribution margin approach.* Under this approach, all joint costs (costs which cannot be directly identified with any business segment) are deducted from the total profit contribution of all the segments to arrive at the total profits of the company as a whole.

Further, separation of direct and indirect costs is useful for certain managerial decisions, such as whether to discontinue a division or a product, whether to make or buy a component, and the like. For example, in deciding whether to discontinue a division, all the costs which will be saved by discontinuing it should be considered. These costs will consist of all the costs directly chargeable to the division.

## SUMMARY

A costing method has three different aspects, and for each aspect two or more alternatives are available. These aspects are (1) job order, process, batch, or operating costing, (2) actual or standard costing, and (3) direct or full-absorption costing. In selecting a costing method for any company, one or more alternatives concerning each aspect should be chosen.

In making the selection among alternatives, their impact on these areas should be considered: (1) cost control; (2) profit determination; (3) price quotation and price determination; (4) costs of designing, implementing, and operating a cost system; (5) nature of the business, (6) data base for profit planning, budgeting, and decision making; and (7) financial accounting and reporting.

# Chapter 8

# Establishing Responsibility Centers and Cost Centers

Everybody's responsibility is nobody's responsibility.

In cost accounting, costs are accumulated not only by the nature of expenses (salaries, wages, rent, electricity, etc.) but also by organizational segments, activities, processes, jobs, products, etc., which for the purposes of cost accumulation are called *cost centers.* When the responsibility accounting system is employed, the entire organization is divided into various organizational segments known as *responsibility centers.* Under this system, costs are charged to and reported by the responsibility centers responsible for incurring them. Thus, in designing a cost system for any purpose, it is necessary to establish cost centers. In addition, when the system of responsibility accounting is to be employed, it is also necessary to establish responsibility centers.

## RESPONSIBILITY ACCOUNTING SYSTEM

Except in a very small organization, the responsibility for the various objectives, functions, operations, or activities of an organization are divided among several individuals. To enable them to discharge their assigned responsibility, they are delegated certain authority. Naturally, management of the organization would like to know how well the designated individuals perform their assigned responsibilities. In other words, the organization needs a system whereby the delegates are able to render accounts of their responsibilities. The system available for this purpose is the *responsibility accounting system.* Under this system, the performance of each responsible individual is measured against some yardstick and reported to that individual as well as to the individual's superior. Thus, the responsibility accounting system is employed for performance measurement and control.

Though the focus of our discussion here is cost control, the application of the responsibility accounting system is not limited to cost control. It can be used, say, for profit control, revenue control, or controlling the cost of converting a manual cost accounting system into a computerized cost system. Further, it can be used in a centralized as well as a decentralized organization and in a profit-seeking as well as a not-for-profit organization.

### Importance of Proper Organization Structure

It is worth emphasizing that cost control is not achieved just by the accumulation and reporting of costs by organizational segments. A proper organization structure is very important for effective cost control and, for that reason, also for achieving any of the company's objectives. By a proper structure is meant not the neatly drawn boxes on the organization chart but the proper division of authority and responsibility and the positioning of each function at the appropriate place in the organization structure.

Proper division of authority and responsibility will avoid gaps or overlapping of responsibilities and authority. Further, for the effective management of a function it is essential that the function be placed in the appropriate department consistent with the organization's objectives. For example, to achieve control over rising costs of materials and inventory, many large manufacturing companies have found it advantageous to create a materials management department under which are put two or more materials management functions of purchasing, production planning, inventory control, distribution, and traffic. The exact arrangement[1] depends upon the importance of various functions and their interrelationship.

Sometimes, it may be necessary to upgrade a function by placing it at a higher level in the organization. This step helps in two ways. First, it is possible to hire better-qualified persons because they can be paid better salaries at a higher level than at a lower level. Second, usually the higher the level at which a function is placed, the more effective it will be.

## TYPES OF RESPONSIBILITY CENTERS

As noted earlier, for responsibility accounting it is necessary to divide the entire organization into responsibility centers and to identify the individ-

[1] See, for example, Jeffrey G. Miller and Peter Gilmour, "Materials Managers: Who Needs Them?" *Harvard Business Review,* July–August 1979, pp. 143–153.

ual in charge of each of the centers and what precisely that individual is responsible for. In any business organization, there usually are four things to be controlled: costs, revenue or sales, profit (profit = revenue − costs), and investment. Hence, conceptually there are four subsets of a responsibility center. If the responsibility center manager (here the term *manager* means a person responsible for a particular organizational segment and does not designate the title) has control over costs, the manager's sphere of responsibility may be called a *cost center.* If the manager has control over revenue, the area of responsibility may be called a *revenue center.* If the manager controls both revenue and costs, the manager's organizational segment may be called a *profit center;* and if the manager controls investment, the responsibility sphere may be called an *investment center.* For example, the purchasing department and the production department are cost centers, a sales branch is a revenue center because the branch manager is responsible for generating sales, and the production department and the electronic data processing (EDP) department are investment centers.

The four-way classification of responsibility centers is essential because for cost control costs are accumulated and reported by cost centers, for revenue control revenue is accumulated and reported by revenue centers, for investment control investment is accumulated and reported by investment centers, and for profit control profits are computed and reported by profit centers.

These four subsets of a responsibility center are *not mutually exclusive.* For example, a sales branch will be a revenue center as well as a cost center because the branch manager will be responsible not only for generating sales but also for the selling and advertising costs incurred by the branch (unless these costs are controlled by the headquarters and the manager is asked just to effect sales). Thus, a revenue center will usually also be a cost center. Similarly, a mechanized production department is both a cost center and an investment center. Further, a profit center generally will be an independent segment of the business responsible for revenue, cost, and investment. Hence, a profit center will comprise one or more revenue centers, cost centers, and investment centers.

**Relationship between Profit Centers and Cost Responsibility Centers** If a company has only one profit center (the company as a whole), there will be one or more cost responsibility centers. If a company has more than one profit center, each profit center will have one or more cost responsibility centers, and there will also be one or more corporate cost responsibility centers. To the corporate cost responsibility center will be charged costs which are not incurred specifically for a particular profit center. For example, corporate advertising expenses will be charged to the appropriate corporate cost responsibility center.

## DISTINCTION BETWEEN RESPONSIBILITY CENTERS AND COST CENTERS

From the preceding discussion, it will be clear that the term *cost center* is used in two senses. In the first sense, it is an *accounting entity* for the accumulation, allocation, and absorption of costs. In the second sense, it is a *responsibility center* set up for cost control. To avoid confusion, it is preferable to use two different terms. For example, in the first sense the term *cost center* or *cost accounting center,* and in the second sense the term *responsibility center, cost responsibility center,* or *cost center* may be used. The commonly used term is responsibility center; it does not create confusion merely because there are different types of responsibility centers. (In fact, every responsibility center is responsible for controlling some costs.) Whenever there is a need to distinguish among different types of responsibility centers, the qualifying words *cost, profit,* etc., may be used.

In this chapter, we use the term *cost center* to denote a cost accounting entity, the term *responsibility center* to denote the organizational segment set up for responsibility accounting (including cost control), and the term *cost responsibility center* only when we want to exclude the other types of responsibility centers.

Responsibility centers and cost centers have different characteristics, their forms are different, and there are also differences in the way the accumulated cost information is allocated and reported. We will examine these differences in the following paragraphs.

### Characteristics of Responsibility Centers and Cost Centers

The following are the important characteristics of a good *responsibility center:*

1. It must always be an organization segment.
2. Some designated individual must be responsible for its performance (i.e., output) as well as for costs (i.e., input) incurred by it.
3. The designated individual must have the necessary authority to carry out the assigned responsibilities. Further, the responsibilities and authority of each responsibility center manager should be clearly demarcated. This provision is essential not only for identifying costs with the proper responsibility centers but also for establishing responsibility for variances.

The following are the important characteristics of a good *cost center:*

1. Every cost center should usually consist of *homogeneous activities* or operations so that uniform cost conditions exist within it. Homogeneity is necessary for allocation of the costs of a cost center on a common basis.

Unlike a responsibility center, a cost center may or may not be an organizational segment, and a designated individual may or may not be responsible for its output and input. For example, though occupancy expenses, insurance, and property taxes are usually accumulated separately, they are only accounting entities and not responsibility centers because generally they are not organizational segments. However, it is possible to set up, say, a separate insurance department headed by some responsible individual, in which case the insurance department may be established as a responsibility center.

2. The activities or operations of each cost center must be well-defined and clearly identifiable. There should be neither ambiguity nor overlapping of activities between centers. This characteristic is essential for proper accumulation of costs.

Because of these differences, there are differences in the forms of responsibility centers and cost centers.

### Forms of Responsibility Centers and Cost Centers

The usual forms of responsibility centers are the entire company, business units, product divisions, sales branches, sales territories, functional departments (production, marketing, administration, etc.) or their subdivisions, and the like.

A cost center may take one or more of the following forms:

- An activity or a group of activities such as billing, credit and collection, etc.
- A piece of equipment or a group of pieces of equipment
- A product or product line or a group of products
- A geographical location or a group of locations
- A branch, division, department, or group thereof (a sales branch, a maintenance department, etc.)
- A group of persons (e.g., a crew of labor performing a certain job)
- An objective expense account (occupancy expenses, employee benefit costs, etc.) which consists of expenses falling under several natural expense accounts
- A project or a program such as a project to convert a manual cost system to a computerized cost system

The Cost Accounting Standards Board, which is responsible for the promulgation of cost accounting standards to be followed by certain defense contractors, uses the term *cost objective* to denote the cost accounting entity. It defines a cost objective as "a function, organizational subdivision, contract, or other work unit for which cost data are desired and for which provision is made to accumulate and measure the cost of processes, projects, jobs, capitalized projects, and so forth."

Despite the fundamental differences between responsibility centers and cost centers, cost responsibility centers and cost centers are interrelated, as explained below.

## RELATIONSHIP BETWEEN COST RESPONSIBILITY CENTERS AND COST CENTERS

A cost responsibility center may itself be a cost center or may consist of several cost centers. For example, a production department performing a single operation will be a responsibility center as well as a cost center. On the other hand, if a production department performing two different types of operations, one manual and the other automated, is in the charge of only one supervisor, it will constitute one cost responsibility center. For cost accumulation, however, it may be divided into two cost centers, one for the manual operation and the other for the automated operation, because the types of costs incurred by the two operations will differ and therefore the bases for cost allocation will also probably differ. Usually, the cost of the manual operation will be allocated on the basis of direct labor–hours and that of the automated operation on the basis of equipment-hours. Further, two different cost centers will (1) facilitate the study of the cost behavior in the two centers, (2) permit direct measurement of the efficiency of the workers in the two centers, and (3) facilitate analysis of the causes of cost variances in the production department. If two different cost centers are set up, the costs of the production department will be accumulated separately in the two centers but only one cost responsibility report will be prepared. The responsibility report, however, may show separately the costs of the two cost centers.

There is a third possibility; i.e., a cost center may consist of several cost responsibility centers. For example, if the plant has been divided into several cost responsibility centers for cost control but a single plantwide overhead rate is used for product costing, the plant as a whole will constitute a single cost center.

If a cost responsibility center consists of several cost centers, costs will be accumulated by cost centers and the costs of the individual cost centers will be separately allocated and absorbed for product costing. For responsibility reporting, however, the costs of the individual centers will be consolidated. If, however, several cost responsibility centers constitute a cost center, costs will be accumulated and reported by cost responsibility centers, but for product costing the costs of all the relevant cost responsibility centers will be consolidated. Thus, costs will be accumulated either by the cost (accounting) center or by the cost (control) center, whichever is at a lower level.

## ESTABLISHMENT OF PROFIT CENTERS

In establishing profit centers, cost control is only one of several considerations. There are other major considerations, a complete discussion of which is beyond the scope of this book. However, because profit centers, cost responsibility centers, and cost centers are interrelated, profit centers are discussed here briefly.

When profit centers, cost responsibility centers, and cost centers are to be established, first profit centers will be established and then cost responsibility centers and cost centers.

### Objectives for Establishing Profit Centers

Profit centers are the centers or segments of an organization by which profits or losses are computed. They are established for the following major reasons:

1. To measure the profit performance of each segment
2. To control costs more effectively by relating costs to profit contributions
3. To measure each segment's contribution to the total profits of the company
4. To enable management to allocate the company's resources according to the contribution (present or potential) of each segment
5. To give greater autonomy to each segment of the organization

### Types of Profit Centers

Profit centers may be real or fictitious. *Real profit centers* are easily identifiable: they sell goods or render services outside the company. In other words, real profit centers earn revenue for the company. Merely because a responsibility center is responsible for revenue and cost, it is not necessarily a profit center. To be a real profit center, it should be responsible for most of the revenue and costs. For example, in a manufacturing company, a sales branch cannot be called a real profit center because it has no control over the cost of goods produced by the production department. On the other hand, a division responsible for production as well as sales is a profit center.

*Fictitious profit centers* are so termed because they are not wholly responsible for generating true profit. They sell goods or render services to other departments of the company and charge the departments receiving the goods or services at some transfer price (at the market rate, on a cost-plus profit basis, etc.). For example, the EDP department can be treated either as a cost responsibility center or as a profit center. If it is treated as a profit center, the departments receiving services from the EDP department will be charged not on a cost basis but on a cost-plus profit basis or at the market rate. The profit or loss generated by the EDP department will be fictitious because it will not affect the overall profits of the company.

Fictitious profit centers are intended to measure truly the profitability of real profit centers. This objective can be achieved only if the transfer price is equal to the market price or the real profit centers are allowed to look outside for less expensive sources for the services provided by the fictitious profit centers.

Fictitious profit centers, however, do not add to the control of the costs which they incur. The same, if not better, results can be achieved by employing the techniques of standard costing and flexible budgeting.

Fictitious profit centers may be either departments rendering services internally (EDP, power generating, etc.) or departments producing goods for internal consumption (e.g., companies manufacturing artificial fiber themselves usually produce the carbon dioxide, sulfuric acid, and caustic soda required for manufacturing the fiber). There is another type of fictitious profit centers. A marketing department or a sales branch may be established as a fictitious profit center to which goods will be transferred by the manufacturing department at some transfer price. The profit of the marketing department will be equal to the sales value of the goods transferred *less* the selling and other expenses incurred by it. The profit of the manufacturing department will be equal to the value of the goods transferred to the marketing department *less* the cost of the goods transferred. Thus, the total profit made by the company is split between the two fictitious profit centers.

If a portion of the goods or services is consumed internally and the balance is marketed outside, the producing department may or may not be treated as a profit center. If a large portion of the goods or services is marketed and only a small portion is consumed internally, the concerned department usually will be treated as a profit center; the internal consumption may be charged at either cost or market price. If, on the other hand, only a small portion is marketed, the concerned department may be deemed a cost responsibility center. For example, one large aluminum company described its practice as follows:

> Certain very large operations—mining, alumina refining, and smelting—are deemed cost centers only, with the small amount of their output that directly enters the market being turned over at a transfer price to those with selling responsibility.

If there are many profit centers, they may be grouped together according to some common characteristic such as a common management, a common plant facility, the same geographical location, etc.

### Actual Company Practices

The following examples (based on a survey conducted by the author among large to medium-size companies) will reveal the widely varying practices in defining profit centers:

- One large multiproduct manufacturing company defines profit centers at the sales level. In most instances, a profit center will be in an "operating division" that also includes final manufacturing responsibility for the product lines sold.
- A large petroleum refinery having a few refineries but a central marketing division treats each refinery and the central marketing division as separate profit centers.
- A company manufacturing and distributing many household products, with sales exceeding $6 billion, treats each product brand as a profit center.
- A company manufacturing telephone communications equipment, with sales exceeding $7 billion, has only two profit centers, "telephone business" and "government business."
- Two large New York banks have respectively about 600 and 210 profit centers (and about 600 and 425 cost centers).

Once the profit centers have been established, the cost responsibility centers and the cost centers are established as explained below.

## HOW TO ESTABLISH COST RESPONSIBILITY CENTERS AND COST CENTERS

Whenever a cost accounting system is established for both cost control and product costing, the cost responsibility centers and the cost centers should either be identical or be so arranged that two or more cost centers constitute a cost responsibility center, or vice versa. Because of this interrelationship between cost responsibility centers and cost centers, the procedure for establishing them is more or less the same. That procedure is explained here and illustrated with the help of the continuing case study of ACME Company.

For establishing cost responsibility centers and cost centers for any company, these *steps and guidelines* may be followed:

1. Study the organization structure, authority-responsibility manual or job description, factory and offices layout, various activities, and production processes and their sequence. This information has already been gathered during the preliminary survey phase. On the basis of this study, list all the operations, functions, activities, and occupations in the company.

2. Give a descriptive title to each operation or activity, and define or briefly describe each operation, activity, etc., if these tasks have not already been carried out by the company.

3. Ask company management if it is contemplating any *reorganization*. Similarly, ask all department heads to review the organization of their own departments. Every reorganization will have some effect on the structure of responsibility and cost centers, budget preparation, cost accumulation, and report preparation. Hence, if a reorganization is being contemplated, it should be carried out before responsibility centers and cost centers are established.

Further, as explained earlier, the existence of a proper organization structure is a key to effective cost control. Hence, on studying the organization structure and the authority-responsibility relationship, the designer may recognize the need for either reorganizing some of the functions or properly defining the authority-responsibility relationship so as to remove any ambiguity in assigning cost and variances to cost centers. If it is beyond the scope of the designer's assignment to recommend the appropriate authority-responsibility relationship, the designer should at least point out to the appropriate executive in the organization the need for redefining the relationship.

The formal organization chart may not reflect the *true authority-responsibility relationship*. If that is the case, the designer should draw up a true organization chart as reflected by the informal lines of authority-responsibility and obtain top management's concurrence to this chart.

4. Once the organization structure has been finalized, break the organization down into *possible* cost responsibility centers and group homogeneous operations or activities into *possible* cost centers. Each cost responsibility center and each cost center should satisfy the characteristics mentioned earlier.

5. The cost responsibility centers and the cost centers thus established should be regarded as tentative or possible centers only. They may be regrouped or reorganized after careful consideration of the following factors:

*a*. The *system objectives* govern the type of cost information required, which, in turn, influences the type and number of cost responsibility centers and cost centers considered desirable. Generally, an organization segment should be set up as a cost responsibility center if its costs are significant enough to be controlled. Similarly, a cost center should be set up whenever there is a need for cost information pertaining to a particular activity, operation, etc., for product costing, planning, or decision making. For example, if the costs of the personnel department and the production planning department of a manufacturing company are not very significant and are more or less fixed in nature, these departments may not be set up as separate cost responsibility centers and may be regarded as a part of, say, the service superintendent's office. However, for product costing the two departments may be set up as separate cost centers if their costs are to be allocated on two different bases.

If a particular activity or a segment is not significant enough to influence the cost information required for planning, control, or decision making, it should be merged with a cost responsibility center or a cost center more closely related to it.

*b.* A cost system should be *flexible* enough, within limits, to provide cost information for occasional requirements. This is possible if the classification of cost centers adopted for cost accumulation is more detailed than that necessary for cost allocation and reporting. To reduce the allocation effort, the related cost centers may then be grouped together. The usual practice is to create a hierarchy or a *pyramid of cost centers,* i.e., to divide a cost center into subcost centers, a subcost center into sub-subcost centers, and so on. The hierarchy method of arranging cost centers greatly facilitates recurring or nonrecurring cost analyses and cost information needs. The hierarchical arrangement of cost centers may take several forms:

| | | |
|---|---|---|
| Company | Company | Company |
| ↓ | ↓ | ↓ |
| Products | Regions | Regions |
| ↓ | ↓ | ↓ |
| Regions | Products | Functional departments |
| ↓ | ↓ | ↓ |
| Functional departments | Functional departments | Subcost centers |
| ↓ | ↓ | ↓ |
| Subcost centers | Subcost centers | Products |

Usually, the arrangement adopted will follow the organization structure of the company.

Similarly, the cost responsibility centers should form a

pyramid. For example, in a manufacturing company, the manufacturing department as a whole will be a cost responsibility center, which will consist of several cost responsibility centers in the form of production shops and service departments.

*c.* The ease in studying cost behavior, allocating costs, measuring performance, and investigating the causes of variances from standards should also be considered in establishing cost centers. (See the example given above in the section "Relationship between Cost Responsibility Centers and Cost Centers.")

*d.* Not only present requirements but also predictable *future requirements* should be considered. If, for example, it is anticipated that a certain department will be significantly expanded in the near future, that department should be established as a separate cost center and also as a separate cost responsibility center even though its costs are not significant at present. This step will eliminate the need for revising the structure of budgeting, cost accounting records, and cost reports within a short time.

*e.* The greater the number of cost responsibility centers and cost centers, the greater the cost of record keeping and reporting will be. Hence, a separate cost responsibility center or cost center should be set up only if the cost of paperwork will be worth the degree of control and other benefits expected from its establishment. Often a trade-off is involved, and therefore discretion is essential. Usually, it is more beneficial to conduct a supplementary analysis to generate certain information than to accumulate the information routinely in a separate cost center.

Another alternative is to record the basic details in the subaccounts of the natural expense account heads. For example, if the only major cost incurred by the cost accounting department is the salaries of cost accountants and if it is not considered worthwhile to set up the department as a separate cost responsibility center or cost center, its salaries may be recorded separately by opening a subaccount, Salaries—Cost Accountants, within the Salary account. Then, all other costs of the cost accounting department may be charged to the general and factory administration cost center. The major cost (salaries) of the cost accounting department can be obtained from the basic records as and when needed.

Further, the organization should not be broken down into cost responsibility centers and cost centers to such an extent that the cost information will be too fragmented to be useful for planning, control, and decision making. For example, though theoretically it is possible to make each direct worker a cost center, in most cases it will be meaningless to do so.

6. The cost centers of a manufacturing department are classified into production centers and service centers.

**EXHIBIT 8-1**

**Manufacturing Organization Chart of ACME Company**

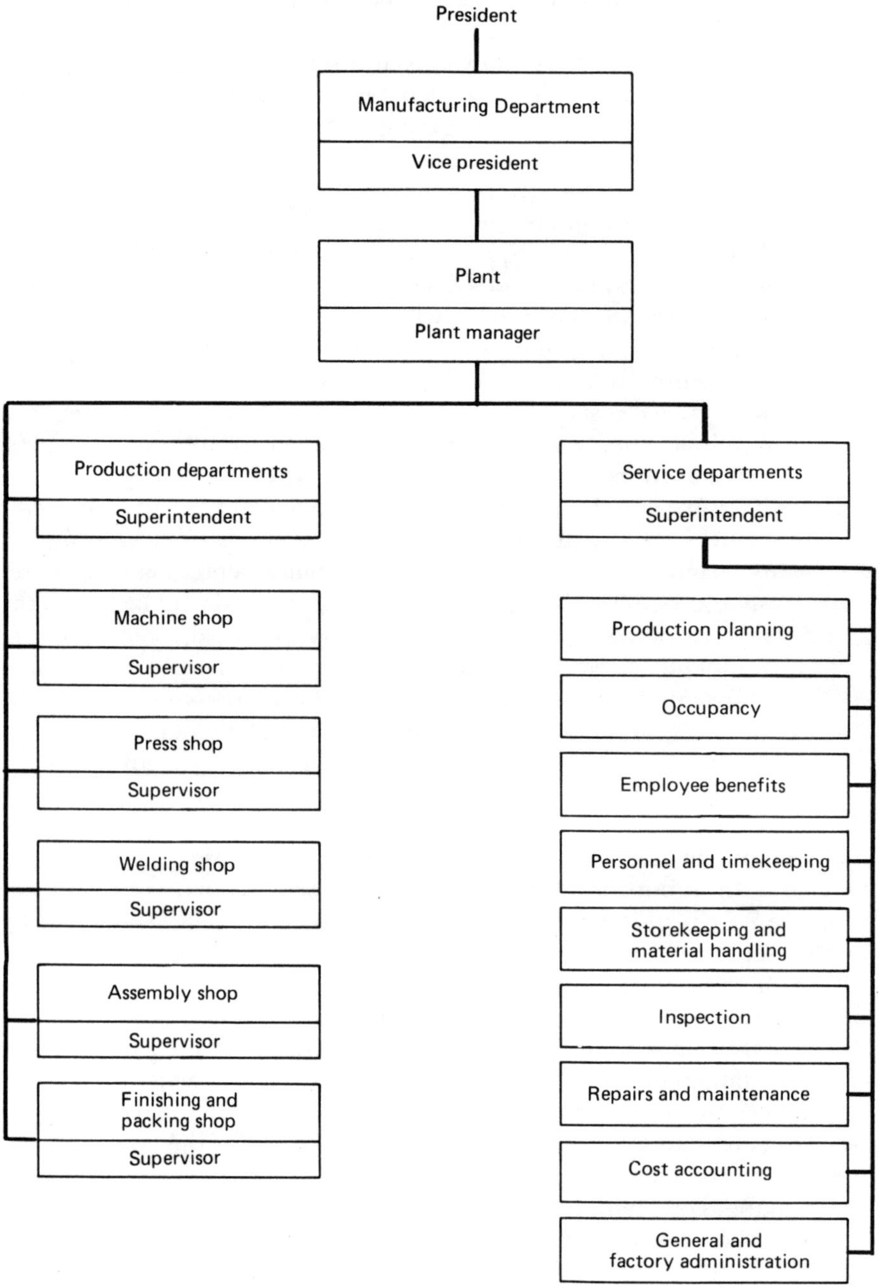

7. After establishing cost centers for the company, it is a good practice to compare them with the list of cost centers of another company in the same or a closely related industry. Further, a list of typical cost centers of any other company may be studied as a guide. The Bibliography contains sources of information on this subject. It should, of course, be noted that different companies may have different operating conditions and organizational setups and, therefore, that different companies even in the same industry may have different cost centers.

8. For convenience in recording, it is preferable to assign code numbers to cost responsibility centers and cost centers. These numbers may be combined with the account numbers.

## Case Study: Establishment of Responsibility Centers and Cost Centers for ACME Company

We will illustrate the above procedure step by step with the help of the continuing case study of ACME Company. For the sake of brevity, we will confine our discussion to the Manufacturing Department.

**Steps 1 and 2** The organization structure of the Manufacturing Department of ACME Company, its plant layout, its activities, its production processes, and their sequence were studied and documented during the preliminary survey stage (see Chapter 3). The organization chart of the Manufacturing Department is reproduced in Exhibit 8-1, which shows all the manufacturing and auxiliary functions and gives a brief descriptive title for each major activity. In a complex organization, it may also be necessary to describe each activity briefly.

**Step 3** On reviewing the organization chart of the Manufacturing Department with the vice president, manufacturing, it was learned that no changes would be necessary to satisfy either present needs or foreseeable future needs.

**Step 4** It is possible to divide the Manufacturing Department into the following cost responsibility centers and cost centers:

| Possible Cost Responsibility Center | Title of Person in Charge |
|---|---|
| 1. Manufacturing Department | Vice president, manufacturing |
| 2. Office of the Vice President, Manufacturing | Vice president, manufacturing |
| 3. Production plant | Plant manager |
| 4. Office of the Plant Manager | Plant manager |
| 5. Production departments as a whole | Production superintendent |
| 6. Office of the Production Superintendent | Production superintendent |
| 7. Machine shop | Supervisor |
| 8. Press shop | Supervisor |

| Possible Cost Responsibility Center | Title of Person in Charge |
|---|---|
| 9. Welding shop | Supervisor |
| 10. Assembly shop | Supervisor |
| 11. Finishing and packing shop | Supervisor |
| 12. Service departments as a whole | Service superintendent |
| 13. Office of the Service Superintendent | Service superintendent |
| 14. Repairs and Maintenance Department | Supervisor |
| 15. Storekeeping and material handling | Storekeeper |
| 16. Production planning | Production planner |
| 17. Inspection Department | Senior inspector |
| 18. Personnel and Timekeeping Department | Personnel administrator |
| 19. Cost Accounting Department | Senior cost analyst |

| Possible Cost Centers | |
|---|---|
| 1–19. | Each of the possible cost responsibility centers |
| 20. | Occupancy expense center |
| 21. | Employee benefits costs |
| 22. | General factory expenses |

It will be noted that occupancy, employee benefits costs, and general factory expenses are listed as possible cost centers but not as possible cost responsibility centers. No purpose will be served by establishing these items as separate cost responsibility centers because each of them falls within the domain of an individual responsibility center manager who is also responsible for other cost items. For example, the responsibility for occupancy expenses and employee benefits costs lies with the plant manager, and therefore these costs will be included in the plant manager's responsibility report. Similarly, the responsibility for general factory expenses lies with the service superintendent, and therefore they will be included in the service superintendent's responsibility report.

Though the above items should not be set up as separate cost responsibility centers, they should be accumulated separately for proper allocation. Further, these cost centers set up for product costing will be useful also for investigating the causes of variances from budgeted costs of the cost items.

**Steps 5, 6, and 7** On the basis of the considerations mentioned earlier, the tentative list of the cost responsibility centers and the cost centers of the Manufacturing Department of ACME Company was finalized. The Cost Accounting Department and the Offices of the Production Superintendent and the Service Superintendent were deleted from the list of responsibility centers as well as from the list of cost centers and were

**EXHIBIT 8-2**

**List of Responsibility Centers and Cost Centers of the ACME Company**

| Center No. | Responsibility Centers and Cost Centers | Responsibility of |
|---|---|---|
| 100 | Manufacturing Department | Vice president, manufacturing |
| 110 | Office of the Vice President, Manufacturing | Vice president, manufacturing |
| 120 | Production Plant | Plant manager |
| 121 | Office of the Plant Manager (consisting of the Office of the Plant Manager, the Cost Accounting Department, and the Offices of the Production Superintendent and the Service Superintendent) | Plant manager |
| 130 | Production departments | Production superintendent |
| 131 | Machine shop | Supervisor |
| 132 | Press shop | Supervisor |
| 133 | Welding shop | Supervisor |
| 134 | Assembly shop | Supervisor |
| 135 | Finishing shop | Supervisor |
| 140 | Service departments | Service superintendent |
| 141 | Repairs and maintenance | Supervisor |
| 142 | Storekeeping and material handling | Storekeeper |
| 143 | Production planning | Production planner |
| 144 | Inspection Department | Senior inspector |
| 145 | Personnel and Timekeeping Department | Personnel administrator |
| 151 | Occupancy Expense Center* | Plant manager |
| 152 | Employee benefits costs* | Plant manager |
| 153 | General factory expenses* | Service superintendent |

* Cost centers only.

merged with the Office of the Plant Manager. The final list of cost responsibility centers and cost centers is given in Exhibit 8-2, which also contains the code numbers of the responsibility centers and the cost centers.

# Chapter 9

# Designing a Direct Material Cost System

> Inanimate things are easier to control than animate things because no feelings are involved.
>
> Pravin P. Shah

## CLASSIFICATION OF COSTS OF A MANUFACTURING COMPANY

The total costs of a manufacturing concern can be classified into direct materials, direct labor, manufacturing overhead, marketing costs, administrative costs, and financial costs. The first three categories of costs are called manufacturing, or production, costs, whereas the last three categories of costs are called nonmanufacturing costs because they do not relate to production. However, some companies also allocate administrative costs to the manufacturing function.

Materials consumed by a company which can be traced directly to individual units of production are termed *direct materials.* In contrast, *indirect materials* are materials which are not a part of the finished product and which cannot be traced to individual production units. Usually, direct materials form an integral part of finished products, whereas indirect materials do not.

Production labor which can be traced directly to individual units of production is termed *direct labor,* and that which cannot be so traced is termed *indirect labor.*

*Manufacturing overhead costs* represent that portion of total manufacturing costs which cannot be traced directly to individual units of production, as can be done for direct materials and direct labor. In other words, benefits from overhead costs are derived jointly by more than one unit of production. Manufacturing overhead costs include indirect materials, indirect labor, maintenance, etc. Traditionally, all manufacturing costs other than direct materials and direct labor are classified as overhead costs. In fact, there may be costs which though not direct materials and direct labor can still be traced to a particular unit of production. An example is rent paid for equipment rented specifically for a particular job in a job order industry. Such costs, if significant, should be charged directly to specific jobs or units of production.

Chapters 9 and 10 deal with the design respectively of a direct material cost system and a direct labor cost system. The process of designing a manufacturing overhead cost system is explained in Chapter 11 and that of nonmanufacturing costs in Chapter 13. Each of these four chapters first enumerates all the tasks involved in designing the respective subcost system. The tasks which are common to the entire cost system and which have been explained in detail in other chapters are only summarized in the four chapters. The remaining tasks and points peculiar to each subcost system are discussed in detail in the respective chapters. The process of designing the first three subcost systems is illustrated with the help of the continuing case study of ACME Company given in Chapter 12. Similarly, in Chapter 13 the case study of ACME Company illustrates the process of designing a marketing cost system.

## IMPORTANCE OF DIRECT MATERIAL COSTS

Direct materials form one of the important components of the cost of a manufacturing company. The worldwide oil crisis has directly or indirectly made many materials more expensive and has adversely affected their supply situation. Hence, materials control now demands greater attention of management than ever before. The following excerpt from an article published in the July–August 1979 issue of the *Harvard Business Review* highlights the problem concerning direct material cost and emphasizes the need for a good material cost control and cost information system:

> The 1973 Arab oil embargo and the subsequent shortages and escalating fuel and materials costs first focused the attention of many manufacturing companies on the importance of materials and transport. . . . [M]any companies discovered that long-term cost structures have shifted and that they could achieve much leverage by concentrating on materials, transport, and inventory costs. Evidence of such shifts includes the following:
>
> - ☐ Data from the *Census of Manufactures* indicate that during the decade . . . materials and transport costs for the average American manufacturing company have increased from 53% to nearly 58% of sales. This means that more profit leverage can be obtained by focusing on materials and transport costs. For example, the average company now has to increase sales by more than 10% (a resource con-

suming activity) in order to generate the same contribution to profit and overhead that a 5% reduction in materials and transport costs (a resource conserving activity) would bring.

- American manufacturers annually reinvest four or five times more capital in inventories than they do in new plants and equipment, according to the *Census of Manufactures.*[1]

In this chapter, we will study the specific points for designing a direct materials cost system. Since indirect materials are treated as a part of manufacturing overhead, they will be dealt with in Chapter 11, "Designing a Manufacturing Overhead Cost System."

## TASKS FOR DESIGNING A DIRECT MATERIAL COST SYSTEM

The process of developing a direct material cost system involves several iterative steps, some of which have already been explained. For completing the picture and for reinforcement, even the completed tasks are summarized here.

### System Analysis Tasks

System analysis precedes system design. Hence, when a designer begins to design a direct material cost system, he will already have completed the following system analysis tasks:

1. The designer will have defined the *objectives* and the scope of the system, particularly the direct material cost system. For example, a direct material cost system may be designed for computing the direct materials consumed for production, inventory valuation, control of direct material costs, product pricing, and various managerial decisions, such as selecting the optimum product mix when different products use the same material in short supply.
2. The designer will have conducted a *survey* of manufacturing operations to gain an understanding of the types of materials consumed, the kinds of material losses suffered, and the direct material functions, such as purchasing, receiving, storage, issue, etc.
3. The designer will have determined, in specific terms, the types of direct material *cost information required* to meet each of the preset objectives.

[1] Reprinted by permission of the *Harvard Business Review.* Excerpt from "Materials Managers: Who Needs Them?" by Jeffrey G. Miller and Peter Gilmour (July–August 1979). 

In actual practice, before beginning to design a direct material cost system, the designer will, at this stage, refer to his file to review these completed tasks.

### System Design Tasks

Once the system analysis phase is over, the system design phase begins. This phase also involves various tasks:

1. Prepare an outline of the direct material cost system.
2. Select appropriate cost methods and techniques for the direct material cost system.
3. Establish responsibility centers and cost centers.
4. Classify direct materials.
5. If a standard cost system is to be employed, set direct material standards.
6. Design a direct material inventory control system.
7. If a budgetary control system is to be employed, design a direct material budgeting system.
8. Design direct material cost reports.
9. Design a cost accounting system for direct materials.

### Task 1: Preparation of Outline of the Direct Material Cost System

Because control over direct material cost is important for many manufacturing organizations, its major features are discussed first. For achieving control over direct material cost, it is necessary to know the aspects of direct materials to be controlled and the control devices.

### Aspects of Direct Material Cost to Be Controlled

Control over direct material cost begins with a proper product design or formula, the selection of proper production equipment and sequence of operations, and appropriate material specifications. For example, the selection of unduly rigid material specifications may involve avoidable direct material cost.

Further, control of direct material cost requires control over each of these important areas: (1) purchasing, (2) receiving, (3) handling, (4) inventory and storage, (5) issue, (6) consumption, and (7) material losses. For example, purchase of the wrong materials, rush buying at premium prices, excessive inventory of materials, failure to detect shortages in materials received from vendors, losses due to theft or an improper storage facility, and excessive waste during production are sources of material costs that are higher than desirable. Hence, all these areas should be controlled to keep material costs down.

## Control Devices

Several control devices are available for exercising control over direct material cost. Usually, a company will need a *multiple* of such devices. The common control devices are as follows:

1. *Organization.* Control is exercised by individuals. Hence, proper structure and staffing of the organization with capable persons are of prime importance for achieving effective control over direct material cost.
2. *Physical control.* Materials received, issued, and in inventory must be properly weighed or counted. Further, control over the loss of material (scrap, waste, etc.) should concentrate on its occurrence, recovery, and disposal: occurrence should be minimal, recovery should be at a maximum, and the maximum quantity recovered should be disposed of at the best available price.[2]
3. *Management policies.* For example, to ensure that purchases are made at the best available prices, management may require that at least three quotations be obtained for high-value items.
4. *Operating or functional systems.* For example, a well-designed material requirements planning system will enable the company to estimate correctly its material requirements for production and inventory and to plan its purchases accordingly. This procedure will reduce or eliminate rush purchases or a buildup of excessive inventory.
5. *Control through standards and budgets.* For effective control over direct material cost, it is essential to establish standards of consumption quantity, purchase price, material losses, inventory quantity, etc., and to prepare budgets for direct material consumption, purchases, and inventory.

The establishment of standards is just the first step of control. The other required steps are:

- Measurement of actual consumption, prices, etc.
- Comparison of actual data against standards and computation of variances
- Reporting of actual data and variances
- Investigation of causes of variances and assignment of responsibility for variances

[2] See Sidney Davidson and Roman L. Weil, *Handbook of Cost Accounting,* McGraw-Hill Book Company, New York, 1978, chap. 17, for an excellent treatment of this subject.

- Taking of corrective or preventive action by the responsible personnel
- Reporting to management the results of corrective action in case of major deviations

Thus, this device emphasizes the need for proper measurement, cost record keeping, and reporting of actual transactions.

6. *Bill of materials.* This important document in controlling direct material cost is prepared separately for each product, part, or assembly. It contains a list of all materials required for a given product, their specifications, and the standard quantity. A bill of materials is prepared by the production planning department; it constitutes authority for the storeroom to issue the specified materials. If the production department requires any material in excess of the quantity specified in the bill of materials, a separate material requisition and even prior approval may be required. Thus, control over issue and consumption is exercised before the issue and consumption of materials. All material requisitions represent excess material consumption and are reported separately in the consumption reports.

In summary, direct material cost control requires *management controls, operational controls,* and *cost accounting controls.* Management as well as the cost system designer should remember that these three controls are interrelated and hence should be well-integrated. For example, merely setting price and quantity standards for direct materials will not achieve control over direct material cost. If, for instance, the material requirements planning system and the purchasing procedure are poor, the company may not be able to buy the required material at the right time and at the right price, and it may have either to place a rush order at a higher price or to buy a superior-quality material at a higher price. Further, unless actual purchases and consumption are properly recorded and compared against standards and unless variances are reported to the responsible personnel, corrective action may not be initiated.

## Role of Designer and Management

Obviously, the cost system designer is not responsible for designing all three types of controls. For example, designing a purchasing system, establishing management policies for levels of inventory, and developing a material requirements planning system are generally not the designer's responsibility, though he may have a role to play in this behalf depending upon his expertise and the scope of his assignment. Similarly, though the designer is primarily responsible for designing a cost control and information system, management also has a role to play in it.

Because of this combined responsibility, the designer should first prepare a list of all relevant aspects of direct material cost. Next, he should identify those items which either are nonexistent or appear to be deficient but essential for controlling direct material cost as well as for product costing. Then, the designer should separate the aspects which are clearly his responsibility from those which are not his responsibility. Usually, the latter aspects will relate to operating systems, management policies, and standards. For those aspects which are not his responsibility, he should ask the appropriate company personnel to review, define, develop, or modify the operating systems, management policies, etc., that have an adverse impact on the direct material cost system.

An illustrative list of the interrelated factors concerning direct materials is given in Exhibit 9-1, which classifies these factors under the three groups of functions relating to direct materials: purchasing and receiving, material handling and inventory, and consumption. This exhibit will also serve as a checklist for the designer.

Even if the designer is designing a cost system from scratch, certain features of the system may be present (e.g., direct materials quantity standards may already have been set), in which case only the remaining aspects need be designed.

In short, this task will enable the designer to define all the steps that should be taken to design a direct material cost system and to integrate it with other aspects of the direct material management system.

### Task 2: Selection of Cost Methods and Techniques

A decision about the type of cost methods and techniques to be used for product costing and responsibility accounting is critical to the subsequent design tasks, and hence the task of selecting cost methods and techniques to be used for the direct material cost system should be undertaken first. Since this is a subject by itself and since this task is common to the entire cost system, it has been dealt with in detail in Chapter 7. However, the important points are summarized here.

The cost methods for direct materials may be any one or more of the following:

- Standard job order costing
- Standard process costing
- Historical job order costing
- Historical process costing

Obviously, the distinction between direct costing and absorption costing is irrelevant for direct materials because direct material costs, being directly identifiable costs, are accorded the same treatment under direct costing and full absorption costing.

**Job Order versus Process Costing** The main difference between a direct material job order cost system and a direct material process cost system lies in the manner of accumulation and charging (to production) of direct material costs. Hence, the selection of job order or process costing has a major impact on tasks 8 and 9. Under the job order cost system, direct material cost is accumulated by jobs or production orders, and direct material cost per unit of production is computed by dividing the total cost of the direct material consumed for a job by the total quantity produced by the job. Under the process cost system, direct material cost is accumulated by processes, and direct material cost per unit of production is computed by dividing the total cost of the direct material consumed for a process during a given period by the total output of that process.

**Historical Costing versus Standard Costing and Budgeting** For controlling direct material cost, some sort of standards or yardsticks against which actual direct material cost can be compared are essential. Though past cost can be used as a yardstick, standard costing based on scientifically oriented standards is far superior and desirable for controlling direct material cost. The other control technique available is budgeting. It may be said that standard costing is useful for day-to-day control over direct material cost, and budgeting is useful for overall control over direct material cost.

Though it is possible to use one technique without the other, in actual practice either both these techniques are used or at least the budgetary control technique is employed. A company will rarely use a standard cost system for direct materials and not prepare direct material budgets.

If budgeting is employed in conjunction with standard costing, direct material quantity and price standards (provided, of course, they are current standards) will form the basis for direct material budgeting. If budgeting is employed without direct material standards, direct material budgets will be based on some sort of estimates of direct material quantity and prices.

Besides being useful for cost control, standard costing is useful for product costing, inventory valuation, product pricing, and various other purposes. Further, even if standard costing is employed, historical costing is used for the accumulation of actual direct material costs.

### Task 3: Establishment of Necessary Responsibility Centers and Cost Centers

For proper cost control, it is necessary to divide the organization into various responsibility centers and to designate persons in charge of the

**EXHIBIT 9-1**

## Five Facets of Direct Materials Control System

| Functions | Standards Required | Management Policies to Be Established | Operating Systems Required | Source Documents and Accounting and Other Records to Be Maintained | Usual Management Reports (Cost and Noncost) |
|---|---|---|---|---|---|
| Purchasing and receiving | Price standards<br>Quantity standards (how much to purchase at a time, i.e., economic order quantity and how much to purchase during a given period)<br>Time standards (reorder points)<br>Quality standards<br>Purchasing budgets | Terms of purchase (e.g., cash or credit)<br>Number of quotations required<br>Make or buy<br>When long-term purchasing commitments are permitted<br>Centralized versus decentralized purchasing departments | Material requirements planning system<br>Purchasing procedure<br>Receiving system<br>Inspection procedure<br>Internal auditing<br>Assignment of responsibility for each function | Purchase requisitions<br>Purchase orders<br>Records of quantity received or returned<br>Accounting for purchasing and incidental costs<br>Purchase price records | Price variance report<br>Purchasing status report: requisitions, orders, deliveries<br>Inspection report<br>Make-or-buy analysis<br>Purchasing performance report showing impact of delays in material procurements, procurement of materials not as per specifications, etc. |
| Material handling and inventory | Inventory quantity levels (safety stocks, minimum-maximum inventory budget) | Resolution of conflict between inventory carrying cost and loss due to stock overrun | Classification and codification of materials<br>Material requirements planning system | Bill of materials or material requisitions<br>Documents for receipts, issues, and transfers of | Inventory status report: book versus physical, actual versus budget<br>Obsolete and slow-moving in- |

| | | | | | |
|---|---|---|---|---|---|
| | Time standards (reordering points)<br>Obsolete quantity standards<br>Standards for loss in storage and handling | In-house versus outside storage<br>Type and space for storage facility<br>Basis for valuation of inventory of direct materials (FIFO, LIFO, etc.)<br>Basis for costing direct materials included in work in process and finished products inventory | Production-planning system<br>Purchasing system<br>Procedures for storage, issues, return to stores, material handling, and security<br>Physical inventory: frequency and procedure<br>Internal auditing<br>Assignment of responsibility for each function | materials<br>Inventory records<br>ABC analysis | ventory report |
| Consumption (production) | Consumption quantity standards<br>Scrap or residual material quantity standards<br>By-products and joint products quantity standards<br>Spoilage and defective work standards<br>Rework materials standards | When use of inferior or better materials permitted<br>Basis for costing consumption (LIFO, FIFO, average, etc.) | Procedures for issue, in-plant transfer, and return to stores<br>Assignment of responsibility for each function | Bill of materials or material requisitions<br>Documents for consumption, transfer, and return of materials<br>Production records<br>Material consumption records | Quantity variance report<br>Scrap report<br>Spoilage and defective report<br>Actual versus budgeted consumption (dollar amount: total and separately for important items) |

individual centers. The responsibility centers for direct material cost control will be from among the following:

- Product design or product engineering department, which will be responsible for material specifications and for setting quantity standards
- Production planning department, which will be responsible for production scheduling and material requirements planning
- Purchasing department, which will be responsible for purchase price, quality, and timely availability of required materials
- Receiving department, which will be responsible for receiving materials from vendors, counting or weighing them, and signing delivery notes
- Inspection department, which will be responsible for inspection and quality control of direct materials, work in process, and finished products
- Material handling and stores department, which will be responsible for receiving, storage, issue, transfer, etc., of materials, work in process, and finished products
- Individual production centers, which will be responsible for consumption, waste, scrap, etc., of direct materials and for spoilage and defective work

For the accounting of direct materials, the relevant cost centers will be various production centers processing direct materials, individual job orders, product lines, or product subassemblies. For instance, in an equipment-manufacturing company (which normally will employ job order costing) direct materials consumed will be accumulated by individual jobs, parts, and assemblies so that the company can compute the cost of each of these items of production.

Since the process of establishing responsibility centers and cost centers has been explained in Chapter 8, it is not repeated here.

### Task 4: Classification of Direct Materials

Since direct materials and indirect materials are accorded different treatments in cost accounting and require different techniques for cost control, the materials consumed by a company must be separated into direct and indirect categories. Materials which can be traced directly to individual units of production are normally classified as direct materials, and other materials are classified as indirect materials. Direct materials include not only raw materials but also parts, components, and assemblies. Even primary packing materials such as bottles to store medicine will also be classified as direct materials. In a book-publishing company, for instance, direct materials will consist of paper, ink, and binding materials such as glue, thread, etc. Indirect materials, on the other hand, will include lubricating oils, greases, cleaning rags, maintenance materials, etc.

**Practical Considerations** On practical considerations, small-value direct materials such as glue, screws, threads, etc., sometimes may be classified as indirect materials. In deciding whether to classify a small-value direct material as a direct or an indirect material, the cost of record keeping should be weighed against the benefit from classifying it as a direct material.

**Uniform Classification** If the same material is used in different departments producing more or less the same products, its classification should be uniform. For example, if a company has three production plants that each manufacture the same product, the material classification at all three plants should be identical. But if the company manufactures different products in different plants, it may classify identical material used for two products differently.

**Material Code Numbers** Each direct material should be clearly described so that one direct material can be readily distinguished from another direct material. If there are many direct materials, they usually are assigned code numbers for ease in cost record keeping.

**Production Units** For product costing, cost control, budgeting, and managerial decision making it is necessary to identify direct materials with various products, parts, and assemblies produced by the company. The prerequisite for this step is that the products, parts, etc., produced by the company be defined and, if they are numerous, that they be assigned code numbers. Next, for control over direct material cost, it is necessary to identify direct materials with production centers, production processes, and operations using or working on direct materials. Further, if a company imports materials from a foreign country, it may be desirable to classify direct materials into imported and domestic materials. Similarly, any other classification which may be relevant in a given case should be adopted.

Though the responsibility for classification and codification of materials lies with the manufacturing department, the designer must guide manufacturing personnel in discharging these tasks and ensure that they have been carried out by a competent person and that there are no apparent ambiguities in the classification and the codification of materials.

## Task 5: Setting Standards for Direct Materials

Obviously, this task is relevant only if a standard cost system is employed and not if a historical cost system is employed. The common points for establishment of a standard cost system were discussed in Chapter 6. In particular, in that chapter we discussed defining the scope of the standard cost system, selecting the kind of standards to be used, responsibility for setting standards and the role of the designer in setting them, general guidelines for setting standards, and revision of standards. Here we will discuss the procedure used in setting direct material standards.

It is worth reemphasizing that responsibility for setting direct material standards lies with purchasing, industrial engineering, process engineering, etc., and not with the cost system designer. However, the designer does have a role to play in setting standards. For example, the designer must specify what standards are to be set and advise management on who should be responsible for setting those standards, and he should provide needed guidance to the persons responsible for setting standards.

### Types of Direct Material Cost Standards

Direct material cost standards consist of quantity and price standards. Quantity standards should be set separately for each of the direct materials for each product in each production center or for each operation. Price standards should be set separately for each distinct direct material. Obviously, the question of setting material price standards by products and production centers does not arise. The resultant direct materials *cost* standards should be expressed by products, by production centers or operations, and by materials.

**Be Selective** Setting standards and updating them involve costs, most important of which is management time. Hence, standards may not be set for less significant items of direct materials, and insignificant standards may not be set even for significant materials. For example, if shrinkage loss is not significant, shrinkage loss standards need not be set.

**Set Priorities** If many standards are to be set, they may be established in a phased manner, usually starting with the more significant standards. For example, initially standards may be set for major materials, assemblies, or products.

**Use ABC Analysis Technique** For setting direct material standards, there are available different methods which provide different degrees of accuracy and require varying amounts of time in establishing standards. To determine the degree of sophistication and effort to be applied in setting direct material standards, the technique of ABC analysis should be used, particularly if many direct materials are used. First, the controller's department or the designer should arrange the direct materials consumed during the last 1 or 2 representative years in the order of value. Then, the designer, manufacturing department, and purchasing department should designate the ABC limits according to the degree of control desired. For example, all materials with an annual consumption in excess of $2 million may be classified as A category materials, those with an annual consumption between $400,000 and $2 million as B category materials, and the rest as C category materials. Usually, auxiliary and small-value materials will fall in C categories. Greater time and effort should be spent on setting standards for A category materials and successively lesser amounts for B and C categories.

## Procedure for Setting Direct Material Standards

The points which the designer should know concerning the procedure for setting direct material standards are discussed below.

**Standardization of Products and Operations** Even if standards are reasonable for one set of circumstances, they may not be appropriate for another set. Hence, before meaningful standards can be set for direct material quantity and price, the following aspects should be standardized:

- Products and product varieties such as packing sizes, deluxe and regular variety, etc.
- Product design, drawings, or formula, for example, the formula for manufacturing a syrup in a pharmaceutical company.
- Direct material specifications, for example, the description and quality of each ingredient required for manufacturing a particular syrup in a pharmaceutical company. Direct material specifications should be prepared separately for each process or operation and for each product, assembly, etc. For direct materials in short supply, specifications should be given also for any substitute materials.
- Production processes and their sequence, plant layout, and physical flow of materials within the plant. This step is necessary not only for setting direct material standards by production processes and production centers but also for assigning responsibility for variances.

**Direct Materials Quantity Standards** For cost control and partly for product costing, direct materials quantity standards should cover the following two kinds of standards:

- Consumption or yield standards
- Material loss standards

**Consumption or Yield Standards** Consumption and yield are two different ways of expressing the quantity of a direct material required per unit of production. We may either say that 10 pounds (4.5 kilograms) of direct material X (input) is required to produce one unit of the finished product (output), or say that 50 gallons (189.3 liters) of gasoline (output) is obtained from 100 gallons (378.5 liters) of crude oil (input). In the latter case, the yield is 50 percent. The term *yield* is used only in the process type of industries, whereas the term *consumption* can be used for all types of industries. In industries producing joint products and by-products, yield standards should specify the yield of each type of joint product and by-product from a given quantity of direct materials.

Several *methods* are available for determining the standard quantity of direct materials required for manufacturing finished products. The most common are as follows:

1. *Engineered standards.* Under this method industrial engineers or product designers estimate the quantity of direct material required on the basis of their study of the product design. This is a scientific method of setting standards.
2. *Laboratory experiments.* Under this method chemists or pharmacists determine the standard quantity required on the basis of laboratory experiments. This also is a scientific method. Obviously, this method can be used only in chemical and pharmaceutical industries.
3. *Test runs under controlled conditions.* Standards are determined by pilot runs of production. This method should be used only for new products, new machinery, or new processes and should be periodically checked for reasonableness.
4. *Standards provided by know-how supplier.* When the process know-how is provided by another company, that company normally will also provide the standards for direct material consumption. These standards may have to be adjusted for differences in climatic conditions, material quality, degree of experience of labor, etc.
5. *Industry standards.* Average consumption figures of the industry as available from a trade association or published data are used. This method is not recommended as a primary method. It may be used as a secondary method to check standards set by other methods. Further, this method can be used only when the industry produces a standard product, using direct materials of standard specifications or material available from a single source, and employs more or less the same type of production equipment. For example, continuous-process industries, such as chemical plants, rayon yarn factories, and oil refineries, may find this method useful.
6. *Past actuals.* Usually, past actuals are unsuitable as standards because it is not known whether or not they represent optimum standards. However, past actuals of a representative period can be used to check standards set by any suitable method: the significant difference between the standards and the past actuals should be analyzed to determine inaccuracies in the standards.

As stated before, the ABC analysis technique should be used to select the methods to be used for setting quantity standards. For A category materials, standards based on engineering studies or laboratory experiments should be used whenever possible. For C category materials, even past actuals adjusted for any known variation may be used as standards. Whatever the method used, the following *factors,* which have an impact on the quantity of direct materials consumed, must be considered in setting consumption standards:

- Product design or formula
- Manufacturing process
- Age and condition of manufacturing equipment
- Plant layout
- Material specifications
- Quality of materials available
- Nature of materials (e.g., the evaporation of some liquids during storage)
- Inspection and quality control standards
- Training and experience of labor
- Supervision
- Storage and material-handling facility available
- Climate

For example, an inexperienced worker will waste more materials than an experienced worker. Hence, in the case of a new product or a heavy turnover of labor, consumption standards may have to provide for additional waste of materials. Similarly, if materials of the required specifications are not available, there may be more waste.

**Material Loss Standards** Material losses consist of the loss of direct materials during handling, storage, issue, and production. For controlling direct material losses, it is desirable to set standards for significant material losses. The process of setting material loss standards is explained step by step:

1. Material losses occurring within the company should be identified. For better understanding they should be classified

   - By type or nature of losses (scrap, residual materials, waste, shrinkage, evaporation, spoiled and defective production, etc.).
   - By products, materials, and cost centers.
   - By causes of loss (handling, issue, storage, obsolescence, production, etc.).
   - By ultimate disposal. Physical loss of material can be dealt with only through an accounting entry. Spoiled material may be re-

usable with or without reprocessing, be salable with or without further processing, or be thrown away.

This information can be obtained from study of a material flowchart (see Exhibit 3-9), analysis of the records of past losses, and discussions with every department handling direct materials at any stage in the flow of materials.

2. Normally occurring significant material losses should then be separated from insignificant material losses. Since standards will be applied to the future period, what is relevant is the expected significant loss of material and not the past significant loss.

3. There is no standard terminology for describing different kinds of material losses. Hence, each significant material loss occurring within the company should be defined unambiguously. For instance, different types of material loss in a textile company may be defined as follows:

- *Waste* signifies loss of direct materials during their handling, storage, issue, or production. Examples are shrinkage of yarn, evaporation of dyes, and damage to yarn.
- *Residual materials* refer to that portion of unusable direct materials which arises during production and which does not require further processing to recover it. All residual materials arising in our company are sold as such. Examples are yarn recovered from the weaving process and dyes recovered from the dyeing process.
- *Defective production* means damaged production which can be either (*a*) reprocessed with or without adding any material and sold as *good production* or as *seconds* or (*b*) sold as such as *seconds*.
- *Spoiled production* refers to that portion of damaged production which can be neither corrected nor sold as such as seconds. Spoiled production in our company usually has a small residual value.

4. For each type of significant material loss, quantity standards allowing for only normal and uncontrollable losses and not for abnormal or controllable losses should be set. The normal-loss level should be set after considering how tightly the standards are to be set, current cost reduction goals, and various factors mentioned in the section "Consumption or Yield Standards." For example, in a company fabricating machine parts, a certain quantity of scrap is inevitable because of boring, cutting, and other operations, and that quantity should be considered the normal scrap level. However, the quantity of scrap which can be avoided, say, by proper supervision should be regarded as controllable and hence not be included in the allowable standard scrap quantity. The classification of a material loss into normal and abnormal categories is not a simple matter and calls for judgment.

In addition to the setting of standards for an acceptable quantity of scrap, waste, spoilage, defective production, etc., standards should be set for the rework materials required for repairing or reconditioning defective production.

5. Next, quantity standards for normal losses should be related to the quantity of direct materials consumed, the production quantity, or the inventory quantity. For example, scrap may be related to the quantity of direct materials consumed and defective production to the quantity of good production.

6. Except for spoiled materials which are thrown away or have insignificant value, standards should also be set for pricing reusable materials or for the sales value of spoiled materials sold outside.

7. The last step is to determine how to treat standard material losses and applicable credits in developing a standard product cost. In resolving these issues, the factors to be considered are the objectives of the cost system, the type of feedback information required for exercising control over material losses, the accounting treatment of material losses, the nature and the significance of the loss, and the nature of the industry. The available alternatives are (*a*) to build into the standard consumption quantity, (*b*) to provide a separate allowance in the product cost, (*c*) to build into the standard material price, (*d*) to charge to the relevant production center as a separate overhead item, and (*e*) to charge to the income statement, i.e., to keep the losses out of the standard product cost. For example, in a continuous-process industry, losses which arise during production and vary with consumption (e.g., scrap) will usually be included in the standard consumption quantity. In a job order industry, this type of losses may be dealt with differently for cost control and product costing. For cost control, it will usually be included in the standard consumption quantity. However, if the losses vary significantly from job to job, for product costing they would be charged to manufacturing overhead and later allocated to all jobs on some equitable basis. Similarly, rework materials, evaporation, and other losses in storage are usually charged to overhead. In a process industry, depending upon the nature of the residual material, the market price of the material is deducted either from the total process cost or only from the direct material cost.

When direct material losses are not built into the standard material quantity, care should be taken to include the loss quantities in the direct material budgets.

**Direct Material Price Standards** In setting direct material price standards, it is necessary to resolve three major issues. They are (1) to determine the type of price standards to be used, (2) to define the composition of direct material prices, and (3) to select the techniques to be used for setting direct material prices.

**Types of Price Standards Used** Depending upon the frequency and the extent of fluctuations in material prices and the objectives of the standard cost system, the standard price of a material could reflect:

- The expected average price for the relevant year, i.e., the cost of (opening inventory + purchases during the year) divided by the quantity of (opening inventory + purchases).
- The expected average price for the relevant month, quarter, or 6 months; i.e., different prices may be set for different months, quarters, etc.
- The expected average price over a period of 2 to 3 years.

For meaningful *cost control,* material price standards should be based on the expected actual price for the relevant period. Hence, if material prices are expected to be stable during the year or if they are subject to wide fluctuations but without a pattern, the first method may be used. If there are wide seasonal fluctuations in the prices of materials during the year, either use the second method or use the first method and analyze the price variances into seasonal and other causes. Normally, the third method is inappropriate for cost control, but if it is used, it will require analyzing the price variances into cyclical and other causes. If there are a number of materials, it may not be practical, unless a computer is used, to set several standard prices for a material to account for seasonal fluctuations.

Irrespective of the method adopted, the standard material price for cost control should be set after considering not only the price trend but also the cost reduction objectives set by management and the planned actions to reduce purchase prices. For example, the impact of the development of alternative sources of supply, entering into long-term contracts, proposed captive production of materials, and other measures should be reflected in the expected actual prices.

In valuing *inventory for income determination,* the first two methods will give the same income on a yearly basis but may give different income in monthly reports. In using the third method for external reporting purposes, the external reporting requirements set by law or generally accepted accounting principles and the requirements of the income tax laws must be considered. Further, management must understand the implication of each of the methods on income determination.

For competitive *pricing,* current cost standards generally will be used. It may, however, be remembered that in setting selling prices for regular sales or competitive bidding, product cost is only one of the considerations, though a very important one. Another major consideration is the company's product-pricing practice. If there are frequent fluctuations in the prices of direct materials but the company does not adjust its finished-product prices with fluctuations in the prices of direct materials, standard material prices may be based on the expected average price for the year. On the other hand, when finished-product prices are adjusted with the variation in the prices of direct materials, material price standards should be revised frequently to reflect current or expected prices at a given time. For setting selling prices, the standard product cost may be revised only by way of memorandum adjustments instead of the standard product cost card itself being revised. For example, for quoting the selling price for a longer-term delivery, the standard product cost should be adjusted to reflect the material prices likely to prevail at the time when the materials will be purchased for satisfying that particular bid (expected actual cost) or at the time of delivery of the product (expected replacement cost).

If a direct material is manufactured in-house, whether for captive consumption or not, it is necessary to set a *transfer price* which may be the standard production cost of that material, the standard selling price of that material, or somewhere in between, depending upon the transfer pricing policy adopted by company management.

**Composition of Direct Material Price** The controller's department must decide the accounting treatment of costs related to purchases. For product costing, a standard material price should consist not only of the basic purchase price but also of the freight in, taxes, insurance, customs duty, and all other incidental costs. Further, quantity discounts and trade discounts should be deducted from the standard purchase prices. However, cash discounts usually are not deducted since they are in the nature of financial credit and hence are shown as income or are offset against interest paid to vendors for the late payment of invoices. When the amounts of freight and transit insurance are small, they may be treated as a purchasing overhead cost.

Purchasing overhead costs, consisting of expenses incurred by the purchasing department and small incidental expenses, may be built into the direct material rates by applying a factor (e.g., if purchasing overhead costs are estimated to be 1 percent of the total estimated material consumption cost, all material prices may be increased by 1 percent) or be treated as manufacturing overhead and allocated to production centers in the ratio of the budgeted direct material consumption of the respective production centers.

When appropriate, two or more incidental purchase costs may be combined with a view to reducing clerical work, and a composite rate adopted for the allocation of those costs to individual products or production centers.

For *cost control,* each major element of purchase cost (basic purchase price, freight in, customs duty, etc.) may be budgeted separately and the actual cost compared with the standard or the budgeted cost. Alternatively, all the related costs may be built into the standard price, but the variances may be analyzed by major elements of purchase cost.

**Techniques for Setting Material Price Standards** Several techniques are available for establishing standard material prices. Hence, it is useful to divide the materials into A, B, and C categories according to their annual consumption as well as the fluctuations in their prices and to apply the more sophisticated techniques to A category materials and successively less sophisticated techniques to B and C category materials. For A category materials, more than one technique may be used. The common techniques available for establishing standard material prices are as follows:

- Study the trend of individual material prices during the last 3 to 5 years, and estimate the prices by looking at that trend.
- Study the meaningful correlations, if any, with the trend of general price levels, farm prices, all industrial material prices, specific industrial material prices, etc., and then estimate the prices of the concerned materials.
- Forecast a long-term price trend by using statistical forecasting techniques.
- Some companies conduct make-or-buy studies even for items not intended to be manufactured in-house so as to estimate vendors' costs and selling prices.
- Obtain price quotations from two or three vendors for future delivery of the relevant direct materials.
- If contracts have been entered into for the purchase of materials, use the contract prices for the duration of the contract.
- For small-value items, use the latest prevailing prices after adjusting them for the known variations or by the percentage increase or decrease based on past experience. Sometimes, even the latest actual purchase prices themselves may be used.

Usually, providing the purchase price forecast is the responsibility of the purchasing department, but when this step is cost-beneficial, the help of an economist may also be solicited.

## Use of Computer in Setting Direct Material Standards

When production, direct material consumption, and purchase price records are already computerized, the establishment of standards is greatly facilitated. The major help will be in the following areas:

1. The computerized data base and the computer will facilitate a detailed analysis of past material consumption and losses to gain an understanding of their variability and their relation to production and different specifications of materials.

2. The computer will also help in preparing a list of annual consumption of direct materials and arranging it in the order of monetary value of consumption. Thus, the application of the ABC technique will be facilitated.

3. Further, the computer will help to generate the price trend of major direct materials and help the material prices by application of mathematical techniques.

4. Since, with the help of the computer, the standard direct material cost can be quickly computed, it is possible to evaluate the impact of alternative material specifications, consumption standards, loss standards, and price standards on the standard product cost. This evaluation enables the company to set direct material cost standards which are not only realistic but also compatible with the company's objectives regarding profit, product quality, and product prices.

## Computation Guidelines

The following guidelines will help to simplify the computation of standard cost and record keeping:

1. Each direct material quantity standard should be expressed in some suitable unit of measurement (numbers, pounds, grams, kilograms, gallons, etc.). Similarly, each direct material price standard should also be expressed in some suitable unit of measurement. Insofar as possible, the unit of measurement used by the purchasing department and that for expressing standard quantity and standard price should be the same for a given material so as to avoid conversion. If, for example, purchases are expressed in kilograms and material standards are expressed in pounds, it will be necessary to convert kilograms into pounds. The unit of measurement used for standard direct material cost should invariably be the unit of measurement used for expressing the relevant unit of production (e.g., if production is measured in dozens of units, the direct material cost standard should also be set for 1 dozen units of production).

2. Direct material quantity and cost standards may be set per single unit of production or some convenient multiple (10, 100, 1000, etc.) thereof, depending upon the volume of production and the usual units of measurement of production and sales.

3. To simplify computation, it is normal to express direct material quantity, price, and cost standards in decimal points. For accuracy of standards, it may be necessary to express standards in several decimal points. For example, if a company manufactures millions of units of a

product and if standard quantities and costs are set per 100 units of the finished product, the standards should be expressed in four or even more decimals.

### Task 6: Designing a Direct Material Inventory Control System

As discussed earlier, proper control over the inventory of direct materials is essential for controlling their total cost. But so also is control over purchasing, receiving, inspection, storage, handling, etc. The cost system designer is usually not responsible for designing an inventory control system just as he is not responsible for designing purchasing, receiving, etc., systems. This is properly a function of the manufacturing department. There is ample literature on this subject.[3] However, the designer should be familiar with the basic requirements of the inventory control system so that he can communicate adequately with manufacturing personnel about this subject. With this view in mind, inventory control is dealt with here only briefly.

For proper control over the inventory of direct materials, it is necessary to establish the following standards:

**Inventory Levels** Usually, minimum and maximum acceptable levels of inventory are established.

**Economic Order Quantity (EOQ)** EOQ means the optimum quantity in which purchases of a particular direct material should be made. It is determined by weighing inventory carrying costs (storage, insurance, interest, etc.) and the potential loss due to stock being out.

**Reorder Point** The reorder point is the point at which an order for replenishing the stock of a particular material should be placed so that the stock will be replenished by the time it reaches the safety stock level. In deciding the reorder point, the desired safety stock level and the lead time for procuring the material are considered.

Proper control over inventory also requires a proper record of inventory and timely submission of inventory reports. The record-keeping aspect is dealt with in Chapter 15 and the reporting aspect in Chapter 14.

### Task 7: Designing a Direct Material Budgeting System

Budgeting is not part of a cost accounting system. However, budgeting and standard costing are interrelated, and budgeting is a useful technique for cost control. Hence, this subject is briefly dealt with here.

[3] A good book on this subject is by James H. Greene (ed.), *Production and Inventory Control Handbook*, McGraw-Hill Book Company, New York, 1970.

Standards are desirable for controlling material consumption per unit of production, individual purchases of materials, and inventory of direct materials. However, for overall control over direct materials, it is desirable to prepare three types of direct materials budgets: a direct materials consumption budget, a direct materials inventory budget, and a direct materials purchase budget. All three budgets should be prepared

- By responsibility centers.
- By product lines.
- By kind of direct materials. If there are a number of direct materials, either they may be suitably grouped or less valuable materials may be expressed in total.
- In quantitative and monetary terms.

When a standard direct material cost system is in use and current standards are employed, standard unit quantities and standard prices of direct materials will be used for preparing direct materials budgets. Otherwise, the production and purchasing departments will have to estimate quantities and prices based on past records and forecast changes. Thus, budget preparation is greatly facilitated and the budget is more reliable if a standard cost system is being used and the system is based on current standards.

Illustrative direct materials budgets for a single-product company are given in Exhibits 9-2 through 9-4. First, the direct materials consumption budget, which contains the total budgeted consumption quantity as well as the dollar amount, is prepared. The budgeted consumption quantity of each material is determined by multiplying the budgeted production and the standard consumption quantity of that material. The budgeted dollar amount of each material is equal to the budgeted consumption quantity multiplied by the standard material price.

For preparing the direct materials inventory budget, it is first necessary to establish standards for inventory levels. Then, the desired ending inventory can be computed by this formula: budgeted consumption quantity for the year times the desired level of inventory in terms of number of months' consumption divided by 12. The desired inventory quantity is valued at the standard material price.

The last step is to prepare the direct materials purchase budget, as illustrated in Exhibit 9-4. The expected opening inventory quantity will be available from the current year's budget, which may be updated for known variations.

Usually, each of these three budgets will be broken down into monthly or quarterly budgets by following the same procedure as that adopted for preparing the yearly budgets.

**EXHIBIT 9-2**

**Direct Materials Consumption Budget: XYZ Company (Product X)**

Budget year ______

| Direct Material | Standard Consumption per Unit of Finished Product | Standard Price per Kilogram of Direct Material | Budgeted Direct Material Consumption for Budgeted Production of 12,000 Units of X | |
|---|---|---|---|---|
| | | | Quantity (Kilograms) | $ |
| A | 2 kilograms | $5 | 24,000 | $120,000 |
| B | 1 kilogram | $6 | 12,000 | 72,000 |
| Total | | | | $192,000 |

## Task 8: Designing Direct Material Cost Reports

There are two types of direct material cost reports: operational control reports and management control reports. Operational control reports are required by the operating people, such as the production shop supervisors, inventory manager, purchasing manager, etc., and their focus is on individual transactions of consumption, losses, etc. In contrast, management control reports are required by upper management, including the vice president, manufacturing, the president, and even the plant manager, depending upon the size of the company and its organization structure. The focus of management control reports is the per-

**EXHIBIT 9-3**

**Direct Materials Inventory Budget: XYZ Company**

Budget year ______

| Direct Material | Budgeted Consumption (See Exhibit 9-2) | Inventory Standards | Desirea Closing Inventory Quantity (Kilograms) | Inventory Value at Standard Price |
|---|---|---|---|---|
| A | 24,000 kilograms | 3 months' consumption | 6,000 | $30,000 |
| B | 12,000 kilograms | 4 months' consumption | 4,000 | 24,000 |
| Total | | | | $54,000 |

**EXHIBIT 9-4**

**Direct Materials Purchase Budget: XYZ Company**

Budget year ______

| | Material A (Kilo-grams) | Material B (Kilo-grams) |
|---|---|---|
| Desired closing inventory (Exhibit 9-3) | 6,000 | 4,000 |
| Add budgeted consumption (Exhibit 9-2) | 24,000 | 12,000 |
| Subtotal | 30,000 | 16,000 |
| Less expected opening inventory (say) | 5,000 | 3,500 |
| Direct materials purchase budget (quantity) | 25,000 | 12,500 |
| Direct materials purchase budget ($ amount at standard prices) | $125,000 | $75,000 |
| Total | $200,000 | |

formance evaluation of a department or a function over a period of, say, a month. For example, operating people will be interested in knowing the daily material consumption and variances from the standards, whereas upper management will be interested in knowing the monthly, or at best the weekly, consumption and variances.

The types of direct material control reports appropriate for a given company will depend upon several factors such as the nature of the business, the significance of direct material cost, organization structure, and so on.

The most common cost control reports for direct materials are listed below.

## Operational Control Reports

1. Daily direct material consumption report comparing actual and standard consumption and showing variances from the standard. In a process industry, input-output reports or yield reports may be prepared.

2. Daily scrap, waste, spoilage, etc., report showing actual and standard quantities of scrap, waste, etc., and variances from the standards.

Both these reports may be prepared by products, parts, production departments, jobs, and processes. In addition, a weekly or monthly summary of variances or the trend of variances may also be shown.

3. Purchase price variance report. This report may be prepared weekly or even monthly. The purchasing department is the prime user.

4. Direct materials inventory report. Usually, this report will be prepared monthly; it will show the actual and the permitted level of inven-

tory and also obsolete or slow-moving materials. This report will be for the use of the production and purchasing departments.

Usually, operational cost control reports will contain either nonmonetary data of input, output, levels of inventory, etc., or monetary as well as nonmonetary data.

### Management Reports

Most management reports usually will be prepared monthly and will contain mainly monetary data and some nonmonetary data. The following are the commonly used management reports for direct materials:

1. Consumption report with analysis of variances into quantity and price and identification of variances with the concerned responsibility centers.
2. Production report, with actual versus planned production by product lines or groups.
3. Inventory report. This report will be more or less the same as that for the operating people but may contain only items in excess of the standards and also show the total dollar amount of actual and standard inventory levels.
4. Scrap, waste, spoilage, etc., report. This report will also be more or less the same as that for the operating people but may be based on the reporting-by-exception principle and may also show the dollar amount of material losses.

### Task 9: Designing Direct Material Cost Records

This task will be explained in Chapter 15.

# Chapter 10

# Designing a Direct Labor Cost System

Unlike materials, labor cannot be stored. Hence, use it or lose it.
Pravin P. Shah

In this chapter, we will discuss the specific points for designing a direct labor cost system. Since indirect labor costs are treated as a part of manufacturing overhead, they will be dealt with in Chapter 11, "Designing a Manufacturing Overhead Cost System."

## HOW TO DESIGN A DIRECT LABOR COST SYSTEM

The process of designing a direct labor cost system involves the iterative steps discussed below, some of which have already been explained. For completing the picture and for reinforcement, even the completed tasks are summarized here. It is useful to note that there is great similarity between the design of a direct labor cost system and that of a direct material cost system.

### System Analysis Tasks

System analysis precedes system design. Hence, when a designer begins to design a direct labor cost system, he will already have completed the following system analysis tasks:

1. The designer will have defined the *objectives* of the cost system, particularly the direct labor cost system.
2. The designer will have conducted a *survey* of manufacturing operations to gain an understanding of various aspects of direct labor, includ-

ing types of labor operations, number of workers in each department, type of wage system, nature of fringe benefits, existing system for controlling direct labor costs, etc. If this survey is not detailed enough, an additional survey should be conducted to gather the relevant information.

3. The designer will have determined, in specific terms, the types of direct labor *cost information required* to satisfy each of the preset objectives.

In actual practice, before beginning to design a direct labor cost system, the designer will, at this stage, refer to his file to review these completed tasks.

### System Design Tasks

Once the system analysis phase is over, the system design phase begins. This phase also involves various tasks:

1. Prepare an outline of the direct labor cost system.
2. Select appropriate cost methods and techniques for the direct labor cost system.
3. Establish responsibility centers and cost centers.
4. Classify direct labor.
5. If a standard cost system is to be employed, set direct labor standards.
6. If a budgetary control system is to be employed, design a direct labor budgeting system.
7. Design direct labor cost reports.
8. Design a cost accounting system for direct labor.

### Task 1: Preparation of Outline of the Direct Labor Cost System

Because control over direct labor cost is important for many manufacturing organizations, particularly labor-intensive organizations, its major features are discussed first. For achieving control over direct labor cost, it is necessary to know the aspects of direct labor cost to be controlled and the control devices.

### Aspects of Direct Labor Cost to Be Controlled

Control over direct labor cost begins with a proper product design or formula, the selection of proper production equipment and sequence of operations, establishment of policy regarding work hours, and appropriate specifications for the level of skills required. For example, setting labor skills required at an unduly high level may involve avoidable direct labor cost.

Further, control of direct labor cost requires control over each of these important areas: (1) recruitment, (2) training, (3) supervision, (4) production scheduling, and (5) utilization of direct labor. For example, recruitment of the wrong type of labor, poor supervision, underutilization of available labor owing to excessive recruitment or faulty production scheduling, and so on are sources of direct labor costs that are higher than desirable. Hence, all these areas should be controlled to keep labor costs down. Unlike direct materials, labor time cannot be inventoried for the future. The company must use it or lose it. Hence, special attention should be given to utilizing most of the available work time.

## Control Devices

Several control devices are available for exercising control over direct labor cost. Usually, a company will need a *multiple* of such devices. The common control devices are as follows:

1. *Organization.* Control is exercised by individuals. Hence, the manufacturing operation should be properly organized, it should be staffed with capable persons, and they should be provided with adequate training.
2. *Physical control.* The attendance, utilization, and movement of the available labor force should be controlled on a day-to-day and hour-by-hour basis. For example, one company in England adopts a glasshouse approach for controlling the idle labor force. It has created a room with glass walls in the center of the plant. All excess workers are sent to the glasshouse, which is clearly visible to the plant manager, who is responsible for reassigning them to other departments where they can be utilized.[1]
3. *Management policies.* Management must decide, for example, about the transfer of excess labor from one operation to another, laying off temporarily excess labor, etc.
4. *Operating or functional systems.* For example, a well-designed manpower requirements planning system will enable the company to estimate correctly its labor requirements for scheduled production and to plan labor recruitment and training accordingly.
5. *Control through standards and budgets.* For effective control over direct labor cost, it is desirable to establish direct labor time and rate standards and to prepare a staffing (manning) table and budgets for direct labor cost.

The establishment of standards and preparation of budgets is just the first step of control. The other required steps are:

[1] Edmund J. McCormick, "Budgetary Control," in H. B. Maynard (ed.), *Industrial Engineering Handbook,* 3d ed., McGraw-Hill Book Company, New York, 1971, p. 8–215.

- Measurement of actual direct labor time, rates, costs, etc.
- Comparison of actual data against standards and computation of variances
- Reporting of actual data and variances
- Investigation of causes of variances and assignment of responsibility for variances
- Taking corrective or preventive action by the responsible personnel
- Reporting to management the results of corrective action in case of major deviation

Thus, this device emphasizes the need for proper measurement, cost record keeping, and reporting of actual transactions.

6. *Process sheet or manufacturing routing sheet.* This sheet is similar to the bill of materials employed for controlling direct material use. A process sheet is prepared separately for each product, part, or assembly. It contains a description of each operation to be performed, the sequence of operations, the production department in which the work is to be performed, the equipment and tools to be used, and the standard direct labor time per unit of each operation. This document is a basis for work force planning, budgeting, and controlling direct labor cost on a day-to-day basis.

In summary, direct labor cost control requires *management controls, operational controls,* and *cost accounting controls.* Management as well as the cost system designer should remember that these three types of controls are interrelated and hence should be well-integrated. For example, merely setting rate and time standards for direct labor will not achieve control over direct labor cost. If, for instance, the labor requirements planning system and the recruitment procedure are poor, the company may not be able to hire the required workers at the right time and at the right wages. Further, unless actual labor time, rates, and costs are properly recorded and compared against standards and unless variances are reported to the responsible personnel, corrective action may not be initiated.

## Role of Designer and Management

Obviously, the cost system designer is not responsible for designing all three types of controls. For example, designing a recruitment system, establishing management policies for laying off temporarily excess labor, and developing a labor requirements planning system are generally not the designer's responsibility, though he may have a role to play in this matter depending upon his expertise and the scope of his assignment.

Similarly, though the designer is primarily responsible for designing a cost control and information system, management also has a role to play in it.

Because of this combined responsibility, the designer should first prepare a list of all relevant aspects of direct labor cost. Next, he should identify those items which either are nonexistent or appear to be deficient but essential for controlling direct labor cost as well as for product costing. Then, the designer should separate the aspects which are clearly his responsibility from those which are not his responsibility. Usually, the latter aspects will relate to operating systems, management policies, and standards. For those aspects which are not his responsibility, he should ask the appropriate company personnel to review, define, develop, or modify the operating systems, management policies, etc., that have an adverse impact on the direct labor cost system.

Even if the designer is designing a cost system from scratch, certain features of the cost system may be present (e.g., direct labor usage standards may already have been set), in which case only the remaining aspects need be designed.

In short, this task will enable the designer to define all the steps that should be taken to design a direct labor cost system and to integrate it with other aspects of the direct labor management system.

### Task 2: Selection of Cost Methods and Techniques

A decision about the type of cost methods and techniques to be used for product costing and responsibility accounting is critical to subsequent design tasks, and hence the task of selecting cost methods and techniques to be used for the direct labor cost system should be undertaken first. Since this is a subject by itself and since this task is common to the entire cost system, it has been dealt with in detail in Chapter 7. However, the important points are summarized here.

The cost methods for direct labor may be any one or more of the following:

- Standard job order costing
- Standard process costing
- Historical job order costing
- Historical process costing

Obviously, the distinction between direct costing and absorption costing is irrelevant for direct labor because direct labor costs are accorded the same treatment under direct costing and full absorption costing.

**Job Order versus Process Costing** The main difference between a direct labor job order cost system and a direct labor process cost system lies in the manner of accumulation and charging (to production) of direct labor costs. Hence, the selection of job order or process costing has a major impact on tasks 7 and 8. Under the job order cost system, direct labor cost is accumulated by jobs or production orders, and direct labor cost per unit of production is computed by dividing the total cost of the direct labor utilized for a job by the total quantity produced by the job. Under the process cost system, direct labor cost is accumulated by processes, and direct labor cost per unit of production is computed by dividing the total cost of the direct labor utilized for a process during a given period by the total output of that process.

**Historical Costing versus Standard Costing and Budgeting** For controlling direct labor cost, some sort of standards or yardsticks against which actual direct labor cost can be compared are essential. Though past cost can be used as a yardstick, standard costing based on scientifically oriented standards is far superior and desirable for controlling direct labor cost. The other control technique available is budgeting. It may be said that standard costing is useful for day-to-day control over direct labor cost and budgeting is useful for overall control over direct labor cost.

Though it is possible to use one technique without the other, in actual practice either both these techniques are used or at least the budgetary control technique is employed. A company will rarely use a standard cost system for direct labor and not prepare direct labor budgets.

If budgeting is employed in conjunction with standard costing, direct labor time and rate standards (provided, of course, they are current standards) will form the basis for direct labor budgeting. If budgeting is employed without direct labor standards, direct labor budgets will be based on some sort of estimate of direct labor time and rates.

Besides being useful for cost control, standard costing is useful for product costing, inventory valuation, product pricing, and various other purposes. Further, even if standard costing is employed, historical costing is used for the accumulation of actual direct labor costs.

### Task 3: Establishment of Necessary Responsibility Centers and Cost Centers

As in the case of direct materials, for proper control over direct labor cost various responsibility centers should be established and the persons responsible for individual centers should be designated. The usual responsibility centers for direct labor cost control will be from among the following:

- Industrial engineering department, which will be responsible for setting direct labor standards

- Personnel department, which will be responsible for direct and indirect labor administration and, to some extent, for the hiring and training of personnel
- Production centers, which will be responsible for efficient and effective use of available direct labor and, in some cases, for the hiring and training of direct labor
- Inspection department, which will be responsible for quality control of the work done by direct labor.

For the accounting of direct labor, the relevant cost centers will be various production centers, individual job orders, product lines or product subassemblies, processes, or operations utilizing direct labor.

Since the process of establishing responsibility centers and cost centers has been explained in Chapter 8, it is not repeated here.

### Task 4: Classification of Direct Labor

Since direct labor and indirect labor are accorded different treatments in cost accounting and require different techniques for cost control, the labor utilized by a company must be separated into direct and indirect categories. Workers whose efforts can be traced directly to individual units of production are normally classified as direct labor, and other workers are classified as indirect labor. Besides indirect labor, there will also be supervisory and clerical personnel whose time cannot be directly traced to individual units of production. In a job order industry, it is easy to identify direct labor and indirect labor, but in a fully automated plant or in continuous-process industries, such as a chemical plant, the distinction between direct labor and indirect labor often is not clear-cut because workers attend to machines but do not manually carry out any production activity. In such cases, the person responsible for classification must use judgment. Similarly, to reduce the cost of record keeping and analysis, workers attending to short operations may be classified as indirect labor.

Further, the time of a worker who works as a direct as well as an indirect worker should be separated into direct and indirect labor time. For example, if a mechanical maintenance worker occasionally operates production equipment, whatever time that worker spends on production should be recorded as direct labor and the remaining time as indirect labor.

Moreover, certain costs related to direct labor may be classified as manufacturing overhead instead of as direct labor costs. For example, overtime premium and employee benefits costs are usually treated as manufacturing overhead.

Direct labor should be classified in three ways, and this classification should be indicated on the manufacturing routing sheet or process sheet:

- By nature of work (welder, assembler, etc.).
- By production cost centers and by operation or production processes.
- By kind of wage system (time-rated, piece-rated, etc.). If different wage rates prevail for the same type of job, labor should also be classified by grades or skills.

If a company has several plants producing the same product, the direct labor classification at all plants should be identical. Further, each classification should be clearly described, and for ease in record keeping an identifying code number may be assigned.

Though the responsibility for classification and codification of labor lies with the manufacturing department, the designer should provide guidance to the department and ensure that these tasks have been carried out by a competent person and that there are no apparent ambiguities in the classification and codification of direct labor.

### Task 5: Setting Standards for Direct Labor

Obviously, this task is relevant only for a standard cost system and not for a historical cost system. The common points for establishment of a standard cost system were discussed in Chapter 6. In particular, in that chapter we discussed defining the scope of the standard cost system, selecting the kind of standards to be used, responsibility for setting standards and the role of the designer in setting them, general guidelines for setting standards, and revision of standards. Here we will discuss the procedure involved in setting direct labor standards.

It is worth reemphasizing that responsibility for setting direct labor standards lies with the manufacturing, industrial engineering, and process engineering departments and not with the cost system designer. However, the designer does have a role to play in setting standards. For example, the designer must specify what standards are to be set and advise management on who should be responsible for setting those standards, and he should provide needed guidance to the persons responsible for setting standards.

### Types of Direct Labor Cost Standards

Direct labor cost standards consist of time and rate standards. Time standards should be set separately for each type of direct labor, for each product, in each production center, or for each operation. Rate standards should be set separately for each type of direct labor, for each product, in each production center, or for each operation. Rate standards should be set separately for each type of direct labor. Obviously, the question of setting direct labor rate standards by products does not arise. The resultant direct labor *cost* standards should be expressed by products, by production centers or operations, and by type of direct labor.

**Be Selective** Setting standards and updating them involve costs, the most important of which is management time. Hence, standards may not be set for less significant operations, and insignificant standards may not be set even for significant operations. For example, if rework time is not significant, rework-time standards need not be set.

**Set Priorities** If many standards are to be set, they may be established in a phased manner, usually by starting with the more significant standards. For example, initially standards may be set for major operations, assemblies, or products.

### Procedure for Setting Direct Labor Standards

The points which the designer should know concerning the procedure for setting direct labor standards are discussed below.

**Standardization of Products and Operations** Even if standards are reasonable for one set of circumstances, they may not be appropriate for another set. Hence, before meaningful standards can be set for direct labor time and rate, the following aspects should be standardized:

- Products and product varieties such as packing sizes, deluxe and regular variety, etc.
- Product design, drawings, or formula, for example, the formula for manufacturing a syrup in a pharmaceutical company.
- Direct labor specifications, i.e., the description of experience and skills for each operation. If appropriate, specifications should be given also for substitute direct labor or substitute operations.
- Production processes and their sequence and plant layout. This step is necessary not only for setting direct labor standards by production processes and production centers but also for assigning responsibility for variances.

**Direct Labor Time Standards** For cost control and partly for product costing based on standards, the following kinds of direct labor time standards should be set:

- Production time standards
- Lost-time standards
- Standard working hours

**Production Time Standards** Direct labor time standards should show the number of direct labor–hours allowed for a given quantity of good production, operation, or job. The standards should be set separately by products, operations, processes, and production cost centers.

In setting direct labor production time (and also lost-time) standards, the following major factors must be considered:

- Product design or formula
- Nature of production processes or operations
- Age and condition of manufacturing equipment
- Plant layout
- Physical work environment
- Training, experience, and degree of skills of direct labor
- Supervision
- Inspection and quality control standards
- Quality of direct materials
- Allowance for fatigue, rest time, and personal needs
- Current goals set by management or claims made by the production department for the improvement of labor productivity

If all direct workers in a particular production center work on equipment, direct labor time will be proportionate to equipment-hours. Hence, it will be necessary to set also standard equipment-hours and express direct labor time standards in terms of direct labor–hours per equipment-hour rather than in hours per unit of product or operation.

Standards should also be established for the setup or adjustment of machines. Since setup time varies with the number of times jobs are changed or stopped and commenced on a machine, it usually is charged to the manufacturing overhead of the relevant production center and is not included in direct labor time standards. Alternatively, for product costing, the standard time per setup may be converted to a standard time per unit of product on the basis of a standard order or lot size.

**Direct Labor Time Loss Standards** The difference between direct labor time available for production and direct labor time utilized for good production is referred to as *lost time.* The process of setting direct labor lost-time standards is explained step by step:

1. Direct labor time losses occurring within the company should be identified. For better understanding they should be classified

- By type or nature of losses (rework time, learning time, idle time, etc.)
- By products, operations, jobs, processes, and production centers
- By causes of loss (e.g., waiting for instructions, waiting for materials, machine breakdown, etc.)

This information can be obtained from the analysis of past records of production and direct labor and from discussions with the respective production centers.

2. Since standards are set only for normal labor time losses, normal labor time losses should be separated from abnormal labor time losses. Further, because standards usually are not set for insignificant losses, normal time losses should be classified into significant and insignificant categories. Since standards will be applied to the future period, all significant losses which are likely to occur during the period for which standards are being set should be considered.

3. For each significant type of normal direct labor time loss, quantity or time standards should be set. The normal-loss level should be set after considering how tightly the standards are to be set and various factors mentioned in the section "Production Time Standards." Usually, standards for direct labor time loss are based on the past 2 or 3 years' experience, adjusted for known or predictable changes and after considering current cost reduction goals regarding direct labor. Standards for learning time may be based on the learning-curve experience of the respective production centers.

4. The standards for direct labor time losses should be related to the direct labor time utilized for good production or to the quantity of good production. Usually, the idle-time standard is expressed as a percentage of the direct labor time utilized or available, and the rework-time standard is expressed as a percentage of standard direct labor–hours allowed for good production because the rework quantity itself is related to the quantity of good production.

5. By multiplying each of these standard time losses by the applicable standard direct labor rate, the standard cost of these losses can be computed. The standard direct labor rates are the rates set for regular time.

6. The last step is to determine how to treat standard direct labor losses in developing a standard product cost. The usual alternatives are (*a*) to build into the standard direct labor time, (*b*) to provide for a separate allowance for these losses, (*c*) to provide losses as a separate item in the overhead budget of the relevant production center (if the losses can be identified with the individual production centers) or in the general plant overhead budget, and (*d*) to charge to the income statement, i.e., to keep the losses out of the standard product cost.

In resolving this issue, the objectives of the cost system, the accounting treatment of direct labor losses, and the type of feedback information required for exercising control over direct labor time losses should be considered. The accounting treatment, in its turn, depends upon the nature and the significance of each of these losses. It is not uncommon to treat these losses as manufacturing overhead.

**Standard Working Hours** For product costing as well as for cost control, it is necessary to set standards for normal working hours. For this purpose, first the net hours available for work and the net time paid for per day, per week, and per worker should be determined from union contracts or management policy. Next, the number of workweeks (or workdays) per year per worker should be computed on the basis of policy and past experience about vacations, holidays, excused absences, and unpaid absenteeism. Then, the net weeks available per year should be multiplied by the net work hours available per week to arrive at the net hours available per year per employee. Similarly, the time paid for but not worked (paid lunch and relief time, holidays, vacations, etc.) should also be computed.

**Direct Labor Rate Standards** It is simpler to set direct labor rate standards than to set direct labor time standards. Often, labor rates are a matter of negotiation between a union and management. Even if there is no union, labor rates are set by management for payroll purposes. In setting standard direct labor rates, the following points should be taken care of:

1. Direct labor rate standards should be set not only for regular time but also for the overtime premium and the shift premium. Though the overtime premium usually is 50 percent of regular-time pay, in some cases the overtime premium for holidays is paid at 100 percent.
2. Direct labor rate standards should also be set for bonus, incentives, etc., if such schemes are in force.
3. Standard direct labor rates should be set by occupations within a cost center. If more than one wage rate prevails for the same occupation within a cost center, a weighted-average hourly rate should be set as the standard direct labor rate for that occupation. However, if there are different grades of labor within an occupation (e.g., a junior mechanic and a senior mechanic), different rates should be set for each grade of labor. A single overall rate should not be set for a cost center or the entire plant unless the difference in wage rates for different occupations or for different cost centers is insignificant.
4. If a crew of operators work on a job, a standard weighted-average labor rate for the crew should be set.
5. For piece-rated workers, standard piece rates should be set. These usually will be the rates at which the piece-rated workers are paid.
6. If a company has decided to treat payroll taxes and benefits applicable to direct labor as a part of direct labor cost and not as a part of manufacturing overhead, direct labor rate standards should include the applicable payroll taxes and costs of employee benefits.

The standard direct labor cost of a production unit or an operation is computed by multiplying the standard direct labor time by the standard direct labor rate.

### Computation Guidelines

The following guidelines will help to simplify the computation of standard cost and record keeping:

1. Direct labor time and cost standards may be set per single unit of production or some convenient multiple (10, 100, 1000, etc.) thereof, depending upon the volume of production and the usual units of measurement of production and sales.
2. To simplify computation, it is normal to express direct labor time, rate, and cost standards in decimal points. For accuracy of standards, it may be necessary to express standards in several decimal points. For example, if a company manufactures millions of units of a product and if standard time and costs are set per 100 units of the finished product, standards should be expressed in four or even more decimals.

### Task 6: Designing a Direct Labor Budgeting System

Budgeting is not part of a cost accounting system. However, budgeting and standard costing are interrelated, and budgeting is a useful technique for cost control. Hence, this subject is briefly dealt with here.

Labor standards are desirable for controlling labor cost per unit of production and, in some cases, for payroll computations. However, for overall control over direct labor cost a staffing (manning) table and a direct labor budget are essential. A staffing table shows the total direct labor–hours required by each production center to meet its production schedule. A direct labor budget shows the direct labor–hours, direct labor rates, and direct labor costs. Both these documents should be prepared

- By responsibility centers.
- By operations or processes, if different from responsibility centers (usually, they will be subclassifications of a responsibility center).
- By grade or skills of direct labor.

When direct labor time and rate standards have been set and they are based on current standards, they should be used in preparing a direct labor budget and a staffing table. Otherwise, direct labor–hours should be estimated from past actuals or from the production department's forecast of labor needs. Thus, budget preparation is greatly facilitated and the budget is more reliable if a standard cost system is being used and the system is based on current standards.

**Preparation of Staffing Table** For preparing a staffing table, first the direct labor–hours, by types of operations per production unit, either are obtained from the time standards or are estimated. Second, the production quantity is obtained from the production budget. Third, total direct labor–hours required are computed by multiplying budgeted production quantity and standard estimated direct labor–hours per production unit. Fourth, total idle hours, rework time, and learning time are derived from standards or are estimated. The last two steps give the total direct labor–hours required by types of labor. A comparison of total direct labor–hours required with available net direct labor–hours separately for each type of labor will show excess or short available hours. This comparison will enable the production or personnel department to determine the need for overtime, additional hiring, additional shifts, laying off of surplus labor, or transfer of surplus labor to other jobs. Thus, a staffing table enables better and timely control over direct labor costs. It should be noted that in preparing a staffing table for direct labor, even direct labor time losses should be included in total direct labor–hours required *irrespective* of whether such losses are treated as a part of direct labor cost or of manufacturing overhead.

**Preparation of Direct Labor Cost Budget** Once the staffing table has been prepared, the direct labor cost budget can easily be prepared. The budgeted total direct labor cost is obtained by multiplying the direct labor–hours required by the standard or estimated direct labor rates. In preparing a direct labor cost budget, direct labor–hours should include direct labor time losses *only if* such losses are treated as a part of direct labor cost. If such losses are treated as a part of manufacturing overhead, they should be included in the manufacturing overhead budget.

For responsibility accounting, direct labor cost budgets should be prepared by responsibility centers so that actual direct labor costs can be compared with budgeted direct labor costs and responsibility for variances established.

Specimens of a staffing table and a direct labor cost budget will be found in the case study of ACME Company given in Chapter 12.

### Task 7: Designing Direct Labor Cost Reports

As in the case of direct materials, there are two types of direct labor cost reports: operational control reports and management control reports. Operational control reports are required by operating personnel, such as production shop supervisors, and their focus is the use of direct labor by jobs, operations, process, and workers. In contrast, management control reports are required by upper management, including the vice president, manufacturing, the president, and even the plant manager, depending upon the size of the company and its organization structure. The focus of management control reports is the performance evaluation of a department or a function in the aggregate. As a result of this difference in focus, operating personnel will be interested in knowing the daily labor efficiency and variances from the standards, whereas management will be interested in knowing the monthly, or at best the weekly, labor efficiency and variances.

The types of direct labor control reports appropriate for a given company will depend upon several factors such as the nature of the business, the significance of direct labor cost, the organization structure, and so on.

The most common cost control reports for direct labor are listed below.

## Operational Control Reports

1. Daily direct labor efficiency report comparing actual and standard direct labor–hours and showing variances from the standard.
2. Daily direct labor idle-time and rework-time reports showing actual and standard idle and rework time, their causes, and variances from the standard.

Both these types of reports may be prepared by products, parts, production departments, jobs, processes, and workers. In addition, a weekly or monthly summary of variances or the trend of variances may also be shown. Further, the reports may show the cumulative data for the month as well as the trend for the recent period.

3. Direct labor rate variance report. This report may be prepared weekly or even monthly.

Usually, operational cost control reports will contain nonmonetary data of input, output, and lost time and may also contain monetary data.

## Management Reports

Most management reports usually will be prepared monthly and will contain monetary and nonmonetary data. The following are the commonly used management reports for direct labor:

1. Direct labor cost report with analysis of variances into time and rate variances and identification of variances with individual responsibility centers.

2. Direct labor efficiency report. This report will be more or less the same as that for operating personnel but may contain only items in excess of standards.

3. Direct labor idle-time and rework-time reports. These reports will also be more or less the same as those for operating personnel but may be based on the reporting-by-exception principle and may also show the dollar amount of direct labor time losses.

## Illustrative Reports

Illustrative direct labor efficiency reports are given in Exhibits 10-1, 10-2, and 10-3. These reports adopt the pyramid approach and use the exception principle in reporting.

Exhibit 10-1 is a *detailed report* for use by production supervisors. It is prepared daily and contains daily and month-to-date direct labor efficiency data for a responsibility center. It also gives the last 3 months' and the last 12 months' high, low, and average efficiency ratios. This report enables a production supervisor to compare daily efficiency ratios with current as well as past efficiency ratios. To save time and paper, the same sheet should be used for a month and be updated every day. If standard hours are set per equipment-hour, instead of the actual production units the actual equipment-hours should be entered in the second column.

Exhibit 10-2 is a *summary report* for use by the plant manager. This report summarizes labor efficiency by responsibility centers and also gives recent past months' comparative data as in the case of a detailed efficiency report. The reports of the individual responsibility centers will *not* be attached to the summary report, but the plant manager can always ask for a copy of the labor efficiency report of a particular center.

In addition, if a responsibility center is unable to achieve at least a 90 percent efficiency ratio three times during a month, a copy of its detailed report, with the efficiency ratios below 90 percent clearly marked, is sent to the plant manager. This report is sent to the plant manager as soon as the center misses the 90 percent mark for the third time during the month and thereafter every time that it misses this mark during that month. This procedure will alert the plant manager to any *continuing* problem in achieving labor efficiency and enable the manager to monitor the concerned supervisor's effort in correcting the problem.

Exhibit 10-3 is an *exception report* for the vice president, manufacturing. It is prepared monthly and shows only the responsibility centers which achieved below 80 percent efficiency during the month. It also shows these centers' ratios for the last 3 months to reveal any declining trend in labor efficiency. In addition, it shows how often these centers missed the 80 percent mark in the last 12 months to reveal any *recurring* problem in achieving 80 percent labor efficiency.

**EXHIBIT 10-1**

**Daily Direct Labor Efficiency Ratio Report**

Responsibility center ____________________ No. ____________

Responsibility of ______________________ Month ____________

| Date | Daily | | | | Month to date | | |
|---|---|---|---|---|---|---|---|
| | Actual production | Standard hours | Actual hours | Efficiency ratio | Standard hours | Actual hours | Efficiency ratio |
| 1 | | | | | | | |
| 2 | | | | | | | |
| 3 | | | | | | | |
| 4 | | | | | | | |
| 5 | | | | | | | |
| 6 | | | | | | | |
| 7 | | | | | | | |
| 8 | | | | | | | |
| 9 | | | | | | | |
| 10 | | | | | | | |
| 11 | | | | | | | |
| 12 | | | | | | | |
| 13 | | | | | | | |
| 14 | | | | | | | |
| 15 | | | | | | | |
| 16 | | | | | | | |
| 17 | | | | | | | |
| 18 | | | | | | | |
| 19 | | | | | | | |
| 20 | | | | | | | |
| 21 | | | | | | | |
| 22 | | | | | | | |
| 23 | | | | | | | |
| 24 | | | | | | | |
| 25 | | | | | | | |
| 26 | | | | | | | |
| 27 | | | | | | | |
| 28 | | | | | | | |
| 29 | | | | | | | |
| 30 | | | | | | | |
| 31 | | | | | | | |

| Last 3 months' efficiency ratio | | | | Last 12 months' efficiency ratio |
|---|---|---|---|---|
| | | | | |
| | | | High<br>Low<br>Average | |

**EXHIBIT 10-2**

**Monthly Direct Labor Efficiency Ratio Report**

Plant ____________ No. ____________

Responsibility of ____________ Month ____________

| Last 12 months (monthly average) | | | Last 3 months (monthly average) | | | Responsibility center | | Current month | Year to date |
|---|---|---|---|---|---|---|---|---|---|
| High | Low | Average | | | | No. | Name | | |
| | | | | | | | | | |

**EXHIBIT 10-3**

**Below 80 Percent Direct Labor Efficiency Ratio Report**

Month ________

| Responsibility center | | Direct labor efficiency ratio | | | | How often below 80 percent efficiency ratio in last 12 months |
|---|---|---|---|---|---|---|
| No. | Name | Current month | Last 3 months (monthly average) | | | |
| Plant: New York | | | | | | |
| Plant: Chicago | | | | | | |

### Task 8: Designing Direct Labor Cost Records

This task will be explained in Chapter 15.

# Chapter 11

# Designing a Manufacturing Overhead Cost System

Facts do not cease to exist because they are ignored.
Aldous Huxley: *Proper Studies*

In a manufacturing company, with the increase in the automation of production and in the size and complexity of a business organization, manufacturing overhead costs, i.e., all manufacturing costs other than direct materials and direct labor, often form a very significant portion of total costs. At the same time, since overhead costs cannot be charged directly to individual units of production, it is necessary to allocate them. Though the process of allocation and accounting of overhead is much more complex, the result is much less exact than that for direct materials and direct labor. These two factors therefore emphasize the need for great care in designing a manufacturing overhead cost system.

Though the term *overhead* can also be identified with selling, distribution, and administrative costs, for the sake of brevity it refers only to manufacturing overhead in this chapter.

To understand properly the process of designing a manufacturing overhead cost system, let us first summarize the manufacturing overhead accounting system.

## DESCRIPTION OF MANUFACTURING OVERHEAD ACCOUNTING

For product costing, all manufacturing costs are ultimately charged to production. Direct materials and direct labor are charged directly to production, whereas overhead costs are applied to production through a process of cost allocation and absorption:

1. Overhead expenses, as incurred, are *accumulated* by their nature or objective.
2. Then, they are assigned or allocated to cost centers, which usually are classified into service centers and production centers. This process is termed *primary allocation* of manufacturing overhead.
3. Next, the costs of service departments are charged to production departments on some equitable bases. This process is called *secondary allocation* of manufacturing overhead.
4. Finally, the overhead costs of production departments are charged or applied to production (jobs, processes, products, etc.). This process is called overhead *absorption*.

Thus, a manufacturing overhead cost system for product costing consists of a system for accumulation, allocation, and absorption of manufacturing overhead costs. For responsibility accounting, accumulation and primary allocation of overhead costs to responsibility centers are the essential steps. Secondary allocation and absorption are not necessary because no element of control is added by reallocation and absorption of overhead costs.

## TASKS IN DESIGNING A MANUFACTURING OVERHEAD COST SYSTEM

Development of a manufacturing overhead cost system involves several *iterative steps,* some of which have already been explained. For completing the picture and for reinforcement, even the completed tasks are summarized here.

### System Analysis Tasks

System analysis precedes system design. Hence, when a designer begins to design a manufacturing overhead cost system, he will already have completed the following system analysis tasks:

1. The designer will have defined the *objectives* of the cost system, particularly the manufacturing overhead cost system.
2. The designer will have conducted a *fact-finding survey* to gather the necessary information relating to manufacturing activities and manufacturing overhead costs. If this survey is not detailed enough, additional inquiries and analyses must now be made to supplement the information already gathered.
3. The designer will have determined, in specific terms, the types of manufacturing overhead *cost information required* to satisfy each of the preset objectives.

In actual practice, before beginning to design a manufacturing overhead cost system, the designer will, at this stage, refer to his file to review these completed tasks.

## System Design Phase

The structure of a manufacturing overhead cost system depends upon whether or not overhead budgets, with or without standard costs, are to be used for responsibility accounting as well as for product costing. If predetermined overhead rates are used for product costing, they are normally based on overhead budgets, though sometimes they may be based on estimated costs. For responsibility accounting, overhead budgets are virtually inevitable.

Because the structure of an overhead cost system is different when overhead budgets are used and when historical overhead costs are used for cost control and product costing, system design tasks also differ. Hence, these tasks are enumerated below by the type of overhead cost system.

## Overhead Cost System Based on Standards and Budgets

1. Determine the cost accounting methods and techniques to be used and decide related key issues.
2. Prepare an outline of the manufacturing overhead cost system and establish an input-output relationship.
3. Establish the necessary responsibility centers and cost centers.
4. Suitably classify manufacturing overhead costs.
5. Select appropriate activity units and determine activity levels for overhead budget preparation.
6. Set standards for individual overhead cost items and develop procedure for the preparation of overhead budgets by responsibility centers.
7. Select bases for primary allocation of overhead.
8. Select bases for secondary allocation of overhead, i.e., allocation of the costs of service centers to production centers.
9. Decide bases and other related issues for overhead absorption.
10. Design a manufacturing overhead reporting system.
11. Design an accounting system for accumulation, allocation, and absorption of overhead.

When predetermined overhead rates are to be based on estimated costs, all the tasks will be the same, except that tasks 5 and 6 will be less systematic and the overhead cost estimates will not be as scientific and reliable as overhead budgets, particularly if the budgets are based on standards.

**Overhead Cost System Based on Historical Costs** When actual overhead costs are used, the questions of selecting activity units, determining activity levels, setting standards, and preparing budgets do not arise. However, all tasks except tasks 5 and 6 will be necessary if historical overhead costs are used for product costing and cost control.

## Task 1: Selection of Cost Accounting Methods and Techniques

Decisions on the following six issues are so fundamental to the design of a manufacturing overhead cost system that they should be made quite early in the design process. (The first four issues have already been discussed more fully in Chapters 6 and 7.)

*a.* What techniques (standard costing, budgeting, etc.) are to be employed for controlling manufacturing overhead costs?

*b.* Will cost accounting be on a historical cost basis or a standard cost basis?

*c.* Will the job order cost method or the process cost method be employed?

*d.* Will product costing be based on *direct costing or full absorption costing?* A company may use one basis for some purposes and the other basis for other purposes, in which case the cost system must be flexible enough to permit the use of both techniques. Further, the concepts of direct costing and full absorption costing are often modified in practice. For example, for divisional performance evaluation, some companies do not allocate corporate joint costs which cannot be allocated except on some questionable or arbitrary basis but allocate the joint costs incurred by a division to its various products.

*e.* If full absorption historical costing is to be used for product costing, will overhead be applied on a *predetermined basis* or an *actual basis?* The absorption of overhead involves two factors: the amount of overhead cost (numerator) to be applied and the basis (denominator) on which the amount of overhead is applied. Hence, theoretically there are four different alternatives, as follows:

| Type of Overhead Rate | Numerator | Denominator |
|---|---|---|
| Pure actual rate | Actual | Actual |
| Mixture of actual and predetermined rates | Actual | Predetermined |
| | Predetermined | Actual |
| Pure predetermined rate | Predetermined | Predetermined |

Usually, however, pure actual or pure predetermined overhead rates are used. In resolving this issue, the objectives of the cost system, the nature of the manufacturing activities, and the type of manufacturing overhead should be considered. For example, if actual cost figures are required, say, for a cost-plus contract, predetermined overhead rates cannot be used. If, during winter months, the heating bill is very high compared with the bill during the remaining months, heating costs will preferably be allocated by taking the annual figure; the basis for allocation may be actual or predetermined. If, on the other hand, production volume fluctuates widely from season to season, the production figures used as a basis for application of fixed overhead should be computed by averaging estimated annual production figures; the fixed overhead amount may be actual or estimated. For eliminating the effect of seasonal fluctuations and for timely computation of product costs, predetermined rates are better than actual rates.

A survey conducted by the National Association of Accountants (NAA) as far back as 1951 reveals that an overwhelming majority of companies employed predetermined rather than historical overhead rates.[1] Further, if predetermined overhead rates are used, they are based on an overhead budget with or without standard costs.

*f.* If, for product costing, the full absorption costing method is used, should a *plantwide single overhead rate* or individual *departmental rates* be used for allocating overhead? When different cost conditions exist in different areas of a plant and more than one product is produced, individual departmental rates normally will give a more accurate cost of production. Even when the process time for different products in each department is the same, departmental rates may be desirable if the volume of production of various products is not the same.

Usually, if a company produces a single product with only one brand and if the production process is very simple, it may not be necessary to use departmental overhead rates. On the other hand, even if a company produces only one product of only one variety (e.g., television sets or automobiles) but the production process involves a number of operations, it may be worthwhile to use departmental rates for make-or-buy analysis, inventory valuation, etc.

### Task 2: Preparation of Outline of a Manufacturing Overhead Cost System

Having determined the requirements, i.e., the output of the manufacturing overhead cost system and the cost methods and techniques to be

[1] "Practice in Applying Overhead and Calculation of Normal Capacity," *NAA Bulletin*, vol. 19, 1951.

used, the designer should answer these questions:

- What is the input (cost and quantitative) information required to develop the required output information?
- How should the input information be processed to generate the desired output information?

To start with, the designer should determine a tentative routing of overhead costs to achieve the desired output information. An illustration will make this point clear.

**Illustration** A company publishes five daily newspapers and eleven magazines and also has a job department which undertakes outside printing and publishing jobs. The company requires a cost accounting system to compute the costs of each newspaper, magazine, and job and of the job department as a whole. The outside consultant determines the tentative routing of the overhead costs as shown in Exhibit 11-1.

The entire manufacturing department is classified into service departments and production departments. The production departments consist of a rotary press where newspapers are printed, a gravure press where magazines are printed, and the job department. Its products are five daily newspapers, eleven magazines, and individual outside jobs.

It is tentatively decided that total manufacturing overhead costs will be allocated to (1) service departments, (2) production departments, (3) individual newspapers (e.g., news-gathering expenses incurred exclusively for individual newspapers), and (4) individual magazines. Certain joint overhead costs will not be allocated.

The costs charged to service departments will be allocated to three production departments and to individual newspapers and magazines. The production departments' costs will be allocated to individual newspapers, magazines, and jobs. Thus, manufacturing overhead costs charged to individual newspapers and magazines will consist of:

- Overhead costs directly charged to them.
- Certain service centers' costs directly charged to them.
- Production departments' costs charged to them. The production departments' costs will consist of directly charged overhead costs as well as costs of service departments allocated to them.

## Summary Tabulation of a Manufacturing Overhead Cost System

Having prepared a conceptual outline of the manufacturing overhead cost system, the designer should prepare a table for summarizing the various components of the system as he designs them. An illustrative tabulation is given in Exhibit 11-2.

**EXHIBIT 11-1**

**Routing of Manufacturing Overhead Costs of a Publishing Company**

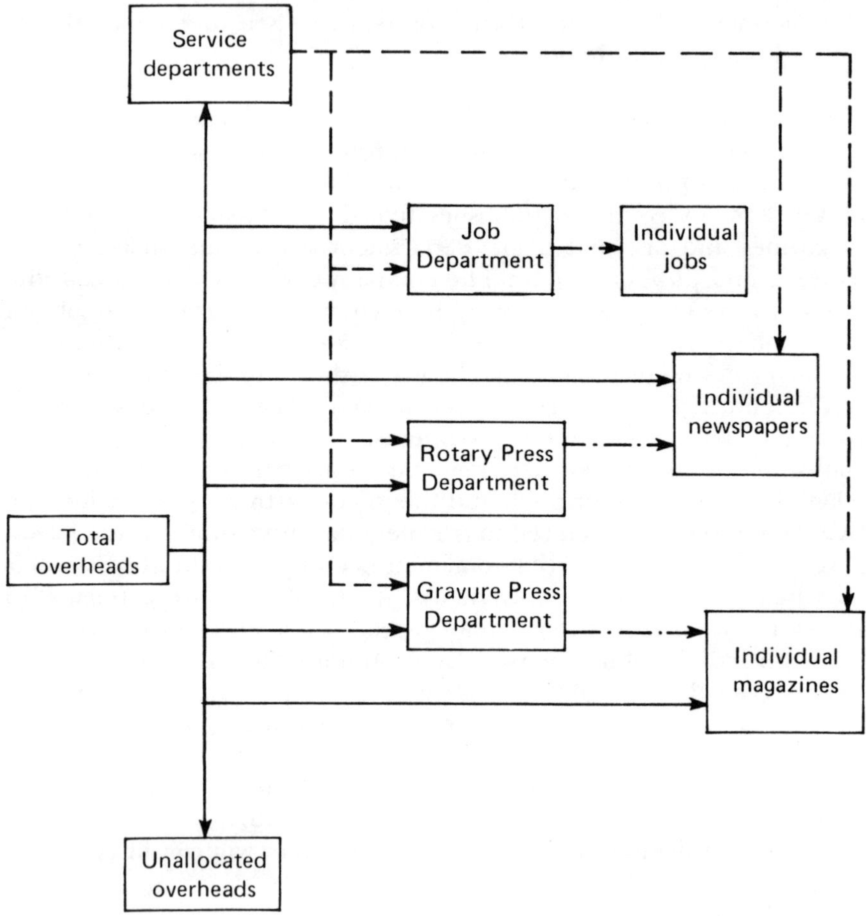


NOTES:

→ = primary allocation.

- - → = secondary allocation.

-·-·→ = overhead absorption.

**EXHIBIT 11-2**

## Summary of a Manufacturing Overhead Cost System (a Publishing Company)

| | | Cost-Responsibility Center (See Task 3) | | | | | | | |
|---|---|---|---|---|---|---|---|---|---|
| | | Service Centers | | | | | Production Centers | | |
| | | Unallocated Costs | Repairs | Inspection | Occupancy | Storeroom | Rotary Press | Gravure Press | Job Department |
| Activity Unit (See Task 5) → | | | | | | | | | |
| Overhead Costs (See Task 4) | Direct Charging or Basis for Allocation (See Tasks 7 and 8) | | | | | | Equipment-Hours | Equipment-Hours | Direct Labor–Hours |
| Supervisory salaries | Direct | | X | | | | | | |
| Clerical salaries | Direct | | | | | | | | |
| Indirect labor | | | | | | | | | |
| Material handlers | | | | | | | | | |
| Mechanics | | | X | | | | | | |
| Electricians | | | X | | | | | | |
| Janitors | | | | | | | | | |
| . . . | | | | | | | | | |
| Indirect materials | From material requisitions | | | | | | | | |
| Maintenance materials | | | X | | | | | | |
| Power | Meters in large cost centers and horsepower ratings or engineering estimates elsewhere | | | | | | | | |
| *Secondary allocation* | | | | | | | | | |
| Repairs Department | Budgeted repair-hours | | | | X | X | X | X | X |
| Inspection Department | Budgeted inspection-hours | | | | | | X | X | X |
| Occupancy | Budgeted floor area occupied | | X | | | X | X | X | X |
| Basis for overhead absorption (see task 9) | | Not applicable | | | | | Standard equipment-hours | Standard equipment-hours | Standard direct labor–hours |

NOTE: Not all the columns in this exhibit have been filled in.

In one form Exhibit 11-2 provides space for summarizing the responsibility centers and cost centers established, classifying manufacturing overhead costs by nature and cost-responsibility centers, activity units for individual centers, bases for primary and secondary allocation of overhead costs, and bases for absorption of overhead costs. It also shows to which departments the cost of each service center will be allocated.

### Task 3: Establishment of Necessary Responsibility Centers and Cost Centers

The process of establishing responsibility centers and cost centers is explained and illustrated in Chapter 8, and hence it is not repeated here. It may, however, be emphasized that if departmental overhead rates are to be used for product costing, individual departments must be established as separate cost centers. Similarly, even if a plantwide single overhead rate is to be used, it may be necessary to set up different cost centers for cost control purposes though not for product costing.

Further, various cost centers of the production department are divided into production centers (departments responsible for the production of goods) and service centers (departments which are auxiliary to production departments).

### Task 4: Classification of Manufacturing Overhead Costs

For standards setting, budgeting, accumulation, allocation, absorption, and reporting, it is necessary to classify manufacturing overhead in a suitable manner. The following are the common ways of classifying manufacturing overhead costs:

- By nature of expenses (supervisory salaries, indirect labor, operating, supplies, rent, etc.)
- By responsibility centers and cost centers
- By cost behavior (separation of variable and fixed costs)
- By controllability (separation of controllable and noncontrollable costs)

Thus, there may be a four-way classification of overhead. For product costing as well as for cost control, all overhead should be classified by the nature of expenses. If departmental overhead rates are to be used for product costing, overhead should also be classified by cost centers. For responsibility accounting or cost control, overhead should be classified by responsibility centers. Further, certain overhead expenses which are common to more than one cost center are accumulated by *objective expense accounts* to facilitate budgeting and allocation of these costs. In effect, these expense accounts are cost centers. Examples of objective expense accounts are building expenses, depreciation, insurance, property taxes, etc.

Whether or not overhead costs should be classified by behavior depends upon (1) whether fixed and variable overhead costs are to be allocated separately for product costing and various cost analyses and (2) whether overhead costs are controlled through variable budgets or fixed budgets. When product costing is based on direct costing, only variable manufacturing overhead costs are included in product costs, and hence separation of fixed and variable overhead is imperative. When product costing is based on full absorption costing, both fixed and variable overhead costs are included in product costs, and hence separation of fixed and variable overhead is not necessary. However, classification of overhead into variable and fixed categories is very helpful for product pricing, profit planning, and various cost-benefit analyses for managerial decision making. Hence, even when full absorption costing is used for product costing, overhead costs are often separated into fixed and variable elements.

Classification of overhead into variable and fixed categories is essential for using a variable budgeting technique for cost control purposes. Without such a classification, it is not possible to provide a proper budget allowance for the level of activity actually attained. For cost control purposes, overhead should be further classified into controllable and noncontrollable categories, as explained in Chapter 6.

To make the cost system flexible enough to satisfy several cost information needs, multiple classification of overhead is advisable, provided the clerical cost of classification and record keeping is not prohibitive. In a computer-based cost system, multiple classification can be achieved without any significant additional cost because once expense vouchers have been properly coded, multiple classification of overhead will be effected by the computer itself.

To achieve proper understanding and to facilitate preparation of overhead budgets, a cost accounts and cost centers matrix classifying overhead expenses by nature of expenses, by cost behavior, and by cost centers should be prepared (see Exhibit 11-2).

## Guidelines for Classification of Overhead by Cost Behavior

The following guidelines will be useful for classifying overhead by cost behavior:

1. Costs are fixed only within a given range of volume of activity, and hence it is necessary to define that range or to estimate costs for more

than one level of activity. Definition of the range of activity within which a cost item is fixed is essential for flexible budgeting, incremental costing, and several other purposes.

2. Not all costs are either strictly variable or strictly fixed. Some costs are semivariable or semifixed, and these should be separated into fixed and variable components by using one or more of these methods: (*a*) scatter diagram, (*b*) regression analysis, (*c*) high-low points method, (*d*) industrial engineering study, and (*e*) judgment method based on analysis and survey.

3. Often, on practical considerations and to avoid undue expense in segregating certain semivariable costs into variable and fixed categories, these costs may be classified as either fixed or variable according to their predominant characteristics.

4. Some costs may increase at one rate with an increase in the volume of activity and decline at another rate with a decrease in the volume of activity.

5. The classification of indirect labor into variable and fixed categories poses some problems. It is governed by the following major considerations:

- Union contract regarding job security, transfer from one work assignment to another, minimum hours of work, overtime, etc.
- Company policy regarding layoffs, transfers, etc.
- Nature of work

Hourly-paid workers who will be laid off with a decrease in the volume of activity should be classified as variable. Employees, hourly-paid or salaried, who can be transferred to alternative work assignments when they do not have enough work should be classified as variable. However, if workers are specialists or if under a contract they cannot be assigned to alternative work, they should be classified as fixed. For example, repair workers usually can be utilized for setup and even for machine operation and hence should be classified as variable. On the other hand, inspectors may not be assignable to other jobs or may be required in a particular department to ensure an even flow of production; in these cases they should be classified as fixed. For better labor cost control, as much indirect labor as possible should be classified as variable.

6. Generally, employee benefits costs should be classified as variable or fixed depending upon whether relevant salaries or wages are classified as variable or fixed. However, one large company classifies employee benfits costs into fixed and variable categories for product costing but regards them all as fixed for cost control purposes.

7. Standby costs (standby power generator, equipment, labor, etc.) are fixed in nature. However, temporary labor and rental of equipment, space, etc., are not necessarily fixed or variable: all depends upon the facts of each case.

8. It is always better to note the relevant range of activities over which costs are fixed or variable and the reasons for classifying expenses as fixed or variable because reclassification may be necessary when conditions change. Reclassification may also be necessary for certain managerial decisions.

## Task 5: Selection of Activity Units and Determination of Activity Levels

For controlling overhead as well as for developing predetermined overhead rates, it is advisable to prepare overhead budgets by cost centers. Under standard costing, the preparation of overhead budgets involves four steps:

*a.* Selection of an appropriate activity unit for each cost center (e.g., kilowatthours for a powerhouse).

*b.* Establishment of standards for each overhead item incurred by a cost center and relating them to the activity unit (e.g., so much per kilowatt of power generated by the powerhouse).

*c.* Determining an activity level for the budget year for each cost center.

*d.* Budgeting an amount for each of the overhead items by multiplying *b* and *c*. If overhead budgets are not based on standard costs, step *b* will involve estimation instead of standards.

Selecting appropriate activity units and determining expected levels of activity for the budget year are necessary not only for development of overhead budgets but also for allocation of overhead costs of service centers to production centers and absorption in product costs of overhead costs of production centers.

The activity unit is selected while the system is being designed; it remains in effect until it is revised. On the other hand, the activity level is determined separately for every budget period.

Steps *a* and *c* are explained below, and steps *b* and *d* are explained under "Task 6: Standards Setting and Budget Preparation."

### Selection of Activity Unit

Two criteria should be used in selecting an activity unit for a cost center: the unit should clearly measure the activity of a cost center, and it should be the most closely related causal factor for overhead in that cost center; i.e., overhead incurred by the cost center should fluctuate with the fluctuations in the activity unit selected. For example, the repairs and maintenance department's costs will vary with the volume of repairs and maintenance jobs, utility consumption, etc. Admittedly, this selection is easier said than done because in a cost center not all costs may vary with one activity base. Hence, care is required in budgeting costs for each cost center.

Some of the commonly used activity units for various *service centers* are maintenance-hours, utility consumption (kilowatthours, gallons, etc.), quantity or value of materials to be handled, inspection-hours, and production-planning time. For service centers, usually an input base (e.g., inspection-hours) is better than an output base (e.g., production volume) because the centers' costs are a function of input and not of output and because input may not always vary proportionately with output.

The commonly used activity units for *production centers* are machine-hours, direct labor–hours, and production volume. In selecting an activity unit for a production cost center, the following points may be noted:

- If production is primarily mechanized, machine-hours may be more appropriate than other activity units. Machine-hours may be computed for individual machines (in this case individual machines become separate cost centers) or for a group of machines, depending upon similarity of operations and machine-hours utilized for various products, jobs, etc.
- If production is predominantly manual, direct labor–hours may be selected as an activity unit.
- What if direct labor and machines are equally predominant? If direct labor–hours are proportionate to machine-hours, either basis may be used. If, however, most direct labor employees work on machines, machine-hours will usually be the better choice. Sometimes, however, direct labor–hours are used because they are easily available. If most direct labor employees do not work on machines, it will probably be better to divide the production department and organize labor-oriented and mechanized operations into two separate production cost centers.
- If the production department produces a single product and a single variety, the production unit is the most equitable and simple activity unit to use.
- Generally, overhead accrues on a time basis, and so also does direct labor. Hence, whenever the choice is not clear, direct labor–hours should be used as a base.

### Activity Level

An activity level may be determined at any one of four levels:

1. *Theoretical capacity.* The installed maximum capacity or the gross available capacity. This level is rarely used.

2. *Practical capacity.* The production capacity which is practical to achieve. It is arrived at by deducting from theoretical capacity the production time lost because of weekends, holidays, plant shutdowns, inventory taking, production jams, waiting, etc.

3. *Expected annual sales volume.* The practical capacity minus the idle or underutilized capacity due to inadequacy of demand. For service centers, expected sales volume means expected utilization (expected utilization of available repair-hours, etc.).

4. *Expected normal sales volume.* The average expected sales volume over a few years. It usually coincides with the business cycle period applicable to the industry under consideration.

If sales volume does not fluctuate from year to year, level 3 will be more or less equal to level 4. If idle capacity is not significant, levels 2, 3, and 4 will be more or less equal.

**Impact of Different Activity Levels** Different activity levels have an impact on overhead rate, overhead variances, product cost, and selling prices based on product cost, each of which is explained below.

1. *Overhead rate.* Different activity levels have an impact only on the fixed overhead rate because only fixed overhead costs do not vary with the volume of activity. For a given year, the fixed overhead rate or the composite overhead rate will vary inversely with the volume of activity selected. For example, it will be higher in the case of expected sales volume and lower in the case of practical capacity. The following illustration will clarify this point:

Data

| | |
|---|---|
| Budgeted fixed overhead | $720,000 |
| Theoretical capacity | 10,000 machine-hours |
| Practical capacity | 9,000 machine-hours |
| Capacity based on expected annual sales volume | 8,000 machine-hours |
| Capacity based on expected normal sales volume | 7,500 machine-hours |

Fixed Overhead Rates on Four Bases

| Theoretical Capacity | Practical Capacity | Expected Annual Sales Volume | Expected Normal Sales Volume |
|---|---|---|---|
| $\frac{\$720,000}{10,000}$ = $72 | $\frac{\$720,000}{9,000}$ = $80 | $\frac{\$720,000}{8,000}$ = $90 | $\frac{\$720,000}{7,500}$ = $96 |

For the sake of clarity, it may be pointed out that the expected annual sales volume may be higher or lower than the expected normal sales volume.

Under theoretical capacity, practical capacity, and expected normal sales volume, the overhead rate from year to year usually will not fluctuate except for the change in the overhead amount. However, if the expected annual sales volume is used as an activity level, the overhead rate may vary from year to year also because of the variation in the activity level.

2. *Volume or utilization variance.* When theoretical or practical capacity is used as an activity level, the underutilization of capacity will be measured through volume variance or underabsorbed fixed overhead. In case of an overhead rate based on expected sales volume, the cost of estimated idle capacity will be built into the standard or budgeted overhead rate. Hence, volume variance will not arise unless the actual production volume is different from the projected production volume based on the expected annual sales volume.

3. *Product cost.* Because of the lower base in the case of expected annual sales volume, the product cost will be higher than that in the case of theoretical or practical capacity. If the expected annual sales volume is lower than the expected normal sales volume, the product cost will be higher under the former, and vice versa.

4. *Price setting.* Because the product cost varies inversely with the size of the base used for computing the overhead rate, selling prices set on the basis of the expected annual sales volume will be higher when the expected sales volume is lower and lower when the expected sales volume is higher.

The choice of an activity level concept is governed by management preference and the purpose for which cost information is required. The designer should explain the implication of each concept and help management select the most appropriate activity level. More than one activity level may be used to meet different objectives, and in this case books of account may be kept on one of the bases and other bases used on a memorandum basis. For example, if the expected annual sales volume is used as a basis for cost-plus contracts, the extent of capacity underulitization and its impact on standard costs may be shown by a report prepared from memorandum records based on practical capacity.

The starting point for setting activity levels for production centers is the production quantity budget, which in turn may be based on the sales quantity budget. From the production quantity of each product, direct labor–hours, etc., are budgeted. Activity levels for service centers are derived from activity levels for production centers; e.g., the activity level for an equipment maintenance center will depend upon budgeted equipment-hours in production centers. Hence, care should be used to ensure that the service center activity levels are consistent with the activity levels of the related production centers.

### Task 6: Standards Setting and Budget Preparation

We saw in Chapter 6 that the techniques of both standard costing and budgeting can be employed to control manufacturing overhead. Further, these two techniques can also be employed to predetermine overhead rates for product costing. For overhead cost control, flexible budgets are usually better than fixed budgets, but for product costing fixed budgets usually are adequate.

As in the case of standards for direct materials and direct labor, standards for overhead are set while a standard cost system is being designed and remain in force until they are revised. When current standards are used, standards are usually reviewed annually and revised whenever necessary. In any case, overhead budgets are prepared separately for each budget period even though there may be no changes in standards.

The general guidelines for setting standards and the designer's role in setting standards explained in Chapter 6 also apply to setting standards for overhead. Here, first, the procedures for setting standards and preparing budgets for service centers and production centers are summarized, and then the process of setting standards and preparing budgets for individual items of overhead is explained.

### Standards Setting and Budget Preparation for Service Centers

Service centers include repairs and maintenance, material handling, storekeeping, utilities, production planning, inspection, quality control, personnel, timekeeping, cost accounting, general factory administration, and the like. The responsibility for controlling the costs of service centers is shared by the service centers providing the various services and the cost centers using or consuming the services. The latter are responsible for the volume of demand for the various services, and the former are responsible for their supply, quality, and unit rates or costs.

Because of this split responsibility, it is advisable to adopt a *sold-service concept* for controlling the costs of service centers. Under this concept, services are sold to the user centers at *predetermined rates;* i.e., users are charged only for actual services consumed at budgeted or standard rates. Thus, a service center is held responsible for variances in the unit cost of providing a service and for the quality of the service but not for an increase in costs caused by an increase in demand for the service by the user centers. Similarly, users are accountable only for the quantity of service consumed and for related costs but not for an increase in costs not caused by an increase in demand for the service. This concept is illustrated later in this chapter for a repairs and maintenance service center.

For product costing, all costs of a service center are eventually charged to the production centers benefiting from it. When budgeting and standard costing are used, predetermined charging rates are employed for this purpose; they are based on service centers' overhead budgets.

To develop a *predetermined charging rate* for a service center, the following steps are necessary:

1. Budget the quantity of the service required during the budget year. This budget may be based on engineered standards (say, so many standard repair-hours per 1000 machine-hours) or on estimates from historical data adjusted for expected changes. As explained earlier, it is better to relate the budgeted quantity of the required service to the input of user departments than to their output.
2. Budget the number, hours, or quantity of supervisory personnel, indirect labor, indirect materials, and other expenses required to provide the budgeted quantity of the service. Again, this budget may be based on engineered standards or on estimates from historical data.
3. Budget the rates or prices for each indirect labor force, material, and expense.
4. Multiply the results of steps 2 and 3 to arrive at the total budgeted cost for each service center.

For some expenses, instead of steps 2, 3, and 4, the total dollar amount itself may be budgeted, the point in case being purchased maintenance.

5. Compute the predetermined charging rate by dividing total budgeted costs by the budgeted quantity of the service. If costs are classified into variable and fixed categories, two separate predetermined rates are computed for product costing. For cost control purposes, fixed costs are allocated at the budgeted amount based on the *budgeted volume* of services required. Variable costs are charged at the predetermined rate for the *actual volume* of services provided.

## Standards Setting and Budget Preparation for Production Centers

Six steps are involved in setting standards and preparing budgets for production centers:

1. Determine the activity level for each production center.
2. Establish standards for indirect materials, indirect labor costs, and

other overhead expenses applicable to each production center. Preferably, separate quantity and rate standards should be established for each cost item.

3. On the basis of the activity level and the standards established, budget indirect labor costs, indirect materials, and other directly applicable overhead expenses for each production center.

4. Allocate budgeted objective expenses (occupancy expenses, insurance, property taxes, etc.) and service center costs to production centers.

5. Depending upon prior decisions, all budgeted overhead for each production center may be separated into variable and fixed expenses as well as into controllable and noncontrollable expenses.

6. For product costing as opposed to cost control, divide the budgeted overhead amount for each center by the activity level and determine the overhead absorption rate. When applicable, overhead absorption rates should be computed separately for variable and fixed expenses. For cost control purposes, budgeted costs are used as a yardstick for actual costs.

## Standards Setting for Indirect Materials: Steps and Guidelines

Indirect materials include operating supplies such as lubricating oils, greases and rags, maintenance materials, small tools, etc. Each of these materials should be identified with individual cost centers.

For estimating the usage of indirect materials in each cost center any one or more of these techniques may be used: engineering study, analysis of historical consumption data, and estimates by the manufacturing department. Care should be taken to select a normal and sufficiently large period. If possible, a trend over a few years should be studied. In the case of a falling trend, the latest usage should be taken as a base figure, which should be adjusted upward or downward for any known changes in material quality, plant condition, and other relevant factors.

Then, as in the case of direct materials, indirect material price standards should be set. If it is not practical or necessary to set quantity and price standards separately, cost standards should be established directly.

Current cost reduction goals or claims should be incorporated in the standards set for indirect materials. Further, variable and semivariable indirect material usage or cost standards should be related to the volume of production, machine-hours, direct labor–hours, maintenance-hours, etc.

## Standards Setting for Indirect or Service Labor: Steps and Guidelines

Indirect or service labor employees include repair and maintenance workers, janitors, production planners, schedulers, production dispatchers, material handlers, storekeepers, quality controllers, and the like. For setting standards for indirect labor, the following procedure may be followed:

1. Identify each service labor category with the cost centers responsible for it and the user cost center.
2. If employees' time cannot be fully utilized on their regular jobs, consider whether they can be assigned to alternative work to utilize their time fully.
3. Set time standards for each type of indirect labor in each cost center by any of the following techniques:
    - Industrial engineering study, i.e., time and motion study
    - Analysis of historical data
    - Estimates by the manufacturing department

In some cases, standards may be set in terms of the number of employees required, e.g., one supervisor, three inspectors, etc. However, even in the case of nontransferable labor, setting the standard time helps in understanding the extent of its utilization. For example, setting the standard inspection time per unit quantity to be inspected helps in understanding the extent of utilization of inspectors' time. This knowledge also helps in increasing or decreasing the labor force with fluctuations in the volume of activity.

4. As in case of direct labor, set indirect labor rate standards.
5. The time and rate standards should incorporate current cost reduction goals or claims.
6. Relate variable and semivariable indirect labor standards to the number of pieces of equipment, volume of production, machine-hours, direct labor–hours, etc. For example, material-handling time may be related to the quantity of material to be handled, janitorial time to floor space to be cleaned, maintenance time to machine-hours, direct labor–hours, or number of pieces of equipment, and so on.
7. As in case of direct labor, prepare a staffing (manning) table of indirect labor whenever indirect labor is significant.

### Standards Setting and Budget Preparation for Direct Labor Costs Chargeable to Manufacturing Overhead

Usually, the following direct labor costs are charged to manufacturing overhead of the relevant production centers:

- Idle time or time lost because of waiting for materials, instructions, etc.
- Rework time, the time required for correcting defective production

- Learning time, the time required by new workers to learn the job
- Overtime premium
- Shift premium
- Transfer labor difference, i.e., the positive or negative difference between the normal labor rate for the production cost center and the rate of excess labor of another cost center utilized by the production cost center

Time standards are fixed for idle time and rework time on the basis of past experience, adjusted for expected changes for the year to which these standards will be applied. Usually, both these standards are expressed as percentages of direct labor–hours.

Learning time is estimated by each cost center every year after considering new hirings and the center's learning-curve experience. Overtime and shift premium rate standards normally are part of a union contract or are established by management. Overtime and shift hours are determined from the staffing table for direct labor after considering, of course, the provisions, if any, in the union contract about overtime and shift hours.

### Standards Setting and Budget Preparation for Objective Expense Accounts

Most overhead costs are budgeted directly in the overhead budgets of the respective cost centers. However, certain overhead costs cannot be directly assigned to individual cost centers and hence are first budgeted separately by objective expense accounts. Common objective expense accounts are as follows:

- Employee benefits
- Utility costs
- Occupancy or building expenses
- Depreciation
- Insurance
- Property taxes

For cost control as well as for product costing, these expenses are budgeted for each budget year and usually are classified into variable and fixed categories.

If possible, for product costing a part of these expenses may be assigned directly to a cost center (e.g., if an insurance premium paid on inventory has been separately computed, it can be assigned directly to the storekeeping cost center). The balance of the expenses is allocated to various cost centers on some equitable basis.

Most of these costs can be controlled in total only by the company and not by individual cost centers. For example, occupancy costs can be controlled in total by the company but not by individual cost centers, although the centers are responsible for effective use of the space occupied by them. Similarly, individual cost centers cannot control the rates of purchased electricity, but they certainly can control electricity consumed by them. These factors should be reflected in the budgets and in the responsibility reports by segregating costs not controllable by individual cost centers from costs controllable by them. The procedure for budgeting each of these expenses is discussed below.

**Employee Benefits Costs** First, define the costs to be classified as employee benefits costs. Usually, employee benefits costs consist of costs related to direct and indirect labor costs incurred by the company, whether or not paid directly to employees and whether or not voluntarily incurred. Examples of employee benefits costs are payroll taxes, vacations, and medical insurance.

Study union contracts, company policy and practices, applicable labor laws, etc., and determine the basis for budgeting each applicable item of employee benefits. Usually, employee benefits costs are budgeted separately for hourly labor and salaried employees because often there are differences in respective benefits and also because there may be differences in their application. For example, some companies treat vacations and holidays as a benefit for hourly labor but as a part of salaries for salaried employees.

Then, on the basis of the labor force budget and the bases for budgeting various employee benefits costs, budget total employee benefits costs. Compute the total cost of benefits for hourly labor as a percentage of budgeted total hourly wages for the budget year. Similarly, compute the cost of benefits for salaried employees as a percentage of total salaries budgeted for the year.

For each cost center, budget employee benefits costs separately for hourly labor and salaried employees by applying the percentages arrived at in the preceding computation to the respective hourly wages and salaries of the cost center. If salaries and wages have been classified into fixed and variable categories, the employee benefits costs budgeted for a cost center should also be so classified.

There is no standard practice for the treatment of employee benefits costs for product costing and cost control. For example, one large company manufacturing consumer products separates employee benefits costs into fixed and variable costs for product costing but treats them as fixed costs for cost control. Some persons even advocate that employee benefits costs should form part of salaries and wages. In the opinion of the author, the best treatment of employee benefits costs *for cost control* is to segregate them into variable and fixed categories and to allocate the variable costs by applying the predetermined rate to the actual labor cost. The fixed costs either may not be allocated or may be allocated at the budgeted amount in the ratio of labor cost. In this way, the higher employee benefits costs due to the higher labor cost will be charged to the cost center using more labor, but the higher employee benefits costs due to other reasons will not be charged to the user cost centers. The latter type of costs will be controlled in the aggregate.

**Utilities** If utilities are purchased, they may be collected under an objective expense account for utilities. If they are generated in-house, a separate cost center may be set up. Depending upon the amount of cost involved and the degree of control desired, subcost centers may be set up for each of the significant utilities. For example, a petroleum refinery may set up separate subcost centers for electricity, gas, steam, compressed air, air conditioning, and water.

Standards for consumption of each significant utility in each of the cost centers should be established by an engineering study, equipment manufacturer's specifications, or an analysis of recent past consumption. These standards should be related to the measure of activity employed in the user cost center. For example, power required for running a machine can be related to equipment-hours.

In setting rate standards for purchased utilities, the basis for charging rates used by the supplier of utilities should be examined. If the utility company's tariff includes any fixed, minimum, or demand charges, there should be two rate standards, one for fixed charges and the other for variable rates applicable to the consumption quantity.

If utilities are generated in-house, the cost of generation may be classified into fixed and variable categories and dual rate standards established.

**Occupancy Expenses** Depending upon the geographic location, size, and layout of premises, several occupancy cost centers may be set up, or an occupancy cost center may be subdivided into several subcost centers. For example, if production facilities are physically located separately and if occupancy expenses are significant, two separate occupancy cost centers may be set up not only for better cost control but also for more accurate allocation of costs for product costing.

**Depreciation** To the extent possible, accounts of depreciable assets in the plant ledger should be maintained by cost centers so that budgeted depreciation can be computed by these centers. If building depreciation cannot be identified by cost centers, it should be included in occupancy expenses. Similarly, depreciation on assets which cannot be identified with specific assets should be included in general factory expenses and allocated with other general factory expenses. For standard or budgeted overhead rates, depreciation usually is computed also on fully depreciated assets and on standby equipment. If depreciation is not computed by cost centers, total budgeted depreciation other than depreciation on buildings should be allocated on the basis of the value of equipment, etc., in the relevant cost centers.

Depreciation expense, being a sunk cost, can best be controlled by proper planning and control over capital expenditures and by proper utilization of fixed assets.

**Insurance and Property Taxes** Both for product costing and for cost control, insurance and property taxes should be budgeted separately. For product costing, whenever insurance and property taxes can be identified with specific cost centers, they should be allocated directly to those centers. For example, inventory insurance premiums can be charged directly to storekeeping, building insurance to the occupancy cost center, and so on. The balance of insurance premiums and property taxes should be allocated to various cost centers on the basis of the value of property in the relevant centers. For cost control, either these two costs are not allocated or, if allocated, are treated as noncontrollable by the individual cost centers. Thus, these costs are controlled in the aggregate.

### Budget Preparation for Repairs and Maintenance and Application of Sold-Service Concept

We saw earlier that because of split responsibility in the case of service centers a sold-service concept is used for charging their costs to user cost centers. We will illustrate this concept for a repairs and maintenance service center. The steps necessary for applying this concept are as follows:

1. All types of repair and maintenance jobs required within the company should be listed and classified by cost centers. For example, they may be classified first into mechanical and electrical maintenance jobs, and then mechanical maintenance jobs may be subclassified into scheduled major maintenance (or planned or preventive maintenance) and emergency repairs.
2. Usually, the activity unit of a maintenance cost center is *maintenance-hours,* and the budgeted number of maintenance-hours (i.e., the activity level) is computed every year.
3. Whenever practicable and desirable, time standards should be established for various types of maintenance jobs separately for each cost center. A company cannot afford to set time standards for all repair jobs, nor does it need such standards. Hence, even when time standards are set for repair jobs, they are confined to a few important jobs.

Time standards may be based on time studies, engineering estimates, or an analysis of historical data. If time standards are set for repair jobs, it becomes necessary to set standards for the number of repair jobs required by each user cost center (e.g., the standards may provide that the machine shop requires two emergency repairs per 1000 equipment-hours and that each repair job requires 10 hours).

As an alternative to setting time standards for individual repair jobs, standards may be set by relating them to the underlying activity in user cost centers (e.g., 20 repair-hours per 1000 equipment-hours).

In either case, budgeted maintenance-hours can easily be computed once we know the budgeted activity level in each of the user cost centers. If neither of these methods is used, budgeted maintenance-hours by cost centers may be estimated from past actuals or on some other basis.

4. If repair and maintenance labor is responsible or available for other jobs such as setup, machine operation, etc., standard time should be established and budgeted hours computed also for those jobs.

5. Depending upon the nature and the volume of maintenance jobs, the number of repair workers available, and past experience, a staffing table showing the labor available and required, regular hours, overtime, idle time, etc., should be prepared.

6. Similarly, standards should be set and total quantity budgeted for materials, utility, and other expenses required for maintenance jobs. These standards, too, should be related to each type of repair job, total budgeted repair-hours, or activity units (equipment-hours, direct labor–hours, etc.) of the user cost centers.

7. Repairs and maintenance labor and materials rate standards should be set as in the case of direct labor and direct materials. In some cases, standards for maintenance supplies, tools, and other indirect materials may be set directly in dollar amounts and not separately for quantity and rates.

8. Cost reduction goals or claims should be incorporated in time and rate standards or in the maintenance budget.

9. On the basis of budgeted maintenance-hours and other maintenance standards, a repairs and maintenance budget should be prepared as follows:

- Maintenance labor-hours (including overtime) are converted into maintenance labor cost at applicable labor rates. (Some companies budget maintenance labor cost in the user cost centers' budgets.)
- Maintenance materials which can be directly identified with individual cost centers are budgeted separately and directly included in the budgets of the respective cost centers. Dollar amounts are computed by multiplying quantity and rates.

- Only common maintenance materials, operating supplies, and small tools are included in the repairs and maintenance budget.
- All other applicable expenses (power, depreciation, etc.) are estimated and included in the repairs and maintenance cost center's budget.
- Purchased maintenance expenses are budgeted directly in the user cost centers if identifiable, or else in the maintenance cost center budget.
- Whenever it is decided to classify costs by cost behavior, maintenance expenses are separated into variable and fixed components.

10. By dividing budgeted repair costs by budgeted repair-hours, the budgeted repair rate should be computed.

11. For preparing user centers' budgets, variable and fixed maintenance expenses are allocated as follows:
    - Variable expenses at the variable maintenance hourly rate multiplied by budgeted maintenance-hours for individual cost centers.
    - Fixed maintenance expenses as a percentage of budgeted variable expenses, or in the ratio of budgeted maintenance-hours. In a monthly budget of a user cost center, yearly fixed maintenance expenses are allocated equally (one-twelfth for each month).

12. The responsibility for controlling maintenance costs falls on the maintenance department as well as on the user departments. The former is responsible for the efficiency of expenditures on each maintenance job and the latter for the volume of maintenance jobs. To enforce this split responsibility, a job ticket is opened for each maintenance job and charged with the actual material cost and variable maintenance cost (either at standard cost per maintenance job or at actual maintenance-hours times the budgeted variable maintenance rate per hour). The total cost according to the job ticket is charged to the user cost center. In addition, each user cost center is charged for the monthly budgeted fixed repairs and maintenance costs.

If cost standards by type of repair jobs are not set, supervisors of the user cost center should control the time spent by repair workers in their departments and also initial repair job tickets, signifying their acceptance of the maintenance time charged to the cost center. If such cost standards are set, the user cost center will be charged at the standard cost for the type of job performed and the maintenance department will bear the excess cost or benefit from the cost savings resulting from the difference between actual and standard maintenance time.

The performance of the *maintenance department* is evaluated by comparing the actual maintenance cost with the flexible budget allowance, i.e., fixed maintenance costs plus variable maintenance costs (computed as explained above). The variances will reflect spending variances in fixed as well as variable costs and, if time standards have been set for individual types of repair jobs, also efficiency variances.

*User cost centers* will be responsible for variances in the actual volume of maintenance jobs from that budgeted and the accompanying costs at the budgeted hourly rate.

The following example will illustrate the last three steps.

**Illustration** The company in this illustration uses flexible budgeting for controlling maintenance costs but does not base its budgets on standard costs. The relevant data for the month of January 1981 for the Maintenance Department and one of the user departments, Department A, are given below.

| Budget Data | Total, Maintenance Department | | Allocation of Repairs and Maintenance Cost to Department A | |
|---|---|---|---|---|
| Machine-hours | | | 2,000 | |
| Repair-hours | 1,200 | | 200 | |
| Fixed costs | $ 6,000 | | $1,000 (200/1200, or one-sixth of $6,000) | |
| Variable costs | 12,000 | | 2,000 (200 × $10) | |
| Total costs | $18,000 | | $3,000 | |
| Variable rate per hour | $10 per maintenance-hour | | $1 per machine-hour | |
| **Actual Data and Flexible Budget Allowance** | **Actual** | **Flexible Budget Allowance** | **Actual** | **Flexible Budget Allowance** |
| Machine-hours | | | 2,300 | 2,300 |
| Maintenance-hours | 1,300 | 1,300[a] | 250 | 230[b] |
| Fixed costs | $ 5,500 | $ 6,000 | $1,000 | $1,000 |
| Variable costs | 14,500 | 13,000 | 2,500 | 2,300 |
| Total costs | $20,000 | $19,000 | $3,500[c] | $3,300 |

NOTES:

*a.* The flexible budget allowance for the Maintenance Department is computed for 1300 maintenance-hours. The allowance for fixed costs remains the same as originally budgeted. The allowance for variable costs is computed by multiplying 1300 hours by the hourly rate of $10.

*b.* The flexible budget allowance for repairs and maintenance costs of Department A is computed for the actual activity level of 2300 machine-hours. The allowance for fixed costs remains the same as originally budgeted, but the allowance for variable costs is increased by $300 because actual machine-hours rose by 300. If budgets were based on standard costs, the allowance for repairs and maintenance costs of Department A would have been computed on the basis of standard machine-hours earned instead of actual machine-hours.

*c.* The total flexible budget allowance of $19,000 for the Maintenance Department will be charged to various user departments; the charge will be reflected as actual costs in the user departments' cost control reports. For example, Department A has been charged $3500 out of the total amount of $19,000.

On the basis of the above data, budget variances for repairs and maintenance costs can be computed as follows:

**Budget versus Actual Comparison**

| Maintenance Department | | | January 1981 | Department A | | |
|---|---|---|---|---|---|---|
| Budget | Actual | Better (or Worse) than Budget | Description | Budget | Actual | Better (or Worse) than Budget |
| 1,200 | 1,300 | 100 | Maintenance-hours | 230 | 250 | (50) |
| $6,000 | 5,500 | 500 | Fixed costs | $1,000 | 1,000 | . . . |
| 13,000 | 14,500 | (1,500) | Variable costs | 2,300 | 2,500 | (200) |
| $19,000 | 20,000 | (1,000) | Total costs | $3,300 | 3,500 | (200) |

The negative variance of $1000 in the Maintenance Department's report reveals that it spent more money than it should have for the actual maintenance activity of 1300 hours. The negative variance of $200 in the control report of Department A reveals that it had more repair work than it should have had for its actual activity of 2300 machine-hours. Thus, the sold-service approach clearly separates responsibility for variances in maintenance costs between the Maintenance Department and the user departments.

## Task 7: Selection of Bases for Primary Allocation of Overhead

Primary allocation of overhead refers to assignment or allocation of overhead which has been classified by the nature or objective of expenses to cost centers for product costing and to responsibility centers for cost control.

For *cost control,* primary allocation of overhead is essential for measuring the performance of each responsibility center and for establishing responsibility for cost variances. These two purposes are achieved by comparing actual and budgeted costs.

For *product costing,* primary allocation is essential for computing overhead rates for ultimately charging overhead to products. Obviously, primary allocation is not required if a plantwide single overhead rate is used for overhead absorption. If, however, departmental overhead rates are used, primary allocation of overhead is necessary irrespective of whether overhead costs are applied to production on an actual basis or a predetermined basis. In the latter case, however, allocation is made of budgeted or predetermined costs, and it is made before the beginning of the period for which overhead rates are determined. In the former case, allocation is made of actual overhead costs, and it is made after they have been incurred.

Both responsibility centers and cost centers for primary allocation consist of service centers and production centers. Further, if responsibility centers and cost centers are the same, the bases for primary allocation of overhead will usually be the same. However, there may be differences in the costs allocated. For example, for responsibility accounting, expenses such as insurance, property taxes, etc., which can be controlled in total only will not be distributed to individual responsibility centers, whereas for product costing even such expenses will be distributed to individual cost centers. Similarly, if product costing is based on direct costing, fixed manufacturing overhead will not be allocated. However, for responsibility accounting even fixed overhead may be allocated.

For allocation of costs, both *monetary* and *nonmonetary cost data* are required. Nonmonetary cost data include the quantity of indirect materials or power, number of employees or direct labor–hours, space occupied, etc. Usually, nonmonetary cost data become the bases for allocation of overhead. Hence, the designer must understand the underlying nonmonetary costs for each of the cost items. To enable the designer to select proper bases for allocation of overhead, practical guidelines and procedure for selection are given below.

## Procedure and Guidelines for Selection of Bases for Primary Allocation

1. If an expense can be identified with a cost center, it should usually be *directly assigned* to that center because direct assignment results in the most equitable allocation of overhead. For example, rent paid for a building which houses only one cost center can be directly charged to the relevant cost center. Similarly, indirect materials usually can also be charged to cost centers consuming them by identifying material requisitions with cost centers; insurance paid for a powerhouse can be directly

charged to the powerhouse; and so on. However, the cost of direct assignment should not exceed the benefit derived from direct assignment.

2. If an expense cannot be identified with a cost center or if the clerical cost of direct assignment will be prohibitive, it should be *prorated* to various cost centers on an appropriate basis. For example, a proper basis for allocation of the cost of power is the quantity of power consumed by each cost center. Power consumption can be measured by installing meters in various cost centers. If this method is expensive or difficult to apply, consumption by each cost center may be estimated by engineers. Though this method will give a little less accurate result than a meter reading, it may be more practical than the direct measurement basis.

3. For selection of appropriate bases for primary allocation of overhead, three ingredients are essential: knowledge of the circumstances and conditions under which each type of expense is incurred, cost accounting knowledge, and sound professional judgment. In addition, either industrial engineering knowledge is required or industrial engineering help must be available.

Knowledge of the circumstances and conditions under which each type of expense is incurred is obtained during the fact-finding survey, particularly while preparing the resource-expense and cost center matrix (see Exhibit 3-6). During that phase, each type of overhead expense was thoroughly examined and related to one or more cost centers benefiting from or responsible for it.

4. In selecting bases for primary allocation, the following *factors* must be considered:

- The bases selected must result in as equitable and fair a distribution of overhead expenses to cost centers as possible. In other words, as far as possible the bases should ensure objective allocation of expenses.
- The bases must be practical or feasible to use.
- As far as possible, the bases must be easy to apply.
- The materiality aspect should also be considered. Relatively insignificant overhead items can be grouped together for the purpose of allocation instead of being allocated separately.

5. To ensure equitable distribution, the bases for overhead allocation should be based on any of the following *principles:*

*a.* Budgeted or actual service rendered by, use made of, or benefit derived from the expenses (for example, the allocation of building expenses in the ratio of space utilized or the allocation of electricity expenses in the ratio of electricity consumption). For the purpose of allocation, the measurement of benefit, use, etc., may be actual or be based on engineering estimates or empirical studies.

*b*. Causal factor. This principle is usually the same as that in Paragraph *a*, but sometimes there may be a difference. Let us take as an example material purchased for a cost center that is to be disposed of at a loss because the center no longer requires it. Since the cost center has received no benefit from that material, following the principle in Paragraph *a*, the center will not be charged for the loss. However, since it caused that loss, it is fair to charge it with the loss. Incidentally, though for product costing such abnormal costs may not be allocated, for responsibility accounting they should be charged to the responsibility centers responsible for their occurrence.

6. If more than one basis for allocation is available, the pros and cons of each basis should be weighed in the light of the guildelines given above, and by the process of elimination the most appropriate basis under the circumstances should be selected. Further, the objective for which cost information is required should always be borne in mind.

In short, first an attempt should be made to find a direct measurement basis, since that normally gives the most equitable apportionment of an expense. If it is not possible or practical to measure precisely the service rendered, use made, or benefit derived, then allocation may be based on engineering estimates or empirical studies.

A review of the usual bases for primary allocation of manufacturing overhead given in Exhibit 11-3 will be helpful in selecting appropriate bases for allocation. The exhibit is illustrative only, and some of the bases may not be appropriate in certain circumstances.

For preparing overhead budgets, all expenses which are directly assignable to cost centers will be budgeted also directly in the budgets of the relevant cost centers. For example, indirect materials will be directly budgeted for each cost center. Expenses (depreciation, insurance, etc.) which are to be allocated on some bases will first be budgeted separately and then allocated on the bases selected for their allocation.

## Task 8: Selection of Bases for Secondary Allocation of Overhead

Secondary allocation of overhead refers to allocation of service departments' costs to production departments. Service departments are auxiliary to production departments, and hence their costs must be included in product costing. Since production does not flow through service departments, the best way to allocate costs of service departments is to apportion them on some equitable bases to various production departments. However, secondary allocation of overhead is necessary only

**EXHIBIT 11-3**

**Usual Bases for Primary Allocation of Manufacturing Overhead**

| Overhead | Basis for Distribution |
|---|---|
| 1. Indirect labor and supervision | Direct to cost centers based on time spent |
| 2. Costs related to indirect labor (payroll taxes, fringe benefits, etc.) | Ratio of indirect labor cost |
| 3. Employee benefit costs related to direct labor | Ratio of direct labor cost |
| 4. Other overhead costs (lost time, overtime premium, etc.) related to direct labor | Direct to cost centers |
| 5. Indirect materials and supplies | Direct to cost centers based on material requisitions |
| 6. Tools | Actual or estimated consumption of tools by each cost center |
| 7. Rework and spoiled or defective work | Direct to cost centers (For responsibility accounting, causes of rework, etc., may be identified with purchasing, inspection, production, or any other department responsible for it.) |
| 8. Power | Meters or horsepower ratings of equipment |
| 9. Fuel (coal, oil, etc.) | Actual measurement or estimated consumption based on technical estimates or past studies |
| 10. Electricity for lighting, etc. | Metered or estimated consumption on survey of lights, fans, etc., in each cost center |
| 11. Water, gas, air, and other utilities | Metered or estimated consumption |
| 12. Rent, taxes, depreciation, maintenance, insurance, security, etc., pertaining to buildings | Floor area occupied by each cost center; common area included in general cost center (At first, all building expenses may be accumulated under occupancy cost center.) |
| 13. Equipment depreciation, insurance, and taxes | Direct to cost centers or allocated in the ratio of value of equipment |
| 14. Equipment maintenance | Purchased maintenance, direct to departments; in-house maintenance, distributed through maintenance cost center |

**EXHIBIT 11-3**

**Usual Bases for Primary Allocation of Manufacturing Overhead (*Continued*)**

| Overhead | Basis for Distribution |
|---|---|
| 15. Workmen's compensation insurance | Direct to cost centers or allocated in the ratio of number of employees (Where different rates are applicable for different occupations within the factory, employees may be grouped by occupations for the purpose of allocation.) |
| 16. Telephone charges based on number of calls made | Actual, if separate bills available from the telephone company (e.g., under a Centrex system it is so done), or estimated calls or number of telephone connections in each cost center |
| 17. Fixed telephone rental | Number of telephone connections |
| 18. Travel and entertainment | Direct to cost centers |

for product costing and *not for responsibility accounting* because cost control is not increased by allocation of costs of one cost center to another cost center. There is one exception to this rule. When the sold-service approach is adopted for controlling the costs of service centers, the costs of the concerned service centers are allocated to other cost centers. Further, even for product costing the question of secondary allocation will not arise if a single plantwide overhead rate is used.

The bases and procedures for secondary allocation of overhead will be the same irrespective of whether overhead costs are applied to production on an actual or a predetermined basis. In the latter case, however, budgeted or estimated overhead costs on budgeted or estimated activity levels are allocated in the beginning of the budget period, and in the former case actual overhead costs on actual activity levels are allocated at some periodical interval.

## Procedure and Guidelines for Selection of Bases for Secondary Allocation

In selecting the bases for secondary allocation of overhead, the following procedure and guidelines will be useful:

1. Thoroughly *examine the activities* of each service center and also of each production center with a view to understanding the nature and type

of services rendered by each service center to other service centers and to various production centers. On the basis of this examination, prepare a matrix showing the interrelationship of the activities of various cost centers. An illustrative matrix is given in Exhibit 11-4. The cost centers to which a service center renders services are indicated by putting an *X* in the columns of the receiving cost centers against that service center. To indicate that a service center receives benefit from and renders services to another center, a circle is put around the *X*. For example, cost center 3, Building, renders services (in terms of space, security, etc.) to cost center 15, Repairs and Maintenance, and the latter provides a maintenance service to the former.

2. Determine whether the cost of one service center is to be allocated to other service centers benefiting from it and, if so, whether a reciprocal

**EXHIBIT 11-4**

**Service Centers and Production Centers Matrix for Secondary Allocation of Overhead**

| Serial No. | Cost center | Serial number of service or production center benefited | | | | | | | | | | | | | | | | |
|---|---|---|---|---|---|---|---|---|---|---|---|---|---|---|---|---|---|---|
| | | 1 | 2 | 3 | 4 | 5 | 6 | 7 | 8 | 9 | 10 | 11 | 12 | 13 | 14 | 15 | 16 | 17 |
| | Production centers | | | | | | | | | | | | | | | | | |
| 1 | Department A | X | X | | | | | | | | | | | | | | | |
| 2 | Department B | X | X | | | | | | | | | | | | | | | |
| | Service centers | | | | | | | | | | | | | | | | | |
| 3 | Building | X | X | | ⊗ | ⊗ | X | | X | X | X | X | X | X | X | ⊗ | ⊗ | ⊗ |
| 4 | Personnel | X | X | ⊗ | | ⊗ | ⊗ | ⊗ | X | X | X | X | X | X | X | X | ⊗ | ⊗ |
| 5 | Timekeeping and payroll | X | X | ⊗ | ⊗ | | ⊗ | ⊗ | X | X | X | X | X | X | X | X | ⊗ | ⊗ |
| 6 | Employee benefits | X | X | ⊗ | ⊗ | X | | ⊗ | X | X | X | X | X | X | X | X | ⊗ | ⊗ |
| 7 | Power and electricity | X | X | | X | X | | | ⊗ | ⊗ | X | X | X | X | X | ⊗ | ⊗ | ⊗ |
| 8 | Water | X | X | | | | | | | | X | X | | | | | | |
| 9 | Fuel | X | X | | | | | ⊗ | | | | | | | | | | |
| 10 | Compressed air | X | X | | | | | ⊗ | | | | ⊗ | | | | | | |
| 11 | Steam | X | X | | | | | | | | ⊗ | | | | | | | |
| 12 | Purchasing | X | X | | | | | | | X | | | | | | | ⊗ | |
| 13 | Receiving and handling | X | X | | | | | | | X | | | | | | | | |
| 14 | Storekeeping | X | X | | | | | | | X | | | | | | | | |
| 15 | Repairs and maintenance | X | X | ⊗ | | | | ⊗ | X | | X | X | | | | | | |
| 16 | Cost accounting | X | X | ⊗ | ⊗ | ⊗ | ⊗ | ⊗ | X | X | X | X | ⊗ | X | X | X | X | ⊗ |
| 17 | Factory administration | X | X | ⊗ | ⊗ | ⊗ | ⊗ | ⊗ | X | X | X | X | X | X | X | X | ⊗ | |

distribution of costs is to be made between two service centers rendering services to each other. In deciding these two issues, the following guidelines would be helpful:

*a.* The objective of distribution of costs is to compute a reasonably accurate product cost. Hence, it can be said, as a general principle, that allocation to other service centers and even a reciprocal allocation should be made *only if* proper cost figures cannot be compiled without such an allocation. For example, usually it will not be worthwhile to allocate the cost accounting department's cost to the building center, but it may be worthwhile to allocate the building center's cost to the cost accounting department.

The aspect of materiality should be judged with reference to the total cost of the cost center (absolute amount and as a percentage of total manufacturing costs of the concern) under consideration and to the impact of nonallocation on the ultimate product cost. The impact can be measured by comparing the basis for allocating the cost of the center rendering services and the basis on which the cost of the center receiving it will be allocated to production departments. For example, if the costs of the personnel department are to be apportioned to the payroll department on the basis of the number of employees and if the costs of the payroll department also are ultimately allocated to production departments on the basis of the number of employees, it is futile to allocate the personnel department's costs to the payroll department. A better course is to combine the costs of the two departments for the purpose of allocation.

Whenever advisable and practical, service centers' costs for a trial period should be allocated on three alternative bases: direct allocation to production centers, nonreciprocal distribution to service centers, and reciprocal distribution to service centers and production centers. Then, a comparison of ultimate product costs on the three bases will show which of the three is preferable. Most often, reciprocal allocation can easily be dispensed with.

*b.* The process of allocation and reallocation should not be complex for two reasons. First, the identity of cost items will be lost, and they will therefore be less useful for managerial decisions. Second, a complex process will be expensive and time-consuming.

*c.* Even if it is decided in principle that allocation to other service departments and reciprocal allocation will be made, it is not necessary to do this in every case. A selective approach may be adopted.

3. If it is decided to make reciprocal distributions of service center costs, one of three methods must be selected: (*a*) step method, or continued distribution method, (*b*) mathematical, or simultaneous equations, method, and (*c*) trial-and-error method. Generally, the first method is preferred because of its simplicity. (Any good textbook on cost accounting will contain an explanation of these three methods.)

4. The bases for secondary distribution are grounded on any of the following *principles:*

   *a. Budgeted actual service received, capacity to use services, or use made of or benefit derived from a service center.* If variable and fixed costs are distributed separately, variable costs are allocated on the basis of budgeted, estimated, or actual usage, and fixed costs (which are usually the costs of capacity to serve) are allocated on the basis of user centers' capacity to use services.

      The measurement of service rendered, use made, etc., can be obtained from direct measurement, engineering studies, analysis or survey of existing conditions, analysis of past records, and estimates by supervisors of the concerned service cost centers.

   *b. Ability to pay.* This principle is based on the principle of "Charge what the traffic can bear." Normally, this type of basis produces an inequitable allocation of costs.

5. The four considerations involved in the selection of bases for primary allocation of overhead apply to the selection of bases for secondary allocation of overhead too. These considerations are equitable distribution of service center costs, practicality, ease in distribution, and materiality. For example, separate distribution rates normally should be computed for the distribution of overhead of separate service centers. However, for simplicity and to save clerical costs, overhead of two or more service centers may be allocated jointly on a common basis if the separate charges of these service centers are not required for managerial or other purposes.

The commonly used bases for allocation of service center costs to the user cost centers are given in Exhibit 11-5, which will be helpful in selecting appropriate bases for secondary allocation. Exhibit 11-5 is illustrative only, and some of the bases may not be appropriate under certain circumstances.

## Task 9: Procedure and Guidelines for Designing Overhead Absorption System

Once all the overhead costs of the manufacturing department have been allocated to production cost centers, it is necessary to charge these overhead costs to individual products passing through the production de-

**EXHIBIT 11-5**

**Usual Bases for Allocation of Service Centers' Overhead**

| Service Center | Basis for Distribution |
|---|---|
| 1. Powerhouse<br>2. Water<br>3. Compressed air<br>4. Steam | Consumption measured by meters, estimates by engineering studies, horsepower ratings of equipment, equipment-hours or direct labor–hours |
| 5. Central heat and air conditioning | Cubic feet of each user department |
| 6. Fuel | Consumption measured from material requisitions or other records or estimated on technical or empirical basis |
| 7. Occupancy | Space occupied |
| 8. Personnel | Rate of labor turnover or labor-hours |
| 9. Timekeeping and payroll | Number of employees in each department or labor-hours |
| 10. Employee benefits | Percent of salaries or wages |
| 11. Cafeteria | Number of employees or person-hours |
| 12. Purchasing | Loading factor applied to material cost on the basis of the number of purchase orders or the value of materials purchased (Purchasing overhead should be allocated also to material bought for resale.) |
| 13. Receiving and handling | Number of material requisitions, weight or volume of material handled, or value of material consumed (if these two functions are segregated, the former can be allocated on the basis adopted for purchasing and the latter on the basis adopted for storekeeping). Allocation should be made also to material bought for resale. |
| 14. Storekeeping | Number of material requisitions or quantity, volume, or value of material issued to each department. Allocation should be made also to material bought for resale. |
| 15. Production planning | Time spent, number of production orders, or production quantity |
| 16. Inspection and quality control | Time spent, number of inspectors assigned, quantity inspected |
| 17. Repairs and maintenance | Number of repair-hours worked or estimated cost incurred |
| 18. Cost accounting<br>19. Factory administration | Usually, it is advisable to allocate these costs only to production departments on the basis of person-hours, direct labor–hours, or quantity, volume, or other measures of production. |

partments. For this purpose, appropriate bases for overhead absorption must be selected. At this stage, the following important issues will have already been decided:

- Predetermined versus actual overhead rates
- Plantwide versus departmental overhead rates
- Separate rates for fixed and variable overhead versus a combined overhead rate

Since the process of designing an overhead absorption system is different for predetermined overhead rates and actual overhead rates, a summary comparison of the steps involved in these two systems is given in Exhibit 11-6, and each of these steps is explained below.

**Bases for Overhead Absorption** The following guidelines will be helpful in selection of an appropriate basis for overhead absorption:

1. The usual bases for overhead absorption are:
   - Machine-hours
   - Direct labor–hours
   - Direct labor cost
   - Units produced
   - Market value or sales prices (normally used in the case of joint products)
   - Direct material cost } These two bases are not very popular.
   - Prime cost }

2. The bases selected should result in an equitable application of overhead, provide reasonably accurate product cost, and be simple and economical to use. So that overhead costs are applied equitably, the base selected must be the most closely related causal factor for overhead costs in the department. Normally, if the base selected relates to the most dominant cost factor in the production department, it will give an equitable application of overhead.

3. If production is *primarily mechanized,* normally a machine-hour rate will be more appropriate than other bases. Machine-hour rates may be computed for individual machines or for a group of machines, depending upon the similarity of operations and the number of machine-hours utilized for various products, jobs, etc.

4. A machine-hour rate may be computed only for manufacturing overhead, or a *composite machine-hour rate* for direct labor and manufacturing overhead may be computed. The composite rate is preferable or essential when it is difficult to trace direct labor cost to individual production units. For example, in the case of rayon yarn, textile, and similar process industries, direct labor cost cannot be traced to individual production units, and hence a composite machine-hour rate is better.

5. If production is *predominantly manual,* direct labor–hours or cost

**EXHIBIT 11-6**

**Comparison of Steps for Developing Predetermined versus Actual Overhead Absorption System**

| Predetermined Overhead Rates | Actual Overhead Rates |
|---|---|
| 1. Select bases for overhead absorption. | Same. |
| 2. Select time period for which overhead (numerator) and base (denominator) will be estimated. | Same except that actual data will be used. |
| 3. At the beginning of the period, estimate overhead costs and activity level of each production center. | Compute actual data and base quantity at the end of the period. |
| 4. Select the time interval in which overhead will be applied. | Same. |
| 5. Determine circumstances under which overhead rates will be revised. | Not applicable. |
| *6. Determine the methods of analysis and disposition of overhead variances. | Not applicable because the question of variances does not arise. |
| *7. Design accounting and reporting systems. | Same except that the nature and the contents will differ. |

* These two topics will be discussed in Chapter 15, "Designing Cost Records and Procedures."

may be selected as a base. Direct labor cost is simpler and more economical to use than direct labor–hours, but it is usually less equitable, particularly when there is a wide difference in the wage rates of different workers within a production department.

6. If direct labor and machines are equally dominant and if labor time is proportionate to machine time, either basis can be used, but it is preferable to use direct labor–hours because these are readily available. If most of the direct labor employees work on machines, the machine-hour rate (preferably, a composite machine-hour rate) may be used. If most of the direct labor employees do not work on machines, it will probably be better to divide the production department and to organize labor-oriented and mechanized operations into two separate production centers.

7. If the production department produces a single product and a single variety, the *production unit method* is the most equitable and simplest basis to use. Usually, this basis is employed by a process industry producing on a mass scale. However, even a process industry cannot use this basis *as such* if more than one variety of the same product or more than

one product is produced. For example, in a company manufacturing rayon yarn, the production time required to produce rayon yarn varies from denier to denier. To apply overhead to the production of individual deniers, two alternative bases are available: (*a*) ratio of actual or estimated spindle-hours utilized for respective deniers and (*b*) ratio of actual or estimated equivalent production of the respective deniers. Equivalent production is computed in terms of the staple denier (120 denier) by applying a weight factor to the production of each denier; the weight factor for each denier is based on the production time difference from the staple denier.

8. Generally, overhead costs accrue on a time basis, and so also does direct labor cost. Hence, in a toss-up situation between direct labor–hours or direct labor cost and other bases, direct labor–hours or direct labor cost should be selected as a base.

9. Often, it is advisable to compute for a representative period product costs on alternative bases of overhead absorption, analyze the implications of the differences in the product costs obtained on different bases, and then make a rational selection of a basis for overhead absorption for each production center.

**Time Period for Computing Overhead and Base Quantity** The time period may be a month, a quarter, a half year, a year, a few years, etc. If the period selected is a year, the resulting overhead rate will eliminate seasonal fluctuations, if any, during the year in the overhead amount and in the base figure. If monthly or quarterly figures are used, there may be fluctuations in the overhead rates from month to month or from quarter to quarter. Further, a time span covering several years will smooth out cyclical fluctuations provided it coincides with the company's business cycle.

The decision is governed by the nature of the industry, the objectives of the cost system, and management preference. Whatever the time period employed, users of the resultant cost information must be aware of the time span used and its impact on the overhead absorbed in the product cost.

**Determine Overhead Amount and Base Quantities** For predetermined overhead rates, overhead amounts and base quantities are usually taken from standards or budgets. In the absence of standards and budgets, a reasonably accurate estimate of both these figures should be made. Since actual overhead rates are computed from historical data, the question of budgeting or estimating the numerator and the denominator does not arise. The question that does arise is how to accumulate these historical data, and this question is relevant also when predetermined rates are used. This aspect is dealt with in detail in Chapter 15.

**Time Interval for Overhead Application** Actual overhead cannot be applied as and when production is completed; it can be applied only at the periodic interval (month, quarter, etc.) at which actual overhead rates are computed. If predetermined overhead rates are used, overhead can be applied on the completion of each job or process or at monthly, quarterly, etc., intervals.

**Revising Overhead Rates** In the case of predetermined overhead rates, it is necessary to decide whether and under which circumstances overhead rates once computed for a period will be revised during that period. It is difficult for any company to lay down specific guidelines on this issue because much depends upon the purposes for which the cost information will be used, the nature of the changes in circumstances causing a potential need for revision, and management preference. If current product cost data are required, predetermined overhead rates should be revised soon after a major change occurs. Similarly, if fire, flood, earthquake, etc., have a material impact on predetermined overhead rates, it will be appropriate to revise them.

### Tasks 10 and 11: Overhead Reporting and Accounting Systems

These two tasks will be explained respectively in Chapters 14 and 15.

# Chapter 12

# Case Study: Design of Direct Material, Direct Labor, and Manufacturing Overhead Cost Systems

An example is better than a precept.
A proverb

In this chapter, with the help of the continuing case study of ACME Company, we will illustrate the process of designing a direct materials cost system, a direct labor cost system, and a manufacturing overhead cost system. This case study covers the major tasks involved in designing a cost system for both product costing and cost control. Further, it highlights the differences between a product cost system and a cost control system. The case study represents a real-life situation. The cost system development project was undertaken in the early part of 1980, and the system was to be effective on January 1, 1981.

## SYSTEM ANALYSIS TASKS

In prior chapters, we discussed the following system analysis steps completed by the designer:

1. *Definition of system objectives.* The two major objectives of the proposed manufacturing subcost system of ACME Company are:

- To provide a mechanism for adequate control over manufacturing costs.
- To develop a product cost system for computing the unit cost

and the total cost of production and for the valuation of inventory of work in process and finished products.

2. *Understanding of ACME Company's business.* The background information gathered by the designer to gain an understanding of ACME Company's business was suitably documented and given in Chapter 3.

3. *Determination of cost system requirements.* The item-by-item requirements of the proposed cost system to meet each of the above-mentioned two objectives were determined and documented in Chapter 4.

## SYSTEM DESIGN TASKS

For designing the cost system, ACME Company has engaged a firm of consultants, and a standard cost committee, consisting of a representative from the consulting firm and the controller and each of the vice presidents of the company, has been set up. The major tasks to be completed for designing an effective manufacturing cost system for the company are summarized below.

1. Select cost control techniques and cost methods.
2. Establish responsibility centers and cost centers.
3. Standardize production processes.
4. Establish product classification.
5. Prepare a flowchart of materials in production departments.
6. Classify manufacturing costs.
7. Set standards for direct materials.
8. Set standards for direct labor and production equipment time.
9. Set standards for idle time, rework time, and learning time of direct labor.
10. Set standards for available work hours.
11. Classify manufacturing overhead costs.
12. Select activity units for production centers and service centers.
13. Establish setup time standards.
14. Set standards for power consumption and rate.
15. Set standards for heat and light.
16. Set standard time for repairs and maintenance.
17. Set standards for repairs and maintenance materials.
18. Set standards for inspection time and quantity.
19. Set standards for other labor.
20. Set standards for rework materials.
21. Determine cost items for which standards will not be set.
22. Select bases for primary allocation of overhead.
23. Select bases for secondary allocation of overhead.

24. Determine the following activity levels for various cost centers for the budget year:
    - Budgeted sales quantity
    - Desired ending inventory
    - Expected opening inventory
    - Budgeted production quantity
    - Normal equipment-hours
    - Direct labor–hours and staffing (manning) table for direct labor
    - Budgeted setup time
    - Budgeted repairs and maintenance–hours
    - Budgeted inspection-hours
25. Prepare the direct materials consumption budget.
26. Prepare the direct labor budget.
27. Prepare the manufacturing overhead cost budgets and make primary and secondary allocation of overhead costs.
28. Compute budgeted overhead absorption rates for each production cost center.
29. Prepare a standard product cost sheet.
30. Prepare a summary of the overhead budgets.

Since the design process is iterative, it will be necessary to complete some of the tasks in two or more installments. Each of these tasks is explained next.

## 1. Selection of Cost Methods and Techniques

In consultation with the controller and the president of ACME Company, the designer selects the full-absorption standard process cost system for product costing and flexible budgeting in conjunction with standard costing for controlling manufacturing costs. For both purposes, "current" standards will be used.

**Product Costing** The standard product cost will be developed for the first time for the year 1981 and revised annually. For developing the standard product cost, each manufacturing cost item will be separated into variable and fixed elements. All manufacturing costs including general factory overhead and expenses of the Office of the Vice President, Manufacturing, will be distributed to all cost centers and products. For allocation of manufacturing overhead costs, individual departmental overhead rates will be used. Whenever possible, standards will be developed, though it is envisaged that the task of establishing standards for some of the overhead items may be phased over 2 to 3 years.

**Cost Control** For cost control purposes, the responsibility accounting system will be used; i.e., the entire Manufacturing Department will be divided into various responsibility centers, and the person responsible for each center will be identified by title and name (which may change from time to time).

Each responsibility center will be responsible only for costs within its control. For this purpose, manufacturing costs incurred by ACME Company will be identified with the individual responsibility centers, and only costs directly incurred by a responsibility center will be considered controllable by it. All allocated costs will be treated as controllable only by responsibility centers primarily incurring them and not by responsibility centers to which such costs have been allocated. The only exception to this rule will pertain to repairs and maintenance costs the responsibility for which is split between the repairs and maintenance cost center and the user cost centers, as explained later on.

For controlling the costs of direct materials and direct labor, a standard cost system exactly the same as that employed for product costing will be used. In addition, for controlling direct material costs and direct labor costs in the aggregate, a direct material budget and a direct labor budget will be prepared.

For controlling manufacturing overhead costs, flexible budgeting in conjunction with standard costing will be used. Each manufacturing cost item will be separated into fixed and variable elements. The standards employed will be the same as those used for product costing. However, it is here that there will be differences in the application of these two techniques for product costing and cost control. The fundamental differences will be as follows:

- Though for product costing, the costs incurred by a cost center will be allocated to other cost centers benefiting from it, for cost control all such cost allocations (except the allocation of repairs and maintenance costs) will be ignored.
- For computing the standard cost of actual production, production units will be multiplied by the standard product cost per unit. Thus, the fixed manufacturing overhead allowance included in the standard cost of actual production will also be adjusted for the actual activity level.
- For computing monthly budget allowances for cost control purposes, only variable costs will be adjusted for the actual activity level, while fixed costs will be taken at the budgeted amount only.

**Cost Control Reports** For cost control purposes, daily, weekly, monthly, and quarterly cost control reports by responsibility centers will be prepared as already documented in Exhibit 4-4. These control reports will compare actual quantitative and dollar amounts with standards or flexible budget allowances as may be appropriate.

### 2. Establishment of Responsibility Centers and Cost Centers

In Chapter 8, we dealt with the establishment of responsibility centers and cost centers for the Manufacturing Department of ACME Company. Hence, that discussion is not repeated here.

### 3. Standardization of Production Processes

Plant layout, production processes, and flow of materials are reviewed and, except for minor alterations, are found to need no change.

### 4. Establishment of Product Classification

ACME Company manufactures only two products, X and Y, which are clearly distinguishable from each other.

### 5. Preparation of Flowchart of Materials in Production Departments

Exhibit 12-1 shows the sequence of operations in the production departments, input of materials at each process, and movement of work in process from one production department to another. In actual practice, often it is also advisable to describe the operations performed by each department. Incidentally, Exhibit 3-9, the material flowchart of ACME Company prepared during the fact-finding survey, depicts the total flow of materials within ACME Company, starting with the receipt of materials from vendors and ending with the dispatch of finished products to customers. Exhibit 12-1 expands only item 7 in Exhibit 3-9. This exhibit is helpful for establishing standards for direct materials and direct labor and, to some extent, standards for manufacturing overhead.

### 6. Classification of Manufacturing Costs into Direct Materials, Direct Labor, and Manufacturing Overhead

Basically, this task involves classifying materials and labor into direct and indirect categories. All indirect materials and labor are treated as manufacturing overhead items.

**Materials** During the fact-finding survey, the designer learned that ACME Company consumes ten materials in addition to packing mate-

**EXHIBIT 12-1**

**Flow of Materials in Production Departments: ACME Company**

| Production Department | Product X | Product Y |
|---|---|---|
| Machine | Input materials B and I ↓ | Input materials B and I ↓ |
| Press | None ↓ | Add material C ↓ |
| Welding | Add materials G and H ↓ | Add materials G and H ↓ |
| Assembly | Add materials A, D, E, and F ↓ | Add materials A, D, E, and F ↓ |
| | Subassembly 1: B, G, H<br>Subassembly 2: A, D, I<br>Subassembly 3: E, F<br>↓ | Subassembly 1: B, H<br>Subassembly 2: C, G, I<br>Subassembly 3: A, D<br>↓ |
| | Final assembly ↓ | Final assembly ↓ |
| Finishing | Add Material J (paint, etc.) ↓ | Add Material J (paint, etc.) ↓ |
| Packing | Packing materials | Packing materials |

NOTE: In an actual case, the operations performed by each department usually will be described step by step, as this helps in setting direct labor standards and also in setting manufacturing overhead standards.

rials. The flowchart of materials in production departments in Exhibit 12-1 shows the materials consumed for each of the two products by the five production departments in which various materials are added. Since all these materials are directly traceable to the finished products and are significant in monetary terms, it has been decided to classify them as *direct materials.*

All other materials, which include operating supplies (oil, grease, cleaning rags, etc.), repairs and maintenance materials, and small tools and equipment, will be regarded as a part of *manufacturing overhead costs.*

**Material Losses** The direct materials required for rework, i.e., for correcting defects in either work in process or finished production, will be charged to manufacturing overhead. All other direct material losses, such as spoiled direct material, spoiled production, and scrap, are not significant and have no resale value. Hence, these losses will be included in the quantity standards for direct materials.

**Composition of Direct Material Price** The controller of ACME Company has decided to account freight in for direct materials, federal, state, and local taxes on purchases of direct materials, and other incidental expenses as a part of the direct material purchase price. Similarly, the trade discount will be deducted from the purchase price, but the cash discount will be treated as miscellaneous income. Receiving, storage, and material-handling costs will be treated as a part of manufacturing overhead costs.

**Labor** All the workers employed in the production departments work directly on the production of the two products. Hence, they will be classified as *direct labor*. The finishing shop includes packing labor, which also will be classified as direct labor.

To be clear, all other employees of the Manufacturing Department will be classified either as *indirect labor* or as *supervisory and clerical personnel.* Indirect labor consists of mechanics, electricians, janitors, and material handlers. Supervisory and clerical personnel consist of production planners, production clerk-dispatchers, supervisor of the Repairs and Maintenance Department, storekeepers, inspectors, timekeepers, personnel administrators, secretaries, cost analysts, service and administration superintendents, the production superintendent, the assistant to the plant manager, the plant manager, and the vice president, manufacturing.

Mechanics from the Repairs and Maintenance Department also do setup work in the Machine and Press Departments. Their setup time will be charged separately (as Indirect Labor—setup) to the manufacturing overhead of these two departments.

Further, the following *costs related to direct labor* will be treated as manufacturing overhead costs and not as direct labor costs:

- Employee benefits costs such as social security taxes, medical coverage, vacations, recreation, etc.
- Idle time, the time of direct workers paid for and available for work but not utilized because of a lack of work, machine breakdown, power shortage, etc.
- Rework time, the time spent by direct labor in correcting defective production.
- Learning time, the time required by new and inexperienced workers to learn the requirements of their jobs. Since initially they will be working at less than their regular efficiency, the wages proportionate to the estimated learning period will be charged to manufacturing overhead costs.

- Overtime premium and second-shift premium.
- Transfer labor difference, the excess wages paid by a production department while utilizing the idle workers of other departments who are paid at a rate higher than that of its own regular workers.

Alternatively these costs can be treated as a part of direct labor costs. For several reasons, however, it is usual to treat them as a part of manufacturing overhead costs. The designer is supposed to know the pros and cons of these two treatments, and hence only one of the major reasons is explained here. Separation of these items from regular direct labor time or cost enhances control over the items. For example, actual rework time will be accumulated separately from other productive time and compared with standard rework time for each production department. Thus, without any further analysis operating personnel and management will know the variances in rework time by production departments. If, on the other hand, rework time is built into standard direct labor time, variances in rework time will not be known without further analysis because in that case actual rework time normally will not be accumulated separately and also because standard rework time will not be available separately.

## 7. Setting Standards for Direct Materials

Following the procedure explained in Chapter 9, direct material quantity and price standards have been set for products X and Y. These standards are summarized in Exhibit 12-2, which shows the standard direct material cost of each of the subassemblies and the finished products. The standard direct material cost for 1981 comes to $76 for product X and $61.90 for product Y.

These standards were audited by the Controller's Department by comparing them with past actuals and analyzing the reasons for differences. Further, the concurrence of the supervisors of the respective production departments about the reasonableness of the quantity standards was obtained because these people will be responsible for variances in actual consumption from the standard quantity.

Both quantity and price standards will be reviewed annually. However, quantity standards are not likely to change from year to year, whereas price standards are likely to change.

## 8. Setting Standards for Direct Labor

Following the procedure explained in Chapter 10, time and rate standards have been set for direct labor in each production department. The time standards have been set separately for products X and Y. These

**EXHIBIT 12-2**

**Standard Direct Material Costs (ACME Company)**

Effective January 1, 1981

| Product and Direct Material | Quantity per Unit of Finished Product | Rate per Unit Quantity ($) | Total Cost per Unit of Product ($) | Standard Direct Material Cost by Production Cost Centers ($) | | | | |
|---|---|---|---|---|---|---|---|---|
| | | | | Machine ($) | Press ($) | Welding ($) | Assembly ($) | Finishing ($) |
| *Product X* | | | | | | | | |
| Material B | 10 kilograms | 3.50 | | 35.00 | | | | |
| Material I | 2 kilograms | 1.00 | | 2.00 | | | | |
| Material G | 0.25 kilogram | 4.00 | | | | 1.00 | | |
| Material H | 3 units | 1.10 | | | | 3.30 | | |
| Material A | 9 units | 2.50 | | | | | 22.50 | |
| Material D | 2 kilograms | 1.25 | | | | | 2.50 | |
| Material E | 2.5 kilograms | 1.00 | | | | | 2.50 | |
| Material F | 14 units | 0.30 | | | | | 4.20 | |
| Material J | 0.5 gallon | 2.00 | | | | | | 1.00 |
| Packing Materials | 1 unit | 2.00 | | | | | | 2.00 |
| Subassembly 1 | B, G, H | | 39.30 | | | | | |
| Subassembly 2 | A, D, I | | 27.00 | | | | | |
| Subassembly 3 | E, F | | 6.70 | | | | | |
| Other | J and packing | | 3.00 | | | | | |
| Total, product X | | | 76.00 | 37.00 | — | 4.30 | 31.70 | 3.00 |

| *Product Y* | | | | | | | | |
|---|---|---|---|---|---|---|---|---|
| Material B | 4 kilograms | 3.50 | | 14.00 | | | | |
| Material I | 1 kilogram | 1.00 | | 1.00 | | | | |
| Material C | 2.9 kilograms | 4.00 | | | 11.60 | | | |
| Material G | 0.25 kilogram | 4.00 | | | | 1.00 | | |
| Material H | 3 units | 1.10 | | | | 3.30 | | |
| Material A | 8 units | 2.50 | | | | | 20.00 | |
| Material D | 1.6 kilograms | 1.25 | | | | | 2.00 | |
| Material E | 2.0 kilograms | 1.00 | | | | | 2.00 | |
| Material F | 12 units | 0.30 | | | | | 3.60 | |
| Material J | 0.7 gallon | 2.00 | | | | | | 1.40 |
| Packing materials | 1 unit | 2.00 | | | | | | 2.00 |
| Subassembly 1 | B, H | | 17.30 | | | | | |
| Subassembly 2 | C, G, I | | 13.60 | | | | | |
| Subassembly 3 | A, D | | 22.00 | | | | | |
| Subassembly 4 | E, F | | 5.60 | | | | | |
| Other | J and packing | | 3.40 | | | | | |
| Total, product Y | | | 61.90 | 15.00 | 11.60 | 4.30 | 27.60 | 3.40 |

Prepared by Production Planning Department (quantity) and Purchasing Department (price)
Audited by Cost Accounting Department
Concurred by Supervisor of each production department
Approved by Production superintendent
Plant manager
Vice president, manufacturing

Date prepared ________ Date approved ________

standards are expressed in decimal numbers and summarized in Exhibit 12-3.

In the Machine and Press Departments, which are predominantly mechanized, direct labor–hours are proportionate to equipment-hours. Hence, first the standard equipment-hours for these two departments are established.

The Production Planning Department, with the help of an outside consulting industrial engineer, has established the standard machine time as follows:

Standard Equipment-Hours per Unit of Finished Product

| Product | Machine Shop | Press Shop |
|---|---|---|
| X | 0.7 hour | 0.5 hour |
| Y | 0.9 hour | 0.6 hour |

For ease in computation, the time is expressed in decimal numbers. For example, the standard time per unit of product X in the press shop is 30 minutes, or 0.5 hour.

In the Machine Department, two workers are required per machine, and therefore standard direct hours will be twice the total of standard equipment-hours. In the Press Department, since one worker is required per machine, standard direct labor–hours will be the same as standard equipment-hours.

The company pays overtime at the rate of time and a half of the regular rate and the premium for the second or third shift at the rate of 6 percent of regular pay. These rates apply to direct as well as indirect labor.

Both the quantity and the rate standards will be reviewed annually. Usually, there will be no change in labor time standards from one year to another, though labor rate standards are likely to change from year to year.

## 9. Setting Standards for Idle Time, Rework Time, and Learning Time of Direct Labor

Drawing on past experience and after considering the cost reduction goals set by company management, the production superintendent has

**EXHIBIT 12-3**

**Direct Labor Standards and Standard Machine Time (ACME Company)**

Effective January 1, 1981

| | Machine | Press | Welding | Assembly | Testing and Painting | Packing |
|---|---|---|---|---|---|---|
| 1. Standard machine-hours per unit of finished product | | | | | | |
| Product X | 0.70 | 0.50 | | | | |
| Product Y | 0.90 | 0.60 | | | | |
| 2. Standard direct labor–hours per unit of finished product | | | | | | |
| Product X | 1.40 | 0.50 | 1.00 | 1.90 | 0.60 | 0.08 |
| Product Y | 1.80 | 0.60 | 1.40 | 2.00 | 0.50 | 0.08 |
| 3. Standard idle time as percentage of standard direct labor–hours | 3 percent | 3 percent | 3 percent | 3 percent | 3 percent | 3 percent |
| 4. Standard rework time as percentage of standard direct labor–hours | 2 percent | 2 percent | 2 percent | 2 percent | 2 percent | . . . |
| 5. Standard learning time | ← To be estimated each year for each department → | | | | | |
| 6. Standard direct labor–hour rate ($) | 7.52 | 7.08 | 7.17 | 8.12 | 8.50 | 6.00 |
| 7. Standard direct labor cost per unit of finished product: | | | | | | |
| Product X ($) | 10.528 | 3.540 | 7.170 | 15.428 | 5.100 | 0.480 |
| Product Y ($) | 13.536 | 4.248 | 10.038 | 16.240 | 4.240 | 0.480 |
| 8. Overtime premium rate | ← 50 percent of normal rate → | | | | | |
| 9. Shift premium | ← 6 percent of normal rate → | | | | | |

Prepared by Production Planning Department with the help of the outside consulting industrial engineer (for time standards) and the Personnel Department (for rate standards).

Audited by Cost Accounting Department

Concurred by Supervisor and workers of each production department

Approved by Production superintendent, plant manager, vice president, manufacturing

Date prepared ______ Date approved ______

set the following standards, which have been approved by the plant manager and the vice president, manufacturing:

| | |
|---|---|
| Standard idle time (arising for various reasons) of direct labor | 3 percent of standard direct labor–hours |
| Standard rework time, the time required to be spent by direct labor to correct damaged or defective production | 2 percent of standard direct labor–hours (No rework time is required in the Packing Department because production is inspected before packing.) |

Since learning time will depend upon new hirings and the extent of training required, learning time for each cost center will be estimated each year at the time of annual budget preparation.

The above standards, too, are included in Exhibit 12-3 with the other direct labor standards.

For cost accounting purposes, idle time, rework time, and learning time of direct labor will be treated as a part of manufacturing overhead costs.

## 10. Setting Standards for Available Work Hours

ACME Company's plant works the first shift from 9.00 A.M. to 5.00 P.M. and the second shift (in the Assembly Department only) from 5.00 P.M. to 1.00 A.M., with an unpaid half hour for lunch and a paid half hour for rest and relief. Thus, the net time available for work is 7 hours per worker per day, or 35 hours per week.

In accordance with company policy, vacation time, paid holidays, and paid excused time on an average aggregate respectively 2 weeks, 2 weeks, and 1 week per year. From past experience, unpaid absenteeism comes to 1 week per year. Thus, a full-time worker works on an average 46 weeks, or 1610 hours (46 weeks × 35 hours per week) per year.

Though a worker works only 1610 hours per year, he is paid for 1912.5 hours per year; i.e., time paid but not worked totals 302.5 hours per worker per year.

These standards are summarized in Exhibit 12-4; they apply also to indirect labor such as material handlers, janitors, etc.

## 11. Classification of Manufacturing Overhead Costs

For product costing and for cost control, it is decided that manufacturing overhead incurred by ACME Company is to be classified by the nature of

**EXHIBIT 12-4**

**Standards for Available Work Hours (ACME Company)**
Effective January 1, 1981

| | Time Available for Work | Time Paid | Time Paid but Not Worked | Charged to |
|---|---|---|---|---|
| Gross hours per day | 8.0 | 8.0 | . . . | |
| Paid rest and relief time (hours) | (0.5) | . . . | 0.5 | Benefits |
| Unpaid lunch time (hours) | (0.5) | (0.5) | . . . | |
| Net hours per day | 7.0 | 7.5 | 0.5 | |
| Net hours per week | 35.0 | 37.5 | 2.5 | |
| Number of weeks in a year | 52 | 52 | | |
| Paid vacation (weeks) | (2) | | 2 | Benefits |
| Paid holidays (weeks) | (2) | | 2 | Benefits |
| Paid excused time (weeks) | (1) | | 1 | Benefits |
| Unpaid absenteeism (weeks) | (1) | (1) | | |
| Net weeks per year | 46 | 51 | 5 | |
| Net hours per year | 1,610 | 1,912.50* | 302.5** | * Cost centers<br>** Benefits |

NOTES:

1. Productive direct labor–hours are charged to production cost centers as direct labor cost.
2. Unproductive direct labor–hours are charged to production cost centers as manufacturing overhead.
3. Productive and unproductive indirect labor–hours are charged to service cost centers as manufacturing overhead.
4. Time paid but not worked is charged to employee benefits.

expenses, cost centers (for product costing and responsibility accounting), and cost behavior. The multiple classification of manufacturing overhead is shown in Exhibit 12-5, "Manufacturing Cost Accounts and Cost Center Matrix." All manufacturing overhead costs incurred by the company are classified by the nature of expenses as listed under the column "Account Title."

For cost control, costs which can be directly identified with a cost center must be separated from costs which are allocated to a cost center. Hence, all manufacturing overhead cost classified by the nature of expenses is grouped into two categories, direct cost center costs and allocated costs. Cost items such as salaries, wages, learning time, rework materials, operating supplies, purchased maintenance, water, leasehold land rent, etc., will be charged directly to the appropriate cost centers. For example, leasehold land rent will be charged to the occupancy cost center, pur-

**EXHIBIT 12-5**

**Manufacturing Cost Accounts and Cost Center Matrix (Classification of Expenses by cost center and by cost behavior)**

| Account No. | Account Title | Machine | | Press | | Welding | | Assembly | | Finishing | |
|---|---|---|---|---|---|---|---|---|---|---|---|
| | Activity Unit → | | | | | | | | | | |
| | Activity Level → | | | | | | | | | | |
| | *Direct cost center costs* | F | V | F | V | F | V | F | V | F | V |
| | Regular salaries | X | | X | | X | | X | | X | |
| | Temporary salaries | | | | | | | | | | |
| | Overtime salaries | X | | | | | | | | | |
| | Direct labor: production | | X | | X | | X | | X | | X |
| | Indirect labor | | X | | X | | | | | | |
| | Setup | | | | | | | | | | |
| | Mechanics | | | | | | | | | | |
| | Electricians | | | | | | | | | | |
| | Material handlers | | | | | | | | | | |
| | Janitors | | | | | | | | | | |
| | Hourly benefits | | X | | X | | X | | X | | X |
| | Salaried benefits | X | | X | | X | | X | | X | |
| | Learning time | | X | | X | | X | | X | | X |
| | Idle time | | X | | X | | X | | X | | X |
| | Rework time | | X | | X | | X | | X | | X |
| | Transfer labor difference | | X | | X | | X | | X | | X |
| | Overtime premium | | X | | X | | X | | X | | X |
| | Shift premium | | X | | X | | X | | X | | X |
| | Rework materials | | X | | X | | X | | X | | X |
| | Operating supplies | | X | | X | | X | | X | | X |
| | Small tools and equipment | | X | | X | | X | | X | | X |
| | Maintenance materials | | X | | X | | X | | X | | X |
| | Purchased power | | X | | X | | X | | X | | X |
| | Heat and light | X | | X | | X | | X | | X | |
| | Telephone and telegram | X | X | X | X | X | X | X | X | X | X |
| | Property taxes | | | | | | | | | | |
| | Insurance | | | | | | | | | | |
| | Depreciation | X | | X | | X | | X | | X | |
| | Travel and entertainment | | | | | | | | | | |
| | Water | | | | | | | | | | |
| | Rent and amortization: land | | | | | | | | | | |
| | *Allocated costs* | | | | | | | | | | |
| | Maintenance charges | X | X | X | X | X | X | X | X | X | X |
| | Insurance | X | | X | | X | | X | | X | |
| | Property taxes | X | | X | | X | | X | | X | |
| | Occupancy expenses | X | | X | | X | | X | | X | |
| | Storekeeping | X | X | X | X | X | X | X | X | X | X |
| | Production planning | X | | X | | X | | X | | X | |
| | Inspection | X | | | | | | X | | X | |
| | General plant expenses | X | X | X | X | X | X | X | X | X | X |

NOTE: F = fixed; V = variable.

| Production Planning | | Inspection | | Repairs and Maintenance | | Personnel and Timekeeping | | Occupancy | | Employee Benefits | | Storekeeping and Material Handling | | All Other | |
|---|---|---|---|---|---|---|---|---|---|---|---|---|---|---|---|
| F | V | F | V | F | V | F | V | F | V | F | V | F | V | F | V |
| X | | X | | X | | X | | | | | | X | | X | |
| | | | | | | | | | | | | X | | X | |
| X | | X | | X | | | X | | | | | | X | | X |
| | | | | | X | | | | | | | | | | |
| | | | | | X | | | | | | | | | | |
| | | | | | | | | | | | | X | | | |
| | | | | | | | | X | | | | | | | |
| | | | | | X | | | | | | X | X | | | |
| X | | X | | X | | X | | | | X | | X | | X | |
| | | | | X | | | | | | | | | | | |
| X | | X | | X | | X | | | | | | X | | X | |
| X | | | | | X | X | X | X | | | | X | X | X | X |
| | | X | | | X | | | | | | | | | | |
| | | | | | | | | X | | | | | | X | X |
| | | | | | X | | | | | | | | | | |
| X | | | | X | | X | | | | | | X | | X | |
| | | | | X | X | | | | | | | X | X | X | X |
| | | | | | | | | | | | | | | X | |
| | | | | | | | | | | | | | | X | |
| X | | | | X | | X | | X | | | | X | | X | |
| | | | | | | | | | | | | | | X | X |
| | | | | | | | | | | | | | | X | X |
| | | | | | | | | X | | | | | | | |
| | | | | | | | | X | | | | | | | |
| X | | | | X | | X | | X | | | | X | X | X | |
| X | | | | X | | X | | X | | | | X | X | X | |
| X | | | | X | | X | | | | | | X | | | |

chased maintenance charges for a weighing scale will be charged to storekeeping and material handling, and all other purchased maintenance for building and of a general nature will be charged to general factory administration. On the other hand, insurance and property taxes will be accumulated as objective expense accounts and then allocated to the relevant cost centers.

All the manufacturing cost centers established earlier are listed horizontally in separate columns. Each cost center column is divided into two subcolumns, F and V, for identifying the fixed and variable expenses applicable to each cost center. Then, these expense items are identified with the respective cost centers by putting an *X* in the appropriate cost center column opposite each expense item. To indicate whether an expense item applicable to a cost center is fixed or variable, an *X* is put in the F or V subcolumn under each column head. Most of the expenses are either fixed or variable. However, fixed expenses remain fixed only within a relevant range of production, and that range varies from item to item. Hence, while each of the fixed expenses is being budgeted for a year, the relevant range of activity within which it is fixed should be examined. Expenses which increase in a step fashion are telephone and telegram (because of the fixed rental plus charges based on use), supplies, maintenance materials, purchased maintenance, travel and entertainment, and water. On the basis of an analysis of these cost items' behavior, they are separated into fixed and variable cost elements and their rates of variability are determined.

This exhibit also shows the cost centers to which the expenses of the service centers will be allocated. Thus, it shows direct and allocated cost items incurred by each cost center and their classification into fixed and variable elements.

Later, after the chart of accounts has been finalized and account codes have been established, the codes will be entered in this exhibit.

## 12. Selection of Activity Units for Production Centers and Service Centers

To budget expenses it is necessary to estimate the volume of activity in each cost center, and to measure the volume of activity it is necessary to select an activity unit for each of the centers. After considering the nature of activities in individual cost centers, the designer has selected an activity unit for each of them. For example, because production processes are mechanized in the Machine and Press Departments, the costs incurred by these departments depend upon the use of equipment in the departments. Hence, equipment-hours (or machine-hours) are selected as the activity unit for these departments. Similarly, expenses incurred by the Repairs and Maintenance Department depend upon the volume of repairs and maintenance–hours. As discussed in Chapter 11, since in a cost center not all costs fluctuate with only one activity base, care is required in budgeting costs for each cost center.

Activity units selected for various cost centers are as follows:

| Cost Center | Activity Unit |
|---|---|
| *Production cost centers* | |
| Machine shop | Equipment- (machine-) hours |
| Press shop | Equipment-hours |
| Welding shop | Direct labor–hours |
| Assembly shop | Direct labor–hours |
| Finishing shop | Direct labor–hours |
| *Service cost centers* | |
| Repairs and maintenance | Repairs and maintenance–hours |
| Storekeeping and material handling | Direct material consumption and inventory and number of material movements |
| Production planning | Production planning time required |
| Inspection | Inspection time required |
| Personnel and timekeeping | Person-hours or direct labor–hours and number of other employees |
| Occupancy | Floor area occupied |
| General factory administration | Person-hours |

The next step is to set quantity and rate standards for individual cost items (listed in Exhibit 12-5) incurred by each cost center. The establishment of equipment-hours for the Machine and Press Departments has been covered in task 8.

## 13. Establishment of Setup Time Standards

From the analysis of past records and expected changes for the coming year, standard setup time has been established as given in Exhibit 12-6. Standard setup time has been expressed in hours for every 100 production units; it will be 1.8 hours in the machine shop and 0.96 hour in the press shop.

## 14. Setting Standards for Power Consumption and Rate

Power is purchased from the outside power company and consumed by each of the production departments and the Repairs and Maintenance

**EXHIBIT 12-6**

**Standard Setup Time (ACME Company)**
Effective January 1, 1981

| | Machine Shop | Press Shop |
|---|---|---|
| Number of setups required per 100 production units | 18 | 12 |
| Setup time per setup | 0.10 hour | 0.08 hour |
| Setup time per 100 production units | 1.8 hours | 0.96 hour |
| Setup to be done by | Mechanics from Repairs and Maintenance Department | |

Department. The standard power quantity required by each of these departments has been established and related to the activity unit in each department; for example, the Machine Department requires 30 kilowatts of power per machine-hour. The standard power rate, being the expected rate for purchased power, is set at 8 cents per kilowatthour. Hence, the standard power cost for the Machine Department is $2.40 per machine-hour. Exhibit 12-7 shows the standard power cost for each of the six departments.

## 15. Setting Standards for Heat and Light

It is estimated that the quantity of electricity consumed for heat and light will be more or less fixed for a year and will not vary with the level of activity in a department. Hence, standard electricity consumption for each department has been expressed as so many kilowatthours per year. The standard electricity rate is set at 8 cents per kilowatthour. These standards are recorded in Exhibit 12-7.

## 16. Setting Standard Time for Repairs and Maintenance

The production plant of ACME Company needs two types of repairs and maintenance work, mechanical and electrical, and hence standards are set separately for each of them.

**Mechanical** There are two types of mechanical repairs and maintenance: scheduled major maintenance and emergency repairs. Scheduled maintenance time varies with the number of pieces of equipment to be

**EXHIBIT 12-7**

## Standards for Power and Electricity*

Effective January 1, 1981

| | Machine | Press | Welding | Assembly | Finishing | Repairs and Maintenance | Storekeeping | Production Planning | Personnel and Timekeeping | General Factory Administration |
|---|---|---|---|---|---|---|---|---|---|---|
| *Standards for power* | | | | | | | | | | |
| 1. Standard quantity of power required (kilowatthours) | 30 per MH | 20 per MH | 3 per DLH | 1.5 per DLH | 1 per DLH | 3 per RH | | | | |
| 2. Power cost per kilowatthour | $0.08 | $0.08 | $0.08 | $0.08 | $0.08 | $0.08 | | | | |
| 3. Standard power cost | $2.40 per MH | $1.60 per MH | $0.24 per DLH | $0.12 per DLH | $0.08 per DLH | $0.24 per RH | | | | |
| *Standards for electricity for heat and light* | | | | | | | | | | |
| 4. Standard quantity of electricity required per year (kilowatthours) | 75 | 50 | 62.5 | 137.5 | 37.5 | 12.5 | 37.5 | 7.5 | 7.5 | 68.75 |
| 5. Power cost per kilowatthour | $0.08 | $0.08 | $0.08 | $0.08 | $0.08 | $0.08 | $0.08 | $0.08 | $0.08 | $0.08 |

* MH = machine-hour; DLH = direct labor–hour; RH = repair-hour.

maintained, whereas emergency repair–hours vary with the activity level (number of equipment-hours or direct labor–hours) in the individual production departments. Standard emergency repair–hours are expressed per 1000 activity units. Standard time for mechanical repairs and maintenance is given in Exhibit 12-8.

**Electrical** There is no scheduled electrical maintenance. Hence, only the standard time for electrical emergency repairs and maintenance has been established, as summarized in Exhibit 12-9. Besides the production departments, the factory buildings also require electrical repairs, the time for which has been estimated at 400 hours per year.

**Overtime** Based on experience, it has been estimated that overtime for electrical and mechanical repairs will be approximately 1 percent of total budgeted repairs and maintenance–hours per year.

**Cost Control** For better control over repairs and maintenance persons' time, it is helpful if a standard time for each type of repair job has been set up. At this stage, however, ACME Company has decided to set standard time only for major mechanical maintenance work and not for the various types of mechanical and electrical repair jobs. Time standards for these jobs may be established once the company has gained more experience with the establishment of time standards and employees get

**EXHIBIT 12-8**

**Standard Person-Hours for Mechanical Repairs and Maintenance (ACME Company)**

Effective January 1, 1981

| | Machine | Press | Welding | Assembly | Finishing (Excluding Packing) |
|---|---|---|---|---|---|
| Scheduled major maintenance | 1. Maintenance of each piece of equipment will be performed twice a year. 2. Each maintenance job will take 40 person-hours per piece of equipment. | | . . . | . . . | . . . |
| *Standard Person-hours for emergency repairs* Based on experience, it is estimated that emergency repair–hours will vary with the activity level at the rate set out here. | 40 person-hours per 1000 equipment-hours | 32 person-hours per 1000 equipment-hours | 15 person-hours per 1000 direct labor–hours | 10 person-hours per 1000 direct labor–hours | 20 person-hours per 1000 direct labor–hours |
| Overtime | Equal to 1 percent of budgeted repairs and maintenance–hours for the year | | | | |
| Established by | Service superintendent and repairs and maintenance supervisor | | | Date ____ | |
| Approved by | Vice president, manufacturing | | | Date ____ | |

**EXHIBIT 12-9**

**Standard Person-Hours for Electrical Repairs and Maintenance (ACME Company)**

Effective January 1, 1981

| | Machine | Press | Welding | Assembly | Finishing (Excluding Packing) | Building (Occupancy Cost Center) |
|---|---|---|---|---|---|---|
| Based on experience, it is estimated that emergency repair-hours will vary with the activity level at the rate set out here. | 35 person-hours per 1000 equipment-hours | 35 person-hours per 1000 equipment-hours | 10 person-hours per 1000 direct labor-hours | 5 person-hours per 1000 direct labor-hours | 5 person-hours per 1000 direct labor-hours | 400 person-hours per year |
| Overtime | Equal to 1 percent of budgeted repairs and maintenance-hours for the year | | | | | |

Established by: Service superintendent and repairs and maintenance supervisor — Date ____

Approved by: Vice president, manufacturing — Date ____

used to the standard costing system. In the interim, the time spent on various repair jobs will be controlled by proper scheduling of repair persons' time and by proper supervision by the Repairs and Maintenance Department supervisor and by the supervisors of the user departments. The supervisor of each user department will be required to sign the repair ticket for each repair job, signifying acceptance of the repair time charged to the department.

For charging all repairs and maintenance costs except maintenance materials, a sold-service concept will be adopted. For this purpose, budgeted fixed costs of repairs and maintenance will be allocated to the user departments on the basis of budgeted repairs and maintenance-hours. For allocating variable costs of repairs and maintenance, a standard variable rate per hour will be established by dividing total budgeted variable repairs and maintenance costs by budgeted repairs and maintenance-hours. User departments will be charged at the standard variable rate for the standard time required for major mechanical maintenance work and for the actual time spent for other repairs and maintenance work.

## 17. Repairs and Maintenance Material Standards

Since repairs and maintenance materials are numerous in variety and relatively small in dollar amount, it has been decided that separate quantity and rate standards will not be set for each type of repairs and maintenance material. Instead, the repairs and maintenance material cost will be budgeted every year on the basis of the preceding 3 years' experience.

## 18. Standards for Inspection Time and Quantity

For establishing standards for inspection, it is necessary to decide four things:

- What products will be inspected?
- At what stage in the production process will they be inspected?
- How much of each product will be inspected?
- How much time will be spent on the inspection of each unit of a product to be inspected?

The answers to these four questions for ACME Company are summarized in Exhibit 12-10. Standard inspection time has been set on the basis of experience and adjusted to reflect the cost reduction goal set by management.

**EXHIBIT 12-10**

**Standards for Inspection (ACME Company)**
Effective January 1, 1981

1. Both product X and product Y will be inspected for quality control.
2. Product X will be inspected in the machine shop after completion of the machine job, in the assembly shop after completion of subassemblies 2 and 3, and in the finishing shop after the final product is ready. In all, 50 percent of the production in the machine shop, 100 percent of that in subassembly 2, 10 percent of that in subassembly 3, and 10 percent of that in the finishing shop will be inspected on a continuous basis. Standard time required for inspection of each unit of product X has been set at 0.10 hour for the machine shop, 0.05 hour for subassembly 2, 0.10 hour for subassembly 3, and 0.12 hour for the finishing shop.
3. Product Y will be inspected in the machine shop after completion of the machine job, in the assembly shop after completion of subassemblies 3 and 4, and in the finishing shop after the final product is ready. The production quantity to be inspected is the same as for product X, except that 100 percent of subassembly 3 and 10 percent of subassembly 4 will be inspected. Standard time required for inspection of each unit of product X has been set at 0.10 hour for the machine shop, 0.05 hour for subassembly 3, 0.10 hour for subassembly 4, and 0.12 hour for the finishing shop.

Prepared by Production superintendent and inspectors — Date ——
Approved by Plant manager — Date ——
Vice president, manufacturing — Date ——

## 19. Standards for Other Personnel

Most of the other labor required by the Manufacturing Department is fixed, and some will increase in step fashion with an increase in the volume of production. It is estimated that in the next 2 to 3 years the total volume of production will be between 35,000 and 70,000 units. Hence, the standards for other personnel have been set for this range of production.

The plant manager, in consultation with the production superintendent and the service superintendent, has established, and the vice president, manufacturing, has approved, that for production volume in the range of 35,000 to 70,000 units the following personnel will be required by the Manufacturing Department:

| Cost Center | Number and Type of Personnel Required |
|---|---|
| General factory administration | 1 plant manager |
| | 1 assistant to plant manager |
| | 1 production superintendent |
| | 1 service superintendent |
| | 2 cost analysts (for volume up to 45,000 units) |
| | 3 cost analysts (for volume between 45,000 and 70,000 units) |
| Machine shop | 1 supervisor |
| Press shop | 1 supervisor |
| Welding shop | 1 supervisor |
| Assembly shop | 2 supervisors (1 each for two shifts) |
| Finishing shop | 1 supervisor |
| Repairs and maintenance | 1 supervisor |
| Personnel and timekeeping | 1 personnel administrator |
| | 2 timekeepers and clerks (for volume up to 50,000 units) |
| | 3 timekeepers and clerks (for volume between 50,000 and 70,000 units) |
| Production planning | 1 production planner |
| | 1 production clerk-dispatcher |
| Storekeeping and material handling | 1 storekeeper |
| | 2 material handlers (for volume up to 40,000 units) |
| | 3 material handlers (for volume between 40,000 and 70,000 units) |
| Occupancy | 2 janitors |

In addition, the Office of the Vice President, Manufacturing, will consist of the vice president, manufacturing, and an executive secretary.

These requirements will be reviewed every year and revised as may be necessary. Salaries and wages will be shown in an annual salary and wage schedule prepared by the plant manager in consultation with the two superintendents. The schedule will be prepared in accordance with the salary increments and promotion guidelines laid down by the company president, and it will be approved by the vice president, manufacturing, and the company president.

## 20. Standards for Rework Materials

On the basis of experience and in consideration of the cost reduction goal set by management, the Production Planning Department has set the standard quantity of rework materials at 1 percent of direct materials consumption in each of the production departments.

## 21. Treatment of Cost Items for Which Standards Are Not Set

For the remaining items of manufacturing overhead costs, standards will not be set either because the costs involved are small or because the costs can be better controlled through overhead budgets. The remaining items are as follows:

*Small-Cost Items*

Small tools and equipment
Water

*Discretionary Costs*

Traveling and entertainment
Purchased maintenance (To some extent, it is essential, but in any event it can be better controlled through the overhead budget.)
Insurance
Telephone and telegram
Voluntary employee benefits costs (recreation, education, etc.)

*Committed (Sunk) Costs*

Depreciation
Rent and amortization of leasehold land

*Involuntary (Mandatory) Costs*

Property taxes
Involuntary employee benefits costs (e.g., social security taxes)

## 22. Selection of Bases for Primary Allocation

Under task 11, the designer identified the overhead costs which can be charged directly to individual cost centers. The following items of expenses which are not directly charged will be allocated to cost centers on the bases mentioned.

| Cost Item | Method and Basis for Primary Allocation |
|---|---|
| Depreciation | Fixed-assets register by cost centers will be maintained, and depreciation will be computed separately for each cost center. Depreciation on assets for general use will be charged to general factory administration. |
| Insurance | Insurance premium for inventory will be charged directly to storekeeping and that for building to occupancy, and the remaining insurance cost will be allocated in the ratio of value of property in the respective cost centers. |
| Property taxes | Same as for insurance. |
| Utilities: power | Metered consumption. Meters are installed in each of the production departments and in the Repairs and Maintenance Department. |
| Utilities: heat and light | Based on an engineering estimate of the electricity requirement for heat and light. |
| Telephone | Fixed rental will be allocated on the basis of the number of telephone connections in each cost center, and call charges will be allocated on an actual basis according to departmental bills submitted by the telephone company. |
| Employee benefits | First, employee benefits cost will be accumulated separately for hourly labor and salaried employees. Then the total amount of the employee benefits cost pertaining to hourly labor will be allocated in the ratio of hourly wages. Similarly, the total amount of the employee benefits costs pertaining to salaried employees will be allocated in the ratio of salaries. |

## 23. Selection of Bases for Secondary Allocation

For *product costing,* service center costs must eventually be allocated to production centers. Management of ACME Company would like to keep the allocation of one service center cost to other service centers and reciprocal allocations to a minimum. Accordingly, the following bases for secondary allocation have been selected:

| Cost Center | Basis for Secondary Allocation |
|---|---|
| Occupancy | Allocated to all cost centers on the basis of the floor area occupied. |
| Repairs and maintenance | Variable repairs and maintenance expenses will be allocated to the occupancy cost center and all production cost centers in the ratio of repair-hours. Budgeted fixed repairs and maintenance expenses will be allocated only to production cost centers in |

| Cost Center | Basis for Secondary Allocation |
|---|---|
| | the ratio of budgeted repairs and maintenance–hours. |
| Storekeeping and material handling | Allocated to production cost centers: variable expenses in the ratio of the value of material consumption and budgeted fixed expenses in the ratio of allocated budgeted variable expenses. |
| Inspection | All expenses are fixed in nature and will be allocated in the ratio of budgeted inspection time. |
| Production planning | All expenses are fixed in nature and will be allocated in the ratio of budgeted production-planning time. |
| General factory administration; personnel and timekeeping | Allocated only to production cost centers, variable expenses in the ratio of direct labor–hours and budgeted fixed expenses in the ratio of allocated budgeted variable expenses. |

## 24. Determination of Activity Level for Each Cost Center for the Budget Year (1981)

It is necessary to determine the activity levels discussed below for the budget year 1981.

**Budgeted Sales Quantity** Sales is a limiting factor in ACME Company. Hence, budgeting sales quantity is the starting point in the preparation of the company's operating budgets. The Marketing Department has budgeted the most likely sales quantity at 24,000 units for product X and 16,200 units for product Y. Sales will be more or less uniform from month to month.

**Desired Ending Inventory** On the basis of experience, it is considered desirable to maintain an inventory of finished products equal to 1 month's sale.

**Expected Opening Inventory** On the basis of forecast sales and production for the remaining months of 1980, it is estimated that 2000 units of product X and 1700 units of product Y will be in inventory at the end of 1980.

**Budgeted Production Quantity** From the above three sales and inventory estimates, deriving the budgeted production quantity is a matter of simple arithmetic, which is summarized in Exhibit 12-11. As in case of sales, production will be more or less uniform from month to month.

**Normal Equipment-Hours** In the Machine and Press Departments production is mechanized. Hence it is necessary to compute available equipment-hours and compare the total with that required to meet the budgeted production. The computation of normal equipment-hours given in Exhibit 12-12 is self-explanatory. Planned equipment-hours rep-

**EXHIBIT 12-11**

**Production Budget (ACME Company)**
Year 1981

| | Reference | Units | |
|---|---|---|---|
| | | Product X | Product Y |
| Sales budget for 1981 | | 24,000 | 16,200 |
| Add desired ending inventory | | 2,000 | 1,500 |
| Subtotal | | 26,000 | 17,700 |
| Less expected opening inventory | | 2,000 | 1,700 |
| Production budget for 1981 | | 24,000 | 16,000 |
| Monthly production (Sales and production will be uniform from month to month.) | | 2,000 | 1,333 |

resent standard equipment-hours (including setup time) required to produce the budgeted production.

**Direct Labor–Hours and Staffing Table for Direct Labor** On the basis of the standards for direct labor (Exhibit 12-3) and budgeted production (Exhibit 12-11), total direct labor–hours required by each production department are estimated and given in Exhibit 12-19. From Exhibit 12-4, we know that the net time available for work per worker is 1610 hours per year. By dividing the total number of direct labor–hours required by 1610, we can arrive at the approximate number of workers required by each production shop and also at the excess or short time. For fuller utilization of direct labor time, excess labor of one department will be transferred to another department. Exhibit 12-13 shows the budgeted number of workers, overtime, transfer time, etc.

**Budgeted Setup Time** Using the data regarding standard setup time (Exhibit 12-6) and budgeted production (Exhibit 12-11), budgeted setup time is computed and given in Exhibit 12-14.

**Budgeted Repairs and Maintenance Hours** Using the data concerning repairs and maintenance standards (Exhibits 12-8 and 12-9), budgeted equipment-hours (Exhibit 12-12), and budgeted direct labor–hours (Exhibit 12-13), budgeted repairs and maintenance–hours, budgeted overtime, and budgeted idle time are computed and given in Exhibits 12-15 and 12-16.

**Budgeted inspection-hours** Using the data regarding inspection standards (Exhibit 12-10) and budgeted production (Exhibit 12-11), budgeted inspection time is computed and given in Exhibit 12-17.

**EXHIBIT 12-12**

**Planned Equipment-Hours (ACME Company)**
Year 1981

| | | Machine Department | Press Department |
|---|---|---|---|
| 1. Gross equipment-hours (52 weeks × 40 hours per week) | | 2,088 | 2,088 |
| 2. Less nonwork hours | | | |
| Holidays | 2 weeks | | |
| Plant shutdown | ... | | |
| | 2 weeks × 40 hours | (80) | (80) |
| 3. Net available hours | | 2,008 | 2,008 |
| 4. Downtime hours (estimated) | | | |
| Maintenance and overhaul | | (150) | (140) |
| Others (inventory, jams, waiting, etc.) | | (36) | (36) |
| 5. Net available hours per piece of equipment | | 1,822 | 1,832 |
| 6. Number of pieces of equipment | | × 18 | × 12 |
| 7. Total available equipment-hours | | 32,796 | 21,984 |
| 8. Planned hours (at expected sales volume) | | | |
| Operating: X = (24,000 × 0.70) | | 16,800 | |
| (24,000 × 0.50) | | | 12,000 |
| Y = (16,000 × 0.90) | | 14,400 | |
| (16,000 × 0.60) | | | 9,600 |
| Subtotal | | 31,200 | 21,600 |
| Setup time (Exhibit 12-16) | | 720 | 384 |
| Total planned hours | | 31,920 | 21,984 |
| 9. Planned idle time due to less use (7 − 8) | | 876 | ...... |

## 25. Preparation of Direct Materials Consumption Budget

Using the data regarding standards for direct materials (Exhibit 12-2) and budgeted production (Exhibit 12-11), the direct materials consumption budget for 1981 is prepared and given in Exhibit 12-18.

## 26. Preparation of Direct Labor Budget

Using the data concerning budgeted direct labor–hours and standard direct labor rates (Exhibit 12-3), the direct labor cost budget for 1981 is prepared as shown in Exhibit 12-19.

**EXHIBIT 12-13**

**Staffing (Manning) Table (ACME Company)**

Year 1981

| | Machine | Press | Welding | Assembly | Testing and Painting | Packing |
|---|---|---|---|---|---|---|
| 1. Budgeted direct labor–hours (Exhibit 12-19) | 62,400 | 21,600 | 46,400 | 77,600 | 22,400 | 3,200 |
| 2. Idle time (at 3 percent of 1) | 1,872 | 648 | 1,392 | 2,328 | 672 | 96 |
| 3. Rework time (at 2 percent of 1) | 1,248 | 432 | 928 | 1,552 | 448 | ..... |
| 4. Learning time (estimated) | 274 | ..... | ..... | ..... | ..... | ..... |
| 5. Total direct labor–hours | 65,794 | 22,680 | 48,720 | 81,480 | 23,520 | 3,296 |
| 6. Number of workers required (at 1610 hours per worker) | 41 | 14 | 30 | 50 (30 + 20) | 15 | 2 |
| 7. Available direct labor–hours (Number of workers × 1610) | 66,010 | 22,540 | 48,300 | 80,500 | 24,150 | 3,220 |
| 8. Excess (or short) hours (7–5) | 216 | (140) | (420) | (980) | 630 | (76) |
| 9. Transferred to: | | | | | | |
| Press | (140) | 140 | ..... | ..... | ..... | ..... |
| Packing | (76) | ..... | ..... | ..... | ..... | 76 |
| Assembly | ..... | ..... | ..... | 630 | (630) | ..... |
| 10. Net excess (or short) hours | ..... | ..... | (420) | (350) | ..... | ..... |
| 11. Overtime necessary | ..... | ..... | 420 | 350 | ..... | ..... |
| *Costs to be charged to overhead ($)* | | | | | | |
| 12. Idle time | 14,077 | 4,588 | 9,981 | 18,903 | 5,712 | 576 |
| 13. Rework time | 9,385 | 3,059 | 6,654 | 12,602 | 3,808 | ..... |
| 14. Learning time | 2,060 | ..... | ..... | ..... | ..... | ..... |
| 15. Overtime premium | ..... | ..... | 1,506 | 1,421 | ..... | ..... |
| 16. Second-shift premium (20 × 1610 × $8.12 × 6 percent) | ..... | ..... | ..... | 15,688 | ..... | ..... |
| 17. Transfer labor rate difference | ..... | 62 | ..... | 239 | ..... | 116 |

**EXHIBIT 12-14**

**Budgeted Setup Time (ACME Company)**
Year 1981

| | Machine Shop | Press Shop |
|---|---|---|
| Each production order to be for 100 units | | |
| Budgeted production for 1981 (Exhibit 12-11) | ← 40,000 units → | |
| Total number of production orders | ← 400 → | |
| Total setup time | 720 hours (400 × 1.8) | 384 hours (400 × 0.96) |

## 27. Preparation of Manufacturing Overhead Budgets

Using the data regarding various standards and budgets previously mentioned, the manufacturing overhead budget for 1981 is prepared separately for each of the following:

- Objective expense accounts, i.e., depreciation, insurance, property taxes, repairs and maintenance materials, power, and heat and light (Exhibits 12-20 through 12-24)
- Service centers (Exhibits 12-25 through 12-31)
- Production centers (Exhibits 12-33 through 12-37)

Initially, these budgets are prepared without making primary and secondary allocations for any costs, including repairs and maintenance costs. The basis for computation of each item is given in the respective budgets. In many cases, the amount is derived from another exhibit or document mentioned opposite the relevant item. Though these budgets are self-explanatory for the most part, the following explanation will help the reader.

**General** The overhead budget for each responsibility center shows among other things:

- Name of the person responsible for it
- Direct and allocated costs separately
- Yearly budgeted amount separated into fixed and variable amounts
- Budget for cost control, i.e., the basis on which the budget allowance for each of the budgeted items will be computed for a monthly comparison of actual and budgeted costs

The budgeted fixed cost is divided equally among 12 months, one-twelfth to each month. For variable budgeted costs, variable overhead rates per activity unit are computed. For cost control, all allocated costs except repairs and maintenance costs are regarded as fixed. As explained earlier, since repairs and maintenance costs are charged to the user cost centers on the sold-service concept, variable repairs and maintenance costs allocated at standard rates are deemed controllable by the user responsibility centers.

The budget allowance for each month for a cost center will be equal to monthly budgeted fixed costs plus variable budget allowance. The variable budget allowance for each cost item will be equal to the activity level achieved times the budgeted variable overhead rate.

### Budgets for Objective Expense Accounts and Their Allocation

The budgets for objective expense accounts are prepared as explained below.

**Depreciation** From the fixed-assets register by cost centers, depreciation is computed by cost centers and summarized in Exhibit 12-20. Depreciation amounts for the individual cost centers are included in the overhead budgets of the respective centers.

**Insurance** First, the insurance premium is budgeted separately for (1) materials, (2) building, and (3) equipment, furniture, etc. Insurance on materials is charged directly to the Storekeeping Department, and insurance on building is charged to the occupancy cost center. Insurance on equipment, furniture, etc., is allocated to various cost centers in the ratio of the value of property. Amounts charged or allocated to individual cost centers are included in the overhead budgets of the respective centers.

Exhibit 12-20 summarizes the total insurance premium and its allocation to various cost centers.

**Property Taxes** Property taxes are budgeted and allocated in the same manner as insurance; they are summarized in Exhibit 12-20.

**Repairs and Maintenance Materials** Different kinds of maintenance materials required for each cost center are estimated from the last 3 years' experience and summarized in Exhibit 12-21.

**Power** On the basis of standards for power cost (Exhibit 12-7) and budgeted machine-hours, direct labor–hours, or repair hours, the power cost at standard is budgeted for various cost centers and summarized in Exhibit 12-21.

**Heat and Light** The budgeted electricity cost for heat and light is computed from the standard cost sheet for heat and light (Exhibit 12-7) and summarized in Exhibit 12-21.

**EXHIBIT 12-15**

**Budgeted Mechanical Repairs and Maintenance–Hours (ACME Company)**

Year 1981

| Description | Mechanical | Press | Welding | Assembly | Finishing (Excluding Packing) | Total |
|---|---|---|---|---|---|---|
| *For scheduled major maintenance* | | | | | | |
| 1. Number of pieces of equipment | 18 | 12 | | | | |
| 2. Budgeted hours for twice-a-year maintenance at the rate of 4 hours per piece of equipment maintained | 1,440 ($18 \times 2 \times 40$) | 960 ($12 \times 2 \times 40$) | | | | 2400 |
| *For emergency repairs* | | | | | | |
| 3. Budgeted equipment-hours (Exhibit 12-12) | 31,200 | 21,600 | | | | |
| 4. Budgeted direct labor–hours (Exhibit 12-13) | | | 46,400 | 77,600 | 22,400 | |

| | | | | | | |
|---|---|---|---|---|---|---|
| 5. Standard person-hours required for repairs for 1000 equipment-hours or 1000 direct labor–hours (Exhibit 12-8) | 40 | 30 | 15 | 10 | 20 | |
| 6. Budgeted emergency repair–hours (3 × 5 or 4 × 5) | 1,310 | 691 | 696 | 776 | 668 | 4141 |
| 7. Total budgeted mechanical repairs and maintenance–hours (2 + 6) | 2,750 | 1,651 | 696 | 776 | 668 | 6541 |
| 8. Setup time (Exhibit 12-14) | 720 | 384 | | | | 1104 |
| 9. Overtime at 1 percent of budgeted repair–hours (1% × 6541) | | | | | | 65 |
| 10. Regular repair–hours (6,541 – 65) | | | | | | 6476 |
| 11. Idle time (balancing figure) | | | | | | 470 |
| 12. Total available effective hours (1610 × 5 + 65 overtime hours) | | | | | | 8115 |

**EXHIBIT 12-16**

**Budgeted Electrical Repairs and Maintenance–Hours (ACME Company)**

Year 1981

| Description | Machine | Press | Welding | Assembly | Finishing (Excluding Packing) | Total |
|---|---|---|---|---|---|---|
| 1. Budgeted equipment-hours (Exhibit 12-12) | 31,200 | 21,600 | | | | |
| 2. Budgeted direct labor–hours (Exhibit 12-13) | | | 46,400 | 77,600 | 22,400 | |
| 3. Standard person-hours required for electrical repairs for 1000 equipment-hours or 1000 direct labor–hours (Exhibit 12-9) | 35 | 35 | 10 | 5 | 5 | |
| 4. Budgeted electrical repair–hours (1 × 3 or 2 × 3) | 1,092 | 756 | 464 | 388 | 112 | 2812 |
| 5. Electrical repairs for building (Exhibit 12-9) | | | | | | 400 |
| 6. Total budgeted electrical repair–hours | | | | | | 3212 |
| 7. Overtime at 1 percent of budgeted repair–hours (1% × 3212) | | | | | | 32 |
| 8. Regular repair–hours (3212 − 32) | | | | | | 3180 |
| 9. Idle time (balancing figure) | | | | | | 40 |
| 10. Total available effective hours (1610 × 2 + 32 overtime hours) | | | | | | 3252 |

**EXHIBIT 12-17**

**Budgeted Inspection-Hours (ACME Company)**

Year 1981

| Production Cost Center | Product X | | | | Product Y | | | | |
|---|---|---|---|---|---|---|---|---|---|
| | | Inspection Quantity | | | | Inspection Quantity | | | |
| | Standard Inspection Time (Hour per Unit) | Standard Percentage of Total Production | Units (= 24,000 × Standard Percentage) | Budgeted Inspection-Hours | Standard Inspection Time (Hour per Unit) | Standard Percentage of Total Production | Units (= 16,000 × Standard Percentage) | Budgeted Inspection-Hours | Total Budgeted Inspection-Hours |
| | 1 | 2 | 3 | 4 (1 × 3) | 5 | 6 | 7 | 8 (5 × 7) | 9 (4 + 8) |
| Machine Assembly | 0.10 | 50 | 12,000 | 1200 | 0.10 | 50 | 8,000 | 800 | 2000 |
| Assembly | | | | | | | | | |
| Subassembly 2 | 0.5 | 100 | 24,000 | 1200 | | | | | 1200 |
| Subassembly 3 | 0.10 | 10 | 2,400 | 240 | 0.05 | 100 | 16,000 | 800 | 1040 |
| Subassembly 4 | | | | | 0.10 | 10 | 1,600 | 160 | 160 |
| Subtotal | | | | 1440 | | | | 960 | 2400 |
| Finishing | 0.12 | 10 | 2,400 | 288 | 0.12 | 10 | 1,600 | 192 | 480 |
| Total | | | | 2928 | | | | 1952 | 4880 |

NOTE: It is estimated that three inspectors are required to keep a continuous flow of production. Available hours = 1610 (Exhibit 12-4) × 3 = 4830. Overtime (4880 − 4830) = 50 hours. Utilization = 101 percent. Production quantity is obtained from Exhibit 12-11.

**EXHIBIT 12-18**

**Direct Materials Consumption Budget (ACME Company)**

Year 1981

| Budgeted production: | Product X 24,000 units |
|---|---|
| | Product Y 16,000 units |

| Direct Materials Consumed by Production Cost Centers | Unit of Measurement | Purchase Price per Unit ($) | Quantity (thousands) | | | Amount ($000) | | |
|---|---|---|---|---|---|---|---|---|
| | | | Product X | Product Y | Total | Product X | Product Y | Total |
| *Machine* | | | | | | | | |
| B | Kilogram | 3.50 | 240 | 64 | 304 | 840 | 224 | 1064 |
| I | Kilogram | 1.00 | 48 | 16 | 64 | 48 | 16 | 64 |
| Subtotal | | | | | | 888 | 240 | 1128 |
| *Press* | | | | | | | | |
| C | Kilogram | 4.00 | . . . | 46.4 | 46.4 | . . . | 185.6 | 185.6 |
| *Welding* | | | | | | | | |
| G | Kilogram | 4.00 | 6 | 4 | 10 | 24 | 16 | 40 |
| H | Number | 1.10 | 72 | 48 | 120 | 79.2 | 52.8 | 132 |
| Subtotal | | | | | | 103.2 | 68.8 | 172.0 |
| *Assembly* | | | | | | | | |
| A | Number | 2.50 | 216 | 128 | 344 | 540 | 320 | 860 |
| D | Kilogram | 1.25 | 48 | 25.6 | 73.6 | 60 | 32 | 92 |
| E | Kilogram | 1.00 | 60 | 32 | 92 | 60 | 32 | 92 |
| F | Number | 0.30 | 336 | 192 | 528 | 100.8 | 57.6 | 158.4 |
| Subtotal | | | | | | 760.8 | 441.6 | 1202.4 |
| *Finishing, testing, and packing* | | | | | | | | |
| J | Gallon | 2.00 | 12 | 11.2 | 23.2 | 24 | 22.4 | 46.4 |
| Packing materials | Number | 2.00 | 24 | 16 | 40 | 48 | 32 | 80 |
| Subtotal | | | | | | 72 | 54.4 | 126.4 |
| Total budgeted direct material cost | | | | | | 1824.0 | 990.4 | 2814.4 |

**EXHIBIT 12-19**

**Direct Labor Cost Budget (ACME Company)**

Year 1981

| Budgeted production: | Product X 24,000 units<br>Product Y 16,000 units |
|---|---|

| | Machine | Press | Welding | Assembly | Finishing and Testing | Packing | Total |
|---|---|---|---|---|---|---|---|
| 1. Standard direct labor–hours per unit (Exhibit 12-3) | | | | | | | |
| X | 1.40 | 0.50 | 1.00 | 1.90 | 0.60 | 0.08 | |
| Y | 1.80 | 0.60 | 1.40 | 2.00 | 0.50 | 0.08 | |
| 2. Total standard direct labor–hours (production x 1): | | | | | | | |
| X | 33,600 | 12,000 | 24,000 | 45,600 | 14,400 | 1920 | |
| Y | 28,800 | 9,600 | 22,400 | 32,000 | 8,000 | 1280 | |
| Total | 62,400 | 21,600 | 46,400 | 77,600 | 22,400 | 3200 | |
| 3. Standard direct labor–hour rate | $7.52 | 7.08 | 7.17 | 8.12 | 8.50 | 6.00 | |
| 4. Standard direct labor cost per unit (Exhibit 12-3) | | | | | | | |
| X | $10.528 | 3.540 | 7.170 | 15.428 | 5.100 | 0.480 | 42.246 |
| Y | 13.536 | 4.248 | 10.038 | 16.240 | 4.250 | 0.480 | 48.792 |
| 5. Total standard direct labor cost ($000) | | | | | | | |
| X | $252.7 | 85.0 | 172.1 | 370.3 | 122.4 | 11.5 | 1014.0 |
| Y | 216.5 | 68.0 | 160.6 | 259.8 | 68.0 | 7.7 | 780.6 |
| Total | 469.2 | 153.0 | 332.7 | 630.1 | 190.4 | 19.2 | 1794.6 |

**EXHIBIT 12-20**

**Budgets for Depreciation, Insurance, and Property Taxes (ACME Company)**
Year 1981

| Objective Expense Account | Basis or Reference | Total | Machine | Press | Welding |
|---|---|---|---|---|---|
| *Depreciation (computed by cost centers)* | | | | | |
| On building | Depreciation | 54,000 | | | |
| On machinery and equipment | worksheets | 294,600 | 132,000 | 96,000 | 24,000 |
| On furniture, fixtures, and office machines | | 19,300 | 300 | 200 | 200 |
| Total | | 367,900 | 132,300 | 96,200 | 24,200 |
| *Insurance* | | | | | |
| Value of property (per cent of total) | Schedule of property value | 100.0 | 42.2 | 30.6 | 7.7 |
| Premium on materials insurance | Direct charge | 20,000 | | | |
| Premium on building insurance | Direct charge | 5,000 | | | |
| Premium on equipment, furniture, etc., insurance | Allocated on value of property | 31,400 | 13,200 | 9,600 | 2400 |
| Total | | 56,400 | 13,200 | 9,600 | 2400 |
| *Property taxes* | | | | | |
| On materials | Direct | 10,000 | | | |
| On building | Direct | 5,000 | | | |
| On equipment, furniture, etc. | Value of property | 15,700 | 6600 | 4800 | 1200 |
| Total | | 30,700 | 6600 | 4800 | 1200 |

| Assembly | Finishing, Testing, and Packing | Occupancy | Repairs and Maintenance | Storekeeping | Production Planning | Personnel and Timekeeping | General Factory Administration |
|---|---|---|---|---|---|---|---|
| | | 54,000 | | | | | |
| 12,000 | 24,000 | | 2000 | 3000 | 1000 | | 600 |
| 400 | 600 | | 200 | 5000 | 1000 | 3000 | 8400 |
| 12,400 | 24,600 | 54,000 | 2200 | 8000 | 2000 | 3000 | 9000 |
| 4.0 | 7.8 | | 0.7 | 2.5 | 0.6 | 1.0 | 2.9 |
| | | | | 20,000 | | | |
| | | 5000 | | | | | |
| 1200 | 2500 | | 220 | 800 | 200 | 300 | 980 |
| 1200 | 2500 | 5000 | 220 | 20,800 | 200 | 300 | 980 |
| | | | | 10,000 | | | |
| | | 5000 | | | | | |
| 600 | 1300 | | 110 | 400 | 100 | 150 | 440 |
| 600 | 1300 | 5000 | 110 | 10,400 | 100 | 150 | 440 |

**EXHIBIT 12-21**

**Budgets for Repairs and Maintenance Materials, Power, Heat, and Light (ACME Company)**

Year 1981

| Objective Expense Account | Basis or Reference | Total | Machine | Press | Welding |
|---|---|---|---|---|---|
| *Repairs and maintenance materials* | | | | | |
| *a.* Equipment maintenance | Estimates | $101,000 | 42,000 | 36,000 | 14,000 |
| *b.* Tool maintenance | based on | $ 21,000 | 6,000 | 6,000 | ...... |
| *c.* Building maintenance | last 3 years' | $ 8,400 | | | |
| *d.* Furniture and fixtures maintenance | experience | $ 12,000 | | | |
| Total | | $142,400 | 48,000 | 42,000 | 14,000 |
| *Utilities: power** | | | | | |
| *a.* Standard kilowatthours per MH, DLH, or RH | | | 30/MH | 20/MH | 3/DLH |
| *b.* Power cost per MH, DLH, or RH at $0.08 per kilowatthour | (*a* × $0.08) | | $ 2.40 | 1.60 | 0.24 |
| *c.* Total, MH, DLH, or RH | Exhibits 12-12, 12-14, 12-17, 12-18 | | 31,920 | 21,984 | 46,400 |
| Total budget costs at standard | (*b* × *c*) | $136,541 | $76,600 | 35,200 | 11,100 |
| *Utilities: heat and light* | | | | | |
| *a.* Standard kilowatthours consumption per year (thousands) | | | 75 | 50 | 62.5 |
| *b.* Standard cost at $0.08 per kilowatthour | (*a* × $0.08) | $ 39,700 | 6000 | 4000 | 5000 |

* MH = machine-hours; DLH = direct labor–hours; RH = repair-hours.

| Assembly | Finishing, Testing, and Packing | Occupancy | Repairs and Maintenance | Storekeeping | Production Planning | Personnel and Timekeeping | General Factory Administration |
|---|---|---|---|---|---|---|---|
| 6,000 | 3000 | | | | | | |
| 6,000 | 3000 | | | | | | |
| | | 8400 | | | | | |
| | | | | | | | 12,000 |
| 12,000 | 6000 | 8400 | | | | | 12,000 |
| 1.5/DLH | 1/DLH | | 3.0/RH | | | | |
| 0.12 | 0.08 | | 0.24 | | | | |
| 77,600 | 25,600 | | 9753 | | | | |
| 9,300 | 2,000 | | 2341 | | | | |
| 137.5 | 37.5 | | 12.5 | 37.5 | 7.5 | 7.5 | 68.75 |
| 11,000 | 3000 | | 1000 | 3000 | 600 | 600 | 5500 |

**Salaries and Indirect Wages Budget** On the basis of budgeted setup time (Exhibit 12-14), budgeted repairs and maintenance–hours (Exhibits 12-15 and 12-16), budgeted inspection-hours (Exhibit 12-17), and standards for other labor (task 19), the labor other than direct labor required by each cost center is budgeted. Then, considering union contracts and policy for raises and promotions, the salary or wage rate for 1981 for each person is estimated. As a next step, the total amount of salaries and indirect wages by cost centers is computed and summarized in Exhibit 12-22. The salaries and wages of individual cost centers are included in the overhead budgets of the respective centers.

**Employee Benefits Costs** On the basis of budgeted direct labor costs (Exhibit 12-19), budgeted salaries and indirect labor costs (Exhibit 12-22), and data regarding the basis of each type of employee benefits cost, the cost of each item of employee benefits is estimated separately for hourly employees and salaried employees. The resultant budget of employee benefits costs is given in Exhibit 12-23.

For the purposes of allocation of employee benefits costs, hourly wages and salaries are first summarized by cost centers in Exhibit 12-24. Next, employee benefits costs pertaining to hourly employees are computed as a percentage of total hourly wages; the figure comes to 30 percent (\$595,946 ÷ \$1,986,554). Similarly, employee benefits costs pertaining to salaried employees are computed as a percentage of total salaries; the figure comes to 25 percent (\$136,500 ÷ \$546,000). Then, the two kinds of employee benefits costs are allocated to individual cost centers by applying the factors of 30 percent and 25 percent respectively to their hourly wages and salaries. For example, the Machine Department's hourly wages and salaries are \$499,200 and \$26,000. Hence, the employee benefits costs allocation comes to \$149,800 (\$499,200 × 30 percent) for hourly employees and \$6500 (\$26,000 × 25 percent) for the salaried employee.

## Budgets for Service Centers

Budgets for the individual service centers and factory administration are given in Exhibits 12-25 through 12-31. During the first iteration, these budgets do not include the allocated costs of other service centers.

In preparing these budgets, most of the data are derived from various exhibits prepared earlier. For example, salaries and indirect wages are taken from Exhibit 12-22, employee benefits costs from Exhibit 12-24, depreciation from Exhibit 12-20, and so on. Certain expense items such as supplies, tools, telephone and telegram, etc., are estimated from the past 2 to 3 years' experience. Further, expense items such as purchased maintenance are estimated from contracts.

Each expense item is separated into fixed and variable categories according to the classification determined under task 11. For example, all occupancy, production-planning, and inspection costs are treated as fixed only.

The preparation of the occupancy budget (Exhibit 12-25) and the repairs and maintenance budget (Exhibit 12-26) deserves special mention because of the reciprocal allocation of these expenses. Since only variable repairs and maintenance expenses are to be allocated to the occupancy cost center and since occupancy expenses are fixed in nature, first the variable repairs and maintenance expense rate is computed, and variable maintenance expenses are allocated to the occupancy cost center. Then, the occupancy cost center budget is completed, and its costs are allocated to various cost centers including repairs and maintenance cost center. Then, the budget of the repairs and maintenance cost center is completed.

### Allocation of Service Centers' Costs to Production Centers

Once the budgets for all the service centers have been completed, the costs of the service centers will be allocated to other service centers and production centers according to the bases for secondary allocation determined under task 23. The result of secondary allocation is summarized in Exhibit 12-32.

### Budgets for Production Centers

Overhead budgets for the individual production centers are given in Exhibits 12-33 through 12-37. In preparing these budgets, most of the data are derived from various exhibits prepared earlier. For example, salaries and indirect wages are taken from Exhibit 12-22, employee benefits costs from Exhibit 12-24, and so on. Certain expense items such as supplies, tools, etc., are estimated from the past 2 to 3 years' experience.

### 28. Computation of Budgeted Overhead Absorption Rates

Once the overhead budgets of the production centers have been completed, overhead absorption rates for each production center are computed. Separate rates are computed for direct and allocated costs as well as for fixed and variable overheads. Overhead absorption rates for production centers are given at the bottom of the respective budgets.

**EXHIBIT 12-22**

**Manufacturing Salaries and Indirect Wages Schedule (ACME Company)**
Year 1981

| | 1981 Budget | | | | |
|---|---|---|---|---|---|
| | Person-Hours | Number of Salaried Employees | Hourly Wage Rate | Total Wages | Total Salaries |
| *Production cost centers* | | | | | |
| Machine supervisor | | 1 | | | 26,000 |
| Press supervisor | | 1 | | | 22,000 |
| Welding supervisor | | 1 | | | 24,000 |
| Assembly supervisor | | 2 | | | 52,000 |
| Finishing supervisor | | 1 | | | 28,000 |
| Production superintendent | | 1 | | | 30,000 |
| Setup wages | (720 + 384) | | 6.15 | 6,800 | |
| Subtotal | 1104 | 7 | | 6,800 | 182,000 |
| *Service cost centers* | | | | | |
| Production planner | | 1 | | | 20,000 |
| Production dispatcher | | 1 | | | 10,000 |
| Storekeeper | | 1 | | | 15,000 |
| Material handlers | }3220<br>176 | 2+ | 5.00<br>6.00 | 16,100<br>1,056 | |
| Inspectors | | 3 | | | 54,000 |
| Repairs supervisor | | 1 | | | 21,000 |
| Mechanics | 7011 | 5 | 6.15 | 43,118 | |
| Electricians | 3252 | 2 | 6.15 | 20,000 | |
| Personnel administrator | | 1 | | | 16,000 |
| Timekeepers-clerks | | 2 | | | 20,000 |
| Janitors | 3220 | 2 | 4.00 | 12,880 | |
| Service superintendent | | 1 | | | 28,000 |
| Subtotal | | 22 | | 93,154 | 184,000 |
| *General* | | | | | |
| Cost analysts | | 2 | | | 32,000 |
| Clerks-secretaries | | 3 | | | 19,000 |
| Assistant to plant manager | | 1 | | | 20,000 |
| Plant manager | | 1 | | | 34,000 |
| Subtotal | | 7 | | | 105,000 |
| *Office of vice president, manufacturing* | | | | | |
| Executive secretary | | 1 | | | 15,000 |
| Vice president, manufacturing | | 1 | | | 60,000 |
| Subtotal | | 2 | | | 75,000 |
| Total | | 38 | | 99,954 | 546,000 |

NOTE: This schedule does not include overtime premium.

Prepared by Plant manager (except salaries of the Office of Vice President, Manufacturing) Date _____

Approved by Vice president, manufacturing Date _____

President Date _____

| 1980 Estimated actual | | | | | |
|---|---|---|---|---|---|
| Person-Hours | Number of Salaried Employees | Hourly Wage Rate | Total Wages | Total Salaries | Percent Increase over 1980 |
| | | Details not given | | | |

**EXHIBIT 12-23**

**Employee Benefits Cost Budget (ACME Company)**
Year: 1981

| Account | Account Title | Basis | For Hourly Employees | For Salaried Employees |
|---|---|---|---|---|
| | *Employee benefits (company's costs)* | | Individual | Individual |
| | FICA Tax | | amounts not | amounts not |
| | Federal unemployment tax | | filled in here | filled in here |
| | State unemployment tax | | because they | because they |
| | Workmen's compensation | | are not rele- | are not rele- |
| | Retirement plan | | vant for the | vant for the |
| | Pension plan | | purpose of | purpose of |
| | Medical insurance | | this case | this case |
| | Life insurance | | study | study |
| | Disability insurance | | | |
| | First aid | | | |
| | Bonus and incentives | | | |
| | Layoff allowance | | | |
| | Uniform allowance | | | |
| | Canteen subsidy | | | |
| | Tuition reimbursement | | | |
| | *Pay for time not worked* | | | |
| | Vacation | | | |
| | Holiday | | | |
| | Sick pay | | | |
| | Excused absence | | | |
| | Military leave allowance | | | |
| | Paid lunch and rest periods | | | |
| | Paid washup and clothes-changing time | | | |
| | *Employee activities* | | | |
| | Social and recreational expenses | | | |
| | Awards | | | |
| | Total budgeted employee benefits | | $ 595,946 | $136,500 |
| | Total wages and salaries (Exhibit 12-24) | | $1,986,554 | $546,000 |
| | Benefits to hourly employees as percentage of wages | | 30 percent | |
| | Benefits to salaried employees as percentage of salaries | | | 25 percent |

## EXHIBIT 12-24

### Allocation of Employee Benefits Costs (ACME Company)

Year 1981

| Cost Center No. | Cost Center | Hourly Wages ($) | | | | | | | Salaries ($) | Allocation of Employee Benefits | |
|---|---|---|---|---|---|---|---|---|---|---|---|
| | | Direct Labor | Indirect Labor | Transfer Labor Difference | Idle Time | Rework Time | Learning Time | Total | | 30 percent of Hourly Wages | 25 percent of Salaries |
| | Exhibit Reference | 12-19 | 12-22 | 12-13 | 12-13, 12-22 | 12-13 | 12-13 | | 12-22 | | |
| | Machine | 469,200 | 4,400 | 100 | 14,100 | 9,400 | 2100 | 499,200 | 26,000 | 149,800 | 6,500 |
| | Press | 153,000 | 2,400 | | 4,600 | 3,100 | | 163,200 | 22,000 | 49,000 | 5,500 |
| | Welding | 332,700 | | | 10,000 | 6,700 | | 349,400 | 24,000 | 104,800 | 6,000 |
| | Assembly | 630,100 | | 200 | 18,900 | 12,600 | | 661,800 | 52,000 | 198,500 | 13,000 |
| | Finishing | 209,600 | | 100 | 6,300 | 3,800 | | 219,800 | 28,000 | 65,900 | 7,000 |
| | Repairs and maintenance | | 59,981 | | 3,137 | | | 63,118 | 21,000 | 18,935 | 5,250 |
| | Storekeeping and material handling | | 17,156 | | ....* | | | 17,156 | 15,000 | 5,147 | 3,750 |
| | Production planning | | | | | | | | 30,000 | | 7,500 |
| | Inspection and quality control | | | | | | | | 54,000 | | 13,500 |
| | Personnel and timekeeping | | | | | | | | 36,000 | | 9,000 |
| | Occupancy | | 12,880 | | ....* | | | 12,880 | | 3,864 | |
| | General factory administration | | | | | | | | 238,000 | | 59,500 |
| | Total | 1,794,600 | 96,817 | 400 | 57,037 | 35,600 | 2100 | 1,986,554 | 546,000 | 595,946 | 136,500 |

* Wages for idle time are not separated from total wages.

**EXHIBIT 12-25**

**Occupancy Expense Budget (ACME Company)**

Responsibility of ________ Responsibility center no. ________

Year 1981

Approved by ________ Date prepared ________

| Account | Expense | Basis for Computation or Reference | 1981 Budget ($) | | Budget for Cost Control ($) | |
|---|---|---|---|---|---|---|
| | | | Fixed | Variable | Fixed Cost per Month | Variable Cost per Activity Unit |
| | Direct cost center costs | | | | | |
| | *Indirect labor* | | | | | |
| | Janitors (2) | Exhibit 12-22 | 12,880 | | 1073 | |
| | *Employee benefits* | 2 × 1610 hours × $4 per hour | | | | |
| | Hourly at 30 percent of wages | Exhibit 12-23 | 3,864 | | 322 | |
| | Supplies | Past experience | 5,000 | | 416 | |

| | | | | | |
|---|---|---|---|---|---|
| Maintenance materials | Exhibit 12-21 | 8,400 | | 700 | |
| Leasehold land: rent and amortization | Contracts, etc. | 12,000 | | 1000 | |
| Depreciation of building | Exhibit 12-20 | 54,000 | | 4500 | |
| Subtotal | | 96,144 | | | |
| Allocated: controllable | | | | | |
| Repairs and maintenance charges | Exhibit 12-32<br>400 hours × $16.477 per hour | 6,600 | | 550 | |
| Subtotal | | 6,600 | | | |
| Total direct costs | | 102,744 | | 8562 | |
| Allocated: other | | | | | |
| Insurance | Exhibit 12-20 | 5,000 | | | |
| Property taxes | Exhibit 12-20 | 5,000 | | | |
| Total allocated costs | | 10,000 | | 833 | |
| Total overhead | | 112,744 | | 9395 | |

NOTES: The basis for allocation is the floor area occupied (see Exhibit 12-32).

Though only variable repairs and maintenance costs are allocated to this cost center, they are treated as fixed costs because they will remain more or less fixed during the year.

**EXHIBIT 12-26**

**Repairs and Maintenance Budget (ACME Company)**

Responsibility of ________ Responsibility center no. ________

Year 1981

Approved by ________ Date prepared ________

| Account No. | Expense | Basis for Computation or Reference | 1981 Budget ($) | | Budget for Cost Control ($) | |
|---|---|---|---|---|---|---|
| | | | Fixed | Variable | Fixed Cost per Month | Variable Cost per Activity Unit |
| | Direct cost center costs | | | | | |
| | Supervisor's salary | 1 × $21,000 (Exhibit 12-22) | 21,000 | | 1750 | |
| | *Indirect labor* | Exhibits 12-17, 12-18, 12-22 | | | | |
| | Mechanics (5) | 6541 hours × $6.15 per hour | | 40,227 | | 4.125 |
| | Electricians (2) | 3212 hours × $6.15 per hour | | 19,754 | | 2.025 |
| | *Idle indirect labor* | Exhibits 12-15, 12-16, 12-22 | | | | |
| | Mechanics | 470 hours × $6.15 per hour | 2,891 | | 240 | |
| | Electricians | 40 hours × $6.15 per hour | 246 | | 20 | |
| | *Employee benefits* | Exhibit 12-23 | | | | |
| | Hourly at 30 percent of wages | 30 percent × 59,981 | | 17,994 | | 1.845 |
| | | 30 percent × 3,137 | 941 | | 78 | |
| | Salaried at 25 percent of salaries | 25 percent × 21,000 | 5,250 | | 437 | |

| | | | | | | |
|---|---|---|---|---|---|---|
| *Overtime premium* | Exhibits 12-15, 12-16, 12-22 | | | | | |
| Mechanics | 65 hours × $6.15 × 50 percent | | | 200 | | 0.031 |
| Electricians | 32 hours × $6.15 × 50 percent | | | 98 | | |
| Operating supplies | Past experience | | | 60,000 | | 6.152 |
| Tools | | | | 14,000 | | 1.435 |
| Power | Exhibit 12-21 | | | 2,341 | | 0.240 |
| Heat and light | Exhibit 12-21 | | 1,000 | | 83 | |
| Telephone and telegram | Past experience | | 905 | 6,086 | 75 | 0.624 |
| Depreciation | Exhibit 12-20 | | 2,200 | | 183 | |
| Total direct costs | | 195,133 | 34,433 | 160,700 | 2870 | 16.477 |
| Allocated costs | | | | | | |
| Insurance | Exhibit 12-20 | | 220 | | | |
| Property taxes | | | 110 | | | |
| Occupancy | Exhibit 12-32 | | 5,637 | | | |
| Total allocated costs | | | 5,967 | ....... | 497 | ...... |
| Total overhead | | 201,100 | 40,400 | 160,700 | 3367 | 16.477 |
| *Repairs and maintenance hour rate* | | | | | | |
| *a.* Planned repair-hours | 9753 | | | | | |
| *b.* Variable repair-hour rate | $160,700 ÷ 9,753 | | | 16.477 | | |
| *c.* Variable repair cost allocated to occupancy cost center | 400 hours × $16.477 (say) | | | 6,600 | | |
| *d.* Fixed repair cost as percentage of remaining variable repair cost | $40,400 ÷ ($160,700 − $6600) | | 26.217 percent | | | |

**EXHIBIT 12-27**

**Storekeeping and Material-Handling Budget (ACME Company)**

Responsibility of ______ Responsibility center no. ______

Year 1981

Approved by ______ Date prepared ______

| Account No. | Expense | Basis for Computation or Reference | 1981 Budget ($) | | Budget for Cost Control ($) | |
|---|---|---|---|---|---|---|
| | | | Fixed | Variable | Fixed Cost per Month | Variable Cost per Activity Unit |
| | Direct cost center costs | | | | | |
| | *Supervisory and clerical salaries* | | | | | |
| | Storekeeper (1) | Exhibit 12-22 | 15,000 | | 1250 | |
| | *Indirect labor* | | | | | |
| | Material handlers (2) | 2 × 1610 hours × $5 per hour | 16,100 | | 1342 | |
| | Extra packing labor time used for material handling and storekeeping | 176 hours × $6 per hour Exhibit 12-22 | 1,056 | | 88 | |

| | | | | | | |
|---|---|---|---|---|---|---|
| *Employee benefits* | Exhibit 12-23 | | | | | |
| Hourly at 30 percent of wages | 30 percent × $17,156 | | 5,147 | | 429 | |
| Salaried at 25 percent of salaries | 25 percent × $15,000 | | 3,750 | | 313 | |
| Supplies | Past experience | | 973 | 2,500 | 81 | 0.00088 |
| Purchased maintenance: Weighing scales | Contracts | | 2,000 | | 167 | |
| Heat and light | Exhibit 12-21 | | 3,000 | | 250 | |
| Telephone and telegram | Past experience | | 500 | 1,500 | 41 | 0.00054 |
| Depreciation | Exhibit 12-20 | | 8,000 | | 666 | |
| Total direct costs | | 59,526 | 55,526 | 4,000 | 4627 | 0.00142 |
| Allocated costs | | | | | | |
| Insurance | } Exhibit 12-20 | | 800 | 20,000 | All allocated costs are treated as fixed for cost control purposes. | |
| Property taxes | | | 400 | 10,000 | | |
| Occupancy expenses | Exhibit 12-32 | | 11,274 | | | |
| Total allocated costs | | 42,474 | 12,474 | 30,000 | 3540 | ....... |
| Total overhead | | 102,000 | 68,000 | 34,000 | 8167 | 0.00142 |

NOTES: The basis for allocation is the dollar amount of direct materials consumed (see Exhibit 12-18).

The variable cost per activity unit for each variable-cost item is computed by dividing the variable-cost amount by $2,814,000, the budgeted direct material consumption (see Exhibit 12-18).

**EXHIBIT 12-28**

**Inspection Budget (ACME Company)**

Responsibility of ________________ Responsibility center no. ________

Year 1981

Approved by ________________ Date prepared ________

| Account No. | Expense | Basis for Computation or Reference | 1981 Budget ($) | | Budget for Cost Control ($) | |
|---|---|---|---|---|---|---|
| | | | Fixed | Variable | Fixed Cost per Month | Variable Cost per Activity Unit |
| | Direct cost center costs | | | | | |
| | *Supervisory and clerical salaries* | Exhibit 12-22 | | | | |
| | Inspectors (3) | 3 × $18,000 | 54,000 | | 4500 | |
| | *Employee benefits* | Exhibit 12-23 | | | | |
| | Salaried at 25 per cent of salaries | | 13,500 | | 1125 | |
| | Small tools, etc. | Past experience | 2,000 | | 166 | |
| | Total direct costs | | 69,500 | | 5791 | |
| | Allocated costs | | ...... | | .... | |
| | Total overhead | | 69,500 | | 5791 | |

NOTE: The basis for allocation is budgeted inspection-hours (see Exhibit 12-17).

**EXHIBIT 12-29**

**Production-Planning Budget (ACME Company)**

Responsibility of ________ Responsibility center no. ________

Year 1981

Approved by ________ Date prepared ________

| Account No. | Expense | Basis for Computation or Reference | 1981 Budget ($) Fixed | 1981 Budget ($) Variable | Budget for Cost Control ($) Fixed Cost per Month | Budget for Cost Control ($) Variable Cost per Activity Unit |
|---|---|---|---|---|---|---|
| | Direct cost center costs | | | | | |
| | *Supervisory and clerical salaries* | Exhibit 12-22 | | | | |
| | Production planner (1) | Salary schedule | 20,000 | | 1667 | |
| | Production clerk-dispatcher (1) | Salary schedule | 10,000 | | 833 | |
| | *Employee benefits* | Exhibit 12-23 | | | | |
| | Salaried at 25 percent of salaries | | 7,500 | | 625 | |
| | Operating supplies | Past experience | 1,045 | | 87 | |
| | Heat and light | Exhibit 12-21 | 600 | | 50 | |
| | Depreciation | Exhibit 12-20 | 2,000 | | 167 | |
| | Total direct costs | | 41,145 | | 3429 | |
| | Allocated costs | | | | | |
| | Insurance | Exhibit 12-20 | 200 | | | |
| | Property taxes | Exhibit 12-20 | 100 | | | |
| | Occupancy expenses | Exhibit 12-32 | 2,255 | | | |
| | Total allocated costs | | 2,555 | | 213 | |
| | Total overhead | | 43,700 | | 3642 | |

NOTE: The basis for allocation is the time spent for planning production of each production department (see Exhibit 12-32).

**EXHIBIT 12-30**

**Personnel and Timekeeping Budget (ACME Company)**

Responsibility of ________ | Responsibility center no. ________

Year 1981

Approved by ________ | Date prepared ________

| Account No. | Expense | Basis for Computation or Reference | 1981 Budget ($) | | Budget for Cost Control ($) | |
|---|---|---|---|---|---|---|
| | | | Fixed | Variable | Fixed Cost per Month | Variable Cost per Activity Unit |
| | Direct cost center costs | | | | | |
| | *Supervisory and clerical salaries* | Exhibit 12-22 | | | | See notes. |
| | Personnel administrator | | 16,000 | | 1333 | |
| | Timekeepers and clerks (2) | 2 × $10,000 | 20,000 | | 1667 | |
| | *Employee benefits* | Exhibit 12-23 | | | | |
| | Salaried at 25 percent of salaries | | 9,000 | | 750 | |
| | Overtime Premium | 2 × 100 hours × 50 percent × $4.80 per hour | | 480 | 40 | |
| | Supplies | Past experience | 200 | | | |
| | Heat and light | Exhibit 12-21 | 600 | | | |
| | Telephone and telegram | Past experience | | 500 | | |
| | Depreciation | Exhibit 12-20 | 3,000 | | | |
| | Total direct costs | 51,280 | 48,800 | 2480 | 4273 | |
| | Allocated costs | | | | | |
| | Insurance | Exhibit 12-20 (Insurance and Property taxes) | 300 | | | |
| | Property taxes | | 150 | | | |
| | Occupancy expenses | Exhibit 12-32 | 2,255 | | | |
| | Total allocated costs | | 2,705 | .... | 225 | |
| | Total overhead | 53,985 | 51,505 | 2480 | 4498 | |

NOTES: The basis for allocation is direct labor–hours (see Exhibit 12-19). These costs are allocated along with general factory administration. Since the total amount of variable costs is not significant, all costs have been treated as fixed for cost control purposes, though they are separated into fixed and variable costs for product costing.

**EXHIBIT 12-31**

**Consolidated Budget of the Office of the Vice President, Manufacturing, Office of the Plant Manager, and General Factory Expenses (ACME Company)**
Year 1981

| | Basis for Computation | Amount ($) Fixed | Variable |
|---|---|---|---|
| Direct cost center costs | | | |
| *Supervisory and clerical salaries* | Exhibit 12-22 | | |
| vice president, manufacturing | | 60,000 | |
| Plant manager | | 34,000 | |
| Assistant to plant manager | | 20,000 | |
| Production superintendent | | 30,000 | |
| Service and administration superintendent | | 28,000 | |
| Cost analysts (2) | 2 × $16,000 | 32,000 | |
| Clerks and secretaries (4) | ($15,000 + $7,000 + $6,000 + $6,000) | 34,000 | |
| *Employee benefits* | Exhibit 12-23 | | |
| Salaried at 25 percent of salaries | 25 percent × $238,000 | | |
| *Overtime premium* | Exhibit 12-23 | | |
| Cost analysts | 240 hours × 2 × 50 percent × $7.69 per hour (regular rate) | | 1,846 |
| Supplies | Past experience | 4,002 | 6,024 |
| Maintenance materials | Exhibit 12-21 | 2,000 | 10,000 |
| Purchased maintenance | Contracts | 500 | 2,000 |
| Heat and light | Exhibit 12-21 | 5,500 | |
| Telephone and telegram | Past experience | 3,000 | 12,000 |
| Travel and entertainment | Past experience | 2,000 | 15,000 |
| Depreciation | Exhibit 12-20 | 9,000 | |
| Water (25 percent fixed, 75 percent variable) | | | |
| First 100,000 gallons | At $5 per 1000 gallons | | |
| Next 200,000 gallons | At $4 per 1000 gallons | | |
| Next 300,000 gallons | At $3 per 1000 gallons ($500 + $800 + $900 = $2200) | 550 | 1,650 |
| Total direct costs | 372,572 | 324,052 | 48,520 |
| Allocated costs | | | |
| Insurance | Exhibit 12-20 | 980 | |
| Property taxes | Exhibit 12-20 | 440 | |
| Occupancy expenses | Exhibit 12-32 | 12,423 | |
| Total allocated costs | | 13,843 | |
| Total overhead | 386,895 | 337,895 | 48,420 |

NOTES: The basis for allocation is direct labor–hours (see Exhibit 12-19).
For responsiblity accounting, there will be separate budgets for:

- Office of the Vice President, Manufacturing
- Office of the Plant Manager (consisting of the Plant Manager's Office, Cost Accounting Department, and the Offices of the Production and Service Superintendents)
- General factory expenses, the responsibility of the service superintendent

For the sake of brevity, the above-mentioned budgets are not shown here separately.

**EXHIBIT 12-32**

**Secondary Distribution of Budgeted Manufacturing Overhead (ACME Company)**

Year 1981

| | Basis or Reference | Total | Machine | Press |
|---|---|---|---|---|
| *Distribution factors* | | | | |
| 1. Floor area (percent of total area) | Schedule* | 100 | 18 | 15 |
| 2. Maintenance hours | | | | |
| Mechanical | Exhibit 12-15 | 6941 | 2750 | 1651 |
| Electrical | Exhibit 12-16 | 2812 | 1092 | 756 |
| Subtotal | | 9753 | 3842 | 2407 |
| 3. Budgeted direct material consumption ($000) | Exhibit 12-18 | $2814 | 1128 | 186 |
| 4. Budgeted direct labor–hours (thousands) | Exhibit 12-13 | 233.6 | 62.4 | 21.6 |
| 5. Budgeted inspection-hours | Exhibit 12-17 | 4880 | 2000 | ... |
| 6. Budgeted production planning time (percent) | Schedule* | 100 | 15 | 30 |
| *Distribution of service center costs* | | | | |
| 1. Occupancy expenses | Floor area | $112,744 | 20,300 | 16,900 |
| 2. Repairs and maintenance | Budgeted maintenance-hours | | | |
| Variable | | $160,700 | 63,300 | 39,700 |
| Fixed | | $ 40,400 | 16,600 | 10,400 |
| 3. Storekeeping and material handling | Budgeted material consumption | | | |
| Variable | | $ 34,000 | 13,600 | 2,300 |
| Fixed | | $ 68,000 | 27,200 | 4,600 |
| 4. Inspection | Inspection-hours | $ 69,500 | 28,500 | |
| 5. Production planning | Time | $ 43,700 | 6,600 | 13,100 |
| 6. General factory administration, including personnel and timekeeping | Direct labor–hours | | | |
| Variable | | $ 51,000 | 13,600 | 4,700 |
| Fixed | | $389,400 | 104,000 | 36,000 |

* For the sake of brevity, these schedules are not given.

| Welding | Assembly | Finishing, Testing, and Packing | Occupancy | Repairs and Maintenance | Storekeeping | Production Planning | Personnel and Timekeeping | General Factory Administration |
|---|---|---|---|---|---|---|---|---|
| 15 | 12 | 10 | .. | 5 | 10 | 2 | 2 | 11 |
| 696 | 776 | 668 | 400 | | | | | |
| 464 | 388 | 112 | ... | | | | | |
| 1160 | 1164 | 780 | 400 | | | | | |
| 172 | 1202 | 126 | | | | | | |
| 46.4 | 77.6 | 25.6 | | | | | | |
| ... | 2400 | 480 | | | | | | |
| 25 | 20 | 10 | | | | | | |
| 16,900 | 13,500 | 11,300 | .... | 5637 | 11,274 | 2255 | 2255 | 12,423 |
| 19,100 | 19,200 | 12,800 | 6600 | | | | | |
| 5,000 | 5,000 | 3,400 | | | | | | |
| 2,100 | 14,500 | 1,500 | | | | | | |
| 4,200 | 29,000 | 3,000 | | | | | | |
| | 34,200 | 6,800 | | | | | | |
| 10,900 | 8,700 | 4,400 | | | | | | |
| 10,100 | 17,000 | 5,600 | | | | | | |
| 77,300 | 129,400 | 42,700 | | | | | | |

## EXHIBIT 12-33

# Manufacturing Overhead Budget (ACME Company)

Production cost center Machine shop
Responsibility center no. ________
Responsibility of ________
Activity level 31,200 machine-hours

Year 1981
Date prepared ________
Approved by ________

| Account No. | Expense | Basis for computation or reference | 1981 budget ($) Fixed | 1981 budget ($) Variable | Budget for cost control ($) Fixed cost per month | Budget for cost control ($) Variable cost per activity unit |
|---|---|---|---|---|---|---|
| | Direct cost center costs | | | | | |
| | Supervisory salaries | Exhibit 12-22 | 26,000 | | 2,166 | |
| | Indirect labor: setup | Exhibits 12-14, 22 | | 4,440 | | 0.141 |
| | Costs related to direct labor | Exhibit 12-13 | | | | |
| | Transfer labor difference | | | ....... | | ..... |
| | Idle time | | | 14,100 | | 0.452 |
| | Rework time | | | 9,400 | | 0.301 |
| | Learning time | | | 2,100 | | 0.067 |
| | Overtime premium | | | ....... | | ..... |
| | Second-shift premium | | | ....... | | ..... |
| | Benefits | Exhibit 12-24 | | | | |
| | Hourly (including direct labor) | At 30 percent of wages | | 149,800 | | 4.801 |
| | Salaried | At 25 percent of salaries | 6,500 | | 542 | |
| | Rework materials | At 1 percent of direct materials | | 11,300 | | 0.362 |
| | Operating supplies | Past experience | | 24,000 | | 0.769 |
| | Small tools and equipment | Past experience | | 30,000 | | 0.962 |
| | Maintenance materials | Exhibit 12-21 | | 48,000 | | 1.538 |
| | Repairs and maintenance charges | Exhibit 12-32 | 16,600 | 63,000 | 1,383 | 2.029 |
| | Power purchased | Exhibit 12-21 | | 76,000 | | 2.455 |
| | Heat and light | Exhibit 12-21 | 6,000 | | 500 | |
| | Telephone and telegram | Past experience | 500 | 3,000 | 42 | 0.096 |
| | Depreciation | Exhibit 12-20 | 132,300 | | 11,025 | |
| | Total direct costs | 623,900 | 187,900 | 436,000 | 15,658 | 13.974 |
| | Allocated costs | | | | | |
| | Insurance | Exhibit 12-20 | 13,200 | | All allocated costs are treated as fixed for cost control purposes. | |
| | Property taxes | Exhibit 12-20 | 6,600 | | | |
| | Occupancy | Exhibit 12-32 | 20,300 | | | |
| | Storekeeping and material handling | Exhibit 12-32 | 27,200 | 13,600 | | |
| | Inspection | Exhibit 12-32 | 28,500 | | | |
| | Production planning | Exhibit 12-32 | 6,600 | | | |
| | General factory administration (including personnel) | Exhibit 12-32 | 104,000 | 13,600 | | |
| | Total allocated costs | 233,600 | 206,400 | 27,200 | 19,467 | ...... |
| | Total overhead | 857,600 | 394,300 | 463,300 | 35,125 | 13.974 |

Budgeted machine-hour rate for product costing

| | Fixed-overhead rate | Variable-overhead rate | Combined-overhead rate |
|---|---|---|---|
| Direct cost center costs | 6.023 | 13.974 | 19.997 |
| Allocated costs | 6.615 | 0.872 | 7.487 |
| Total overhead | 12.638 | 14.846 | 27.484 |

## EXHIBIT 12-34

# Manufacturing Overhead Budget (ACME Company)

Production cost center Press shop
Responsibility center no. ______
Responsibility of ______
Activity level 21,600 machine-hours

Year 1981
Date prepared ______
Approved by ______

| Account No. | Expense | Basis for computation or reference | 1981 budget ($) Fixed | 1981 budget ($) Variable | Budget for cost control ($) Fixed cost per month | Budget for cost control ($) Variable cost per activity unit |
|---|---|---|---|---|---|---|
| | Direct cost center costs | | | | | |
| | Supervisory salaries | Exhibit 12-22 | 22,000 | | 1,833 | |
| | Indirect labor: setup | Exhibits 12-14, 22 | | 2,400 | | 0.111 |
| | Costs related to direct labor | Exhibit 12-13 | | | | |
| | Transfer labor difference | | | 100 | | 0.005 |
| | Idle time | | | 4,600 | | 0.213 |
| | Rework time | | | 3,100 | | 0.143 |
| | Learning time | | | ..... | | ..... |
| | Overtime premium | | | ..... | | ..... |
| | Second-shift premium | | | ..... | | ..... |
| | Benefits | Exhibit 12-24 | | | | |
| | Hourly (including direct labor) | At 30 percent of wages | | 49,000 | | 2.269 |
| | Salaried | At 25 percent of salaries | 5,500 | | 458 | |
| | Rework materials | At 1 percent of direct materials | | 1,900 | | 0.088 |
| | Operating supplies | Past experience | | 12,000 | | 0.556 |
| | Small tools and equipment | Past experience | | 15,000 | | 0.694 |
| | Maintenance materials | Exhibit 12-21 | | 42,000 | | 1.944 |
| | Repairs and maintenance charges | Exhibit 12-32 | 10,400 | 39,700 | 867 | 1.838 |
| | Power purchased | Exhibit 12-21 | | 35,200 | | |
| | Heat and light | Exhibit 12-21 | 4,000 | | 333 | 1.630 |
| | Telephone and telegram | Past experience | 500 | 3,000 | 42 | |
| | Depreciation | Exhibit 12-20 | 96,200 | | 8,017 | 0.139 |
| | Total direct costs | 346,600 | 138,600 | 208,000 | 11,550 | 9.630 |
| | Allocated costs | | | | | |
| | Insurance | Exhibit 12-20 | 9,600 | | All allocated costs are treated as fixed for cost control purposes. | |
| | Property taxes | Exhibit 12-20 | 4,800 | | | |
| | Occupancy | Exhibit 12-32 | 16,900 | | | |
| | Storekeeping and material handling | Exhibit 12-32 | 4,600 | 2,300 | | |
| | Inspection | Exhibit 12-32 | | | | |
| | Production planning | Exhibit 12-32 | 13,100 | | | |
| | General factory administration (including personnel) | Exhibit 12-32 | 36,000 | 4,700 | | |
| | Total allocated costs | 92,000 | 85,000 | 7,000 | 7,667 | ..... |
| | Total overhead | 438,600 | 223,600 | 215,000 | 19,217 | 9.630 |

Budgeted machine-hour rate for product costing

| | Fixed-overhead rate | Variable-overhead rate | Combined-overhead rate |
|---|---|---|---|
| Direct cost center costs | 6.417 | 9.630 | 16.047 |
| Allocated costs | 3.935 | 0.324 | 4.259 |
| Total overhead | 10.352 | 9.954 | 20.306 |

## EXHIBIT 12-35

## Manufacturing Overhead Budget (ACME Company)

| | |
|---|---|
| Production cost center: Welding shop | Year: 1981 |
| Responsibility center no. ______ | Date prepared ______ |
| Responsibility of ______ | Approved by ______ |
| Activity level: 46,400 direct labor-hours | |

| Account No. | Expense | Basis for computation or reference | | 1981 budget ($) Fixed | 1981 budget ($) Variable | Budget for cost control ($) Fixed cost per month | Budget for cost control ($) Variable cost per activity unit |
|---|---|---|---|---|---|---|---|
| | Direct cost center costs | | | | | | |
| | Supervisory salaries | Exhibit 12-22 | | 24,000 | | 2,000 | |
| | Indirect labor: setup | | | | | | |
| | Costs related to direct labor | Exhibit 12-13 | | | | | |
| | Transfer labor difference | | | | ....... | | ..... |
| | Idle time | | | | 10,000 | | 0.216 |
| | Rework time | | | | 6,700 | | 0.144 |
| | Learning time | | | | ....... | | ..... |
| | Overtime premium | | | | 1,500 | | 0.032 |
| | Second-shift premium | | | | ....... | | |
| | Benefits | Exhibit 12-24 | | | | | |
| | Hourly (including direct labor) | At 30 percent of wages | | | 104,800 | | |
| | Salaried | At 25 percent of salaries | | 6,000 | | 500 | ..... |
| | Rework materials | At 1 percent of direct materials | | | | | 2.259 |
| | | | | | 1,700 | | |
| | Operating supplies | Past experience | | | 20,000 | | 0.036 |
| | Small tools and equipment | Past experience | | | 12,000 | | 0.431 |
| | Maintenance materials | Exhibit 12-21 | | | 14,000 | | 0.259 |
| | Repairs and maintenance charges | Exhibit 12-32 | | 5,000 | 19,100 | 417 | 0.301 |
| | Power purchased | Exhibit 12-21 | | | 11,100 | | 0.412 |
| | Heat and light | Exhibit 12-21 | | 5,000 | | 417 | 0.239 |
| | Telephone and telegram | Past experience | | 500 | 3,000 | 42 | 0.065 |
| | Depreciation | Exhibit 12-20 | | 24,200 | | 2,016 | |
| | Total direct costs | | 268,600 | 64,700 | 203,900 | 5,392 | 4.394 |
| | Allocated costs | | | | | All allocated costs are treated as fixed for cost control purposes. | |
| | Insurance | Exhibit 12-20 | | 2,400 | | | |
| | Property taxes | Exhibit 12-20 | | 1,200 | | | |
| | Occupancy | Exhibit 12-32 | | 16,900 | | | |
| | Storekeeping and material handling | Exhibit 12-32 | | 4,200 | 2,100 | | |
| | Inspection | Exhibit 12-32 | | ...... | | | |
| | Production planning | Exhibit 12-32 | | 10,900 | | | |
| | General factory administration (including personnel) | Exhibit 12-32 | | 77,300 | 10,100 | | |
| | Total allocated costs | | 125,100 | 112,900 | 12,200 | 10,425 | ..... |
| | Total overhead | | 393,700 | 177,600 | 216,100 | 15,817 | 4.394 |

**Budgeted direct labor-hour rate for product costing**

| | Fixed-overhead rate | Variable-overhead rate | Combined-overhead rate |
|---|---|---|---|
| Direct cost center costs | 1.395 | 4.394 | 5.789 |
| Allocated costs | 2.433 | 0.263 | 2.696 |
| Total overhead | 3.828 | 4.657 | 8.485 |

## EXHIBIT 12-36

## Manufacturing Overhead Budget (ACME Company)

Production cost center: Assembly shop
Responsibility center no. ______
Responsibility of ______
Activity level: 77,600 direct labor-hours

Year: 1981
Date prepared ______
Approved by ______

| Account No. | Expense | Basis for computation or reference | | 1981 budget ($) Fixed | 1981 budget ($) Variable | Budget for cost control ($) Fixed cost per month | Budget for cost control ($) Variable cost per activity unit |
|---|---|---|---|---|---|---|---|
| | Direct cost center costs | | | | | | |
| | Supervisory salaries | Exhibit 12-22 | | 52,000 | | 4,333 | |
| | Indirect labor: setup | | | | | | |
| | Costs related to direct labor | Exhibit 12-13 | | | | | |
| | Transfer labor difference | | | | 200 | | 0.003 |
| | Idle time | | | | 18,900 | | 0.243 |
| | Rework time | | | | 12,600 | | 0.162 |
| | Learning time | | | | ....... | | ..... |
| | Overtime premium | | | | 1,400 | | 0.018 |
| | Second-shift premium | | | | 15,700 | | 0.202 |
| | Benefits | Exhibit 12-24 | | | | | |
| | Hourly (including direct labor) | At 30 percent of wages | | | 198,500 | | |
| | Salaried | At 25 percent of salaries | | 13,000 | | 1,083 | 2.558 |
| | Rework materials | At 1 percent of direct materials | | | 12,000 | | 0.155 |
| | Operating supplies | Past experience | | | 6,000 | | 0.077 |
| | Small tools and equipment | | | | 12,000 | | 0.155 |
| | Maintenance materials | Exhibit 12-21 | | | 12,000 | | 0.155 |
| | Repairs and maintenance charges | Exhibit 12-32 | | 5,000 | 19,200 | 417 | 0.247 |
| | Power purchased | Exhibit 12-21 | | | 9,300 | 917 | 0.120 |
| | Heat and light | | | 11,000 | | | |
| | Telephone and telegram | Past experience | | 500 | 1,000 | 42 | |
| | Depreciation | Exhibit 12—20 | | 12,400 | | 1,033 | 0.013 |
| | Total direct costs | | 412,700 | 93,900 | 318,800 | 7,825 | 4.108 |
| | Allocated costs | | | | | | |
| | Insurance | Exhibit 12-20 | | 1,200 | | All allocated costs are treated as fixed for cost control purposes. | |
| | Property taxes | | | 600 | | | |
| | Occupancy | Exhibit 12-32 | | 13,500 | | | |
| | Storekeeping and material handling | | | 29,000 | 14,500 | | |
| | Inspection | | | 34,200 | | | |
| | Production planning | | | 8,700 | | | |
| | General factory administration (including personnel) | | | 129,400 | 17,000 | | |
| | Total allocated costs | | 248,100 | 216,600 | 31,500 | 20,675 | . . . . |
| | Total overhead | | 660,800 | 310,500 | 350,300 | 28,500 | 4.108 |

**Budgeted direct labor-hour rate for product costing**

| | Fixed-overhead rate | Variable-overhead rate | Combined-overhead rate |
|---|---|---|---|
| Direct cost center | 1.210 | 4.108 | 5.318 |
| Allocated costs | 2.791 | 0.406 | 3.197 |
| Total overhead | 4.001 | 4.514 | 8.515 |

## EXHIBIT 12-37

# Manufacturing Overhead Budget (ACME Company)

Production cost center: Finishing, testing and packing shop
Responsibility center no. ______
Responsibility of ______
Activity level: 25,600 direct labor-hours

Year 1981
Date prepared ______
Approved by ______

| Account No. | Expense | Basis for computation or reference | | 1981 budget ($) | | Budget for cost control ($) | |
|---|---|---|---|---|---|---|---|
| | | | | Fixed | Variable | Fixed cost per month | Variable cost per activity unit |
| | Direct cost center costs | | | | | | |
| | Supervisory salaries | Exhibit 12-22 | | 28,000 | | 2,333 | |
| | Indirect labor: setup | | | | | | |
| | Costs related to direct labor | Exhibit 12-13 | | | | | |
| | Transfer labor difference | | | | 100 | | 0.004 |
| | Idle time | | | | 6,300 | | 0.246 |
| | Rework time | | | | 3,800 | | 0.148 |
| | Learning time | | | | ...... | | |
| | Overtime premium | | | | ...... | | |
| | Second-shift premium | | | | ...... | | |
| | Benefits | Exhibit 12-24 | | | | | |
| | Hourly (including direct labor) | At 30 percent of wages | | | 65,900 | | 2.574 |
| | Salaried | At 25 percent of salaries | | 7,000 | | 583 | |
| | Rework materials | At 1 percent of direct materials | | | 500 | | 0.020 |
| | Operating supplies | } Past experience | | | 27,000 | | 1.055 |
| | Small tools and equipment | | | | 21,000 | | 0.820 |
| | Maintenance materials | Exhibit 12-21 | | | 6,000 | | 0.234 |
| | Repairs and maintenance charges | Exhibit 12-32 | | 3,400 | 12,800 | 283 | 0.500 |
| | Power purchased | } Exhibit 12-21 | | | 2,000 | | 0.078 |
| | Heat and light | | | 3,000 | ...... | 250 | |
| | Telephone and telegram | Past experience | | 500 | 4,000 | 42 | |
| | Depreciation | Exhibit 12-20 | | 24,600 | | 2,050 | 0.156 |
| | Total direct costs | | 215,900 | 66,500 | 149,400 | 5,542 | 5.836 |
| | Allocated costs | | | | | | |
| | Insurance | } Exhibit 12-20 | | 2,500 | | All allocated costs are treated as fixed for cost control purposes. | |
| | Property taxes | | | 1,300 | | | |
| | Occupancy | | | 11,300 | | | |
| | Storekeeping and material handling | } Exhibit 12-32 | | 3,000 | 1,500 | | |
| | Inspection | | | 6,800 | ..... | | |
| | Production planning | | | 4,400 | ..... | | |
| | General factory administration (including personnel) | | | 42,700 | 5,600 | | |
| | Total allocated costs | | 79,100 | 72,000 | 7,100 | 6,591 | ..... |
| | Total overhead | | 295,000 | 138,500 | 156,500 | 12,133 | 5.836 |

**Budgeted direct labor-hour rate for product costing**

| | Fixed-overhead rate | Variable-overhead rate | Combined-overhead rate |
|---|---|---|---|
| Direct cost center costs | 2.598 | 5.836 | 8.434 |
| Allocated costs | 2.812 | 0.277 | 3.089 |
| Total overhead | 5.410 | 6.113 | 11.523 |

### 29. Compilation of Standard Product Cost Sheet

Standard costs for product X and product Y are summarized in Exhibit 12-38. All the data for Exhibit 12-38 are derived from prior exhibits. Standard direct material and direct labor costs are obtained directly from Exhibits 12-2 and 12-3. For computing standard manufacturing overhead costs, (*a*) overhead absorption rates for each production center are obtained from its production budget, and (*b*) the standard machine-hour or direct labor–hour required per unit of finished product is obtained from Exhibit 12-3.

Standard manufacturing overhead cost for each product in each of the production centers is obtained by multiplying *a* by *b*. For example, in the Machine Department, 0.70 machine-hour is required per unit of product X, and the variable overhead rate is $14.846 per machine-hour. Hence, the standard variable manufacturing overhead cost in the Machine Department for product X is $10.392 ($14.846 × 0.70 hour) per unit. Similarly, the standard fixed overhead cost is $8.847 ($12.638 × 0.70) per unit.

The total of the three cost elements gives the total standard product cost, which for product X is $180.138 and for product Y is $183.202. Exhibit 12-38 also shows the percentage of direct materials, direct labor, and manufacturing overhead of the total product cost.

The standard variable cost of product X is $151.006 ($76 + 42.246 + 32.760), or 84 percent of the total cost, and that of product Y is $149.118 ($61.900 + 48.792 + 38.426), or 82 percent of the total cost.

### 30. Summary of Manufacturing Overhead Budgets

For management information purposes, the manufacturing overhead budgets of various cost centers are summarized in Exhibit 12-39, which shows direct and allocated costs separately. In actual practice, each of these budgets may be broken up into months or quarters, and a monthly or quarterly summary of total manufacturing overhead costs may be shown.

## MONTHLY COST CONTROL REPORTS

To illustrate how cost control reports are prepared when standard costs and budgets are used, a cost control report for the Welding Department is prepared by using hypothetical data for the month of January 1981. The cost control report is given in Exhibit 12-40, and its working is given in Exhibit 12-41.

## EXHIBIT 12-38

### Standard Product Cost Sheet (ACME Company)*

Date prepared ________
Cost analyst ________
Approved by F. J. Harkins
Date ________

Effective date January 1, 1981

| | Exhibit Reference | Total $ | Total Percent of Total | Machine ($) | Press ($) | Welding ($) | Assembly ($) | Finishing, Testing, and Packing ($) |
|---|---|---|---|---|---|---|---|---|
| Machine-hour or direct labor–hour rates (overhead rates) | | | | MHR (Exhibit 12-33) | MHR (Exhibit 12-34) | DLHR (Exhibit 12-35) | DLHR (Exhibit 12-36) | DLHR (Exhibit 12-37) |
| Variable | | | | 14.846 | 9.954 | 4.657 | 4.514 | 6.113 |
| Fixed | | | | 12.638 | 10.352 | 3.828 | 4.001 | 5.410 |
| *PRODUCT X* Machine-hour or direct labor–hour per unit of finished product | 12-3 | | | 0.70/ MH | 0.50/ MH | 1.00/ DLH | 1.90/ DLH | Finishing and testing = 0.60 DLH packing = 0.08 DLH |

| | | | | | | | | |
|---|---|---|---|---|---|---|---|---|
| Direct materials | 12-2 | 76.000 | 42 | 37.000 | ..... | 4.300 | 31.700 | 3.000 |
| Direct labor | 12-3 | 42.246 | 24 | 10.528 | 3.540 | 7.170 | 15.428 | 5.580 |
| Manufacturing overhead | | | | | | | | |
| Variable | | 32.760 | 18 | 10.392 | 4.977 | 4.657 | 8.577 | 4.157 |
| Fixed | | 29.132 | 16 | 8.847 | 5.176 | 3.828 | 7.602 | 3.679 |
| Subtotal | | 61.892 | 34 | 19.239 | 10.153 | 8.485 | 16.179 | 7.836 |
| Total costs | | 180.138 | 100 | 66.767 | 13.693 | 19.955 | 63.307 | 16.416 |
| *PRODUCT Y* | | | | | | | | |
| Machine-hour or direct labor–hour per unit of finished product | 12-3 | | | 0.90/ MH | 0.60/ MH | 1.40/ DLH | 2.00/ DLH | Finishing and testing = 0.50 DLH packing = 0.08 DLH |
| Direct materials | 12-2 | 61.900 | 34 | 15.000 | 11.600 | 4.300 | 27.600 | 3.400 |
| Direct labor | 12-3 | 48.792 | 27 | 13.536 | 4.248 | 10.038 | 16.240 | 4.730 |
| Manufacturing overhead | | | | | | | | |
| Variable | | 38.426 | 21 | 13.361 | 5.972 | 6.520 | 9.028 | 3.545 |
| Fixed | | 34.084 | 18 | 11.374 | 6.211 | 5.359 | 8.002 | 3.138 |
| Subtotal | | 72.510 | 39 | 24.735 | 12.183 | 11.879 | 17.030 | 6.683 |
| Total costs | | 183.202 | 100 | 53.271 | 28.031 | 26.217 | 60.870 | 14.813 |

* MHR = machine-hour rate; DLHR = direct labor–hour rate.

**EXHIBIT 12-39**

## Manufacturing Overhead Budget by Cost Centers (ACME Company)

(In thousands of dollars)
Year 1981

| | Machine Shop | Press Shop | Welding Shop | As-sembly Shop | Finish-ing Shop |
|---|---|---|---|---|---|
| **Exhibit Reference** | | | | | |
| *Direct cost center costs* | | | | | |
| Supervisory and clerical salaries | 26.0 | 22.0 | 24.0 | 52.0 | 28.0 |
| Indirect labor | 4.4 | 2.4 | .... | ..... | .... |
| Costs related to direct labor | 25.6 | 7.8 | 18.2 | 48.8 | 10.2 |
| Overtime: indirect; salaried | ..... | .... | ..... | ..... | .... |
| Employee benefits costs | 156.3 | 54.5 | 110.8 | 211.5 | 72.9 |
| Rework materials | 11.3 | 1.9 | 1.7 | 12.0 | 0.5 |
| Operating and other supplies | 24.0 | 12.0 | 20.0 | 6.0 | 27.0 |
| Small tools and equipment | 30.0 | 15.0 | 12.0 | 12.0 | 21.0 |
| Maintenance materials | 48.0 | 42.0 | 14.0 | 12.0 | 6.0 |
| Purchased maintenance | .... | .... | ..... | ..... | .... |
| Purchased power | 76.6 | 35.2 | 11.1 | 9.3 | 2.0 |
| Heat and light | 6.0 | 4.0 | 5.0 | 11.0 | 3.0 |
| Telephone and telegram | 3.5 | 3.5 | 3.5 | 1.5 | 4.5 |
| Travel and entertainment | ..... | .... | ..... | ..... | .... |
| Rent and amortization: leasehold land | ..... | .... | ..... | ..... | .... |
| Water | ..... | .... | ..... | ..... | .... |
| Depreciation | 132.3 | 96.2 | 24.2 | 12.4 | 24.6 |
| Insurance | ..... | .... | ..... | ..... | .... |
| Property taxes | ..... | .... | ..... | ..... | .... |
| Total direct costs | 544.0 | 296.5 | 244.5 | 388.5 | 199.7 |
| *Allocated costs* | | | | | |
| Repairs and maintenance charges | 79.9 | 50.1 | 24.1 | 24.2 | 16.2 |
| Insurance | 13.2 | 9.6 | 2.4 | 1.2 | 2.5 |
| Property taxes | 6.6 | 4.8 | 1.2 | 0.6 | 1.3 |
| Occupancy | 20.3 | 16.9 | 16.9 | 13.5 | 11.3 |
| Storekeeping and material handling | 40.8 | 6.9 | 6.3 | 43.5 | 4.5 |
| Inspection | 28.5 | .... | ..... | 34.2 | 6.8 |
| Production planning | 6.6 | 13.1 | 10.9 | 8.7 | 4.4 |
| Other general factory administration, including personnel | 117.6 | 40.7 | 87.4 | 146.4 | 48.3 |
| Allocation to other cost centers | | | | | |
| Total allocated costs | 313.5 | 142.1 | 149.2 | 272.3 | 95.3 |
| Total overhead after allocation | 857.5 | 438.6 | 393.7 | 660.8 | 295.0 |

| Sub-total | Occu-pancy | Repairs and Main-tenance | Store-keeping and Material Handling | In-spection | Pro-duction Plan-ning | Per-sonnel and Time-keeping | All Other | Total |
|---|---|---|---|---|---|---|---|---|
| | 12-25 | 12-26 | 12-27 | 12-28 | 12-29 | 12-30 | 12-31 | |
| 152.0 | .... | 21.0 | 15.0 | 54.0 | 30.0 | 36.0 | 238.0 | 546.0 |
| 6.8 | 12.9 | 63.1 | 17.1 | .... | .... | .... | ..... | 99.9 |
| 110.6 | .... | .... | .... | .... | .... | .... | ..... | 110.6 |
| ..... | .... | 0.3 | .... | .... | .... | 0.5 | 1.9 | 2.7 |
| 606.0 | 3.9 | 24.2 | 8.9 | 13.5 | 7.5 | 9.0 | 59.5 | 732.5 |
| 27.4 | .... | .... | .... | .... | .... | .... | ..... | 27.4 |
| 89.0 | 5.0 | 60.0 | 3.5 | .... | 1.1 | 1.7 | 10.0 | 170.3 |
| 90.0 | .... | 14.0 | .... | 2.0 | .... | .... | ..... | 106.0 |
| 122.0 | 8.4 | .... | .... | .... | .... | .... | 12.0 | 142.4 |
| ..... | .... | .... | 2.0 | .... | .... | .... | 2.5 | 4.5 |
| 134.2 | .... | 2.3 | .... | .... | .... | .... | .... | 136.5 |
| 29.0 | .... | 1.0 | 3.0 | .... | 0.6 | 0.6 | 5.5 | 39.7 |
| 16.5 | .... | 7.0 | 2.0 | .... | .... | 0.5 | 15.0 | 41.0 |
| ..... | .... | .... | .... | .... | .... | .... | 17.0 | 17.0 |
| ..... | 12.0 | .... | .... | .... | .... | .... | ..... | 12.0 |
| ..... | .... | .... | .... | .... | .... | .... | 2.2 | 2.2 |
| 289.7 | 54.0 | 2.2 | 8.0 | .... | 2.0 | 3.0 | 9.0 | 367.9 |
| ..... | .... | .... | .... | .... | .... | .... | 56.4 | 56.4 |
| ..... | .... | .... | .... | .... | .... | .... | 30.6 | 30.6 |
| 1673.2 | 96.2 | 195.1 | 59.5 | 69.5 | 41.2 | 51.3 | 459.6 | 2645.6 |
| 194.5 | 6.6 | ... | .... | .... | ... | ... | .... | 201.1 |
| 28.9 | 5.0 | 0.2 | 20.8 | .... | 0.2 | 0.3 | 1.0 | 56.4 |
| 14.5 | 5.0 | 0.1 | 10.4 | .... | 0.1 | 0.1 | 0.4 | 30.6 |
| 78.9 | ... | 5.7 | 11.3 | .... | 2.2 | 2.3 | 12.4 | 112.8 |
| 102.0 | ... | ... | .... | .... | ... | ... | .... | 102.0 |
| 69.5 | ... | ... | .... | .... | ... | ... | .... | 69.5 |
| 43.7 | ... | ... | .... | .... | ... | ... | .... | 43.7 |
| 440.4 | ... | ... | .... | .... | ... | ... | .... | 440.4 |
| | (112.8) | (201.1) | (102.0) | (69.5) | (43.7) | (54.0) | (473.4) | (1056.5) |
| 972.4 | ( 96.2) | (195.1) | ( 59.5) | (69.5) | (41.2) | (51.3) | (459.6) | ...... |
| 2645.6 | ..... | ..... | ..... | .... | .... | .... | ..... | 2645.6 |

## EXHIBIT 12-40

# Cost Control Report (ACME Company)

Responsibility center Welding Department
Responsibility of Mr. T. S. Parekh
Month January 1981

No. ____________

| Year to date: Budget | Year to date: Actual | Year to date: Better (worse) than budget | Account or cost center No. | Description | Current month: Budget | Current month: Actual | Current month: Better (worse) than budget |
|---|---|---|---|---|---|---|---|
| | | | | Direct cost center costs | | | |
| | | | | Supervisory salaries | 2,000 | 2,000 | ..... |
| | | | | Indirect labor: setup | ..... | ..... | ..... |
| | | | | Costs related to direct labor | | | |
| | | | | Transfer labor difference | | | |
| | | | | Idle time | 878 | 115 | 763 |
| | | | | Rework time | 586 | 717 | (131) |
| | | | | Learning time | ..... | ..... | ..... |
| | | | | Overtime premium | 130 | 359 | (229) |
| | | | | Second-shift premium | ..... | ..... | ..... |
| | | | | Benefits | | | |
| | | | | Hourly (including direct labor) | 9,185 | 10,165 | (980) |
| | | | | Salaried | 500 | 500 | ..... |
| | | | | Rework materials | 146 | 200 | (54) |
| | | | | Operating supplies | 1,753 | 2,233 | (480) |
| | | | | Small tools and equipment | 1,053 | 1,181 | (428) |
| | | | | Maintenance materials | 1,224 | 808 | 416 |
| | | | | Repair and maintenance charges | 2,092 | 3,251 | (1,159) |
| | | | | Power purchased | 972 | 1,042 | (70) |
| | | | | Heat and light | 417 | 457 | (40) |
| | | | | Telephone and telegram | 306 | 356 | (50) |
| | | | | Depreciation | 2,016 | 2,016 | ..... |
| | | | | Total direct costs | 23,258 | 25,400 | (2,142) |
| | | | | Allocated costs | 10,425 | 10,425 | ..... |
| | | | | Total overhead | 33,683 | 35,825 | (2,142) |

Performance Summary

| | Standard | Actual | Better (worse) than standard | Actual as percent of standard |
|---|---|---|---|---|
| Direct labor-hours | 4,066 | 4,366 | (300) | 107 |
| Direct labor rate | $7.17 | $7.57 | $(0.50) | 106 |
| Direct labor cost | $29,153 | $33,051 | $(3,898) | 113 |
| Direct material cost | $15,192 | $14,892* | $(300) | 98 |
| Equipment-hours | ...... | ...... | ..... | ... |
| Direct overhead | $23,258 | $25,400 | $(2,142) | 109 |

| Overhead Variance Analysis | Efficiency variance | Variable-overhead spending variance | Fixed-overhead spending variance |
|---|---|---|---|
| | $ | $ | $ |

*At standard rate to show only quantity variance.

**EXHIBIT 12-41**

**Worksheet for Calculating Variable Budget Allowances (ACME Company)**

Responsibility center Welding Department — No. ______

Activity unit Direct labor–hours — Budget: J 3867, F, M, A — Standard: J 4066, F, M, A — Actual: J 4366, F, M, A

| Account No. | Expense | Monthly fixed overhead | Variable-overhead rate | January Variable overhead | January Total budget (1) + (3) | February Variable overhead | February Total budget (1) + (5) | March Variable overhead | March Total budget (1) + (7) | April Variable overhead | April Total budget (1) + (9) |
|---|---|---|---|---|---|---|---|---|---|---|---|
| | Direct cost center costs | 1 | 2 | 3 | 4 | 5 | 6 | 7 | 8 | 9 | 10 |
| | Supervisory salaries | 2,000 | | | 2,000 | | | | | | |
| | Indirect labor: setup | ..... | | | ..... | | | | | | |
| | Costs related to direct labor | | | | | | | | | | |
| | Transfer labor difference | | | | ..... | | | | | | |
| | Idle time | | 0.216 | 878 | 878 | | | | | | |
| | Rework time | | 0.144 | 586 | 586 | | | | | | |
| | Learning time | | | | ..... | | | | | | |
| | Overtime premium | | 0.032 | 130 | 130 | | | | | | |
| | Second-shift premium | | | | ..... | | | | | | |
| | Benefits | | | | | | | | | | |
| | Hourly (including direct labor) | | 2.259 | 9,185 | 9,185 | | | | | | |
| | Salaried | 500 | | | 500 | | | | | | |
| | Rework materials | | 0.036 | 146 | 146 | | | | | | |
| | Operating supplies | | 0.431 | 1,753 | 1,753 | | | | | | |
| | Small tools and equipment | | 0.259 | 1,053 | 1,053 | | | | | | |
| | Maintenance materials | | 0.301 | 1,224 | 1,224 | | | | | | |
| | Repair and maintenance charges | 417 | 0.412 | 1,675 | 2,092 | | | | | | |
| | Power purchased | | 0.239 | 972 | 972 | | | | | | |
| | Heat and light | 417 | | | 417 | | | | | | |
| | Telephone and telegram | 42 | 0.065 | 264 | 306 | | | | | | |
| | Depreciation | 2,016 | | | 2,016 | | | | | | |
| | Total direct costs | 5,392 | 4.394 | 17,866 | 23,258 | | | | | | |
| | Allocated costs | 10,425 | ..... | ..... | 10,425 | | | | | | |
| | Total overhead | 15,817 | 4.394 | 17,866 | 33,683 | | | | | | |

The worksheet is used for calculating the variable budget allowance for the level of activity achieved. Since the activity unit of the Welding Department is direct labor–hours, budgeted, standard, and actual direct labor–hours are first ascertained. Standard direct labor–hours are computed by multiplying actual production of the Welding Department by the standard direct labor–hour per unit of finished product. Budgeted direct labor–hours represent direct labor–hours planned while preparing the 1981 budget.

Monthly fixed overhead amounts and variable overhead rates are obtained directly from the last two columns of the manufacturing overhead budget of the Welding Department given in Exhibit 12-35. The variable overhead amounts in column 3 are arrived at by multiplying standard direct labor–hours by the respective variable overhead rates. For example, the variable allowance of $878 for idle time is computed by multiplying 4066 standard direct labor–hours by $0.216, the variable overhead rate. The total budget allowance is given in column 4 and reproduced in the current month's "Budget" column of the cost control report (Exhibit 12-40). Actual costs are listed opposite budget allowances. Actual costs for all the cost items except employee benefits and repairs and maintenance are derived directly from the cost records.

Employee benefits costs are computed at the rate of 30 percent of *actual* hourly wages and 25 percent of *actual* salaries of the Welding Department. By allocating employee benefits costs at the standard rates of 30 and 25 percent, excess (or short) employee benefits costs arising as a result of excess (or short) salaries and wages compared with the budget are charged to the respective cost centers because the centers are responsible for the variance. Also, a consolidated report comparing the actual cost and flexible budget allowance for each item of employee benefits will be computed. The variance in this report will reflect the responsibility of the person in charge of the employee benefits costs center. Thus, this approach segregates the responsibility for variances in employee benefits costs between the employee benefits center and the other centers.

The repairs and maintenance charges shown in the "Actual" column are computed as explained under task 16. Allocated costs are shown at the budgeted amount only because the Welding Department is not responsible for controlling them. The report shows that for the month of January 1981 the Welding Department exceeded its budget by $2142, of which the itemized portions are given in the last column.

The "Performance summary" section of the report summarizes the performance of the Welding Department in controlling direct labor, direct materials, and manufacturing overhead costs. Space is also provided for showing an analysis of the overhead variance.

# Chapter 13

# Designing Nonmanufacturing Cost Systems

Leave no stone unturned.
Euripides

Nonmanufacturing costs consist of marketing costs, general and administrative costs, and financial expenses. These costs are incurred both by manufacturing and nonmanufacturing concerns. The process of designing a cost system for each type of nonmanufacturing cost is considered separately in this chapter. In particular, the complex process of designing a marketing cost system is explained at length.

## CHARACTERISTICS OF NONMANUFACTURING COSTS

In designing a nonmanufacturing cost system, the following characteristics of nonmanufacturing costs should be noted:

1. Nonmanufacturing costs are not relevant for product costing because they are not incurred in manufacturing a product, but they are relevant for income determination, planning, and cost control. In designing a nonmanufacturing cost system, the main focus is on the need for different kinds of cost analysis and cost control.
2. The basic cost accounting of nonmanufacturing costs is usually less complex than that of manufacturing costs.
3. Fundamental cost accounting principles are common to both manufacturing and nonmanufacturing cost accounting. There may, however, be differences in application. Similarly, the basic design process is common to both types of cost systems, though there are differences in application, as shown later in this chapter.

## DESIGNING A MARKETING COST SYSTEM

Marketing costs consist of costs incurred on advertising, market research, warehousing, selling, order processing, transportation, billing, credit, collection, and similar functions. These costs are also referred to as *distribution costs.* Sometimes these costs are grouped into *order-getting* and *order-filling* categories. Organizationally, not all the listed functions may be under marketing. For example, warehousing and transportation may be a part of the separate material-handling function, and billing, credit, and collection may be set up either as a separate department or as a part of the administration department.

## SUMMARY OF THE ITERATIVE PROCESS

The process of designing a marketing cost system, like that of any other cost system, requires a high level of creativity, and the design process therefore cannot be reduced to rigid rules or self-contained steps. The process is essentially iterative and involves a series of successive approximations. Nonetheless, the creative effort will be more productive if it is properly disciplined. For example, by identifying the major tasks involved in designing a cost system, the creative design effort can be made goal-directed.

The major tasks performed in developing a marketing cost system are explained below. For completing the picture and for reinforcement, even tasks which have been explained earlier are summarized here.

### System Analysis Tasks

When the designer begins to design a marketing cost system, the following system analysis tasks will already have been completed:

1. The designer will have defined the *objectives* of the marketing cost system, which can be one or more of the following:
    - *a.* To ascertain the costs of marketing, in total and separately for each function, each product, each marketing channel, and other segments of marketing.
    - *b.* To provide information for controlling marketing costs.
    - *c.* To furnish information for measuring marketing performance for the company as a whole and also by territories, channels, products, and other aspects of marketing.
    - *d.* To provide a data base for preparing a marketing expense budget.
    - *e.* To provide information for marketing planning and decision making, such as:

- Strategic and tactical marketing decisions in general
- Selection of sales promotion methods, distribution channels, geographical areas of marketing operations, etc.
- Determination of the total advertising budget and its breakdown by various markets, products, and media
- Product price determination
- Decision on whether to increase or decrease selling prices
- Special-order pricing
- Decision on whether to add or drop a product line, territory, sales channel, distribution channel, class of customers, particular order sizes, and so on
- Justifying, under the Robinson-Patman Act, price discrimination based on cost differentiation

Since the procedure for defining the objectives of a cost system has been explained in Chapter 2, it is not repeated here.

2. The designer will have conducted a *fact-finding survey* to gather the necessary information relating to the marketing function, marketing costs, and the existing marketing cost system, if any. If this survey is not detailed enough, additional inquiries and analyses must be made to supplement the information already gathered.

3. The designer will have determined the specific *cost information* required to satisfy each of the preset objectives of the marketing cost system.

In actual practice, before beginning to design a marketing cost system, the designer will, at this stage, refer to his file to review the tasks mentioned above.

## System Design Tasks

Having determined the specific requirements of the marketing cost system, the designer now must translate them into the appropriate system. This phase involves the following tasks:

1. Select the cost accounting methods and techniques to be employed.
2. Establish responsibility centers and cost centers.
3. Establish the marketing cost input-output relationship.
4. Classify marketing costs.
5. Separate direct and indirect marketing costs.
6. Select proper bases for allocation of marketing costs.
7. If standard costs are to be used, develop standards for marketing costs. If a budgetary control system is to be employed, design a procedure for developing a marketing cost budget.

8. Design a marketing cost reporting system.
9. Design marketing cost records and procedures.

## Task 1: Selection of Cost Accounting Methods and Techniques

Since these two issues are pertinent to the entire cost system, they are usually resolved quite early in the design process. Hence, they have been discussed more fully in Chapters 6 and 7, and only a summary of relevant points is given here:

- Marketing cost accounting is in the nature of operating costing because each type of marketing operation or activity is costed separately.
- Theoretically, the basis of accounting may be either historical costs or standard costs, though the use of historical costs is more feasible and prevalent.
- For marketing cost computations and analysis, the technique of either direct costing or total costing may be employed.
- Marketing costs are usually controlled through budgeting with or without standard costing. Among the techniques used for marketing decision making and planning, the more common are the cost-volume-profit relationship, break-even analysis, and the contribution margin approach.

## Task 2: Establishment of Necessary Responsibility Centers and Cost Centers

For the purposes of accumulation, allocation, and analysis of marketing expenses, marketing cost centers are required. For the purpose of controlling marketing costs and performance, marketing responsibility centers are required. Marketing responsibility centers will be functional departments such as advertising, sales, warehousing, transportation, etc. The number and the type of responsibility centers will depend upon the marketing organization structure and the division of authority-responsibility among various organizational segments. Often responsibility centers and cost centers will be the same, but in some cases a responsibility center may consist of several cost centers. The process of establishing responsibility centers and cost centers has been explained in Chapter 8 and hence is not repeated here.

## Task 3: Establishment of Marketing Cost Input-Output Relationship

Once the types of marketing cost information required have been specified, the designer should determine the input cost data necessary to provide the required output cost information. For example, if a company distributing two products uses various media for advertising each product, the types of input cost data required for computing and analyzing the advertising costs for these products will be:

- Advertising costs by media
- Common advertising costs such as salaries and other expenses of the advertising department
- Some estimate of sales generated from advertisements in each of the various media

From the marketing cost matrix (see Exhibit 3-12), it is easy to determine the input data necessary to generate each item of the required output information.

### Task 4: Classification of Marketing Costs

After the input marketing expenses required to generate the desired output information have been established, it is essential to determine the kind of classification of marketing expenses needed for standards setting, budgeting, accumulation, distribution, and reporting of costs. Marketing expenses can be classified in one or more of the following ways:

- *By nature of expenses,* e.g., salaries, traveling, transportation, rent, electricity, commission, brokerage, and so on
- *By cost behavior,* i.e., separation of variable and fixed costs
- *By marketing functions,* e.g., warehousing, sales, advertising and sales promotion, market research, distribution, billing, credit, and collection
- *By marketing segments,* e.g., departments of marketing, sales territories, product divisions, customer divisions, sales representatives, and the like
- *By marketing methods,* e.g., sales channels, distribution channels, advertising media, and the like
- *By other aspects of marketing,* e.g., order sizes, size of customer accounts, credit terms, and sales terms

Each of these classifications can be arranged in several ways; for example, marketing functions may be classified into order-getting and order-filling functions only. Similarly, billing, credit, and collection may be treated either as three separate functions or grouped under one heading. Within each classification, there may be subclassification and sub-subclassification. For example, a product division may be divided into product lines, each product line into individual products, each product into different brands, each brand into different packing sizes, and so on.

Factors determining the kind of classification required include types of expenses incurred, significance of various cost factors, requirements of the marketing cost system, type of cost allocation and analyses required, marketing organization, methods of marketing operation, and preferences of the designer and management. The requirements of the marketing cost system dictate the *minimum* classification required, while the other factors influence the decision regarding further classification to be made. Because of the multiplicity of factors, determination of the appropriate classification of marketing expenses demands considerable attention and imagination.

### Task 5: Separation of Direct and Indirect Marketing Costs

Each input marketing cost item should be separated into *direct expenses,* those expenses which can be charged or assigned directly to individual marketing segments (or cost centers) without apportionment, and *indirect expenses,* those expenses which cannot be charged to individual marketing segments without some apportionment because they are incurred for more than one segment. The objective of this classification is to determine which expenses can be directly charged to cost centers and which expenses need allocation.

The following guidelines will be helpful in separating marketing expenses into direct and indirect categories:

1. As a general rule, more accurate cost figures are obtained by direct assignment of costs than by allocation of costs, and consequently the goal should be to *identify directly as much cost as possible.* There are two exceptions to this general rule. First, direct assignment, though possible, may either not be worthwhile because it it too expensive or not be necessary because apportionment will give more or less the same result as direct assignment will give. For example, if postage expenses are insignificant, it may be worthwhile to classify them directly by functions. The second exception is found when a more accurate cost can be obtained by allocation than by direct assignment. For example, ordinarily it is more equitable to allocate the cost of packing overtime to all the packing sizes used by a company than to charge that cost to only those packing sizes which were packed during the overtime period.

2. The separation of expenses into direct and indirect categories is *relative* and not absolute. For example, a branch manager's salary is direct to the branch but indirect to the various products sold by that branch. However, if a branch sells only one product, the branch manager's salary will be direct to the branch as well as to the product, but it will still be

indirect to the various functions performed by the branch. Thus, every expense will be *direct to at least one cost center* and may be indirect to one or more cost centers.

3. Since the same expense can be direct to one segment and indirect to another segment, it is essential to classify marketing expenses into direct and indirect categories separately for *each* segment.

In other words, irrespective of the order in which marketing expenses are allocated to various segments (e.g., nature of expenses ⟶ functions ⟶ territories ⟶ products ⟶ customers), the distinction between direct and indirect expenses should be observed throughout the process of allocation. For example, once marketing expenses have been allocated, say, to various functions, the total cost of each function should not be allocated to territories on a single basis; whatever cost under each function can be allocated directly to territories should be so assigned, and only the balance cost should be allocated.

The best way to depict direct and indirect expenses of each segment is to prepare a marketing cost matrix (see Exhibit 3-12).

## Task 6: Selection of Bases for Allocation of Indirect Marketing Expenses

Once the designer has identified indirect expenses for each segment, the next task is to select an equitable basis for allocating each indirect expense. The allocation bases should be selected very carefully because improper bases will give an inaccurate distribution of costs that may lead to incorrect decisions. Further, for cost control, indirect costs may not be allocated if they can be better controlled in the aggregate. Similarly, for cost control, the costs of one segment should not be allocated to another segment unless the *sold-service concept* explained in Chapter 11 is adopted.

### Selection Guidelines

A few useful guidelines for the selection of proper bases for allocation are given below.

**Should Fixed and Variable Costs Be Distinguished?** In the first place, the designer should decide whether or not to allocate fixed and variable portions of a given cost factor separately. For more accurate allocation of costs, variable and fixed portions of a given cost factor must be allocated on different bases. For example, if sales representatives are remunerated on a salary-plus-commission basis, commission may be identified directly with the individual products or be allocated in the ratio of the sales value of the products sold, and salaries may be allocated in the ratio of the time devoted to, or the budgeted sales value of, the various products.

Another factor which influences the decision on this issue is the type of techniques used for controlling marketing expenses. For instance, if a fixed budgetary control method is employed, there is no need to classify expenses by their variability. But if a flexible budgetary control method is employed, it is essential to classify expenses by their variability in conformity with the classification adopted for budget preparation.

**Should Joint Costs Be Allocated?** The second issue is whether all indirect costs are to be allocated or whether indirect costs which can be allocated only on some arbitrary basis are not to be allocated. Advocates of direct costing or the contribution margin approach contend that joint costs should not be allocated, whereas advocates of absorption costing disagree. From a practical viewpoint, this issue should be resolved with regard to the objectives of cost allocation. For example, for statutory rate making or product price setting, all joint costs should be apportioned or somehow be taken into account. But in deciding, say, whether to continue or to drop a product line, joint costs which will not vary even if that product line is discontinued should not be apportioned to products.

If it is decided to allocate joint costs, it is better to highlight the total cost of a segment with and without allocation of joint costs.

**Actual or Predetermined Basis** The third issue to be resolved is whether marketing expenses are to be allocated on an actual basis or a predetermined basis. This question applies to the numerator (marketing expenses to be allocated) as well as to the denominator (basis for allocation). However, some expenses may be allocated on an actual basis, and others may be allocated on a predetermined basis. The pros and cons of the actual versus the predetermined basis applicable to manufacturing overhead (discussed in Chapter 11) are also applicable to marketing expenses.

**Primary and Secondary Allocations** Sometimes an indirect expense can be allocated to either of two cost centers which are at different levels in the hierarchy of cost centers. In such cases, primary allocation should be made to the level that is more appropriate under the circumstances. For example, let us assume that a company advertises two products, X and Y, in two magazines having circulation in two regions. In the first magazine, combined advertisements for both products are run, and in the second magazine separate advertisements for products X and Y are run. The cost of running advertisements in the first magazine should be allocated primarily to the regions, whereas that in the second magazine should be allocated primarily to the individual products in each region. In the former case, the advertising cost allocated to each region must be further allocated to products. In the latter case, the question of secondary allocation will not arise because the advertising cost for each region can be determined by summarizing the costs primarily allocated to individual products in each region. The following table will aid in clarifying this point:

| | Type of Advertisement | Primary Allocation | Secondary Allocation |
|---|---|---|---|
| Magazine A | Combined advertisements for both products | To regions | To products |
| Magazine B | Separate advertisements for products X and Y | To products | Does not arise |

**Principles of Allocation** The principles underlying the selection of equitable bases for the allocation of manufacturing overhead (discussed in Chapter 11) are also applicable to marketing expenses. The existence of a cause-and-effect relationship between the basis selected and the expense to be allocated is essential for an equitable allocation of expenses. For example, it is inequitable to allocate warehousing cost on the basis of the value of each product stored; the proper basis is the space utilized because warehousing cost is a function of space. Thus, the major criteria used in selecting the bases for allocation are the benefits received, the service or facilities provided or utilized, cost responsibilities, and the basis on which the supplier of the service charges for the service (e.g., if freight is charged on the basis of volume, freight expenses should be allocated in the ratio of the volume of products shipped).

To find a cause-and-effect relationship, the designer should analyze each cost factor by using correlation analysis, multiple-regression analysis, and simple observance techniques. Next, the designer should consider all the alternative bases for allocating each cost factor and select that basis which will allocate cost fairly without undue expense of allocation.

### Common Bases for Allocation of Indirect Marketing Expenses

To facilitate the designer's work of selecting appropriate bases for allocation, a list of the commonly used bases for allocation of indirect marketing expenses is given below (the illustrations given for each basis refer only to the indirect portion of the relevant expenses).

- Space utilized (e.g., for allocation of warehousing expenses to various products stored).
- Number of sales visits (e.g., for allocation of traveling expenses for

order getting or sales promotion to products, territories, or customers).

- Number of invoice lines (e.g., for distributing billing, credit and collection, accounting, etc., expenses).
- Number of sales orders (e.g., for apportioning order-handling expenses).
- Circulation in each territory for allocation of newspaper and magazine advertising expenses to territories.
- Population or estimated number of viewers or listeners in the respective territories for allocation of television or radio advertising expenses to territories.
- Budgeted or actual sales (e.g., for prorating common advertising expenses or sales office expenses to territories or products).
- Weight, volume, or quantity of products handled, shipped, stored, or sold (e.g., for distributing packing, handling, shipping, etc., expenses).
- Number of credit customer accounts, number of delinquent accounts, or amount covered by delinquent accounts (e.g., for apportioning credit and collection expenses to products, territories, class of customers, etc.).
- Number of service calls or time devoted (e.g., for allocation of after-sales expenses to territories, products, customers, etc.).
- Number of actual or potential customers (e.g., for prorating the cost of catalogs distributed to customers in different regions).
- Value of equipment (e.g., for allocation of expenses on insuring property or taxes on property located in different regions or departments).
- Sales value (e.g., for allocating joint marketing expenses which cannot be allocated on any other basis). This is based on the principle of charging what the traffic can bear, and therefore it is inequitable. In some cases, *budgeted sales value* is a better basis than *actual sales value.* For example, advertising expenses usually are incurred to achieve a certain volume of sales, and consequently it is proper to allocate indirect advertising expenses on the basis of budgeted sales.

## Matrix of Marketing Cost Allocation

Once the bases for allocation of marketing expenses have been determined, it is necessary to document them. Here again a matrix is preferable to a narrative form. A specimen is given in Exhibit 13-1. A careful review of the matrix will reveal any omissions or inconsistencies in allocation. Further, the matrix will also serve as a reference document for the cost accounting department.

**EXHIBIT 13-1**

**Specimen Matrix of Marketing Cost Allocation**

| Marketing Costs Classification by Marketing Functions and Nature of Expenses | Bases for Allocation to | | Not to Be Allocated |
|---|---|---|---|
| | Regions | Products | |
| A. *Advertising* | | | |
| Media: Common to regions but direct to individual products | 2. Ratio of estimated circulation | 1. Direct | |
| Media: Common to products but direct to individual regions | 1. Direct | 2. Budgeted sales | |
| Media: Common to regions as well as products | 1. Circulation | 2. Budgeted sales | |
| . . . | | | |
| B. *Warehousing and distribution* | | | |
| Costs common to regions but direct to products (e.g., central packing material purchasing department's costs) | 2. Consumption of packing material | 1. Direct | |
| Costs common to products but direct to regions: | | | |
| ■ Own trucking costs | 1. Direct | 2. Volume of products transported | |
| ■ Occupancy, salaries, etc. | 1. Direct | 2. Space utilized | |
| Costs common to regions | 2. Units sold | 1. Space utilized | |
| C. . . . | | | |
| D. . . . | | | |
| E. . . . | | | |
| F. *Central marketing division's costs* | | | |
| Common to all functions, regions, and products | 1. Budgeted sales | 2. Budgeted sales | For special-order pricing |

NOTE: The serial numbers indicate the order of allocation between regions and products.

## Task 7: Standards Setting and Budget Preparation for Marketing Expenses

Marketing expenses are controlled with the help of marketing expense budgets, and standard costing is not well-suited for controlling marketing expenses because it is difficult to set standards for many marketing expenses, such as advertising and salaries. Many marketing expenses are discretionary, and hence the best way to control marketing expenses is to set marketing goals (in terms of market share, sales volume, etc.) and then budget the resources required to achieve the goals. In addition, whenever possible, standards may be set and used in budgeting marketing expenses. The following are some of the standards which may be set:

- Sales quota per sales representative, territory, etc.
- Dollar amount of advertising expenses (by media) to generate a unit sale
- Cost per ton-mile of products delivered

For setting standards for transportation, order processing, and clerical functions, the work measurement technique may be used. However, this technique is not suitable, for example, for advertising and sales promotion expenses, which are based on management's discretion. For these types of expenses, standards may be set by analyzing historical data adjusted for known changes. For certain expenses, a combination of these two methods may be used. For example, in setting a sales quota for controlling selling expenses, quantitative standards may be established for the number of calls or sales visits that a sales representative should make per day, but the amount of sales that the representative should generate may be based on past performance adjusted for changes in market conditions. For instance, normally a sales quota will be lower when the market is near saturation than when it is rapidly rising.

When it is difficult to set standards for the preparation of budgets, the cost behavior of various expenses should be studied to determine the rate of variation in each expense with the volume of related activity. For example, expenses such as traveling and telephone are semivariable, and the rate of variation of the variable portion of these expenses can be estimated by studying their past behavior. Expenses such as office rent and depreciation are more or less fixed.

Usually, two types of budgets are used for controlling marketing expenses:

- Appropriation-type budget for controlling market research and advertising expenses which are left to management's discretion and then are limited to a certain percentage of sales
- Flexible budget for controlling other expenses

Marketing expense budgets should be prepared by marketing responsibility centers and by the nature of expenses. For example, an advertising budget should be classified by media and by locations.

The guidelines for setting standards and preparation of budgets for manufacturing overhead given in Chapter 11 apply to setting standards and preparation of budgets for marketing expenses, too, and hence are not repeated here.

### Tasks 8 and 9: Designing Marketing Cost Reporting and Accounting Systems

For cost control purposes, the marketing cost report compares actual costs with budgets or some predetermined amounts. When flexible budgeting is used, budget allowances are adjusted for the volume of activity actually attained. For discretionary costs such as market research, advertising, etc., not only are actual costs compared with the fixed budget but actual results are compared with predetermined goals.

Besides cost control reports, various marketing-oriented cost analysis reports are prepared. A detailed exposition of the process of designing cost reports and cost records will be found in Chapters 14 and 15.

## SUMMARY

In this chapter, we show how to establish an input-output relationship for marketing costs, classify marketing costs, select bases for allocation of indirect marketing costs, set standards, and develop a budget for marketing costs. In Chapter 14, we will discuss the subject of cost reports, in chapter 15 the subject of cost records and procedures, and in Chapter 16 the subject of a chart of accounts.

It is obvious that a computerized marketing cost system will greatly facilitate the multiple marketing cost analyses required. The way to achieve multiple classification and analyses of marketing costs is to code the source documents properly.

## DESIGNING AN ADMINISTRATIVE COST SYSTEM

Administrative costs are not incurred specifically for the manufacturing function or the selling and distribution function but are incurred for the organization as a while. These costs are those incurred on general management, legal, accounting, auditing, personnel, finance, treasury, public relations, and similar activities. Designing an administrative cost system involves the following major tasks:

**Two Issues** As in the case of manufacturing and marketing cost systems, an administrative cost system may be designed for cost control and for cost determination. Consequently, it is necessary to resolve two issues: (1) How are administrative costs to be controlled? (2) How are administrative costs for product costing to be treated?

**Cost Control Method** The designer must determine the exact method that is to be used or is already being used for *controlling* administrative costs. Most of the administrative costs are policy, discretionary, or managed costs; e.g., the public relations cost is influenced by a policy decision about the nature and the type of public relations desired. Hence, the use of budgets is the best method of controlling administrative costs. Further, since most administrative costs do not vary with the volume of activities, fixed budgets are appropriate, and there is no need to use flexible budgets.

Usually, administrative activities are classified into a few logical functional groupings, depending upon the importance of each function and the type of organization. For example, some functional groupings could be top management, legal, accounting, personnel, finance and treasury, auditing, and public relations. The costs incurred on each of these functions are classified also by nature of expenses such as salaries, traveling, entertainment, telephone, telex, depreciation, insurance, rent, etc. The dual classification of administrative expenses facilitates control over such expenses in two ways. First, it enables management to budget administrative expenses by functions. Generally, it is easier to evaluate the reasonableness of administrative expenses when they are budgeted by functions than when they are budgeted by nature of expenses. Second, actual costs can be compared with budgeted costs by functions as well as by nature, and responsibility for variances can be pinpointed.

Despite the fact that a budget is the best way to control administrative expenses, standards can be set for certain repetitive administrative work such as billing, typing, and bookkeeping. The work measurement technique is used to set standards for these types of work. For example, for the billing function standards are first set for each of the steps (typing, calculation, checking, etc.) involved in preparing a bill. Then these standards are converted into dollar amounts per so much quantity of each step, and ultimately the cost of preparing a bill is determined. For instance, if a clerk can prepare, on an average, 10 bills of 10 lines each per hour, and if the clerk earns $5 per hour, standard billing cost will be 50 cents per bill. If different bills have different numbers of lines, the standard cost will vary. In this case, the standard cost will have to be set separately for bills of different lengths.

There are two problems in setting standards for clerical work. First, usually a person performs more than one type of work, and hence it is necessary to keep a record of the time spent by a clerk on different types of work. Second, counting the quantity of actual work performed (e.g., the number of lines typed by a typist) is difficult or time-consuming. Despite these difficulties, many companies do use with advantage standards for controlling the cost of repetitive clerical work.

**Treatment for Product Costing** In cost accounting, administrative costs are commonly dealt with as follows:

1. They are treated as policy costs and hence are *directly charged to the profit and loss account* without allocating them to products or any other segment of the business. It should, however, be noted that administrative costs which can be identified with any particular segment of the business should be directly charged to it. For example, legal expenses incurred for the collection of outstanding accounts receivable should be charged to the division for which they are incurred.
2. They are *charged to products* as a separate charge, similarly to manufacturing and marketing expenses. The charge may be made on any one of the following bases:
   - Production cost (i.e., direct material plus direct labor plus manufacturing overhead)
   - Production units (actual or estimated)
   - Sales units (actual or estimated)
   - Cost of sales (i.e., manufacturing costs plus distribution costs)
3. At first they are *allocated to manufacturing and selling functions* and then are dealt with as are other manufacturing and distribution costs.

There are several pros and cons for each alternative, and therefore the selection should be made after considering the purpose of product costing and the facts of each case. For example, for managerial decisions such as whether to continue or to drop a product line, administrative costs which will not vary under either alternative should not be allocated to products or divisions. However, for a cost-plus contract administrative costs should be charged on some basis.

**Accumulation and Allocation Procedure** Having settled on administrative cost control and product costing methods, the designer must develop cost accumulation and allocation procedures. The accumulation procedure is the same as in the case of general accounting, except that in cost accounting administrative expenses are accumulated by functions as well as by nature of expenses. The type of administrative cost classification required depends upon the cost control and product costing methods adopted for administrative costs. The general ledger may contain, in addition to the individual accounts for various administrative costs, a control account for administrative costs. To record accumulation of administrative costs by functions, there may be memorandum records, or there may be ledger accounts by functions. The record of allocation of administrative costs for product costing is usually kept on a memorandum basis.

## FINANCIAL EXPENSES

There are pros and cons for treating financial expenses as a part of the total cost. However, the designer should know the bases for allocation if financial expenses are to be allocated. Possible bases for allocation of financial expenses are as follows:

- Net assets employed.
- Net working capital employed.
- Direct charge; e.g., if a loan is arranged for a particular division, interest and related expenses may be charged directly to that division. This method is suitable when the incremental-cost approach is adopted. Otherwise, it is unfair to charge interest expenses based on the loan amount and not to charge any amount for other sources of finance such as equity capital, reserves, etc.
- Cost of production.
- Total costs excluding financial expenses.

The procedure for financial cost accumulation is simple. These expenses are recorded by nature (interest, brokerage, commission, etc.) and later are allocated on a memorandum basis. To control financial expenses, it is necessary to control the amount of borrowing and procure financing from the least expensive sources possible.

## RESEARCH AND DEVELOPMENT COSTS

In the case of research and development costs also, the procedure for accumulation is fairly simple. Such costs are usually accumulated by nature of expenses. However, the main issue is how to treat such costs for product costing. These costs may be treated as a part of the cost of production, marketing costs, or general and administrative expenses or be charged directly to the profit and loss account, depending upon the purpose for which they are incurred, the objectives of cost analysis, and management preference.

Research and development costs are *managed costs,* and hence they are best controlled by appropriation-type budgets.

## CASE STUDY: DESIGNING A MARKETING COST SYSTEM (ACME COMPANY)

We will illustrate the process of designing a marketing cost system with the help of the continuing case study of ACME Company.

## System Analysis Tasks

**Task 1: Objective of the Proposed Cost System** In the preceding chapters we showed that one of the major objectives of the proposed cost system of ACME Company is to control the costs of marketing, particularly the costs of distribution and selling. It is also the objective of the company to develop the necessary cost information for product pricing and profit measurement by profit centers.

**Task 2: Relevant Background Information** From the fact-finding survey and further inquiries, the following relevant background information is gathered:

1. ACME Company warehouses and distributes its finished products X and Y from two distribution centers (Center I and Center II), which are located in New York and Memphis respectively. (See Exhibit 3-11.)
2. Each center is in the charge of the local center manager, who reports to the director, warehousing and distribution, at the New York office, who in turn reports to the vice president, marketing.
3. The company distributes its products throughout the United States by its own trucks, outside trucking companies, or rail, as may be appropriate. All sales are ex customer's premises.
4. Each center has four company-owned trucks.
5. The company, as a matter of policy, insofar as possible uses its own trucks for delivering its products before employing public transportation. However, this policy is not based on any cost-benefit analysis.
6. For controlling distribution expenses, the company compares each of the last three months' distribution expenses as percentages of sales. However, it often finds unexplainable variations in percentages from month to month.
7. There are two sales regions, located in New York and Memphis respectively, each in the charge of a manager who reports to the sales director at the corporate office. Sales are effected through sales representatives and through response to direct inquiries. However, each sales representative is assigned certain customer accounts and is paid a commission on total sales to all the representative's accounts.

**Task 3: System Requirements** It has been determined that the proposed cost system should generate the following reports:

1. Weekly sales reports separately for each region showing:
   *a.* Sales quantity and dollar amounts by products and customer types
   *b.* Comparison with budgeted sales

   Within a week, the regional sales managers should explain the causes of variances and how they propose to correct and prevent them.

2. Monthly summary of weekly sales reports with the causes of variances.

3. Weekly distribution cost reports separately for each distribution center showing:

   *a.* Costs by mode of distribution and cost factors
   *b.* Cost per unit of product distributed separately for each mode of distribution

The reports should show actual and budgeted costs and variances from budgeted costs. Within a week, the distribution center managers should explain the causes of variances and how they propose to correct and prevent them.

4. Monthly summary of weekly distribution cost reports with the causes of variances.
5. Monthly warehousing cost reports by centers.
6. Monthly consolidated warehousing and distribution cost reports.
7. Monthly selling expense reports, consolidated and separate for each region.
8. Monthly advertising expense reports.
9. Monthly marketing cost reports showing:
   *a.* Details of costs by various marketing segments
   *b.* Comparison with the flexible budget
10. Various statistical reports and graphs pertaining to the marketing function.

In addition, the proposed cost system should facilitate the preparation of marketing cost budgets.

## System Design Tasks

The major tasks to be completed for designing an effective marketing cost system for ACME Company are as summarized below:

1. Select cost control techniques and cost methods.
2. Establish responsibility centers and cost centers.
3. Determine marketing input data required to generate the required information.
4. Determine classification of marketing costs.
5. Separate direct and indirect marketing costs.
6. Select bases for allocation of indirect marketing costs.
7. Lay down procedure for preparation of marketing cost budgets.
8. Design marketing cost reporting system.
9. Design marketing cost accounting system.

We will explain the major points of only the first eight of these tasks.

**Task 1: Selection of Cost Accounting Methods and Techniques** In consultation with the controller and the president of ACME Company, the designer selects (*a*) the full absorption historical marketing cost system for product costing, product pricing, and profit determination by segments and (*b*) the flexible and appropriation types of budgets for controlling marketing costs. For cost control purposes, a responsibility reporting system similar to the one used for controlling manufacturing costs and explained in Chapter 12 will be used.

**Task 2: Establishment of Marketing Responsibility Centers and Cost Centers** Following the procedure explained in Chapter 8, the following responsibility centers have been established:

| Center No. | Responsibility-Cost Center | Responsibility of |
|---|---|---|
| 200 | Corporate Marketing Department | Vice president, marketing |
| 201 | Office of Vice President, Marketing | Vice president, marketing |
| 210 | Advertising and Market Research | Director, advertising and market research |
| 220 | Sales Department | Director, sales |
| 221 | Office of Director, Sales | Director, sales |
| 222 | Sales Region 1 | Manager, Region 1 |
| 223 | Sales Region 2 | Manager, Region 2 |
| 230 | Warehousing and Distribution Department | Director, warehousing and distribution |
| 231 | Office of Director, Warehousing and Distribution | Director, warehousing and distribution |
| 232 | Center I | Manager, Center I |
| 233 | Center II | Manager, Center II |
| X | Product X* | |
| Y | Product Y* | |

* Cost center only.

**Task 3: Determination of Input Data Required** The types of input data necessary to provide the required output information for cost control and product costing are as follows:

### Input Data Regarding Distribution Expenses

1. Own trucking expenses, separately for each truck, classified by cost elements, centers, and average per unit-miles traveled

2. The following quantitative data separately for each truck and each distribution center:

   *a.* Number of trips undertaken
   *b.* Total miles traveled
   *c.* Total units of each product delivered
   *d.* Total unit-miles traveled

3. Outside truck freight and rail freight by distribution centers and products

4. Total units of each product delivered from each distribution center separately by outside truck and rail

5. Total unit-miles involved in delivering through outside trucks and rail separately by distribution centers and products

**Input Data Regarding Warehousing Expenses**

1. Warehousing expenses classified by cost elements, distribution centers, and products
2. Warehousing space allocated for each product
3. Production quantity of each product

**Input Data Regarding Selling Expenses**

1. Selling expenses classified by cost elements, sales regions, and products
2. Sales quantity and dollar amounts by sales regions, products, customers, and sales representatives

**Input Data Regarding Advertising Expenses**

1. Advertising expenses by cost elements, media, sales regions, and products
2. Sales quantity by regions and products

**Input Data Common to All Functions** Corporate marketing costs classified into cost elements and distribution centers or sales regions and products.

**Task 4: Classification of Marketing Costs** It is decided to classify marketing expenses as follows:

- By nature of expenses
- By marketing functions
- By marketing segments
- By distribution channels

**Task 5: Separate Direct and Indirect Marketing Costs** Each of the marketing expenses should be classified into direct and indirect categories as illustrated below for distribution expenses. Since distribution costs are to be reported by distribution centers and products, each of the input distribution expenses should be classified into direct expenses and indirect expenses relative to distribution centers and products. The marketing cost matrix (see Exhibit 3-12) clearly shows the following:

- Distribution expense items which are direct to individual distribution centers but common to products
- Distribution expense items which are direct to individual distribution centers as well as to products
- Other marketing cost items which are common to more than one marketing function

All outside trucking and rail freight are clearly identifiable with individual products and hence should be classified as direct to the products. Among the company's own trucking expenses, only a portion of gasoline, oil, and tolls can be identified with individual products when deliveries by a particular truck involve only a single product. Since usually every truck delivers both products in one trip, a substantial portion of own truck expenses is not identifiable with individual products, and it will not be worthwhile to identify the small portion of these expenses with individual products. Hence, all own truck expense items are classified as direct to distribution centers but indirect to individual products.

The expenses which are common to the distribution function and one or more other marketing functions consist of the following:

- Certain expenses at each distribution center are common to warehousing and distribution functions, as both functions are located on the same premises.
- Expenses of the Office of the Director, Warehousing and Distribution, are common not only to the two functions but also to the two distribution centers.
- Expenses of the Office of the Vice President, Marketing, are common to all four marketing functions.

**Task 6: Selection of Proper Bases for Allocation of Indirect Expenses** For the sake of brevity, this task is explained only for distribution expenses. The designer, in consultation with ACME Company's management, has reached the following decisions for allocation of indirect distribution expenses:

1. For controlling distribution costs, *joint costs* of distribution and other functions will not be allocated either to individual products or to individual centers because no element of control is added by allocating such costs. Such joint costs will be shown in the appropriate cost center reports as follows:

- Costs which are incurred jointly for warehousing and distribution functions will be shown in the cost control report of the warehousing and distribution cost center, for which the director, warehousing and distribution, is responsible.
- Expenses of the Office of the Vice President, Marketing, will be shown in the vice president's responsibility report.

However, for determining *distribution costs in total* and *per unit* of each product, all the above joint costs will be allocated on some equitable basis.

2. For the purposes of allocation of indirect expenses, *fixed and variable costs* will not be allocated on separate bases. Only own truck expenses include indirect variable costs such as gasoline, oil, tolls, a portion of repairs and maintenance, etc. To allocate these variable costs on the most equitable basis, it is necessary to compute total unit-miles for each product. Having regard to the amount of such expenses, it was decided that the cost of computing total unit-miles for each product would far exceed the benefits from such a refinement. Hence, on practical considerations all own truck expenses will be allocated to products as if all these expenses were fixed.

3. Indirect expenses will be allocated on predetermined bases as opposed to actual bases.

4. The following bases have been selected for allocation of indirect expenses only for product pricing and for determining profit by segments on a full-absorption basis (as will be noted, most of the bases are arbitrary):

| Indirect Expenses | Basis |
|---|---|
| *a.* Own truck expenses of each center | Allocate to products on the basis of the number of units of each product delivered. (Though unit-miles would be a more equitable basis, its adoption would not be cost-beneficial.) |
| *b.* Occupancy expenses at each center | Allocate to warehousing and distribution functions in the ratio of space utilized. |
| *c.* Salaries and related expenses of center manager and the manager's secretary | Allocate to warehousing and distribution functions on the basis of the estimated time devoted.<br>Allocate to products in the ratio of the number of units of the two products delivered. |
| *d.* Other distribution expenses of each center | Allocate to products on the basis of the number of units of each product delivered. (Alternatively, the ratio of distribution expenses, excluding other distribution expenses, of each product may be used, but it is not as simple as the first choice.) |

| Indirect Expenses | Basis |
| --- | --- |
| *e.* Salaries and other expenses of the director, warehousing and distribution, and assistants | Expenses such as traveling which can be identified directly with individual centers should be allocated on a direct basis.<br>Other expenses, mainly salaries and related expenses, should be allocated to the two centers on the basis of the estimated time devoted.<br>The above expenses allocated to each center should be reallocated to the two functions at each center in the ratio of the estimated time devoted for each function.<br>Reallocate the joint distribution expenses of each center to products in the ratio of the number of units distributed. |
| *f.* Expenses of the Office of the Vice President, Marketing | Expenses such as traveling which can be identified directly with any function, region, or center should be so allocated.<br>The remaining expenses should be allocated to the four marketing functions on the basis of the time devoted.<br>Allocate the amount apportioned to distribution expenses to the distribution centers and products on the same bases as mentioned in *e*. |

**Task 7: Development of Procedure for Preparation of Marketing Cost Budgets** For controlling discretionary expenses such as market research, advertising, and sales promotion, ACME Company has decided that appropriation-type budgets should be used. In developing these budgets, the following factors will be considered:

- Marketing goals such as market shares, budgeted sales volume, new product or territory to be developed, etc.
- Profitability of the company
- Cost of desired advertising, sales promotion, etc., programs

In developing these budgets, management judgment obviously will play an important role.

For controlling volume-related marketing expenses such as warehousing, distribution, and selling expenses, ACME Company has decided to use flexible budgets without standard costing. However, to understand the cost behavior of various expenses and their rate of variation with the volume of relevant activity, the past 3 years' expenses will be analyzed.

The procedure for preparing marketing expense budgets is similar to that for preparing manufacturing overhead budgets illustrated in Chapter 12 and hence is not repeated here.

**Task 8: Designing Marketing Cost Reporting System** For cost control purposes, the designer has designed the following responsibility reports pertaining to marketing costs:

**EXHIBIT 13-2**

**Marketing Cost Report (ACME Company)**

Responsibility center Corporate Marketing Department  No. 200

Responsibility of Vice president, marketing  Month ______

<table>
<tr><th colspan="2">Actual</th><th colspan="2">Description</th><th colspan="2">Better (worse) than budget</th></tr>
<tr><th>Current month</th><th>Year to date</th><th>Account or cost center no.</th><th>Expense item or cost center</th><th>Current month</th><th>Year to date</th></tr>
<tr><td></td><td></td><td>201<br>210<br>220<br>230</td><td>Office of the Vice President, Marketing<br>Advertising and market research<br>Sales Department<br>Warehousing and Distribution Department</td><td></td><td></td></tr>
<tr><td></td><td></td><td></td><td>Total marketing costs</td><td></td><td></td></tr>
<tr><td colspan="6">Details of expenses of Office of Vice President, Marketing</td></tr>
<tr><td></td><td></td><td></td><td></td><td></td><td></td></tr>
<tr><td colspan="6">Performance summary</td></tr>
<tr><td></td><td></td><td></td><td>Sales ($)<br>Product X<br>Product Y</td><td></td><td></td></tr>
<tr><td></td><td></td><td></td><td>Total</td><td></td><td></td></tr>
<tr><td></td><td></td><td></td><td>Marketing costs as percentage of sales<br>Product X<br>Product Y</td><td></td><td></td></tr>
<tr><td></td><td></td><td></td><td>Total</td><td></td><td></td></tr>
</table>

**EXHIBIT 13-3**

**Consolidated Sales Expense Report (ACME Company)**

Responsibility center Sales Department　　　　Center no. 220

Responsibility of Sales director　　　　Month ____

| Actual | | Description | | Better (worse) than budget | |
|---|---|---|---|---|---|
| Current month | Year to date | Account or cost center no. | Expense item or cost center | Current month | Year to date |
| | | 221 | Office of Sales Director | | |
| | | 222 | Sales Region 1 | | |
| | | 223 | Sales Region 2 | | |
| | | | Total selling costs | | |
| Details of expenses of Office of Sales Director | | | | | |
| | | | | | |
| Performance summary | | | | | |
| | | | Sales ($) | | |
| | | | Sales Region 1 | | |
| | | | Sales Region 2 | | |
| | | | Total sales | | |
| | | | Selling costs as percentage of sales | | |
| | | | Sales Region 1 | | |
| | | | Sales Region 2 | | |
| | | | Total | | |

**EXHIBIT 13-4**

**Sales Expense (Sales Region) Report (ACME Company)**

Responsibility center <u>Sales Region 1</u> Center no. <u>222</u>

Responsibility of <u>Regional sales manager</u> Month ______

| Actual | | Description | | Better (worse) than budget | |
|---|---|---|---|---|---|
| Current month | Year to date | Account or cost center no. | Expense item or cost center | Current month | Year to date |
| | | | Salaries—management<br>Salaries—sales representatives<br>Commission<br>Allowances<br>Traveling<br>Rent<br>Telephone<br>Other expenses | | |
| | | | Total selling expenses | | |
| Performance summary | | | | | |
| | | | Sales ($)<br>Product X<br>Product Y | | |
| | | | Total | | |
| | | | Selling costs as percentage of sales<br>Product X<br>Product Y | | |
| | | | Total | | |
| | | | Selling costs per unit of sale<br>Product X<br>Product Y | | |

- Sales performance report: weekly and monthly
- Marketing cost report: monthly
- Advertising and market research report: monthly
- Consolidated sales expense report: monthly
- Sales expense reports by regions: monthly
- Consolidated warehousing and distribution cost report: monthly
- Warehousing cost reports by centers: monthly
- Distribution cost reports by centers: weekly and monthly

In addition, there will be statistical reports and special-purpose reports.

For the sake of brevity, only the specimen formats of the reports for marketing costs, consolidated sales expense, and regional sales expense reports are given respectively in Exhibits 13-2, 13-3, and 13-4. An outline of the distribution cost report has already been given in Exhibit 4-7. All these reports use the integrated reporting structure explained in Chapter 14.

Exhibit 13-4 gives a breakdown of sales expenses by their nature. The actual expenses for the current month and the year to date are compared with budgeted expenses, and variances are also shown. The report enables the regional sales manager to pinpoint variances in individual expense items. Since selling expenses are incurred to procure sales, they should be controlled by relating them to sales quantity and sales value. The "Performance summary" section of the report provides two overall measures of the cost effectiveness of the expenses incurred by the sales region. These measures are selling costs as a percentage of sales and selling costs per unit of sale. To compute these two measures separately for products X and Y, selling costs must be allocated to the two products.

Exhibit 13-3 is compiled from the sales expense reports of the two regions (Exhibit 13-4) and details of the expenses of the Office of the Sales Director. Exhibit 13-2 is compiled from the consolidated cost center reports of individual market segments and is similar to the report in Exhibit 13-3.

# Chapter 14

# Designing Effective Cost Reports

Ignorance is the night of the mind, a night without moon or star.
Confucius

Management reports are the lifeblood of any organization, providing upward, downward, and lateral communications channels. Reports are an important requisite to delegation of authority because through reports subordinates account for the authority and duties delegated to them. They are also a vehicle for providing direction to subordinates, for evaluating their performance, and for controlling operations. Without management reports, management may fail to take timely action or will have to base its decisions on ignorance and hunches. Thus, management reports are an internal intelligence system and are essential for effective management of any organization.

Cost reports are an important species of management reports. Chapter 4, "Determining Requirements of the Cost System," discusses how to ascertain what information is required from a cost information system. Chapters 5 through 13 and Chapters 15 and 16 explain how to design a cost information system so as to provide the requisite information. A culminating point of the cost information system is the reporting of cost information, the subject of this chapter. A cost accounting system exists to support a cost reporting system. Since the design of cost records, procedures, and a chart of accounts follows the design of cost reports, the order of Chapters 14 through 16 is logical.

This chapter deals with the following major issues which arise in designing a cost reporting system:

1. Reporting principles and guidelines
2. Selection of reports to be prepared
3. Report form design
4. Procedure for report preparation
5. Specimen cost reports

## PRINCIPLES AND GUIDELINES FOR AN EFFECTIVE REPORTING SYSTEM

To design an effective reporting system, the designer must know the principles of a good reporting system. Many of these principles are interrelated or overlapping in nature. The major principles and guidelines are given below:

**1. Purpose-Oriented Character** Every report should have a useful and well-defined purpose: a report should not exist for its own sake. A related principle is that not only should a report be useful but users should use it. It is not adequate for the designer to be convinced that a report is useful; the users should feel the same way. Unless users feel that a report will be useful, they will not use it. This does not necessarily mean that the designer should design only reports which users want, but it emphasizes the need for convincing users not that they must use a particular report because it exists but that it exists because it will be useful to them. Thus users must be sold on the utility of the report to them.

**2. Relevancy** A report must contain data which are relevant to the person to whom it is submitted and to the purpose for which it is required. For example, a report for cost control should contain only information which relates to the person to whom it is submitted, and it should either show only controllable costs or separate controllable and noncontrollable costs. Similarly, in a report prepared to enable management to choose between alternatives (make or buy, replace or repair, etc.), only costs which would vary between the alternatives should be reported, or at least attention should be focused on them. Since a computer can generate large amounts of data at a high speed, there is a tendency toward too much reporting. Hence, in the case of a computerized cost system, the designer should be particularly careful in sifting relevant and irrelevant information.

**3. Materiality** Data included in a report should not only be relevant but also be significant enough to be reported, and all significant data should be properly highlighted or red-flagged. If insignificant data are included in a report to complete a picture, they should be grouped appropriately and not shown individually. For example, a cost control report or a product cost report should show all significant items separately and group less significant items.

**4. Reporting by Exception** Whenever appropriate and feasible, the principle of reporting by exception should be adopted. According to this principle, only items which are out of line with normal expectations and which merit management attention are reported. To explain this principle, one writer has made a distinction between *data* and *information*. According to him, information is that portion of data which informs (serves as news to) the recipient about something not known to the recipient. For example, if the standard cost of a given product is $5 and the actual cost is also $5, reporting this fact provides no new information to management. However, if the actual cost is $5.50, under the exception-reporting principle management may be informed that the actual cost is 50 cents, or 10 percent, above the standard product cost.

Reporting by exception consumes less time of the recipient in reading the report and understanding the situation. Further, it makes the recipient aware that the business is not as usual and that the report must be attended to as soon as possible. Thus, exception reports are *quick action–oriented* and make *management by exception* possible.

A principle related to the exception principle is that emphasis should be placed on *selectivity* and not on condensation or summarization. For example, in a responsibility report to the plant manager, instead of a summary of costs incurred by the individual production shops, significant cost variances by production shops should be reported.

The extent to which the exception principle can be adopted depends upon the purpose of reporting, the levels of management to which reports are submitted, and the costing methods and techniques employed. For example, cost control reports may contain only variances from standards, budgets, or estimates, whereas product cost reports for inventory valuation or product pricing will usually contain complete data.

Similarly, exception reporting is better suited to a higher level than a lower level because lower-level management requires detailed reports for day-to-day operations and upper management needs to know only significant deviations from planned or expected results.

Further, to use the exception-reporting principle, it is essential to predetermine monetary and nonmonetary amounts so that deviations in actual amounts from predetermined amounts can be determined and reported. For example, if material usage and price standards are established, then only the areas of deviation from these standards can be reported. If, however, these standards are not established, it will be necessary to report material usage and price data for all materials and all products. Though past costs may be used as a basis for comparison, they often do not provide a valid basis for comparison.

With computers, it is easy to generate exception reports because computers can automatically and speedily match, sort, and select appropriate data from a mass of data.

**5. Pyramid Structure of Reporting** The pyramid structure of reporting can be adopted for both a single report and reports submitted at different levels of management. For example, if a report contains a large number of data, first the summary should be given and then the details should be given either on the same or on following pages. The reverse order—starting with the details and ending with a summary—is usually not advisable because a recipient who has first read the summary will have a proper perspective while reading the details and will be able to skip those details that are not relevant.

Similarly, cost reports submitted at different levels of management should vary in details inversely with the level of management, as shown diagrammatically in Exhibit 14-1. Operating management needs details of individual transactions. Middle management needs a summary of

**EXHIBIT 14-1**

**Pyramid Structure of Reporting**

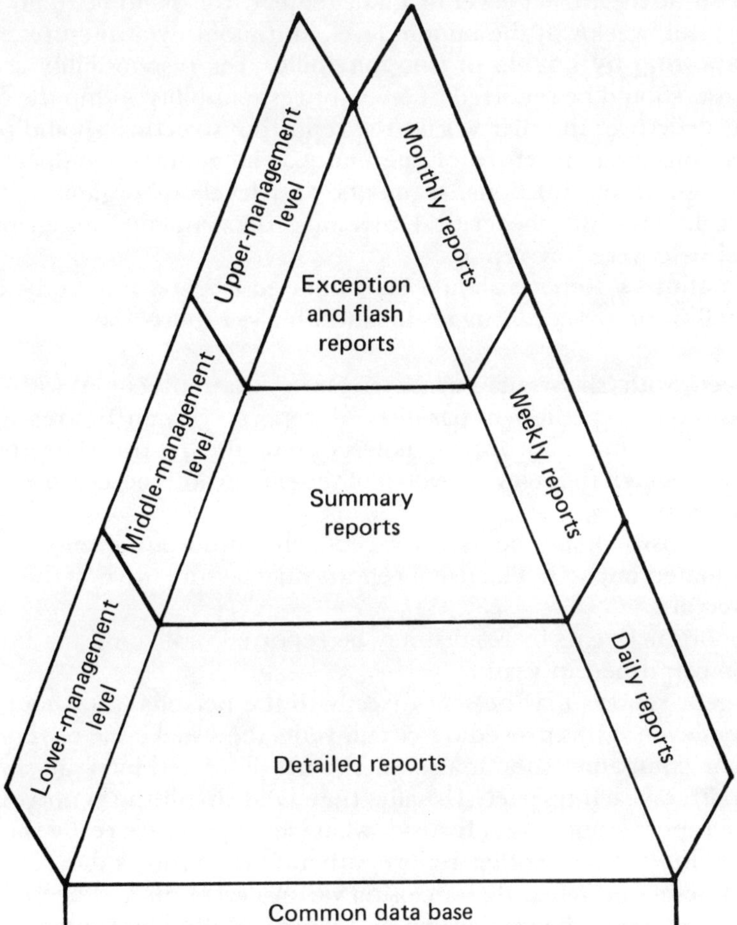

individual transactions, and upper management is interested only in key items, highlights, or exceptional items for overall control. These reports should be prepared from the same data base, and the lower-level report should support the higher-level report on the same item. For example, reports submitted to departmental supervisors should support the report submitted to the production manager. This does not mean that the report to the production manager should contain no more than totals of the individual reports to supervisors. The report to the production manager may contain additional information, but the information which is also included in the supervisor's reports should be consistent with the information included in the manager's report. An offshoot of this principle is that reports should be more frequent at the lower level and less frequent at the higher level of management, for example, daily at the lower level, weekly at the middle level, and monthly at the upper level.

**6. Reporting by Levels of Responsibility** For responsibility accounting, costs should be reported by levels of responsibility within the organization structure. In other words, the reporting structure should parallel the organization structure of the entity. The reports should cover as many significant functions, segments, and levels of organization as is practical. At least, the critical divisions, departments, and functions should be covered by reports.

**7. Timeliness** Reports should be submitted in good time to be useful. The following practical suggestions will make reports timely:

- Speed with slight inaccuracy is better than precision with delay. Hence, to expedite preparation of reports, certain figures may be estimated and appropriate notes put in the report. The designer should weigh the relevant worth of timeliness and the sacrifice of some accuracy.
- *Flash reports* should be used for reporting important events and their estimated impacts. The usual reports may be submitted at the regular intervals.
- Important events or results may be reported orally and the information confirmed in writing.
- Urgent reports may be sent directly to the persons who should have them even if this procedure circumvents the usual cycle of reporting.
- Some companies submit a set of reports at a fixed interval, say, each month or each quarter. Usually, they hold up all the reports if even one report is not ready. Instead, whatever reports are ready should be submitted and the other reports submitted as soon as they are ready.
- A time-bound schedule for closing various accounts and preparing an analysis should be established and vigorously followed up.

**8. Accuracy** The quality of decisions and actions based on reports depends upon the accuracy of the information contained in them. Further, wrong reports may mislead management. To ensure accuracy, the designer must provide for built-in checks and cross-checks in the system. Further, the person who prepares reports should exercise great care and always review reports before submitting them.

**9. Clarity** A report should be clear, unambiguous, and easy to read and understand. Either it should be self-explanatory or appropriate explanations should be attached to it. To achieve clarity, the following points may be noted:

- Use the language of the user or educate the user to the language of the report.
- Standardize terminologies of all regularly used reports so that a given term means the same thing to all persons.
- Use proper headings and subheadings, underline key words, arrange contents in a logical order, and add necessary explanations.
- Show variances as "better (worse) than standard or budget," and write negative variances in parentheses instead of showing "increase (decrease) compared with standard or budget" or "over (under) standard or budget." In the "better (worse) than" technique, all amounts in parentheses, whether revenue, costs, or profits, convey unfavorable variances, and all variances not in parentheses convey favorable variances. Thus, this technique eliminates the confusion which arises when the other two techniques are used. It will be obvious that the "better (worse) than" technique can be used for comparison not only with standards or budgets but also with past actuals or other entities' data for the same period.
- Review the report form with the user to get the user's reaction to it.
- Observance of the relevancy principle will also help achieve clarity.
- On the face of the report clearly indicate the period of the report, units of measurement (e.g., "$000," "quantities in tons," etc.), assumptions made, and other relevant information.

**10. Simplicity** A report should be as simple as possible. This goal can be achieved by observing the following rules:

- Use only relevant information.
- Select the techniques and tools of reporting with discretion. The designer should consider, for example, whether comparative figures are necessary and, if so, whether these figures are to be given in both monetary terms and percentages.
- Properly design the form of each report.

**11. Comprehensiveness** The principles of clarity and comprehensiveness are interrelated. To make a report more comprehensive, the following points may be noted:

- A logical grouping of products, departments, divisions, territories, etc., reduces the mass of information to be digested.
- Go from summary to details, not vice versa.
- Large figures should usually be rounded off, say, to thousands, millions, billions, etc.
- A logical classification of cost data will increase its comprehensiveness. If a multiple classification is to be adopted, the designer should consider whether to use a complex classification (a classification within a classification) or a separate classification. For example, a distribution cost report may be prepared by using complex multiple classification, as shown in Exhibit 14-2, or it may be broken down into two or more reports. For example, two separate reports may be prepared, one showing classification of costs by functions and nature and the other showing classification of costs by nature and behavior.
- Further, data should be so arranged that they will quickly apprise the reader of the message. For example, if in a cost variance report variances are arranged in the order of magnitude (either dollar amounts or percentages), the reader will quickly know the major variances. Similarly, comprehension can be increased by placing comparative data as close to one another as possible.

**12. Analysis and Narrative Interpretation** Insofar as possible, the report should not leave analysis and interpretation to the reader, particularly when the report is meant for several readers or for upper management. There are several reasons for this stricture. First, the preparer often is in the best position to analyze and interpret the report. Second, upper management does not have the time to analyze and interpret it. Management needs distilled facts which can be quickly assimilated. Third, if a report meant for several readers does not give analysis and interpretation, it will waste valuable time because each reader will have to analyze and interpret it. Fourth, numbers on a sheet of paper cannot convey the message as effectively as words can.

**13. Two-Way Communication, or Feedback Principle** Reporting should be a two-way street. A subordinate who submits a report to a superior should be informed of the superior's reactions. Similarly, the superior should keep the subordinate apprised of decisions made or actions taken on the basis of that report.

**14. User-Oriented Reports** Since reports are meant for use by their recipients, the designer should give weight to the users' preference re-

**EXHIBIT 14-2**

**Illustrative Distribution Cost Reports Using Complex Multiple Classification**

| Costs | Company as a Whole | North | | | East | | | South | | | West | | |
|---|---|---|---|---|---|---|---|---|---|---|---|---|---|
| | | A | B | Total | C | D | Total | E | F | Total | G | H | Total |
| Classified as follows:<br>1. By functions<br>2. Within each function, by behavior (fixed and variable)<br>3. Within fixed and variability categories, by nature of expenses | | | | | | | | | | | | | |

garding the format, arrangement of items, etc. Of course, convenience in preparing a report should also be considered.

**15. Integrated Reports** Insofar as possible, an integrated reporting structure, in which related reports are tied to one another, should be adopted. Such a structure offers the advantages of greater accuracy in reporting, integrity of management decisions, coordination among different functions, promptness in reporting, and prompt further investigation if necessary.

Integration can be achieved for levels of management reporting, periods of reporting, and objectives of reporting. For example, the pyramid structure of reporting explained earlier in this chapter is an example of integrated reporting. Similarly, daily reports should be the basis of or support weekly reports, and weekly reports should support monthly reports.

Further, cost reports for cost control, product costing, product pricing, decision making, etc., should be integrated by ensuring that the definitions and sources of monetary and quantitative data are the same. This does not preclude conscious decisions to accord different treatment to the same item for different purposes. For example, one large company treats fringe benefits as fixed for cost control purposes but segregates them into fixed and variable categories for product costing. But this difference in treatment is by design and not by ignorance.

Similarly, cost and noncost reports should be integrated. For example, production data used for cost reports should be the same as those used for production management, materials management, etc.

In a computerized cost system, the integrated reporting structure can be adopted by using the technique of data base or integrated-file structure.

**16. Tailor-Made Reports** Most of the above principles lead logically to the principle that every report should be tailor-made and not just copied. Certain precautions will ensure that reports are custom-made. First, do not define reporting requirements in terms of *reports to be prepared;* instead, define them in terms of information required, and then determine in which reports the required information should be included. Second, even if ready-made forms are to be used, modify them whenever necessary; i.e., adapt them to the particular concern's requirements.

**17. Cost-Benefit Analysis** The cost of reporting should not exceed the benefits likely to be derived from the reports. Hence, the designer should conduct a cost-benefit analysis at least for reports which do not seem to offer much benefit or for those which involve significant cost.

In conducting a cost-benefit analysis, not only the cost of preparation but also the costs of typing, reproduction, binding, distribution, reading, discussions, storage, and disposal should be considered. Often, this type of analysis gives shocking results. Because of the various costs involved besides the cost of report generation, such a cost-benefit analysis should also be conducted for computer-prepared reports.

**18. Keeping the System Up to Date** As and when major changes occur in an organization or in any aspect of its business, its reporting system should be reviewed to eliminate unnecessary reports or reporting procedures or to add to or modify existing reports to take care of the changed circumstances. In addition, it is a healthy practice to review periodically the entire reporting system in order to keep it current with new developments in reporting techniques and tools.

**19. Balancing** It will be obvious that some of these principles conflict with one another. Hence, the principles should be balanced by making trade-off decisions whenever appropriate.

## SELECTION OF REPORTS TO BE PREPARED

Since different persons require different information at different times and for different purposes, all the required information cannot be submitted in one report. Hence, the designer should divide the information to be reported into several reports. In this task, the designer may use the following guidelines.

1. The aim should be to have as few reports as necessary. Hence, whenever appropriate, two or more reports should be combined into one report. Usually, the same data relating to the same time period can be put into one report even though they are required by different persons for different purposes. For example, product cost data required for both inventory valuation and product pricing may be put in one report. On the other hand, information required for product costing and cost control will differ in nature and characteristics and therefore should be included in separate reports.

If different sections or departments are preparing reports furnishing various information, it is better to consolidate their data and submit a combined report. For example, to report the quantity and cost of material scrap and waste during each month, first the production shops or the stockroom may fill out the quantitative information in a predesigned combined form, and then the cost accounting department may enter the cost data on the form and submit the report to the interested parties.

2. The designer should avoid the common pitfall of first determining the reports to be prepared and then deciding other aspects such as the contents of each report, the persons to whom the report should be distributed, and the time when it should be prepared. The correct approach is just the reverse.

In Chapter 4, we showed how to determine cost information requirements in terms of why, what, by whom, when, etc. At this stage, the designer must finalize the type of reports in which this information should be included.

3. Once the various reports to be prepared have been determined, each report should be checked for completeness. A report has five facets, or aspects, which should be defined for each report:

- A report is always prepared for some activity of a business (production, sales, etc.).
- The activity relates to some segment of a business (company as whole, individual production departments, cost centers, etc.).
- The report treats one or more aspects of business activities, such as performance, status, use, efficiency, responsibility accounting, etc.
- The activities are expressed in terms of events and/or results.
- The events and results are expressed in monetary and/or quantitative terms (quantity and cost of material consumed, units sold, profits made, etc.).

4. A list of the *common types of reports* is given below (this classification is not mutually exclusive):

- Performance reports, e.g., production by divisions, sales by territories, etc.
- Status reports, e.g., a monthly report on the status of inventory of direct materials and finished products by items and locations.
- Use reports, e.g., machine utilization, labor utilization, material usage, etc.
- Efficiency reports, e.g., labor efficiency, production efficiency, etc.
- Responsibility reports, e.g., cost by responsibility centers and sales and profits by profit centers.
- Budget reports or variance reports, e.g., reports comparing actual costs, sales, profits, production, etc., with budgeted, standard, or estimated figures. These reports include a material usage variance report, a material price variance report, a labor utilization variance report, overhead variance reports, etc.
- Cost reports, e.g., product cost reports, process cost sheets, etc.
- Analysis reports, e.g., variance analysis, idle-time analysis, analysis of cost per sales call, etc.
- Progress reports, e.g., cost of plant under construction.
- Material loss and product loss reports, e.g., scrap, wastage, and defective-production reports.
- Profitability reports.
- Quality control reports.

5. It is also proper to consider whether any currently prepared cost reports should be discontinued.
6. Management's approval should be obtained for introducing each proposed report and for dropping any of the current reports.

## GUIDELINES FOR REPORT FORM DESIGN

For effective communication of any information, it is necessary to use a proper report form. A good form will make the report easy to read and understand, will take less time for preparation, will be pleasing to the eyes, and, above all, will not lack clarity. The techniques and principles of form design constitute a subject by itself, and their complete discussion therefore is beyond the scope of this book. However, a few practical suggestions will be useful:

1. For each report, first list its contents and think of the best way to arrange them. Usually, the best arrangement is arrived at by trial and error. Try to arrange the information in the order in which the reader would like to read it. At the same time, convenience in preparation should be borne in mind.
2. Insofar as possible, the report size should be standardized; usually 8½ by 11 inches is considered a standard business size.
3. Worksheets and report sheets should be separated.
4. Necessary references and cross-references should be given. For example, if two items in a report are added, this fact should be indicated in parentheses beside them.
5. All headings, subheadings, and particulars should either be self-explanatory or be suitably explained on the face of the report itself.
6. Report headings, subheadings, and contents should be as concise as possible. For example:

Undesirable heading:

XYZ Company

Statement Showing Cost of Production of Rayon Yarn of 120 Denier for the Month of March 1981

Better heading:

XYZ Company

Cost of Production of Rayon Yarn (120 Denier)

Month: March 1981

7. If different columns and lines in a report are separated by blocks, the report is more readable. For example, the report form given in Exhibit 14-4 is more effective than that given in Exhibit 14-3.

**EXHIBIT 14-3**

**Specimen Cost Report Not Using Block Form**

Cost of Production

Month March 1981

$ 000

| Cost elements | Actual | | Budget | | Variance | |
|---|---|---|---|---|---|---|
| | Current month | Year to date | Current month | Year to date | Current year | Year to date |
| Direct materials | 100 | 750 | 120 | 800 | 20 | 50 |
| Direct labor | 50 | 400 | 50 | 450 | .. | 50 |
| Manufacturing overhead | | | | | | |
| Department A | 35 | 275 | 40 | 290 | 5 | 15 |
| Department B | 25 | 220 | 20 | 210 | (5) | (10) |
| Subtotal (A + B) | 60 | 495 | 60 | 500 | .. | 5 |
| Total cost of production | 210 | 1645 | 230 | 1750 | 20 | 105 |

NOTE: Unfavorable variances are shown in parentheses.

8. Consider whether adding some cost information on existing non-cost accounting reports will eliminate the need for an additional cost report.

9. Use appropriate reporting techniques and tools such as tables, charts, graphs, decision trees, diagrams, curves, and narratives.

10. Test the suitability of each form by filling it in with actual data for any of the past months or with assumed data to see if any difficulty will arise in preparing it.

## PROCEDURAL ASPECTS

Having decided what reports should be prepared and having designed their forms, the designer should lay down the procedure for their preparation and distribution and provide the necessary instructions and explanations. Usually, it is better to attach the following particulars to each report form:

Explanations

Report title: (e.g., Manufacturing Overhead Costs Statement)
Prepared by: (Cost Accounting Department)
Purpose: (To compare monthly actual and budgeted manufacturing overhead costs separately for each of the production departments for cost control and to arrive at the actual departmental manufacturing overhead rates for computing overhead variances.)
When prepared: (The report for each month should be ready by the tenth of the following month.)
Distribution: (1. Supervisor of the respective production departments)
(2. Production manager)

Instructions

(Give here the necessary instructions for completing each item of the report from beginning to end, indicating, in particular, the source of each item of information, method of computing each item, assumptions, if any, to be made, basis of comparison, etc.)

**EXHIBIT 14-4**

**Specimen Cost Report Using Block Form**

Cost of Production

Month March 1981

$ 000

| Cost elements | Actual | | Budget | | Better (worse) than budget | |
|---|---|---|---|---|---|---|
| | Current month | Year to date | Current month | Year to date | Current month | Year to date |
| 1. Direct materials | 100 | 750 | 120 | 800 | 20 | 50 |
| 2. Direct labor | 50 | 400 | 50 | 450 | . . | 50 |
| 3. Manufacturing overhead | | | | | | |
| Department A | 35 | 375 | 40 | 290 | 5 | 15 |
| Department B | 25 | 220 | 20 | 210 | (5) | (10) |
| Subtotal (A + B) | 60 | 495 | 60 | 500 | . . | 5 |
| 4. Total cost of production | 210 | 1645 | 230 | 1750 | 20 | 105 |

NOTE: Unfavorable variances are shown in parentheses.

The cost accounting and reporting systems should be so thoroughly integrated that the periodic reports are produced routinely. For this purpose, the designer should prepare a complete plan of reports preparation (beginning with business transactions, data accumulation, allocation, etc., and going all the way through report preparation) on paper to check any loose ends.

**Guidelines for Expediting Report Preparation** To ensure timely preparation of reports, it is necessary to prepare schedules of closing and reporting, showing by what dates various books of account and memorandum records should be ready and also showing who should do what. The strength of a chain is the strength of its weakest link. To ensure that the schedule is adhered to, there should be provision that every delay be explained by the person responsible for it so that either the bottlenecks may be removed or a more realistic schedule may be prepared.

Given below are a few practical suggestions or methods to cut the closing time (it is assumed that reports are required monthly).

1. Whatever work can be done during the month should not be deferred until the end of the month. For example, monthly depreciation based on the balances of fixed assets at the beginning of the month can be computed during the month. Similarly, budgeted figures or figures of a previous period can be filled out in advance. Further, to the extent possible even worksheets should be filled out in advance.
2. Instead of closing journals at the end of the month, they may be closed a few days before, and the remaining entries for the month may be passed through a general journal or be taken to the next month if they are not significant.
3. For recurring billing or any other work, a cycling procedure may be adopted to spread the work evenly throughout the month.
4. The trial balance may be prepared a few days prior to the month end, and a separate trial balance be prepared for the entries for the last few days.
5. For internal reports, instead of waiting for some information, the information may be estimated, and if it is significant, the necessary note may be made. When actual figures are available, a supplementary report may later be issued if the actuals differ significantly from the estimated figures.

## SPECIMEN COST REPORTS

A few specimen cost reports are given throughout the book. Here are a few additional reports.

## Executive Summary Reports

Exhibits 14-5, 14-6, and 14-7 comprise the actual executive summary report designed by the author for XYZ Company. Prior to the design of this report, this company distributed a monthly administrative report containing operating reports of some fifty different organizational units (area offices, cities, service shops, etc.). The entire administrative report for a month is now summarized into a three-page executive summary report. The following are the benefits of this report:

1. It is *brief* but adequate for the purpose. Anyone who is interested in details can refer to the administrative report.
2. It is based on the principle of *reporting by exception* because it throws a spotlight on deviations in revenue, expenses, and operating income by individual items, by cities, by areas, and for the company as a whole. Consequently, it makes *management by exception* possible.
3. It provides *information* and not just *data.* Unlike the administrative report, it does not require every reader to analyze it.
4. It is *action-oriented* because it calls not only for explanations of negative deviations but also for planned or actual corrective and/or preventive actions from the persons responsible for negative deviations.

A brief explanation of the three pages of the report follows.

**Exhibit 14-5: Key Items Summary by Areas** This report gives a bird's-eye view of operating results, together with variances from the budgets, by areas. It highlights *areas* which *missed budgets* for either the current month or the year to date and points out whether the trouble lies in achieving revenue or in controlling a particular group of costs. It also shows each area's contribution to profits in dollar amounts and in percentage.

**Exhibit 14-6: Performance Report by Cities** All cities and service shops are listed here and classified as underachievers and others. All cities and service shops with lower than budgeted revenue or operating income for the current month or the year to date are listed here. The *number of times* each city or service shop *missed* the budget during the year is mentioned beside each city's name to identify cities with a persistent problem in meeting the budgets. These cities should be constantly and closely monitored.

**Exhibit 14-7: Variance Explanation and Action Report** First, the Controller's Department should prepare this report listing, separately *for each city,* negative variances in revenue and individual items of expenses exceeding the following limits:

- Revenue: when the year-to-date total revenue for a city is under budget by more than $5000

**EXHIBIT 14-5**

**Key Items Summary by Areas (XYZ Company)**

Month September 1980

| | XYZ Consolidated | Areas I | Areas II | Areas III | Corporate |
|---|---|---|---|---|---|
| 1. *Current month* | | | | | |
| 2. *Actual* | | | | | |
| 3. Revenue ($000) | 1069 | 312 | 552 | 205 | . . . |
| 4. Operating income ($000) | 176 | 49 | 187 | 81 | (141) |
| 5. *Better (worse) than budget* | | | | | |
| 6. Revenue ($000) | 66 | (4) | 48 | 22 | . . |
| 7. Cost of service ($000) | (43) | (16) | (27) | (14) | 14 |
| 8. Selling expenses ($000) | (18) | (2) | (12) | . . | (4) |
| 9. General and administrative expenses ($000) | (66) | (13) | (4) | 4 | (53) |
| 10. Operating income ($000) | (61) | (35) | 5 | 12 | (43) |
| 11. Operating income as percentage of revenue | 16 | 16 | 34 | 40 | . . |
| 12. Operating income as percentage of total operating income | 100 | 28 | 106 | 46 | (80) |
| 13. *Net additions in units* | | | | | |
| 14. Actual | 990 | 214 | 497 | 279 | . . |
| 15. Better (worse) than budget | 25 | 15 | (10) | 20 | . . |
| 16. | | | | | |
| 17. *Year to date* | | | | | |
| 18. *Actual* | | | | | |
| 19. Revenue ($000) | 8596 | 2599 | 4417 | 1589 | . . . . |
| 20. Operating income ($000) | 1273 | 354 | 1541 | 633 | (1255) |
| 21. *Better (worse) than budget* | | | | | |
| 22. Revenue ($000) | 291 | Details not shown here | | | |
| 23. Cost of service ($000) | (130) | | | | |
| 24. Selling expenses ($000) | 34 | | | | |
| 25. General and administrative expenses ($000) | (498) | | | | |
| 26. Operating income ($000) | (303) | | | | |
| 27. Operating income as percentage of revenue | 15 | 14 | 35 | 40 | . . |
| 28. Operating income as percentage of total operating income | 100 | 28 | 120 | 50 | (98) |
| 29. *Net additions in units* | | | | | |
| 30. Actual | | Not shown here | | | |

**EXHIBIT 14-5**

**Key Items Summary by Areas (XYZ Company) (*Continued*)**

Month September 1980

| | XYZ Con-soli-dated | Areas | | | Corpo-rate |
|---|---|---|---|---|---|
| | | I | II | III | |
| 31. Better (worse) than budget | | Not shown here | | | |
| 32. Number of units in service | 45,758 | 11,575 | 24,582 | 9601 | |
| 33. Number of employees: actual | 298 | 123 | 95 | 34 | 46 |
| 34. Better (worse) than budget | (10) | (2) | 2 | (3) | (7) |
| 35. Accounts receivable: total ($000) | 745 | 223 | 401 | 121 | .. |
| 36. Due in 90 days or more ($000) | 197 | 62 | 116 | 19 | .. |

- Expenses: when the year-to-date total of *any items of expense* is over budget by more than $1000

Then, the report should be distributed without completing "explanations" and "planned actions" columns. The concerned areas managers should be asked to explain the causes of negative variances and to explain what corrective and/or preventive actions they have planned or taken. Copies of reports with the last two columns filled in should then be distributed.

As a follow-up, the current month's variance report should be checked with prior months' variance reports to see if the same variances occur month after month.

## Analysis of Sales Calls

Exhibit 14-8 is a specimen report for analyzing the effectiveness of each sales representative in generating sales and for measuring efficiency in spending resources. The report is self-explanatory.

## Analysis of Direct-Mail Advertisement Cost

Exhibit 14-9 measures the effectiveness of the direct-mail advertisement campaign. The hypothetical numbers reveal the following facts:

1. During the current month, the direct-mail advertisement cost per unit of sales generated through direct mail was $10 as against $7.50 for

**EXHIBIT 14-6**

**Performance by Cities (XYZ Company)**

Month ______________ $000

| Current month | | | | | Year to date | | | | |
|---|---|---|---|---|---|---|---|---|---|
| Actual | | Better (worse) than budget | | | Actual | | Better (worse) than budget | | |
| Revenue ($) | Operating income ($) | Revenue ($) | Operating income ($) | City or service shop | Revenue ($) | Operating income ($) | Revenue ($) | Operating income ($) | Operating income as percent of revenue |
| | | | | Underachievers<br>(List those having actual revenue or operating income for the current month or the year to date less than that budgeted. Arrange in the order of the highest year to date worse than budgeted operating income. In parentheses write the number of times under budget during the year.) | | | | | |
| | | | | Others<br>(Arrange in the order of the highest year to date better than budgeted operating income. In parentheses, write the number of times worse than budget during the year.) | | | | | |

**EXHIBIT 14-7**

**Variance Explanation and Action Report (XYZ Company)**

Month ______________

(NOTE: For each city or service shop, list year-to-date negative variances when variances are (1) $5000 in total revenue and (2) $1000 in an individual item of expense.)

| Revenue or expense by cities | Year to date | | Variance explanation and corrective or preventative actions planned or taken |
|---|---|---|---|
| | Actual ($) | Negative budget variance ($) | |
| (City) | | | |
| . . . | | | |
| . . . | | | |
| (City) | | | |
| . . . | | | |
| . . . | | | |
| (City) | | | |
| . . . | | | |
| . . . | | | |

the year to date. Since there was no change in the cost per piece of direct mail, the higher cost per unit of sales generated must be due to lower sales (in units).

2. The direct-mail advertisement cost as a percentage of sales increased from 8.3 percent for the year to date to 11.1 percent for the current month. Since there was no change in the sale price or unit cost of direct mail, the higher percentage must be the result of lower sales (in units).

**EXHIBIT 14-8**

**Analysis of Sales Calls**

Month February 1981 Number of working days 20

| Sales representative | Sales generated ($000) | Number of sales calls made | Direct selling expenses* | Ratios | | |
|---|---|---|---|---|---|---|
| | | | | Sales per sales call | Direct selling expenses per sales call | Sales per $1 of selling expenses |
| A | $20,000 | 50 | $ 5,000 | $400 | $100 | $4.00 |
| B | 17,000 | 50 | 4,500 | 340 | 90 | 3.78 |
| C | 15,000 | 40 | 4,200 | 375 | 105 | 3.57 |
| Total | $52,000 | 140 | $13,700 | $371 | $ 98 | $3.71 |

*Direct selling expenses consist of sales salaries, commissions, car allowance, travel, and telephone.

3. Both the above conclusions are supported by the fact that during the current month the number of units of sales generated per $100 of direct-mail advertisement declined to 10 units from 13.3 units for the year to date.

Thus, this one report measures the effectiveness of the direct-mail advertisement campaign for the current month as compared with (*a*) the year-to-date performance of the current year, (*b*) the same month last year, and (*c*) the year to date of the last year.

**EXHIBIT 14-9**

**Analysis of Direct-Mail Advertisement Cost**

Month June 19XX

| Last year | | | | | | | Current year | | | | | |
|---|---|---|---|---|---|---|---|---|---|---|---|---|
| Current month | | | Year to date | | | | Current month | | | Year to date | | |
| $ | Units | $ per unit | $ | Units | $ per unit | | $ | Units | $ per unit | $ | Units | $ per unit |
| | | | | | | 1. Direct-mail advertisement cost | 10,000 | 20,000 | 0.50 | 60,000 | 120,000 | 0.50 |
| | | | | | | 2. Sales from direct-mail advertisement | 90,000 | 1,000 | 90.00 | 720,000 | 8,000 | 90.00 |
| | | | | | | 3. Sales per $100 of advertisement cost | 900 | 10 | ☒ | 1,200 | 13.3 | ☒ |
| | | | | | | 4. Advertisement cost per unit sold | ☒ | ☒ | 10.00 | ☒ | ☒ | 7.50 |
| | | | | | | 5. Advertisement cost as percent of sales | 11.1 | ☒ | ☒ | 8.3 | ☒ | |

# Chapter 15

# Designing Cost Records and Procedures

Cost records are the backbone of a cost control and information system.
Pravin P. Shah

In this chapter, we will discuss the process of designing cost records and procedures for accumulation, allocation, and absorption of costs for product costing and responsibility accounting. Since the designer is presumed to know cost accounting procedures, they are not explained here, but they are discussed from the system design viewpoint.

This chapter is divided into the following five sections:

1. System analysis tasks
2. Basic decisions involved in designing cost records
3. Designing cost records and procedures for historical costing
4. Designing cost records and procedures for standard costing
5. Designing computerized cost records and procedures

## SYSTEM ANALYSIS TASKS

For designing cost records, the designer should gather information on the following factors (discussed in Chapters 2 through 4) as they affect the design of cost records of any concern:

**Objectives of Cost System** Different objectives require different kinds of cost information, which, in turn, may cause differences in classification, accumulation, allocation, and absorption of costs and, consequently, in cost records and procedures.

**Nature of Business and Operations** A manufacturing company's cost accounting system will be different from that of a service company. Similarly, even in the same type of industry, differences in operations, equipment, plant layout, organization structure, etc., may cause variation in the cost accounting systems of different concerns. For example, when operations are manual, direct labor cost records will form an important part of a cost accounting system, and when operations are fully automated, manufacturing cost records will center in equipment operation and utilization.

**Organization Structure** Usually, a cost accounting system corresponds to the organization structure of a company not only for reporting purposes but also for the recording of input cost data.

**Functional Systems** An effective cost accounting system should be an integral part of various functional systems such as purchasing, material handling, storekeeping, distribution, etc. Hence, various functional procedures and operating controls also influence the design of a cost accounting system.

**Management Preferences and Attitude** In several areas, two or more equally acceptable alternatives may be available. For example, direct materials can be costed on FIFO, LIFO, average, or other cost bases. Selection will depend upon the preferences of management, the controller, and the designer.

**External and Internal Constraints** For example, a cost accounting system designed to comply with a statutory or a regulatory requirement must incorporate those features which are expressly laid down by the statute or the regulation. Internal constraints such as the education, experience, and training of cost accounting and other persons associated with the system also affect the ultimate design of the system.

## BASIC DECISIONS INVOLVED

Before designing cost records and procedures, either the designer or company management should decide the following major issues:

**Selection of Method of Costing** The design of a cost accounting system under historical costing is significantly different from that under standard costing. Similarly, there are differences in cost records between job order and process costing, on the one hand, and direct costing and full absorption costing, on the other hand. Since we have already discussed the subject of selection of methods of costing at length, it is not repeated here.

**Integrated or Separate Cost and Financial Accounting Systems** A concern may employ either separate financial accounting and cost accounting systems or an integrated financial and cost accounting system. Two chief merits of an integrated system are avoidance of duplication of accounting work and more accurate cost records. In financial accounting, expenses are classified according to their nature, such as salaries, wages, materials, freight, and packing.

In cost accounting, expenses are *additionally* classified by various segments of the concern (divisions, departments, locations, etc.), by cost behavior, by controllability of costs, etc. But this classification is essentially of the same expenses and is in *addition* to classification by nature of expenses. Thus, integration of the two records avoids duplicate record keeping. Second, because cost records will be integrated with financial records, the possibility of errors will be greatly reduced.

When the two systems are separate, accuracy of cost records should be ensured by periodical reconciliation of the two records.

The ultimate decision is influenced by several factors such as the competence of the accounting staff, the controller's preference, the objectives of the cost system, and the cost of record keeping under the two alternatives.

**Extent of Automation of Accounting** There are some significant differences in the design of cost records and procedures under an automated system and a manual system. For example, under a manual system, a source document will have to be classified and recorded in more than one way to generate information required for different purposes. In contrast, under an automated system, by using a proper coding system multiple classification and recording of the same source document can be avoided. These differences are explained in detail later in this chapter.

**Uniform Cost Accounting System** When such a system has been developed and recommended by a trade association, management must decide whether and to what extent to adopt it.

**Organization of the Cost Accounting Function** The cost accounting function may be centralized or decentralized. Though selection of the centralized versus the decentralized cost accounting function per se may not affect cost records, it will certainly have an impact on cost procedures. In a large organization with a manual or semiautomated cost system, decentralization of the cost accounting function often becomes inevitable. In a large organization with a computerized cost system, though it is possible to centralize the cost accounting function, it is not uncommon to find decentralized cost accounting functional.

## DESIGNING COST RECORDS AND PROCEDURES FOR HISTORICAL COSTING

The design of a historical cost accounting system involves the following aspects:

- Source documents to be used or prepared for recording various expenses
- Procedure for classification of source documents

- Records and procedure for recording expenses from source documents
- Procedure and records for charging direct material and direct labor costs to production units and responsibility centers
- Procedure and records for accumulation, allocation, and absorption of manufacturing overhead
- Procedure and records for accumulation and allocation of marketing and administrative expenses
- Procedure and records for inventory
- Procedure and records for accumulation of quantitative data
- Procedure and worksheets for various analyses for preparing required cost reports

## Source Documents

Source documents authenticate or support transactions within an organization or with a third party. The steps to be taken by the designer in regard to cost accounting source documents are as follows:

1. Determine the source documents required for recording each type of cost transaction. Some of the documents may be purely accounting documents (e.g., job cost card), but most of them (purchase orders, material requisitions, etc.) will be common to functional systems, the cost accounting system, and the financial accounting system. Insofar as possible, the documents already being used for various functional systems should be used also for cost accounting purposes. The documents or vouchers may be prepared internally or be received from a third party (a vendor, contractor, etc.). The commonly used source documents are listed in Exhibits 15-1 through 15-5.
2. When documents already being used for various functional systems are to be used also for cost accounting purposes, determine whether they must be modified to meet the requirements of cost accounting. Modifications may be required in respect of contents, arrangement of contents, procedure for preparation, sources of information to be used for preparation, number of copies to be prepared, distribution or routing procedure, etc. Depending upon the scope of the assignment, the designer may have to redesign the concerned forms or to recommend the required changes to the appropriate departments within the company.
3. Design the documents required exclusively for cost accounting purposes. In designing each of these documents,
    - Decide its function or purpose.
    - Determine its contents.
    - Determine its distribution or routing.

- Design its form after considering the desired arrangement of contents, size of the form, number of copies, color scheme, etc.
- Set forth the instructions for preparation, which should include the purpose of preparation, the time when the form is prepared, by whom it is prepared, how it is prepared (how the required input data will be obtained, mechanical devices, if any, to be used, etc.), and any approval authority required).
- Lay down the flow of papers, i.e., the distribution or routing of each copy of the document.

4. For all *internally generated documents,* the following points may be noted:

*a.* The form of each document must be tailor-made to suit the needs of the company and not just be copied from a specimen. The contents should be arranged in a logical order to facilitate the form's preparation and processing. However, whenever possible, standard forms may be used.

*b.* To the extent possible, the form should be self-explanatory. And whenever necessary, instructions for preparation and distribution of a document preferably should be given on the document itself. If a document is to be sent to a third party, instructions should be printed on the file copy. Other instructions such as processing, filing, the retention period, etc., may be given in the procedure manual.

*c.* Space should be provided for writing the account title or code and, if applicable, even the responsibility area or cost center name or code.

*d.* The form of a document should be uniform throughout the company. In one case, the author found that seven different locations were using five different forms of a material transfer memorandum without any justification for the differences.

*e.* For better control, forms should be prenumbered.

*f.* Usually, it is better to test each type of document by completing one or two documents, using actual or assumed transactions. The test-run procedure usually will reveal any difficulties in preparing a document and the need for modifying it.

*g.* A particular type of document should be readily distinguishable from other types of documents. The distinction can be achieved in several ways, e.g., by changing the size, color, or design. For example, the accounts department's copy of the sales invoice may be blue, and the purchase order may be green.

*h.* If a prepared document is required by more than one department, decide whether the original document itself should be routed among various departments or copies of it be distributed. For example, material requisitions prepared by the production departments are required by the storekeeper for making entries on stock cards as well as by the cost accounting department for recording consumption of materials. Some accountants advocate using the original material requisition for recording a material issue by the storekeeper and for making entries by the cost accounting department. Under this procedure, after recording the issue of material on the relevant stock card, the storekeeper writes the balance according to storekeeping records on the material requisition and sends it to the cost accounting department. The cost accounting department is instructed not to make entries from a material requisition unless the balance according to stock records is written on it and unless the balance agrees with the balance in the department's own records. However, this procedure may not be either feasible or convenient in all cases, for example, if storerooms are decentralized.

*i.* In some cases, the cost accounting department may find it expedient to use two separate copies of the same document, one for product costing and the other for responsibility accounting. However, it then becomes necessary to reconcile the two records or to provide some form of cross-checking to ensure the reliability of both records.

*j.* Certain accounting documents may also be required for nonaccounting purposes. In such cases, the nonaccounting requirements should be considered while these forms are being designed.

5. For each *external document,* the designer should specify how it is to be processed and disposed of for accounting purposes.

6. It should be ensured that documents pass along the normal operational flow and that the flow of documents and record keeping follow a logical sequence so that needless back-and-forth movements of documents are avoided. A flowchart of each high-volume document will pinpoint avoidable back-and-forth movements.

7. For better control and greater accuracy of records, accounting documents and related nonaccounting documents should, as far as possible, be interlinked through cross-referencing, etc.

## Specifying Procedure for Classification of Source Documents

Before recording in cost records the information from source documents, these documents should be properly classified. For this purpose, the designer should specify *how, when,* and *by whom* the various source documents will be classified. The answers to these questions depend upon the types of cost classification required and the procedure adopted for accumulation, allocation, absorption, and analyses of costs.

The extent of classification of source documents is governed not only by the chart of accounts or the ledger accounts maintained but also by the memorandum cost records and analyses prepared. As a general rule, source documents should be classified in sufficient detail to fulfill later requirements. At a minimum, documents should be classified by nature of expense, by cost centers, and by responsibility centers. Usually, direct material requisitions and direct labor time tickets are identified with the relevant jobs, operations, or processes by the preparers themselves. Overhead expenses may be classified into fixed and variable categories.

To indicate the classification of source documents, the account code or name and the cost center code or name usually are written on the source document itself. Preferably, the entire classification should be made before a document is recorded. However, for reasons of expediency, particularly when multiple classification of a document is made by more than one person or department, only the basic classification of a document may be made initially and additional classification made after the document has been recorded in the books. In a computerized cost system, it is imperative to make the entire classification of a source document before it is recorded.

The designer should also ensure that departments, cost centers, and production units (job, process, etc.) to which various costs are to be charged are well-defined and that a system of identifying them exists.

## General Design of Cost Records

First, the following four interrelated questions should be resolved:

1. What records will be maintained to accumulate costs from the source documents for each type of cost?

2. How will the accumulated costs be charged to responsibility centers for cost control and to production units for product costing? For product costing, direct materials and direct labor are charged to jobs or processes. For cost control, these costs are charged to responsibility centers. However, for both cost control and product costing, manufacturing overhead is allocated to cost centers consisting of service centers and production centers. Further, for product costing alone, service center costs are allocated to production centers, and production center overhead eventually is charged to production units.

3. How much of these records will be on the books of account, and how much will be maintained on a memorandum basis? In other words,

to what extent will double-entry bookkeeping be employed? The purpose of double-entry bookkeeping is to ensure arithmetical accuracy of accounting records, which is achieved by passing a debit entry and a corresponding credit entry for every transaction. In a full-fledged double-entry cost system, the costing source documents are recorded in the books of original entries from which transactions are posted to subsidiary or general ledgers. Further, journal entries are passed even for primary and secondary allocation of overhead.

Though a double-entry-bookkeeping system is indispensable for financial accounting, it is complicated, cumbersome, and time-consuming and hence is less useful for developing information for cost control, planning, cost analysis, and even product costing. At the same time, unless cost records and reports are tied with the financial accounts in some way, users will question the integrity of the cost data. Hence, the best course is to employ the double-entry-bookkeeping system only for the basic cost records and to develop various types of cost information by suitable analysis and by summarization of data obtained from the basic cost records.

4. How will the double-entry-bookkeeping records be divided into journals, subsidiary ledgers, and the general ledger? As a general rule, if many accounts are to be maintained, only control accounts may be maintained in the general ledger and detailed records be kept either in the subsidiary ledgers or in memorandum records. For example, a chemical company using a few direct materials and producing a few products may not need a direct material control account. But a pharmaceutical company using many direct materials and producing several products will usually maintain a direct material control account in the general ledger and detailed accounts in a subsidiary ledger called a direct materials ledger.

The answers to these questions depend upon:

- The kind of cost information required.
- The volume of cost accounting transactions.
- The number of products manufactured or dealt in.
- The method of costing employed. The main differences in cost records under job order costing and process costing concern product costing and not responsibility accounting. Under job order costing, cost records are maintained by jobs and under process costing by processes.

Once the above four questions have been resolved, design each of the records to be maintained. For this purpose:

- Determine its form.
- Determine its size and whether it will be in bound or loose-leaf format.

- Set out the procedure for record preparation.
- Establish the relationship, if any, with other records, for example, reconciliation of the balance according to stock cards with that in the stock ledger when these two records are maintained.

## Designing Cost Records for Direct Materials

Direct materials cost records relate to receipts, issues, consumption, and wastage of direct materials. Exhibit 15-1 shows the usual cost records and source documents maintained for direct materials.

Generally, direct materials inventory records are maintained by the cost accounting department as well as by the storeroom. The storeroom may maintain only quantity records, whereas the accounting department's inventory records show both quantity and value. However, these two records should be reconciled periodically.

For product costing, bills of materials, material requisitions, or material consumption documents are analyzed by jobs, processes, or products, and for responsibility accounting these documents are classified by responsibility centers.

If minimum use is to be made of double-entry bookkeeping, the general ledger will contain only a work-in-process control account, and records of direct material consumption by types of materials will be kept in a stock ledger and records by production units in production cost sheets (job order cost sheet, process cost sheet, assembly cost sheet, etc.). Though theoretically possible, it is unusual to keep accounts of direct material consumption by departments and production units in the general ledger or in a subsidiary ledger.

In deciding whether a separate material price register should be maintained or prices be obtained from the stock ledger, expediency, convenience, the accuracy of records, and the cost of separate record keeping should be considered.

Further, records should also be designed to record direct material losses such as scrap, wastage, and rework materials. The exact records for these items will depend upon their accounting treatment.

The controller or the designer must also determine the following *accounting issues* if they have not already been determined:

- Cost flow assumption (FIFO, LIFO, weighted-average, etc.) for valuation of direct material inventory
- Treatment of various material losses

**EXHIBIT 15-1**

Cost Records for Direct Materials

| Transaction | Supporting Documents | Books of Original Entries and/or Memorandum Records | Subsidiary Ledgers | General Ledger Entries | Remarks |
|---|---|---|---|---|---|
| Materials purchase and receipt from vendor | Purchase invoice and materials received note | Purchase journal or accounts payable voucher summary<br>Stores cards (by storeroom)<br>Price register (optional; by cost clerk) | Stores ledger: in receipt columns of individual direct material accounts (by cost clerk) | Direct Materials Control account<br>Vendors accounts | |
| Issue of materials to production: job order costing | Bill of materials or material requisition | Material requisition analysis (for identifying direct material consumption by jobs and cost centers)<br>Stores cards<br>General journal | Stores ledger: in issue columns of individual direct material accounts<br>Job cards (posting done from material requisition analysis) | Work-in-Process Control account<br>Direct Materials Control account | Job cards serve as a subsidiary ledger to Work-in-Process Control account in the general ledger. |
| Issue of materials to production: process costing | Consumption report, bill of materials, or material requisition | Material requisition analysis (for identifying direct material consumption by processes and cost centers)<br>Stores cards<br>General journal | Stores ledger<br>Process Cost Control account | Work-in-Process Control account<br>Direct Materials Control account | 1. Process cost sheets serve as a subsidiary ledger to Work-in-Process account.<br>2. Separate work-in-process control accounts may be maintained for separate processes. |

## Designing Cost Records for Direct Labor

Direct labor cost records relate to attendance, accumulation of direct cost incurred, and the charging of direct labor costs to production and responsibility centers. Exhibit 15-2 shows the usual cost records and source documents maintained for direct labor.

**Direct Labor Source Documents** For product costing, work tickets or job cards are summarized by jobs, processes, or products, and for responsibility accounting these documents are classified by responsibility centers.

Direct labor is controlled in terms of *time* as well as *cost.* Direct labor cost by departments will be readily available from the payroll record if it is departmentalized. This approach will avoid duplicate record keeping and separate analysis for cost control purposes. For controlling direct labor time, it is necessary to analyze time tickets, work tickets, job tickets, or attendance sheets and summarize them by productive time and unproductive time. Unproductive time may be analyzed into normal and abnormal idle time and also by causes of unproductive time.

For product costing as well as for cost control, the source documents may be either directly posted to job cards, production cost cards, process cost sheets, etc., or first analyzed separately by departments, operations, jobs, products, processes, etc., and the summary totals then posted to various production and responsibility cost records. An illustrative direct labor cost analysis is presented in Exhibit 15-3, which shows total direct labor costs by departments and, within the departments, by operations, jobs, and individual workers.

Further, a procedure for reconciling direct labor costs according to payroll sheets and costs according to direct labor cost analysis should be instituted.

Production people dislike paperwork, and therefore they must be made to do as little paperwork for cost accounting as possible. Hence, whenever justified, a cost clerk should be assigned to the production department. This approach will also increase the reliability and timeliness of direct labor time records.

**Internal Control over Direct Labor Documents** In accumulating direct labor–hours, care should be taken to ensure that workers or supervisors do not deliberately account for actual labor time wrongly. For example, excess production time may be recorded as time lost due to stoppage, material fault, etc., or excess time on one job may be distributed to a few jobs so that consistency in variances can be attributed to external factors or variances on each job be reduced to an acceptable level. To discourage such practices, surprise checks should be made and cumulative variances computed.

**EXHIBIT 15-2**

**Cost Records for Direct Labor**

| Transaction | Supporting Documents | Books of Original Entries or Memorandum Records | Subsidiary Ledgers | General Ledger Entries | Remarks |
|---|---|---|---|---|---|
| Recording of attendance and payroll computation and distribution | Clock or time cards or attendance register | Payroll registers or sheets by cost centers<br>Journal | | For accrued payroll:<br>Direct Labor Control account<br>Accrued Payroll | |
| For charging cost of direct labor to production | *Job order industries*<br>1. Job or work tickets: time worked by each worker on each job recorded on separate job or work tickets<br>2. Job cards: separate card prepared for each job and travels with the job<br>3. Piece-rate cards or work tickets for piece-rated workers | Direct labor costs analysis by cost centers<br>Journal | Job cards | Work-in-Process Control account<br>Direct Labor Control account | In both types of industries, analysis of costs by responsibility centers should be made for cost control. |
| | *Process industries*<br>Same as attendance records. To record transfers of workers from one process to another process, transfer tickets may be used. | Journal | Process cost sheets | Same. There may be a separate Work-in-Process Control account for each process. | |

**EXHIBIT 15-3**

**Illustrative Multiple Direct Labor Cost Analysis**

| Department A | | | | | |
|---|---|---|---|---|---|
| **Operation No. 1** | | | | | |
| Employee | Job No. | Labor Cost | Job Subtotals | Job Totals | Employee Totals |
| 131 | 15 | $ 425 | | | |
| | 16 | 320 | | | |
| 132 | 15 | 225 | $ 650 | | |
| | 17 | 130 | 130 | | |
| 133 | 16 | 140 | 460 | | |
| | 18 | 250 | 250 | (18) 250 | 390 |
| Operation No. 1 total | | $1490 | $1490 | | |
| **Operation No. 2** | | | | | |
| 131 | 15 | $ 190 | 190 | (15) 840 | 1215 |
| | 17 | 280 | | | |
| 132 | 17 | 260 | | | |
| | 20 | 320 | 320 | (20) 320 | 935 |
| 134 | 16 | 120 | 120 | (16) 580 | |
| | 17 | 160 | 700 | (17) 830 | 280 |
| Operation No. 2 total | | $1330 | $1330 | | |
| Department A total | | $2820 | $2820 | $2820 | $2820 |

**Direct Labor Cost Records** If for direct labor cost accounting minimum use is to be made of double-entry bookkeeping, the general ledger will contain only a work-in-process control account to which direct labor cost will be debited and the corresponding credit will be given to the direct labor control account. Otherwise, accounts for direct labor by departments may be maintained in the general ledger or in a subsidiary ledger, with a control account in the general ledger.

**Direct Labor Accounting Issues** The controller or the designer must resolve the following cost accounting issues:

1. What treatment should be accorded to payroll taxes and fringe benefits related to direct labor costs? Some companies treat these costs as a part of direct labor cost, while others treat them as a part of manufacturing overhead.
2. Should overtime paid to direct labor be treated as a part of direct

labor cost or of manufacturing overhead? The pros and cons of each alternative are too well known to cost accountants to be discussed here.

## Designing Cost Records for Manufacturing Overhead Costs

Manufacturing overhead cost records consist of four types:

- Initial recording of manufacturing overhead
- Primary allocation of manufacturing overhead
- Secondary allocation of manufacturing overhead
- Absorption of manufacturing overhead

The alternative manufacturing overhead accounting plans for each of these types are shown in Exhibit 15-4.

Usually, manufacturing overhead costs are accumulated by nature of expenses and by cost centers or responsibility centers. Overhead costs which can be directly identified with cost centers should be charged to the cost centers on a direct basis, and only the remaining costs should be allocated. For example, the following expenses usually can be charged directly as explained against each item:

| Expense Item | How Charged to Cost Centers |
|---|---|
| Salaries, wages, learning time, idle time, rework time, overtime premium, and shift premium | Payroll records and time tickets will be maintained by cost centers so that all salaries and wages can be charged to concerned cost centers. |
| Rework materials, operating supplies, tools, maintenance materials, and office supplies | These will be charged to respective cost centers from the issue requisitions. |
| Telegrams, travel, and entertainment | These will be directly charged to cost centers from the expense vouchers. |
| Purchased maintenance | Outside maintenance for weighing scales will be charged to the storekeeping and material-handling cost center; all other outside maintenance for building and of a general nature will be charged to general factory administration. |

For primary and secondary allocations and absorption of overhead, it is necessary to design worksheets and provide instructions for preparing each worksheet.

The procedure must also provide for the times when initial recording, primary allocation, and secondary allocation will be made and when

**EXHIBIT 15-4**

**Cost Records for Manufacturing Overhead**

| Transaction | Supporting Documents | Books of Original Entries and/or Memorandum Records | Subsidiary Ledgers | General Ledger Entries |
|---|---|---|---|---|
| 1. *Initial recording of manufacturing overhead (accumulation)* | | | | |
| *a.* Indirect materials | Material requisitions or purchase invoices | Material requisition analysis<br>Purchase or expense journal<br>General journal | Stock ledger (may not be maintained for small-value items) | Debit Indirect Materials account. |
| *b.* Indirect labor | Work tickets, time cards, or attendance sheets | Payroll analysis<br>General journal | Alternative 1: no subsidiary ledger } (b and c) | Debit Indirect Labor account and various expense accounts. |
| *c.* Other overhead expenses | Expense statements, invoices, etc. | Columnar expense journal<br>Cashbook | Alternative 2: manufacturing overhead expense ledger } (b and c) | Debit Manufacturing Overhead Control account. |
| 2. *Allocation of overhead expenses to cost centers (primary allocation)*<br>*a.* Indirect materials<br>*b.* Indirect labor<br>*c.* Other overhead | Depreciation schedule, repair orders, spoiled work tickets, scrap report, etc. | Material requisition analysis<br>Payroll analysis<br>Overhead analysis (Various expense vouchers are analyzed by cost centers, and objective expense accounts are distributed to cost centers.) | Alternative 1: no subsidiary ledger | Make no entry for primary allocation. |
| | | | Alternative 2: no subsidiary ledger | Debt individual cost center accounts.<br>Credit individual expense accounts. |
| | | | Alternative 3: credit individual expense accounts in the manufacturing overhead expense ledger. | Debit individual cost center accounts.<br>Credit Manufacturing Overhead Control account. |

| | | | |
|---|---|---|---|
| | | Alternative 4: cost center ledger with or without manufacturing overhead expense ledger | Debit Cost Center Control account. Credit individual expense accounts or Manufacturing Overhead Control account. |
| 3. *Allocation of service centers' cost to production centers (secondary allocation)* | Allocation worksheets | Alternative 1: no subsidiary ledger | Make no entry for secondary allocation. Usually this alternative is combined with alternative 1 under "primary allocation records." |
| | | Alternative 2: no subsidiary ledger | Debit individual production center accounts. Credit individual service center accounts. Usually, this alternative is combined with alternative 2 or 3 under "primary allocation records." |
| | | Alternative 3: cost center ledger | Debit and credit entries in the Cost Center Control account. Usually this alternative is combined with alternative 4 under "primary allocation records." |
| 4. *Application of manufacturing overhead to production (absorption)* | *a.* Production records<br>*b.* Worksheets for computing production department overhead application rates | *a.* Job cost cards<br>*b.* Process cost sheets | |

**EXHIBIT 15-4 (*Continued*)**

**Cost Records for Manufacturing Overhead**

| Transaction | Supporting Documents | Books of Original Entries and/or Memorandum Records | Subsidiary Ledgers | General Ledger Entries |
|---|---|---|---|---|
| | | *c.* Manufacturing overhead absorption analysis showing allocation of overhead to various production units | *c.* Batch cost sheets (entries made in "Applied overhead" columns) plus | |
| | | | Alternative 1: no subsidiary ledger | No general ledger entry |
| | | | Alternative 2: no subsidiary ledger | Debit Manufacturing Overhead Applied account. Credit Manufacturing Overhead Control account *or* individual manufacturing overhead expense accounts *or* individual production center accounts *or* Cost Center Control account. (The credit entry will depend upon the records maintained for accumulation and allocation of overhead.) |
| | | | Alternative 3: cost center ledger | Same as for alternative 2 |

overhead will be applied to production. It should also eventually specify who will handle each of these functions.

The following two design issues should be resolved for overhead records:

1. Should manufacturing overhead by nature of expenses be maintained in the general ledger or in a subsidiary ledger?
2. Should overhead cost accumulation by cost centers be recorded in the general ledger, a subsidiary ledger, or memorandum records?

If only a few overhead expense accounts are involved, they may be maintained in the general ledger itself, and there is no need for a separate subsidiary ledger for manufacturing overhead expenses. However, if there are many overhead expense accounts, it will be worthwhile to maintain a separate subsidiary ledger for recording overhead expenses.

## Designing Cost Records for Marketing and Administrative Expenses

Marketing expenses are accumulated by nature of expenses and, in addition, may be accumulated or compiled by cost centers, responsibility centers, marketing functions, marketing methods, etc. The major design issue to be resolved is how to divide these records among the general ledger, subsidiary ledgers, and memorandum records. As a general rule, the more complex the marketing cost analyses required, the greater the use of memorandum records.

In the books of account, indirect marketing expenses are accumulated by nature of expenses or by objective expense accounts. Direct marketing expenses are usually accumulated by nature of expenses and may also be accumulated by major cost centers (functions, territories, products, etc.).

In decentralized accounting, some cost classifications are obtained automatically. For example, if separate books of account and other records are kept by individual sales territories, costs are automatically accumulated by territories.

The alternative accounting plans for accumulation and allocation of marketing expenses are the same as those for manufacturing overhead except for the differences caused by differences in the nature of expenses and in cost centers. Hence, only the usual records and source documents maintained for the initial recording of marketing expenses are given in Exhibit 15-5.

Accounting records for administrative expenses are more or less similar to those for marketing expenses except that they are simpler. Ad-

**EXHIBIT 15-5**

**Initial Recording of Marketing Expenses**

| Expense | Document | Books of Original Entries | Subsidiary Ledgers and Other Records | General Ledger Debit or Credit |
|---|---|---|---|---|
| Salaries | Attendance sheets | Payroll register by marketing segments<br>General journal | | Debit Salaries—Marketing. |
| Wages | Time cards | Payroll register by marketing segments<br>General journal | | Debit Wages—marketing. |
| Rent, electricity, gas, outside repairs, freight, etc. | Vendors' invoices, payment receipts | Columnar expense journal | | Debit Various Expenses—Marketing. |
| Depreciation | | General journal | Depreciation schedule | Debit Depreciation—Trucks (similarly for other assets). |
| Property taxes | Tax returns and schedules | General journal | | Debit Property Taxes—Marketing. |
| Traveling expenses | Expense statements and invoices | General journal | | Debit Traveling Expense—Marketing. |

ministrative expenses are accumulated by nature of expenses and by functions or responsibility centers.

The usual source documents for marketing and administrative expenses are vendors' invoices, expense vouchers, the payroll register, commission statements, etc. Most of these documents are also required for financial accounting and hence need not be designed specially for cost accounting.

## Designing Inventory Records

The inventory of a manufacturing concern may consist of direct materials, components, parts, work in process, and finished products. Separate inventory records should be maintained not only for each of these categories but also for its subdivisions. For example, separate inventory records should be kept for each direct material, finished product, etc.

**Inventory Records for Direct Materials** Inventory records for direct materials have been dealt with under the heading "Designing Cost Records for Direct Materials."

**Inventory Records for Components and Parts** Inventory records for bought-out components and parts will be similar to those for direct materials, and records for own-manufactured components and parts will be similar to those for finished products discussed below.

**Inventory Records for Work in Process** Usually, quantitative records of work in process are not maintained. For income determination, the work-in-process inventory is taken at the end of the period for which the income is to be determined.

In a job order industry, the quantity of work in process can be easily measured at any time from the job cards. Direct materials and direct labor costs will also be available from the job cards. If manufacturing overhead costs are to be included in valuing the work-in-process inventory, they should be applied to each job in process on some suitable basis.

In a process industry, for valuation of work in process it is essential to convert it into *equivalent completed units.* This conversion will be made by the engineers or the production personnel. Often, it is necessary to compute the equivalent completed units separately for direct materials and direct labor. For example, if the entire direct material is added at the beginning of the process, work in process will be 100 percent complete as to direct material but only partially complete as to direct labor.

**Inventory Records for Finished Products** The inventory records for finished products should show opening balances, receipts of finished products from production departments or from vendors if purchased, dispatch to customers, sales depot, etc., and closing balances. These records should also show defective products received back from customers and returned to production departments or vendors. For valuation of the finished products inventory, the unit product cost will be available from the product cost statements.

### Designing Procedures and Records for Accumulation of Quantitative Data

Quantitative data are required for allocation and absorption of costs, computing unit product cost, variance analysis, and various other cost analyses. Usually, there are three sources of quantitative data:

- Operating departments' records, e.g., for machine-hours, person-hours, production, sales, inventory, number of sales invoices, number of employees, scrap, wastage, etc.
- Statistical studies employing some sort of work measurement or industrial engineering techniques, e.g., to compute the volume of products handled, service calls or sales visits, etc. If a complete count is difficult, a sampling technique may be used.
- External records, e.g., for data on population or the circulation of newspapers or magazines.

Whenever possible, existing records of the various departments should be used, and additional records should be designed only for quantitative data which are otherwise not available from internal or external sources. If existing records are to be used, the designer should consider whether the existing documents and records and the procedures for their preparation should be modified to simplify allocation work. For example, if, instead of using a single serial numbering system for sales invoices, a separate numbering series is used for each territory and, within each territory, customer division codes and product codes are used, the total number of sales invoices by territories, by customer divisions within a territory, and by products within a customer division will be readily available. Similarly, if the sales journal, the sales order book, and other records are suitably classified by territories, divisions, products, etc., the task of obtaining the base data required for cost allocation will be simplified.

## DESIGNING COST RECORDS AND PROCEDURES FOR STANDARD COSTING

Most of the discussion concerning historical cost records and procedures applies also to standard cost records. Hence, only additional points or distinguishing points of standard cost records are discussed here.

### Selection of an Accounting Plan

For standard cost record keeping, three alternative accounting plans are available: (1) partial plan, (2) single plan, and (3) dual plan. A comparative analysis of these three plans is given in Exhibit 15-6. Since the journal entries passed under each of these plans will be available from any standard textbook on cost accounting, they are not given here. Exhibit 15-6 will enable the designer to select an appropriate accounting plan. In making this selection, the major decision is whether to have standard cost records on a double-entry-bookkeeping basis (first two plans) or on a memorandum basis. Obviously the preference of the controller will be a major decisive factor in this choice.

### Variance Analysis

From the system design viewpoint, the issues concerning variance analysis are (1) types of variances to be computed, (2) selection of a method of computing variances, and (3) selection of a method of disposal of variances. Each of these issues is discussed separately below.

**Types of Variances** One or more of the following variances may be computed:

- Net total variance between actual cost and standard cost.
- Variances by cost elements such as direct material cost variance, direct labor cost variance, overhead variance, etc.
- Direct materials variance may be separated into price and quantity variances, direct labor variance into rate and time variances, and overhead variance into volume or utilization variance, spending variance, and efficiency variance. A volume variance arises only in the case of fixed overhead and not in the case of variable overhead.
- The above variances may be computed separately for each major responsibility center.

Formulas for computing these variances are available from any standard textbook on cost accounting and hence are not given here.

The decision regarding the type of variances to be computed is governed by the objectives of the variance analysis and the significance of various cost factors. For example, for cost control a detailed cost variance analysis is desirable, but for product costing the net variance may be sufficient. Further, even for cost control insignificant variances need not be computed or reported.

**Method of Computing Variances** Variances may be computed at the time of recording various costs or at the end of a period. Under the first method, variances are computed from the source documents. For example, purchase price variances are recorded from purchase invoices while the purchase transactions themselves are being recorded. Under the second method, variances are computed from analysis of accounts and memorandum cost records. For example, material quantity variances are

**EXHIBIT 15-6**

**Comparison of Three Accounting Plans for Standard Costing**

| Partial Plan | Single Plan | Dual Plan |
|---|---|---|
| 1. This is an *output method* because the Work-in-Process (WIP) account is debited at actual cost and credited at standard cost of finished goods and work in process. | This is an *input method* because the WIP account is debited and credited at standard cost. | As the name suggests, this method is a combination of the first two plans, and records therefore are maintained on actual as well as standard costs. In practice, there are several variations of this plan. For example, both types of cost records may be maintained in the double-entry-bookkeeping system, or one of the two records may be maintained on a memorandum basis. |
| 2. The balance in the WIP account equals variance. | The balance in the WIP account equals the WIP inventory at standard cost, and variance equals actual cost less standard cost debited to WIP account. | |
| 3. The plan uses current standards. | The plan uses current standards. | |
| 4. Finished goods and WIP inventory are valued at current standard cost. | Finished goods and WIP inventory are valued at current standard cost. | |
| 5. Variances can be computed only periodically. | Analysis of variances is made on a continuous basis from source documents except that variances in manufacturing expenses are analyzed periodically. | |
| 6. Analysis of variances is difficult because the relevant information is not readily available in the accounts; it is necessary to go to the source documents. | Variance analysis is easy because analysis is made from the source documents while transactions are being recorded. | |
| 7. The plan requires physical inventory of WIP for income determination and variance analysis. | The plan does not require a physical inventory because the balance in the WIP account is the WIP inventory at standard cost. | |
| 8. There may be difference in profit computed by these two methods because under the partial plan material price variances are recorded on a consumption basis and under the single plan they are computed at the time of recording purchases. | | |
| 9. The plan is useful if a relatively simple analysis of variances is desired. | The plan is favored if a detailed variance analysis is desired. | |
| 10. The plan is easy to design and install. | Because of analysis of variances at the source, this method requires more groundwork in design and implementation. | |

NOTE: There are no standard terminologies for the accounting plans for recording standard costs. The terms *partial plan, single plan,* and *dual plan* are used by R. I. Dickey in *Accountants' Cost Handbook,* 2d ed., The Ronald Press Company, New York, 1960, sec. 16.

computed by comparing the actual quantity of materials consumed for a period or a job with the standard consumption quantity for the period or the job.

The designer should ensure that nonmonetary records such as material loss records, lost-time records, etc., will facilitate computation and analysis of variances. Further, the necessary worksheets for computing variances should be designed. Exhibit 15-7 is an illustrative worksheet for computing variances in direct labor–hours and machine-hours. It will facilitate computing variances by production cost centers, products, and production orders.

**Disposal of Variances** Variances may be disposed of in either of these two ways:

- They are closed to profit and loss account.
- They are distributed to inventory and cost of goods sold.

The first method results in showing inventory and cost of goods sold at standard cost, whereas the second method shows them at actual cost. In selecting the method of disposal of variances, generally accepted accounting principles, income tax requirements, and management's preference should be taken into account.

## DESIGNING A COMPUTERIZED COST SYSTEM

The tasks in designing a computerized cost system are more or less the same as those for designing a manual cost system. However, because of the computer's involvement, the computer-based cost system gives rise to certain additional features and considerations. Broadly speaking, the following are the tasks involved in designing a computerized cost system:

1. Output design
2. Design of data organization and storage
3. Input design
4. Design of processing and control

The following discussion on each of these tasks focuses on the role of the cost system designer.

### Task 1: Output Design

From the viewpoint of the computer-based cost system, output consists of three types:

- Management reports (responsibility reports, product cost reports, etc.)
- Cost accounting output (journal, trial balance, expense ledger, cost allocation details, etc.)

**EXHIBIT 15-7**

**Form for Computing Variances in Direct Labor–Hours and Machine-Hours**

Production cost center ______________ No. ______________

Responsibility of ______________ Period ______________

| Products → | | | | | | | |
|---|---|---|---|---|---|---|---|
| Production order no. → | | | | | | | |
| Time ticket | Equipment no. | Direct labor–hours | Machine-hours | Direct labor–hours | Machine-hours | Direct labor–hours | Machine-hours |
| | | | | | | | |
| 1. Total hours | | | | | | | |
| 2. Actual production quantity | | | | | | | |
| 3. Standard direct labor–hours or machine-hours at – units per machine-hour | | | | | | | |
| 4. Variances (show excess hours in parentheses) | | | | | | | |

Prepared by __________ Date ______ Reviewed by _______ Copy to _____

- Computer control reports which show the errors in input revealed during automatic editing of input

In designing the first two types of reports, the cost system designer has a major role to play, while the design of computer control reports is mainly the responsibility of the computer specialist.

**Design of Management Reports** The following tasks are involved in designing computer-prepared management reports:

1. Define the cost information needs in terms of why, what, by whom, for what period, at what frequency, and when.
2. Define the report heading, column descriptions, and line descriptions.
3. Specify the information to be used in generating a report. This information is specified by indicating the relevant account numbers or cost center codes for each line, responsibility center, etc., and by indicating the time period for each column.
4. Specify the calculations to be performed.
5. Determine the sequence and positioning of information on the report.
6. Define the subtotals, totals, and exception parameters used for exception reporting.

Though these tasks are necessary also in a manual system, greater care is required in a computerized cost system because a computer will do exactly what it is told to do and cannot supply a missing link. For example, an accountant need not be told that to compute profit costs should be deducted from revenue, but the computer must be provided with that logic. Further, all output devices, such as the printer and CRT screens, have width limitations. In a manual system, such limitations can be easily overcome by using a bigger-size paper and smaller type.

Report formats should be specified for all known reports. In addition, provision should be made for generating *user-designed reports;* i.e., the user should be allowed to define the contents, arrangement of contents, control totals, subtotals, etc., of a report. For cost control and managerial decision making, it is often necessary to analyze cost information in a variety of ways, all of which cannot be defined in advance. For example, in addition to the usual actual versus budget reports, management may want to know all expense items which are over the budget, say, by $500 or more during the year. If the capability of generating user-designed reports is available, this report can be prepared very easily. Thus, this capability is a very valuable tool for users.

**Design of Cost Accounting Output** As mentioned before, cost accounting output includes costing journals, allocation records, an expense ledger, etc., which are meant primarily for use by the cost accounting department and the auditors. The design of this output is similar to the cost records in a manual system, but a computer-based cost system offers the flexibility of printing either all details or only subtotals and totals.

**Design of Computer Control Reports** To ensure the integrity of input data, a computerized system provides for various types of editing of input data and for the reporting of errors detected during the editing. At a minimum, the account numbers or cost center codes used should be validated. Similarly, the total of the individual entries should be reconciled with the batch totals, and any discrepancy should be printed on the error report. Usually, narrative error messages also are shown on the report.

## Task 2: Design of Data Organization and Storage

The design of data organization and storage is mainly the responsibility of the computer specialist; hence, only its major points are summarized here.

Data organization and storage involves the arrangement, creation, storage, and maintenance of data in and off the computer. In computer terminology, all data related to a particular item or objective constitute a *record.* For example, all the data relating to movement of material A will constitute a record of material A. In a manual system, corresponding names for a record are a stock card, a ledger account, etc. Each record consists of several data elements called *fields.* For example, fields in an inventory record will include the transaction data, the source document reference, ins and outs, the balance, etc. In designing a record, it is necessary to define the elements to be included in each record and the length of each field.

A group of related records makes up a *file.* For example, records for the movement of all materials are called an inventory file. In a manual system, the corresponding names for a file are ledger, journal, etc. Thus, in a manual system, cost and noncost data are recorded in journals, subsidiary ledgers, general ledgers, memorandum records, reports, etc., and in a computerized cost system these data are recorded in files. Even in a computerized cost system, there will be files of journals, ledgers, trial balances, etc. However, in contrast to a manual system, the distinction between memorandum records and double-entry-bookkeeping records is irrelevant for the records generated by a computer because all computerized cost accounting records will be a part of the double-entry-bookkeeping system.

Files may be classified into *master files* and *transaction files.* A master file contains a complete record of transactions, whereas a transaction file contains only transactions pertaining to a particular period. For example, the master file of inventory of material will include the opening balance, receipts, issues, and closing balance of each material in stock. Processing all the transactions relating to movement of materials during, say, a month, creates a material transaction file for the month which contains ins and outs records of only those materials which have been received or issued during the month. With the help of the transaction file and an appropriate computer program, the old master file is updated and a new master file is created. Thus, a transaction file is *temporary* in nature. Depending upon the period for which data are included in the transaction file, it may be called a *current* transaction file, a *month-to-date* transaction file, a *year-to-date* transaction file, etc.

### Kinds of Master Files

In a computerized cost system, master files will be of three kinds: static files, dynamic files, and historical files, as explained below.

**Static Files** Static files will contain data which remain more or less static and change only occasionally. The following are the commonly used static files:

1. *Chart of accounts file,* containing the numbers and description of various accounts used by the system.

2. *Cost and responsibility center files,* containing cost and responsibility center names and codes.

3. *Relationship, or pointer, file,* showing the relationship between various account numbers for summarization. For example, if four direct materials are consumed for two products, there will be eight accounts of direct material consumption. The relationship file may show that these accounts will be summarized (*a*) by materials and within each material by products and (*b*) by products and within each product by materials. Similarly, the relationship file will show which cost centers should be included in a particular report. For example, if the production department consists of three production shops, the relationship file will show that the report for the production department should include all relevant data for the three production shops.

4. *Allocation or formula file,* containing all the allocation formulas required for product costing and responsibility accounting. The allocation formulas will automatically perform several functions, such as passing recurring journal entries, allocating specified costs to relevant cost centers, applying overhead rates, and computing the product cost. Allocations can be performed by using budget or actual data. This feature will eliminate manual work on repetitive calculations, entries, etc., and also improve accuracy and turnaround time.

5. *Report files,* containing predesigned report formats as well as information for generating nonstandard reports.

6. *Product cost file,* containing products definitions, bills of materials by products, production process descriptions, standard costs data, etc.

7. *Employee file,* containing basic data about employees.

**Dynamic Files** Dynamic files are files which contain current transaction data and therefore are frequently updated. Examples of dynamic files used by a computerized cost system are as follows:

1. Direct materials inventory file
2. Direct materials cost (quantity and price) file
3. Direct materials purchase file
4. Direct labor cost (time and rate) file
5. Manufacturing overhead file
6. Job cost or process cost file, containing production quantity and costs by current job orders or processes
7. Finished-goods inventory file
8. Marketing cost file
9. General and administrative cost file

Dynamic files may simultaneously contain actual, budget, and standard data by any chosen time interval (daily, weekly, monthly, etc.). For example, if the accounting year is divided into months, each accounting record should provide for entering data for at least twelve periods and should also provide an additional space for year-end adjustments.

**Historical Files** In fact, historical files are not separate types of files. These files consist of any dynamic or static files, except that they contain past data instead of current data. A large volume of past data must be stored for planning, budgeting, reporting, and accounting purposes. Since historical files have already been created, the main design issues are what, how long, and where data should be stored and how the data contained in historical files will be retrieved. The cost system designer should specify what data should be stored and for how long. The designer should also specify how frequently and for what purposes past data will be required. The computer specialist will then be responsible for designing the storage and retrieval aspects of the historical files.

### Integrated versus Separate Files

There are two ways to arrange the files: separately or in an integrated manner. For example, separate files may be maintained for accounts payable, the general ledger, inventory control, direct material costs, direct labor costs, manufacturing overhead costs, etc., or all these files may be integrated to constitute one *data base.* In a data-base management system, each data item is entered only once, and it can be accessed for any application throughout the company. When separate files are maintained, the same data item may have to be entered more than once and stored in more than one file for different applications. Thus, in a separate application system, there will be duplication of records.

Exhibit 15-8 illustrates a part of the manufacturing data base and shows by means of arrows the relationship between information contained in separate areas of the data base. One input will update all the related records and thus obviate the need for the successive updating of different records.

### Organization of Records in a File

Records in a file may be arranged in *sequential, indexed sequential,* or *random* order. These arrangements also refer to the methods used for accessing the records in a file. In a sequential file, records are arranged in a numerical sequence (e.g., by account numbers) or an alphabetical sequence. In an indexed sequential file, there is no set order of arrangement of records, but the file contains an index through which a particular record can be accessed. In a random file, there is neither a set order of arrangement nor an index, but data are accessed by means of an identifier.

The file structure and the method of accessing records in a file have a far-reaching influence on storage media, processing, retrieval, response time, and computer programs. Hence, these two aspects should be carefully designed.

### Storage of Data

Data may be stored on magnetic tape, disks, diskettes, cards, etc. At least a part of the data will be stored in the computer itself, and additional data may be stored off the computer. Since the data are stored for future use, the storage device and the method of accessing the data should be selected with regard to the frequency of retrieval of various data.

### Task 3: Input Design

In designing an input system, both the cost system designer and the computer specialist have roles to play. The cost system designer's role is very similar to that in a manual cost system. The computer specialist's role is confined mainly to the computer aspect of the system.

The major tasks involved in input design are as follows:

1. As in a manual system, the designer must define the cost and non-cost input data required for generating the desired output. The designer

**EXHIBIT 15-8**

**Illustration of Computerized Data-Base Cost System**

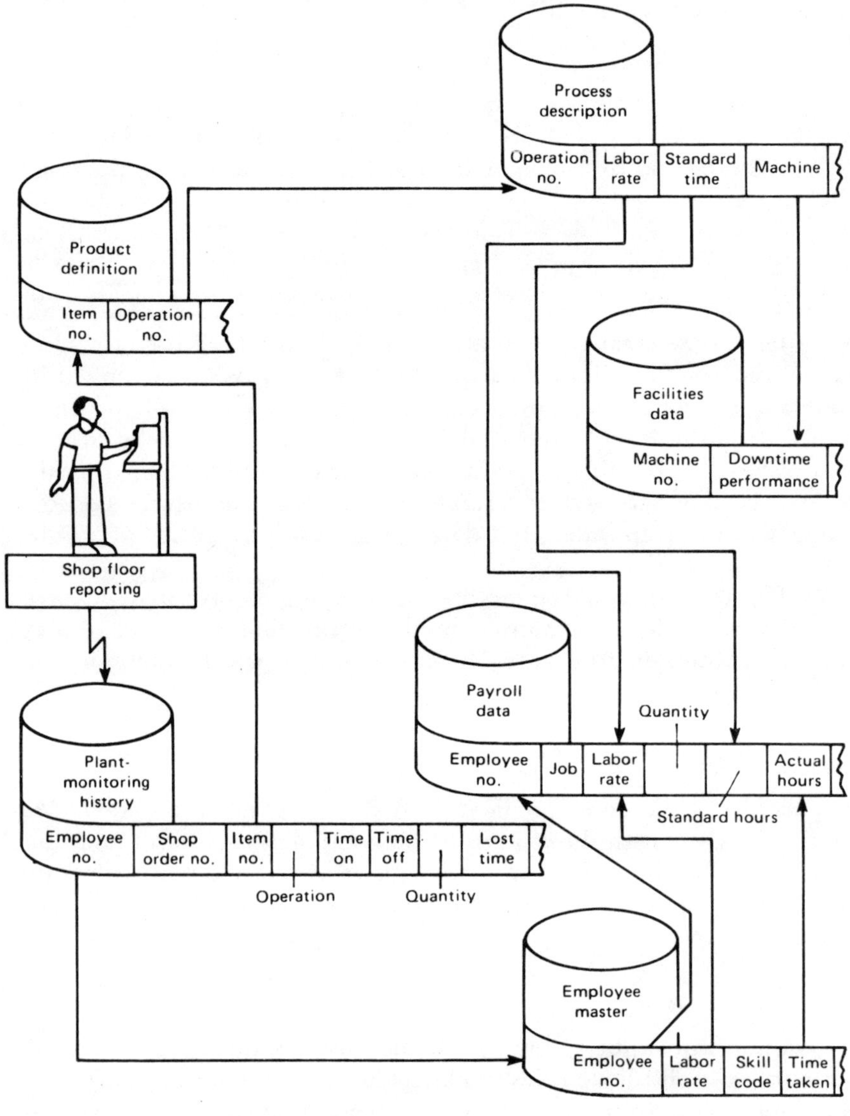


When plant monitoring and control provides completed operation transactions, information required by finance can be immediately available.

Courtesy of International Business Machines Corporation, reprinted from *Communications Oriented Production Information and Control System,* March 1972, Figure 1, page 6, Chapter 12.

must also determine the source of each of the input data items. As in a manual system, the input data may be generated outside the computerized cost system, or it may be an output of some computer subsystem. For example, for allocating manufacturing overhead, the input used is the overhead amount generated by the computer system from the recording and posting of expense vouchers.

2. Insofar as possible, the source documents required for various operating systems (purchasing, inventory control, etc.) and the computer system should be common.

3. Input data which originate outside the system may have to be prepared in a computer-readable form, depending upon the data entry system used. Further, depending upon the system used, it may be necessary to select an appropriate input medium and a data preparation device.

Punch cards, paper tapes, magnetic tapes, and disks are the commonly available input media. For the preparation of these media, a data-encoding system such as a key punch, a keyboard, etc., is required. Then, for the transfer of data from the input medium to the computer, a data entry system such as a card reader, an optical reader, etc., is required. In some cases, one or both of these steps may be eliminated. For example, in the case of an on-line keyboard or a CRT terminal, data are entered into the computer system directly from source documents such as expense vouchers, direct labor time tickets, etc. Similarly, large department stores have a point-of-sale system under which sales data entered in a cash register by a cashier are automatically transferred to the computer. Further, an optical scanner, known as an optical character recognition (OCR) device, can read documents prepared on a typewriter.

4. Input data may be entered as they arise or in batches. Even in an on-line system (in which the input device is connected to the central processing unit of the computer and input enters the computer directly), input data may be entered in batches. In a real-time system (in which the processing of input data and of requests for output data is done instantaneously), usually the input device will be on-line and input data will be entered as they occur. The choice is governed by the objective of cost information. For example, for inventory control it is advantageous to enter each inventory transaction as it arises provided the system is on real time, but for control over manufacturing overhead costs, which usually are controlled through monthly budgets, entering input in batches usually is adequate.

5. It is also necessary to decide on the method of transferring data from the data-generating locations to the data entry center. The usual alternatives are hand delivery, mailing, locating a data entry system in each of the major data-generating locations and then sending the disks,

**EXHIBIT 15-9**

**Illustrative Decision Chart for Exception Reporting**

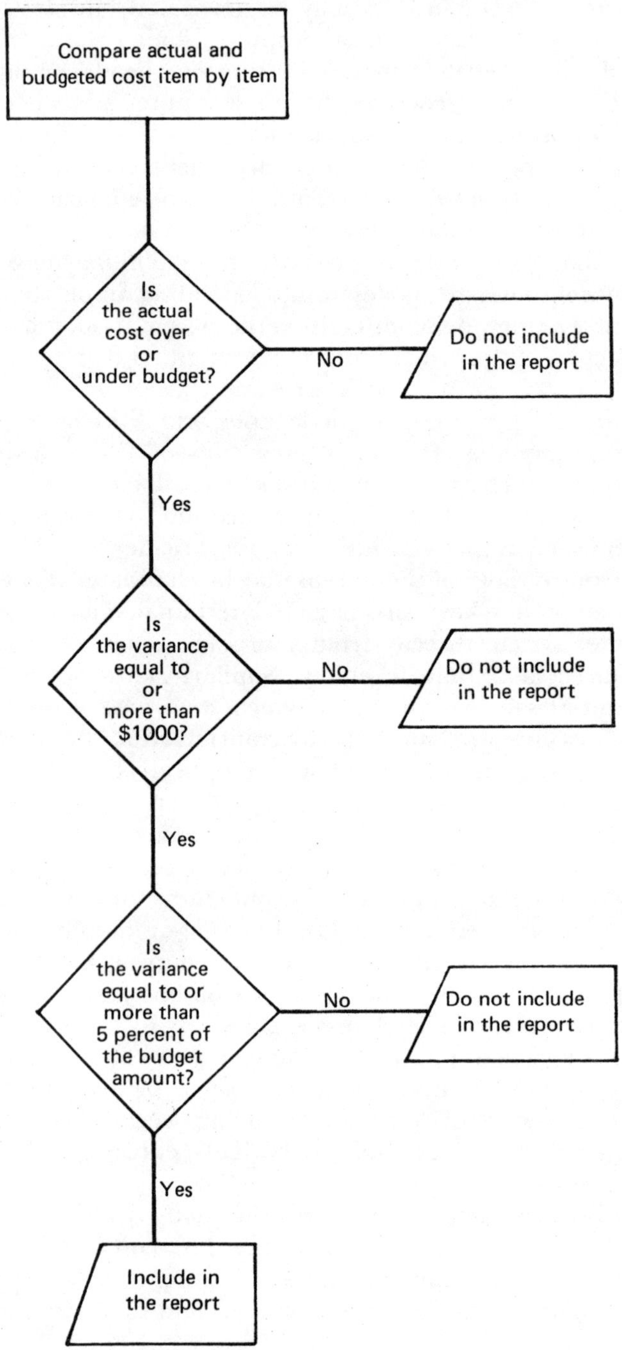

diskettes, etc., to the computer, and using a telecommunications network.

6. To ensure the integrity of the output generated by the computer, several checks, called *editing of input,* are provided. Editing of input may be manual or computerized, or both. Many methods of input editing are available, among them use of a check digit to validate account numbers, cost center codes, and other numbers, batch totals (i.e., comparing manual and computerized totals of significant data in a batch), etc.

7. Further, a procedure should also be developed for reporting and correcting errors detected through input control. Designing various editing techniques and the error correction procedure is the responsibility of the computer specialist.

### Task 4: Design of Processing and Control

A computer functions through a series of *programs,* each of which contains a set of instructions for accomplishing a given objective (allocation of overhead, generation of a report, etc.). Usually, computer programs are developed by the computer programmer on the basis of the system specifications developed by the system analyst with the help of the cost system designer. The role of the cost system designer is to specify the various steps involved in achieving a given objective.

The following are the major items which the *cost system designer* should specify:

1. The input data to be used for each computer job or routine and their sources.
2. The calculations to be performed, comparisons to be made, and decision rules to be followed. For example, for generating an exception report for cost control, the decision rules may be specified as illustrated in Exhibit 15-9. In this case, it is decided to include on the cost control report (prepared on an exception basis) all actual costs which were under or over budget both by at least $1000 and by 5 percent of the budget amount.
3. Totals, subtotals, and cross-totals to be accumulated.
4. Output contents, layout, and medium.

For controlling computer operations, several manual and computerized controls are exercised on input, output, processing, and the use of the computer. Designing these controls is the responsibility of the computer specialist.

# Chapter 16

# Developing a Comprehensive Chart of Accounts

Though this be madness, yet there is method in't.
William Shakespeare: *Hamlet*

A chart of accounts contains a list of accounts used by a concern for recording its business transactions. Such a chart for financial accounting consists of accounts for expenses, revenue, income, assets, and liability, and one for cost accounting consists of accounts for expenses only. However, the classification of expenses for cost accounting is more detailed and complex than that for financial accounting. In the case of integrated cost and financial accounting, the chart of accounts will be a combination of the two separate charts of accounts after duplicate account heads have been eliminated.

## HOW TO DEVELOP A CHART OF ACCOUNTS

The die of the chart of accounts is cast when the designer has determined the classification of costs while designing individual subcost systems and has decided on the type of cost records to be maintained. At this stage, the designer must arrange these cost accounts in some suitable order and finalize the chart of accounts. For completing the picture, all the steps to be taken and the guidelines to be followed for developing a chart of accounts are given below.

1. The subject of *classification* of each of the subcosts was discussed in Chapters 9 through 13. By referring to these prior steps, the designer should first prepare a list of the desired classifications of various costs. At

this stage, the list should consist of the entire cost classification without consideration of whether or not a particular cost classification is to be recorded in the books of account.

2. As we showed earlier, *cost records* may be divided among memorandum records, subsidiary ledgers, and the general ledger. A chart of accounts contains a list of accounts required for double-entry records and, in addition, may contain a list of accounts required for memorandum records (in this case it should clearly separate the two lists). Similarly, a chart of accounts must distinguish general ledger accounts from subsidiary ledger accounts. For each subsidiary ledger, a general ledger control account should be established.

3. In the classification and arrangement of accounts, the *organization structure* of the concern should be borne in mind because a cost accounting system should parallel the organization structure. For example, if a concern has three branches, there will be three accounts for each type of expense directly incurred by the branches. Since for responsibility accounting the organization structure is divided into responsibility centers and cost centers, the list of responsibility centers and cost centers should be kept on hand while a chart of accounts is being designed.

4. If cost and financial accounting *systems* are to be *integrated,* the classification of expenses, revenue, assets, and liabilities for financial accounting and the types of financial records to be kept should also be considered. Even if cost and financial accounting systems are not integrated, it is necessary to classify properly accounts for revenue, assets, and liabilities because the information on them may be necessary for proper allocation of costs (for example, for allocating insurance expense in the ratio of fixed assets).

5. An appropriate account title (preferably self-defining) should be selected for each account.

6. Each account should be adequately defined, and its use (the transactions to be debited and credited to it) should be specified.

7. The account titles should be arranged in some logical order. Generally, account titles are arranged under broad groups of assets, liabilities, revenue, and expenses. Within each of these broad groups, accounts are arranged in some order, normally that in which the items appear in balance sheets, income statements, and various reports. Accounts should be so arranged that it is convenient to use the chart and record the transactions; one alternative is to place similar or related account titles adjacent to one another. The classification and arrangement of accounts is discussed later in this chapter.

8. For multiple classification, consistency, uniformity, and convenience, code numbers should be given to account titles. This aspect also is discussed later in this chapter.

9. Normally, it is advantageous, and in decentralized accounting and in a large organization it is almost inevitable, to have an accounts manual containing the following:

- Chart of accounts
- Account codes
- Description and explanation on use of each account
- Accounting policies
- Accounting procedures

To keep the manual up to date, it should be reviewed and appropriately revised whenever there is a change in the nature of the business, the organization structure, cost items, cost definitions, etc.

## CLASSIFICATION AND ARRANGEMENT OF COSTS

In determining the extent of cost classification, the following points may be noted:

1. The nature and extent of classification of costs will depend upon the objectives of the cost system, the nature of the business, the types of costs incurred, and the extent of automation of accounting records.
2. When an accounting system is prescribed by a regulatory agency or a statute or voluntarily by an industry association, the chart of accounts should contain the minimum classification prescribed in the relevant accounting system.
3. There are three recognized methods of classifying costs of a manufacturing concern:

| By Functions or Departments | By Identification of Expenses with Products | By Behavior of Costs |
|---|---|---|
| *a.* Prime costs:<br>Direct materials<br>Direct labor<br>Direct expenses<br>*b.* Manufacturing overhead:<br>Production departments<br>Service departments<br>*c.* Administrative overhead<br>*d.* Distribution overhead<br>*e.* Financial overhead | *a.* Direct material costs<br>*b.* Direct labor costs<br>*c.* Direct expenses<br>*d.* Indirect materials<br>*e.* Indirect labor<br>*f.* Indirect expenses | *a.* Fixed costs<br>*b.* Variable costs<br>*c.* Semivariable or semifixed costs |

These three methods are not mutually exclusive: the same expense may be classified in more than one way.

4. In any cost system, expenses ultimately are identified with areas of responsibility and cost centers. For example, expenses relating to sales may be classified by territories, customers, products, etc., whereas manufacturing expenses may be classified by operations, equipment, divisions, products, etc. Hence, whenever feasible, it is better to accumulate expenses by cost centers and areas of responsibility at the source itself. And the chart of accounts should provide account heads for such expenses by cost centers and areas of responsibility. However, allocation of common or joint costs should not be attempted while they are being recorded. Such costs should be accumulated under objective expense accounts and later allocated on a suitable basis.

When a responsibility accounting system is employed, separate accounts, called *cross-charge* accounts or *transfer* accounts, are maintained to record the expenses transferred from one cost center to another cost center for product costing. This approach enables allocated costs to be excluded from responsibility reporting. An additional benefit of this method is that it is possible to avoid pyramiding expenses in total consolidation; hence, the basic accounts themselves can be used for external reporting.

5. There are several ways in which a multiple classification of expenses may be arranged. For example, primary classification of all expenses may be by nature of expenses (salaries, related costs, material, etc.), and each expense, in turn, may be classified by divisions, locations, etc. Alternatively, expenses may be recorded separately by divisions and subclassified by locations, nature, etc. The choice is dictated by several considerations, such as the organization structure, whether the accounts department is centralized or decentralized, and whether the accounting system is manual or automated.

6. The classification should be unambiguous, and separate accounts should be opened for separate types of costs.

7. Undoubtedly, the more detailed the classification of costs, the better equipped the cost system will be to provide information easily for a nonroutine analysis or decision. However, the more detailed the cost records, the greater the cost of record keeping. Further, as the extent of classification of costs increases, its accuracy generally may decrease because the elements of estimation, judgment, and even arbitrariness increase. Therefore, the optimum classification of costs should be arrived at by balancing the merits and demerits of detailed classification.

8. In decentralized accounting or even in centralized accounting when accounts are classified by cost centers, departments, divisions, locations, etc., classification should be uniform throughout the organization to facilitate intrafirm comparisons and consolidation of accounts. For exam-

ple, throughout the organization fringe benefits should be treated either as a part of direct labor cost or as a part of manufacturing overhead.

## ACCOUNT CODES

Account codes are used for multiple classification, consistency, uniformity, and convenience. Though the coding system can be numerical, mnemonic (i.e., using key letters of the account title or symbols), or alphanumerical, the numerical system is the most widely used method for coding a chart of accounts.

**Types of Numerical Codes** The numerical coding system has several variations, the most common of which are as follows:

1. *Sequential coding.* This type starts with 1 and contains blank numbers for adding new account titles in the future. It is suitable for a small company having a simple accounting structure and few account titles.

2. *Block coding.* A block of numbers is assigned to assets, liabilities, revenue, and expenses, and within each category a smaller block of numbers is assigned to each major class of assets, expenses, etc. The following is an example of block coding:

| | |
|---|---|
| Current assets | 000–099 |
| Fixed assets | 100–199 |
| Other assets | 200–299 |
| Liabilities | 300–499 |
| Sales and discounts | 500–599 |
| Other income | 600–699 |
| Manufacturing costs | 700–799 |
| Administrative and selling expenses | 800–899 |
| Nonoperating expenses | 900–999 |

This system does not permit a detailed subclassification and sub-subclassification of accounts.

3. *Decimal system.* An account bearing a whole number indicates the prime account head, and accounts with decimal numbers indicate its subdivisions. The following is an example of a decimal coding system:

10.0 Manufacturing costs
    10.1 Materials
        10.11 ABC
        10.12 XYZ
    10.2 Labor
        10.21 Wages

10.22 Payroll taxes
10.23 Fringe benefits
10.3 Manufacturing overhead
10.31 Salaries
10.32 Wages
. . .
. . .
. . .
20.0 Selling costs
. . .
. . .
. . .
30.0 Warehousing and transportation costs
. . .
. . .
. . .
40.0 Administrative costs
. . .
. . .
50.0 General expenses
. . .
. . .
. . .

The chief advantage of this method is that it is easy to add subaccounts or sub-subaccounts.

4. *Combination of a control account number and a subsidiary account number and even a detail account number of the subsidiary account number.* The number may be written as one combined number or be separated by dashes or semicolons:

| Control No. | Subsidiary No. | Detail No. |
|---|---|---|
| 0 | 000 | 00 |
| written as<br>135325<br>1-353-25, or<br>1:353:25, or<br>1353:25 | | |

**Cost Center Codes** Codes may also be used to denote locations, areas of responsibility, divisions, cost centers, product families, etc. Cost center codes may be combined with account codes.

**Preferred Coding System** Usually, a coding system which requires the least number of digits is preferable because it is less time-consuming and reduces the possibility of error in writing codes on documents and entries. This goal is accomplished by using a decimal system as illustrated in the following example.

Let us assume that the company requires 875 basic accounts and that some of these accounts require subaccounts, not exceeding 25 per basic account. Again, some of the subaccounts require sub-subaccounts, not exceeding 9 per subaccount. The company can use a coding system as follows:

| Basic Account No. | Subaccount No. | Sub-subaccount No. |
|---|---|---|
| 000: | 00: | 0 |

All basic accounts not having a subaccount will be designated only by three-digit codes. Basic accounts requiring subaccounts will be designated by five-digit codes with a colon after three digits: 123:01, 123:02, 123:03, etc. An account with sub-subaccounts will be written, for example, as 126:01:1, 126:01:2, 126:01:3, 126:02:1, 125:02:2, etc. A total of all sub-subaccounts starting with 123:01 will give the total amount for the subaccount 123:01. Similarly, a total of all subaccounts starting with 123 will give the total amount for the basic account 123.

Whatever the coding system used, it should be flexible enough to permit adding new accounts in the future.

## CHART OF ACCOUNTS IN A COMPUTERIZED COST SYSTEM

In developing a chart of accounts for a computerized cost system, the basic procedure is the same as described above, but there are some distinguishing or additional features:

1. A chart of accounts in a computerized cost system can be made much more detailed than that in a manual system because the computer can quickly sort and summarize detailed accounts.
2. The use of account coding or account numbers is imperative. As in case of a manual system, the account coding system may be numerical, mnemonic, or alphanumerical, though the numerical system is the most prevalent. Account numbers should include a mathematically computed check digit to validate the numbers.
3. There are two ways to arrange a chart of accounts. The first is to structure the chart so that subaccounts appear under a basic, or a parent,

account. However, a structured chart of accounts is inflexible and difficult to change when circumstances change.

The second and better alternative is to establish a relationship between subaccounts and parent accounts through a *relationship file,* or a *pointer file.* Here also the accounts are arranged in a logical order, but the user can determine any other relationship and obtain a summary of any accounts in the chart of accounts. This approach makes the chart very flexible and facilitates generation of nonstandard reports. Because of the importance of this method, it is illustrated below with a detailed example.

**Illustration** Innovative, Inc., has three product divisions. Each division uses various materials of which one material is used by all the divisions. The company's chart of accounts contains the following accounts for direct materials consumed:

| Account No. | Account Description |
|---|---|
| 40-30-00 | Direct materials—all divisions |
| 40-31-00 | Direct materials—Division X |
| 40-31-10 | Material A |
| 40-31-20 | Material B |
| 40-32-00 | Direct materials—Division Y |
| 40-32-10 | Material A |
| 40-32-30 | Material C |
| 40-33-00 | Direct materials—Division Z |
| 40-33-10 | Material A |
| 40-33-40 | Material D |

Innovative, Inc., usually requires summarization of direct materials consumed by divisions and for the company as a whole. Hence, in the relationship file, this relationship is expressed as shown in Exhibit 16-1. Summarization of amounts charged to detailed accounts into the parent account is done automatically.

Now, let us suppose that management of Innovative, Inc., also wants to know the total amount of direct material A consumed by all three divisions. This information can be developed simply by adding a new parent account, Direct Material A—All Divisions, to the chart of accounts and by establishing the relevant relationship for it as shown in Exhibit 16-2. This new parent account is given the account number 40-40-00. With every amount posted to 40-31-10, 40-32-10, or 40-33-10, the account 40-40-00 will be automatically updated along with the other parent accounts shown in Exhibit 16-1.

Thus, a computerized cost system that provides for user-determined summarization of accounts greatly enhances the usefulness of cost data.

**EXHIBIT 16-1**

**Chart of Accounts Relationship File**

| Parent Account | Detailed Account |
|---|---|
| 40-30-00 | 40-31-00 |
| 40-30-00 | 40-32-00 |
| 40-30-00 | 40-33-00 |
| 40-31-00 | 40-31-10 |
| 40-31-00 | 40-31-20 |
| 40-32-00 | 40-32-10 |
| 40-32-00 | 40-32-30 |
| 40-33-00 | 40-33-10 |
| 40-33-00 | 40-33-40 |

**EXHIBIT 16-2**

**Relationship File for New Parent Account**

| Parent Account | Detailed Account |
|---|---|
| 40-40-00 | 40-31-10 |
| 40-40-00 | 40-32-10 |
| 40-40-00 | 40-33-10 |

## ACTUAL COMPANY PRACTICES REGARDING THE CHART OF ACCOUNT AND ACCOUNT CODING

The coding systems used by some of the large companies surveyed by the author are given below.

### Company Manufacturing Packaging Products

The coding system used by this company (sales over $2.8 billion) illustrates perhaps the most complex system. This is a multicompany, multiplant, multiproduct company with plants all over the world. Its organization structure is as shown on page 467.

The company employs an integrated cost and financial accounting system which is uniformly adopted for all its operations. It compiles costs separately for *product costing* and *cost control.* The cost centers and subcost centers shown here in the organization chart are established for the dual purpose of developing rates to be applied to products and of plac-

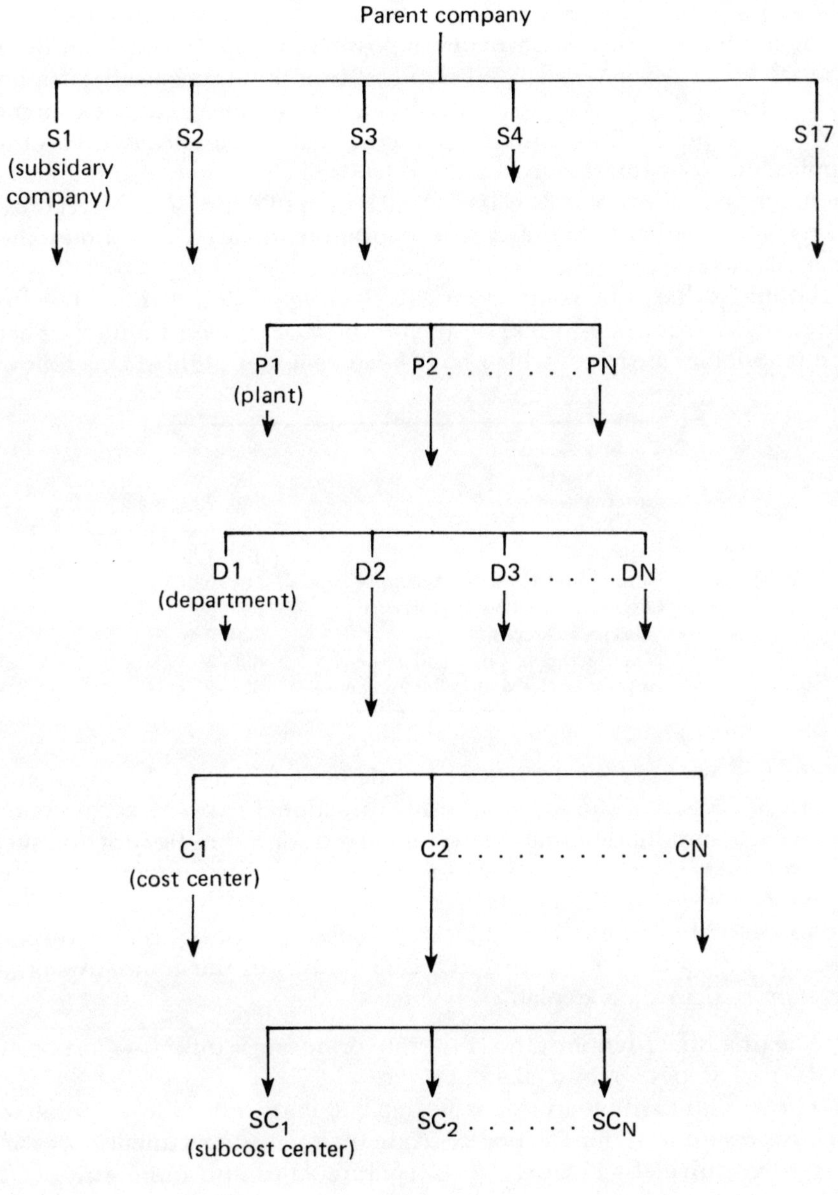


NOTE: For each subsidiary company, the structure is as shown for S3. The same is true for each plant, department, etc.

ing responsibility for controlling costs. For cost control purposes, the company assigns all costs, whenever possible, to the lowest level of responsibility *without allocation.* When a cost cannot be specifically assigned to a responsibility level without allocation, it is assigned to the next higher level of responsibility. Costs of one cost center are allocated to other applicable cost centers only for the purpose of product costing. Therefore, the company not only classifies each item of expense to be recorded by its nature but also identifies it as to location and area of responsibility, as explained below.

**Account Codes** The company uses a five-digit account code. The first three digits from 000 to 999 designate the *basic account* number. There are ten major categories which have been assigned numbers, as follows:

| | |
|---|---|
| Current Assets | 000–099 |
| Fixed Assets | 100–199 |
| Other Assets | 200–299 |
| Liabilities | 300–399 |
| Capital | 400–499 |
| Closing and Clearing Accounts | 500–599 |
| Other Income and Deductions | 600–699 |
| Sales and Discounts | 700–799 |
| Manufacturing Costs and Expenses | 800–899 |
| Administrative and Selling Expenses | 900–999 |

The last two digits of the five-digit code designate a subclassification of the basic account. The *subaccounts* are functional expense accounts because each amount designates a cost incurred for a specific function such as inspection, packing, etc. A sample page from the company's chart of accounts is given in Exhibit 16-3.

**Responsibility Codes** A six-digit code is used to distinguish the responsibilities within the corporate and business units of the company's organization structure, as explained below:

- The first digit identifies the corporate or business unit: 0—Corporate, 4—Packaging, 7—Miscellaneous, etc.
- The second digit identifies major departments under the corporate or business unit: under Corporate (code 0), major department codes are 0—Executive, 1—Finance, 2—Corporate Administration, etc.
- The third digit identifies units of cost control in major departments: under Corporate Finance Department (01), units of cost control are 1—Comptroller's Department, 2—Treasurer's Department, 3—Tax Department.
- The last three digits identify further detailed units of cost control.

A sample page from the responsibility codes is given in Exhibit 16-4.

**EXHIBIT 16-3**

**Sample Page from a Chart of Accounts**

| Accounting Policy and Procedures Manual<br>Issued by Accounting Methods and Systems | Index Code 5-5<br>Page 1 of 42<br>Date 1/1/76<br>Authority<br>Replaces 5-5-1<br>dated 1/1/75 |
|---|---|

Chart of Accounts Manufacturing Cost and Expense Accounts

| Account number | | | | Account name and definition |
|---|---|---|---|---|
| Labor | | Material and expenses | | |
| Basic | Sub | Basic | Sub | |
| 700 | XX | 800 | XX | SALARIES (OWN P/R 700 PURCHASED 800): SEE SUBACCOUNTS |
| | 01 | | 01 | REGULAR: ALL SALARIES EXCEPT MAINTENANCE AND TEMPORARY SALARIED (OUR P/R) PAID THROUGH SALARY ROLLS FOR REGULAR EXEMPT AND NONEXEMPT (FOR NORMAL PAY) EMPLOYEES 700.01: PURCHASED 800.01<br>PLANTS MAY USE SUBACCOUNTS AS REQUIRED FOR INDIVIDUAL OPERATIONS BUT WILL "CLOSE" TO THIS ACCOUNT(S) FOR FAR |
| | 02 | | 02 | OVERTIME: TOTAL SALARY PAID, DUE TO EXCESS OF NORMAL HOURS, FOR WORK PERFORMED BY NONEXEMPT PLANT SALARIED EMPLOYEES (700.02): PURCHASED (800.02) |
| | 03 | | | TEMPORARY SALARIED EMPLOYEES ON OUR PAYROLL |
| | 04 | | | EXTENDED EFFORT AWARD OR EXEMPT EMPLOYEES OVERTIME PAYMENTS |
| | 10 | | | SHIFT PREMIUM: SALARIES PAID IN EXCESS, DUE TO SHIFT DIFFERENTIAL, OF THAT CALCULATED ON BASE SHIFT RATE(S) |
| | 23 | | | MAINTENANCE DEPARTMENT, NONCLERICAL |
| | 26 | | | MAINTENANCE DEPARTMENT, CLERICAL |
| | 30 | | | SEPARATION ALLOWANCE: SALARIED EMPLOYEES |
| | 31 | | | PRERETIREMENT ALLOWANCE: SALARIED EMPLOYEES; JOB ELIMINATION |
| | 32 | | | PRERETIREMENT ALLOWANCE: SALARIED EMPLOYEES; OTHER |
| | 33 | | | SPECIAL RETIREMENT ALLOWANCE: SALARIED EMPLOYEES; JOB ELIMINATION |
| | 34 | | | SPECIAL RETIREMENT ALLOWANCE: SALARIED EMPLOYEES; OTHER |
| | 99 | | | OTHER SALARIES |
| 701 | XX | 801 | XX | DIRECT LABOR: WAGES PAID EMPLOYEES DIRECTLY ASSIGNED TO THE PRODUCTION OF SALABLE PRODUCT AND/OR NECESSARY ASSOCIATED PARTS. SUCH LABOR WILL INCLUDE BUT NOT BE LIMITED TO FEEDING, OPERATING, CUTTING, FORMING, PACKING, AND OFF-BEARING EQUIPMENT SUCH AS SLITTERS, PRESSES, BODYMAKERS, PRINTING AND COATING EQUIPMENT, SCROLL SHEARS, TUB FORMERS, WINDERS, I.S. MACHINES, CARTON AND BAG MAKING, EXTRUDERS, CUP FORMERS, PACKERS AND PALLETIZERS, MACHINE AND BELT OPERATION, SEAMERS, TUB-BOTTOM BLANKERS, ETC.; SEE SUBACCOUNTS. |
| | 01 | | 01 | OPERATION: WAGES PAID FOR LABOR IMMEDIATELY IDENTIFIED WITH OPERATING EQUIPMENT IN THE PRODUCTION OF SALABLE PRODUCT AND/OR NECESSARY ASSOCIATED PARTS<br>FOR READYING OF EQUIPMENT, SEE ACCOUNT 701.02; FOR PRODUCTION MECHANIC, SEE ACCOUNT 702.02 |
| | | | | OPERATIONS MAY USE SUBACCOUNTS IN PAYROLL BUT WILL "CLOSE" TO THIS ACCOUNT(S) FOR FAR |
| | 02 | | 02 | PREPARATION: WAGES PAID IN THE READYING OF EQUIPMENT DUE TO CHANGE OR ALTERATIONS NECESSARY TO PRODUCE A DIFFERENT SIZE, STYLE, COLOR, PACKAGE OR PART: ALSO, START-UP SHOULD BE CHARGED TO THEIR RESPECTIVE FUNCTIONAL ACCOUNTS |
| | 03 | | 03 | EXTRA LABOR—RESORTED PLATE: WAGES TO COVER LABOR EXPENDED OVER AND ABOVE NORMAL STANDARD(S) AS CAUSED BY THE SECONDARY MATERIAL |

## Company Manufacturing Household Electrical Appliances and Selling Them to Large Stores

This company (sales over $1.4 billion) uses an integrated mechanized standard cost system. Its chart of accounts, explained below, is comparatively simple.

The company uses four-digit code numbers to designate *uniform base accounts,* as follows:

| | |
|---|---|
| Balance Sheet Accounts | 1000–2999 |
| Sales | 3000–3199 |
| Returns and Allowances | 3200–3399 |
| Cost of Sales | 3400–3599 |
| Cost of Sales Variances | 3600–3799 |
| Corporate Assessed Expenses | 3800–3999 |
| Various Expense Accounts (Salaries, Wages, Supplies, etc.) | 4000–8199 |

**EXHIBIT 16-4**

## Sample Page from Responsibility Center Codes

| | Accounting Policy<br>and<br>Procedures Manual<br>Issued by Accounting Methods and Systems | Index Code 5-3<br>Page 4 of 39<br>Date 1/1/76<br>Authority<br>Replaces 1/1/75 |
|---|---|---|
| Chart of Accounts | Chart of Accounts: A&S Responsibility Codes | |

| Responsibility code | | | | | | Responsibility title |
|---|---|---|---|---|---|---|
| Operation | Department | | Cost Center | | | Corporate (Operation) CC 19-38<br>Finance: See below (Department) CC 39-58<br>Cost Center CC 59-78 |
| 7 | 8 | 9 | 10 | 11 | 12 | |
| 0 | 1 | 0 | 0 | 0 | 1 | SENIOR VICE PRESIDENT, FINANCE |
| | | | | | | COMPTROLLER'S DEPARTMENT |
| 0 | 1 | 1 | 0 | 0 | 1 | VICE PRESIDENT AND COMPTROLLER'S ADMINISTRATION |
| 0 | 1 | 1 | 1 | 0 | 1 | CORPORATE OPERATIONS ANALYSIS AND CONTROL |
| 0 | 1 | 1 | 2 | 0 | 1 | GENERAL ACCOUNTING |
| 0 | 1 | 1 | 2 | 1 | 1 | GENERAL ACCOUNTING |
| 0 | 1 | 1 | 2 | 1 | 2 | ACCOUNTS PAYABLE, GENERAL ACCOUNTING |
| | | | | | | |
| | | | | | | |
| 0 | 1 | 1 | 5 | 0 | 1 | INSURANCE ADMINISTRATION |
| 0 | 1 | 1 | 5 | 0 | 2 | INSURANCE: WORKMEN'S COMPENSATION; SELF-INSURED |
| 0 | 1 | 1 | 5 | 0 | 3 | CLOSED PLANTS: WORKMEN'S COMPENSATION; SELF-INSURED |
| 0 | 1 | 1 | 6 | 0 | 1 | INTERNAL AUDITING |
| 0 | 1 | 1 | 7 | 0 | 1 | RETIREMENT AND INSURANCE FUNDS |
| | | | | | | TREASURER'S DEPARTMENT |
| 0 | 1 | 2 | 0 | 0 | 1 | TREASURY SERVICE |
| 0 | 1 | 2 | 0 | 0 | 2 | SHAREHOLDER RECORDS |
| | | | | | | TAX DEPARTMENT |
| 0 | 1 | 3 | 0 | 0 | 1 | TAX GENERAL: GREENWICH |
| | | | | | | |

Code numbers 3000 to 3999 are *subdivided* by suitable three-digit codes; for example, Cost of Sales (3400–3599) is subclassified as follows:

| | |
|---|---|
| Standard Material | 001 |
| Standard Labor | 002 |
| Standard Burden—Variable | 003 |
| | . . . |
| | . . . |
| | . . . |
| Changeover Costs | 142 |

## Newspaper-Publishing Company

This company (sales over $355 million) uses the following six-digit numerical codes:

For revenue and expenses:

| Control Account No. | Department No. | Detail No. |
|---|---|---|
| 0<br>(Revenue—4, Expenses—5) | 00 | 0000 |

For assets and liabilities:

| Control Account No. | Subcontrol Account No. | Detail No. |
|---|---|---|
| 0<br>(Assets—1, Liabilities—2, Equity—3) | 00 | 0000 |

## Aircraft-Manufacturing Company

The chart of accounts of this company (sales over $1.2 billion) is the simplest possible, as will be evident from the following:

| General ledger accounts | Subsidiary ledger accounts | Analysis accounts |
|---|---|---|
| 0000 | 0000 | 00 |

If a general ledger account is a control account, its last two digits are 00 (zero-zero). A subsidiary ledger account number always begins with the first two digits of the general ledger control account number. Analysis accounts are used only when necessary. An example follows.

| General Ledger Account | | Subsidiary or Analysis Accounts | |
|---|---|---|---|
| Number | Title | Number | Title |
| 7200 | Sales, Commercial | 7210 | Industry—Domestic |
| | | 7211 | Industry—Export |
| | | 7220 | Intercompany |
| 5700 | Other Taxes | 5723 | Accrued State Retail Sales Tax |
| | | | *Analysis* |
| | | | 05 California |
| | | | 10 Florida |
| | | | 99 All States |

# Phase III

# System Implementation

After a cost accounting system has been designed and before its actual implementation begins, certain essential steps must be completed. Similarly, after the system has been implemented, certain follow-up steps must be taken to ensure that the system meets the preset objectives. Preimplementation, implementation, and postimplementation steps are discussed in Chapters 17 through 19. These chapters are divided into the following subjects:

- Synthesis, i.e., coordination of various subcost systems as well as various system blocks
- System testing
- System presentation and acceptance
- System implementation or conversion
- Follow-up and consolidation
- Refinements and sophistications
- Maintenance
- Review and revision

# Chapter 17

# Synthesis and Testing

The proof of the pudding is in the eating.

In this chapter, we will explain two important preimplementation tasks, synthesis and testing.

## SYNTHESIS

The various steps in the design of a cost accounting system are not separate and distinct but iterative. It is only for the sake of convenience in designing a cost sytem that the proposed system is divided into various building blocks, components, parts, or subsystems (material cost accounting system, labor cost accounting system, chart of accounts, cost centers, etc.). These subsystems cannot operate independently because they are part and parcel of a single cost accounting system. Hence, the designer must ensure that various subsystems and components of the proposed cost accounting system mesh properly with one another to make a unified system.

Second, a cost accounting system does not exist in a vacuum or in isolation from various functional systems (purchasing, receiving, production, sales, etc.). In fact, it should be an integral part of various functional systems and not be superimposed on them.

For these reasons, it is essential to bring together various subsystems, coordinate various parts, and iron out any wrinkles in the system or give it an artist's finishing touch. In this respect, the process of designing a cost accounting system can be likened to an assembly-line operation of a job order industry.

Different approaches may be adopted for synthesizing various subsystems and aspects of a cost accounting system. One approach is to prepare a table of typical cost accounting transactions showing, for each transaction, the documents to be prepared, their routing, the cost accounting records to be prepared, and other relevant points. This approach will uncover any loose ends, ambiguity, and other weaknesses in the system. Alternatively or additionally, the designer may prepare consolidated flowcharts of various subsystems showing the movement of each item from the input to the output stage. Also, when the procedure is reduced to writing, the deficiencies in the system will be revealed.

## TESTING

Before the proposed cost accounting system is implemented, it must be tested to make sure that it will meet the objectives for which it is designed and that it is technically sound. The designer should prepare a comprehensive plan of system testing before proceeding to test the system. A comprehensive test plan should cover the following aspects:

- Testing for what, i.e., the purposes of testing.
- What areas of the cost accounting system are to be tested?
- Who should test the system?
- Methods and procedures of testing.
- When should testing be conducted?
- Procedure for the reporting and correction of deficiencies revealed during testing.

### Purposes of Testing

There are several design criteria which the designer must keep in mind while designing a cost acounting system. At this stage, the designer should check whether or not all these criteria have been met. Below is a list of questions which the designer can use as a checklist (there is some duplication or overlapping in the questions, but this is not redundant).

- ☐ Does the system satisfy all the objectives for which it has been designed? (Refer to the list of objectives prepared for the company.)
- ☐ Will all the system requirements be met by this system? (Refer to the list of system requirements prepared for the company.) To be more specific,
  - ☐ Will all the required information be available from this system?
  - ☐ Will it be available at the specified time?
  - ☐ Will it be available in a form which meets the users' requirements?

- ☐ Is this system technically sound? To be more specific,
  - ☐ Is it as nearly complete as it ought to be?
  - ☐ Are there any loose ends?
  - ☐ Do all parts of this system or various subsystems properly and effectively coordinate with one another?
  - ☐ Does this system interface properly with various operating (functional) systems?
  - ☐ Are there any inconsistencies in this system?
  - ☐ Can this system be made sounder?
- ☐ Is it practical or feasible? To be more specific,
  - ☐ Will it fit the environment or culture of the company?
  - ☐ Does it take into account various predictable constraints, or is this system workable despite predictable constraints? (Refer to the list of system constraints prepared for the company.)
  - ☐ Does it require more personnel or accounting machines than are presently available? If so, is management willing to allocate the necessary resources for them?
  - ☐ Will there be any difficulty in operating any aspect of this system?
  - ☐ Will such difficulties be temporary or transitory?
  - ☐ Can this system be made more practical?
- ☐ Is this system reliable? To be more specific,
  - ☐ Is this system capable of giving dependable and accurate information and achieving other objectives at the specified time?
  - ☐ Will this system operate satisfactorily under normal as well as abnormal conditions?
  - ☐ In what conditions or situations is this system vulnerable?
  - ☐ Can this system be made more reliable?
- ☐ If under the new system any feature of the existing system is proposed to be deleted, is it proper to delete it?
- ☐ Are there any avoidable duplications or overlapping?
- ☐ Are there any unnecessary features in this system?
- ☐ Can this system be made more efficient?
- ☐ Can this system be simplified?
- ☐ Can this system be made less expensive?

## Areas to Be Tested

As we saw earlier, a cost accounting system consists of several components, such as forms of documents, forms of records, forms of reports, procedures, flow of papers, flow of information, a time schedule, internal checks, and policies. Hence, theoretically each of these aspects should be tested, following the proverbial wisdom that the strength of a chain is the strength of its weakest link. However, in a chain every link has equal importance because each link performs the same function, whereas different aspects of a cost accounting system do not have the same function and therefore their importance is not the same. Hence, it is possible to be selective and check only those aspects which are vital to the successful functioning of the system. Here, we should remember that aspects which may be important for one system may not be equally important for another system.

By the time that the design of the system has been completed, the designer will have a feel for the system and will probably know which aspects are essential to its success. As a general rule, vital aspects will be related to major cost factors, major objectives of the cost system, key factors affecting the business of the company, and system constraints. For example,

- When a particular cost factor forms an insignificant part of total costs, the basis on which it is allocated or the method by which it is charged to cost of production will not matter much. The reverse is also true.
- If the cost accounting department lacks a well-trained or well-educated staff, the designer should carefully check whether the system is too sophisticated for staff members and whether too much is being done too rapidly. It is better to soft-pedal changes in such a situation.

For each of the areas selected for testing, satisfactory answers should be sought for the relevant questions from the checklist given earlier.

### Who Should Conduct Testing?

The methods to be adopted for testing the proposed cost accounting system and the persons who should test it are interrelated. A cost accounting system may be tested by one or more of the following persons:

- Designer
- Controller or chief accountant
- Cost accountant and assistants
- Persons who must furnish input data
- Users of the system, i.e., recipients of the information generated by it
- Other persons affected by the system such as those whose performance will be evaluated by it

The designer may face a dilemma if users and other persons who either have to furnish input data or are affected by the system must be involved. The dilemma is: should the system first be accepted by company management before it is tested, or should it be tested before it is accepted? This dilemma is discussed later in this chapter under the heading "When to Test."

**Designer** Obviously, the designer should test the entire system on paper. Usually, the designer will not be responsible for checking the system by using a simulation technique or for operational testing, but he may have to assist others in testing it by using these two techniques. The precise role the designer will have to play will depend upon the scope of his work. If he is an outside consultant, this question becomes very important. Usually, it is in the best interest of the company and the designer to make the designer responsible for system testing. If the designer is not responsible for implementation of the system, he usually will not take part in testing the proposed system by employing the last two methods.

If the designer is responsible for system testing, his role may be as follows:

- To recommend and explain the methods to be adopted for testing the proposed system
- To recommend the timing of testing it
- To recommend the persons who should be involved in testing it
- To guide the persons involved in testing
- To check the results of testing and modify the system if necessary

**Controller or Chief Accountant** A review of the proposed cost accounting system by the controller or chief accountant may range anywhere from a cursory review to a thorough review, depending upon the importance attached to the proposed system, the competence of the designer, the complexity of the proposed system, and the capability of the cost accounting staff.

**Cost Accountant** The cost accountant and assistants should thoroughly review the proposed system because they are the persons who ultimately must operate it. Particularly, they should try to visualize the difficulties likely to be encountered in operating it and consider the feasibility of meeting various time schedules. They will have to play an important role in operational testing as well as in simulation testing.

**Suppliers of Input Data** Suppliers of input data will be people from production, services, marketing, and various other departments. Depending upon the importance of the proposed system concerning them and their capability, they may be asked to review the relevant portion of the system. At one extreme of the scale, they may be asked, say, whether they will have any difficulty in filling the necessary forms or complying with a particular procedure. At the other end of the scale, they may be asked, say, whether in their opinion the system is practical or feasible, and if not, why not and how the impracticalities may be removed. Unless the suppliers of input data are trained to think forward, they may misunderstand the latter types of questions and their confidence in the system may be shaken. On the other hand, if they are professional people, they may feel that they are being ignored if their comments are not solicited. Hence, the designer should be careful in deciding the extent of involvement of suppliers of input data in system testing.

**Users of the System** Invariably, the output of the proposed system must be reviewed with the internal users before it is implemented, even if many comments are not expected from them. They are the persons for whose benefit or use the proposed system is designed, and they must feel that it answers their needs. Hence, it is logical that their opinions be asked. Sometimes they may have valuable comments, too. Even if they don't have any comments, at least they will not be hostile to the new system later on.

**Others** The system may be reviewed with other persons who may be concerned with it in any way. For example, in the case of a standard cost system, various standards may be discussed with the persons whose performance will be measured against those standards. The question which may arise here is: how far down the organization should one go? For example, should direct labor standards be discussed only with supervisors or also with workers? Answers to this type of question depend upon management's preference, the requirements for successful operation of the system, the level of understanding of the people in the lower echelons of the organization, and similar factors.

### Testing Methods

Broadly speaking, there are three methods of testing a proposed cost accounting system: on-paper testing, simulation testing, and operational testing.

**On-Paper Testing** Every system should be tested on paper before any other testing method is used. For this purpose, the checklist given earlier will be useful. On-paper testing should obviously be done by the designer, but it may also be done by any of the persons mentioned earlier.

Another way to test the system on paper is to draw a flowchart of various subsystems and see whether they are complete and whether they interface properly with one another as well as with various functional systems.

**Simulation Testing** The proposed cost accounting system may be tested under simulated conditions; i.e., hypothetical data resembling the real-life situation in the company may be used to test the system. Either the entire system or only the complicated or difficult portions may be tested. Further, hypothetical data may cover every typical situation occurring in the company or only situations which are not easy to understand in operating the proposed system. For example, preparation of basic cost accounting records may not be tested or illustrated by using hypothetical figures, but reports and supporting statements may be tested with hypothetical data.

The effectiveness of this test depends upon the hypothetical data selected. If the hypothetical data include all the complex and difficult situations actually occurring in the company, simulation testing will be very effective and, at the same time, less time-consuming and less expensive than operational testing.

Simulation testing may be conducted by the designer or the cost accounting staff and the suppliers of input data. It is preferable to involve all or some of the persons who will actually have to operate the system so that they can get some training in operating the system. The output or reports prepared under simulation testing may be shown to would-be users for comments.

**Operational Testing** While hypothetical data used for simulation testing may resemble real-life data, the main shortcoming of this testing is that it is not conducted in a *real operational environment.* Therefore, though the technical soundness of the system can be tested, its feasibility and reliability cannot be tested. Operational testing can overcome this shortcoming because it tests the system by using actual data, in the actual environment, and by the very persons who will operate it ultimately. Since the persons testing the system may be inexperienced with the system, initially there may be difficulties in understanding the system and meeting the time schedule. However, operational testing will highlight potential trouble spots and areas in which training may be necessary.

Basically, there are three forms of operational testing:

1. By using a past period's data (last month, last quarter, etc.), the new system should be operated from input through output stages. If a cost accounting system already exists in some form, the results obtained with the help of the new system should be compared with that of the existing system. In addition, the results should be checked against the system objectives. Sometimes, comparison with the existing system may not be meaningful if there is a significant difference in the objectives of the new and the existing systems.

2. Using the current period's data, the system should be operated from input through output stages, and the results should be compared as explained in Paragraph 1. If a cost accounting system already exists, it should be continued until the new system is fully implemented because at this stage the new system is only being tested and not implemented.

3. In partial testing, the new system is tested in only one of the divisions, branches, locations, etc. Partial testing may be carried out by using

a past or current period's data. It can also be handled with reference to only certain aspects of a cost system. For example, only the material and labor cost accounting systems may be tested operationally.

**Combination of Testing Methods** In actual practice, some combination of these three methods will be used. Preferably, whatever can be tested on paper should be tested on paper, and whatever cannot be tested on paper may be tested by the simulation technique or the operational technique, in that order. Usually, technical soundness can be tested on paper. System feasibility and reliability can better be tested by the simulation or the operational testing method. Further, for different phases to be tested, different testing methods may be used. For example, simple procedural aspects, forms, etc., may be tested on paper only, while the actual filling out of forms and their clarity may be tested by the simulation method. Complex procedures involving the interaction of several persons and several subsystems or functional systems can best be tested by operational testing.

**Considerations** In selecting the method or methods of testing, the following are the relevant considerations:

- Complexity of the system.
- Capability of the persons who have to operate the system.
- Whether the system is being implemented for the first time or is only a revision of the existing system.
- Experience and competence of the designer.
- Time available and required for testing.
- Cost involved in using different testing methods.
- Consequences of errors or defects in the system. For example, if a system is being designed for voluntary or statutory price setting, the consequences of errors may be significant, and hence it is advisable to test it thoroughly. But if the system is being designed only for internal performance evaluation, the consequences of defects will not be serious unless management is prone to rash decision making.

### When to Test

The manufacturer of an assembly-type product does not defer testing the quality of the product until the end but does in-process testing. Similarly, a cost accounting system should usually be tested at several points while it is being designed. For example, the adequacy of a chart of accounts or a cost center classification may be tested before the entire system design has been completed. In-process testing is less time-consuming and more effective because it is carried out while things are fresh in the mind of the designer.

However, the designer may be faced with a chicken-and-egg type of dilemma: which should precede—company management's approval of the system or system testing? Though the answer depends upon the facts of each case, the following general guidelines will be useful:

1. The designer must make a distinction between testing alone and testing when users and other persons are to be involved. The designer should not attempt in-process testing with users or cost accounting staff too early in the design phase. Further, the users or others should not be involved in the in-process testing work unless they can be given a complete picture of the portion of the system concerning them and how that portion fits in the total system. Otherwise, they are apt to be misled and to react unfavorably. However, if several equally valid alternatives are available for some aspects of the system, the designer may discuss the alternatives with the concerned company employees with a view to ascertaining their preferences and prejudices.
2. If the proposed cost accounting system involves major changes in the organization structure, operating procedures, or any other area, then before testing the system it is advisable to present its essential points to company management, pointing out clearly essential changes and recommended changes, and obtain its approval. The reasons for this step are simple. The changes may not take place if company management disapproves of them. Second, the premature disclosure of forthcoming major changes may upset company management. Third, unless a proper strategy has been developed for communicating major changes, the designer may face insurmountable resistance from those affected by the changes.
3. In any case, the entire system should be tested at the end. Of course, it is not necessary to repeat tests which have been performed earlier unless subsequently significant changes have been made in the portion of the system already tested.

## Procedure for Feedback

The designer should lay down precisely how, when, and by whom he will be informed of deficiencies, difficulties, or suggestions for improvement revealed while the proposed system is being tested. This step is all the more important if several persons are involved in testing and if the test period extends beyond a few weeks.

After the deficiencies, troubles, etc., have been revealed, the designer must evaluate whether they can be eliminated or reduced and, if not, why not. The designer's pride should not come in the way of accepting the deficiencies, difficulties, or suggestions and of modifying the system whenever necessary.

# Chapter 18

# Successful Implementation, Operation, and Modification

It is comforting to know that it [change in human nature] can be done and has been done. The problem . . . is to find out how.

Ralph Linton: *The Study of Man,* 1936

This chapter treats system presentation and acceptance, system implementation, follow-up and consolidation, refinement and sophistication, system maintenance, and review and revision.

## SYSTEM ACCEPTANCE

Every new or revised system involves some changes. These changes may be in the organization structure, operating procedures, forms, contents, timing of reporting, or some other respect. Further, human beings by their very nature resist changes. Hence, the designer should not presume that company personnel will accept the system or the recommendations as gospel truth. The designer must recognize that the proposed cost accounting system must be sold to its potential users, the cost accounting department, and other persons concerned with it. System selling is essential even if the system is designed by an outside consultant of high standing.

Before the system is accepted by the users, the designer must first present it to them and then overcome any objections they may have.

### Presentation of the System

In deciding how to present the system, the designer must resolve the following interrelated issues:

1. Should the presentation be oral or in writing?

2. Should a written presentation be in the form of a lengthy written report or a summary report explaining the system? Should the written report be accompanied be a complete systems manual?

3. At an oral discussion, should the entire system or only the main features be presented? Should audiovisual equipment or even simple flip charts be used for presentation?

4. Should a written presentation precede or succeed an oral discussion?

There is no one best answer to each of these questions. The presentation technique must be suited for the company for which it is intended. The discussion that follows will be useful as a guide. A complete system cannot be presented orally, but the main features (e.g., cost reports) can be presented orally. Unless a system is very complex, an oral presentation usually should precede a written report. At best, only an *interim report* or a discussion memorandum should be submitted before the proposed system is approved. An interim report should cover the major changes proposed or the main features of the system, the advantages and disadvantages of each of them, and, when appropriate, the reasons for selecting a particular alternative among several possibilities. Sometimes, the various alternatives that have been considered may only be mentioned, leaving the reasons for their rejection for oral discussion. The interim report may be used as an agenda and basis of discussion at a meeting. It should be finalized on the basis of users' reactions.

5. Should the system be presented first to higher management, first to lower management, or to all concerned simultaneously? The answer to this question depends upon the wishes of the person who has the authority to accept or reject the system. If the person with authority for final approval is very conscious of the feelings of others, he will first like to know the views of users and others. If, on the other hand, he likes to reserve all important decisions for himself, he will prefer at least to be the first to know the system. In any event, the principles of exception and selectivity can be applied here. Those features of the system which affect several departments of the company, involve major changes, or have significant impact may first be presented to higher management, leaving details for the employees directly concerned with them. Second, though the main features, concepts, and ideas underlying the system may be discussed with users at exploratory meetings, the major changes should not be disclosed prematurely to employees in the lower echelons of the company. Third, sometimes it may be advisable to divide the persons into two or more groups if many individuals are involved or if they are in widely separated locations.

6. What will the contents of the presentation be? In part, the answer to

this question will depend upon decisions on the issues discussed above. In any case, the presentation must be comprehensive, concise, and nontechnical. Particularly in a computer-based cost system, simple terms should be used instead of computer jargon. As someone has put it, system implementation involves 20 percent technique and 80 percent education. To sell the system to users and others, the designer must explain (*a*) the system, (*b*) the ways in which it will meet preset objectives, (*c*) its benefits to the company, (*d*) its benefits to various users and others, and (*e*) any shortcomings. When shortcomings are expressly recognized by the designer, users will not suspect the quality of the system and will give it better credibility. Further, it is not enough to show advantages to the company only: advantages must also be related to the individual users. The designer must clearly spell out the benefits from the system in terms of effective cost control, better managerial decisions, work simplification, better tools for performance evaluation, etc., and be able to illustrate each advantage. For example, the designer may make these points:

*a.* The system makes a distinction between product costing and responsibility accounting. The product cost system will enable company management to estimate cost accurately for proper price quotation and thus will increase the potential for improving profits. The responsibility accounting system will accumulate and report costs by levels of responsibility within the company. It benefits the company because it makes cost control more effective, and it benefits individual responsibility center managers because they will be held responsible only for the costs controllable by them.

*b.* A shortage of critical materials is a recurring problem in your company. This system provides information for measuring the effect of changes in price, mix, volume, and cost on profits by products and regions. Hence, during the shortage of a critical material, by using the information provided by this system you will be able to select the most profitable product mix. (This point may be illustrated with hypothetical data.)

*c.* Our recommendations include assigning two cost clerks to the production department to reduce the load of paperwork relating to cost accounting on production personnel. This step will increase the accuracy of cost information and make the information available on a timely basis. These two benefits will more than recover the additional costs of employing two cost clerks.

Every system hinges on some key ingredients which determine its success or failure. The designer must identify the key ingredients of the system and bear in mind that these must be accepted by management if the system is to succeed.

### How to Prevent and Overcome Users' Resistance

The guidelines given here will be useful in handling users' resistance. First, the designer must recognize that users' resistance is a normal phenomenon. It is said that a sale begins *when the customer says "No."* When the customer raises objections, the sales representative gets an opportunity to understand the customer's mind and to overcome the objections to close the sale. The representative must, therefore, anticipate areas of resistance and persons who are likely to resist. According to the psychologist Lawrence K. Williams of Harvard University,

> The whole concept of resistance to change, to a large degree, can be recorded as a problem of attitudes. . . . The middle level manager can and often does offer more resistance to systems change than all the employees reporting to him.[1]

This may be so because a system usually affects the manager more than the subordinates.

Next, the designer should analyze the likely causes of each type of resistance. Normally, users' resistance stems from fear of the unknown. Common questions in users' minds are:

- Will the system demand better performance from them?
- Will there be tighter control, closer supervision, or greater accountability?
- Will there be more paperwork for them or their subordinates?
- Will the system affect them adversely in any way, particularly their job security, their position in the organization, their authority, and their pay?
- Will they have to learn new things?
- Will they have to depend upon computer specialists?
- Will their subordinates be able to understand and operate the system?
- Will they have to hire or fire people?
- Will the cost of the system outweigh its benefits?

In addition, if the system is to replace an existing system, the ego of originators of the existing system may be hurt unless they are handled properly.

Then, the designer should prepare a strategy for preventing resistance whenever possible and for overcoming it if it should arise. Users' resistance can be prevented or reduced by securing their cooperation. Let us first discuss how the designer can obtain users' cooperation and then how the designer can overcome their resistance.

[1] Lawrence K. Williams, "The Human Side of a Systems Change," *Systems and Procedures Journal* [now *Journal of Systems Management*], July–August 1964, pp. 40–43.

## How to Obtain Users' Cooperation

Securing users' cooperation will prevent users' resistance. Thus, this is a preventive rather than a curative step, and as the saying goes, "Prevention is always better than a cure." A designer who understands human behavior can prevent or at least reduce users' resistance. Here are time-tested, practical suggestions to secure users' cooperation:

1. From the beginning, the designer should ensure that continuous *support from top management* will be available. Top management's support increases the confidence and morale of employees about the importance of the system. For this reason, it is usually better to have top management make the announcement about the project for design of the system. Further, top management must be involved in important decisions concerning the system. Moreover, its assistance may be necessary even for achieving interdepartmental cooperation.

2. One of the major sources of resistance to a new system is the absence or inadequacy of communication about the new system. Consequently, users feel that they are being left out. Thus, their involvement in all phases of the system project is very important to its success. First, users must be informed of the decision to undertake the project for designing a cost accounting system soon after the decision has been made. Thereafter, they must be encouraged to participate in system analysis, system design, and system implementation. In earlier chapters ways of involving users during system analysis and system design phases have been explained. While designing the system, the designer should use, whenever possible, client employees' suggestions and give credit to them for these suggestions. If equally valid alternatives are available and users prefer a particular alternative, that alternative should be adopted. If their suggestions are not acceptable, the designer should explain why they are not acceptable.

Users' participation has several advantages. First, users contribute their firsthand knowledge and ideas, receive training in the cost accounting techniques involved, and become sufficiently familiar with the system to understand and operate it once it has been implemented. Second, once users understand the system, their fear of the unknown is reduced, and so also is their resistance to change. Third, they have a greater sense of commitment to a system in whose development they have participated. Fourth, when the designer is an outside consultant, this approach allows the designer to provide expertise and know-how rather than personnel, which also helps to keep his fees to a minimum.

3. The designer should retain the good features of the existing system. Further, he should be tactful in pointing out reasons for replacing or deleting any features of that system. Instead of criticizing the existing

system, the designer should compare the two systems and point out the additional advantages from the new or the revised system. When appropriate, he should point out that replacement or deletion is necessary because of changed circumstances, such as the growth or reorganization of the company, the development of new cost control and cost accounting techniques, etc. The designer should also point out to users that in a progressive company periodical updating of systems is normal.

4. Whatever factors are essential for the success of the system, such as the need for additional personnel, training, reorganization, or procurement of certain accounting machines, must be stated categorically.

5. Whenever necessary, provision should be made for the education and training of the persons involved. The cost accounting people must be trained in operating the system. Suppliers of input data must be taught how to furnish the required data. Recipients of cost reports must be educated on how to interpret and use these reports.

6. The designer must inform company management of the *realistic time* when it can expect the system to be fully operational. This time should be determined after the time required for overcoming inertia to change, for training and education of concerned employees, and foı solving teething problems have been taken into account. Obviously, the realistic time will depend upon the complexity of the system, the attitude of employees and management, and the organization structure of the company. It is best to be conservative in estimating the realistic time and to provide a liberal contingency margin. This will allay the anxieties of the users because they will know that they will not be rushed with the new system. A conservative estimate also works to the designer's advantage because company management will not judge success or failure of the system prematurely.

## How to Overcome Users' Resistance

Even after taking all the precautions to prevent users' resistance, the designer may not be able to eliminate it altogether. Hence, he must know how to handle resistance if it should arise. The following guidelines would be helpful in overcoming users' resistance:

The designer must recognize that resistance is not rejection but a refusal to accept the system because the designer has not given users adequate reasons for accepting it. Thus, a right attitude is imperative.

The designer must also do his homework thoroughly. He must have justifications for those features of his system which are likely to cause significant resistance. For example, if the system involves more paperwork, the designer must ask himself, "Are there enough justifications for it?" If not, the system must be modified. Similarly, if users must educate themselves, the designer should consider whether the required education consists of brief orientation or detailed study extending over several months. For the former, he should advise users of that fact as early as possible. For the latter, the designer should not only have proper justifications for the system but also show users how the system will benefit them. For instance, when appropriate, the designer may explain to users how the system provides them with an opportunity to grow and broaden themselves while increasing their contributions to the company.

However, it is worthwhile again to quote the psychologist Lawrence K. Williams:

> There is a complete literature on attitude formation and attitude change which suggests that attitudes are not formed in a logical manner nor are they changed in a logical manner. To a large degree, an attitude is a matter of emotion and not logic.[2]

Hence, the designer should not rely on logic alone to sell his system. He must also give due consideration to the aspects of human behavior and motivation.

Master sales representatives use a five-step approach for overcoming sales resistance. The same approach, with due modifications, can be used by the designer for overcoming resistance in selling the system. The five steps[3] are as follows:

1. The designer should listen patiently and carefully to an objection so as to understand it and to show the user that he cares about the user's objection.
2. The designer should use a softening statement or an ego-building statement for a deference transition. However, this does not mean that the designer should agree with the user's point. He may say, for example, "Your point needs consideration." Such a statement pacifies the objector.
3. The designer should convert the objection to a question. For example, if a user says that the system involves too much paperwork, the designer may say, "Then, what you are saying, Ms. ———, is that there should not be unnecessary paperwork. Is that correct?" There are three advantages to this approach. First, it helps the user clarify her thinking (e.g., more paperwork by itself is not objectionable; it is only unnecessary paperwork which is objectionable). Second, it enables the designer to discover the real reason for the objection. Third, once the objection has

[2] Ibid.

[3] Adapted from side 2 of the record "Magic Formula for Personal Achievement: How to Overcome Stalls and Objections" by Paul J. Meyer and Tom Norfleet. Copyright © Success Motivation Institute, Inc., 1967.

been converted to a question, the designer has to answer the question and not rebut the objection. Thus, this step avoids arguments.

4. The designer should answer the question concisely and fully. Sometimes it may be necessary to ask further questions. For example, in the illustration in Paragraph 3, it would be appropriate to say, "Let us consider where we can eliminate unnecessary paperwork. Do you have some specific suggestions in mind?" The designer should be open-minded and accept worthwhile suggestions made by users and others. At times it may be a good idea to ask users to give the system a fair trial before modifying or rejecting it. Thus users will not feel committed.

5. After answering the question, the designer should ask a closing question, for example, "Now that we have discussed this point [or eliminated unnecessary paperwork], do you think that the system involves only essential paperwork?" After handling all the objections in this manner, the designer must ask the final closing question to gain the user's acceptance of the entire system.

## IMPLEMENTATION

Once the system has been accepted, it must be implemented (installed). Many well-designed systems have failed because of inadequate attention to system implementation. Often, system implementation receives inadequate attention because either the designer or company management does not appreciate the importance of proper implementation.

For successful system implementation, the implementation task should be divided into the following three subtasks: planning, preliminary work, and actual implementation.

### Implementation Planning

A comprehensive implementation plan should cover the following interrelated strategic and tactical decisions:

- Is the entire system to be installed at one time or in phases?
- What are all the steps to be taken?
- How is each of the steps to be accomplished?
- In what sequence are the various steps to be taken?
- Who should be responsible for and involved in implementation?
- When should the system be implemented?

Each of these aspects is discussed below.

**Phases of Implementation** The following are three possible ways of implementing a system:

1. *Installation of the entire system at one time.* The existing system, if any, is scrapped. (Even if a cost accounting system is being designed for the first time, there may be some features of such a system in existence.)
2. *Phased implementation.* The new system is implemented in stages, and the existing system is scrapped simultaneously. For example, if the company has several divisions, the system may be implemented first in one division, usually a simple one. Similarly, the system may be confined to one of the product lines, regions, channels of sales, or even cost items (raw materials, labor, manufacturing overhead, marketing overhead, etc.). This approach will educate company management and other employees concerned with the system. The designer will also learn from this partial implementation, and it will not disrupt the business of the company. A phased implementation is desirable in a large organization or for a complex system.
3. *Parallel installation.* The new system is installed without scrapping the existing system, which is continued until the new system starts operating satisfactorily. The new system may be implemented at one time or in phases. In converting a manual cost system to a computerized cost system, a parallel installation usually is advisable.

The correct speed of implementation should be determined with regard to the complexity of the system, the education and experience of concerned employees, time availability, management's priorities, and other relevant factors.

**Steps Involved** First, the designer should list all the steps to be taken for implementing the system. These steps can be divided into preliminary work and actual implementation. They are explained later in this chapter.

Then, the designer should decide how each of these steps will be accomplished. "How" will involve choosing between alternatives. In reaching a final decision, the designer must consider management's preference. Since most of the steps will be interdependent or interrelated and since several persons will be involved, it is necessary to lay down the sequence in which various steps must be accomplished. In the case of a complex system, a PERT chart (see Appendix for a specimen chart) may be prepared. It is also necessary to provide the means whereby the progress of implementation will be checked against that planned.

**By Whom Is the System to Be Implemented?** Whether or not the designer will be responsible for implementation depends upon whether he is an in-house consultant or an outside consultant. If the designer is an in-house consultant, he normally will be a part of the implementation team. If he is an outside consultant, the policy of his firm and the scope of his engagement will decide the issue. Some consulting firms lack capability for assisting the client company in implementing a system designed by them. On the other hand, because of cost considerations the client company may not want the outside consultant to implement the system.

For several reasons, it is best not to leave implementation to client personnel. First, they may lack the necessary motivation, time, and experience for proper implementation. Second, they may misunderstand certain portions of the system. Third, the cost accounting department may not be successful in gaining top management's support and cross-departmental cooperation. Fourth, if the system is not properly implemented, it may not have the desired success, which, in turn, may affect the consultant's reputation. Hence, even when implementation time is not billable, the outside consultant is well-advised to supervise implementation or to conduct a postimplementation checkup to correct any misunderstandings.

Even when the outside consultant is responsible for implementation, he should not do everything himself. He should act as a team leader and let client personnel do as much as possible. The consultant should assist personnel in developing an implementation plan, provide the necessary guidance, train and educate the concerned employees, supervise the implementation, and correct any misunderstandings about the system. Usually, the company employees to be involved in implementation are those who will ultimately be responsible for operating the system. However, users of the output of the cost system should also be invited to attend briefing sessions.

**When Should the System Be Implemented?** A proper time for implementation should be selected so that there is minimum disruption of normal activity. Usually, a system should be implemented in a department when work is slack in that department, and the implementation work or a major portion of it should be over before the busy season begins. For example, a cost accounting system may be installed in production and sales departments during the off-peak season. Unless a proper time is selected for installation, concerned employees may not be able to devote adequate time and attention to implementing the system. Further, the system should preferably be implemented for the period beginning with the company's accounting year.

## Preliminary Work

Before actual implementation begins, certain preliminary work must be done. The exact nature of this work depends upon whether the cost system is manual or computerized. Lists of typical preliminary work under manual and computerized cost systems follow:

*Preliminary Work under Manual Cost System*

1. Inform all concerned of the implementation timetable and task schedule along with the necessary instructions. Usually, the announcement should come from as high-ranking an executive as possible.
2. It is desirable to prepare a systems manual containing at least the essential aspects of the system.
3. Procure the necessary forms, records, etc.
4. Hire additional personnel.
5. Train existing and new personnel—cost accountants as well as users.
6. Buy all equipment (accounting machines, calculators, etc.) necessary for operating the system.

*Preliminary Work under Computerized Cost System*

1. *Announcement.* An announcement about system implementation should be made as in the case of the manual cost system.
2. *Equipment*
   - Order EDP, peripheral, and communications equipment.
   - Prepare site for location of this equipment.
   - Receive delivery and install the equipment.
   - Test the equipment.
3. *Communications facility.* If the data processing function is not centralized and the various data processing centers are to be linked by a telecommunications facility, it is necessary to arrange for the required facility with the company providing data communications services.
4. *Purchased software.* If preexisting software available from a software house is to be used, it often must be customized. Hence, an arrangement for its purchase and customizing should be made in good time for the target implementation date. Further, the customized software should be tested to ensure that it will meet the company's requirements.
5. *Personnel*
   - Determine the number and type of personnel (cost accountants, computer operators, etc.) required.
   - Hire the necessary personnel if they are not already available in-house.
   - Train existing and new personnel. For this purpose, it is necessary to determine separately for each person the type of training required, the providers and location of that training, and the duration, timing, and cost of the training.
6. *Documentation.* Prepare the cost system manual as in the case of the manual system. In addition, prepare necessary instruction manuals regarding the computerized system for use by computer operators and users.

7. *Forms.* Procure the necessary forms, records, etc.

As mentioned before, it is necessary to specify who will do what and by what time. Second, the progress of the preliminary work should be checked periodically.

### Actual Implementation

Once all the preliminary work has been completed, actual implementation of the system begins. Usually, there are a greater number of logistic problems in replacing the existing system with a new system than in implementing a system for the first time because the new system is to be phased in and the existing system phased out. However, even if no formal cost system is in existence, there may be some features of a cost system which should either be phased out or be integrated with the new system.

In implementing a cost system, the following guidelines will be helpful:

1. There are two stages in implementation:
   a. *Static conversion.* Existing records are converted into the new forms. For example, it is necessary to record opening balances in the new record forms.
   b. *In-process conversion.* While the new system is being implemented, there will be some business operations in process, the records of which may have to be changed under the new system. For example, in the production department there will be production in progress. If, under the new system, labor time and cost are to be recorded differently from the method in the existing system, the problem of how to record labor time and cost for the completed part of in-process production will arise. The designer should recognize in advance all such problems and determine their solutions.

In the case of a computerized cost system, it is essential to set up the necessary master files. For this purpose, the designer should determine the type and sources of data to be entered in these files. If the source data are spread out in several records and at several locations, it may be necessary to prepare the existing data in a form suitable for entering them in the master files.

2. It is necessary to select a *cutoff date* from which system implementation will begin and to announce it well in advance. From that date on all business transactions of the segment in which the system is being implemented should be recorded in the new source documents, books of account, and other records. Once the entire system is operational, the implementation phase ends.

During the implementation stage, precautions should be taken to ensure that no data are recorded in both systems and that no data are left to be recorded in either system. The best way is to convert the existing system to the new system over a weekend, on a holiday, or at night or, in the case of a computerized system, by using several data entry terminals.

3. It is also necessary to specify important implementation rules, for example:

*a.* How will difficulties encountered during implementation be handled? That is, who will report those difficulties to whom, when, and in what manner?

*b.* While system implementation is going on, new ideas for improving the system will occur to different persons. If changes in the system are made hastily, the system may become a patchwork of pieces, some overlapping, some duplicating, and some working at cross-purposes. Hence, it is essential to make it a rule that no changes be made in the system after its implementation begins and until it is fully operational, unless the changes required are so vital that they must be made immediately. All ideas for improvements should be noted separately and considered after implementation is over.

## FOLLOW-UP AND CONSOLIDATION

Once the system becomes operational, many problems initially may arise mainly because company personnel are learning and because the system does have some defects. Hence, after the system is operational, it is advisable to conduct a postimplementation checkup, basically to make sure that the system is doing what it should.

The following are specific checkpoints or areas of inquiry (some are overlapping):

- Is the system achieving its objectives?
- Is the required information being generated on a timely basis?
- Do the recipients understand the information they receive?
- Do the recipients use the information they receive?
- Is the system operating as it should?
- Is it operating efficiently?
- Do the persons operating the system properly understand it?
- Do they find it difficult to operate the system in any respect, as in meeting time schedules, managing the flow of paper, managing the workload, etc?
- Is the system reliable?

- Have all the unnecessary features of the existing system been eliminated?
- Have any unexpected problems cropped up?

Most of these questions are the same as those raised during the testing stage, which was discussed in Chapter 17. Any problems which come to light during postinstallation review are resolved by modifying the system, by correcting the misunderstanding, or in any other appropriate way. Thus, the follow-up gives the company an opportunity to consolidate the system.

**By Whom?** A postinstallation checkup should be conducted by one or more of the following: the person who implemented the system, the designer, the cost accountant, and the controller. If the system has been designed by an outside consultant, it is in his own interest to arrange with the client, before accepting the engagement, for a postinstallation review by him. Further, to protect his reputation, the consultant should do the review even if his time is not billable. The additional cost will be more than recovered by having a satisfied client.

**When?** Once the system has been implemented, it should be watched closely for a few weeks and as necessary thereafter. If recurring problems are encountered, it may be necessary to watch the system more frequently; otherwise the frequency can be reduced. But the follow-up should continue until the entire cost accounting cycle has been completed. Thereafter, a follow-up should be undertaken only to check whether the specific problems have been resolved.

## REFINEMENT AND SOPHISTICATION

The designer should think big but start small. Even if he can design an ideal system, more often than not he cannot implement it at one time. Hence, first the designer should build the foundation and include only the essential features in the system. Once the basic system is operating satisfactorily, refinements may be introduced. These refinements may take several forms; for instance, objectives may be added to those of the present system, cost reports may be made more detailed, reports may be prepared more frequently, the timing of submission of reports may be expedited, overhead may be allocated on a more scientific basis, cost variance analysis may be extended, and so on.

The potential areas of sophistication or refinement may be identified while the system is being designed and implemented, or they may be sought after the system is operating satisfactorily. In any case, before any refinements are introduced, their need and suitability should be carefully examined.

## SYSTEM MAINTENANCE

Even after the system is fully operational, it must be maintained during its life cycle. Maintenance is necessary because business environments do not remain static. For example, there may be changes in the organization structure or the cost structure, new activities may be added, and so on. These changes may require modifications in any aspect of the cost system, such as its chart of accounts, cost center classification, cost allocation method, flow of paper, form design, etc.

To ensure that the cost system is always kept current, the following steps should be taken:

1. Whenever there is a major change in any aspect of the company's business, the person responsible for operating the cost accounting system should ask this question of himself and of others: "What is the likely effect of this change on the cost accounting system?"
2. Various persons concerned with the system must be encouraged to predict the effect of any change on the system, and a procedure should be provided to take care of their suggestions.

It is not always necessary to change the system as soon as it becomes evident that a change is necessary. While major changes should be made as soon as possible, minor changes may be deferred and made later with some major changes.

## REVIEW AND REVISION

In the life cycle of any cost system, several changes will occur. If there have been many changes, the system may become a patchwork of pieces, some connecting with others, some duplicating, some overlapping, and some working at cross-purposes. Second, even if the system is maintained regularly, there may be some needed changes which may not be feasible without a major overhaul of the system. There may be other signals for undertaking a review: inaccurate reports generated by the system, recurring problems of compliance with the time schedule, major modernization of the production processes, the addition of a new division, a major reorganization, etc. There may be still another reason for revising the cost system. A company may change its system to keep pace with development and improvement in cost accounting and cost control techniques, such as the development of the technique of zero-base budgeting. Thus, any number of internal and external changes may make a review necessary. Hence, it is better to review a cost system at certain intervals, say, every 3 to 5 years.

The best way to conduct a successful review is to proceed with all the steps for system development. For example, check whether there is any change in the system objectives, in what respect business environments have changed, what modifications in the cost information are required, etc. It is also necessary to consider any existing problems. Then, consider whether and in what respect the system needs to be updated to take care of changed circumstances. Often revision will affect the classification of expenses, the chart of accounts, the structure of responsibility centers and cost centers, allocation bases, and reporting requirements. Since the objective here is to tackle changes only, these steps will take considerably less time than that required for designing a cost system from scratch, provided the existing system is properly documented.

Once the areas of revision have been determined, the next step is to redesign the system and then to follow all the steps for system testing, acceptance, and implementation.

# Chapter 19

# Systems Manual

Writing clarifies thinking.
A saying

A systems manual contains the cost system designed for the company. Usually, it is prepared after the cost system has been designed and before the system is implemented. In this chapter we will discuss the need for a systems manual, set forth its usual contents, and illustrate some of its aspects.

## NEED FOR A SYSTEMS MANUAL

The following are the major reasons why it is desirable to have a manual:

*1. Means of communication.* Usually, a cost system involves an interface of several departments and many persons. A systems manual becomes a medium of communication about the system to all concerned. The need for a manual increases because over the years neither the system nor the organization remains static. The system may be revised from time to time, and the organization may be modified. Employees move up or leave the company, and new people are hired. Hence, a manual becomes a good means of communicating the system and the changes in it to the concerned employees.

The need for a systems manual becomes still greater if the company has several locations or divisions. The manual ensures uniformity in the system throughout the company. Similarly, the more complex the system, the greater the need for a systems manual as a means of communicating the system.

*2. Clarification of the system.* A written system is better than an oral system with respect to clarity of procedures and the like. In the first place, writing clarifies thinking. When a system is reduced to writing, most of its inconsistencies or ambiguities will become apparent. Second, oral procedures are apt to be misunderstood. The more complex the cost system, the greater the need for a systems manual to clarify various aspects of the system.

3. *Reference document.* A systems manual becomes a useful source of reference. Even if a cost system is well-understood, it may be necessary to check certain of its aspects. A manual serves as a good source of reference.

4. *Starting point for implementation.* Before implementing a cost system, company personnel must be educated and trained in the system. A manual of the cost system is very useful for this purpose.

5. *Documentation of system revisions.* If a cost accounting system is documented, the manual usually provides for a procedure for making changes in the system and requires those changes also to be documented. In such a case, not only will unauthorized changes not be made but all changes that are made will be communicated to all concerned.

## CONTENTS AND ARRANGEMENT OF A SYSTEMS MANUAL

There are different types of systems manual. Some manuals are only *action manuals,* setting forth who is to do what and when. At the other end of the scale is a comprehensive manual, and between these two extremes there is a wide variety of manuals.

A *comprehensive manual* of a cost system will contain most of the following details:

1. Title page
2. Table of contents
3. Explanation of how to use the manual. To facilitate locating the contents of the manual, two devices should be provided in addition to the table of contents for the entire manual:
    *a.* Table of contents of each section or chapter of the manual
    *b.* Quick-reference subject index with appropriate explanations for using it.
4. Objectives of the system. Once employees understand the objectives, they will better appreciate their role in the operation of the system.
5. Scope of the system, i.e., whether the system is companywide or applies to only particular organizational segments, functions, expenses, etc.
6. Scope of the manual, i.e., whether this is the only manual or other manuals or documents are also to be consulted in operating the system. For example, some companies have separate manuals for budgeting, cost accounting, and reporting which are interlinked by cross-referencing. In

a computerized cost system there may be two separate manuals, one dealing with cost accounting aspects and the other with the computer aspect of the system.

7. Plan of the manual:
   *a.* Contents of the manual and their arrangement.
   *b.* Format of the pages of the manual. For example, Exhibit 19-1 is a specimen page from a systems manual prepared by the author.
   *c.* Person or persons who may be consulted whenever a difficulty arises in interpreting any portion of the manual.
   *d.* Procedures for suggesting and effecting a revision of any part of

**EXHIBIT 19-1**

**Specimen Systems Manual Page**

| Section no. // | |
|---|---|
| Subject | Page no. |
| | Effective |

Section number and title are written in the top block. Paragraph number and title are written in the "Subject" block. Page number is written in the "Page no." block. Each section of the manual is numbered consecutively starting with 1. If a page later is inserted between two pages, it is given the number of the succeeding page, suffixed by the letter A. If two or more pages are inserted, they are suffixed by A, B, etc. For example, if three pages are inserted between pages 5 and 6, they are numbered 6A, 6B, and 6C.

If a page is revised, the page number shall be prefixed by the letter R, and the number of the revision shall be indicated by a figure before R. For example, if there is a third revision of page 5, it will be given the page number 3R5. This numbering system enables keeping track of all revisions.

The date from which each page is effective is written in the block "Effective." If the system is implemented in phases, the different sections of the manual will be effective from different dates. In case of revision of any page of the manual, the effective date will refer to the date from which the revision is effective.

the manual and the methods of communicating revisions to all concerned.

8. Brief description of the cost accounting and reporting system used by the company. For example, the manual should specify whether the system is a standard or an actual cost system, a job order or a process cost system, etc., and explain the system selected.

9. Systems flowcharts or diagrams as aids in understanding the system.

10. Organization chart of the company.

11. List of profit centers and cost centers and the cost center coding system, if any.

12. Explanations and instructions on each aspect of the cost system or each subcost system (material cost accounting, labor cost accounting, etc.). Explanations and instructions should cover the following:

*a.* All relevant procedures from beginning to end

*b.* Expense control policies and procedures (see Exhibit 19-2)

*c.* Internal documents to be prepared together with forms and instructions for preparing them

*d.* Cost accounting treatment of all the relevant transactions (see Exhibit 19-3)

13. Cost reports to be prepared together with specimen forms and instructions for their preparation and distribution. Exhibit 19-4 illustrates the portion of a manual regarding cost reports.

14. Chart of accounts with explanations of the account coding system and each account head: its purpose, debits and credits to be made to it, etc.

15. Financial and cost accounting policies and principles to be followed.

16. Closing and reporting schedules, i.e., who is to do what and when.

17. A computerized cost system will contain computer-operating procedures and specify the order of processing runs. For example, the manual will specify what type of data will be submitted by the user departments to the EDP department, in what form, and when; how, when, and by whom the input data will be entered in the data entry system and verified; what error reports will be generated by the computer, what they indicate, and how the errors reflected by the error reports will be corrected; what transaction files will be generated, using what input data and programs and when; when and how each master file will be updated; what reports will be prepared, using what master files, when, and in what formats; and so on.

18. Costing techniques such as break-even analysis, incremental costing, etc., to be used with explanations on their purpose and how they are to be employed.

**EXHIBIT 19-2**

**Illustrative Traveling Expense Control Policy and Procedure (Partial)**

The *Cost Control and Information Systems Manual* of ACME Company contains the following policy and procedure on the incurrence of traveling expenses.

## PERMITTED TRAVELS

Travels shall be undertaken only for purposes of the company's business, such as the following:

*a.* Meeting present or prospective suppliers of equipment, goods, or services
*b.* Meeting present or prospective customers of the company
*c.* Travel by company personnel from one company location to another company location for any necessary business purpose
*d.* Interviewing an out-of-town job applicant (travel either by the company employee or by the applicant)

Travel will be undertaken only when necessary, i.e., only if the business cannot be transacted effectively and economically by correspondence or by telephone.

Travel for the purposes mentioned in Paragraph *d* shall be undertaken in accordance with the company's policy on "Recruitment" (see Section D of this manual) and "Reimbursement of expenses on business conventions, etc." (see Section H of this manual).

## TRAVEL BY WHOM

Traveling expenses should be incurred for traveling by the company's employees, customers, or suppliers, prospective job applicants, statutory auditors, and such other people (e.g., company's guests) as may be approved by the appropriate authority. When an employee's family members accompany the employee while he or she is on business travel, the traveling expenses of the family members shall not be charged to the company except in the following cases:

- When an employee has been permitted to be accompanied by a spouse at a business convention, etc., in accordance with the company's policy on "Reimbursement of Expenses on Business Conventions, etc."
- When a sick employee has to undertake a business trip and a doctor advises that he or she be accompanied by someone.

## APPROVAL PROCEDURE

All domestic travels should be approved by the immediate supervisor, and if the immediate supervisor is below the rank of manager, also by the manager of the department.

**EXHIBIT 19-2**

**Illustrative Traveling Expense Control Policy and Procedure (Partial) (*Continued*)**

All international travels should be approved by the department head as well as by the company president.

All travels should be approved before they are undertaken. Approval for domestic travels may be oral or written; approval for foreign travels should be in writing in accordance with the rules set forth in this manual.

While approving any travel, the approving authority should be informed or be aware of the purpose of the travel, by whom to be undertaken, the approximate duration of the travel, transportation if it is not of a type normally permitted according to the company's rules, and special expenditure, if any, to be incurred during the business trip. The approving authority should ensure that the proposed travel is in accordance with the rules set forth in this manual.

While approving a business trip, the approving authority should also try to ensure that the traveling expenses incurred by his or her department will not exceed budgeted traveling expenses for his or her department for the current month, year to date, and year. Hence departments which undertake considerable travel should plan their travel for the whole year and constantly monitor actual travel expenses.

After a business trip the employee shall submit a travel expense report on the prescribed form "TER," which shall be approved by the same approving authority which approved the travel in the first place. The approving authority should carefully scrutinize all travel expenses and ensure that they have been incurred for the purposes of the business and are within the limits set forth in this manual.

Before reimbursing travel expenses, the Controller's Department should scrutinize the travel expense report to ensure compliance with the company's travel rules as set forth in this manual. It should also ensure that all relevant vouchers in support of the expenses are attached to the report and that the report contains the requisite details.

## LIMITATIONS ON TRAVEL EXPENSES

Except as otherwise specified, only those traveling expenses which are actually and properly incurred as set forth in this manual shall be paid or reimbursed. The following limits shall apply:

### Mode and Class of Transportation

**Below the Rank of Managers** All domestic travel shall be by the most economical mode of transportation available. For example, for travel within 300 miles, if trains are available and are economical compared with air travel, the travel shall be undertaken by train.

**Managers and Above** Air travel by coach or train by first class is permitted. The president and the vice presidents are permitted first-class air travel. Local travel by taxi is permitted.

**EXHIBIT 19-2**

**Illustrative Traveling Expense Control Policy and Procedure (Partial) (*Continued*)**

**Reimbursement of Motor Car Rental or Mileage Allowance** Whenever it is economical or necessary to travel by the employee's own car or in a rented car, the necessary expenses will be reimbursed as specified here. Car rental expenses including gasoline, toll charges, and parking charges for a subcompact, compact, or a middle-size car will be reimbursed. If an employee uses his or her own car for company business as permitted by this manual, the company will reimburse him or her at the flat rate of 18 cents per mile plus actual toll and parking charges. No reimbursement will be made for gasoline, oil, or any other expenses. Further, in either case, the company will not be responsible for any traffic or parking violation or for any loss caused to a third party or sustained by the employee, except to the extent covered by medical or any other coverage provided by the company.

### Lodging and Boarding Expenses

**Below the Rank of Managers** Stay should be in a reasonably good economical hotel but not beyond a three-star hotel. Daily expenses on lodging and board should not exceed $80.

**Managers and Above** Though there are no limitations on the type of accommodation to be used, discretion is required in every case. In addition, daily expenses should not exceed $100 in small cities and $120 in big cities.

### Incidental Travel Expenses

All incidental travel expenses such as telephone, telegram, postage, laundry, etc., shall be reasonable and be properly incurred for the company's business. Applicable taxes and tips shall be treated as a part of transportation or lodging and board expenses, as the case may be.

### Travel Advances

Travel advances shall be within the limits of estimated travel expense *less* those expenses (air, train, etc., fares) to be paid directly by the company. A request for travel advances shall be made on the "Payment request" form and approved by the authority approving the travel.

### Exceptions to Limits on Travel Expenses

All exceptions to the above rules shall be specifically approved by the approving authority, and when the amount involved for such special approval exceeds $200, by the immediate supervisor of the approving authority.

**EXHIBIT 19-3**

**Illustrative Form for Recording Accounting Treatment of Typical Cost Accounting Transactions**

| Transaction | Documents to be prepared | | | Routing or distribution | Book of original entry | General ledger entry | Entries in subsidiary or memorandum cost records |
|---|---|---|---|---|---|---|---|
| | Title | Number of copies | Prepared by | | | | |
| 1. Purchase of raw materials | | | | | | | |
| 2. Purchase of supplies | | | | | | | |
| 3. Purchased material sent directly to production department | | | | | | | |
| 4. Purchased supplies sent directly to factory for consumption | | | | | | | |
| 5. Materials returned to factory | | | | | | | |
| 6. Supplies returned to vendors | | | | | | | |
| 7. Issue of raw materials for production | | | | | | | |
| 8. Issue of supplies to factory | | | | | | | |
| 9. Raw materials returned from production to stockroom | | | | | | | |
| 10. Supplies returned from factory to stockroom | | | | | | | |
| 11. Transfer of raw materials from one production department to another | | | | | | | |
| 12. Distribution of labor costs | | | | | | | |
| 13. Purchase or payment of factory services (e.g., utilities, insurance, rent, etc.) | | | | | | | |
| 14. Depreciation of fixed assets | | | | | | | |

**EXHIBIT 19-3**

**Illustrative Form for Recording Accounting Treatment of Typical Cost Accounting Transactions (*Continued*)**

| Transaction | Documents to be prepared | | | Routing or distribution | Book of original entry | General ledger entry | Entries in subsidiary or memorandum cost records |
|---|---|---|---|---|---|---|---|
| | Title | Number of copies | Prepared by | | | | |
| 15. Allocation of service centers' costs to production centers | | | | | | | |
| 16. Application of production overhead costs to production | | | | | | | |
| 17. Defective or spoiled work | | | | | | | |
| 18. Packing | | | | | | | |
| 19. Transfer from production to warehouse | | | | | | | |
| 20. Sale of intermediary or finished products | | | | | | | |
| 21. Payment for marketing costs (individual items to be listed separately) | | | | | | | |
| 22. Payment for distribution costs (to be listed by individual items) | | | | | | | |
| 23. Payment for administrative costs (listed individually) | | | | | | | |
| 24. Cost of sales | | | | | | | |
| 25. Overhead variance analysis and disposition | | | | | | | |
| 26. Closing of costing profit and loss account | | | | | | | |

**EXHIBIT 19-4**

**Illustrative Instructions for Preparing Monthly Flash Report**

**Report 10A:** Sample Telex for Monthly Flash Reporting by Regional Controller

| | |
|---|---|
| **To** | A. B. Careful (corporate controller) |
| **From** | I. M. Punctual (regional controller) |
| **Date** | |
| **CC** | U. R. Boss (regional manager) |
| **Re** | Western Region: Monthly Flash Report |

| | | **$ (in 000)** | | | | | |
|---|---|---|---|---|---|---|---|
| | | **Current month** | | | **Year to date** | | |
| | | Actual (estimated) | Budget | Prior year, actual | Actual (estimated) | Budget | Prior year, actual |
| 1. Revenue | $ | | | | | | |
| 2. Cost of goods sold | $ | | | | | | |
| 3. Selling and administration expenses | $ | | | | | | |
| 4. Operating income (1 − 2 − 3) | | | | | | | |
| 5. Operating income percent (4 ÷ 1) | | | | | | | |
| 6. Sales: units | | | | | | | |
| 7. Orders on hand: units | | | | | | | |
| 8. Production: units | | | | | | | |
| 9. Work in process: units | | | | | | | |
| 10. Finished product inventory: units | | | | | | | |
| 11. Inventories | $ | | | | | | |
| 12. Receivables | $ | | | | | | |
| 13. Employees: number | | | | | | | |
| 14. Direct wages | $ | | | | | | |
| 15. Direct materials consumed | $ | | | | | | |
| 16. Capital expenditures | $ | | | | | | |

**EXHIBIT 19-4**

**Illustrative Instructions for Preparing Monthly Flash Report (*Continued*)**

| Reliable Products, Inc. | |
|---|---|
| Section No. 10 | Management Reports |
| Subject: 10.3 Monthly Flash Reports | Page 4<br>Effective January 1, 1981 |

## EXPLANATIONS

### PURPOSE

The purpose of the monthly flash report is to provide top management with key financial and cost data at an early date while regular reports are being prepared. The monthly flash report is the basis of discussion at the first weekly management meeting of the month.

### RESPONSIBILITY FOR PREPARATION

The corporate controller is responsible for compiling the consolidated flash report from the regional flash reports received from the three regions. The regional controllers are responsible for preparing flash reports for their respective regions.

### DUE DATE

Flash reports for each month from the regional controllers are due in corporate headquarters in New York no later than 1:00 P.M. New York time on the second working day of the following calendar month. The corporate controller is responsible for submitting to top management a monthly consolidated flash report by the third working day of the following month. The timeliness of this report is crucial.

### DISTRIBUTION

The regional controllers should send their flash reports by telex to the corporate controller and send a copy to the respective regional managers.

The corporate controller will submit the monthly consolidated flash report to the chairman and chief executive officer, the president, and each vice president.

## INSTRUCTIONS

### FORMATS

The regional controllers will send their flash reports in the sample telex form given in Report 10A, and the corporate controller will submit the consolidated flash report in the specimen form given in Report 10B.

Many of the items on these two forms are self-explanatory. The remaining items are explained below.

#### Current Month and Year to Date

All flash data should be for the current month and year to date.

**EXHIBIT 19-4**

**Illustrative Instructions for Preparing Monthly Flash Report (*Continued*)**

**Actual (Estimate)**

The current month's actual data should be submitted when available (except as otherwise specified below). However, as the timeliness of this report is crucial, the regional controllers should, in consultation with the regional managers, provide the best estimate when actual data for the current month are not available.

Year-to-date actual data should be the total of the actual data up to the preceding month and actual or estimated data for the current month.

**Budget**

Budget data as in the finally approved budget should be entered here. In other words, no adjustment should be made for the difference in the level of activity actually attained.

**Cost of Goods Sold**

Cost of goods sold for the current month should be computed at the standard cost of production of the quantity sold. Cost of goods sold for the year to date should be the total of the actual cost of goods sold up to the preceding month and the cost of goods sold for the current month at the standard cost.

**Orders on Hand**

Include only those orders which you have accepted to deliver.

**Production Units**

Show only good production units.

**Inventories**

Show all inventories less obsolete inventories.

**Receivables**

Show receivables net of the reserve for doubtful accounts.

**Employees**

Show equivalent full-time employees.

**Direct Materials Consumed**

For current month, value the quantity of direct materials consumed at standard prices. For the year-to-date actual amount, add to the current month's amount the actual amount for the year up to the preceding month.

**By Regions**

List, by regions, only those items for which a region had more than 20 percent positive or negative variance from the budget for the current month or the year to date. For example, if the Western Region was under budget on revenue by more than 20 percent, this should be reported under the Western Region. If the variances in other items were less than 20 percent, they should not be reported here.

**Comments**

The regional controllers' flash reports should be accompanied by appropriate comments on significant variances. At a minimum, an explanation of all variances in excess of 10 percent should be provided.

Similarly, the corporate controller's flash report should also include a necessary explanation of all significant variances.

**EXHIBIT 19-4**

## Illustrative Instructions for Preparing Monthly Flash Report (*Continued*)

**Report 10B:** Specimen Monthly Consolidated Flash Report by the Corporate Controller

**Reliable Products, Inc.**

**Monthly Consolidated Flash Report**

**Month** ____________

| | | $ (in 000) | | | | | |
|---|---|---|---|---|---|---|---|
| | | **Current month** | | | **Year to date** | | |
| | | Actual (estimated) | Budget | Prior year, actual | Actual (estimated) | Budget | Prior year, actual |
| **Consolidated** | | | | | | | |
| 1. Revenue | $ | | | | | | |
| 2. Cost of goods sold | $ | | | | | | |
| 3. Selling and administration expenses | $ | | | | | | |
| 4. Operating income (1 − 2 − 3) | $ | | | | | | |
| 5. Operating income percent (4 ÷ 1) | | | | | | | |
| 6. Sales: units | | | | | | | |
| 7. Orders on hand: units | | | | | | | |
| 8. Production: units | | | | | | | |
| 9. Work in process: units | | | | | | | |
| 10. Finished product inventory: units | | | | | | | |
| 11. Inventories | $ | | | | | | |
| 12. Receivables | $ | | | | | | |
| 13. Employees: number | | | | | | | |
| 14. Direct wages | $ | | | | | | |
| 15. Direct materials consumed | $ | | | | | | |
| 16. Capital expenditures | $ | | | | | | |
| **BY REGIONS** | | | | | | | |
| (Show only those items for which a region had more than 20 percent plus or minus deviations from the budget) | | | | | | | |
| **Western Region** | | | | | | | |
| **Central Region** | | | | | | | |
| **Eastern Region** | | | | | | | |

### Arrangement of a Systems Manual

The arrangement of a systems manual will depend upon the nature of the cost system and the existence of only one manual or two or more manuals. Normally, the arrangement of the contents will be more or less as listed above, except that items 12 through 16 will be arranged by types of subcost systems (direct materials, manufacturing overhead costs, etc.). In other words, all aspects from source documents to report preparation relating to, say, direct materials will be contained in one section.

# Other Aspects

# Chapter 20

# Designing Cost Systems for Nonmanufacturing and Nonprofit Organizations

The United States economy is a service economy.

Until now our discussion has centered in the design and implementation of a cost system for a manufacturing business. The United States economy is said to be a service economy; i.e., more than 50 percent of its gross national product is derived from the service sector. In recent years, even service organizations are realizing the usefulness of cost control and information systems. Hence, in this chapter we will discuss the special points for designing a cost system for nonmanufacturing businesses and nonprofit organizations.

## DESIGNING COST SYSTEMS FOR NONMANUFACTURING ORGANIZATIONS

Nonmanufacturing businesses include banks, insurance companies, stock brokers, transportation and communications companies, hotels, restaurants, retail stores, department stores, wholesalers, repair shops, professional firms, and so on. These businesses provide some kind of services or buy and sell products, as opposed to the manufacturing and selling of goods undertaken by a manufacturing organization.

The *process* of designing a cost system for a nonmanufacturing business is similar to that for a manufacturing business, except that there are differences in *applications,* as explained in this chapter. The distinguishing points are discussed separately for each task under system analysis, system design, and system implementation.

At the outset, it will be helpful if we regard the services provided by a nonmanufacturing business as products. Unlike the products of a manufacturing business, the services provided by a nonmanufacturing business are intangible. For example, a commercial bank's various products may be checking accounts, savings accounts, term deposit accounts, personal loans, business loans, and the like. It will also be helpful to understand at the outset the product cost structure of a multiproduct nonmanufacturing company. Exhibit 20-1 diagrammatically explains such a

**EXHIBIT 20-1**

**Product Cost Structure of a Multiproduct Nonmanufacturing Business**

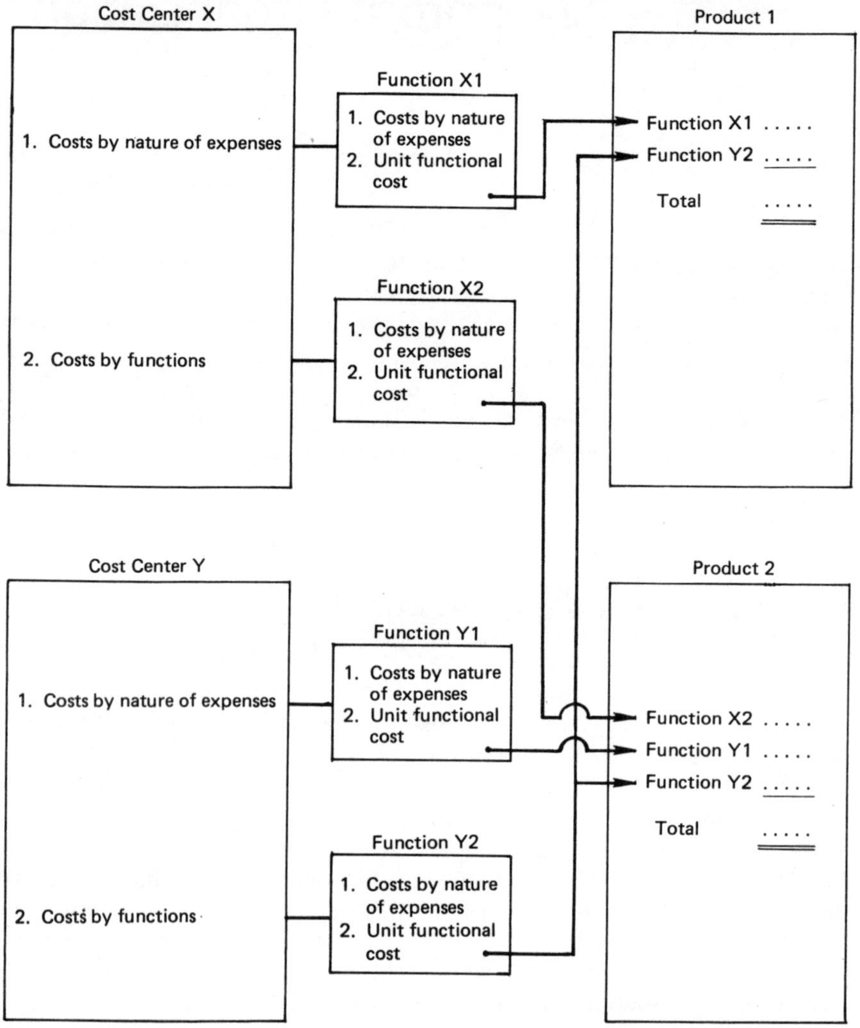

structure. For product costing, cost centers are established. A cost center may perform only one type of function (or activity, operation, etc.) or two or more types. From the costs of a cost center, unit functional costs are computed, and by combining the relevant unit functional costs, unit product costs are computed. In some businesses, a product cost may include certain direct costs besides functional costs. For example, in an appliance repair business, the cost of repairing an appliance will include the cost of parts.

For cost control, responsibility centers are established and costs are computed by levels of responsibility as in a manufacturing organization.

## System Analysis Phase

The distinguishing points of the system analysis phase for nonmanufacturing businesses, as compared with those for manufacturing businesses, are described below.

**Defining System Objectives** The objectives will be more or less the same as in a manufacturing business except that many nonmanufacturing businesses do not consume direct materials and hence valuation of inventory will not be a relevant objective. In the case of retailers, wholesalers, and other traders, however, valuation of inventory may be one of the objectives of designing a cost system.

A nonmanufacturing business incurs costs, and hence it has as great a need for controlling costs as a manufacturing business has. Further, a nonmanufacturing business needs cost information for managerial decision making, profit planning, determining rates or charges for its services or products, profitability analysis by line of business, and so on.

**Gathering Background Information** This task is similar to that in a manufacturing company. There will, however, be a difference in the items of background information to be gathered. For example, instead of the sequence of a manufacturing process, the sequence of a service operation will be studied. Second, except in retail and merchandising businesses, material cost usually does not form a significant part of total costs, and hence it will not be studied in detail. On the other hand, labor cost forms a significant portion of total costs, and hence labor operations will be studied more carefully.

**Determining Cost System Requirements** Because of the differences in cost elements, the major difference is in the items of cost information required. For example, in a commercial bank, the most important cost factor is the cost of funds, or interest expenses. Excluding interest, salaries and employee benefits costs account for the major portion of the total operating expenses of a bank. This point will be clear from the following cost structure of a large commercial bank in New York:

| Cost Structure (Excluding Interest) | |
|---|---|
| | Percent |
| Salaries and employee benefits costs | 57 |
| Occupancy, depreciation, advertising, and publicity | 14 |
| All other operating expenses | 29 |
| Total operating expenses | 100 |

Similarly, in other service industries such as insurance companies, communications businesses, brokerage houses, etc., there is a preponderance of personnel costs in total operating expenses. Hence, it is essential that their cost accounting systems focus on personnel costs. It may, however, be noted that in contrast to practice in a manufacturing business, personnel costs in a nonmanufacturing business usually are not classified into direct and indirect labor costs.

For cost control, costs are identified by areas of responsibility and by nature of expenses. For cost analysis for managerial decision making and also for cost control, costs are computed for each function or activity and for each product or group of products.

## System Design Phase

The distinguishing points of the system design phase for nonmanufacturing businesses as compared with those of the manufacturing businesses are as described below.

**Selection of Appropriate Cost Methods** Operational or functional costing is appropriate for most nonmanufacturing businesses. For example, a bank will compute the average cost of each of its major functions, such as processing a check, processing a deposit ticket, etc. However, businesses providing customized services may use a sort of job order costing. For example, an automobile repair center may compute the cost of repairing each car.

Further, as in the case of a manufacturing business, a nonmanufacturing business also must choose between (1) standard costing and historical costing and (2) direct costing and full absorption costing. Though nonmanufacturing businesses use standard costs for cost control and various other managerial purposes, cost records are usually maintained on a historical cost basis and not on standard costs.

For cost control, both budgeting and standard costing can be used. Traditionally, budgeting is more widely used than standard costing in nonmanufacturing businesses. Of late, however, standard costing has become popular even among banks and insurance companies. Undoubtedly, budgeting is more effective in controlling costs when budgets are based on scientifically established standards. Further, both fixed and flexible budgets can be used. Flexible budgeting is more appropriate for costs which bear a relation to the volume of work. For example, labor cost for encoding checks in a bank varies with the number of checks encoded, and therefore flexible budgeting is more appropriate for controlling the costs of a check-encoding center. On the other hand, fixed budgeting is more appropriate for discretionary costs such as advertising and publicity and for controlling committed costs such as depreciation. As in the case of manufacturing businesses, standard costs are better than actual costs for planning, managerial analysis, profitability evaluation by lines of business, and product pricing.

In a service business, the concepts of direct costing and full-absorption costing can be used for costing its products (or services). However, since in a service business the question of valuation of inventory of finished products and work in process does not arise, these concepts are used for managerial cost analysis and not for recording costs in the books of account. For example, for line-of-business profitability evaluation, all costs, including joint costs, may be allocated to various business lines, or only the overhead costs from which the business lines derive benefits may be so allocated.

**Establishment of Responsibility Centers and Cost Centers** As in the case of a manufacturing business, it is necessary to establish responsibility centers for cost control and cost centers for cost accumulation, allocation, and functional costing. Further, the process of establishing responsibility centers and cost centers is the same as in a manufacturing business, but the types of responsibility centers and cost centers will differ. For example, nonmanufacturing businesses do not have production cost centers. Further, for most nontrading nonmanufacturing businesses, purchasing, material-handling, and inventory control centers will not be significant. For chain department stores, however, purchasing is a very important responsibility center.

Banks and insurance companies usually compute profitability by lines of business. For example, one insurance company computes profitability by these lines of business: industrial, ordinary life, ordinary annuities, personal health, group life, group health, group annuities, credit life, and credit health.

Usually, the lines of business will constitute responsibility centers, which may be subdivided into smaller responsibility centers consisting of product lines, geographic subdivisions, etc. For example, a bank's personal loan department may have products such as automobile loans, housing loans, educational loans, unsecured loans, etc.

The business lines and their subdivisions will also be cost centers for cost accumulation and allocation. These cost centers may be further subdivided or grouped as may be appropriate. In addition to these cost centers, there will be cost centers providing support services such as maintenance, janitorial service, administrative service, accounting, treasury, etc.

Various responsibility or cost centers can also be classified into *operating centers* and *support service centers*. Operating centers are those which interface with customers or provide services to customers, and support centers are those which provide services to the operating centers. Examples of support service centers are the occupancy cost center, the maintenance department, and the accounting and EDP departments.

Once the cost centers have been established, the major functions or activities performed by each cost center should be identified. For example, in a bank various functions may be processing deposit and withdrawal tickets, check encoding, check sorting by branches, pickup and delivery of mail, filing, etc.

Then, the functions should be related to products; i.e., various functions performed for individual products should be identified. For better understanding, a matrix of cost centers, functions, and products should be prepared. A specimen matrix for a bank is given in Exhibit 20-2, in which functions applicable to each product will be indicated by putting an *X* in the appropriate columns.

**Cost Classification** Costs of a nonmanufacturing business may be classified into one or more of the following categories, depending upon the objectives of its cost system and the nature of its business:

1. Nature of expenses (salaries, employee benefits costs, rent, electricity, etc.).
2. Lines of business, such as checking accounts, term deposit accounts, personal loan accounts, etc., in the case of banks.
3. Cost behavior, i.e., separation of variable, fixed, and semifixed costs.
4. Controllability, i.e., separation of controllable and noncontrollable costs. This classification is essential only for cost control.
5. Functions or activities, such as processing new insurance applications, sending renewal notices, processing claims for automobile insurance, medical insurance, annuities, etc., in the case of insurance companies. Unit functional or activity costs constitute the building blocks for product costing and various other purposes. It will be obvious that because there is no manufacturing function, the question of classifying costs by manufacturing activities does not arise.
6. Products. Usually, unit product costs are compiled from unit func-

**EXHIBIT 20-2**

**Matrix of Cost Centers, Functions, and Products of a Bank**

| | Products | | | | | |
|---|---|---|---|---|---|---|
| Cost Centers and Functions | Check Cashing | Deposit Ticket Processing | Loan Accounts | | | |
| *Headquarters* | | | | | | |
| (List functions) | | | | | | |
| *Branch* | | | | | | |
| Process loan applications | | | | | | |
| Paying and receiving debits | | | | | | |
| Proof control debits | | | | | | |
| . . . | | | | | | |
| *Check processing* | | | | | | |
| Encoding | | | | | | |
| Tape conversion | | | | | | |
| Sorting checks by branch | | | | | | |
| . . . | | | | | | |
| *Central delivery* | | | | | | |
| Pickup and delivery | | | | | | |
| Other | | | | | | |
| *Other cost centers* | | | | | | |
| (To be specified) | | | | | | |

tional costs. Even when a cost item is incurred exclusively for a particular product, it will be accumulated by the nature of the cost item and may also be accumulated by function.

**Cost Matrix** For better understanding, a matrix showing cost classification by nature, functions, etc., should be prepared. Exhibit 20-3 is an illustrative matrix of cost items and functions in a bank. To complete this exhibit, it is first necessary to determine the cost items applicable to each function. Then, to indicate the cost items applicable to individual functions, place an *X* in the appropriate columns against each cost item.

**Selection of Units of Measurement** For computing actual as well as standard costs of various products and functions and for developing budgets, a unit of measurement must be selected for each product and function. The unit of measurement often reflects the workload or volume of activity of a cost center and is its performance determinant. For example, the unit of measurement for a check-encoding section of a bank will be the number of checks encoded, which on the one hand influences the amount of cost incurred by the encoding section and on

**EXHIBIT 20-3**

**Matrix of Cost Items and Functions in a Bank**

| Cost Items | Functions: Processing Loan Appli-cations | Loan Approval | Encod-ing | Sorting Checks by Branch | | | | | |
|---|---|---|---|---|---|---|---|---|---|
| Supervisory salaries | | | | | | | | | |
| Clerical salaries | | | | | | | | | |
| Encoding | | | | | | | | | |
| Sorting | | | | | | | | | |
| Typing | | | | | | | | | |
| Filing | | | | | | | | | |
| . . . | | | | | | | | | |
| Equipment rental | | | | | | | | | |
| Encoding | | | | | | | | | |
| Accounting | | | | | | | | | |
| Security | | | | | | | | | |
| Duplicating | | | | | | | | | |
| Printing and stationery | | | | | | | | | |
| . . . | | | | | | | | | |

the other hand is also a measure of its performance. For instance, by comparing the actual time taken to encode a given number of checks against the predetermined time, the efficiency of the encoding section can be measured. Hence, for selecting the appropriate unit of measurement, the designer should determine what factor or factors govern the costs incurred by a cost center.

The following are the commonly used measurements in nonmanufacturing businesses:

1. *Number of items involved for item-oriented activities.* Usually, routine activities which require more or less constant but small units of time to perform them and the volume of which fluctuates fall in this category. For this type of activities the unit of measurement will be the number of items involved. For example, for the filing of cards, the unit of measurement will be the number of cards filed; and for the encoding of checks, the number of checks encoded. A hotel will compute the cost per room, a restaurant will compute the cost per meal, a mining company will compute the cost per ton of mining product mined, and so on.

2. *Time involved for time-oriented activities.* If the time required to complete a job fluctuates from one job to another and the time unit is rea-

sonably large, the unit of measurement will be the time spent. Usually, this factor is required for nonstandard jobs; for example, in an appliance repair shop different types of repair jobs may require different amounts of time, and hence it is appropriate to select time (hour, day, etc.) as a unit of measurement. However, if each type of repair job is regarded as a separate product, the number of repair jobs of each type performed can be selected as a unit of measurement.

3. *Distance for distance-oriented activities.* For a trucking department, the unit of measurement may be the number of miles traveled.

4. *Weight, volume, or space.* For a warehousing function, the weight or volume of goods warehoused may be the unit of measurement. For a crating company, the unit of measurement may be the volume, i.e., the cubic measurement of the cargo crated. A department store will compute the sales, cost, and profit per square feet of space utilized by various products.

5. *Combination of units of measurement.* When more than one factor is the determinant of the cost of a product or a function, a combination of two (rarely more than two) factors may be used as a unit of measurement. For example, a trucking company normally computes the cost per ton-mile traveled, a passenger transportation company usually computes the cost per passenger-mile traveled, and so on.

**Development of Standards and Budgets** The process of setting standards and developing budgets is more or less the same in manufacturing and nonmanufacturing businesses. In nonmanufacturing businesses, there is often a preponderance of labor costs, and therefore labor standards assume importance. The procedures for developing standards and budgets for labor and other costs are explained below.

**Labor Cost Standards** For developing labor standards it is essential to select an appropriate performance measurement factor, workload factor, or determinant for each cost center or for each function if a cost center performs more than one function. For this purpose, it is useful to classify various activities into three categories as follows:

1. *Item-oriented activities.* Usually, routine activities which require more or less constant but small units of time to perform them and the volume of which fluctuates fall in this category. For example, for such activities as the filing of cards, the encoding of checks, etc., labor standards will be expressed as so many items per time unit, which may be an hour or a day.

2. *Time-oriented activities.* If the time required to complete a job fluctuates from one job to another and the time unit is reasonably large, the time standards will be set in terms of so much time per job. For example, in an appliance repair shop, different types of repair jobs require differ-

ent amounts of time, and hence it is appropriate to set time standards in terms of so many hours for each type of job.

3. *Programmed activities.* Activities which do not fall in the first two categories will usually be classified as programmed activities. Normally, these types of activities require set amounts of time and have a more or less constant workload. For example, activities such as pickup and delivery of mail fall in this category. Standards of this type are set in terms of so many persons to do a job. For example, standards may provide that for up to three deliveries and pickups of mail two persons will be required and that for three or more deliveries and pickups three persons will be required.

The establishment of standards is the most difficult task in the entire process of developing a cost system. Standards for the first two types of activities may be based on time study, work measurement, or supervisors' estimates. In recent years, many banks and insurance companies have used the techniques of time study and work measurements for the establishment of standards. For the third type of activity, standards can be based on time study, but the more common method is to use supervisors' estimates.

By multiplying the labor quantity standards by the standard labor rate, the standard labor cost can be determined. For the first two types of activities, the total costs of which vary with the volume of work, the standard cost for a single unit of activity is set; e.g., the standard cost of check encoding may be 2 cents per check, or that of servicing a typewriter may be $10 per typewriter, etc. For the third type of activity, the standard cost is set in total for the job; e.g., the standard labor cost for two deliveries and pickups of mail is $24,000 per month.

As in the case of a manufacturing business, employee benefits costs such as vacations, holidays, medical benefits, employment taxes, etc., may be included as a part of the labor cost or treated as a separate cost item. The second alternative is better for cost control as well as for managerial decision making.

**Labor Budget.** Once the standard costs for labor have been set, preparation of the labor budget is comparatively easy. First, it is necessary to estimate the volume of activity for each responsibility center and, on the basis of the standards, to budget the total number of employees of various types required by it. Then, the labor required is converted into dollars by multiplying it by the standard or estimated labor rates (fixed salaries or hourly rates). If a flexible budget is used, fixed and variable labor costs will be shown separately.

**Standards for Other Costs** For the development of predetermined unit nonlabor costs for various activities, fixed or flexible budgets are used. The procedure is similar to that followed for the development of predetermined manufacturing overhead rates.

If flexible budgeting is used, the costs are separated into fixed and variable categories. Second, the activity unit, measurement factor, workload factor, or determinant is selected for each activity, as explained above in the section "Selection of Units of Measurement." Third, an activity level or range of activity levels is selected. Fourth, for each expense item, the total amount for the budgeted level of activity is estimated. Whenever possible and worthwhile, these estimates should be based on scientific standards. For example, engineered standards can be set for repairs and maintenance materials and quantity of power consumption. Of course, there are very few nonlabor costs which are amenable to scientific standards setting. For fixed costs, predetermined amounts are expressed as dollar values per time unit: space rental of $1200 per month, equipment maintenance at the rate of $100 per piece of equipment per month, and so on. For variable costs, the quantity and the rate may be developed separately, or the cost amounts themselves may be estimated, but in either case they are expressed per activity unit of the relevant cost center. For example, for the personal loan department of a bank, cost standards may be set per loan application processed.

**Budgets for Other Costs** From the data developed during the preceding steps, the total expense budget for the planned activity level can be prepared for managerial planning. Further, for preparing the monthly actual-to-budget comparison reports, the flexible budget allowance can also be computed easily from these data.

If fixed budgeting is used, fixed and variable costs will not be separated, the budget will be prepared for one activity level, and a single predetermined overhead rate will be set for the activity level selected.

**Procedures for Cost Allocation, Functional Costing, and Product Costing** For computing product costs as well as functional or activity costs, costs which can be identified with individual cost centers are charged directly to them, and the other costs are allocated. For example, occupancy, maintenance, and general administration expenses will first be accumulated under objective expense accounts and then allocated to various cost centers; this step is similar to primary allocation of the manufacturing overhead costs. Then, the costs allocated to the support service centers will be distributed to the operating centers; this procedure is similar to secondary allocation of manufacturing overhead costs.

By dividing the total cost of each activity center by the total volume of its activity, the unit functional or activity cost can be computed. For example, if the encoding department normally encodes 200,000 checks per month at the standard cost of $4000, the standard cost for check encoding will be set at 2 cents ($4000 ÷ 200,000) per check. If a cost center performs more than one function, its cost must be allocated among various functions. Costs which can be identified directly with a function should be charged directly to that function. Costs common to several functions should be allocated on some equitable basis, usually in the ratio of the relevant volume of activity.

From the unit functional costs, the unit products cost can be computed by totaling the costs of the functions relevant to the product. The hypothetical example given in Exhibit 20-4 will illustrate the point.

The objective of Exhibit 20-4 is to compute the standard unit cost of the product "education loan." The unit of measurement selected for this product is the number of education loan accounts opened because that factor truly controls the cost of the education loan product. The first column lists all the functions relevant to this product, and they are arranged by the cost centers in which they are performed. For each function, the unit of measurement and the standard unit functional cost are separately determined. The standard unit functional costs are set separately for fixed and variable costs.

For converting each function's unit cost to the unit product cost, it is necessary to determine the conversion factor. The conversion factor represents the number of units of a function required for a single unit of the product under consideration. For example, for every five education loan applications received, four loan accounts are opened, and therefore for the functions of (1) preliminary discussion and paperwork and (2) review application the conversion factor is 1.25 (5 ÷ 4). What this means is that though the unit functional cost for review application is $0.0232 in fixed cost and $0.1036 in variable cost, the amounts to be included in the unit product cost are 1.25 times these amounts.

By adding up the unit product cost for each function, the total unit product cost can be arrived at. In the hypothetical example given in Exhibit 20-4, the standard cost of opening and maintaining an education loan account comes to $8.3250, which consists of $3.4250 in fixed costs and $4.9000 in variable costs.

There are several advantages of this modular approach to product costing. For functions which are common to several products, it is not necessary to compute the unit functional cost separately for each product unless the time and other costs required for various products vary from product to product. For example, the time required for receiving applications and checking credit for a home mortgage loan would be much greater than that for an educational loan or an automobile loan. Hence, standard costs will be developed separately for the home mortgage loan product and other personal loan products. However, the unit functional cost for credit administration (collection, follow-up, etc.)

**EXHIBIT 20-4**

**Standard Product Cost Sheet**

Date effective ________

Product description: Education Loan

Product code: EL-124

Unit of measurement: Number of loan accounts opened

| Cost centers and functions | Unit of measurement | Standard unit functional cost | | Conversion factor | Unit product cost | | |
|---|---|---|---|---|---|---|---|
| | | Fixed | Variable | | Fixed | Variable | Total |
| Branch | | | | | | | |
| Preliminary discussion and paperwork | Number of applications received | $0.3632 | $0.2412 | 1.25 | $0.4540 | $0.3015 | $0.7555 |
| Review application | Number of applications received | 0.0232 | 0.1036 | 1.25 | 0.0290 | 0.1295 | 0.1585 |
| . . . | | | | | | | |
| . . . | | | | | | | |
| Set up loan account | Number of loan accounts opened | 0.3254 | 0.6892 | 1.0 | 0.3254 | 0.6892 | 1.0146 |
| . . . | | | | | ____ | ____ | ____ |
| Credit administration | | | | | | | |
| . . . | | | | | | | |
| . . . | | | | | ____ | ____ | ____ |
| Accounting | | | | | | | |
| . . . | | | | | | | |
| . . . | | | | | | | |
| Total | | | | | $3.4250 | $4.9000 | $8.3250 |

may be the same for various types of personal loans. In that case, only one unit functional cost will be developed for this function.

Further, if the standard cost of a particular function changes, only that cost factor will have to be changed in the individual product costs. Similarly, if a particular function applicable to a product is added or deleted, the new product cost can easily be recomputed. Thus, the modular, or building-block, approach helps in developing the initial product cost and in keeping the product cost current.

Lastly, the building-block approach facilitates variance analysis and other cost analyses for various managerial decisions. Variances in costs can be tracked down to cost items, functions, and products, and consequently responsibility for cost variances can be assigned. For managerial decision making, it is necessary to segregate the cost items affected by the alternatives being considered and to compare them. The modular approach to unit product costing obviously facilitates this type of cost analysis and comparison.

**Cost Reports** Cost reports of a nonmanufacturing business consist of (1) responsibility reports for cost control and (2) functional cost reports and product cost reports for planning, budgeting, cost control, and managerial decision making, such as product pricing, choosing whether to continue or to drop a product line, formulating marketing strategies, etc.

There is practically no difference in the cost control reports of a nanufacturing business and a nonmanufacturing business. A cost control report of a responsibility center should include only the costs controllable by it. If the report includes the allocated costs too, they should be clearly designated as allocated costs. Further, the techniques of flexible budgeting and standard costing can be used to show variances of actual costs against predetermined costs. The report should show the relevant quantitative data, such as workload or activity volumes, labor efficiency ratio, performance achievement ratio, etc. The variances should be shown by each significant cost item or a group of cost items. Usually, in a nonmanufacturing business there is a preponderance of *labor costs,* and hence they are reported separately and even subclassified when appropriate. The variances can be analyzed by causes such as volume variance, efficiency variance, and spending variance. Obviously, the reports should be submitted to the responsibility center managers, who should be asked to explain the variances and also to explain what actions they have taken or planned to correct or prevent the deviations.

Functional and product cost reports may be prepared regularly or as and when needed. If a standard costing system is employed, standard functional and product costs are established once and then updated either periodically or as and when a significant change occurs.

All the reporting principles, guidelines, and techniques discussed in Chapters 6 and 14 apply to cost reports of a nonmanufacturing business too.

**Cost Records** As stated before, nonmanufacturing businesses usually keep cost records on an actual cost basis even when standard costing is employed. Further, cost classification by nature of expenses is maintained in the books of account. In addition, all costs directly identifiable with individual lines of business or functions may be recorded separately if the amount involved is significant. For example, salaries will usually be recorded separately by cost centers. However, in contrast to a manufacturing business, most of the costs in a nonmanufacturing business are incurred for several lines of business or products, and hence they cannot be directly identified with individual lines of business or products. Consequently, most of the cost records are by nature of expenses. Functional and product cost computations are handled on a memorandum basis.

The procedure for designing cost records is similar to that applicable to the marketing and administrative costs of a manufacturing business. In particular, to facilitate the multiple classification of costs (by nature, by functions, etc.) proper coding of source documents should be provided.

### System Implementation Phase

The system implementation phase will be identical to that of a manufacturing business. However, in most nonmanufacturing businesses, labor cost will form a significant part of total costs. Hence, the designer should be more cautious about human relations while implementing a cost system in a nonmanufacturing business.

## DESIGNING COST SYSTEMS FOR NONPROFIT ORGANIZATIONS

Though theoretically nonprofit organizations can run any kind of business or activity, the usual types of businesses and activities handled by nonprofit organizations are hospitals, schools, colleges, universities, churches, relief work, business, professional, and vocational associations, charities, labor unions, social clubs, health and welfare organizations, and the like. What distinguishes a nonprofit organization from a profit-seeking organization is the absence of a profit motive. However, even a nonprofit organization may carry on revenue- and profit-earning activities. For example, a university may make profit from its book-publishing activity. It should be noted that the activities mentioned here are not exclusive to nonprofit organizations. For example, there are for-profit hospitals and educational institutions.

Since most nonprofit organizations are engaged in providing some kind of services, the process of designing a cost system for a nonprofit organization is more or less similar to that for a nonmanufacturing business. There may, however, be differences in applications, as explained below. The distinguishing points are explained separately for each task under system analysis, system design, and system implementation.

## System Analysis Phase

**Defining System Objectives** The following are some of the major objectives of a cost system for a nonprofit organization:

1. Cost control.
2. Selection of the most effective programs and allocation of resources among the selected programs.
3. Setting rates or prices for services or products which are not provided free of charge. For example, a hospital must set the prices for recovering its charges for various services from patients or third parties such as insurance companies, Medicare, etc.
4. Providing cost information for managerial decision making, such as choosing whether to continue or to drop a program or to automate a clerical function, selecting the most cost-effective fund-raising methods, etc.
5. Providing cost information to comply with statutory requirements. For example, OMB Circular A-21, "Cost Principles for Educational Institutions," issued by the Office of Management and Budget on March 6, 1979, requires all federal agencies that sponsor research and development and training to apply the provisions of the circular in determining the costs incurred for such work. This circular establishes the principles for segregating costs into direct and indirect categories and for distributing indirect costs.
6. Determining what percentage of resources is spent on the objectives of the organization and what percentage is spent on support activities.

A profit-seeking organization should control its costs to enhance its profits, which is its objective. Similarly, every nonprofit organization should control its costs to achieve its objectives at the least possible cost so that with the available resources it can serve more people or better serve a given number of people and will not be required to seek more funds.

For most nonprofit organizations, the resources available are limited, and the program or activities which fit within their mission are many.

Hence, they must be careful in selecting programs and allocating resources among them so that they can achieve maximum goals with minimum resources. For example, a hospital must select the types of medical and surgical facilities to be provided and decide about the resources to be allocated for each of the selected facilities. Cost is one of the important considerations in reaching this decision. Similarly, for deciding the rates to be charged for various paid services, a nonprofit organization needs cost data by type of services which it provides.

**Gathering Background Information** This task is similar to that in a profit-seeking nonmanufacturing business. Here also, labor costs will form a significant portion of total costs, as will be clear from the following cost structure of a large hospital in New Jersey:

Cost Structure of a New Jersey Hospital

| | Percent |
|---|---|
| Employees' salaries and benefits | 63 |
| Patient supplies | 9 |
| Professional fees | 6 |
| Food and drugs | 5 |
| Malpractice insurance | 5 |
| Utilities and maintenance | 3 |
| Depreciation | 3 |
| General and administrative | 6 |
| Total | 100 |

Hence, labor operations should be studied carefully.

**Determining Cost System Requirements** Since there is a preponderance of labor costs, it is essential that a nonprofit organization's cost system focus on these costs. However, in contrast to the labor costs of a manufacturing business, labor costs of a not-for-profit organization usually are not classified into direct and indirect labor.

For cost control, costs are identified by areas of responsibility and by nature of expenses. For cost analysis for managerial decision making and also for cost control, costs are computed for each function or activity and each program. A program is similar to a product or service provided by a profit-seeking organization. For example, a hospital's programs may include educating the community about preventive health care with a view to containing the cost of providing health care services.

## System Design Phase

The distinguishing points of the system design phase for nonprofit organizations as compared with those of the profit-seeking manufacturing and nonmanufacturing businesses are as follows:

**Selection of Appropriate Cost Methods** The options available to nonprofit organizations regarding cost methods are the same as those available to profit-seeking organizations. For example, a hospital, whether it is a for-profit or a not-for-profit entity, will employ functional or operational costing. Further, nonprofit organizations traditionally maintain their cost records on a historical cost basis and not on a standard cost basis.

For cost control, both budgeting and standard costing can be used. For example, a hospital can use standard costing for controlling recurring costs of the dietary department, the nursing department, etc. However, the scope for using standard costing for controlling costs in hospitals, schools, churches, etc., is very limited. Hence, budgeting is more widely used than standard costing. Further, both fixed and flexible budgets can be used. Flexible budgeting is more appropriate for costs which bear a relation to the volume of activity. For example, since costs related to patient care in a hospital vary with the number of patients admitted to the hospital, flexible budgeting is more appropriate for controlling those costs. Fixed budgeting is more appropriate when the volume of activity can be forecast fairly accurately, as in the case of a school, and for controlling discretionary costs such as advertising and publicity and committed costs such as depreciation, rent, etc.

In a nonprofit organization, the concepts of direct costing and full absorption costing can be used for costing its programs, products, or services. For example, for managerial decision making, various programs may be on a direct cost basis or a full absorption cost basis.

**Establishment of Responsibility Centers and Cost Centers** The process of establishment of responsibility centers and cost centers is the same as in the case of a profit-seeking organization. Further, most of the responsibility centers and cost centers of a not-for-profit organization will be more or less the same as those of a for-profit organization, provided their activities and setup are the same. For example, in a nonprofit organization fund-raising activity may be set up as a separate responsibility center, which would be absent in a for-profit organization.

Various responsibility or cost centers can be classified into (1) mission centers, or operating centers, (2) support service centers, or ancillary service centers, and (3) general and administration centers. Mission centers are directly concerned with achieving the organization's objectives, and the support service centers provide services to the operating centers or are indirectly concerned with achieving the organization's objectives. Some of the responsibility centers and cost centers of a typical hospital would be as follows:

*Operating Centers*

Medical (may be classified into various divisions)
Surgical (may be classified into various divisions)

*Support Service Centers*

Nursing
X-ray
Laboratory
Dietary department
Medical supplies
Drugs
Social services

*General and Administration Centers*

Communications
Laundry
Business offices
Housekeeping and maintenance
Security
Medical records department

Some of these operating centers and support service centers are revenue centers and profit centers, too. For example, medical, surgical, x-ray, etc., centers are revenue centers.

Once the cost centers have been established, the major functions or activities performed by each center should be identified. Then, the functions should be related to various programs or services. For example, a nurse may assist a physician in medical examination, surgery, and physical therapy, in which case the nursing function should be identified with each of these services. Further, if the patients are classified according to the mode of recovery of the charges (third-party reimbursement, direct, free, etc.), various services pertaining to each category of patients should also be identified. For better understanding, a matrix of cost centers, functions and programs or services should be prepared as shown in Exhibit 20-2.

**Cost Classification** Costs of a nonprofit organization may be classified into one or more of the following categories, depending upon the objectives of its cost system and the nature of its mission:

1. Nature of expenses (salaries, employee benefits costs, rent, electricity, etc.). In almost all cases, costs are classified by nature of expenses.
2. Missions, major programs, or service lines.
3. Cost behavior.
4. Controllability, i.e., separation of controllable and noncontrollable costs.
5. Functions or activities; for example, various functional classifications in a school will be instruction, attendance, health, transportation, food service, administration, and so on.

**Cost Matrix** For better understanding, a matrix showing cost classification by nature, functions, missions, etc., should be provided as illustrated in Exhibit 20-3.

**Selection of Units of Measurement** For computing costs of various services, programs, and functions and for developing budgets, a unit of measurement must be selected for each service, program, and function. The unit of measurement often reflects the workload or volume of activity of a cost center and is its performance determinant.

Units of measurement could be the number of items involved, time involved, weight, volume or space, etc. Some units of measurement are as follows:

Number of personnel (full-time equivalent)
Number of students, patients, etc., admitted
Inpatient days
Average length of stay
Emergency room visits
Clinic visits
Outpatient visits
Cost per bed-day or patient-day
Cost of meals per day
Cost per student
Cost per patient admitted
Cost per case

When the cost per case is used, the cost of health care is computed not by averaging the charges by patient-days but by measuring the resources utilized by a particular patient or a group of patients. This is known as *diagnosis-related groups system.*

**Development of Standards and Budgets** Though standard costing usually is not used in a nonprofit organization, the process for developing it is more or less the same as that for a for-profit organization. Hence it is not discussed in detail here.

Though the process of developing an expense budget for a nonprofit organization is more or less the same as that for a profit-seeking organization, there is one important difference. In a profit-seeking organization, costs are incurred to generate revenue and ultimately profits. In a nonprofit organization, costs are incurred to achieve its mission or objectives, and revenues or funds are secured to meet those costs. Hence, in preparing its budget, a nonprofit organization can adopt two approaches:

1. It can first determine how much funds it can raise and then determine what programs it can undertake.
2. It can first determine what programs it wants to undertake to achieve its goals and then determine the funds needed to undertake those programs and the sources of raising the required funds. If it cannot raise the required funds, it will have to amend its programs.

The second approach is essential for public schools, which have no choice but to educate all those students of the community who wish to go to public schools. The first approach may be adopted by relief organizations, charitable organizations, hospitals providing free or concessional health care services, etc.

**Procedures for Cost Allocation, Functional Costing, and Program Costing** For computing product or program costs as well as functional or activity costs, costs which can be identified with individual cost centers should be charged directly to them, and the other costs should be allocated. The procedures involved and the bases for allocations are more or less the same as for a profit-seeking organization.

If the number of programs or services is more than one, cost allocations will be complex. For example, computing the cost per student educated by a high school is simpler than that per student educated by a college having several different types of educational programs.

The important point is that some nonprofit organizations must make cost allocations in accordance with the principles or guidelines laid down in statutes, rules, government circulars, etc. For example, OMB Circular No. A-21, referred to earlier, lays down the principles for determining the costs of a sponsored agreement, i.e., any grant, contract, or other agreement between a federal agency and the educational institution.

According to this circular, in computing the cost of a sponsored agreement, total costs incurred by an educational institution should be divided into direct and indirect costs. Direct costs are costs which can be identified specifically with a particular sponsored agreement. Indirect costs are costs that are incurred for common or joint objectives and cannot be readily and specifically identified with a particular sponsored project or with any other activity of the educational institution. The procedure for allocation of indirect costs is shown diagrammatically in Exhibit 20-5.

First, all indirect costs are normally classified under the seven *cost categories* shown in Exhibit 20-5. Within each cost category, costs of like nature are grouped together, and one or more cost groupings are established. Next, the costs accumulated under each cost grouping are allocated to the institution's *functions* in the order and according to the rules mentioned in Exhibit 20-5. Functions of the educational institution consist of instructions, organized research, other sponsored activities, and institutional activities. Then, for each function, single or multiple indirect cost rates are arrived at which are used to distribute the indirect costs of a function to individual sponsored agreements of that function.

**Cost Reports** Cost reports of a nonprofit organization consist of (1) responsibility reports for goal achievement and cost control and (2) functional cost reports and program cost reports for planning, budgeting, cost control, and managerial decision making such as determining service charges, choosing whether to continue or drop a program, etc.

There is practically no difference between the responsibility reports of a profit-seeking business and those of a nonprofit organization. A responsibility report would show the relevant quantitative data and other information, such as objectives sought to be achieved, activity volume, performance achievement ratio, etc. Whenever practical, the budget allowances for cost control purposes should be adjusted for the volume of activity achieved. For example, if the number of patients admitted is more than that budgeted, the budget allowance for variable expenses should be increased suitably to make a valid comparison between actual and budgeted costs. Since there is a preponderance of *labor costs,* they are reported separately. Though generally it is not done, it is possible for hospitals, schools, and similar organizations to analyze variances by causes such as volume variance and spending variance. The reports should be submitted to the responsibility center managers, who should be asked to explain variances and also explain what actions they have taken or planned to correct or prevent the unfavorable variances. In a nonprofit organization, the factor which makes cost control difficult is the attitude of personnel toward costs. In a profit-seeking organization, cost control is related directly to its objective of profit maximization, and hence it is comparatively easy to introduce cost-consciousness. In a nonprofit organization cost control is not directly related to its objective, say, of health care, relief work, or education, and hence it is comparatively difficult to enforce cost control discipline.

The functional and program cost reports of a nonprofit organization will depend upon the nature of the organization, its cost structure, and the objectives of cost compilations. The reporting principles and guide-

**EXHIBIT 20-5**

**Scheme for Distribution of Indirect Costs to Sponsored Agreements between Educational Institution and Government Agency**

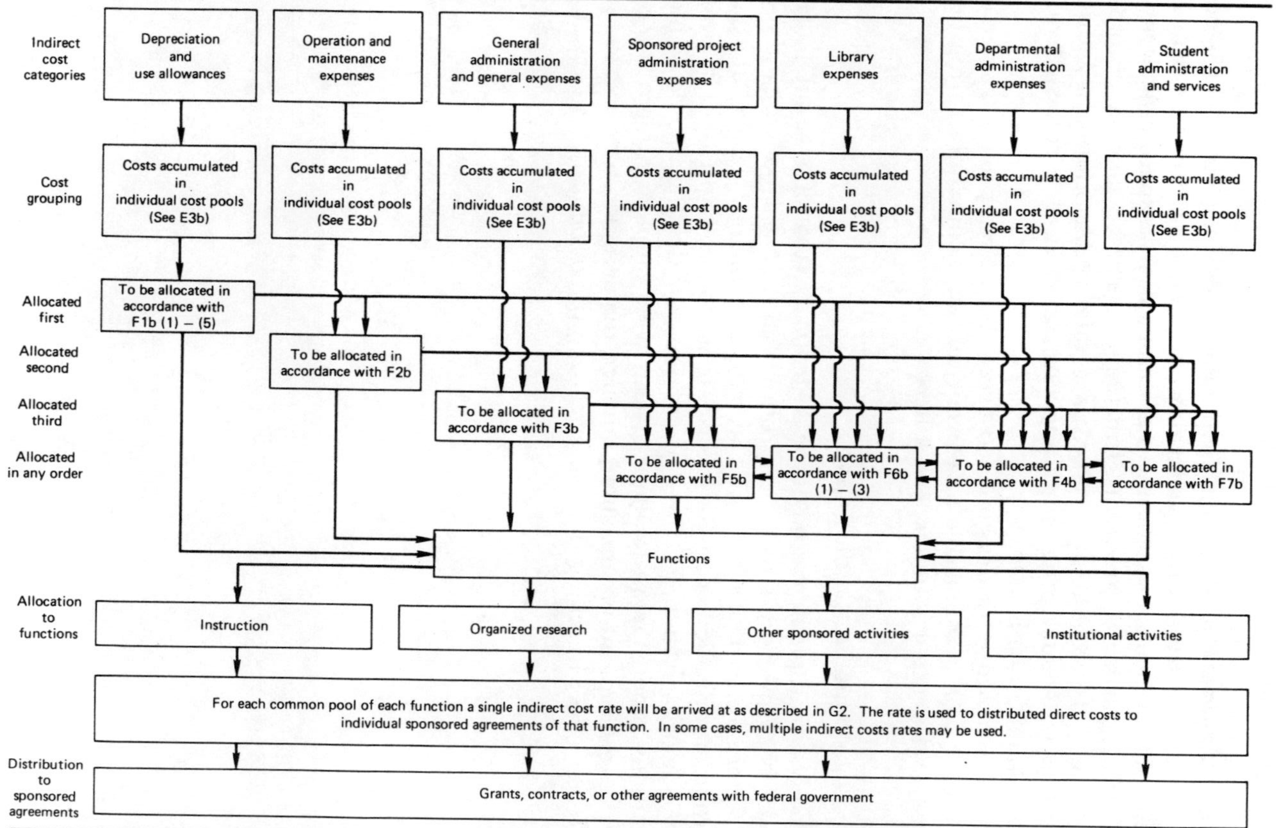


SOURCE: Except for some modifications made by the author, this diagram was prepared by Mrs. Judith Weiss, manager, Continuing Professional Education Division of the American Institute of Certified Public Accountants, New York. It is reproduced here with her permission.

lines applicable to profit-seeking organizations discussed earlier also apply to nonprofit organizations.

**Cost Records** Usually nonprofit organizations keep cost records on a historical cost basis. Cost classification by nature of expenses is maintained in the books of account. In addition, all costs specifically identifiable with particular programs, functions, or services may be recorded separately if the amount involved is significant. Allocation of indirect costs to individual programs, functions, or services is recorded on a memorandum basis only.

The procedure for designing cost records of a nonprofit organization is similar to that applicable to a profit-seeking nonmanufacturing business, and hence it is not repeated here.

### System Implementation Phase

The system implementation phase is identical to that of a manufacturing business. However, in most nonprofit organizations, labor cost will form a significant part of total costs. Second, as explained earlier, in a nonprofit organization, cost-consciousness is not as high as in a profit-seeking organization. For these two reasons, the designer should be more cautious about human relations aspects when implementing a cost system in a nonprofit organization. Further, the designer may have to exert greater effort in selling the cost system to the organization's personnel.

# Epilogue

In this book we have discussed the procedure for designing and implementing an effective cost system. From that discussion, it will be obvious that there are a multiplicity of factors which are responsible for or influence the successful design and implementation of a cost system. It is worthwhile to summarize those factors here:

1. The designer must have knowledge and experience in cost accounting techniques, methods, and procedures, bookkeeping and general accounting procedures, and internal controls.
2. The designer must also know how to design and implement a cost accounting system.
3. The designer must be able to put the theoretical knowledge mentioned in Paragraphs 1 and 2 into practice; i.e., he must be able to apply his knowledge to designing a cost system for a given organization. It is here that experience is of great help.
4. The designer must have a good business overview.
5. The designer must have good oral and written communications skills.
6. The designer must be skillful in managing system projects and in working as a team leader.
7. The designer must possess such personal qualities as a positive attitude, an analytical mind, creativity, good judgment, project orientation, and insight, and he must be people-oriented.
8. The designer must be solution-oriented and not technique-oriented. That is, he should focus attention on the problems at hand and design a system to solve these problems instead of emphasizing techniques and designing a system around them. For example, the designer should not proceed with a foregone conclusion that a manufacturing organization should have a standard cost system because even if a standard cost system is ideal for the organization, it may not be practical for the time being.

9. The designer must select the right method of costing and costing techniques.
10. There must be continuous and adequate support from top management.
11. The attitude and capability of company personnel, particularly key personnel concerned with the cost system, are also important factors.

Some of these factors may be critical to the success of the system; others may have only healthy or damaging effects. Much depends upon the facts of each case. It is also well to reemphasize that the payoff from a good cost system will come only when the system is properly operated and management uses the information generated by it.

# APPENDIX

# Specimen PERT Charts for Designing and Implementing a Standard Cost System

As explained in Chapter 1, PERT (program evaluation and review technique) charts are very useful in managing the project of a cost system. This appendix contains four PERT charts[1] with underlying lists of events for designing and implementing a standard cost system. Though these charts are not exhaustive, they include most of the major events which take place in designing and implementing a standard cost system.

These four charts depict the events and their interrelationships for developing respectively (1) standard product costs, (2) variances related to procurement and material usage, (3) variances related to labor and productivity, and (4) miscellaneous variances and maintaining the general ledger. These charts are not separate and independent of one another. They are parts of a single chart but are divided into four charts for convenience. From these charts, the minimum time required to complete a project can be determined.

[1] PERT charts and lists of events are reproduced, with the permission of Price Waterhouse & Company, from "A Program for Designing and Installing a Standard Cost System" in the 1974 *MAS/PACE Cost Accounting System* (a Price Waterhouse & Company manual for continuing education programs).

## APPENDIX CHART 1

### Developing Standard Product Costs

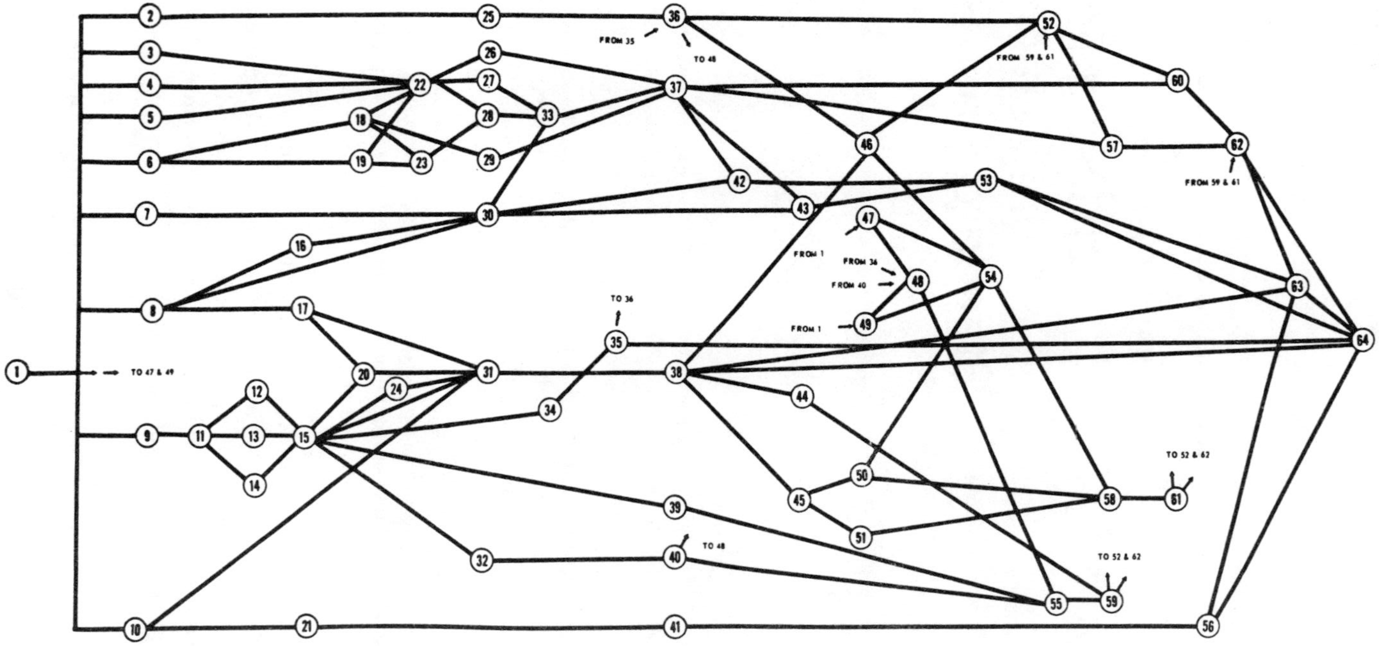

# List of Events

1 Preliminary survey of organization and methods completed
2 Product numbers assigned
3 Accounting treatment of cash discount decided
4 Direct labor defined
5 Accounting treatment of freight-in decided
6 Organization charts reviewed and revised as necessary
7 Normal workweek determined
8 Machine groups established
9 Parts numbering system established
10 Standard labor grades established
11 Parts numbers assigned
12 Unit-of-measure codes assigned
13 Engineering-level codes assigned
14 Source codes assigned
15 Parts number identification files set up
16 Standard downtime allowances set
17 Standard manning tables prepared
18 Service centers established
19 Production centers established
20 Standard production rates set
21 Wage rate ranges assigned to labor grades
22 Expense account classes reviewed and revised
23 Factors of variability selected
24 Raw material content determined: piece parts
25 Annual sales forecasted
26 Procurement burden analysis completed
27 Bases for amortizing capacity costs revised as necessary
28 Fixed-variable expense analyses made
29 Bases for redistributing service center costs determined
30 Practical capacity determined
31 Operation sheets available
32 Vendors chosen for purchased parts
33 Flexible budgets prepared
34 Bills of material available
35 EDP bill-of-material file established
36 Annual parts requirements determined
37 Budgeted costs in service centers redistributed
38 EDP operation sheet data file established
39 Standard freight rates set for purchased parts
40 Tentative standards set for purchased parts
41 Standard labor rates set for all grades
42 Variable manufacturing burden rates computed
43 Fixed manufacturing burden rates computed
44 Standard prices set for outside operations
45 Vendors chosen for raw materials
46 Annual raw-material requirements established
47 Inventory carrying costs estimated
48 Economic order quantities established: purchased parts
49 Cost of placing a purchase order estimated
50 Tentative standards set for raw materials
51 Standard freight rates set for raw materials
52 Standard cost of annual purchases computed
53 EDP file, manufacturing burden rates, established
54 Economic order quantities established: raw materials
55 Standard prices determined: purchased parts
56 EDP file, standard labor rates, established
57 Standard procurement burden rates set: raw materials
58 Standard prices determined: raw materials
59 EDP file, standard cost of purchased parts and outside operations (excluding procurement burden), established
60 Standard procurement burden rates set: purchased parts
61 EDP file, standard cost of raw materials (excluding procurement burden), established
62 Procurement burden added and standard purchase price files combined
63 EDP file, standard cost of fabricated parts, established
64 EDP file, standard cost of assemblies, established

## APPENDIX CHART 2

### Determining Variances Related to Procurement and Material Usage

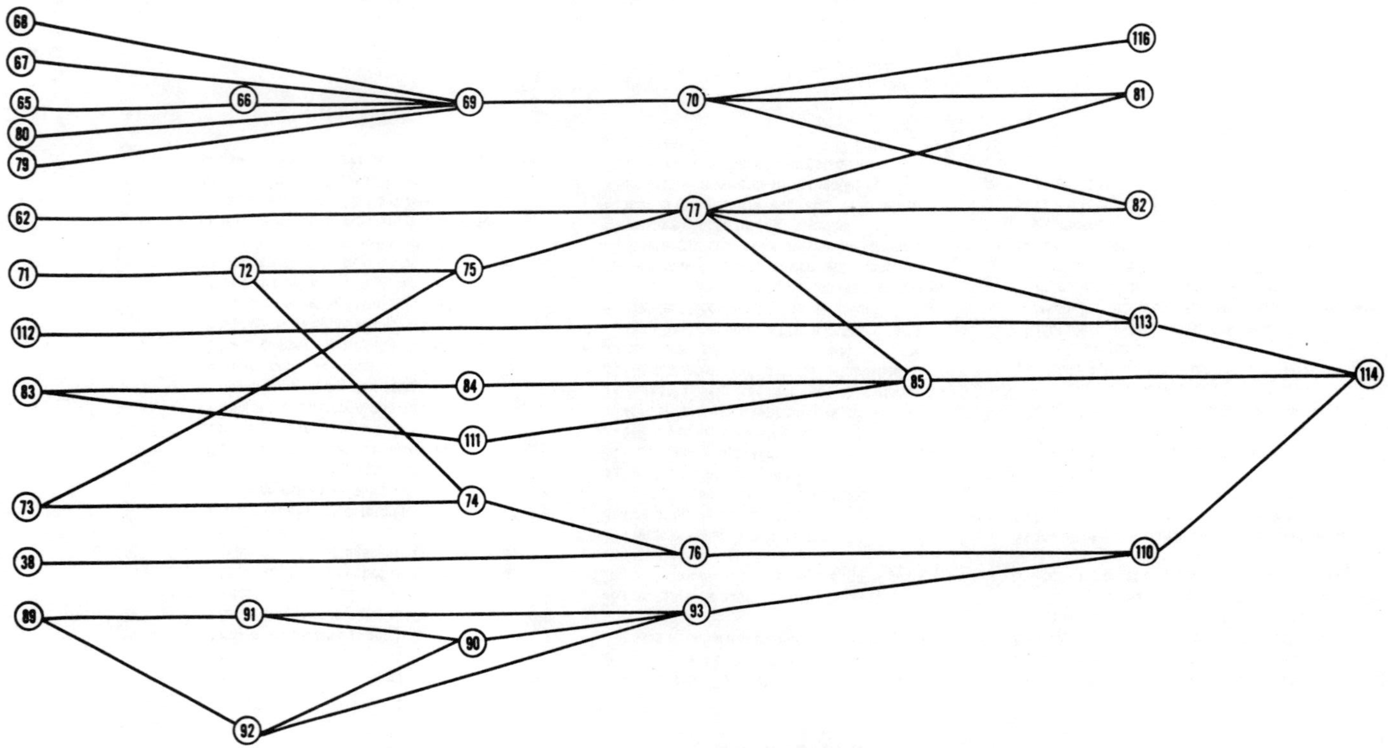

## List of Events

38 EDP operation sheet data file established
62 Procurement burden added and standard purchase price files combined
65 Basis for valuing vendor returns established
66 Procedures for making vendor returns established
67 Procedures for accounting for materials in hands of vendors revised
68 Format and frequency of purchase price variance report determined
69 Procedures established for determining purchase price variance and applying procurement burden
70 Purchase transactions for current period coded and keypunched
71 Engineering change control system established
72 Engineering release review system established
73 Methods change review system established
74 Procedures developed for updating EDP operation sheet data file
75 Procedures developed for updating EDP file of standard purchase prices
76 EDP file, operation sheet data, updated currently
77 EDP file, standard purchase prices, updated currently
79 Inventory and cost of goods sold account classes reviewed and revised
80 Accounting procedures for tooling costs reviewed and revised
81 Standard cost of purchases and applied procurement burden determined
82 Purchase price variance reports prepared
83 Procedures established for preparing material requisitions
84 Procedures established for pricing material requisitions at standard
85 Standard cost of requisitioned material available
89 Use of automatic data collection equipment evaluated
90 Timekeeping system modified as necessary
91 Job ticket preparation procedures revised as necessary
92 Production reporting procedures revised as necessary
93 Labor-hours spent and units produced summarized
110 Standard cost of standard material quantities determined
111 Material requisitions coded and keypunched
112 Procedures for recording and pricing inventories revised
113 Month-end inventories recorded and priced
114 Material usage variance computed
116 Value of noninventory purchases determined

## APPENDIX CHART 3

### Determining Variances Related to Labor and Productivity

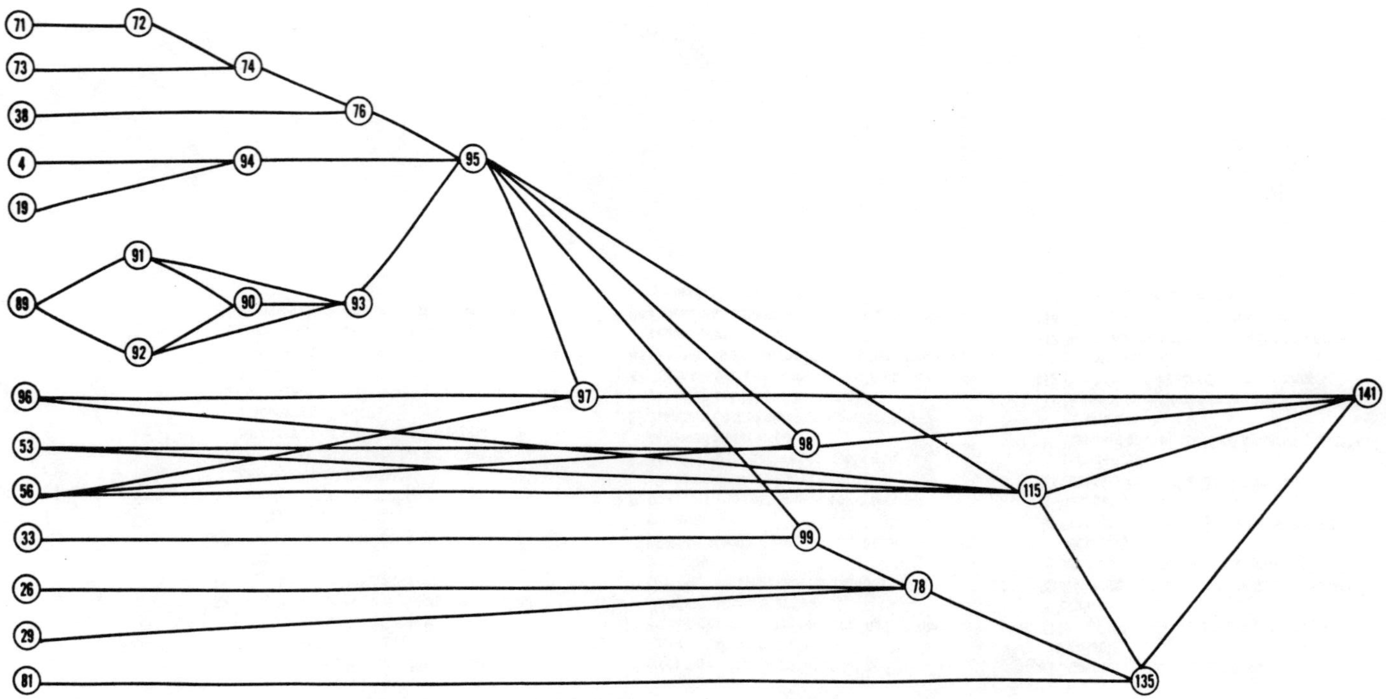

## List of Events

4 Direct labor defined
19 Production centers established
26 Procurement burden analysis completed
29 Bases for redistributing service center costs determined
33 Flexible budgets prepared
38 EDP operation sheet data file established
53 EDP file, manufacturing burden rates, established
56 EDP file, standard labor rates, established
71 Engineering change control system established
72 Engineering release review system established
73 Methods change review system established
74 Procedures developed for updating EDP operation sheet data file
76 EDP file, operation sheet data, updated currently
78 Adjusted budget apportioned between manufacturing and procurement
81 Standard cost of purchases and applied procurement burden determined
89 Use of automatic data collection equipment evaluated
90 Timekeeping system modified as necessary
91 Job ticket preparation procedures revised as necessary
92 Production reporting procedures revised as necessary
93 Labor-hours spent and units produced summarized
94 Labor performance reporting system designed
95 Labor performance reports available
96 EDP file, employee actual labor rates, established
97 Amount of labor rate variance determined
98 Amount of efficiency variance calculated
99 Flexible budgets adjusted for current level of activity
115 Labor costs and applied burden distributed to accounts
135 Volume variances calculated
141 Labor and burden summarized for input to ledger

## APPENDIX CHART 4

### Determining Miscellaneous Variances and Maintaining General Ledger

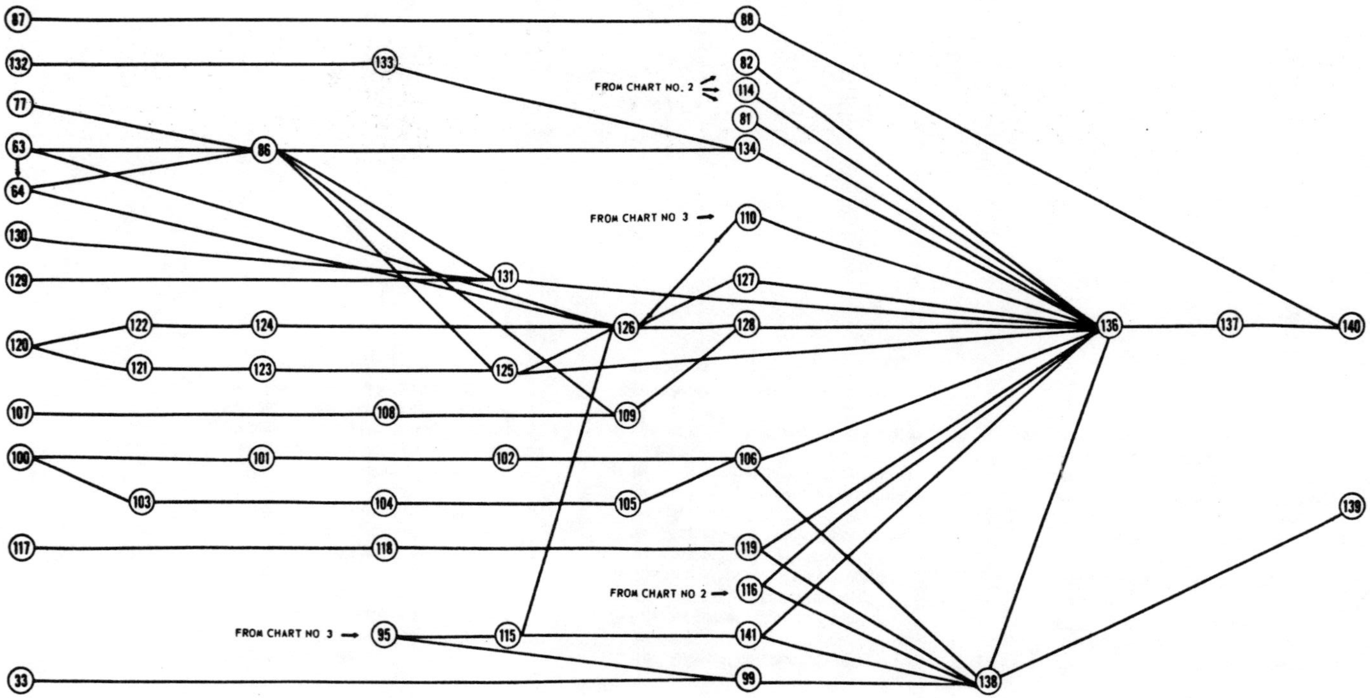

## List of Events

33 Flexible budgets prepared
63 EDP file, standard cost of fabricated parts, established
64 EDP file, standard cost of assemblies, established
77 EDP file, standard purchase prices, updated currently
81 Standard cost of purchases and applied procurement burden determined
82 Purchase price variance reports prepared
86 Standard cost data stored for computer use
87 Operating reports and financial statements redesigned
88 Procedures established for preparing operating reports and financial statements
95 Labor performance reports available
99 Flexible budgets adjusted for current level of activity
100 Statistical sampling of maintenance and operating supplies completed
101 Standard prices set for inventoriable supplies
102 EDP file, standard supply prices, established
103 Physical controls, standard supply items, established
104 Supply requisitioning procedures established
105 Supply pricing procedures revised as necessary
106 Supply requisitions priced, extended, and summarized
107 Scrap reporting procedures reviewed and revised
108 Current month's scrap reports coded and keypunched
109 Current month's scrap losses determined
110 Standard cost of standard material quantities determined
114 Material usage variance computed
115 Labor costs and applied burden distributed to accounts
116 Value of noninventory purchases determined
117 Miscellaneous journal entries prepared (mainly amortizing capacity costs)
118 Miscellaneous journal entries keypunched
119 Summary listing of miscellaneous journal entries prepared
120 Work authorization system reviewed and revised
121 Procedures revised for documenting deliveries of parts to stores
122 Job-closing procedures revised
123 Accounting procedures for costing stores deliveries revised
124 Accounting procedures for completed job orders revised
125 Standard cost of completed parts determined
126 Cost analyses of completed jobs prepared
127 Engineering and methods change variance computed
128 Scrap variance calculated
129 Procedures for revaluing opening inventory at standard established
130 Accounting policy on inventory revaluation adjustment set
131 Opening inventories revalued at standard
132 Procedures for determining cost of goods sold revised
133 Sales transactions coded and keypunched
134 Standard cost of goods sold determined
136 General and expense ledgers posted
137 Trial balance available
138 Spending variance calculated
139 Budget expense comparisons prepared
140 Financial statements prepared
141 Labor and burden summarized for input to ledger

# Bibliography


## General

1. Davidson, Sidney, and Roman L. Veil (eds.): *Handbook of Cost Accounting,* McGraw-Hill Book Company, New York, 1978.
2. Black, Homer A., and James D. Edwards (eds.): *The Managerial & Cost Accountant's Handbook,* Dow Jones-Irwin, Inc., Chicago, 1979.
3. Dickey, Robert I. (ed.): *Accountants' Cost Handbook,* 2d ed., The Ronald Press Company, New York, 1960.
4. Prentice-Hall editorial staff: *Encyclopedia of Cost Accounting Systems,* Prentice-Hall, Inc., Englewood Cliffs, N.J., 1965.
5. Pescow, Jerome K. (ed.): *Encyclopedia of Accounting Systems,* Prentice-Hall, Inc., Englewood Cliffs, N.J., 1976.
6. National Society of Public Accountants: *Portfolio of Accounting Systems for Small and Medium-Sized Businesses,* Prentice-Hall, Inc., Englewood Cliffs, N.J., 1977.
7. Gillespie, Cecil: *Accounting Systems, Procedures and Methods,* 3d ed., Prentice-Hall, Inc., Englewood Cliffs, N.J., 1971.
8. Heckert, Brooks J., and Harry D. Kerrigan: *Accounting Systems, Design and Installation,* 3d ed., The Ronald Press Company, New York, 1967.
9. Lasser, J. K. (ed.): *Handbook of Cost Accounting Methods,* D. Van Nostrand Company, Inc., New York, 1949.
10. Anton, Hector R., and Peter A. Firmin (eds.): *Contemporary Issues in Cost Accounting,* 2d ed., Houghton Mifflin Company, Boston, 1972.

## Chapters 2 through 4: System Analysis Phase

11. Glans, Thomas B., and others: *Management Systems,* Holt, Rinehart and Winston, Inc., New York, 1968.

## Chapter 6: Cost Control System

12. Anthony, Robert N., John Deardon, and Richard F. Vancil: *Management Control Systems, Cases and Readings,* Richard D. Irwin, Inc., Homewood, Ill., 1965.
13. National Association of Accountants (U.S.A.) publications:
    a. *Control of Maintenance Cost,* 1964.
    b. *Accounting for Cost of Capacity,* 1963.
    c. *Separating and Using Costs as Fixed and Variable,* Research Report 39.
    d. *How Standard Costs Are Being Used Currently,* Research Reports 11–15.

14. Welsch, Glenn A.: *Budgeting, Profit Planning and Control,* 4th ed., Prentice-Hall, Inc., Englewood Cliffs, N.J., 1976.
15. Jones, R. L., and H. George Trentin: *Budgeting: Key to Profit Planning and Control,* American Management Association, New York, 1966.
16. Pyhrr, Peter A.: *Zero-Base Budgeting: A Practical Management Tool for Evaluating Expenses,* Wiley-Interscience, New York, 1973.
17. Austin, Allan L., and Logan M. Cheek: *Zero-Base Budgeting: A Decision Package Manual,* American Management Association, New York, 1979.

## Chapter 7: Costing Methods

18. McNesby, Edward J.: *Direct and Full Absorption Cost Control,* Prentice-Hall, Inc., Englewood Cliffs, N.J., 1969.
19. *Direct Costing,* Research Series No. 23, NACA Bulletin, vol. 34, 1953.

## Chapter 8: Responsibility Centers and Cost Centers

20. Solomons, David: *Divisional Performance Measurement and Control* (Financial Executive Research Foundation, New York), Richard D. Irwin, Inc., Homewood, Ill., 1965.
21. Shillinglaw, Gordon: *Cost Accounting: Analysis and Control,* Richard D. Irwin, Inc., Homewood, Ill., 1961.

## Chapters 9 through 13: Manufacturing and Marketing Cost Systems

22. Institute of Cost and Works Accountants of India publications on cost audit and cost accounting record rules for the following industries:

- Bicycles
- Cement
- Automobile batteries
- Tyres and tubes
- Tractors
- Motor vehicles
- Room air conditioners
- Refrigerators
- Electric lamps
- Electric fans
- Caustic soda
- Electric motors
- Aluminum
- Bulk drugs
- Infant milk foods
- Industrial alcohol
- Sugar
- Paper
- Cotton textiles
- Nylon
- Soda ash
- Dye

23. Henrici, S. B.: *Standard Costs for Manufacturing,* 3d ed., McGraw-Hill Book Company, New York, 1960.
24. NAA publications:
    a. *Analysis of Non-Manufacturing Costs for Managerial Decisions.*
    b. *Accounting for Labor Costs and Labor-Related Costs,* 1957.
25. Maynard, H. B. (ed.): *Industrial Engineering Handbook,* secs. 2, 3, 4, 5, and 8, 3d ed., McGraw-Hill Book Company, New York, 1971.

## Chapter 14: Cost Reports

26. Lewis, R. B.: *Management Control Techniques for Improving Profits,* Prentice-Hall, Inc., Englewood Cliffs, N.J., 1962.
27. Lewis, R. B.: *Financial Controls for Management,* Prentice-Hall, Inc., Englewood Cliffs, N.J., 1961.
28. Joplin, Bruce, and James W. Pattillo: *Effective Accounting Reports,* Prentice-Hall, Inc., Englewood Cliffs, N.J., 1969.
29. Shillinglaw, Gordon: "Guides to Internal Profit Measurement," *Harvard Business Review,* vol. 35, no. 2, March–April 1957, pp. 82–94.
30. Deardon, John: "Problems in Decentralized Profit Responsibility," *Harvard Business Review,* vol. 38, no. 3, May–June 1960, pp. 79–86.

## Chapter 15: Cost Records and Procedures

31. Gillespie, Cecil: *Accounting Procedure for Standard Costs,* The Ronald Press Company, New York, 1952.
32. Cushing, Barry E.: *Accounting Information Systems and Business Organizations,* Addison-Wesley Publishing Company, Reading, Mass., 1974.
33. *Standard Costs & Variance Analysis,* National Association of Accountants.
34. *Standard Expense Center Accounting Manual* (for use of the distributive trades for classifying and controlling expenses).
35. Minnich, Charles K., and Oscar Nelson: *Systems Management for Greater Profits and Growth,* Prentice-Hall, Inc., Englewood Cliffs, N.J., 1966.
36. *Uniform System of Accounts for Restaurants,* National Restaurant Association, Chicago, 1968.
37. *Uniform System of Accounts and Expense Dictionary for Motels–Motor Hotels, Small Hotels,* American Hotel and Motel Association, New York, 1962.

## Chapter 16: Chart of Accounts

38. Whiteside, Conon Doyle: *Accounting Systems for Small and Medium-Sized Business,* Prentice-Hall, Inc., Englewood Cliffs, N.J., 1961.
39. *Uniform Classification of Accounts for Motels or Motor Hotels,* Motel/Motor Inn Journal, 1972.
40. *Classification and Coding Techniques to Facilitate Accounting Operations,* Research Series 34, National Association of Accountants, New York, 1959.

## Chapter 19: Systems Manual

41. *Uniform Accounting Manual for Electrical Manufacturing Industry,* National Electrical Manufacturers Association, U.S.A.
42. *Basic Cost System for Gray Iron Foundries,* Gray Iron Founders' Society, Inc., U.S.A.
43. *Uniform Accounting Manual for the Plastic Industry,* Society of the Plastic Industry, U.S.A.

## Chapter 20: Nonmanufacturing Businesses and Nonprofit Organizations

44. Anthony, Robert N.: *Management Control Systems in Non-Profit Organizations,* Richard D. Irwin, Inc., Chicago, 1979.
45. Horwath, E. B., Louis Toth, and J. D. Lesure: *Hotel Accounting,* The Ronald Press Company, New York, 1978.

4442 McGraw
"Shah index"
Msp. 1-8
Maureen 1-8-81 ET1
oc Maureen 1-14-81 ET1

Responsibility center Sales Department — Center no. 220

Responsibility of Sales director — Month ____

| Actual | | Description | | Better (worse) than budget | |
|---|---|---|---|---|---|
| Current month | Year to date | Account or cost center no. | Expense item or cost center | Current month | Year to date |
| | | 221 | Office of Sales Director | | |
| | | 222 | Sales Region 1 | | |
| | | 223 | Sales Region 2 | | |
| | | | Total selling costs | | |
| Details of expenses of Office of Sales Director | | | | | |
| | | | | | |
| Performance summary | | | | | |
| | | | Sales ($) | | |
| | | | Sales Region 1 | | |
| | | | Sales Region 2 | | |
| | | | Total sales | | |
| | | | Selling costs as percentage of sales | | |
| | | | Sales Region 1 | | |
| | | | Sales Region 2 | | |
| | | | Total | | |

# INDEX

Pravin P. Shah, B. Com. (Hons.), Grad. C.W.A., F.C.A., Chartered Accountant, is Assistant Vice President, WUI, Inc. (a wholly owned subsidiary of Xerox Corporation), responsible for providing internal consulting services. Before joining WUI, he was a Principal with the Management Consulting Division of S. V. Ghatalia & Co., a firm of CPAs in Bombay, India. He has handled a wide variety of consulting projects in many industries, including the design and implementation of cost systems, financial accounting systems, and planning, budgeting, and management reporting systems. He has written a self-study course for the Continuing Professional Education Division of the American Institute of Certified Public Accountants. He has also published articles and given talks on the design and implementation of management accounting systems.